ARCTIC OCEAN
50-51

Greenland
50-51

Alaska &Western Canada
22-23

CONTINENTAL MAP:
NORTH AMERICA
20-21

C A N A D A

Eastern Canada
24-25

Pacific
States
36-37

Central &
Mountain States
32-33

Great Lakes
30-31

Northeastern
States
26-27

U N I T E D   S T A T E S
O F   A M E R I C A

PACIFIC OCEAN
128-129

Southwestern
States
34-35

Southern States
28-29

ATLANTIC
OCEAN
52- 53

Mexico
38-39

Central America &
the Caribbean
42-43

Northern
South America
44-45

CONTINENTAL MAP:
CENTRAL & SOUTH AMERICA
40-41

Brazil
46-47

CONTINENTAL MAP:
OCEANIA
130-131

New Zealand
134

Southern
South America
48-49

ANTARCTICA
50-51

THE EYEWITNESS

ATLAS
OF THE
WORLD

THE EYEWITNESS

ATLAS
OF THE
WORLD

DK PUBLISHING, INC.

CONSULTANTS

Consultant editor
Dr. David R. Green, Department of Geography, King's College

Digital mapping consultant
Professor Jan-Peter A. L. Muller, Professor of Image Understanding and Remote Sensing,
Department of Photogrammetry and Surveying, University College London

Digital base map production
Department of Photogrammetry and Surveying, University College London:
Philip Eales (Producer) • Kevin Tildsley • David Rees •
James Pearson • Peter Booth • Tim Day • Planetary Visions Ltd

Contributors
Peter Clark, Former Keeper, Royal Geographical Society, London •
Martin McCauley, Senior Lecturer in Politics,
School of Slavonic and East European Studies, University of London

Dorling Kindersley would also like to thank
Dr. Andrew Tatham, Keeper, and the Staff of the Royal Geographical Society, London,
for their help and advice in preparing this Atlas

Project art editor: Nicola Liddiard
Project editors: Elizabeth Wyse and Caroline Lucas
Project cartographer: Julia Lunn

Editorial: Jayne Parsons • Phillip Boys • Chris Whitwell • Donna Rispoli •
Margaret Hynes • Ailsa Heritage • Sue Peach • Laura Porter

Design: Lesley Betts • Rhonda Fisher • Paul Blackburn • Jay Young

Cartography: Roger Bullen • Michael Martin • James Mills-Hicks • James Anderson •
Yahya El-Droubie • Tony Chambers • Simon Lewis • Caroline Simpson

Illustrations: John Woodcock • Kathleen McDougall • Mick Gillah • David Wright

Photography: Andy Crawford • Tim Ridley • Steve Gorton

Picture research: Clive Webster • Charlotte Bush •
Sharon Southren • Frances Vargo • Caroline Brook

Editorial director: Andrew Heritage
Art director: Chez Picthall
Production: Susannah Straughan
U.S. Editor: Charles A. Wills

A DK PUBLISHING BOOK

Revised Edition
2 4 6 8 10 9 7 5 3

Published in the United States by DK Publishing, Inc.,
95 Madison Avenue, New York, NY 10016

Library of Congress Cataloging-in-Publication Data
DK Publishing, Inc.
The eyewitness atlas of the world. – Revised edition
p. cm.
Includes index

1. Atlases. I. Title. II. Title: Atlas of the world
G1021.D65 1993 <G&M>
912-dc20   93-18572 CIP MAP

CONTENTS

THE EARTH IN SPACE

THE EARTH IS ONE OF NINE PLANETS that orbit a large star – the Sun. Together they form the solar system. All life on Earth – plant, animal, and human – depends on the Sun. Its energy warms our planet's surface, powers the wind and waves, drives the ocean currents and weather systems, and recycles water. Sunlight also gives plants the power to photosynthesize – to make the foods and oxygen on which organisms rely. The fact that the Earth is habitable at all is due to its precise position in the solar system, its daily spin, and its annual journey around the Sun at a constant tilt. Without these, and the breathable atmosphere that cloaks and protects the Earth, it would be as barren as our near-neighbors Venus and Mars.

Asteroid belt

Mars 687 days *Jupiter 12 years*
Uranus 84 years *Mercury 88 days* *Earth 365 days (1 year)*
Venus 225 days
Saturn 29 years
Neptune 165 years
Pluto 248 years

THE SOLAR SYSTEM
Although the planets move at great speeds, they do not fly off in all directions into space because the Sun's gravity holds them in place. This keeps the planets circling the Sun. A planet's "year" is the time it takes to make one complete trip around the Sun. The diagram shows the length of the planet's year in Earth-days or Earth-years.

THE SUN
The Sun is 865,000 miles (1,392,000 km) across. It has a core temperature of 25 million°F (14 million°C).

Saturn -292°F (-180°C)

Jupiter -238°F (-150°C)

YOU CAN USE THIS SENTENCE TO REMEMBER THE SEQUENCE OF PLANETS: MANY VERY EAGER MOUNTAINEERS JOG SWIFTLY UP NEW PEAKS.

Venus 870°F (465°C) *Mars -9.5°F (-23°C)*

Mercury Day: 806°F (430°C) Night: -292°F (-180°C) *Earth 60°F (15°C)*

Pluto -382°F (-230°C)

Venus 67,200,000 miles (108,200,000 km) *Jupiter 483,000,000 miles (778,330,000 km)*

Uranus -346°F (-210°C) *Neptune -364°F (-220°C)*

Above: *The relative sizes of the Sun and planets, with their average temperature.*

| Mercury 36,000,000 miles (57,910,000 km) | Earth 92,900,000 miles (149,500,000 km) | Mars 141,600,000 miles (227,940,000 km) | Saturn 886,700,000 miles (1,426,980,000 km) | Uranus 1,783,000,000 miles (2,870,990,000 km) | Neptune 2,800,000,000 miles (4,497,070,000 km) | Pluto 3,670,000,000 miles (5,913,520,000 km) |

Above: *The planets and their distances from the Sun.*

THE LIFE ZONE: THE EARTH SEEMS TO BE THE ONLY HABITABLE PLANET IN OUR SOLAR SYSTEM. MERCURY AND VENUS, WHICH ARE CLOSER TO THE SUN, ARE HOTTER THAN AN OVEN. MARS, AND PLANETS STILL FARTHER OUT, ARE COLDER THAN A DEEP FREEZE.

Huge solar flares, up to 125,000 miles (200,000 km) long, lick out into space

THE FOUR SEASONS
The Earth always tilts in the same direction on its 590 million-mile (950 million-km) journey around the Sun. This means that each hemisphere in turn leans toward the Sun, then leans away from it. This is what causes summer and winter.

It takes 365 days, 6 hours, 9 minutes, and 9 seconds for the Earth to make one revolution around the Sun. This is the true length of an Earth "year."

To North Star

The Earth takes 23 hours, 56 minutes, and 4 seconds to rotate once. This is the true length of an Earth "day."

DECEMBER 21ST (SOLSTICE)
Summer in the Southern hemisphere; winter in the Northern hemisphere. At noon, the Sun is overhead at the Tropic of Capricorn. The South Pole is in sunlight for 24 hours, and the North Pole is in darkness for 24 hours.

MARCH 21ST (EQUINOX)
Spring in the Northern hemisphere; autumn in the Southern hemisphere. At noon, the Sun is overhead at the Equator. Everywhere on Earth has 12 hours of daylight, 12 hours of darkness.

The Earth travels around the Sun at 66,600 miles per hour (107,244 km per hour).

Sun

JUNE 21ST (SOLSTICE)
Summer in the Northern hemisphere; winter in the Southern hemisphere. At noon, the Sun is overhead at the Tropic of Cancer. The North Pole is in sunlight for 24 hours, and the South Pole is in darkness for 24 hours.

South Pole

SEPTEMBER 21ST (EQUINOX)
Autumn in the Northern hemisphere; spring in the Southern hemisphere. At noon, the Sun is overhead at the Equator. Everywhere on Earth has 12 hours of daylight, 12 hours of darkness.

24 HOURS IN THE LIFE OF PLANET EARTH
The Earth turns a complete circle (360°) in 24 hours, or 15° in one hour. Countries on a similar line of longitude (or "meridian") usually share the same time. They set their clocks in relation to Greenwich Mean Time (GMT). This is the time at Greenwich (London, England), on longitude 0°. Countries east of Greenwich are ahead of GMT. Countries to the west are behind GMT.

Noon everywhere on this meridian

	0°	15°W	30°W	45°W	60°W	75°W	90°W	105°W	120°W	135°W	150°W	165°W
Noon at:	Greenwich	Dakar	E. Greenland	Rio de Janeiro	Caracas	New York	Mexico City	Calgary	Los Angeles	E. Alaska	Honolulu	(Pacific Ocean)
Greenwich time:	1200 hrs	1100 hrs	1000 hrs	0900 hrs	0800 hrs	0700 hrs	0600 hrs	0500 hrs	0400 hrs	0300 hrs	0200 hrs	0100 hrs

MOON AND EARTH

The Moon is a ball of barren rock 2,156 miles (3,476 km) across. It orbits the Earth every 27.3 days at an average distance of 238,700 miles (384,400 km). The Moon's gravity is only one-sixth that of Earth's – too small to keep an atmosphere around itself, but strong enough to exert a powerful pull on the Earth. The Moon and Sun together create tides in the Earth's oceans. The period between successive high tides is 12 hours, 25 minutes. The highest (or "spring") tides occur twice a month, when the Moon, Sun, and Earth are in line.

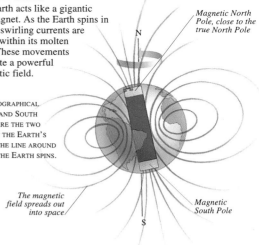

Craters made by collision with meteors

The Moon's surface temperature falls from 220°F (105°C) in sunlight to 247°F (155°C) when it turns away from the Sun

MAGNET EARTH

The Earth acts like a gigantic bar magnet. As the Earth spins in space, swirling currents are set up within its molten core. These movements generate a powerful magnetic field.

Magnetic North Pole, close to the true North Pole

THE GEOGRAPHICAL NORTH AND SOUTH POLES ARE THE TWO ENDS OF THE EARTH'S AXIS – THE LINE AROUND WHICH THE EARTH SPINS.

The magnetic field spreads out into space

Magnetic South Pole

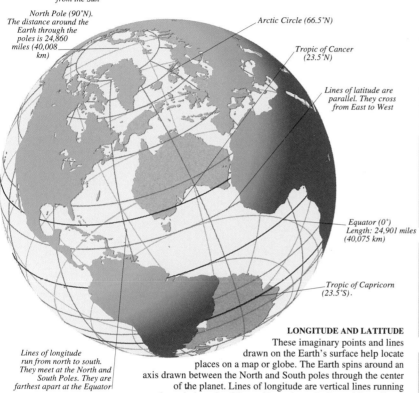

North Pole (90°N). The distance around the Earth through the poles is 24,860 miles (40,008 km)

Arctic Circle (66.5°N)

Tropic of Cancer (23.5°N)

Lines of latitude are parallel. They cross from East to West

Equator (0°) Length: 24,901 miles (40,075 km)

Tropic of Capricorn (23.5°S).

Lines of longitude run from north to south. They meet at the North and South Poles. They are farthest apart at the Equator

LONGITUDE AND LATITUDE

These imaginary points and lines drawn on the Earth's surface help locate places on a map or globe. The Earth spins around an axis drawn between the North and South poles through the center of the planet. Lines of longitude are vertical lines running through the poles. Lines of latitude are horizontal lines drawn parallel to the Equator, the line around the middle of the Earth.

DIAMETER OF EARTH AT EQUATOR: 7,927 MILES (12,756 KM). DIAMETER FROM POLE TO POLE: 7,900 MILES (12,714 KM). MASS: 5,988 MILLION, MILLION MILLION TONS (TONNES).

THE ATMOSPHERE

An envelope of gases such as nitrogen and oxygen surrounds our planet. It provides us with breathable air, filters the Sun's rays, and retains heat at night.

Height in miles (km)

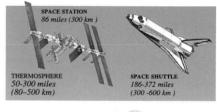

INTERPLANETARY SPACE

COMMUNICATIONS AND SOME ASTRONOMICAL SATELLITES 22,295 miles (5,880 km)

EXOSPHERE 300-1,240 miles (500–2,000 km) ()

25,000 (40,000)

SPACE STATION 86 miles (300 km)

THERMOSPHERE 50-300 miles (80–500 km)

SPACE SHUTTLE 186-372 miles (300 -600 km)

300 (500)

MESOSPHERE 31-50 miles (50–80 km)

WEATHER BALLOON up to 31 miles (50 km)

50 (80)

31 (50)

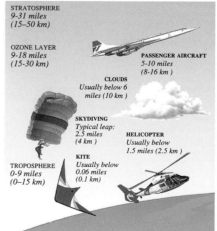

STRATOSPHERE 9-31 miles (15–50 km)

OZONE LAYER 9-18 miles (15-30 km)

PASSENGER AIRCRAFT 5-10 miles (8-16 km)

CLOUDS Usually below 6 miles (10 km)

SKYDIVING Typical leap: 2.5 miles (4 km)

HELICOPTER Usually below 1.5 miles (2.5 km)

KITE Usually below 0.06 miles (0.1 km)

TROPOSPHERE 0-9 miles (0–15 km)

Sea level

WINDS AND CURRENTS

The world's winds and ocean currents are caused by the way the Sun heats the Earth's surface. More heat energy arrives at the Equator than at the poles because the Earth is curved and tilted. Warm air and warm water carry much of this energy toward the poles, heating up the higher latitudes. Meanwhile, cool air and water moves back toward the Equator, lowering its temperature.

Cold air descends from the poles toward the Equator

Warm air and water travel to the poles from the Equator

Air circulates between the poles and the Equator in stages called "cells"

Winds and currents do not move in straight lines because the Earth spins

180°	165°E	150°E	135°E	120°E	105°E	90°E	75°E	60°E	45°E	30°E	15°E	0°
Wellington 2400 hrs	(Pacific Ocean) 2300 hrs	Sydney 2200 hrs	Tokyo 2100 hrs	Manila 2000 hrs	Jakarta 1900 hrs	Dacca 1800 hrs	Karachi 1700 hrs	Muscat 1600 hrs	Baghdad 1500 hrs	Cairo 1400 hrs	Berlin 1300 hrs	Greenwich 1200 hrs

THE EARTH'S STRUCTURE

IN SOME WAYS, the Earth is like an egg, with a thin shell around
a soft interior. Its hard, rocky outer layer – the crust – is up to 45
miles (70 km) thick under the continents, but less than 5 miles
(8 km) thick under the oceans. This crust is broken into gigantic
slabs called "plates," in which the continents are embedded.
Below the hard crust is the mantle, a layer of rocks so hot that
some melt and flow in huge swirling currents. The Earth's plates
do not stay in the same place. Instead, they move, carried along
like rafts on the currents in the mantle. This motion is very slow
– usually less than 2 in (5 cm) a year – but enormously powerful.
Plate movement makes the Earth quake and volcanoes erupt,
causes immense mountain ranges such as the Himalayas to grow
where plates collide, and explains, how over millions of years,
whole continents have drifted across the face of the planet.

Pangaea

DRIFTING CONTINENTS
Currents of molten rock deep
within the mantle slowly
move the continents. Over
time, they appear to "drift"
across the Earth's surface.

200 MILLION YEARS AGO
All of today's continents were
joined in one supercontinent,
called Pangaea. It began to break
up about 180 million years ago.

"Africa"

"India"

"Atlantic
Ocean"
opening up

"North
America"   "Asia"

"India"

120 MILLION YEARS AGO
The Atlantic Ocean splits
Pangaea into two. India has
broken away from Africa.

"Australia"   North America

Europe

Asia

India

South
America

Australia

Africa

Antarctica

"Antarctica"

40 MILLION YEARS AGO
India is moving closer to
Asia. Australia and
Antarctica have separated.

TODAY
India has collided with
Asia, pushing up the
Himalaya Mountains.

**50 MILLION YEARS
IN THE FUTURE?**
If today's plate movements continue,
the Atlantic Ocean will be 775 miles (1,250
km) wider. Africa and Europe will fuse, the
Americas will separate again, and Africa east of
the Great Rift Valley will be an island.

*Great Rift Valley,
now sea*

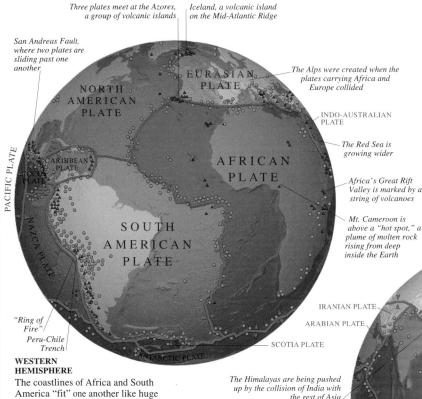

*Three plates meet at the Azores,
a group of volcanic islands*

*Iceland, a volcanic island
on the Mid-Atlantic Ridge*

*San Andreas Fault,
where two plates are
sliding past one
another*

EURASIAN
PLATE

NORTH
AMERICAN
PLATE

*The Alps were created when the
plates carrying Africa and
Europe collided*

INDO-AUSTRALIAN
PLATE

CARIBBEAN
PLATE

COCOS
PLATE

AFRICAN
PLATE

*The Red Sea is
growing wider*

*Africa's Great Rift
Valley is marked by a
string of volcanoes*

PACIFIC PLATE

SOUTH
AMERICAN
PLATE

*Mt. Cameroon is
above a "hot spot," a
plume of molten rock
rising from deep
inside the Earth*

NAZCA PLATE

"Ring of
Fire"

*Peru-Chile
Trench*

ANTARCTIC PLATE

SCOTIA PLATE

**WESTERN
HEMISPHERE**
The coastlines of Africa and South
America "fit" one another like huge
jigsaw pieces. This is because they were
once joined. About 180 million years
ago, a crack appeared in the Earth's
crust. Hot liquid rock (magma) rose
through the crack and cooled, forming
new oceanic crust on either side. As the
ocean grew wider, the continents moved
apart. The process continues today.

*The Ring of Fire passes
through Japan.*

*Mariana Trench, 6.8 miles
(11,033 m) deep, where
an ocean plate dives
into the mantle*

EURASIAN
PLATE

IRANIAN PLATE

ARABIAN PLATE

PHILIPPINE
PLATE

PACIFIC
PLATE

*The Himalayas are being pushed
up by the collision of India with
the rest of Asia*

AFRICAN PLATE

*The Java Trench, 4.6 miles
(7,450 m) deep, runs parallel
to a long chain of active
volcanoes in Southeast Asia*

INDO-AUSTRALIAN
PLATE

ANTARCTIC PLATE

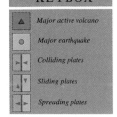

KEYBOX

▲	*Major active volcano*
●	*Major earthquake*
►┤	*Colliding plates*
▼	*Sliding plates*
►┤	*Spreading plates*

THE ATLANTIC OCEAN IS
GROWING WIDER BY
1 IN (2.5 CM) A YEAR –
ABOUT THE SAME SPEED
THAT FINGERNAILS GROW.
THE NAZCA PLATE IS
SLIDING THREE TIMES
FASTER UNDER SOUTH
AMERICA, PUSHING UP
THE ANDES.

EASTERN HEMISPHERE
Most earthquakes and volcanoes
occur around the edges of crustal plates
(or plate margins). Australia, in the middle
of the Indo-Australian plate, has no active
volcanoes and is rarely troubled by earthquakes.
Things are very different in neighboring New Zealand and
New Guinea, which lie on the Pacific "Ring of Fire". The ring is an area
of intense volcanic activity which forms a line all the way round the
Pacific rim, through the Philippines, Japan, and North America, and
down the coast of South America to New Zealand.

*The Hawaiian
islands lie over
a "hot spot"*

*Highly volcanic New
Zealand lies on the
"Ring of Fire"*

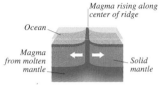

THE LAYERED EARTH
The Earth has layers, like an egg. The core is made of metals such as iron and nickel. This is surrounded by a rocky mantle and a thin crust.

Crust (solid)

Mantle (solid rock and liquid magma)

Inner core (solid)

Outer core (liquid)

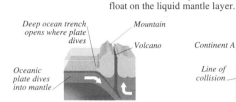

Ocean

Oceanic crust, 3-5 miles (5-8 km) thick

Solid mantle, up to 30 miles (50 km) thick

Liquid mantle

Continental crust, up to 45 miles (70 km) thick

Lithosphere (all crust plus solid layer of mantle). Up to 75 miles (120 km) thick

CRUST
The Earth's crust is of two kinds: continental and oceanic. Continental crust is older, thicker and less dense. Beneath the crust is a solid layer of mantle. Together, these form the lithosphere, which is broken into several plates. These float on the liquid mantle layer.

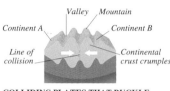

59°F (15°C)	5,400°F (3,000°C)	7,200°F (4,000°C)	8,100°F (4,500°C)	
CRUST	MANTLE	OUTER CORE	INNER CORE	

3,955 miles (6,370 km)

3,1000 miles (5,000 km)

1,850 miles (3,000 km)

Sea level

TEMPERATURE AND DEPTH
Our planet is a nuclear-powered furnace, heated from within by the breakdown of radioactive minerals such as uranium. Temperature increases with depth: 60 miles (100 km) down it is 2,460°F (1,350°C), hot enough for rocks to melt.

Magma rising along center of ridge

Ocean

Magma from molten mantle

Solid mantle

SPREADING PLATES
When two plates move apart, molten rock (magma) rises from the mantle and cools, forming new crust. This is called a constructive margin. Most are found in oceans.

Deep ocean trench opens where plate dives

Mountain

Volcano

Oceanic plate dives into mantle

COLLIDING PLATES THAT DIVE
When two ocean plates or an ocean plate and a continent plate collide, the denser plate is forced under the other, diving down into the mantle. These are destructive margins.

Valley   Mountain

Continent A

Continent B

Line of collision

Continental crust crumples

COLLIDING PLATES THAT BUCKLE
When two continents collide, their plates fuse, crumple, and push upward. Mountain ranges like the Himalayas and the Urals have been formed in this way.

Fault

Plate

Plate

SLIDING PLATES
When two plates slide past one another, intense friction is created along the "fault line" between them, causing earthquakes. These are called conservative margins.

ICELAND, MID-ATLANTIC RIDGE
Most constructive margins are found beneath oceans, but here in volcanic Iceland one comes to the surface.

VOLCANO, JAVA
Diving plates often build volcanic islands and mountain chains. Deep ocean trenches form offshore.

FOLDING STRATA, ENGLAND
The clash of continental plates may cause the Earth to buckle and twist far from the collision zone.

SAN ANDREAS FAULT
A huge earthquake may one day occur somewhere along California's San Andreas Fault, seen here.

EXPLOSIVE VOLCANO
About 50 of the world's 600 or so active volcanoes erupt each year. Explosive pressure is created by the buildup of magma, gases, or superheated steam.

Crater

Cloud of ash, gases, and steam

Lava flows

Main vent (opening)

Cone of ash and lava from old eruptions

SOME MAJOR QUAKES AND ERUPTIONS
This map shows some of the worst natural disasters in recorded history. Over one million earthquakes and about 50 volcanic eruptions are detected every year. Most are minor or occur where there are few people, so there is no loss of human life or great damage to property. But crowded cities and poorly-constructed buildings are putting ever-greater numbers at risk.

Direction of ocean plate movement

HOT SPOT, HAWAII
Hawaii is on a "hot spot" in the Earth's crust. This is a plume of hot magma that rises from the mantle and breaks through the thin ocean crust to feed a volcano. As the crust moves, the volcano is carried away, but the hot spot stays, forming a new volcano.

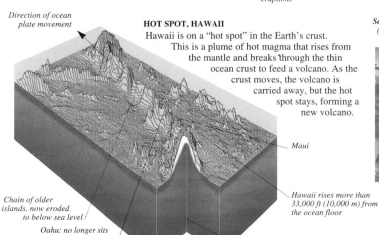

Chain of older islands, now eroded to below sea level

Oahu: no longer sits over the hot spot. No volcanic eruptions for over 2 million years

Maui

Hawaii rises more than 33,000 ft (10,000 m) from the ocean floor

Hot spot

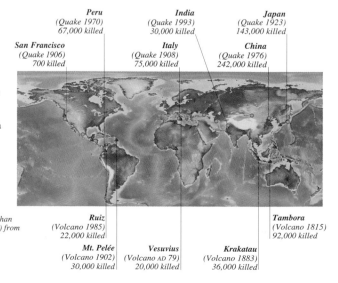

Peru
(Quake 1970)
67,000 killed

India
(Quake 1993)
30,000 killed

Japan
(Quake 1923)
143,000 killed

San Francisco
(Quake 1906)
700 killed

Italy
(Quake 1908)
75,000 killed

China
(Quake 1976)
242,000 killed

Ruiz
(Volcano 1985)
22,000 killed

Tambora
(Volcano 1815)
92,000 killed

Mt. Pelée
(Volcano 1902)
30,000 killed

Vesuvius
(Volcano AD 79)
20,000 killed

Krakatau
(Volcano 1883)
36,000 killed

SHAPING THE LANDSCAPE

LANDSCAPES ARE CREATED AND CHANGED – even destroyed – in a continuous cycle. Over millions of years, constant movements of the Earth's plates have built up continents, islands, and mountains. But as soon as new land is formed, it is shaped (or "eroded") by the forces of wind, water, ice, and heat. Sometimes change is quick, as when a river floods and cuts a new channel, or a landslide cascades down a mountain slope. Usually, however, change is so slow that it is invisible to the human eye. Extremes of heat and cold crack open rocks and expose them to attack by wind and water. Rivers and glaciers scour out valleys, the wind piles up sand dunes, and the sea attacks shorelines and cliffs. Eroded materials are blown away or carried along by rivers, piling up as sediments on valley floors or the seabed. Over millions of years, these may be compressed into rock and pushed up to form new land. As soon as the land is exposed to the elements, the cycle of erosion begins again.

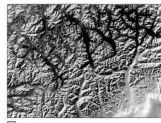

ICE ACTION, ALASKA
Areas close to the North Pole are permanently covered in snow and ice. Glaciers are rivers of ice that flow toward the sea. Some glaciers are more than 40 miles (60 km) long.

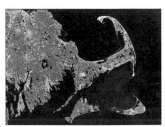

SEA ACTION, CAPE COD
Cape Cod, a sandy peninsula 65 miles (105 km) long, juts out like a beckoning finger into the Atlantic Ocean. Its strangely curved coastline has been shaped by wave action.

KEYBOX

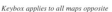

Area covered in ice today	Area drained by major river
Ice and snow 18,000 years ago	Protected coastline
Desert	Coast affected by tidal swell
Wind direction (simplified)	Coast affected by storm waves

Keybox applies to all maps opposite

THE "ROOF OF NORTH AMERICA"
Steeply sloping Denali (also called Mt. McKinley), Alaska, is North America's highest mountain at 20,320 ft (6,194 m). It is a fairly "young" mountain, less than 70 million years old. The gently sloping Appalachians in eastern North America are much older. Once, they were probably higher than Denali is today. But more than 300 million years of ice, rain, and wind have ground them down.

WIND ACTION, DEATH VALLEY
Death Valley is the hottest, driest place in North America. Its floor is covered in sand and salt. Winds sweeping across the valley endlessly reshape the loose surface.

THIS SECTION OF THE GLOBE SHOWS NORTH AMERICA AND THE DIFFERENT FORCES WORKING ON ITS LANDSCAPE. THE LANDSCAPE IN EVERY PART OF THE WORLD IS CHANGED BY THE ACTION OF ICE, RUNNING WATER, SEA WAVES, AND WIND.

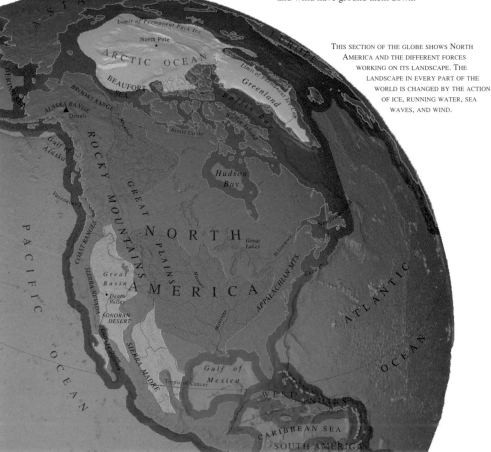

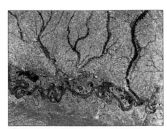

WATER ACTION, MISSISSIPPI
The Mississippi River and its many tributaries frequently change course. Where two loops are close together, the river may cut a new path between them, leaving an "oxbow lake."

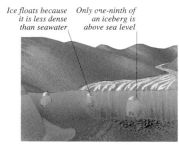

Ice floats because it is less dense than seawater

Only one-ninth of an iceberg is above sea level

A GLACIER REACHES THE SEA
When a glacier enters the sea, its front edge, or "snout," breaks up and forms icebergs – a process called calving. These "ice mountains" are then carried away by ocean currents.

ICE COVER *See keybox opposite*

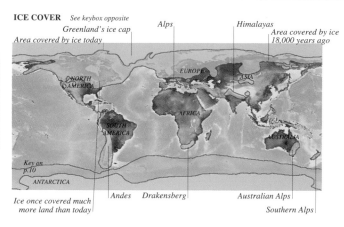

Greenland's ice cap *Alps* *Himalayas*
Area covered by ice today *Area covered by ice 18,000 years ago*

NORTH AMERICA   EUROPE   ASIA
AFRICA
SOUTH AMERICA
AUSTRALIA

Key on p.10
ANTARCTICA

Ice once covered much more land than today *Andes* *Drakensberg* *Australian Alps* *Southern Alps*

NORDFJORD, NORWAY
One sign of glacial action on the landscape is the fjord. These long, narrow, steep-sided inlets are found along the coasts of Norway, Alaska, Chile, and New Zealand. They mark the points where glaciers once entered the sea.

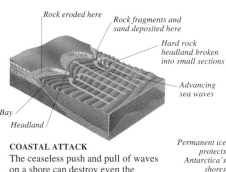

Rock eroded here *Rock fragments and sand deposited here*
Hard rock headland broken into small sections
Advancing sea waves
Bay
Headland

COASTAL ATTACK
The ceaseless push and pull of waves on a shore can destroy even the hardest rocks. The softest rocks are eroded first, leaving headlands of hard rock that survive a little longer.

COASTAL EROSION *See keybox opposite* *Northwest Europe's shorelines are heavily eroded by Atlantic storms*

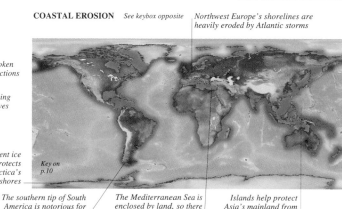

Permanent ice protects Antarctica's shores
Key on p.10
The southern tip of South America is notorious for its devastating storms *The Mediterranean Sea is enclosed by land, so there is little coastal erosion* *Islands help protect Asia's mainland from advancing waves*

WAVE POWER
The powerful action of waves on an exposed coast can erode a coastline by several feet a year.

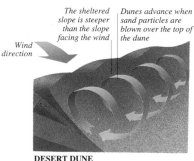

The sheltered slope is steeper than the slope facing the wind *Dunes advance when sand particles are blown over the top of the dune*
Wind direction

DESERT DUNE
Dunes are slow-moving mounds or ridges of sand found in deserts and along some coastlines. They form only when the wind's direction and speed is fairly constant.

THE GREAT DESERTS *See keybox opposite* *Kara Kum*
Great Basin *Sahara* *Arabian* *Takla Makan*

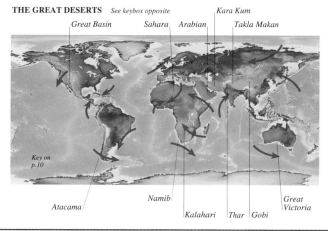

Key on p.10
Atacama *Namib* *Great Victoria*
Kalahari *Thar* *Gobi*

NAMIB DESERT, SOUTHERN AFRICA
The sand dunes seen in the center of the picture are about 160 ft (50 m) high. Winds are driving them slowly but relentlessly toward the right. Not all deserts are sandy. Wind may blow away all the loose sand and gravel, leaving bare rock.

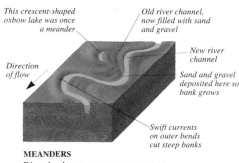

This crescent-shaped oxbow lake was once a meander *Old river channel, now filled with sand and gravel*
New river channel
Direction of flow
Sand and gravel deposited here so bank grows
Swift currents on outer bends cut steep banks

MEANDERS
River banks are worn away most on the outside of bends, where water flows fastest. Eroded sand and gravel are built up into banks on the inside of bends in slower-moving water.

THE LARGEST RIVER BASINS *See keybox opposite* *Lena* *Amur*
Mackenzie *Mississippi* *Ob'* *Yenisey*

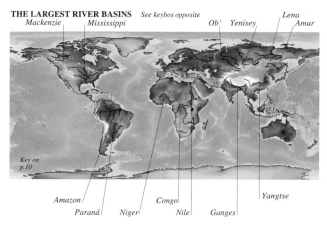

Key on p.10
Amazon *Congo* *Yangtse*
Paraná *Niger* *Nile* *Ganges*

WINDING RIVER, ALASKA
The more a river meanders across a plain, the longer it becomes and the more slowly it flows.

CLIMATE AND VEGETATION

THE EARTH IS the only planet in our solar system which supports life. Most of our planet has a breathable atmosphere and sufficient light, heat, and water to support a wide range of plants and animals. The main influences on an area's climate are the amount of sunshine it receives (which varies with latitude and season), how close it is to the influence of ocean currents, and its height above sea level. Since there is more sunlight at the Equator than elsewhere, and rainfall is highest here, too, this is where we find the habitats which have more species of plants and animals than anywhere else: rain forests, coral reefs, and mangrove swamps. Where rainfall is very low, and where it is either too hot, such as in deserts, or too cold, few plants and animals can survive. Only the icy North and South Poles and the frozen tops of high mountains are practically without life of any sort.

WEATHER EXTREMES
Weather is a powerful influence on how we feel, the clothes we wear, the buildings we live in, the plants that grow around us, and what we eat and drink. Extreme weather events – heat waves, hurricanes, blizzards, tornadoes, sandstorms, droughts, and floods – can be terrifyingly destructive.

TORNADO
Tornadoes are whirlwinds of cold air that develop when thunderclouds cross warm land. They are extremely violent and unpredictable. Windspeeds often exceed 180 miles (300 km) per hour.

TROPICAL STORMS
These devastating winds develop when air spirals upward above warm seas. More air is sucked in and the storm begins to move. They bring torrential rain, thunder and lightning, and destruction.

DROUGHT
Long periods without water kill plants. Stripped of its protective covering of vegetation, the soil is easily blown away.

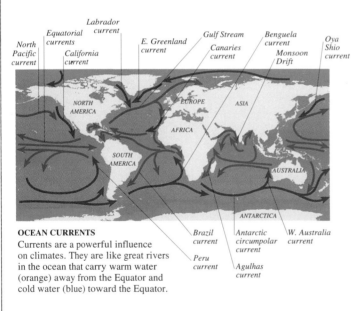

OCEAN CURRENTS
Currents are a powerful influence on climates. They are like great rivers in the ocean that carry warm water (orange) away from the Equator and cold water (blue) toward the Equator.

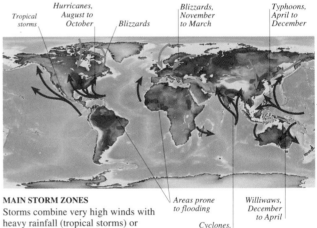

MAIN STORM ZONES
Storms combine very high winds with heavy rainfall (tropical storms) or driving snow (blizzards). Typhoons, cyclones, hurricanes, and williwaws are regional names for tropical storms.

TEMPERATURE
Average temperatures vary widely around the world. Areas close to the Equator are usually hot (orange on the map); those close to the Poles are usually cold (deep blue). The hottest areas move during the year from the Southern to the Northern hemispheres.

Average January temperature

Average July temperature

Arctic Circle

Tropic of Cancer

Equator

Tropic of Capricorn

Antarctic Circle

Highest: (136°F), 58°C Saharan Libya

Lowest: -129°F (-89°C), Antarctica

Average January rainfall

Average July rainfall

RAINFALL
The wettest areas (gray) lie near the Equator. The driest are found close to the tropics, in the center of continents, or at the poles. Elsewhere, rainfall varies with the season, but it is usually highest in summer. Asia's wet season is known as the monsoon.

Arctic Circle

Tropic of Cancer

Equator

Tropic of Capricorn

Antarctic Circle

Highest in 1 year: 460 in (11.68 m), Hawaii

Lowest: No rain in more than 14 years, Atacama

BROADLEAF FOREST

Temperate climates have no great temperature extremes, and drought is unusual. Forests usually contain deciduous (broadleaved) trees, such as beeches or oaks, that shed their leaves in autumn.

TUNDRA

As long as frozen soil melts for at least two months of the year, some mosses, lichens, and ground-hugging shrubs can survive. They are found around the Arctic Circle and on mountains.

NEEDLELEAF FOREST

Forests of coniferous (needleleaf) trees, such as pines and firs, cover much of northern North America, Europe, and Asia. They are evergreen and can survive long frozen winters. Most have tall, straight trunks and down-pointing branches. This reduces the amount of snow that can settle on them. The forest floor is dark because leaves absorb most of the incoming sunlight.

TRAVELING SOUTHWARD FROM THE NORTH POLE, A NUMBER OF DISTINCT LIFE ZONES OR "BIOMES" CAN BE SEEN. PLANT AND ANIMAL LIFE IS CLOSELY ADAPTED TO LOCAL CLIMATE.

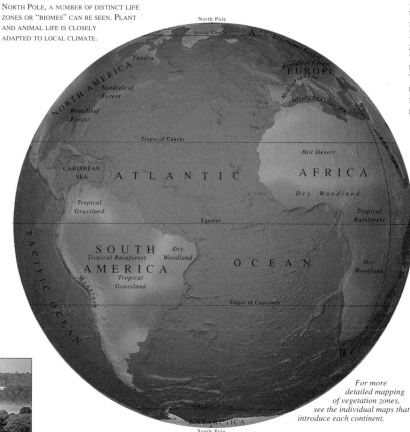

MEDITERRANEAN

The hot dry summers and warm wet winters typical of the Mediterranean region are also found in small areas of Southern Africa, the Americas, and Australia. Mediterranean-type vegetation can vary from dense forest to thinly spread evergreen shrubs like these.

MOUNTAIN

Vegetation changes with height because the temperature drops and wind increases. Even on the Equator, mountain peaks can be covered in snow. Although trees may cloak the lower slopes, at higher altitudes they give way to sparser vegetation. Near the top, only tundra-type plants can survive.

For more detailed mapping of vegetation zones, see the individual maps that introduce each continent.

TROPICAL RAIN FOREST

The lush forests found near the Equator depend on year-round high temperatures and heavy rainfall. Worldwide, they may contain 50,000 different kinds of trees, and support several million other plant and animal species. Trees are often festooned with climbing plants, or covered with ferns and orchids that have rooted in pockets of water and soil on trunks and branches.

DRY WOODLAND

Plants in many parts of the tropics have to cope with high temperatures and long periods without rain. Some store water in enlarged stems or trunks, or limit water losses by having small, spiny leaves. In dry (but not desert) conditions, trees are widely spaced, with expanses of grassland between, called savannah.

HOT DESERT

Very few plants and animals can survive in hot deserts. Rainfall is low – under 4 in (10 cm) a year. Temperatures often rise above 104 °F (40°C) during the day, but drop to the freezing point at night. High winds and shifting sands can be a further hazard to life. Only specially adapted plants, such as cacti, can survive.

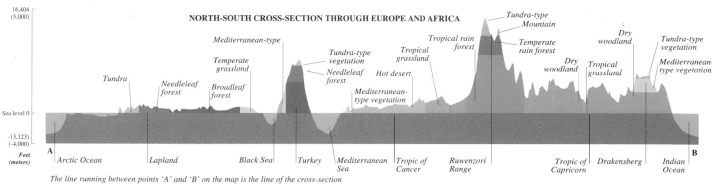

NORTH-SOUTH CROSS-SECTION THROUGH EUROPE AND AFRICA

The line running between points 'A' and 'B' on the map is the line of the cross-section

PEOPLE AND PLANET

SOON, THERE WILL BE 6 billion people on Earth, and numbers are rising at the rate of about 1 million every week. The Earth's population is not distributed evenly. Some areas, such as parts of Europe, India, and China, are very densely populated. Other areas – particularly deserts, polar regions, and mountains – can support very few people. Almost half of the world's people now live in towns or cities. Until 1800, most people lived in small villages in the countryside and worked on the land. But since then, more and more people have lived and worked in much larger communities. A century ago, most of the world's largest cities were in Europe and North America, where new industries and businesses were flourishing. Today, the most rapidly growing cities are in Asia, South America, and Africa. People who move to these cities are usually young adults, so the birth rate among these new populations is very high.

A CROWDED PLANET?
If the 5.5 billion people alive today stood close together, they could all fit into an area no larger than the small Caribbean island of Jamaica. Of course, so many people could not live in such a small place. Areas with few people are usually very cold, such as land near the poles and in mountains, or very dry, such as deserts. Areas with large populations often have fertile land and a good climate for crops. Cities can support huge populations because they are wealthy enough to import everything they need.

THERE ARE JUST OVER 400 MILLION PEOPLE IN NORTH AMERICA. NEARLY 7 IN 10 LIVE IN A CITY (METROPOLITAN AREA).

NORTH AMERICA

New York 14.6 million

Los Angeles 10.1 million

Mexico City 20.9 million

JAMAICA

Rio de Janeiro 11.7 million

SOUTH AMERICA

São Paulo 18.7 million

Buenos Aires 11.7 million

THERE ARE ABOUT 300 MILLION PEOPLE IN SOUTH AMERICA. MORE THAN 7 IN 10 LIVE IN A CITY.

KEYBOX

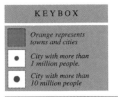

Orange represents towns and cities

● *City with more than 1 million people.*

● *City with more than 10 million people*

London

MILLIONAIRE CITIES 1900
Less than a century ago there were only 13 cities with more than 1 million people living in them. All the cities were in the Northern hemisphere. The largest was London, with 7 million people.

New York

MILLIONAIRE CITIES 1950
By 1950, there were nearly 70 cities with more than one million inhabitants. The largest was New York City.

WORLD POPULATION GROWTH 1500–2020
Each figure on the graph represents 500 million people.

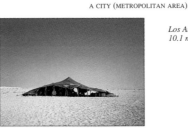

SAHARA, AFRICA
The Sahara, like all deserts, is thinly populated. The Tuareg of the northern Sahara are nomads. They travel in small groups because food sources are scarce. Their homes have to be portable.

AMAZONIA, SOUTH AMERICA
The Yanomami people gather plants in the rain forest and hunt game, but they also grow crops in small forest gardens. Several families live together in a "village" under one huge roof.

MONGOLIA, ASIA
Traditionally, Mongolia's nomadic people lived by herding their animals across the steppe. Today, their felt tents, or *gers*, are often set up next to more permanent houses.

MALI, AFRICA
The Dogon people of Mali use mud to construct their elaborate villages. Every family has its own huts and walled areas in which their animals are penned for the night.

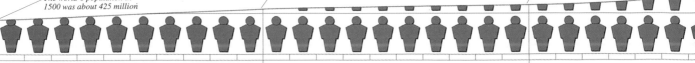

The world's population in 1500 was about 425 million

The world's population in 1600 was about 545 million

The world's population in 1700 was about 610 million.

1500   *1600*   *1700*

POOR SUBURB
Densely-populated "shantytowns" have grown on the fringes of many cities in the developing world. Houses are usually built from discarded materials.

RICH SUBURB
Cities are often surrounded by areas where the richest people live. Population densities are low, and the houses may be luxurious, with large gardens or swimming pools. People in these suburbs rely on their cars for transportation. This allows them to live a great distance from places of work and leisure in the city center.

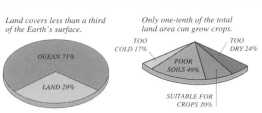

Land covers less than a third of the Earth's surface.

OCEAN 71%

LAND 29%

Only one-tenth of the total land area can grow crops.

TOO COLD 17%
TOO DRY 24%
POOR SOILS 49%
SUITABLE FOR CROPS 10%

CULTIVATION
Only a small portion of the Earth's surface can grow crops. It may be possible to bring more land – such as deserts – into production, but yields may be costly.

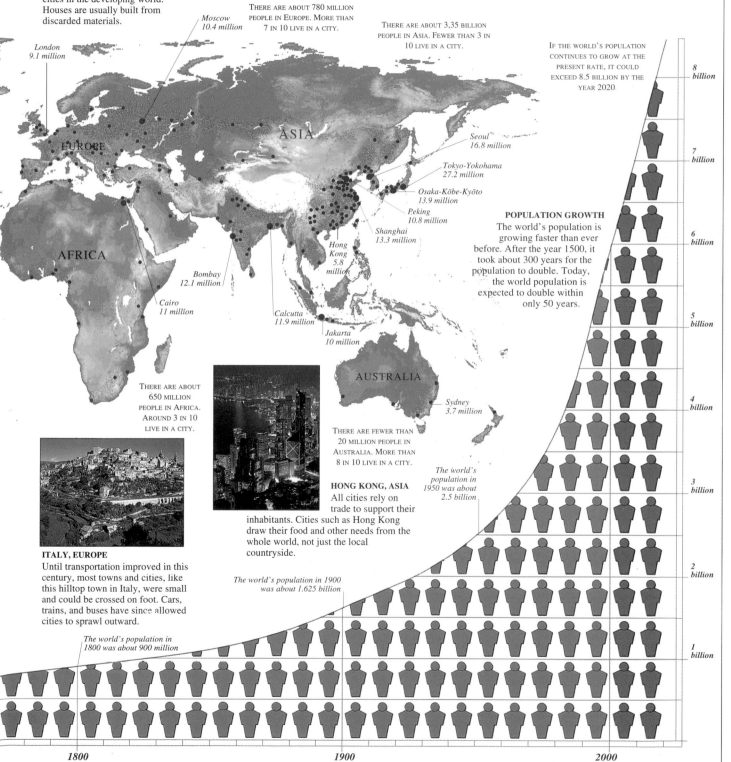

Moscow 10.4 million

THERE ARE ABOUT 780 MILLION PEOPLE IN EUROPE. MORE THAN 7 IN 10 LIVE IN A CITY.

THERE ARE ABOUT 3,35 BILLION PEOPLE IN ASIA. FEWER THAN 3 IN 10 LIVE IN A CITY.

London 9.1 million

EUROPE

ASIA

Seoul 16.8 million

Tokyo-Yokohama 27.2 million

Osaka-Kōbe-Kyōto 13.9 million

Peking 10.8 million

Shanghai 13.3 million

AFRICA

Hong Kong 5.8 million

Bombay 12.1 million

Cairo 11 million

Calcutta 11.9 million

Jakarta 10 million

AUSTRALIA

THERE ARE ABOUT 650 MILLION PEOPLE IN AFRICA. AROUND 3 IN 10 LIVE IN A CITY.

Sydney 3.7 million

THERE ARE FEWER THAN 20 MILLION PEOPLE IN AUSTRALIA. MORE THAN 8 IN 10 LIVE IN A CITY.

HONG KONG, ASIA
All cities rely on trade to support their inhabitants. Cities such as Hong Kong draw their food and other needs from the whole world, not just the local countryside.

ITALY, EUROPE
Until transportation improved in this century, most towns and cities, like this hilltop town in Italy, were small and could be crossed on foot. Cars, trains, and buses have since allowed cities to sprawl outward.

IF THE WORLD'S POPULATION CONTINUES TO GROW AT THE PRESENT RATE, IT COULD EXCEED 8.5 BILLION BY THE YEAR 2020.

8 billion
7 billion
6 billion
5 billion
4 billion
3 billion
2 billion
1 billion

POPULATION GROWTH
The world's population is growing faster than ever before. After the year 1500, it took about 300 years for the population to double. Today, the world population is expected to double within only 50 years.

The world's population in 1950 was about 2.5 billion

The world's population in 1900 was about 1.625 billion

The world's population in 1800 was about 900 million

1800
1900
2000

THE WORLD TODAY

THERE ARE 192 INDEPENDENT countries in the world today. With the exception of Antarctica, every land area of the Earth's surface belongs to, or is claimed by, one country or another. In 1950, there were only 82 countries. Since then, many former colonies of the European countries have gained independence. The final stage in this process was the breakup of the Soviet Union after 1990. The world's nations vary enormously in size and shape. The largest country in the world is the Russian Federation; the smallest is Vatican City.

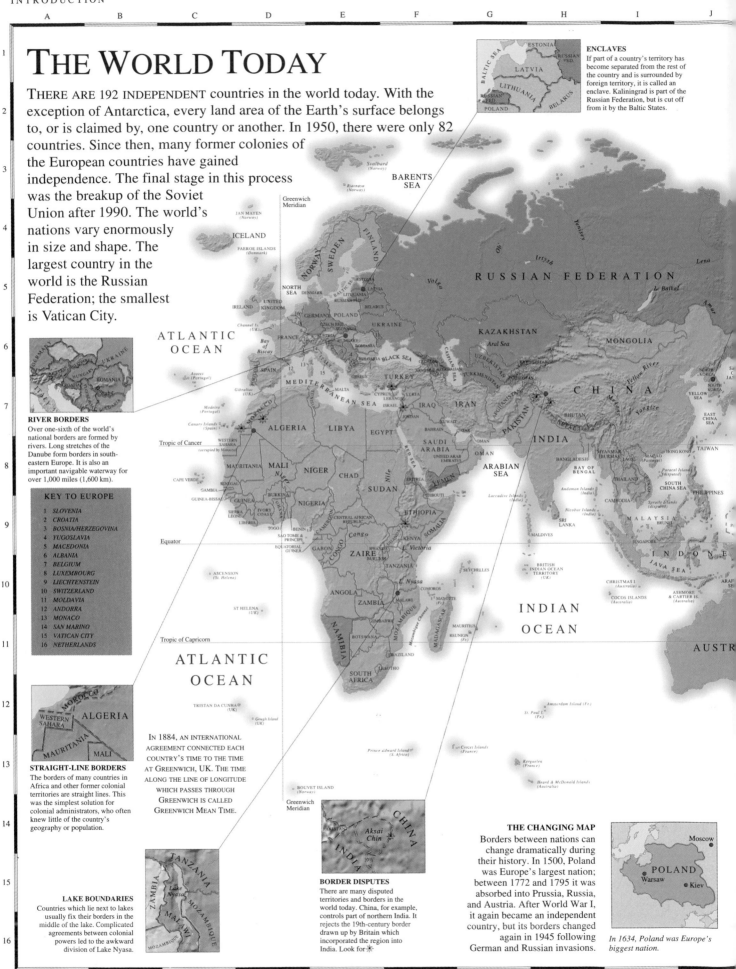

ENCLAVES
If part of a country's territory has become separated from the rest of the country and is surrounded by foreign territory, it is called an enclave. Kaliningrad is part of the Russian Federation, but is cut off from it by the Baltic States.

RIVER BORDERS
Over one-sixth of the world's national borders are formed by rivers. Long stretches of the Danube form borders in south-eastern Europe. It is also an important navigable waterway for over 1,000 miles (1,600 km).

KEY TO EUROPE
1 SLOVENIA
2 CROATIA
3 BOSNIA/HERZEGOVINA
4 YUGOSLAVIA
5 MACEDONIA
6 ALBANIA
7 BELGIUM
8 LUXEMBOURG
9 LIECHTENSTEIN
10 SWITZERLAND
11 MOLDAVIA
12 ANDORRA
13 MONACO
14 SAN MARINO
15 VATICAN CITY
16 NETHERLANDS

STRAIGHT-LINE BORDERS
The borders of many countries in Africa and other former colonial territories are straight lines. This was the simplest solution for colonial administrators, who often knew little of the country's geography or population.

IN 1884, AN INTERNATIONAL AGREEMENT CONNECTED EACH COUNTRY'S TIME TO THE TIME AT GREENWICH, UK. THE TIME ALONG THE LINE OF LONGITUDE WHICH PASSES THROUGH GREENWICH IS CALLED GREENWICH MEAN TIME.

LAKE BOUNDARIES
Countries which lie next to lakes usually fix their borders in the middle of the lake. Complicated agreements between colonial powers led to the awkward division of Lake Nyasa.

BORDER DISPUTES
There are many disputed territories and borders in the world today. China, for example, controls part of northern India. It rejects the 19th-century border drawn up by Britain which incorporated the region into India. Look for ✳.

THE CHANGING MAP
Borders between nations can change dramatically during their history. In 1500, Poland was Europe's largest nation; between 1772 and 1795 it was absorbed into Prussia, Russia, and Austria. After World War I, it again became an independent country, but its borders changed again in 1945 following German and Russian invasions.

In 1634, Poland was Europe's biggest nation.

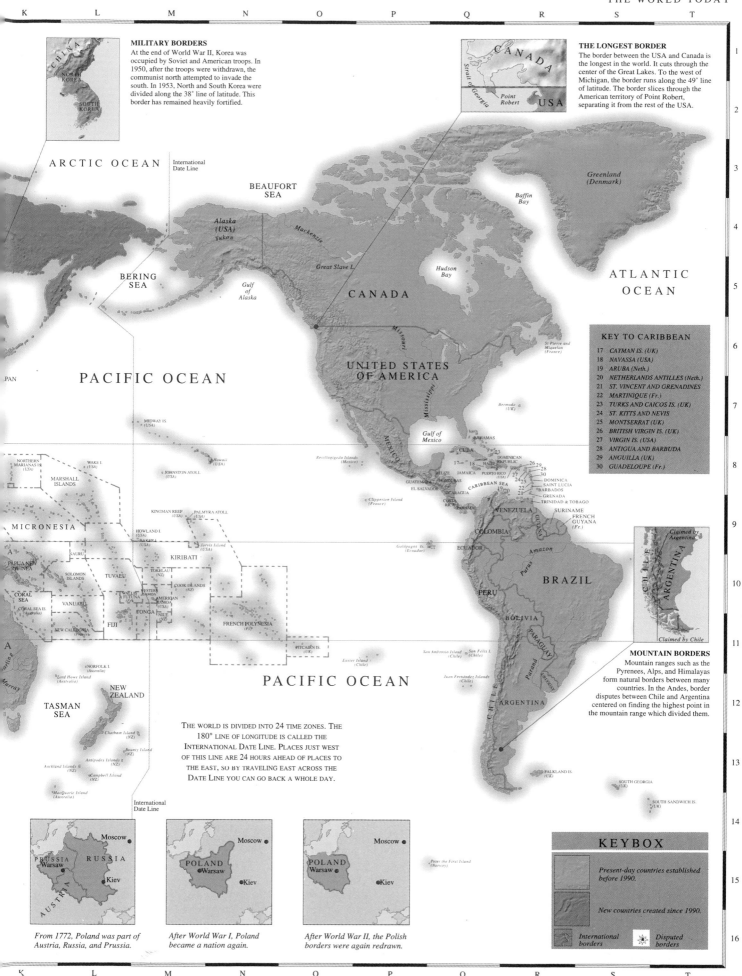

MILITARY BORDERS
At the end of World War II, Korea was occupied by Soviet and American troops. In 1950, after the troops were withdrawn, the communist north attempted to invade the south. In 1953, North and South Korea were divided along the 38° line of latitude. This border has remained heavily fortified.

THE LONGEST BORDER
The border between the USA and Canada is the longest in the world. It cuts through the center of the Great Lakes. To the west of Michigan, the border runs along the 49° line of latitude. The border slices through the American territory of Point Robert, separating it from the rest of the USA.

CANADA
Strait of Georgia
Point Robert
USA

ARCTIC OCEAN

International Date Line

BEAUFORT SEA

Alaska (USA) Yukon

Mackenzie

Great Slave L.

Greenland (Denmark)

Baffin Bay

Hudson Bay

CANADA

BERING SEA

Gulf of Alaska

ATLANTIC OCEAN

PACIFIC OCEAN

Missouri

UNITED STATES OF AMERICA

St-Pierre and Miquelon (France)

KEY TO CARIBBEAN

17 CAYMAN IS. (UK)
18 NAVASSA (USA)
19 ARUBA (Neth.)
20 NETHERLANDS ANTILLES (Neth.)
21 ST. VINCENT AND GRENADINES
22 MARTINIQUE (Fr.)
23 TURKS AND CAICOS IS. (UK)
24 ST. KITTS AND NEVIS
25 MONTSERRAT (UK)
26 BRITISH VIRGIN IS. (UK)
27 VIRGIN IS. (USA)
28 ANTIGUA AND BARBUDA
29 ANGUILLA (UK)
30 GUADELOUPE (Fr.)

Mississippi

Bermuda (UK)

Gulf of Mexico

MEXICO

BAHAMAS

CUBA

JAPAN

MIDWAY IS. (USA)

Hawaii (USA)

Revillagigedo Islands (Mexico)

BELIZE JAMAICA
GUATEMALA HONDURAS
EL SALVADOR
NICARAGUA
CARIBBEAN SEA
COSTA RICA PANAMA

DOMINICAN REPUBLIC
HAITI PUERTO RICO (USA)
DOMINICA
SAINT LUCIA
BARBADOS
GRENADA
TRINIDAD & TOBAGO

NORTHERN MARIANAS IS. (USA)

WAKE I. (USA)

JOHNSTON ATOLL (USA)

MARSHALL ISLANDS

Clipperton Island (France)

VENEZUELA
SURINAME
FRENCH GUYANA (Fr.)

KINGMAN REEF (USA) PALMYRA ATOLL (USA)

MICRONESIA

HOWLAND I. (USA)
BAKER I. (USA)

Jarvis Island (USA)

COLOMBIA

Galápagos Is. (Ecuador)

Amazon

ECUADOR

Purus

BRAZIL

NAURU

PAPUA NEW GUINEA

SOLOMON ISLANDS

TUVALU

KIRIBATI

TOKELAU (NZ)

WALLIS & FUTUNA (Fr.)

WESTERN SAMOA

AMERICAN SAMOA (USA)

COOK ISLANDS (NZ)

PERU

Claimed by Argentina

ARGENTINA

CHILE

Claimed by Chile

CORAL SEA

CORAL SEA IS. (Australia)

VANUATU

TONGA

NIUE (NZ)

FIJI

NEW CALEDONIA (France)

FRENCH POLYNESIA (Fr.)

BOLIVIA

PARAGUAY

Paraná

Uruguay

MOUNTAIN BORDERS
Mountain ranges such as the Pyrenees, Alps, and Himalayas form natural borders between many countries. In the Andes, border disputes between Chile and Argentina centered on finding the highest point in the mountain range which divided them.

PITCAIRN IS. (UK)

Easter Island (Chile)

San Ambrosio Island (Chile) San Félix I. (Chile)

PACIFIC OCEAN

Juan Fernández Islands (Chile)

NORFOLK I. (Australia)

Lord Howe Island (Australia)

Murray

NEW ZEALAND

TASMAN SEA

Chatham Island (NZ)

Bounty Island (NZ)

Antipodes Islands (NZ)

Auckland Islands (NZ)

Campbell Island (NZ)

Macquarie Island (Australia)

CHILE

ARGENTINA

THE WORLD IS DIVIDED INTO 24 TIME ZONES. THE 180° LINE OF LONGITUDE IS CALLED THE INTERNATIONAL DATE LINE. PLACES JUST WEST OF THIS LINE ARE 24 HOURS AHEAD OF PLACES TO THE EAST, SO BY TRAVELING EAST ACROSS THE DATE LINE YOU CAN GO BACK A WHOLE DAY.

International Date Line

FALKLAND IS. (UK)

Peter the First Island (Norway)

SOUTH GEORGIA (UK)

SOUTH SANDWICH IS. (UK)

KEYBOX

Present-day countries established before 1990.

New countries created since 1990.

International borders

Disputed borders

Moscow
PRUSSIA
RUSSIA
Warsaw
Kiev
AUSTRIA

Moscow
POLAND
Warsaw
Kiev

Moscow
POLAND
Warsaw
Kiev

From 1772, Poland was part of Austria, Russia, and Prussia.

After World War I, Poland became a nation again.

After World War II, the Polish borders were again redrawn.

HOW TO USE THIS ATLAS

THE MAPS IN THIS ATLAS are organized by continent: North America; Central and South America; Europe; Africa; North and West Asia; South and East Asia; Oceania. Each section of the book opens with a large double-page spread introducing you to the physical geography – landscapes, climate, animals, and vegetation – of the continent. On the following pages, the continent is divided by country or group of countries. These pages deal with the human geography; each detailed map is supplemented by photographs, illustrations, and landscape models. Finally, a glossary defines difficult terms used in the text, and the index provides a list of all place names in the Atlas and facts about each country.

CONTINENT SPREAD

Key to symbols: *This keybox lists major physical features which appear on the continental maps*

Key to natural vegetation: *The world is broken up into areas which are defined by the plants and animals which live there*

Locator map: *This world map shows where the continent is located*

Image key: *This natural vegetation color and symbol box locates the type of landscape on the map to which the photograph refers*

! Threatened species: *This symbol indicates that the future of certain plants and animals is uncertain*

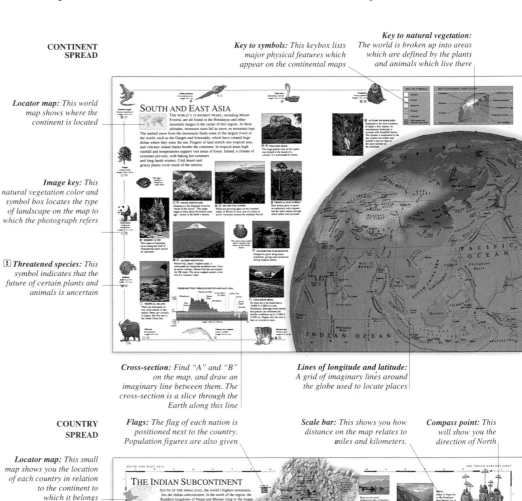

Cross-section: *Find "A" and "B" on the map, and draw an imaginary line between them. The cross-section is a slice through the Earth along this line*

Lines of longitude and latitude: *A grid of imaginary lines around the globe used to locate places*

COUNTRY SPREAD

Locator map: *This small map shows you the location of each country in relation to the continent to which it belongs*

Reference grid: *The letters and numbers around this grid help you to locate places listed in the index. For an explanation on how to use the grid, see Index, page 137*

Keybox: *A keybox on each spread lists the symbols which appear on the map. These symbols have been chosen to illustrate particularly important or interesting aspects of the country*

Flags: *The flag of each nation is positioned next to the country. Population figures are also given*

Scale bar: *This shows you how distance on the map relates to miles and kilometers.*

Compass point: *This will show you the direction of North*

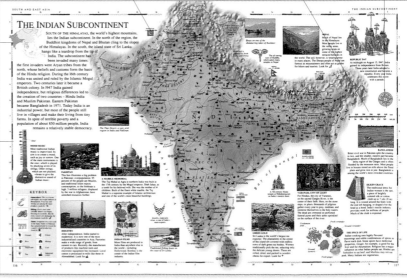

HOW THIS ATLAS WAS MADE

MAKING UP-TO-DATE and accurate maps of the world is a complicated process which draws upon the skills of geographers, researchers, cartographers (or map-makers), and designers. The maps in *The Eyewitness Atlas of the World* are completely new. They have been created using the latest computerized techniques. At the heart of this process was the development of a computerized model of the Earth. Computers store vast amounts of information. Cartographers used this technology to create precise maps, which may be regarded as the most accurate representation of the Earth's surface achieved in atlas form.

MAPS AND PROJECTIONS

Mapmakers have a problem: the Earth is round, but a map is flat. In order to represent a curved surface on a flat page, the image of the Earth's surface needs to be stretched and distorted. The mathematical way of achieving this is by using a projection. There are three main types of projection used in this atlas.

CYLINDRICAL PROJECTION

This is most commonly used to make maps of the whole world. The image is rolled out to form a rectangular shape. The image becomes distorted as it moves away from the Equator toward the poles.

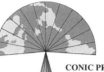

CONIC PROJECTION

This is useful for making regional maps and is most often used in this atlas. Distortion occurs as lines converge as they move away from the center of the map.

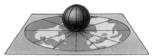

ORTHOGRAPHIC PROJECTION

This kind of projection is useful for mapping polar regions. The image appears as though you were looking at the Earth from Space. Distortion increases as you move away from the center of the map.

THE EARTH MODEL

To create a faithful representation of the Earth's relief – the shape of coastlines, mountains, valleys, and plains – an enormous model of the Earth (called a "terrain model") was constructed using a computer. This was achieved by combining and processing various sets of data. Then other features, such as roads, railroads, place names, and colored vegetation areas, were added to complete each map.

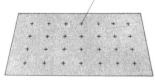

Points on the grid represent height values

HEIGHT DATA

A grid was created which covers the whole of the Earth's surface. Each point on the grid has an accurate height value. The grid was fed into the computer to form the basic framework for the terrain model.

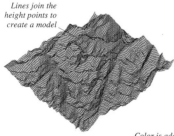

Data record the height of individual hills and mountains

LARGE SCALE MAPS

For large-scale maps, this basic framework was combined with a data set of land heights, which record the height of the summit of every hill and mountain. This produced a much more detailed framework for the terrain model.

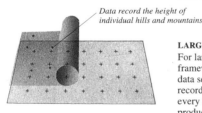

Lines join the height points to create a model

PRODUCING THE TERRAIN MODEL

The computer then transformed these elevation points into a basic terrain model known as a wire-frame model. The computer does this by joining the individual height points with lines, creating a realistic image of the Earth's surface.

Color is added to the wire-frame model

THEMATIC MODELS

Models such as these appear on various pages throughout the Atlas. By adding various layers of extra information and annotations, they are a useful diagrammatic way of showing how the landscape of a particular region works.

Artificial light source, imitating the action of the Sun

A SMOOTH SURFACE

To create the main maps, the computer processed these models even further. First, a smooth surface to the model was created (a process known as interpolation). An artificial light source within the computer was then used to create the effect of hill-shading. This light source imitates the action of the Sun, casting highlights and shadows across the landscape. The coastline was then added to the map.

The terrain model after interpolation

COLORING THE MAP

The coloring of the maps in this atlas gives an impression of vegetation and land use. Using both satellite imagery and ground survey information, a color base map was made by our cartographers. It was then scanned into the computer, where it was projected over the hill-shaded model of the landscape to form the fully colored base map.

Color is projected over the terrain model within the computer

THE COMPLETE MAP

Finally, the remaining map information – rivers, roads, railroads, borders, place names, and other symbols – were carefully compiled from the most up-to-date sources. These were traced into the computer and combined with the colored landscape image to create the finished map.

Roads and railroads are added to the colored terrain model

Raccoon
Procyon lotor
Length: 26 in (66 cm)

NORTH AMERICA

NORTH AMERICA LOOKS LIKE a gigantic downward-pointing triangle out of which two bites have been taken – Hudson Bay and the Gulf of Mexico. Huge parallel mountain chains run down the eastern and western sides. The oldest are the Appalachians to the east, which have been worn away by wind and rain for so long that they are now considerably lower than the younger Rockies to the west. The vast landscape between the mountain chains is mostly flat. There are large forests in the north, while the central Great Plains are covered by grasslands on which huge herds of buffalo once roamed. North America is a continent of climatic extremes. In the farthest north, temperatures drop to a freezing -87°F (-66°C), and a dome of ice up to 2 miles (3 km) thick covers Greenland. In the hot deserts of the southwest, temperatures can soar to 134°F (57°C).

Triceratops, a vegetarian dinosaur that lived in western North America 70 million years ago.

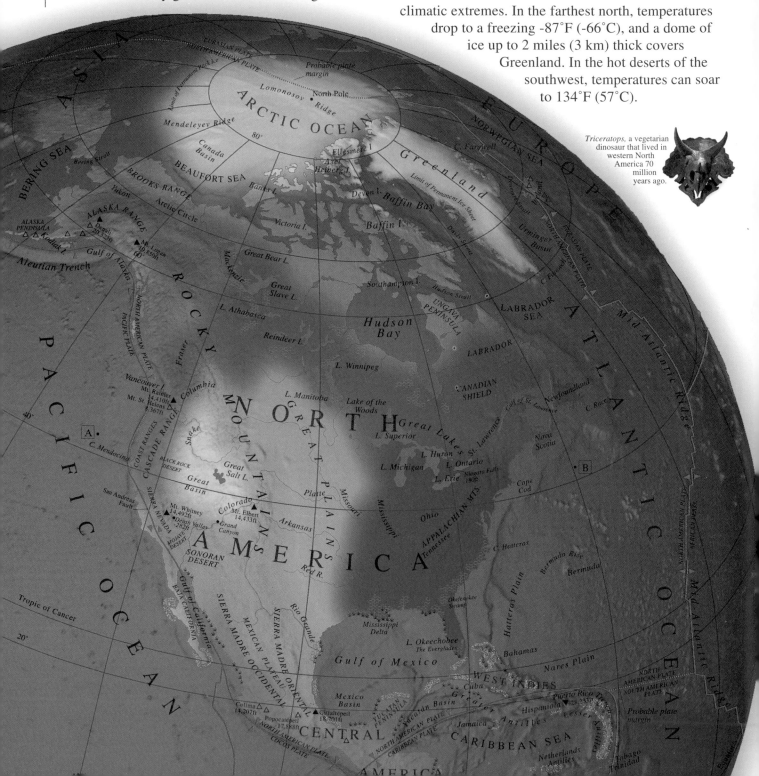

Douglas fir cone
Pseudotsuga menziesii
Length: 3 in (8 cm)

Road runner
Geococcyx californianus
Length: 2 ft (60 cm)

Loggerhead turtle
Caretta caretta
Length: 4 ft (1.2 m)

AUTUMN IN ALASKA
Only short grasses, low shrubs, and small trees can survive the climate of the northern tundra. In the brief Alaskan summer, plants burst into bloom, changing color in autumn.

THE ROOF OF AMERICA
When water-laden ocean air rises over the Alaska Range, moisture freezes and falls as snow. It is so cold that mountain slopes as low as 3,000 ft (900 m) are always snow-covered.

Eutrephoceras, which lived in North America 100 million years ago. It swam by squirting water out of its body cavity.

VOLCANIC ACTIVITY
The volcanic island of Iceland lies above the Mid-Atlantic Ridge. Intense heat generated deep underground creates bubbling hot mud pools and hot springs.

Coast redwood
Sequoia sempervirens
Height: 330 ft (100 m)

Priscacara, a perch that swam in North America's lakes and rivers 50 million years ago.

RAIN FORESTS
Temperate rain forests thrive between the Pacific and the Coast Ranges. Heavy rainfall carried inland by moist ocean winds makes their lush growth possible.

RIVERS, TREES, AND GRASSLAND
For millions of years, rivers flowing east from the Rockies have deposited silt on the Great Plains. This has helped to create a deep and very fertile soil which supports huge areas of grassland.

NORTHERN FORESTS
Forests grow across most of the northern region and on cold mountain slopes. These contain mostly coniferous trees which are well suited to growing in cold conditions.

Bald eagle
Haliaeetus leucocephalus
Wingspan: 7 ft (2.2 m)

DRY WINDS AND SAND DUNES
Dry winds blowing from the center of the continent, combined with the lack of rain, are responsible for the extensive deserts in the southwest. Because the climate is so dry, vegetation is sparse.

OKEFENOKEE SWAMP
The Okefenokee Swamp is part of the complex river system of the southeast. This large wetland area has a warm climate, providing a haven for reptiles such as alligators and snakes. It is also an important resting place for many migratory birds.

American beaver
Castor canadensis
Length: 5 ft (1.6 m)

KEY TO SYMBOLS

▲	*Mountain*
△	*Volcano*
⁂	*Mangroves*
▦	*Wetlands*
▨	*Coral reef*
▰	*Plate margins showing direction of movement*

DESERT RIVER
The brown silt-laden waters of the Colorado River have cut a spectacular gorge through solid rock – the Grand Canyon – nearly 6,135 ft (2 km) deep.

DESERT TREES
With searing temperatures and low rainfall, deserts are home to plants which are adapted to conserve water, like cacti and the Joshua trees shown here.

KEY TO NATURAL VEGETATION

- Mountain
- Temperate rain forest
- Cold desert
- Mediterranean-type
- Hot desert
- Dry woodland
- Tundra
- Needleleaf forest
- Temperate grassland
- Broadleaf forest
- Tropical rain forest

CROSS-SECTION THROUGH NORTH AMERICA

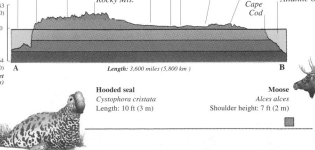
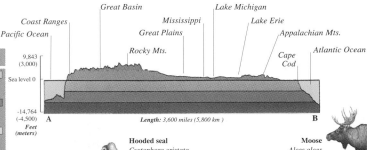

Coast Ranges
Pacific Ocean
Great Basin
Great Plains
Rocky Mts.
Mississippi
Lake Michigan
Lake Erie
Appalachian Mts.
Cape Cod
Atlantic Ocean

9,843 (3,000)
Sea level 0
-14,764 (-4,500)
Feet (meters)

A

Length: 3,600 miles (5,800 km)

B

Hooded seal
Cystophora cristata
Length: 10 ft (3 m)

Moose
Alces alces
Shoulder height: 7 ft (2 m)

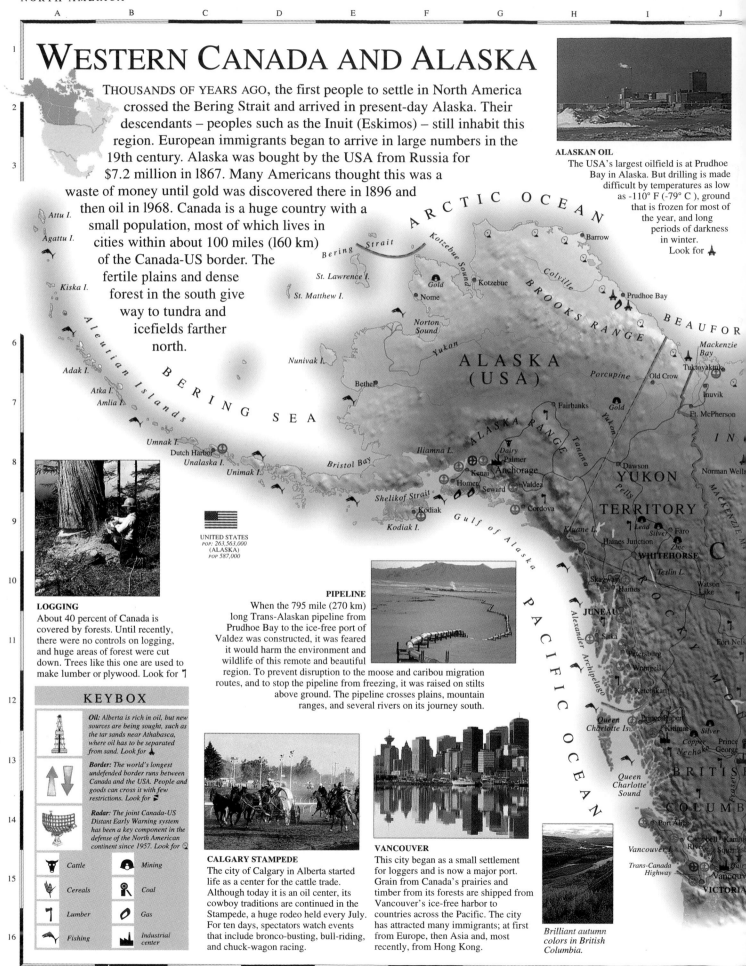

WESTERN CANADA AND ALASKA

THOUSANDS OF YEARS AGO, the first people to settle in North America crossed the Bering Strait and arrived in present-day Alaska. Their descendants – peoples such as the Inuit (Eskimos) – still inhabit this region. European immigrants began to arrive in large numbers in the 19th century. Alaska was bought by the USA from Russia for $7.2 million in 1867. Many Americans thought this was a waste of money until gold was discovered there in 1896 and then oil in 1968. Canada is a huge country with a small population, most of which lives in cities within about 100 miles (160 km) of the Canada-US border. The fertile plains and dense forest in the south give way to tundra and icefields farther north.

ALASKAN OIL
The USA's largest oilfield is at Prudhoe Bay in Alaska. But drilling is made difficult by temperatures as low as -110° F (-79° C), ground that is frozen for most of the year, and long periods of darkness in winter.
Look for ⚒

LOGGING
About 40 percent of Canada is covered by forests. Until recently, there were no controls on logging, and huge areas of forest were cut down. Trees like this one are used to make lumber or plywood. Look for ⌐

UNITED STATES
POP: 263,563,000
(ALASKA)
POP 587,000

KEYBOX

Oil:	Alberta is rich in oil, but new sources are being sought, such as the tar sands near Athabasca, where oil has to be separated from sand. Look for ⚒
Border:	The world's longest undefended border runs between Canada and the USA. People and goods can cross it with few restrictions. Look for ⇅
Radar:	The joint Canada-US Distant Early Warning system has been a key component in the defense of the North American continent since 1957. Look for ◖

♞ Cattle	⛏ Mining
🌾 Cereals	☆ Coal
⌐ Lumber	◊ Gas
🐟 Fishing	■ Industrial center

PIPELINE
When the 795 mile (270 km) long Trans-Alaskan pipeline from Prudhoe Bay to the ice-free port of Valdez was constructed, it was feared it would harm the environment and wildlife of this remote and beautiful region. To prevent disruption to the moose and caribou migration routes, and to stop the pipeline from freezing, it was raised on stilts above ground. The pipeline crosses plains, mountain ranges, and several rivers on its journey south.

CALGARY STAMPEDE
The city of Calgary in Alberta started life as a center for the cattle trade. Although today it is an oil center, its cowboy traditions are continued in the Stampede, a huge rodeo held every July. For ten days, spectators watch events that include bronco-busting, bull-riding, and chuck-wagon racing.

VANCOUVER
This city began as a small settlement for loggers and is now a major port. Grain from Canada's prairies and timber from its forests are shipped from Vancouver's ice-free harbor to countries across the Pacific. The city has attracted many immigrants; at first from Europe, then Asia and, most recently, from Hong Kong.

Brilliant autumn colors in British Columbia.

Map labels

ARCTIC OCEAN
Barrow
Colville
Kotzebue Sound
BROOKS RANGE
BEAUFOR(T)
Prudhoe Bay
Bering Strait
Kotzebue
Gold
Nome
St. Lawrence I.
St. Matthew I.
Norton Sound
Nunivak I.
Yukon
ALASKA (USA)
Porcupine
Old Crow
Mackenzie Bay
Tuktoyaktuk
Attu I.
Agattu I.
Kiska I.
Bethel
Inuvik
Ft. McPherson
Adak I.
Fairbanks
Gold
Yukon
IN(UVIK?)
Aleutian Islands
Atka I.
Amlia I.
ALASKA RANGE
Tanana
Dawson
YUKON
Norman Wells
BERING SEA
Umnak I.
Dutch Harbor
Unalaska I.
Unimak I.
Bristol Bay
Iliamna L.
Dairy
Palmer
Anchorage
Kenai
Homer
Seward
Valdez
Pelly
TERRITORY
MACKENZIE M(TS)
Shelikof Strait
Cordova
Lead
Silver
Faro
Zinc
Kodiak
Kodiak I.
Gulf of Alaska
Kluane L.
Haines Junction
WHITEHORSE
C(OAST?)
Teslin L.
Watson Lake
Skagway
Haines
PACIFIC OCEAN
JUNEAU
Sitka
Alexander Archipelago
Fort Nels(on)
Petersburg
Wrangell
ROCKY MO(UNTAINS)
Ketchikan
Queen Charlotte Is.
Prince Rupert
Kitimat
Silver
Copper
Prince George
Nechako
Queen Charlotte Sound
BRITISH
COLUMB(IA)
Port Alice
Fraser
Campbell River
Kamloops
Squamish
Vancouver I.
Trans-Canada Highway
Vancouver
VICTORIA

Mountains are mirrored in Lake Louise, Alberta.

Caribou roam the northern parts of Canada and Alaska.

TRANSPORTATION

In a country as vast as Canada, transportation is vital. When the Canadian Pacific Railway was completed in 1885, the country's east and west coasts were linked for the first time. Roads like the Trans-Canada Highway also helped to open up the country, especially the wilderness areas. Here, a highway crosses a spectacular part of Alberta.

SALMON FISHING

The main fish caught on Canada's west coast is the Pacific salmon. The bulk of the catch is canned. The cans are made at aluminum smelting plants like the one at Kitimat; the plant is powered by hydroelectricity produced by the damming and reversing of the Nechako River. Look for

Pacific salmon

Edmontonia, a dinosaur once found in Alberta.

KWAKIUTL

The Kwakiutl were skilled artisans and among the first peoples to settle along Canada's west coast. Families displayed their wealth and prestige in totem poles carved with animal and human figures. Other carved pieces were created for the potlach, a celebration of gift-giving. When this was banned in 1884, many artifacts were destroyed. Since the 1950s, native artists have revived the traditional techniques.

SNOWSHOES

Snowshoes, made from wooden frames strung with animal gut or leather strips, were once essential for winter travel. They are still used in areas where vehicles, such as snowmobiles, cannot maneuver.

THE PRAIRIES

Grain production on the vast prairies of western Canada is highly mechanized; one farmer can harvest several hundred hectares single-handed. After the grain is cut, it is stored in huge grain elevators like these before being sent by rail to cities or ports. Railroads were the key to the development of farming on the prairies. Look for

Harvesting grain on the fertile prairies of Saskatchewan.

CANADA
POP: 29,248,000
(WESTERN CANADA)
POP: 8,062,000

100 200 300 400 500 600 700 KM
50 100 150 200 250 300 350 400 MILES

PIONEER

Map labels

Nares Strait
Ellesmere I.
Axel Heiberg I.
Queen Elizabeth Islands
Baffin Bay
Mackenzie King I.
Bathurst I.
Lead
Devon I.
Parry Is.
Melville I.
Cornwallis I.
Zinc
Resolute
Lancaster Sound
McClure Strait
Viscount Melville Sound
Somerset I.
Banks I.
Prince of Wales I.
Gulf of Boothia
BAFFIN
Baffin I.
Davis Strait
Amundsen Gulf
Victoria I.
McClintock Channel
Prince Charles I.
Pangnirtung
Cumberland Sound
King William I.
Foxe Basin
KITIKMEOT
Coppermine
Iqaluit
Frobisher Bay
NORTHWEST TERRITORIES
Southampton I.
Hudson Strait
Great Bear L.
Coppermine
Contwoyto L.
Garry L.
Gold
KEEWATIN
Coats I.
FORT SMITH
Lac la Martre
Dubawnt L.
Chesterfield Inlet
CANADA
Rankin Inlet
Fort Simpson
YELLOWKNIFE
Great Slave L.
Nonacho L.
Eskimo Pt.
Hudson Bay
Hay River
Fort Resolution
Fort Smith
Uranium City
Seal
Churchill
Churchill
L. Athabasca
Uranium
Wollaston L.
Copper
Silver
Fort Vermilion
Cree L.
Uranium
MANITOBA
Fort McMurray
Reindeer L.
Zinc
Lynn Lake
Nelson
Dawson Creek
Lesser Slave L.
Frobisher L.
Gold
Nickel
Hayes
Grande Prairie
Beef
Potassium
Thompson
Athabasca
Copper
Fort St. John
SASKATCHEWAN
Flin Flon
ALBERTA
The Pas
L. Winnipeg
ONTARIO
Jasper
Edmonton
Lloydminster
Saskatchewan
Leduc
North Battleford
Prince Albert
Wetaskiwin
Wheat
Red Deer
Dairy
Saskatoon
Yorkton
Drumheller
Wheat
L. Winnipegosis
L. Louise
Wheat
Potash
Trans-Canada Highway
Calgary
Swift Current
Melville
Selkirk
Vernon
Trans-Canada Highway
Wheat
REGINA
Brandon
WINNIPEG
Beef
Medicine Hat
Moose Jaw
Penticton
Lethbridge
Trans-Canada Highway
Weyburn
Dairy
Copper
Beef
Estevan
Cranbrook
Beef
UNITED STATES OF AMERICA

EASTERN CANADA

THE VIKINGS WERE THE FIRST Europeans to visit eastern Canada, in about AD 986. Then, in the 15th and 16th centuries, two expeditions, one from England and one from France, reached Canada and each claimed it. Traders and fur trappers from the two countries followed, setting up rival trading posts and settlements. The struggle for territory led to war between Britain and France. The French were forced to give up their Canadian territories to Britain in 1763, but the French language is still spoken in the province of Quebec today. Canada eventually achieved effective independence from Britain in 1867. Today, southern Quebec and Ontario form eastern Canada's main industrial region, containing most of its population and two of its largest cities – Montreal and Toronto. The Hudson Bay area, while rich in minerals, is a wilderness of forests, rivers, and lakes. Snowbound for much of the year, it is sparsely inhabited except by Inuit in the far north.

The Toronto Sky Dome, a huge stadium which seats 50,000.

FRENCH / ENGLISH
Most Canadians speak English, but the country is officially bilingual – as can be seen from the use of both French and English on this stamp which commemorates the province of New Brunswick.

The sap of the sugar maple tree is made into syrup and sugar. The maple leaf is Canada's national symbol.

CANADA
POP: 29,248,000
(EASTERN CANADA)
POP: 19,738,000

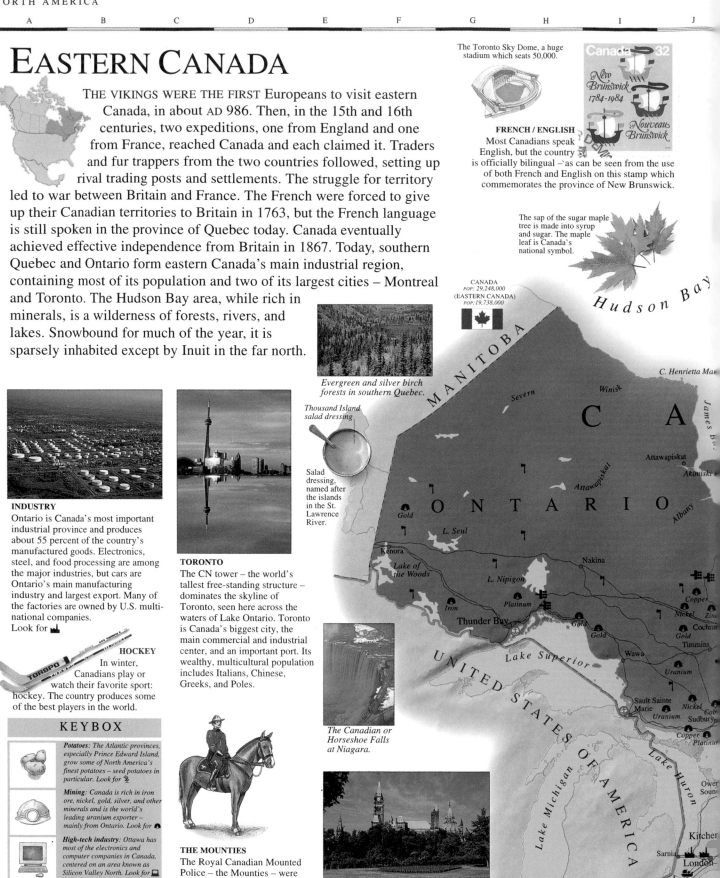

Evergreen and silver birch forests in southern Quebec.

Thousand Island salad dressing

Salad dressing, named after the islands in the St. Lawrence River.

INDUSTRY
Ontario is Canada's most important industrial province and produces about 55 percent of the country's manufactured goods. Electronics, steel, and food processing are among the major industries, but cars are Ontario's main manufacturing industry and largest export. Many of the factories are owned by U.S. multi-national companies.
Look for ⚒

TORONTO
The CN tower – the world's tallest free-standing structure – dominates the skyline of Toronto, seen here across the waters of Lake Ontario. Toronto is Canada's biggest city, the main commercial and industrial center, and an important port. Its wealthy, multicultural population includes Italians, Chinese, Greeks, and Poles.

HOCKEY
In winter, Canadians play or watch their favorite sport: hockey. The country produces some of the best players in the world.

The Canadian or Horseshoe Falls at Niagara.

KEYBOX

Potatoes: *The Atlantic provinces, especially Prince Edward Island, grow some of North America's finest potatoes – seed potatoes in particular. Look for* ⚘

Mining: *Canada is rich in iron ore, nickel, gold, silver, and other minerals and is the world's leading uranium exporter – mainly from Ontario. Look for* ⬤

High-tech industry: *Ottawa has most of the electronics and computer companies in Canada, centered on an area known as Silicon Valley North. Look for* 💻

Mixed fruits	Shellfish
Timber	Hydro-electricity
Fishing	Industrial center

THE MOUNTIES
The Royal Canadian Mounted Police – the Mounties – were established in 1873 during the opening of the vast areas in the west to trade and industry. Today, they are one of the world's most efficient and sophisticated police forces, with their headquarters in Ottawa.

OTTAWA
The Parliament Buildings in Ottawa, Canada's capital city, were inspired by the British Houses of Parliament. Many older buildings reflect the city's British origins. Others, such as the National Gallery, are thoroughly modern.

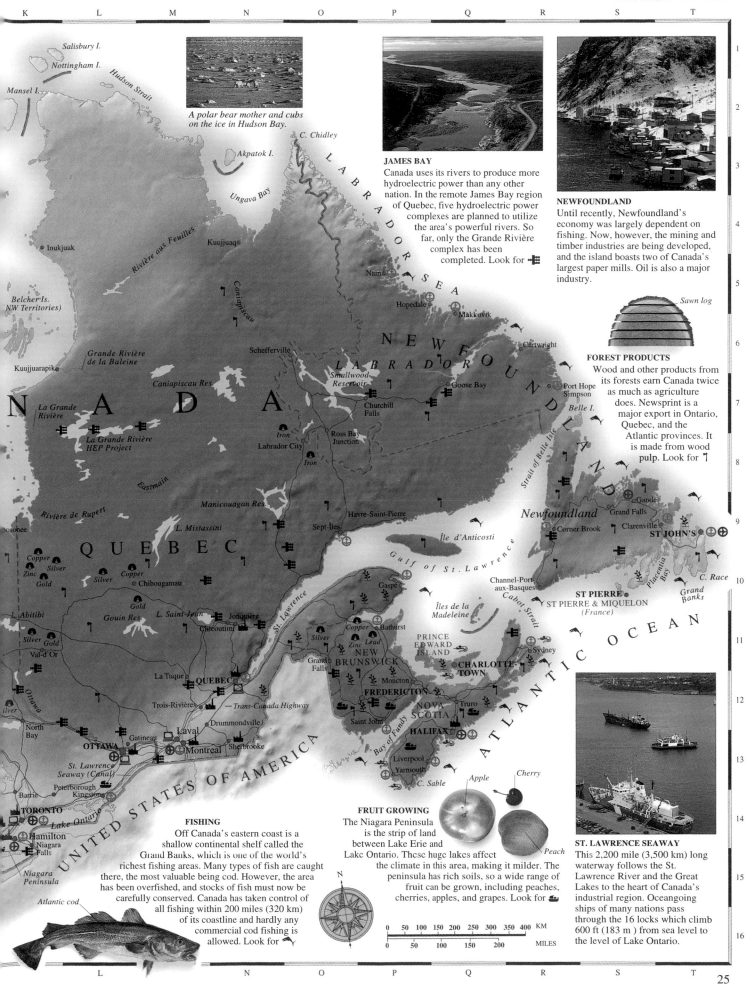

A polar bear mother and cubs on the ice in Hudson Bay.

JAMES BAY
Canada uses its rivers to produce more hydroelectric power than any other nation. In the remote James Bay region of Quebec, five hydroelectric power complexes are planned to utilize the area's powerful rivers. So far, only the Grande Rivière complex has been completed. Look for

NEWFOUNDLAND
Until recently, Newfoundland's economy was largely dependent on fishing. Now, however, the mining and timber industries are being developed, and the island boasts two of Canada's largest paper mills. Oil is also a major industry.

Sawn log

FOREST PRODUCTS
Wood and other products from its forests earn Canada twice as much as agriculture does. Newsprint is a major export in Ontario, Quebec, and the Atlantic provinces. It is made from wood pulp. Look for

FISHING
Off Canada's eastern coast is a shallow continental shelf called the Grand Banks, which is one of the world's richest fishing areas. Many types of fish are caught there, the most valuable being cod. However, the area has been overfished, and stocks of fish must now be carefully conserved. Canada has taken control of all fishing within 200 miles (320 km) of its coastline and hardly any commercial cod fishing is allowed. Look for

Atlantic cod

FRUIT GROWING
The Niagara Peninsula is the strip of land between Lake Erie and Lake Ontario. These huge lakes affect the climate in this area, making it milder. The peninsula has rich soils, so a wide range of fruit can be grown, including peaches, cherries, apples, and grapes. Look for

Apple

Cherry

Peach

ST. LAWRENCE SEAWAY
This 2,200 mile (3,500 km) long waterway follows the St. Lawrence River and the Great Lakes to the heart of Canada's industrial region. Oceangoing ships of many nations pass through the 16 locks which climb 600 ft (183 m) from sea level to the level of Lake Ontario.

N

| 0 | 50 | 100 | 150 | 200 | 250 | 300 | 350 | 400 | KM |

| 0 | 50 | 100 | 150 | 200 | MILES |

Map labels:
Salisbury I.
Nottingham I.
Mansel I.
Hudson Strait
C. Chidley
Akpatok I.
Ungava Bay
LABRADOR SEA
Belcher Is. (NW Territories)
Inukjuak
Rivière aux Feuilles
Kuujjuaq
Caniapiscau
Nain
Hopedale
Makkovik
Kuujjuarapik
Grande Rivière de la Baleine
Caniapiscau Res.
Schefferville
NEWFOUNDLAND
LABRADOR
Smallwood Reservoir
Goose Bay
Cartwright
Port Hope Simpson
Belle I.
NADA
La Grande Rivière
La Grande Rivière HEP Project
Iron
Ross Bay Junction
Churchill Falls
Labrador City
Iron
Eastmain
Strait of Belle Isle
Gander
Grand Falls
Rivière de Rupert
Manicouagan Res.
L. Mistassini
Havre-Saint-Pierre
Newfoundland
Corner Brook
Clarenville
ST JOHN'S
osoonee
QUEBEC
Sept-Îles
Île d'Anticosti
Gulf of St. Lawrence
Channel-Port-aux-Basques
Placentia Bay
C. Race
Copper
Silver
Zinc
Gold
Silver
Copper
Chibougamau
Gold
Gaspé
Îles de la Madeleine
Cabot Strait
ST PIERRE
ST PIERRE & MIQUELON (France)
Grand Banks
ATLANTIC OCEAN
L. Abitibi
Gouin Res.
Gold
L. Saint-Jean
Jonquière
Chicoutimi
Copper
Bathurst
Silver
Zinc Lead
PRINCE EDWARD ISLAND
Sydney
Silver Gold
Val-d'Or
Grand Falls
NEW BRUNSWICK
CHARLOTTE-TOWN
La Tuque
QUEBEC
Moncton
Ottawa
ilver
Trois-Rivières
Trans-Canada Highway
FREDERICTON
NOVA SCOTIA
Truro
North Bay
Drummondville
Laval
Sherbrooke
Saint John
HALIFAX
OTTAWA
Gatineau
Montreal
Bay of Fundy
St. Lawrence Seaway (Canal)
Liverpool
Barrie
Peterborough
Kingston
Yarmouth
C. Sable
TORONTO
Lake Ontario
Hamilton
Niagara Falls
Niagara Peninsula
UNITED STATES OF AMERICA
St. Lawrence

NORTHEASTERN UNITED STATES

THE MOST DENSELY populated, heavily industrialized, and ethnically diverse region of the USA, the Northeast can be divided into New England – Maine, New Hampshire, Vermont, Massachusetts, Rhode Island, and Connecticut – and the Mid-Atlantic states – New York, New Jersey, Pennsylvania, and Delaware. The terrain of the region ranges from the near-wilderness of New York's Adirondack Mountains to the rocky coastline of northern New England and the rolling hills of Pennsylvania; climate is temperate, with cold winters and warm summers. First settled in the early 1600s, the region's good harbors, mineral resources, fast-flowing rivers, and rich coastal fishing grounds contributed to its early economic development; by the American Revolution, New York City, Boston, and Philadelphia were leading cities. Rapid industrialization after about 1800 brought millions of immigrants from Europe and elsewhere. In recent decades, a decline in manufacturing and a population shift toward the "Sun Belt" states of the South and West has weakened the Northeast's economy, but high-tech and service industries have taken up some of the slack. Today, New York is the nation's largest city and a financial, communications, and artistic center for the world.

THE HUDSON-MOHAWK GAP

New York became the East Coast's leading port thanks to its fine harbor and its location at the mouth of the Hudson River. The Hudson connects with the Mohawk River, giving the city access to the continent's interior; mineral resources and industrial products were transported along this route.

The spectacular Niagara Falls near Buffalo, New York.

THE AMISH

This isolated Amish farm near Lancaster, Pennsylvania, is run without any modern technology. The Amish are a Protestant sect who came to America from Switzerland in the 18th century. They live by farming, make all their own clothes and use horses for transport.

PUMPKINS

Pumpkins are grown all over New England, and pumpkin pie is a favorite American dish. Pumpkins are also hollowed out to make Jack-O'-Lanterns for Halloween.

TOMATO SOUP

Many of the fruits and vegetables for the region's big cities, especially New York, are grown on the fruit and vegetable farms, called market gardens, of New Jersey (known as "the Garden State"). Tomatoes are grown in huge quantities, and made locally into canned tomato soup. Look for 🐄

Severe winter weather is common in New England.

KEYBOX

Sailing: *Yachting is a popular pastime on New England's Atlantic coast. The Bermuda Race starts from Rhode Island. Look for* ⛵

Universities: *There are more centers of further education and research and development in New England than in any other part of the USA. Look for* 🎓

Maple syrup: *Both sugar and syrup are obtained from the sap of maple trees. Vermont is the USA's main producer. Look for* 🍁

🐂	Cattle	🚢	Fishing port
🐓	Poultry	⚜	Coal
🛒	Market gardening	🏭	Industrial center
🐟	Fishing	💻	High-tech industry

NEW ENGLAND BERRIES

Cranberries and blueberries both came from New England and large quantities are grown there. Cranberries are used in sauces, especially to go with roast turkey at Thanksgiving. Blueberries are sweeter and are often used in pies.

Blueberries

Cranberries

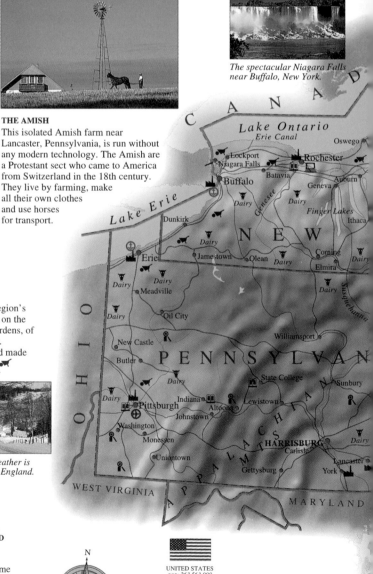

Adirondack Mts.
Albany
Hudson Valley
Utica
Hudson R.
Mohawk R.
Syracuse
Rochester
N
Long Island
L. Ontario
New York City
Appalachian Mountains

Lake Ontario
Erie Canal
Oswego
Lockport
Niagara Falls
Rochester
Buffalo
Batavia
Auburn
Dairy
Geneva
Dairy
Finger Lakes
Dunkirk
Genesee
Ithaca
NEW
Erie
Jamestown
Olean
Dairy
Corning
Elmira
Dairy
Dairy
Dairy
Meadville
Dairy
Oil City
Williamsport
Susquehanna
New Castle
Butler
PENNSYLVAN
Dairy
State College
Sunbury
Dairy
Pittsburgh
Indiana
Altoona
Lewistown
OHIO
Johnstown
Washington
Monessen
HARRISBURG
Dairy
Uniontown
Carlisle
Lancaster
Gettysburg
York
WEST VIRGINIA
APPALACHIAN MTS
MARYLAND
CANADA

UNITED STATES
POP: 263,563,000
(NORTHEASTERN STATES)
POP: 51,806,000

N

0	25	50	75	100	125	150	175	KM
0	25	50	75		100			MILES

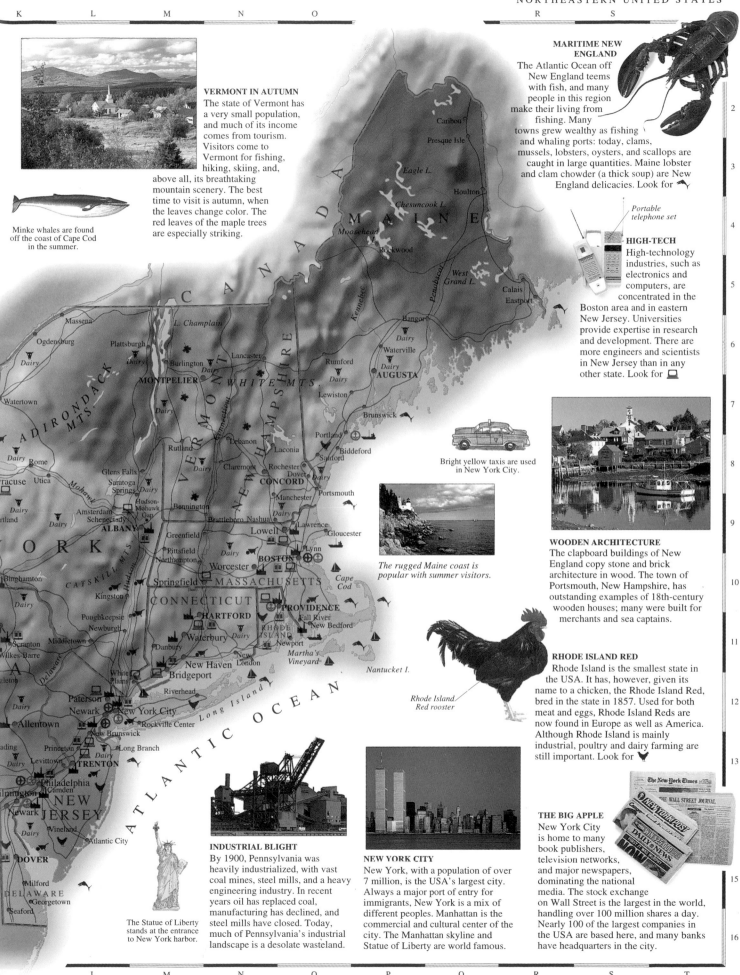

VERMONT IN AUTUMN
The state of Vermont has a very small population, and much of its income comes from tourism. Visitors come to Vermont for fishing, hiking, skiing, and, above all, its breathtaking mountain scenery. The best time to visit is autumn, when the leaves change color. The red leaves of the maple trees are especially striking.

Minke whales are found off the coast of Cape Cod in the summer.

MARITIME NEW ENGLAND
The Atlantic Ocean off New England teems with fish, and many people in this region make their living from fishing. Many towns grew wealthy as fishing and whaling ports: today, clams, mussels, lobsters, oysters, and scallops are caught in large quantities. Maine lobster and clam chowder (a thick soup) are New England delicacies. Look for

Portable telephone set

HIGH-TECH
High-technology industries, such as electronics and computers, are concentrated in the Boston area and in eastern New Jersey. Universities provide expertise in research and development. There are more engineers and scientists in New Jersey than in any other state. Look for

Bright yellow taxis are used in New York City.

The rugged Maine coast is popular with summer visitors.

WOODEN ARCHITECTURE
The clapboard buildings of New England copy stone and brick architecture in wood. The town of Portsmouth, New Hampshire, has outstanding examples of 18th-century wooden houses; many were built for merchants and sea captains.

RHODE ISLAND RED
Rhode Island is the smallest state in the USA. It has, however, given its name to a chicken, the Rhode Island Red, bred in the state in 1857. Used for both meat and eggs, Rhode Island Reds are now found in Europe as well as America. Although Rhode Island is mainly industrial, poultry and dairy farming are still important. Look for

Rhode Island Red rooster

INDUSTRIAL BLIGHT
By 1900, Pennsylvania was heavily industrialized, with vast coal mines, steel mills, and a heavy engineering industry. In recent years oil has replaced coal, manufacturing has declined, and steel mills have closed. Today, much of Pennsylvania's industrial landscape is a desolate wasteland.

The Statue of Liberty stands at the entrance to New York harbor.

NEW YORK CITY
New York, with a population of over 7 million, is the USA's largest city. Always a major port of entry for immigrants, New York is a mix of different peoples. Manhattan is the commercial and cultural center of the city. The Manhattan skyline and Statue of Liberty are world famous.

THE BIG APPLE
New York City is home to many book publishers, television networks, and major newspapers, dominating the national media. The stock exchange on Wall Street is the largest in the world, handling over 100 million shares a day. Nearly 100 of the largest companies in the USA are based here, and many banks have headquarters in the city.

Map labels:
CANADA, MAINE, Caribou, Presque Isle, Eagle L., Houlton, Chesuncook L., Moosehead L., Rockwood, West Grand L., Calais, Eastport, Bangor, Waterville, AUGUSTA, Rumford, Lewiston, Brunswick, Portland, Biddeford, Sanford, Dover, Portsmouth, Manchester, Nashua, Lawrence, Gloucester, Lynn, BOSTON, Worcester, Cape Cod, Martha's Vineyard, Nantucket I., Massena, Ogdensburg, Plattsburgh, L. Champlain, Burlington, Lancaster, MONTPELIER, WHITE MTS., NEW HAMPSHIRE, VERMONT, Watertown, Rutland, Lebanon, Laconia, Concord, Rochester, Claremont, Bennington, Brattleboro, Greenfield, Pittsfield, Northampton, Springfield, MASSACHUSETTS, CONNECTICUT, HARTFORD, Waterbury, Danbury, New Haven, Bridgeport, New London, PROVIDENCE, Fall River, New Bedford, Newport, RHODE ISLAND, Rome, Utica, Syracuse, ADIRONDACK MTS., Mohawk, Glens Falls, Saratoga Springs, Amsterdam, Schenectady, ALBANY, Hudson-Mohawk Gap, Kingston, Poughkeepsie, Newburgh, Middletown, CATSKILLS, YORK, Binghamton, White Plains, Riverhead, Long Island, Scranton, Wilkes-Barre, Hazleton, Delaware, Paterson, Newark, New York City, Rockville Center, New Brunswick, Long Branch, Allentown, Princeton, TRENTON, Levittown, Reading, Philadelphia, Camden, Wilmington, NEW JERSEY, Newark, Vineland, Atlantic City, DOVER, DELAWARE, Milford, Georgetown, Seaford, ATLANTIC OCEAN

THE SOUTHERN STATES

THE SOUTH'S GEOGRAPHY includes the Tidewater along the Atlantic coast, the Piedmont extending to the coal-rich Appalachian Mountains, the Mississippi River Valley, and the subtropical coastal belt along the Gulf of Mexico. The region was settled mostly by British colonists, beginning with the founding of Jamestown, Virginia, in 1607. The South soon developed an agricultural economy based on tobacco, rice, indigo, and especially cotton, grown by African-American slaves. The American Civil War (1861-65) left the region devastated. The war ended slavery, but a system of legal segregation (separation by race) lasted into the 1960s in much of the South. Today, the South's economy is more varied, thanks to the discovery of oil reserves in the Gulf region and the development of industry. Florida, first colonized by Spain in 1565, has experienced great growth in recent years, becoming the fourth-largest state in the 1980s. Its population includes retirees from other states and refugees from Cuba, the Caribbean, and Latin America.

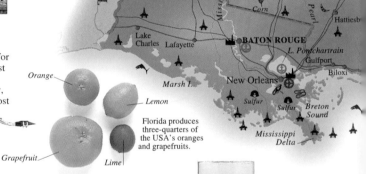

Horses graze on a Kentucky farm in the Bluegrass country.

ATLANTA

The commercial center of the region is Atlanta, which is the hub of the South's transport network, and has one of the world's busiest airports. Raw materials flood into Atlanta and manufactured goods pour out: clothes, books, iron and steel products, and Coca-Cola are all made here.

DERBY DAY

Kentucky is called the "Bluegrass State" after the grasslands around the city of Lexington, which provide superb grazing for livestock. This area has the world's greatest concentration of stud farms for breeding thoroughbred horses. The Kentucky Derby, held at Louisville, is one of the world's famous horse races.

Orange

Lemon

Grapefruit

Lime

Florida produces three-quarters of the USA's oranges and grapefruits.

KEYBOX

Soybeans: The main crop in the South is the soybean. Used for oil, margarine, and livestock feed, it has found both domestic and export markets. Look for 🌱

Coal: Coal, mined from the rich reserves of the Appalachian Mountains, is being overtaken by oil and gas. Look for ⛏

High-tech industry: The South, with its skilled labor force and good communications, is attracting many high-tech industries. Look for 💻

Space center: The Space Shuttle is launched from the Kennedy Space Center, the launch site of the U.S. Space program. Look for 🚀

🌾	Cereals	🐬	Fishing
🍋	Citrus fruit	⛽	Oil
🥜	Peanuts	⛏	Mining
🌿	Cotton	🏭	Industrial center
🌱	Tobacco	✍	Tourism

JAZZ

Jazz saxophone

Jazz developed in New Orleans in the early 1900s. Originally it was the music of the bands who marched through the streets, playing at funerals and weddings. Jazz combined many influences – blues and spirituals (sung by slaves) and popular songs. Wind instruments are accompanied by drums, piano, and double bass.

BOURBON

Corn is one of Kentucky's major crops. It is used for making Bourbon whiskey, which is a worldwide export.

MISSISSIPPI

Steamboats carry tourists on scenic trips along the Mississippi, one of the world's busiest waterways. Barges transport heavy cargoes from the industrial and agricultural regions near the Great Lakes to the Gulf Coast.

KING COTTON

Cotton, grown on large plantations using slave labor, was once the basis of the Southern economy. Today, it is still grown on farms in some parts of the South. Look for 🌿

Okra

Shrimp

Gumbo is a spicy seafood and vegetable stew from Louisiana.

RETIREMENT STATE

Nearly 30 percent of Florida's inhabitants are over 55 years old. Large numbers of people retire to Florida, lured by its climate and sports facilities. Many settle in retirement developments or in the coastal cities.

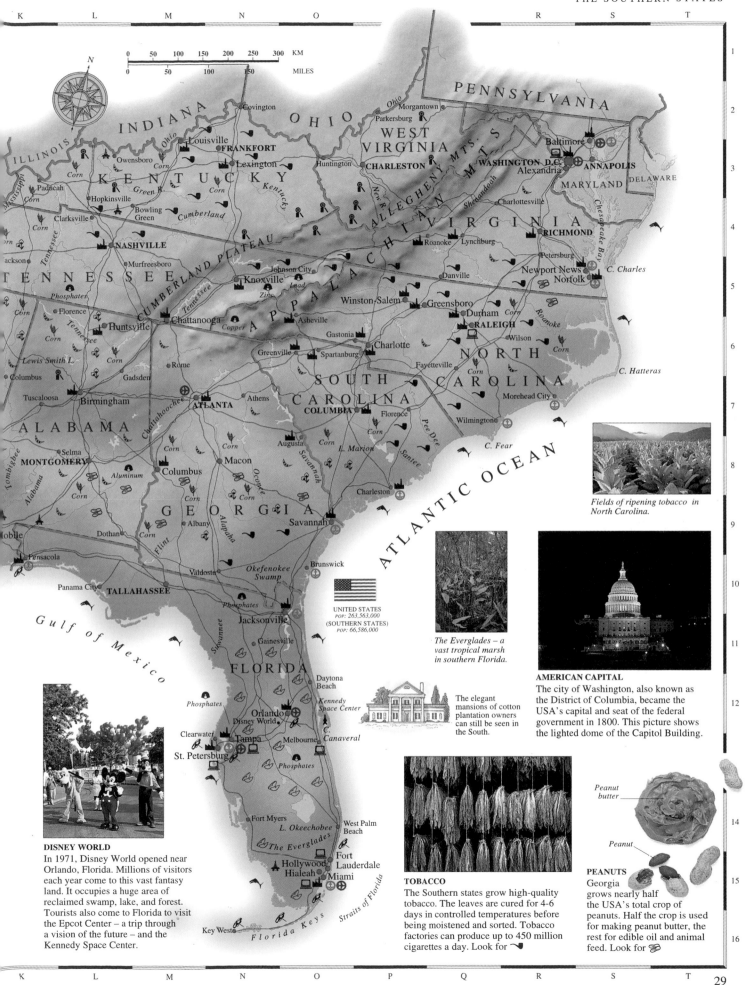

0 50 100 150 200 250 300 KM
0   50   100   150 MILES

N

K L M N O R S T
1
2
3
4
5
6
7
8
9
10
11
12
14
15
16

ILLINOIS
INDIANA
OHIO
PENNSYLVANIA
Covington
Morgantown
Parkersburg
Ohio
WEST
VIRGINIA
CHARLESTON
Baltimore
Louisville
FRANKFORT
Lexington
Huntington
WASHINGTON D.C.
ANNAPOLIS
Owensboro
Corn
Alexandria
MARYLAND
DELAWARE
KENTUCKY
Paducah
Corn
Green R.
Corn
Kentucky
Charlottesville
Hopkinsville
Shenandoah
Chesapeake Bay
Clarksville
Bowling
Green
Cumberland
VIRGINIA
RICHMOND
Corn
NASHVILLE
Roanoke
Lynchburg
Petersburg
C. Charles
Jackson
Murfreesboro
Johnson City
Danville
Newport News
Norfolk
TENNESSEE
Knoxville
Winston-Salem
Greensboro
Phosphates
Zinc
Lead
Asheville
Durham
RALEIGH
Florence
Chattanooga
Copper
Gastonia
Wilson
Corn
Huntsville
Corn
Charlotte
NORTH
Roanoke
Corn
Lewis Smith L.
Corn
Greenville
Spartanburg
CAROLINA
Columbus
Rome
Fayetteville
C. Hatteras
Tuscaloosa
Gadsden
Athens
SOUTH
Corn
Birmingham
ATLANTA
CAROLINA
Morehead City
ALABAMA
Florence
Corn
Selma
COLUMBIA
Wilmington
MONTGOMERY
Augusta
Corn
C. Fear
Corn
Corn
L. Marion
Aluminum
Macon
Savannah
ATLANTIC OCEAN
Columbus
Santee
Corn
Corn
Charleston
Pee Dee
GEORGIA
Albany
Oconee
Savannah
Mobile
Dothan
Corn
Alapaha
Flint
Pensacola
Valdosta
Okefenokee
Swamp
Brunswick
Panama City
TALLAHASSEE
Gulf of Mexico
Phosphates
Suwannee
Jacksonville
Gainesville
Daytona
Beach
Kennedy
Space Center
Phosphates
Orlando
Disney World
Clearwater
Tampa
Melbourne
Canaveral
St. Petersburg
FLORIDA
Phosphates
Fort Myers
West Palm
Beach
L. Okeechobee
The Everglades
Hollywood
Hialeah
Fort
Lauderdale
Miami
Straits of Florida
Key West
Florida Keys

UNITED STATES
POP: 263,563,000
(SOUTHERN STATES)
POP: 66,586,000

Fields of ripening tobacco in North Carolina.

The Everglades – a vast tropical marsh in southern Florida.

AMERICAN CAPITAL
The city of Washington, also known as
the District of Columbia, became the
USA's capital and seat of the federal
government in 1800. This picture shows
the lighted dome of the Capitol Building.

The elegant
mansions of cotton
plantation owners
can still be seen in
the South.

DISNEY WORLD
In 1971, Disney World opened near
Orlando, Florida. Millions of visitors
each year come to this vast fantasy
land. It occupies a huge area of
reclaimed swamp, lake, and forest.
Tourists also come to Florida to visit
the Epcot Center – a trip through
a vision of the future – and the
Kennedy Space Center.

TOBACCO
The Southern states grow high-quality
tobacco. The leaves are cured for 4-6
days in controlled temperatures before
being moistened and sorted. Tobacco
factories can produce up to 450 million
cigarettes a day. Look for

*Peanut
butter*

Peanut

PEANUTS
Georgia
grows nearly half
the USA's total crop of
peanuts. Half the crop is used
for making peanut butter, the
rest for edible oil and animal
feed. Look for

THE GREAT LAKES

THE FIVE GREAT LAKES of North America – Ontario, Erie, Huron, Michigan, and Superior – together form the largest area of fresh water in the world. The states of Indiana, Illinois, Michigan, Ohio, Wisconsin, and Minnesota, all of which border on one or more of the lakes, are often called the industrial and agricultural heartland of the United States. This region is rich in natural resources, including coal, iron, copper, and timber, and there are large areas of fertile farmland on the flat plains of the prairies. First explored by French traders, fur trappers, and missionaries in the 17th century, the region began to attract large numbers of settlers in the early 1800s. Trading links were improved by the opening of the Erie Canal in 1825, which connected the region to the Atlantic Coast, while the Mississippi and other rivers gave access to the Gulf of Mexico and the rest of the continent. When railroads reached the region in the 1840s, cities such as Chicago grew and prospered as freight-handling centers. Steel production and the car industry later became the main industries in the region. In recent years, a decline in these traditional industries has led to high unemployment in some areas.

HOG
In the 19th century, huge numbers of animals from all over this region were sent to the stockyards in Chicago for slaughter and processing. Rearing livestock is still important in Illinois. Corn and soybeans, both grown locally, are used as animal feed. Look for 🐖

HAMBURGERS
Hamburgers are America's own fast food, first produced on a massive scale in Illinois in the 1950s. It has been calculated that in every second of the day, 200 Americans are eating a hamburger. American-style hamburgers and fast food can now be found all over the world.

Cherries: *One-third of the world cherry crop is grown along the shores of Lake Michigan. Look for* 🍒

Iron ore: *Iron ore deposits are found around the shores of Lake Superior. It is mined, processed, then shipped to industrial centers in pellet form. Look for* ⬤

🐂	Cattle	🌙	Soybeans
🐖	Hogs	⛏	Coal
🌾	Cereals	🛢	Oil
🍠	Sugar beets	🏭	Industrial center
🛒	Market gardening	🚗	Vehicle manufacture

Baseball and fielder's glove. Baseball is the USA's national game.

MILWAUKEE BEER
The Great Lakes region has attracted many immigrants, especially from Germany, the Netherlands, and the Scandinavian countries. Milwaukee, where many Germans settled, is home to several of the USA's largest breweries.

COLD WINTERS
The Great Lakes region has severe winters, and Minnesota, in particular, suffers from heavy snowstorms. Parts of the Great Lakes themselves can freeze over in winter, and lakeside harbors can be frozen from December to early April.

PRAIRIE LANDS
The fertile soil and hot, humid summers make the flat expanses of the Midwestern prairies ideal for farming. Nearly half of the world's corn crop is grown on the huge farms in this region.

THE WINDY CITY
Chicago is situated at the southern tip of Lake Michigan. It gets its nickname – the Windy City – from the weather conditions in this area. Chicago was ideally positioned for trading with the Midwest region and quickly became a wealthy modern city. By 1900 it had vast complexes of lumber mills, meat processing factories, railroad yards, and steel mills.

An isolated farm on the open prairies of Illinois.

CORNFLAKES
Food processing is a major industry throughout this agricultural region. Wisconsin, for example, is the major producer of canned peas and sweet corn in the USA. Corn and wheat-based breakfast cereals are exported all over the world from Battle Creek, Michigan. Look for 🌾

Walleyes live in the Great Lakes, but their numbers are falling due to pollution.

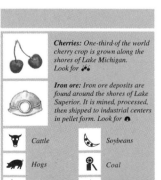

Map labels

CANADA

Lake of the Woods

Wheat

Wheat

Upper Red L.

Red Lake R.

Lower Red L.

Iron

NORTH DAKOTA

MINNESOTA

Bemidji

Iron

Iron

Virginia

Hibbing

Wheat

Leech L.

Moorhead

Duluth

Superior

Chequamegon Bay

Manganese

Fergus Falls

Brainerd

WISCONSIN

Wheat

Iron

Mille Lacs L.

Chippewa L.

Dairy

Dairy

St Cloud

SOUTH DAKOTA

Wheat

Willmar

Minneapolis

Stillwater

Beef

Dairy

Eau Claire

Corn

ST. PAUL

Bloomington

Red Wing

Marshfield

Iron

Corn

New Ulm

Dairy

Faribault

Wisconsin Rapids

Mankato

Owatonna

Winona

Dairy

Wheat

Rochester

La Crosse

Corn

Fairmont

Albert Lea

Austin

Dairy

Dairy

Wisconsin

IOWA

Beef

Br... Free...

Rock Island

Kewan...

Galesburg

Macomb

Canton

ILL...

Quincy

Jacksonville

Illinois

MISSOURI

East S... Loui...

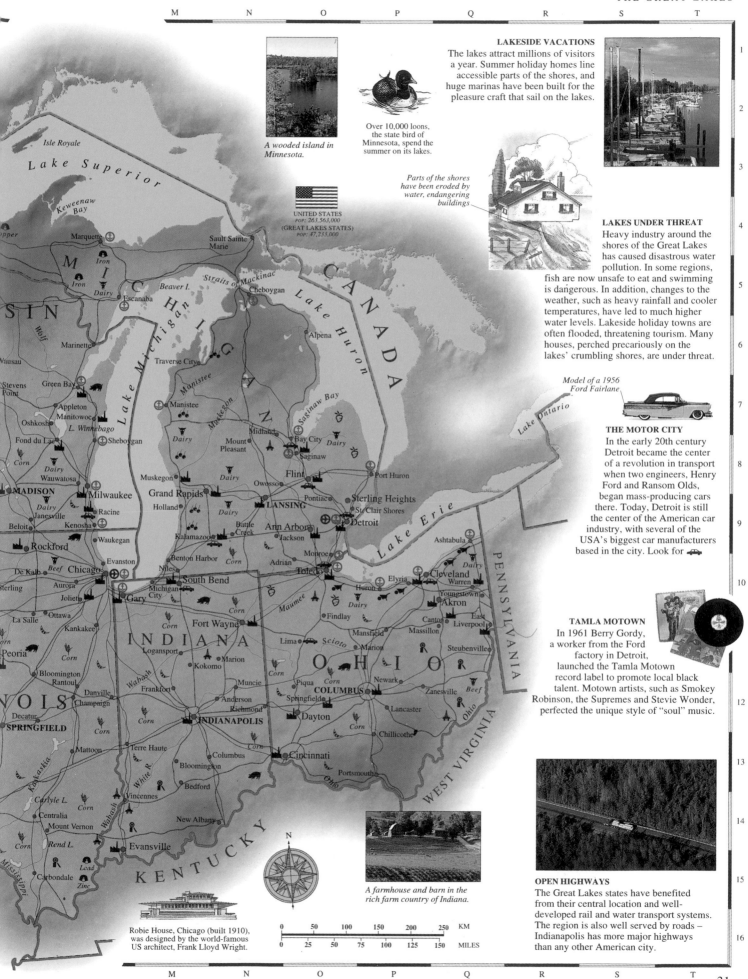

LAKESIDE VACATIONS

The lakes attract millions of visitors a year. Summer holiday homes line accessible parts of the shores, and huge marinas have been built for the pleasure craft that sail on the lakes.

A wooded island in Minnesota.

Over 10,000 loons, the state bird of Minnesota, spend the summer on its lakes.

Parts of the shores have been eroded by water, endangering buildings

UNITED STATES
POP: 263,563,000
(GREAT LAKES STATES)
POP: 47,233,000

LAKES UNDER THREAT

Heavy industry around the shores of the Great Lakes has caused disastrous water pollution. In some regions, fish are now unsafe to eat and swimming is dangerous. In addition, changes to the weather, such as heavy rainfall and cooler temperatures, have led to much higher water levels. Lakeside holiday towns are often flooded, threatening tourism. Many houses, perched precariously on the lakes' crumbling shores, are under threat.

Model of a 1956 Ford Fairlane

THE MOTOR CITY

In the early 20th century Detroit became the center of a revolution in transport when two engineers, Henry Ford and Ransom Olds, began mass-producing cars there. Today, Detroit is still the center of the American car industry, with several of the USA's biggest car manufacturers based in the city. Look for

TAMLA MOTOWN

In 1961 Berry Gordy, a worker from the Ford factory in Detroit, launched the Tamla Motown record label to promote local black talent. Motown artists, such as Smokey Robinson, the Supremes and Stevie Wonder, perfected the unique style of "soul" music.

OPEN HIGHWAYS

The Great Lakes states have benefited from their central location and well-developed rail and water transport systems. The region is also well served by roads – Indianapolis has more major highways than any other American city.

A farmhouse and barn in the rich farm country of Indiana.

Robie House, Chicago (built 1910), was designed by the world-famous US architect, Frank Lloyd Wright.

N

| 0 | 50 | 100 | 150 | 200 | 250 | KM |
| 0 | 25 | 50 | 75 | 100 | 125 | 150 | MILES |

31

CENTRAL AND MOUNTAIN STATES

The foothills of the snow covered Rockies in Montana.

THIS REGION INCLUDES the lowlands on the west bank of the Mississippi River, the vast expanses of the Great Plains, and the majestic Rocky Mountains. In climate, it is a region of extremes: hot summers alternate with cold winters, and hailstorms, blizzards, and tornadoes are frequent events. Once home to large numbers of Native Americans and great herds of buffalo, the plains were settled in the 19th century; the Native Americans were pushed onto reservations and the buffalo slaughtered. Originally dismissed as a desert because of low rainfall and lack of trees, the Great Plains proved to be one of the world's great agricultural regions; today, vast amounts of cereals are grown on mechanized farms, and cattle are grazed on huge ranches. The Rockies are rich in minerals, and reserves of coal, oil, and natural gas are being exploited.

Shredded wheat

AGRICULTURAL INDUSTRIES

A great range of cereals are grown in the Midwest and transported to local cities for processing. Iowa has the largest cereal processing factory in the world, and it is in the cities of this region that many cereals are prepared for the world's breakfast tables. Cities also provide storage facilities for grain and cereals, as well as markets for grain, livestock, and farm machinery.

Corn flakes *Oats* *Puffed rice*

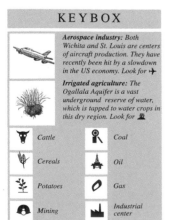

COWBOYS

Cattle are raised on the Great Plains and foothills of the Rocky Mountains. Ranches often have thousands of cattle. In summer, mounted cowboys herd cattle to upland pastures and drive them back to the ranch for the winter. Cattle are then taken to markets in nearby towns for cattle auctions. Look for ⛉

KEYBOX

✈	**Aerospace industry:** Both Wichita and St. Louis are centers of aircraft production. They have recently been hit by a slowdown in the US economy. Look for ✈
🌾	**Irrigated agriculture:** The Ogallala Aquifer is a vast underground reserve of water, which is tapped to water crops in this dry region. Look for 🌱

🐂	Cattle	⚒	Coal
🌾	Cereals	🛢	Oil
🥔	Potatoes	⬭	Gas
⛏	Mining	🏭	Industrial center

WYOMING COAL

Wyoming now leads the USA in coal production. Coal from the West is in demand because it has a lower sulfur content than coal mined in the East and causes less pollution when burned. Shallow coal reserves are extracted from open-pit mines, like this one, which spoil the landscape. Look for ⚒

Fossils of dinosaurs, such as *Tyrannosaurus*, have been found in the foothills of the Rockies.

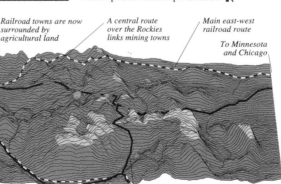

Railroad towns are now surrounded by agricultural land

A central route over the Rockies links mining towns

Main east-west railroad route

To Minnesota and Chicago

Snake River valley: potato farming on fertile floodplain

MODEL OF ROCKY MOUNTAINS

The Rocky Mountains divide the North American continent in two; rivers to the west of the range flow toward the Pacific, while those to the east drain into the Arctic and Atlantic oceans and the Gulf of Mexico. First explored by fur trappers and traders in the 19th century, the mountain passes were used by settlers on their way west. Miners followed the settlers, and the mining towns of Montana were established. By 1869, the Transcontinental railroad had crossed the Rockies, linking the Pacific Coast with the rest of the country.

FARMING

Corn is the main crop in Iowa, while wheat is more important in the center of this region. Nearer the Rockies, the rainfall decreases and wheat farming gives way to cattle ranching. Farming in the Midwest is large-scale and mechanized. These vast wheat fields in Nebraska stretch to the far horizon. Farmers often produce more than they can sell. Look for 🌾

Map labels

CANADA

WASHINGTON OREGON NEVADA UTAH

MONTANA IDAHO WYOMING

ROCKY MOUNTAIN RANGE BITTERROOT WIND RIVER RANGE BIGHORN MTS GRAND TETON MTS

Wheat Shelby Barley L. Elwell Havre
Zinc Lead Kalispell Beef Fort Peck
Coeur d'Alene Flathead L. Barley Wheat Missouri
Silver Silver Beef Great Falls
Missoula MONTANA
Lewiston Canyon Ferry L. Beef
HELENA
Salmon Anaconda Copper Butte Beef Beef
Dillon Bozeman Billings Yellowstone Beef Bighorn
Beef Beef Sheridan
Beef Cody Yellowstone L. BIGHORN MTS
BOISE Jackson L. GRAND TETON MTS
Nampa Worland
Idaho Falls Wheat Uranium
Phosphate Pocatello Iron
Beef Twin Falls Snake WYOMING
Beef Wheat Pathfinder Res.
Green R. Rock Springs Rawlins
Flaming Gorge Res.

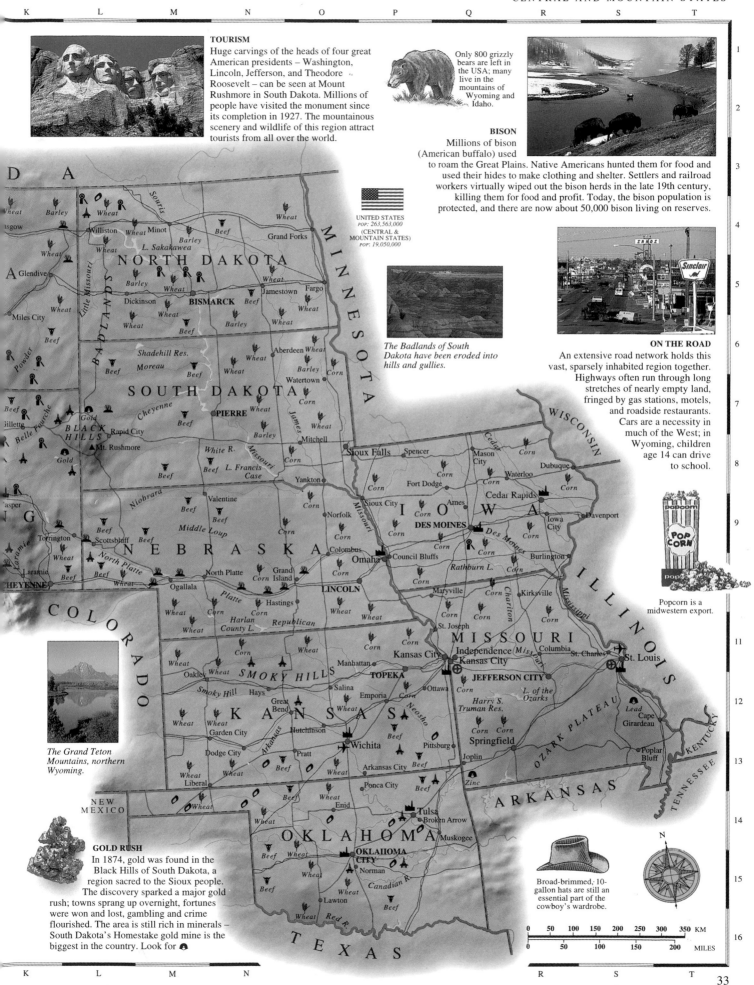

TOURISM
Huge carvings of the heads of four great American presidents – Washington, Lincoln, Jefferson, and Theodore Roosevelt – can be seen at Mount Rushmore in South Dakota. Millions of people have visited the monument since its completion in 1927. The mountainous scenery and wildlife of this region attract tourists from all over the world.

Only 800 grizzly bears are left in the USA; many live in the mountains of Wyoming and Idaho.

BISON
Millions of bison (American buffalo) used to roam the Great Plains. Native Americans hunted them for food and used their hides to make clothing and shelter. Settlers and railroad workers virtually wiped out the bison herds in the late 19th century, killing them for food and profit. Today, the bison population is protected, and there are now about 50,000 bison living on reserves.

UNITED STATES
POP: 263,563,000
(CENTRAL & MOUNTAIN STATES)
POP: 19,050,000

The Badlands of South Dakota have been eroded into hills and gullies.

ON THE ROAD
An extensive road network holds this vast, sparsely inhabited region together. Highways often run through long stretches of nearly empty land, fringed by gas stations, motels, and roadside restaurants. Cars are a necessity in much of the West; in Wyoming, children age 14 can drive to school.

Popcorn is a midwestern export.

The Grand Teton Mountains, northern Wyoming.

GOLD RUSH
In 1874, gold was found in the Black Hills of South Dakota, a region sacred to the Sioux people. The discovery sparked a major gold rush; towns sprang up overnight, fortunes were won and lost, gambling and crime flourished. The area is still rich in minerals – South Dakota's Homestake gold mine is the biggest in the country. Look for

Broad-brimmed, 10-gallon hats are still an essential part of the cowboy's wardrobe.

0 50 100 150 200 250 300 350 KM
0 50 100 150 200 MILES

33

THE SOUTHWESTERN STATES

THE SOUTHWESTERN USA is a region of deserts and high tablelands, broken by the ridges of the southern Rocky Mountains. Many different Native American peoples lived in the Southwest. The region still has the country's largest concentration of Native Americans. The first Europeans to settle in this region were the Spanish who came north from Mexico. This mixed Spanish and Native American heritage is reflected in the region's folk art, architecture, and foods. American settlers in Texas rebelled against Mexican rule in 1836, and Texas was annexed to the USA a decade later. The rest of the region became part of the USA after the Mexican War of 1846-48. Gold and silver mining and cattle ranching attracted settlers to the region in the late 19th century, and oil became a major part of Texas's economy in the 20th century. The region's natural beauty draws tourists from all over the world.

Jordan Mormon Temple, Utah

MORMON CITY
Salt Lake City in Utah is the headquarters of the Latter-day Saints, or Mormons. They settled in Utah in the 1840s, after fleeing from the eastern states, where they had been persecuted for their beliefs. There are now more than six million Mormons worldwide.

NAVAJO RUGS
Many Navajo people live on a vast reservation in Arizona and New Mexico. They still practice weaving, pottery, silverworking, and other traditional crafts. Navajo rugs are woven into geometric patterns, and colored with natural dyes such as juniper and blackberry.

The Saguaro cactus thrives in the deserts of Arizona.

An 11th-century pottery bowl, made by the Mogollon people.

KEYBOX

High-tech industry: The space program has attracted high technology industries to the area. Look for 💻

Irrigated agriculture: Sprinklers fixed on central pivots create circular oases of green fields in the arid landscape. Look for 🌱

Dams: Acute water shortages are being remedied by the construction of dams on the region's rivers. Look for 🏞

Military bases: The first nuclear bombs were tested in New Mexico and Nevada. Military installations are common in the region. Look for III

🐂	Cattle	🛢	Oil
🌾	Cereals	◍	Gas
⚓	Cotton	🏭	Industrial center
⛏	Mining	🎿	Skiing

THE GREAT OUTDOORS
Riding, hiking, canoeing, skiing, and fishing are just some of the outdoor activities which draw tourists to the Southwest. But the region's main attraction is the Grand Canyon. About 10,000 visitors each year navigate the Canyon's dangerous waters on rubber rafts, and many others explore it on foot or by donkey.

TAOS
The *pueblo*, or village, of Taos in New Mexico is built of unbaked clay brick, called *adobe*. This style of building dates back to the Pueblo people, who lived in the region a thousand years ago, farming corn, cotton, beans, and squash.

These strangely shaped rocks in Monument Valley, Arizona, have been carved by the wind.

THE GRAND CANYON
Over the last million years, the Colorado River has cut its way through the rocky plateaus of northern Arizona. At the same time, the plateaus have risen. This combined action has formed the largest land gorge in the world – the Grand Canyon. It is more than 1 mile (1.6 km) deep, and 220 miles (350 km) long. Some of the oldest rocks in North America have been found at the base of the canyon.

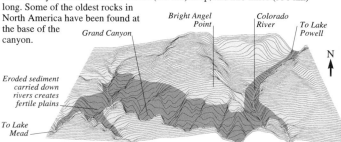
Bright Angel Point
Colorado River
To Lake Powell
Grand Canyon
Eroded sediment carried down rivers creates fertile plains
To Lake Mead
N

Map labels

OREGON
IDAHO
BLACK ROCK DESERT
Mercury
Beef
Bear L.
Winnemucca
Beef
Great Salt L.
Brigham City
Logan
Rye Patch Res.
GREAT
Ogden
Pyramid L.
Gold
Humboldt
Bountiful
SALT LAKE CITY
Elko
Reno
Sparks
BASIN
Tooele
Zinc
L. Utah
Orem
Provo
CARSON CITY
L. Tahoe
Copper
NEVADA
Silver
Walker L.
Ely
Beef
UTAH
Sevier L.
Salina
CALIFORNIA
Beef
Bryce Canyon
Nellis Air Force Range
Uranium
Iron
L. Powell
Glen Canyon Dam
Uranium
Nevada Test Site
Monument Valley
North Las Vegas
L. Mead
Grand Canyon
Bright Angel Point
PAINTED DESERT
Las Vegas
Henderson
Hoover Dam
COLORADO PLATEAU
Davis Dam
Flagstaff
Colorado
ARIZONA
Beef
Parker Dam
Prescott
Theodore Roosevelt L.
Salt
SONORAN
Glendale
Scottsdale
PHOENIX
Mesa
Copper
Copper
Yuma
Imperial Dam
Central Arizona Project
Colorado Project
Luke Air Force Range
Casa Grande
Copper
Silver
Copper
Tucson
DESERT
Santa Cruz
Beef
Copper
Dougla

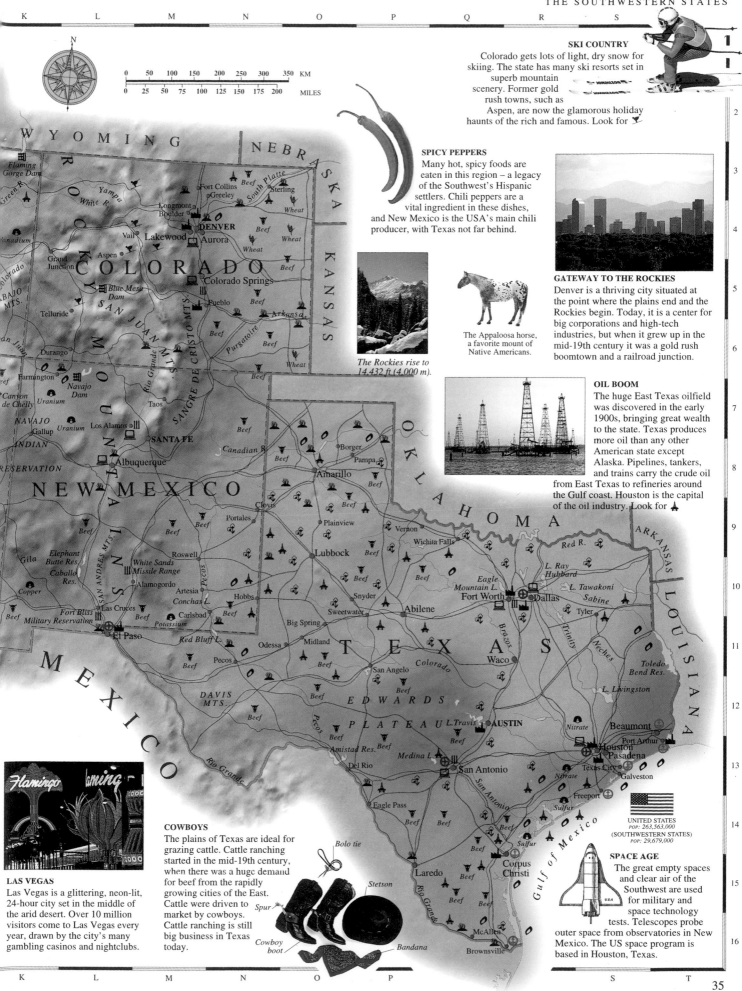

SKI COUNTRY
Colorado gets lots of light, dry snow for skiing. The state has many ski resorts set in superb mountain scenery. Former gold rush towns, such as Aspen, are now the glamorous holiday haunts of the rich and famous. Look for 🎿

SPICY PEPPERS
Many hot, spicy foods are eaten in this region – a legacy of the Southwest's Hispanic settlers. Chili peppers are a vital ingredient in these dishes, and New Mexico is the USA's main chili producer, with Texas not far behind.

The Rockies rise to 14,432 ft (4,000 m).

The Appaloosa horse, a favorite mount of Native Americans.

GATEWAY TO THE ROCKIES
Denver is a thriving city situated at the point where the plains end and the Rockies begin. Today, it is a center for big corporations and high-tech industries, but when it grew up in the mid-19th century it was a gold rush boomtown and a railroad junction.

OIL BOOM
The huge East Texas oilfield was discovered in the early 1900s, bringing great wealth to the state. Texas produces more oil than any other American state except Alaska. Pipelines, tankers, and trains carry the crude oil from East Texas to refineries around the Gulf coast. Houston is the capital of the oil industry. Look for ⚒

LAS VEGAS
Las Vegas is a glittering, neon-lit, 24-hour city set in the middle of the arid desert. Over 10 million visitors come to Las Vegas every year, drawn by the city's many gambling casinos and nightclubs.

COWBOYS
The plains of Texas are ideal for grazing cattle. Cattle ranching started in the mid-19th century, when there was a huge demand for beef from the rapidly growing cities of the East. Cattle were driven to market by cowboys. Cattle ranching is still big business in Texas today.

Bolo tie

Stetson

Spur

Cowboy boot

Bandana

UNITED STATES
POP: 263,563,000
(SOUTHWESTERN STATES)
POP: 29,679,000

SPACE AGE
The great empty spaces and clear air of the Southwest are used for military and space technology tests. Telescopes probe outer space from observatories in New Mexico. The US space program is based in Houston, Texas.

THE PACIFIC STATES

THE PACIFIC COAST STATES boast some of the most varied scenery in the USA. California, for example, contains the snow-capped peaks of the Sierra Nevada Mountains and the lowest point in North America – Death Valley. Much of California is arid, with farming dependent on irrigation, while vast forests and well-watered fertile valleys are characteristic of Washington and Oregon. American settlers began to cross the Rockies to the Pacific Coast in the 1840s. California became part of the USA as a result of the Mexican-American War (1846-48), and the discovery of gold in 1848 led to its rapid settlement. All three states are now major agricultural producers and centers of high-technology industry. In the early 1960s, California became the USA's most highly populated state. Despite recent problems, the state's economy rivals those of many wealthy nations.

AGRICULTURE

California alone produces half of the USA's fruit and vegetables. Fertile soils and a warm climate have contributed to the state's success, but dry conditions mean that much of the state's farmland has to be irrigated. California's main crops are cotton and grapes. Look for 🍇

Almond

Avocado

Peach

Plum

TIMBER

Oregon and Washington are the USA's major timber producers. The region's cedar and fir forests supply one-third of the country's softwood timber. The trees are cut into logs at one of the thousands of sawmills in the forests and then floated down rivers on rafts to the large coastal cities. Some of the wood is made into paper at pulp mills like the one pictured here. Much of the region's timber is exported to Japan. Logging has reduced the region's stocks of mature trees; efforts are now being made to plant more trees. Look for 🌲

AEROSPACE

The Boeing Corporation, the world's largest aircraft manufacturer, is based in Seattle. Boeing is the city's main employer, and any decline in orders can result in unemployment. California is a major producer of military aircraft; cuts in U.S. defense spending have badly affected this region. Look for ✈

Boeing 767 aircraft

California redwoods are evergreen trees which can reach 330 ft (100 m).

Washington's Mount Rainier is permanently snow-covered.

Fortune cookie served in San Francisco's Chinese restaurants

IMMIGRATION

California attracts many immigrants from Asia and South America. Many Chinese immigrants have settled in San Francisco's Chinatown. This area of the city is a magnet for the Chinese community and is famous for its shops and restaurants. Immigrants from Latin America, especially Mexico, make up a growing part of the state's population.

SILICON VALLEY

Santa Clara Valley south of San Francisco has one of the largest concentrations of high-technology industry in the world. Over 3,000 area firms specialize in microelectronics and computer hardware and software. U.S. manufacturers face increasing competition from Asia. Look for 💻

Computer disks capable of storing vast amounts of information

SAN FRANCISCO

San Francisco is located on one of the world's finest natural harbors and is the West Coast's trade and shipping center. The city is built on a hilly peninsula, with some of the steepest streets in the world. San Francisco suffers from frequent earthquakes because it is situated on the San Andreas Fault. The city's large skyscrapers are specially designed to withstand earthquakes.

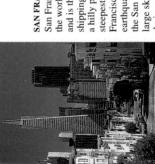

Waves batter the rugged Pacific coast of Oregon.

CANADA

IDAHO

WASHINGTON

OREGON

Spokane
Uranium
Gold
Ross L.
L. Chelan
Banks L.
Moses Lake
Bellingham
Everett
Snohomish
Edmonds
Bellevue
Seattle
Tacoma
OLYMPIA
Riffe L.
Longview
Vancouver
Portland
SALEM
Albany
Corvallis
Eugene
Springfield
Roseburg
Coos Bay
Bandon
Newport
Astoria
Aberdeen
Hillsboro
Port Angeles
Olympic National Park
San Juan Is.
Bremerton
Columbia
Snake
Yakima
Ellensburg
Richland
Kennewick
Walla Walla
Pendleton
The Dalles
John Day
Bend
La Grande
Baker City
Burns
Malheur L.
Harney L.
Owyhee
BLUE MOUNTAINS
△ Mt. Rainier
Strait of Juan de Fuca

PA

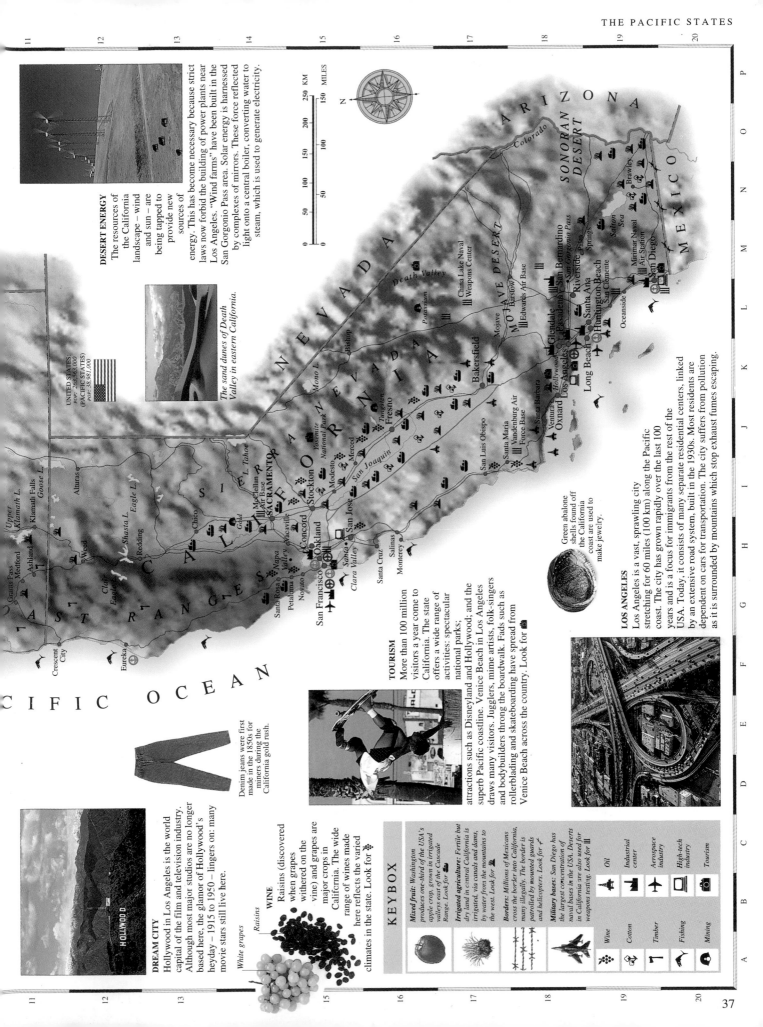

DESERT ENERGY

The resources of the California landscape – wind and sun – are being tapped to provide new sources of energy. This has become necessary because strict laws now forbid the building of power plants near Los Angeles. "Wind farms" have been built in the San Gorgonio Pass area. Solar energy is harnessed by complexes of mirrors. These force reflected light onto a central boiler, converting water to steam, which is used to generate electricity.

The sand dunes of Death Valley in eastern California.

UNITED STATES:
POP: 263,563,000
(PACIFIC STATES)
POP: 38,981,000

DREAM CITY

Hollywood in Los Angeles is the world capital of the film and television industry. Although most major studios are no longer based here, the glamor of Hollywood's heyday – 1915 to 1950 – lingers on: many movie stars still live here.

HOLLYWOOD

Denim jeans were first made in the 1850s for miners during the California gold rush.

WINE

Raisins (discovered when grapes withered on the vine) and grapes are major crops in California. The wide range of wines made here reflects the varied climates in the state. Look for 🍇

White grapes
Raisins

TOURISM

More than 100 million visitors a year come to California. The state offers a wide range of activities: spectacular national parks; attractions such as Disneyland and Hollywood; and the superb Pacific coastline. Venice Beach in Los Angeles draws many visitors. Jugglers, mime artists, folk-singers and bodybuilders throng the boardwalk. Fads such as rollerblading and skateboarding have spread from Venice Beach across the country. Look for 📷

LOS ANGELES

Los Angeles is a vast, sprawling city stretching for 60 miles (100 km) along the Pacific coast. The city has grown rapidly over the last 100 years, and is a focus for immigrants from the rest of the USA. Today, it consists of many separate residential centers, linked by an extensive road system, built in the 1930s. Most residents are dependent on cars for transportation. The city suffers from pollution as it is surrounded by mountains which stop exhaust fumes escaping.

Green abalone shells found off the California coast are used to make jewelry.

KEYBOX

Mixed fruit: Washington produces one-third of the USA's apple crop, grown in irrigated valleys east of the Cascade Range. Look for 🍎

Irrigated agriculture: Fertile but dry land in central California is irrigated, via canals and dams, by water from the mountains to the west. Look for 🌾

Borders: Millions of Mexicans cross the border into California, many illegally. The border is patrolled by mounted guards and helicopters. Look for ⚜

Military bases: San Diego has the largest concentration of naval bases in the USA. Deserts in California are also used for weapons testing. Look for ✈

Wine	🍇
Cotton	🌿
Timber	🪓
Fishing	🎣
Mining	⛏

Oil	🛢
Industrial center	🏭
Aerospace industry	✈
High-tech industry	💻
Tourism	📷

PACIFIC OCEAN

Map labels: ARIZONA, SONORAN DESERT, MEXICO, NEVADA, CALIFORNIA, SIERRA NEVADA, COAST RANGES, Colorado, Death Valley, MOJAVE DESERT, China Lake Naval Weapons Center, Edwards Air Base, Barstow, San Bernardino, San Gorgonio Pass, Riverside, Palm Springs, Salton Sea, Miramar Naval Air Station, San Diego, Oceanside, San Clemente, Santa Ana, Huntington Beach, Long Beach, Los Angeles, Hollywood, Glendale, Pasadena, Oxnard, Ventura, Santa Barbara, Vandenburg Air Force Base, Santa Maria, San Luis Obispo, Bakersfield, Mojave, Fresno, Tunisters, Merced, Modesto, San Joaquin, Yosemite National Park, Stockton, Concord, Oakland, San Francisco, San Jose, Santa Clara Valley, Salinas, Monterey, Santa Cruz, Potarium, Bishop, Mono L., L. Tahoe, SACRAMENTO, McClellan Air Base, Vacaville, Napa Valley, Santa Rosa, Petaluma, Novato, Chico, Clear L., Eagle L., Redding, Weed, Shasta L., Goose L., Eagle L., Alturas, Klamath Falls, Upper Klamath L., Ashland, Medford, Grants Pass, Crescent City, Eureka

KM MILES
250
200
150
100
50
0

N

A B C D E H I J

MEXICO

THE LAND OF MEXICO consists of a dry plateau crossed by broad valleys and enclosed to the west and east by mountains, some of which are volcanic. Baja California, the Yucatan Peninsula, and the country's coasts are the main low-lying areas. Mexico was once home to civilizations such as the Maya and Aztec, who built magnificent cities containing plazas, palaces, and pyramids. Lured by legends of fabulous hoards of gold and silver, Spanish conquistadores invaded Mexico in 1519 and destroyed the Aztec Empire. For 300 years the Spanish ruled the country, unifying it with their language and the Roman Catholic religion. Mexico succeeded in winning its independence from Spain by 1821. Today, most Mexicans are *mestizo* – which means they are descendants of the native peoples and the Spanish settlers. Although half the population lives in towns, many people still inhabit areas only accessible on horseback, but rail and air transport are improving. So much of the country is mountainous or dry that only 12 percent of the land can be used for farming. Mexico has vast oil reserves and mineral riches, but suffers from overpopulation and huge foreign debts. The North American Free Trade Agreement (NAFTA) adopted in 1993 promised to strengthen Mexico's economy.

MEXICO
POP: 95,365,000

Tijuana
Mexicali
Colorado
Ensenada
UNITED ST
Nogales
Millet
Copper
Ángel de la Guarda I.
Tiburón I. Hermosillo
Millet
Cedros I.
Guaymas
SIERRA MADRE OC
Lead
Zinc
Mill
Conchos
Santa Rosalia
Ciudad Obregón
Zinc
Silver
Manganese
Los Mochis
Carmen I.
Santa Catalina I.
San José I.
Culiacán
Espíritu Santo I.
Cerralvo I.
La Paz
Millet
Mazatlán

Cedros Island, off the northwest coast of Mexico.

THE DAY OF THE DEAD
Mexicans believe that life is like a flower; it slowly opens and then closes again. During the annual festival of the Day of the Dead, the streets are decorated with flowers, and ghoulish skeletons are everywhere.

Skeleton made of papier-mâché

TEXTILES
Although many fabrics are now machine-made, some Mexicans still practice their traditional art of hand-weaving colorful textiles. This *sarape*, part of the traditional Mexican dress for men, is worn over the shoulder.

Teeth made of shell

Aztec mask, inlaid with turquoise, depicting a god.

AGRICULTURE
Although Mexico is rapidly industrializing, over half the working population still makes its living from farming. They grow crops like corn, beans, and vegetables, and raise cattle, sheep, pigs, and chickens.

Cacti growing on Mexico's dry central plateau.

Corn
Marías Is.

SPIKED DRINKS
The desert and dry regions of Mexico are home to many varieties of the spiny-leaved *agave* plant. Juice from two varieties is used to make the alcoholic drinks *tequila* and *mezcal*. The *agave* plant is grown on plantations, then cooked, crushed, and fermented. The drink is exported worldwide.

KEYBOX

Tourism: Resort cities like Acapulco attract thousands of visitors to Mexico each year. Tourism is now a vital source of foreign currency. Look for

Maquiladora: American raw materials are brought across the border to supply factories, or maquiladora, where labor costs are lower. Look for

Cereals		Fishing	
Sugarcane		Mining	
Coffee		Oil	
Cotton		Industrial center	
Forest products		Archaeological site	

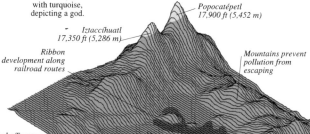

Popocatépetl
17,900 ft (5,452 m)

Iztaccíhuatl
17,350 ft (5,286 m)

Ribbon development along railroad routes

Mountains prevent pollution from escaping

Lake Texcoco

Uncontrolled expansion of suburbs

Limit of urban area

Center of Mexico City

N

MEXICO CITY
The Aztec capital, Tenochtitlán, was built on islands in Lake Texcoco. The city was destroyed by the Spanish, but modern-day Mexico City is built on the ruins. By AD 2000 it is expected to be the world's largest city, containing over 20 million people. Mexico City is very polluted because it is surrounded by a ring of mountains which trap polluted air from cars and factories.

A B C D E G H I J

HOT DISHES
Mexicans eat a wide variety of foods. Chili peppers are an important ingredient and are used to add spice and fire to many dishes. Pancakes, or *tortillas,* form the basis of most meals. They are made from corn or wheat flour and can be filled with meat, vegetables, and cheese.

Green pepper

Maize

Avocado

Chili

Red snapper is a favorite dish, fried or grilled.

SILVER
Mexico is rich in minerals. Spanish settlers discovered silver in the mountains of the Sierra Madre in the 16th century. Today, Mexico supplies one-fifth of the world's silver, some of which is made into fine jewelry. Look for

Silver brooch

MUSIC
Traditional folk music is very popular in Mexico. *Mariachi* bands like these wear colorful clothes and play and sing in cafés and plazas all over the country.

SOUVENIR SELLERS
Thousands of people find ways of making a living in the crowded streets of Mexico City. Vendors sell food, clothes, and lottery tickets; small boys earn a few *pesos* as fire-eaters while others sell souvenirs to tourists.

THE CHEW IN GUM
In the forests of Mexico grows the wild sapodilla tree, from which a milky white sap called *chicle* is extracted. When processed, the sap becomes a gum, the vital ingredient that makes chewing gum chewy.

SUPER SADDLERY
Many horses are bred on the northern grasslands. Horses were brought to Mexico by the Spanish in the 16th century. Many Mexicans are expert riders. They use leather saddles made by local craftsmen.

Saddle horn

Straps for saddle packs

Leather stirrup

LURE OF THE PAST
This 12th-century Mayan pyramid in the city of Chichén Itzá is one of the many buildings left by the ancient civilizations which once inhabited Mexico. Four stairways lead up to a beautifully carved temple. Look for

Pyramid steps

Temple platform

Cozumel Island, off the coast of the Yucatán Peninsula.

BLACK GOLD
Mexico's rich reserves of oil and natural gas are vital to its economy. Oil is found mainly along the Bay of Campeche and sent to refineries like this one. Look for

Popocatépetl is a dormant snow-covered volcano.

Colossal stone head made by the Olmec people, the first Central American civilization.

K L M N O P Q R S T

0 50 100 150 200 250 300 350 400 KM

0 50 100 150 200 MILES

Toco toucan
Ramphastos toco
Length: 24 in (60 cm)

Emerald tree boa
Corallus caninus
Length: 6 ft (1.8 m)

Geoffroy's spider monkey
Ateles geoffroyi
Length: 5 ft (1.5 m)

CENTRAL AND SOUTH AMERICA

SOUTH AMERICA is shaped like a giant triangle that tapers southward from the Equator to Cape Horn. A huge wall of mountains, the Andes, stretches for 4,500 miles (7,250 km) along the entire Pacific coast. Until 3 million years ago, South America was not connected to North America, so life there evolved in isolation. Several extraordinary animal groups developed, including sloths and anteaters. Many unique plant species originated here, too, such as the potato and tomato. South America has the world's largest area of tropical rain forest, through which run the Amazon River and its many tributaries. Central America is mountainous and forested.

TROPICAL TOBAGO
Coconut palms grow along the shores of many Caribbean islands. Palms have flexible trunks that enable them to withstand tropical storms.

Mahogany
Swietenia macrophylla
Height: 82 ft (25 m)

VOLCANIC ISLANDS
One of the extinct volcanic craters of the Galápagos island group breaks the surface of the Pacific Ocean. Like other isolated regions of the world, many unique species have evolved here, such as the giant tortoise 4 ft (1.2 m) long.

SEA-DWELLING TREES
Mangroves grow along tropical coastlines. The tangled roots of Pinuelo mangroves create ideal homes for tiny aquatic species.

PAMPAS
Giant grasses up to 10 ft (3 m) high grow on Argentina's dry southern Pampas. Here, further north, more plentiful rainfall supports a few scattered trees.

Alpaca
Lama pacos
Height: 5 ft (1.5 m)

Archaeogeryon, a crab that lived in this region 20 million years ago.

THE FOREST FLOOR
Tropical rain forest trees form such a dense canopy that little sunlight or rain can reach the ground 200 ft (70 m) below. Rain forest soils are easily washed away when the trees and plants are removed.

THE BLEAK SOUTH
Patagonia's cold desert environment contrasts starkly with the lush hot forests of Amazonia. Plants take root in the cracks of bare rock and grow close to the ground to survive icy winds.

VOLCANIC ANDES
Steam and smoke rises from Villarrica, an active volcano. Many peaks in the Andes are active or former volcanoes. Despite the intense heat within these lava-filled mountains, the highest are permanently covered in snow – even those on the Equator.

Passionflower
Passiflora caerulea
Across bloom: 6 in (15 cm)

BIRTH OF A RIVER
The snow-capped peaks of the Andes are the source of the Amazon, the world's second longest river. It is 4,080 miles (6,570 km) long.

CROSS SECTION THROUGH SOUTH AMERICA

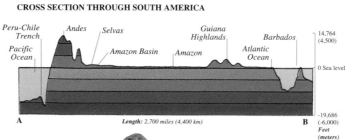

Peru-Chile Trench — Andes — Selvas — Guiana Highlands — Barbados
Pacific Ocean — Amazon Basin — Amazon — Atlantic Ocean
14,764 (4,500)
0 Sea level
-19,686 (-6,000)
Feet (meters)
A — *Length: 2,700 miles (4,400 km)* — B

DRY ATACAMA DESERT
The Atacama Desert is the world's driest place outside Antarctica. Rain has not fallen in some areas for hundreds of years. Winds that pass over cold coastline currents absorb no moisture.

Giant anteater
Myrmecophaga tridactyla
Length: 7 ft (2 m)

Galápagos fur seal
Arctocephalus galapagoensis
Length: 6 ft (1.8 m)

Ocelot
Felis pardalis
Length: 6 ft (1.7 m)

The triton shell can be found from Central America to Brazil.

GREAT WATERS
The Iguaçu Falls in Brazil are spectacular. Water thunders over the rim from November to March, but at other times slows to almost a trickle.

Common Chilean tarantula
Grammostola spatulatus
Length: 4 in (10 cm)

KEY TO SYMBOLS

▲ Mountain
△ Volcano
⚜ Mangroves
▦ Wetlands
▨ Coral reef
▦ Plate margins and direction of movement

KEY TO NATURAL VEGETATION

□ Tropical grassland
□ Mountain
□ Mediterranean-type
□ Broadleaf forest
□ Cold desert
□ Tropical rain forest
□ Dry woodland
□ Temperate rain forest
□ Temperate grassland
□ Hot desert

A B C D E F G H I

CENTRAL AMERICA
AND THE CARIBBEAN

THE TROPICAL REGION OF Central America and the Caribbean was settled by
hunters and farmers many thousands of years ago. By 300 BC the
Maya had established a sophisticated civilization on the
mainland – ruins of their pyramids and temples can
still be seen deep in the forests of Guatemala.
The Maya, as well as the native peoples who
lived on the Caribbean islands, were almost wiped out
by European explorers who arrived in the 15th century. From this
time, European nations, in particular the British, French, Spanish, and
Dutch, competed for control of the region
and some countries did not gain independence
until recently. Europeans brought slaves
from Africa to work on vast sugar
plantations. In the last few
decades, tourism has enriched
the Caribbean, but in Central
America, poverty and civil
wars are still major problems.

*A Jamaican beach devastated
by a hurricane.*

CUBA
POP: 11,172,000

HAVANA
(LA HABANA)
Matanzas
Copper Pinar del Río
I. de la Juventud
(I. of Pines)
Cienfuegos
Santa Clara
Camagüey
Jardines de la Reina

GUATEMALA
POP: 10,000,000

Tikal
Altun Ha
Belize City
BELMOPAN
San Ignacio
Belize
Flores

BELIZE
POP: 200,000

G R E A T E R
Little
Cayman
GEORGETOWN Grand Cayman Brac
Cayman
CAYMAN ISLANDS
(UK)
Gulf of Guacanayab

JAMAICA
POP: 2,572,000

M E X I C O

G U A T E M A L A

Cobán
Huehuetenango
Quezaltenango Nickel
Sololá L. Izabal
Mazatenango
GUATEMALA
CITY
Escuintla
Copán
Santa Rosa
Puerto Barrios
Zacapa
Puerto Cortés
San Pedro
Sula
La Ceiba
Trujillo

B E L I Z E

Gulf of Honduras

HONDURAS
POP: 5,600,000

Conches from
the shallow
waters of the
Caribbean
are edible.

Savanna-la-Mar
Montego
Bay
JAMAICA
Spanish Tow

C A R I B B E A N

H O N D U R A S

Caratasca
Lagoon

EL SALVADOR
POP: 5,400,000

Santa Ana
La Libertad
SAN SALVADOR
La Esperanza
Comayagua
TEGUCIGALPA
Juticalpa
Patuca
Coco

San Miguel
EL SALVADOR
San Lorenzo
Choluteca
Somoto
Gold
Copper
Puerto
Cabezas

Chinandega
Corinto
Estelí
Jinotega
Matagalpa
León
L. Managua
Boaco
MANAGUA
Juigalpa
Granada
L. Nicaragua
Rivas
Bluefields

N I C A R A G U A

Río Grande

NICARAGUA
POP: 4,100,000

NICARAGUA
Since Nicaragua
became independent in
1838 it has been
devastated by civil war
and foreign
interference. During
the 1980s, a desperate conflict took place between the Marxist
government and the right-wing *Contras,* supported by the
USA. Although democracy has now been restored, little
progress has been made in fighting the huge problems of
poverty, ill-health, and homelessness.

*The ancient Maya temple of
Altun Ha is hidden deep in the
rain forest of Belize.*

RURAL MARKETS
Many Guatemalans live in
small villages, growing corn
and beans and making
brightly colored cloth,
baskets, pottery, and wood
carvings. These goods, as
well as fruit and tobacco, are
sold at local markets.

KEYBOX

*Archaeological sites: Great
civilizations, such as the Maya,
flourished in Central America
from 300 BC. They built temples,
palaces, and cities. Look for* ▲

*Shellfishing: Shrimp and
lobsters thrive in the mangrove
swamps on the coasts of Central
America, which provide rich
feeding grounds. Look for*

*Shipping registry: Ships from all
over the world fly Panama's flag.
They register there because of
low fees and limited controls on
the labor force. Look for* ▰

↓	Sugarcane	🌿	Tobacco
	Bananas	🔧	Timber
	Coffee	⬤	Mining
	Cocoa		Industrial center
⚓	Cotton		Tourism

San Carlos
Liberia
San Juan
Puntarenas
C O S T A
Alajuela
SAN JOSE
Cartago
Puerto Limón
Gulf
of Nicoya
R I C A

COSTA RICA
POP: 3,300,000

*Swamps near the
Honduran coast.*

N

0 50 100 150 200 250 300 350 400 KM
0 50 100 150 200 MILES

Bocas del Toro
Mosquito
Gulf
Colón
Panama Canal
P A N A M A
David
Copper
Peñonomé
PANAMA CITY
Gulf of
Chiriquí
Santiago
San José I.
Gulf of Panama
Gulf of
Darien
Coiba I.
Chitré
Isla del Rey
Las Tablas
La Palma

Hot pepper
sauce, made
with spicy
chilis, is
used all over
the region.

PANAMA
POP: 2,600,000

C O L O M B I A

42

PACIFIC OCEAN

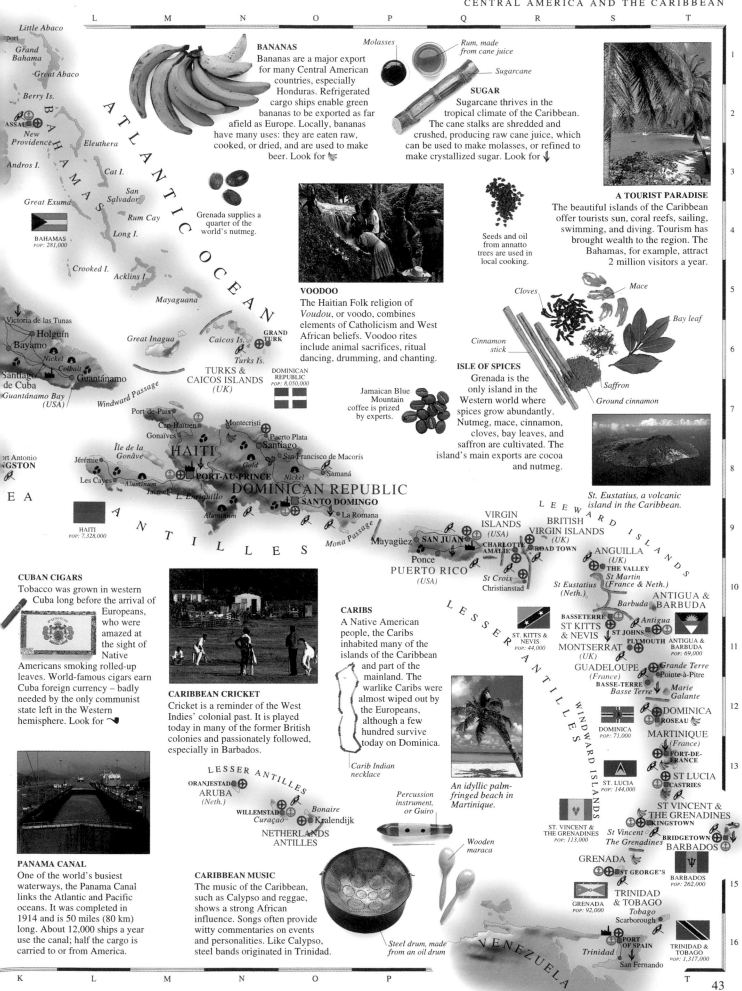

BANANAS

Bananas are a major export for many Central American countries, especially Honduras. Refrigerated cargo ships enable green bananas to be exported as far afield as Europe. Locally, bananas have many uses: they are eaten raw, cooked, or dried, and are used to make beer. Look for 🍌

Molasses

Rum, made from cane juice

Sugarcane

SUGAR

Sugarcane thrives in the tropical climate of the Caribbean. The cane stalks are shredded and crushed, producing raw cane juice, which can be used to make molasses, or refined to make crystallized sugar. Look for ⬇

Little Abaco

port

Grand Bahama

Great Abaco

Berry Is.

NASSAU
New Providence

Eleuthera

Andros I.

Cat I.

San Salvador

Rum Cay

Long I.

Great Exuma

BAHAMAS
POP: 281,000

Crooked I.

Acklins I.

Mayaguana

ATLANTIC OCEAN

BAHAMAS

Grenada supplies a quarter of the world's nutmeg.

A TOURIST PARADISE

The beautiful islands of the Caribbean offer tourists sun, coral reefs, sailing, swimming, and diving. Tourism has brought wealth to the region. The Bahamas, for example, attract 2 million visitors a year.

Seeds and oil from annatto trees are used in local cooking.

VOODOO

The Haitian Folk religion of *Voudou*, or voodo, combines elements of Catholicism and West African beliefs. Voodoo rites include animal sacrifices, ritual dancing, drumming, and chanting.

Cloves

Mace

Cinnamon stick

Bay leaf

Victoria de las Tunas

Holguín

Bayamo

Nickel

Cobalt

Santiago de Cuba

Guantánamo

Guantánamo Bay (USA)

Windward Passage

Great Inagua

Caicos Is.

GRAND TURK

Turks Is.

TURKS & CAICOS ISLANDS (UK)

DOMINICAN REPUBLIC *POP: 8,050,000*

Saffron

Ground cinnamon

ISLE OF SPICES

Grenada is the only island in the Western world where spices grow abundantly. Nutmeg, mace, cinnamon, cloves, bay leaves, and saffron are cultivated. The island's main exports are cocoa and nutmeg.

Jamaican Blue Mountain coffee is prized by experts.

Port Antonio

KINGSTON

Port-de-Paix

Cap-Haïtien

Montecristi

Gonaïves

Puerto Plata

HAITI

Île de la Gonâve

Santiago

San Francisco de Macorís

Jérémie

Gold

PORT-AU-PRINCE

Nickel

Samaná

Les Cayes

Aluminum

DOMINICAN REPUBLIC

St. Eustatius, a volcanic island in the Caribbean.

Jacmel

L. Enriquillo

SANTO DOMINGO

HAITI *POP: 7,328,000*

Aluminum

ANTILLES

La Romana

Mona Passage

Mayagüez

SAN JUAN

Ponce

PUERTO RICO (USA)

St Croix

Christianstad

VIRGIN ISLANDS (USA)

CHARLOTTE AMALIE

BRITISH VIRGIN ISLANDS (UK)

ROAD TOWN

St Eustatius (Neth.)

ANGUILLA (UK)

THE VALLEY

St Martin (France & Neth.)

LEEWARD ISLANDS

ANTIGUA & BARBUDA

Barbuda

Antigua

LESSER ANTILLES

CARIBS

A Native American people, the Caribs inhabited many of the islands of the Caribbean and part of the mainland. The warlike Caribs were almost wiped out by the Europeans, although a few hundred survive today on Dominica.

Carib Indian necklace

BASSETERRE

ST. KITTS & NEVIS *POP: 44,000*

ST KITTS & NEVIS

ST JOHNS

MONTSERRAT (UK)

PLYMOUTH

ANTIGUA & BARBUDA *POP: 69,000*

GUADELOUPE (France)

Grande Terre
Pointe-à-Pitre

BASSE-TERRE
Basse Terre

Marie Galante

DOMINICA

ROSEAU

DOMINICA *POP: 71,000*

CUBAN CIGARS

Tobacco was grown in western Cuba long before the arrival of Europeans, who were amazed at the sight of Native Americans smoking rolled-up leaves. World-famous cigars earn Cuba foreign currency – badly needed by the only communist state left in the Western hemisphere. Look for 🚬

CARIBBEAN CRICKET

Cricket is a reminder of the West Indies' colonial past. It is played today in many of the former British colonies and passionately followed, especially in Barbados.

WINDWARD ISLANDS

LESSER ANTILLES

MARTINIQUE (France)

FORT-DE-FRANCE

ST LUCIA

CASTRIES

ST LUCIA *POP: 144,000*

ORANJESTAD

ARUBA (Neth.)

Bonaire

WILLEMSTAD

Curaçao

Kralendijk

NETHERLANDS ANTILLES

An idyllic palm-fringed beach in Martinique.

Percussion instrument, or Guiro

ST VINCENT & THE GRENADINES

KINGSTOWN

St Vincent The Grenadines

ST. VINCENT & THE GRENADINES *POP: 113,000*

BRIDGETOWN

BARBADOS

Wooden maraca

GRENADA

ST GEORGE'S

BARBADOS *POP: 262,000*

PANAMA CANAL

One of the world's busiest waterways, the Panama Canal links the Atlantic and Pacific oceans. It was completed in 1914 and is 50 miles (80 km) long. About 12,000 ships a year use the canal; half the cargo is carried to or from America.

CARIBBEAN MUSIC

The music of the Caribbean, such as Calypso and reggae, shows a strong African influence. Songs often provide witty commentaries on events and personalities. Like Calypso, steel bands originated in Trinidad.

Steel drum, made from an oil drum

GRENADA *POP: 92,000*

TRINIDAD & TOBAGO

Tobago
Scarborough

Trinidad

PORT OF SPAIN

San Fernando

TRINIDAD & TOBAGO *POP: 1,317,000*

VENEZUELA

NORTHERN SOUTH AMERICA

THIS REGION IS DOMINATED BY the volcanic peaks and mountain ranges of the Andes. The powerful Incas ruled much of this area in the 15th century, and large numbers of their descendants still live in Peru, Bolivia, and Ecuador today. In the 16th century, Spanish *conquistadores* reached South America, swept the Incas and other native peoples aside, and colonized the region from Venezuela to Bolivia. Although areas to the east were later settled by the French, Dutch, and British. All the countries except French Guiana are now independent republics, independence has brought many problems, such as military dictatorships, high inflation, organized crime, the illegal drug trade, and huge foreign debts. Many of the cities are overcrowded, but large numbers of people still flock there from the countryside, looking for jobs.

MARKET DAY
Brightly dressed in their traditional Andean clothes and hats, local people display their wares in the market of the Peruvian town of Pisác. They sell fruit and vegetables, together with pottery and clothes produced for the tourist trade.

Hammered gold
A figure made by ancient Colombian craftsmen.

CARACAS
The discovery of oil in 1917 made Venezuela the richest country in the region. Its capital, Caracas, was built with oil money. Modern highways and skyscrapers dominate the city, but many people live in shantytowns on the surrounding hillsides.

The lush Caribbean coastline of northern Venezuela.

SHRIMP
Shrimp living in the muddy waters of Ecuador's mangrove swamps have become the country's second most important source of foreign currency, after oil. But as the industry expands, it is destroying the mangroves – the shrimps' natural habitat. Look for 🦐

EMERALDS
Some of the world's finest emeralds are mined near Bogotá, the capital of Colombia. Long before the Spanish invaded the country in search of gold, native peoples mined the emeralds for their gold jewelry and ceremonial objects. Look for 💚

Emerald

Cinchona leaves
Quinine from the bark of the Peruvian *cinchona* tree is used to treat malaria.

The ancient Inca city of Machu Picchu in the Peruvian Andes.

KM MILES

VENEZUELA
POP: 20,490,000

SURINAME
POP: 470,000

GUYANA
POP: 845,000

COLOMBIA
POP: 35,624,000

ECUADOR
POP: 12,063,000

FRENCH GUIANA (France)

SURINAME

GUYANA

VENEZUELA

COLOMBIA

BRAZIL

ECUADOR

PANAMA

CARIBBEAN SEA

PACIFIC OCEAN

CAYENNE
Kourou
Gold
St Laurent-du-Maroni
Albina
PARAMARIBO
Brokopondo
Aluminum
Kabalebo Res.
New Amsterdam
Fort Wellington
Georgetown
Bartica
Gold
Aluminum
Mazaruni
Diamonds
Essequibo
Suddie
Lethem
Beef
Santa Elena
Diamonds
Gold
Maburuma
Ciudad Guayana
Gold
Aluminum
Guri Res.
Orinoco
Iron
Ciudad Bolívar
Tucupita
Maturín
Cumaná
Barcelona
La Asunción
Margarita I.
San Juan de los Morros
Maracay
Valencia
Puerto Cabello
San Felipe
Coro
Barquisimeto
Trujillo
Barinas
San Carlos
Guanare
San Fernando de Apure
Puerto Ayacucho
Puerto Carreño
Puerto Inírida
Mitú
Leticia
Amazon
Caquetá
Napo
Iquitos
Putumayo
Morona
Marañón
Cabimas
Maracaibo
L. Maracaibo
Mérida
San Cristóbal
Cúcuta
Arauca
Arauca
Yopal
Bucaramanga
Meta
Villavicencio
San José del Guaviare
Guaviare
Riohacha
Santa Marta
Barranquilla
Cartagena
Valledupar
Sincelejo
Montería
Gulf of Darién
Magdalena
Cauca
Medellín
Bello
Quibdó
Gold
Manizales
Pereira
Armenia
Ibagué
Emeralds
BOGOTÁ
Tunja
Buenaventura
Palmira
Cali
Neiva
Florencia
Popayán
Mocoa
Pasto
Ibarra
QUITO
Latacunga
Ambato
Riobamba
Santo Domingo de los Colorados
Esmeraldas
Manta
Portoviejo
Montecristi
Bahía
Milagro
Cuenca
Guayaquil
Gulf of Guayaquil
Machala
Loja
Sullana
Piura

Gulf of Venezuela
Couantyne
Marowijne
Berbice

HIGHEST RAILROAD

Peru's railroads are the highest in the world. The single-track railroad from Lima to Huancayo in the Andes zigzags through tunnels and over wooden bridges, reaching an altitude of 15,885 ft (4,843 m) where it crosses one of the passes.

OTAVALO PEOPLE

Rug decorated with llamas, the traditional Andean pack animals

Woolen rugs woven by the Otavalo people from Ecuador are sold all over the Americas and Europe. The Otavalo have developed new techniques, such as replacing traditional natural dyes with synthetic ones.

ANDEAN CULTIVATION

On the steep hillsides of the Andes, every scrap of soil must be made to work efficiently. Like their Inca ancestors, Andean farmers suit the crop to the temperature, which gets lower higher up the mountains. This region is the original home of the potato, which can be grown successfully at high altitudes.

Inland river valleys: sugar, coffee

Permanent snow and ice

9,850 ft (3,000 m)

6,550 ft (2,000 m)

3,280 ft (1,000 m)

Altiplano: high plateaus between mountains used for grazing animals

Peru-Chile Trench: c.19,686 ft (6,000 m) below sea level

Highland areas: barley, potatoes, wheat

Temperate zone: coffee, tobacco, corn

Coastal lowland: sugar, cacao, bananas, rice

Pacific Ocean floor

N

Sea level

BOLIVIA
POP: 8,256,000

COCAINE

The steep slopes of the Andes are ideally suited to growing the coca bush. The native peoples have always chewed coca leaves to protect themselves against cold and altitude sickness. But the drug cocaine, made from the leaves, is now a major world problem. Today, Colombia's economy is virtually dependent on the illegal export of cocaine.

Coca leaves

Clay body

Strap handle

Water jar, found at the ancient Inca city of Cusco in Peru.

Llamas grazing on the high plains of the Andes in Bolivia.

PERU
POP: 24,314,000

LAKE TITICACA

Stretching across the border between Bolivia and Peru is the world's highest lake, Lake Titicaca, 13,000 ft (4,000 m) above sea level. The Uru people sail on the lake in boats of woven reeds.

The native peoples of the Andes were the first to grow potatoes.

The Andes are the world's longest chain of mountains.

CORPUS CHRISTI

Every town commemorates its patron saint with a festival. Events such as this colorful procession on Corpus Christi Day in Cusco, Peru, combine the religious beliefs of the native peoples with Christian ceremonies.

PANAMA HATS

Panama hats are made of fiber from a palm tree that grows in the coastal forests of Ecuador. One hat can take up to three months to make.

LIMA

Pizarro, a leader of the Spanish conquistadores, founded Peru's capital city in the 16th century, and his bones are buried in the cathedral on the Plaza de Armas, the main square in the city's center.

Lima Cathedral

KEYBOX

Bananas: Bananas are grown as a cash crop in Ecuador's tropical lowlands. Ecuador is now the world's main exporter. Look for 🍌

Oil: Oil is vital to Venezuela's economy; today the country's oil revenues account for 80 percent of its export earnings. Look for 🗼

Archaeological sites: The remains of many magnificent ancient cities and temples can still be seen in the Andes. Look for 🏛

Space center: The European Space Agency launches its rocket, Ariane, from its rocket base at Kourou, French Guiana. Look for 🚀

🐂 Cattle	🌾 Rice	➤ Sugarcane	☕ Coffee
🌲 Timber	🦐 Shellfishing	⛏ Mining	🏭 Industrial center

Map labels

PACIFIC OCEAN

PERU

BOLIVIA

BRAZIL

CHILE

ARGENTINA

PARAGUAY

A N D E S

Cajamarca
Chiclayo
Trujillo
Chimbote
Cerro de Pasco
Yungay
Huánuco
Pucallpa
La Oroya
Lima
Callao
Huancayo
Ayacucho
San Juan
Nazca
Ica
Juliaca
Mollendo
Arequipa
Tacna
Cusco
Machu Picchu
Ollantaytambo
Pisac
Puno
L. Titicaca
LA PAZ
Oruro
Cochabamba
Sucre
Potosí
Uyuni
Tarija
L. Poopó
Trinidad
Santa Cruz
San Miguel
Cobija
Ucayali
Madre de Dios
Beni
Mamoré

Beef
Silver
Copper
Lead
Zinc
Iron
Silver
Tin
Tungsten
Copper

BRAZIL

OCCUPYING NEARLY HALF of South America, Brazil possesses the greatest river basin in the world. The Amazonian rain forest, which covers some two-thirds of the country, is a vast storehouse of natural riches, still largely untapped. But land is needed for agriculture, ranching, and new roads, and each year vast tracts of forest are cleared. The Portuguese colonized the country in the 16th century, intermarrying with the local population. They planted sugar in the northeast, working the plantations with slaves brought from Africa. With a further influx of Europeans, Brazil is now one of the world's most populous and ethnically diverse democracies. A land of opportunity for some – like those in the industrial region around São Paulo – it is one of poverty and deprivation for many, especially in the northeast. In spite of improved industrial output, Brazil still has high unemployment and huge foreign debts.

NATIVE PEOPLES

There were once some two million native people in Amazonia. Today only about 240,000 survive. This Xingu girl is fortunate: she was born into a tribe which lives in a protected area of the Amazon rain forest. The well-being of many peoples is threatened by the ever-shrinking rain forest and by disease, logging, farming, and gold prospecting.

BRAZIL NUTS

Nuts fit into shell, like segments of an orange

Shelled nut

Sometimes known as the *inferno verde*, or green hell, Brazil's vast rain forest is home to an astonishing variety of animals and plants from which products – such as chemicals, drugs, and rubber – can be made. Scattered through the forest are Brazil nut trees. Their nuts can be eaten or crushed to make an oil used in cosmetics. Look for 🌲

SOCCER

Soccer is an all-consuming passion for millions of Brazilians. It is played in every back street and on every open space, even on the beach at Rio. Sometimes the ball is only a coconut. During the World Cup, Brazil comes to a standstill.

Conga drum

DANCE MUSIC

Transported to the north-eastern region of Brazil to work on the sugar plantations, African slaves brought the musical rhythms of their homelands with them. Their music has blended with other musical influences to produce the music for dances, such as the *samba* and the *lambada*. The instruments include this drum, called a *conga*.

A stretch of coast near Salvador in the northeast.

Grandillas, one of the many exotic fruits found in Brazil.

A huge tree trunk deep in the Brazilian rain forest.

BRAZIL
POP: 163,577,000

ATLANTIC OCEAN

B R A Z I L

FRENCH GUIANA (France)

SURINAME

GUYANA

VENEZUELA

COLOMBIA

PERU

A M A Z O N I A

PLATEAU OF MATO GROSSO

SERRA GRANDE

SERRA PELADA

Fortaleza
Mossoró
Sisal
Sisal
Tungsten
Sisal
Campina Grande
C. de São Roque
Natal
João Pessoa
Recife
Maceió
Beef
Beef
Beef
Juazeiro
Beef
Parnaíba
São Luís
Aluminum
Teresina
Picos
Beef
Sobradinho Res.
Carolina
Gold
Gold
Beef
Palmas
Belém
Aluminum
Macapá
Manganese
Jari
Tucuruí Res.
Gold
Iron
Iron
Xingu
Gold
Santarém
Tapajós
Gold
Teles Pires
Aluminum
Balbina Res.
Manaus
Madeira
Boa Vista
Gold
Gold
Rio Negro
Tin
Purus
Porto Velho
Tin
Gold
Brazil Nuts
Rubber
Rubber
Juruá
Amazon
Brazil Nuts
Rio Branco
Cruzeiro do Sul
Rubber
Brazil Nuts
Rubber
Amazon
Parnaíba
Paraguaí
Araguaia
Xingu
RONCADOR

COLONIAL LEGACY

When the Portuguese arrived in Brazil in the 16th century, they brought their distinctive style of architecture. At the heart of many towns and cities in modern Brazil lie cobbled streets, squares, and churches. The historic town of Ouro Prêto – center of the 18th-century gold rush – remains today as a perfect example of a 16th-century town.

CARNIVAL

Every year, just before Lent, Rio de Janeiro erupts into carnival. Often called "The Biggest Party on Earth," carnival involves five days of music and dance. The main event is the competition to find the most outrageous costumes and best decorated floats as they parade through the city to the sound of samba music.

Guanabara Bay provides access to the sea

Suburbs have grown rapidly

Rio-Niterói Bridge

Rio de Janeiro

Favelas lacking sanitation and other amenities

From Rio, good road and rail routes lead inland

Favelas on steep slopes vulnerable to heavy rain

RIO DE JANEIRO

Once the capital of Brazil, the beautiful city of Rio de Janeiro sprawls among the bays, islands, and hills around Guanabara Bay. The city acts like a magnet, drawing people from poor rural areas who come in search of work. A severe lack of housing has given birth to endless shanty towns, called favelas, which creep up the hillsides and crowd every piece of land unfit for other development.

The huge statue of Christ the Redeemer which towers over Rio de Janeiro.

STEEL

Attracted by Brazil's steel industry, cheap labor, and plentiful electricity, several multinational companies have invested money in the country. US and European car manufacturers have established successful factories around São Paulo. Look for 🚗

Brazilian-made Fiat sedan

BRASILIA

In the mid-1950s, the government of Brazil decided to build a new capital city in the sparsely inhabited central plateau region. Built in the shape of an airplane, the futuristic city of Brasilia became the country's official capital in 1960. The wide boulevards and open spaces contain spectacular buildings like this cathedral.

ORANGE JUICE

Oranges are grown in the region around São Paulo, where the climate is frost-free. Over a million tons are picked each year. Most of it is processed into orange juice concentrate. Brazil now supplies 85 percent of the world's orange juice, exporting it mainly to the USA and Europe. Look for 🍊

The Iguaçu River as it drops over the Iguaçu Falls.

COFFEE

Coffee originated in Africa, but Brazil is now the world's largest producer. When the trees have shed their white blossoms, the green berries ripen into red "cherries." Each cherry contains two seeds, or coffee beans, which are washed, dried, and roasted. Look for 🟤

The wings of the Morpho butterfly are often used to decorate jewelry.

GOLD MINING

Brazil has vast mineral reserves. This huge human anthill is the result of a gold rush which began in the 1980s near the Serra Pelada. Thousands of prospectors – called garimpeiros – burrow into the hillsides hoping to find gold. Look for 🟡

KM MILES
600 / 500 / 400 / 300 / 200 / 100 / 0
300 / 200 / 100 / 0

SOUTHERN SOUTH AMERICA

ALL FOUR COUNTRIES in this region were colonized in the 16th century by Spain. With the exception of Argentina, their populations are almost entirely *mestizo* – people of mixed Spanish and Native American descent. In Argentina, 85 percent of the population is descended from European settlers, as the native peoples were killed or driven out by the immigrants. Argentina falls into three regions: the hot, damp lands of the Gran Chaco in the north, the grasslands of the Pampas in the center, and the barren plateau of Patagonia in the south. Argentina gets its wealth from the rich soil of the Pampas, where cereals are grown and vast herds of sheep and cattle graze. The Pampas spills into neighboring Uruguay, where sheep provide the country with its main export, wool. Paraguay's economy is mainly dependent on agriculture. Chile lies stretched like a snake along the western side of the Andes, its head in the mineral-rich Atacama Desert and its tail in the icy wastes of the south. These countries all suffer from high inflation, unstable governments, and poverty.

THE PEOPLES OF THE CHACO
Only five percent of Paraguay's population live in the grasslands and swamps of the Gran Chaco. The main people still living there are the Guaranís, the first inhabitants of Paraguay. A smaller group, the Macá, make money by selling colorful hand-woven cloth and goods, like this bag, to tourists.

ASUNCION
Plaza Constitución is just one of many squares where beautiful Spanish buildings still stand in Asunción, Paraguay's capital and only large city.

MAINLY MEAT
In the late 19th century, processing and packing meat became an important industry in Uruguay. Today, canned meats, such as corned beef, are still a major export. Look for ▼

Tomatoes were first grown in South America.

URUGUAY
POP: 3,240,000

ITAIPU DAM
On the mighty Paraná River is one of the world's largest hydro-electric projects, the Itaipú Dam. This joint venture between Brazil and Paraguay boosted Paraguay's economy, creating jobs for thousands of people. Look for ✠

PARAGUAY
POP: 4,576,000

COPPER
Near Calama, Chile, shining orange metal is extracted from the largest open-pit copper mine in the world. Giant trucks remove thousands of tons of ore a day. However, the world price of copper is now falling, causing severe economic problems in Chile. Look for ⬤

The Atacama Desert in Chile is the driest place on earth.

Map labels

PACIFIC OCEAN

BRAZIL

PARAGUAY

URUGUAY

BOLIVIA

CHILE

GRAN CHACO

A R G E N T I N A

A N D E S

ATACAMA DESERT

PERU

Itaipú Dam
Ciudad del Este
Salto del Guairá
Pedro Juan Caballero
San Pedro
Concepción
Fuerte Olimpo
Mayor Pablo Lagerenza
General Eugenio A. Garay
Dr Pedro P. Peña
Filadelfia
Pozo Colorado
ASUNCION
Paraguarí
Villarrica
Caazapá
San Juan Bautista
Encarnación
Pilar
Posadas
Formosa
Corrientes
Resistencia
Vera
Santa Fe
Paraná
Rosario
San Nicolás de los Arroyos
BUENOS AIRES
La Plata
Colonia
MONTEVIDEO
Melo
Treinta y Tres
Rocha
Artigas
Rivera
Tacuarembó
Paysandú
Mercedes
Fray Bentos
Durazno
Florida
Salto
Concordia
Colón
Gualeguaychú
Villa María
Río Cuarto
Córdoba
La Rioja
Catamarca
Santiago del Estero
San Miguel de Tucumán
Salta
San Salvador de Jujuy
Calama
Chuquicamata
Tocopilla
Antofagasta
Chañaral
Copiapó
Vallenar
La Serena
Coquimbo
Ovalle
Illapel
La Ligua
San Felipe
Quillota
Viña del Mar
Valparaíso
San Juan
Mendoza
Godoy Cruz
San Luis
Mercedes
Iquique
Arica

River Negro
Mirim Lagoon
Paraguay
Pilcomayo
Bermejo
Salado
Paraná
Uruguay
Plate
L. Mar Chiquita
Pan-American Highway

Beef
Wheat
Dairy
Silver
Lead
Zinc
Iron
Copper
Lapis lazuli

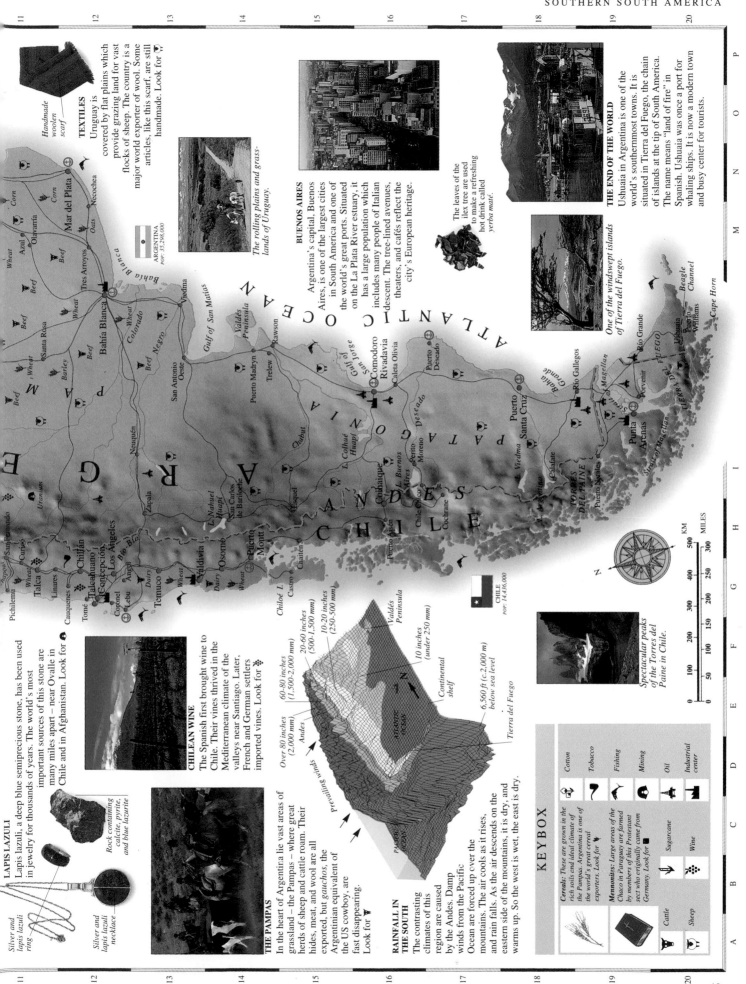

TEXTILES

Uruguay is covered by flat plains which provide grazing land for vast flocks of sheep. The country is a major world exporter of wool. Some articles, like this scarf, are still handmade. Look for ![scarf]

Handmade woolen scarf

The rolling plains and grass-lands of Uruguay.

ARGENTINA
POP: 35,298,000

BUENOS AIRES

Argentina's capital, Buenos Aires, is one of the largest cities in South America and one of the world's great ports. Situated on the La Plata River estuary, it has a large population which includes many people of Italian descent. The tree-lined avenues, theaters, and cafés reflect the city's European heritage.

The leaves of the ilex tree are used to make a refreshing hot drink called yerba maté.

THE END OF THE WORLD

Ushuaia in Argentina is one of the world's southernmost towns. It is situated in Tierra del Fuego, the chain of islands at the tip of South America. The name means "land of fire" in Spanish. Ushuaia was once a port for whaling ships. It is now a modern town and busy center for tourists.

One of the windswept islands of Tierra del Fuego.

LAPIS LAZULI

Lapis lazuli, a deep blue semiprecious stone, has been used in jewelry for thousands of years. The world's most important sources of this stone are many miles apart – near Ovalle in Chile and in Afghanistan. Look for ![mining]

Silver and lapis lazuli ring

Silver and lapis lazuli necklace

Rock containing calcite, pyrite, and blue lazurite

CHILEAN WINE

The Spanish first brought wine to Chile. Their vines thrived in the Mediterranean climate of the valleys near Santiago. Later, French and German settlers imported vines. Look for ![wine]

THE PAMPAS

In the heart of Argentina lie vast areas of grassland – the Pampas – where great herds of sheep and cattle roam. Their hides, meat, and wool are all exported, but *gauchos*, the Argentinian equivalent of the US cowboy, are fast disappearing. Look for ![cattle]

RAINFALL IN THE SOUTH

The contrasting climates of this region are caused by the Andes. Damp winds from the Pacific Ocean are forced up over the mountains. The air cools as it rises, and rain falls. As the air descends on the eastern side of the mountains, it is dry, and warms up. So the west is wet, the east is dry.

CHILE
POP: 14,436,000

Spectacular peaks of the Torres del Paine in Chile.

Over 80 inches (2,000 mm)

60-80 inches (1,500-2,000 mm)

20-60 inches (500-1,500 mm)

10-20 inches (250-500 mm)

10 inches (under 250 mm)

Andes

prevailing winds

PACIFIC OCEAN

ATLANTIC OCEAN

Continental shelf

Valdés Peninsula

6,560 ft (c.2,000 m) below sea level

Tierra del Fuego

KM 0 100 200 300 400 500
MILES 0 50 100 150 200 250 300

N

KEYBOX

Cereals: These are grown in the rich soils and ideal climate of the Pampas. Argentina is one of the world's great cereal exporters. Look for ![cereals]

Mennonites: Large areas of the Chaco in Paraguay are farmed by members of this Protestant sect who originally came from Germany. Look for ![bible]

![cattle] Cattle	![cotton] Cotton
![sheep] Sheep	![tobacco] Tobacco
![sugarcane] Sugarcane	![fishing] Fishing
![wine] Wine	![mining] Mining
	![oil] Oil
	![industrial] Industrial center

Place names on map:
Corn, Corn, Wheat, Oats, Beef, Beef, Beef, Wheat, Wheat, Barley, Beef, Wheat, Beef, Wheat, Dairy, Dairy, Wheat, Uranium, Wheat

Necochea, Mar del Plata, Olavarría, Azul, Tres Arroyos, Bahía Blanca, Santa Rosa, Neuquén, Zapala, Viedma, San Antonio Oeste, Valdés Peninsula, Rawson, Trelew, Puerto Madryn, Comodoro Rivadavia, Caleta Olivia, Puerto Deseado, Puerto Santa Cruz, Río Gallegos, Río Grande, Porvenir, Punta Arenas, Puerto Williams, Ushuaia, Cape Horn, Beagle Channel, Strait of Magellan, Bahía Grande

Pichilemu, Curicó, Talca, Linares, Cauquenes, Tomé, Coronel, Lebu, Concepción, Talcahuano, Los Angeles, Angol, Temuco, Valdivia, Osorno, Puerto Montt, Castro, Chiloé I., Chaitén, Coihaique, Esquel, San Carlos de Bariloche, L. Nahuel Huapí, L. Colhué Huapí, Cochrane, Puerto Aisén, Perito Moreno, L. Buenos Aires, Cochrane, Torres del Paine, Puerto Natales, Calafate, Viedma, Bahía Blanca

M PAMPAS, ARGENTINA, PATAGONIA, ANDES, CHILE, TIERRA DEL FUEGO

Bahía Blanca, Río Negro, Colorado, Chubut, Deseado, Río Chico, Río Santa Cruz, Río Argentino

Gulf of San Matías, Gulf of San Jorge, Strait of Magellan

THE ANTARCTIC

THE CONTINENT OF ANTARCTICA has such a cold, harsh climate that no people live there permanently. The land is covered by a huge sheet of ice up to 1.2 miles (2 km) thick, and seas around Antarctica are frozen over. Even during the short summers, the temperature barely climbs above freezing, and the sea ice only partly melts; in winter, temperatures can plummet to -112° F (-80° C). Few animals and plants can survive on land, but the seas around Antarctica teem with fish and mammals. The only people on the continent are scientists working in the Antarctic research stations and tourists, who come to see the dramatic landscape and the unique creatures that live here. But even these few people have brought waste and pollution to the region.

KRILL
Krill are the main food of the baleen whale. Japanese and Russian ships catch about 400,000 tons of krill each year, threatening the whales' food supply. Mainly used for animal feed, krill are also considered a delicacy in Japan. Krill gather in such huge numbers that they are visible from airplanes or even satellites.

Adélie penguins live in huge colonies on rocks or Antarctic pack ice.

Icebergs are huge blocks of ice which float in the sea.

Crozet Is. (France)

VARIOUS NATIONS CLAIMED TERRITORY IN ANTARCTICA WHEN IT WAS FIRST DISCOVERED IN THE 19TH CENTURY. THESE CLAIMS HAVE BEEN SUSPENDED UNDER THE 1959 ANTARCTIC TREATY (SIGNED BY 39 NATIONS). STATIONS CAN BE SET UP FOR SCIENTIFIC RESEARCH, BUT MILITARY BASES ARE FORBIDDEN.

Kerguelen I. (France)

Heard I. (Australia)

ATLANTIC OCEAN

SCOTIA SEA

South Orkney Is. (UK)

Elephant I. (UK)

South Shetland Is. (UK)

Drake Passage

Fimbul Ice Shelf

Riiser-Larsen Ice Shelf

Novolazarevskaya (Russian Fed.)

Georg van Neumayer (Germany)

QUEEN MAUD LAND

Lutzow-Holm Bay

Syowa (Japan)

ENDERBY LAND

INDIAN OCEAN

Larsen Ice Shelf

Halley (UK)

Belgrano II (Argentina)

Filchner Ice Shelf

WEDDELL SEA

Mawson (Australia)

C. Darnley

Anvers I. (USA)

PALMER LAND

Ronne Ice Shelf

Amery Ice Shelf

Mackenzie Bay

Prydz Bay

Lambert Glacier

West Ice Shelf

Fishing fleets are reducing stocks of Antarctic cod.

Siple (USA)

ELLSWORTH MTS.

SOUTH POLAR PLATEAU

TRANSANTARCTIC MTS.

DAVIS SEA

Peter the First I. (Norway)

BELLINGSHAUSEN SEA

• South Pole
Amundsen-Scott (USA)

Mirnyy (Russian Fed.)

Shackleton Ice Shelf

These mountains are on Anvers Island, which lies off the Antarctic peninsula.

MARIE BYRD LAND

AMUNDSEN SEA

Vostok (Russian Fed.)

Getz Ice Shelf

Ross Ice Shelf

Vincennes Bay

Scott Base (New Zealand)

VICTORIA LAND

Cape Poinsett

ANTARCTIC TOURISM
Cruise liners have been bringing tourists to the Antarctic region since the 1950s. Several thousand visitors each year observe the harsh beauty of the landscape and its extraordinary wildlife from the comfort of cruise ships. Look for 📷

C. Colbeck

McMurdo Sound

WILKES LAND

Porpoise Bay

PACIFIC OCEAN

ROSS SEA

C. Adare

Dumont d'Urville (France)

Balleny Is.

| 0 | 250 | 500 | 750 | 1000 | 1250 | 1500 | KM |
| 0 | 250 | 500 | 750 | | 1000 | | MILES |

WHALES
Whales thrive in the seas around the Antarctic, which are rich in plankton and krill, their main food sources. Large-scale whale hunting started in the 20th century, and the numbers of whales soon fell. In 1948 the International Whaling Commission was set up to regulate the numbers and species of whales killed and to create protected areas. Look for ⌁

Blue whale

POLLUTION
The Antarctic research stations have yet to find effective ways of disposing of their waste. Although some of it is burned, cans, bottles, machine parts, and chemicals are often simply dumped near the bases, spoiling the area's natural beauty. The only solution to the problem is to take the rubbish out of Antarctica. Look for ☠

RESEARCH
The scientific base in this picture is the U.S. Amundsen-Scott station, which is built underground at the South Pole. Scientists at the Antarctic research stations are monitoring changes to the weather and environment. Look for ◗

KEYBOX

Oil: Much of the Arctic region is rich in oil, but the difficulty of drilling and moving oil, as well as environmental concerns, have slowed exploitation. Look for ⚒

Penguin grounds: Penguin breeding grounds are found near Antarctic coasts. Some are being disturbed by tourists, airstrips and construction. Look for ⬥

⬥	Fishing	◗	Polar research center
🪨	Coal	☠	Pollution
📷	Tourism	⌁	Whales

THE ARCTIC

THE ARCTIC OCEAN IS covered by drifting ice up to 98 ft (30 m) thick, which partially melts and disperses in the summer. Much of the surrounding land is tundra – plains and moorlands that are carpeted with moss and lichens, but permanently frozen beneath the surface. People have lived around the Arctic for thousands of years, hunting the mammals and fish that live in the ocean. This region has large deposits of oil, but the harsh climate makes it difficult to extract from the ground.

FISH STICKS
Large numbers of cod, haddock, halibut, and other fish live in the Arctic Ocean. Cod and haddock are taken to fish-processing factories in Greenland. Here they are frozen, canned or – in the case of cod – made into fish sticks and exported to the markets of the USA and Europe. Look for ➤

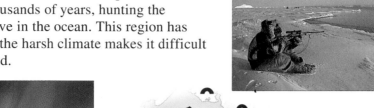

ARCTIC PEOPLES
Traditionally, the people of the Arctic survived by hunting animals. They used sealskin for boats and clothing and seal fat (blubber) for fuel. Today, tools, clothes, and buildings are made from modern materials. Rifles now replace harpoons and snow-mobiles are used for transport.

The northern lights can be seen over the Arctic at night.

ICE-BREAKER
About half the Arctic Ocean is covered with ice in winter, but special ships called ice-breakers can still sail across it. In 1969, a large tanker, the *SS Manhattan*, penetrated the pack ice of the Northwest Passage from eastern Canada to Alaska for the first time.

Polar bears spend summers on the Arctic ice. They move farther south in winter.

GREENLAND
The first Europeans to explore and settle Greenland were Vikings, who arrived in about 986. Greenland later came under Danish rule and is now a self-governing part of Denmark.

The Arctic tern migrates every year between the Arctic and Antarctica.

Mountains on Svalbard reflected in a melted ice pond.

ARCTIC COAL
The island of Spitsbergen has rich deposits of minerals, especially coal. It is part of Norway, but other countries are allowed to mine there. The Norwegian coal town of Longyearbyen is 620 miles (1,000 km) from the mainland. It can be reached by sea for only eight months a year, making it difficult and expensive to ship coal out. Coal screes and long, severe winters make this a desolate place. Look for ⚒

Map labels

ALASKA (USA)
CHUKCHI SEA
RUSSIAN FEDERATION
EAST SIBERIAN SEA
Pevek
Ambarchik
Wrangel I. (Russian Fed.)
Barrow
Prudhoe Bay
BEAUFORT SEA
Limit of Permanent Pack Ice
New Siberian Is. (Russian Fed.)
LAPTEV SEA
Tiksi
Cape Kellett
Banks I. (Canada)
Prince Patrick I. (Canada)
Melville I. (Canada)
Mould Bay
Nordvik
ARCTIC OCEAN
TAYMYR PENINSULA
Queen Elizabeth Is.
Limit of Permanent Pack Ice
CANADA
Resolute
Axel Heiberg I. (Canada)
North Pole
Severnaya Zemlya (Russian Fed.)
Dikson
Devon I. (Canada)
Ellesmere I. (Canada)
Alert
Limit of Permanent Pack Ice
KARA SEA
Dundas
Thule
Baffin I. (Canada)
PEARY LAND
Franz Josef Land (Russian Fed.)
Baffin Bay
KNUD RASMUSSEN LAND
North Station
SVALBARD (Norway)
BARENTS SEA
Pangnirtung
GREENLAND (Denmark)
Upernavik
Ny Ålesund
LONGYEARBYEN
Spitsbergen (Norway)
Davis Strait
Godhavn
Søndre Strømfjord
GODTHÅB (NUUK)
GREENLAND SEA
Frederikshåb
Narssarsuaq
Julianehåb
Scoresbysund
Jan Mayen (Norway)
Ammassalik
Denmark Strait
C. Farvel
ATLANTIC OCEAN
ICELAND

| 0 | 250 | 500 | 750 | 1000 |
| 0 | 100 | 200 | 300 | 400 | 500 |

THE ATLANTIC OCEAN

THE WORLD'S OCEANS cover almost three-quarters of the Earth's surface. Beneath the surface of the Atlantic Ocean lie vast, featureless plains and long chains of mountains called ridges. The Mid-Atlantic Ridge is one of the world's longest mountain chains; some of its peaks are so high that they pierce the surface as volcanic islands, such as the Azores. A huge rift valley 15-30 miles (24-48 km) wide runs down the ridge's center. The deepest part of the Atlantic is 5 miles (8 km) below the surface. On average, the Atlantic has the warmest and saltiest waters of any ocean. Before regular shipping routes were established, the Atlantic isolated the Americas from the countries of Europe, but today it is crossed by some of the world's most important trade routes. The North Atlantic has always been one of the world's richest fishing grounds, but it has been overfished, and fish stocks are now dangerously low.

LAND OF ICE AND FIRE
There are more than 100 volcanoes on Iceland. Many of them are still active. Beneath the island's harsh, rocky surface lie vast natural heat reserves. This energy is used to provide hot water and central heating for much of the population. Iceland's economy is based on fishing, which accounts for about 70 percent of its exports.

TIDAL ENERGY
Electricity can be generated from the sea in areas where there is a big difference between high and low tide levels. A barrage, like this one at La Rance in France, has to be built across the estuary. Water passing backward and forward through the barrage drives the turbines. Look for ⚡

Tomatoes and other fruit are grown in the warm climate of the Canary Islands.

Puffins breed on rocky islands, like the Faeroes.

FISHING
Catches of cod, herring, and haddock in the North Atlantic have been severely reduced by overfishing. Fishing fleets must now travel long distances and remain at sea for months at a time. The fish are processed on the fleet's factory ship to keep them fresh. Look for ⌐

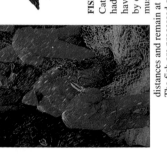

WHALING
Whaling has been going on in the world's oceans for hundreds of years. But with the invention of the explosive-tipped harpoon, catches increased rapidly. Today some species of whales are threatened with extinction. Attempts are being made to ban whaling worldwide until numbers recover. Look for 🦈

British aircraft carrier

NATO
The North Atlantic Treaty Organization (NATO) is an association of North American and European countries established in 1949 to defend its members – principally against the former Soviet Union. Look for ▥

An extinct volcano on an island in the West Indies.

ICELAND
POP: 300,000

CAPE VERDE
POP: 400,000

TOURISM

A number of islands in the Atlantic, including the Canaries and Madeira, are great tourist attractions, especially during winter in the Northern Hemisphere. The Canaries are a chain of seven mountainous islands; some areas are green and lush, others volcanic. The volcanic lava produces dramatic black landscapes. Look for ✍

SAILING

Areas of the Atlantic have become pleasure grounds. Sailing is one of the main activities, especially in the warm seas of the Caribbean. Long-distance races are increasingly popular, some of them transatlantic. Boats range from yachts sailed single-handed to ships like this tea clipper, sailed by large crews.

CABLES

Cables snake across the ocean floor carrying many forms of modern communication, such as telephone calls and fax messages. The first transatlantic cable was laid in 1866. The cables are laid by special ships, like this one in the North Atlantic.

Lobsters are caught in lobster pots baited with dead fish.

Massive icebergs drift among the pack ice, a threat to shipping in the Atlantic.

KM						
0	50	100	150	200	250	300
0	50	100	150			
MILES						

N

SALMON

The early years of an Atlantic salmon are spent in the river where it was born. Then it swims downriver to the ocean. It rapidly gains weight in the rich feeding grounds of the North Atlantic. When it is ready to breed, the salmon's amazing homing ability enables it to return to its native river. Here, on their long, hard journey upriver, salmon negotiate a waterfall. Few salmon survive this endurance test to breed a second time.

Fish like these live among the sargassum weed

SARGASSO SEA

At the center of three great North Atlantic currents lies the Sargasso Sea – an area of calm water, covered with *sargassum* weed. Sailors once believed their ships would be trapped by the weeds.

POLLUTION

There are very few laws to control the way the world's oceans are used. The North Atlantic is one of the busiest and most polluted oceans. Many ships discharge oil and chemicals and dump radioactive waste. Some stretches of the northeast coast of America are so polluted that signs warn people not to swim. Plastic containers litter the world's coasts. International action to control this pollution is long overdue. Look for ☣

An isolated settlement on the island of West Falkland in the South Atlantic.

KEYBOX

Underwater wrecks: *Marine archaeology and location of wrecks was greatly advanced by the development of deep-sea diving equipment. Look for* ⚓

Pollution: *Oil rig blowouts and spills from oil tankers along the coastlines and around the Gulf of Mexico are a major problem in the Atlantic. Look for* ☣

Hurricane: *The warm Atlantic waters off the north coast of Brazil are the gathering grounds for hurricanes, which then sweep northwestward. Look for* 🌀

⚡ Alternative power	✍ Tourism	
🎣 Fishing	⚓ Fishing ports	⛨ Military bases
⛽ Oil	⬮ Gas	➤ Whales

Map labels

OCEAN

AFRICA

Niger

Lagos

Congo

Gulf of Guinea Libreville

São Tomé Príncipe

Guinea Basin

Walvis Bay

Lüderitz

Port Nolloth

Cape Town

Cape of Good Hope

Guinea Basin

ASCENSION ISLAND (UK)

ST HELENA (UK)

TRISTAN DA CUNHA (UK)

Gough Island (UK)

Cape Basin

Angola Basin

Mid-Atlantic Ridge

Atlantic Indian Ridge

BOUVET ISLAND (Norway)

Atlantic Indian Antarctic Basin

ATLANTIC OCEAN

Cape Verde Basin

Sierra Leone Basin

Guyana Basin

Fernando de Noronha I. (Brazil)

Brazil Basin

Trindade (Brazil)

Argentine Basin

SOUTH AMERICA

Cayenne

Georgetown

La Guaira

Cartagena

Panama City

Amazon

Fortaleza

Recife

Salvador

Rio de Janeiro

Buenos Aires

Mar del Plata

Bahía Blanca

Cape Horn

FALKLAND ISLANDS (UK)

SCOTIA SEA

South Shetland Is. (UK)

South Orkney Is. (UK)

SOUTH GEORGIA (UK)

SOUTH SANDWICH ISLANDS (UK)

WEDDELL SEA

ANTARCTICA

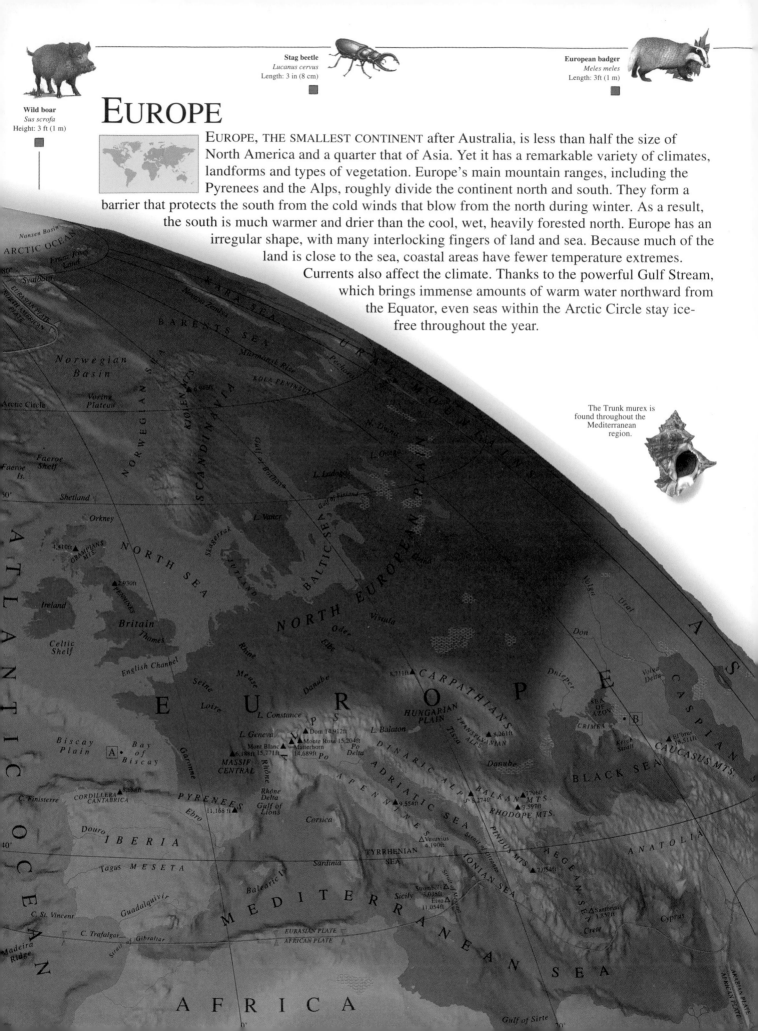

Wild boar
Sus scrofa
Height: 3 ft (1 m)

Stag beetle
Lucanus cervus
Length: 3 in (8 cm)

European badger
Meles meles
Length: 3ft (1 m)

EUROPE

EUROPE, THE SMALLEST CONTINENT after Australia, is less than half the size of North America and a quarter that of Asia. Yet it has a remarkable variety of climates, landforms and types of vegetation. Europe's main mountain ranges, including the Pyrenees and the Alps, roughly divide the continent north and south. They form a barrier that protects the south from the cold winds that blow from the north during winter. As a result, the south is much warmer and drier than the cool, wet, heavily forested north. Europe has an irregular shape, with many interlocking fingers of land and sea. Because much of the land is close to the sea, coastal areas have fewer temperature extremes. Currents also affect the climate. Thanks to the powerful Gulf Stream, which brings immense amounts of warm water northward from the Equator, even seas within the Arctic Circle stay ice-free throughout the year.

The Trunk murex is found throughout the Mediterranean region.

Map labels:

Nansen Basin
ARCTIC OCEAN
Franz Josef Land
80°
Svalbard
KARA SEA
Novaya Zemlya
BARENTS SEA
Norwegian Basin
Arctic Circle
Vøring Plateau
KOLA PENINSULA
Murmansk Rise
Pechora
URAL MOUNTAINS
Faeroe Shelf
Faeroe Is.
N. Dvina
60°
Shetland
L. Onega
Orkney
L. Ladoga
Gulf of Bothnia
NORWEGIAN SEA
SCANDINAVIA
KJOLEN MTS.
Gulf of Finland
L. Vänern
ATLANTIC
4,410ft
GRAMPIANS MTS.
NORTH SEA
JUTLAND
BALTIC SEA
NORTH EUROPEAN PLAIN
Volga
Ural
CASPIAS
2,930ft
PENNINES
Skagerrak
Oder
Vistula
Don
Ireland
Britain
Elbe
Dnieper
Celtic Shelf
Thames
Rhine
Volga Delta
English Channel
Danube
8,711ft
CARPATHIANS
Meuse
Seine
HUNGARIAN PLAIN
SEA OF AZOV
EUROPE
Loire
L. Constance
Tisza
TRANSYLVANIAN ALPS
8,261ft
CRIMEA
B
El'brus 18,511ft
Biscay Plain
Bay of Biscay
A
L. Geneva
Dom 14,912ft
Monte Rosa 15,204ft
L. Balaton
DINARIC ALPS
Kerch Strait
CAUCASUS MTS.
Mont Blanc
Matterhorn
9,554ft
Danube
BLACK SEA
6,188ft 15,771ft
14,689ft Po
Po Delta
BALKAN MTS.
7,796ft
MASSIF CENTRAL
Rhône
APENNINES
8,274ft
9,597ft
RHODOPE MTS.
CORDILLERA CANTABRICA
6,588ft
PYRENEES
Rhône Delta
Gulf of Lions
ADRIATIC SEA
PINDUS MTS.
AEGEAN SEA
ANATOLIA
C. Finisterre
11,168 ft
Ebro
Corsica
7,054ft
40°
Douro
IBERIA
Vesuvius 4,190ft
AEGEAN SEA
Tagus MESETA
Sardinia
TYRRHENIAN SEA
IONIAN SEA
Cyprus
Balearic Is.
Sicily
Crete
Guadalquivir
Stromboli 3,038ft
Strait of Otranto
Santorini 1,850ft
C. St. Vincent
MEDITERRANEAN
Etna 11,054ft
Strait of Messina
C. Trafalgar
Strait of Gibraltar
EURASIAN PLATE
AFRICAN PLATE
Madeira Ridge
OCEAN
MEDITERRANEAN SEA
ARABIAN PLATE AFRICAN PLATE
AFRICA
Gulf of Sirte
0°

EURASIAN PLATE
NORTH AMERICAN PLATE

Siberian tit
Parus cinctus
Length: 5 in (13 cm)

Green toad
Bufo viridis
Length: 4 in (10 cm)

Osprey
Pandion haliaetus
Wingspan: 5 ft (1.6 m)

BOGLANDS
Bogs cover many of northern Europe's wettest areas. Mosses and reeds are among the few plants that grow in waterlogged soils. Wetlands take thousands of years to develop, because plants grow so slowly there.

Ammonites, fossil relatives of today's octopus, were once found in Europe. They died out 65 million years ago.

PIONEERING BIRCH
Light-loving birches are often the first trees to appear on open land. Although quick to grow, they are short-lived. After a few years, birches are replaced by trees that can survive shade, such as oaks.

WAVE POWER
Waves can wear away the shore, creating odd landforms. This seastack off the Orkneys in the British Isles is 450 ft (135 m) high.

English oak
Quercus robur
Height: 130 ft (40 m)

BARE MOUNTAIN
Ice, rain, wind, and gravity strip steep slopes of all soil. Rocks pile up at the foot of peaks, where plants can take root.

FJORDS
Glaciers have cut hundreds of narrow inlets, or fjords, into Scandinavia's Atlantic coastline. The water in the inlet is calmer than in the open sea.

NEEDLELEAF FOREST
Cone-bearing trees such as pines, larches, and firs cover Scandinavia. Most are evergreen: they keep their needlelike leaves even when covered in snow for many months of the year.

TREELESS TUNDRA
Arctic summers are so cool that only the topmost layer of frozen soil thaws. Only shallow-rooted plants can survive in the tundra.

Pine marten
Martes martes
Length: 20 in (52 cm)

ANCIENT WOODLANDS
Relics of Europe's ancient forests, such as these oaks stunted by the rain and wind, are found only in a few valleys in southwest Britain.

This fossil of *Stauranderaster*, a starfish once found in this region, dates from around 70 million years ago.

DRY SOUTH
Crete is a mountainous Mediterranean island with hot dry summers. Many plants survive the summer as underground bulbs, blooming briefly in the wet spring.

YOUNG MOUNTAINS
The Alps include some of western Europe's highest mountains. They are part of an almost continuous belt that stretches from the Pyrenees in the west to the Himalayas in Asia. The Alps are still rising because of plate movements in the Mediterranean region.

Sweetbriar
Rosa rubiginosa
Height: 10 ft (3 m)

CROSS-SECTION THROUGH EUROPE

Massif Central · Dinaric Alps · Alps · Adriatic Sea · Bay of Biscay · Atlantic Ocean · Hungarian Plain · Transylvanian Alps · Black Sea · Crimea · Kerch Strait

9,843 (3,000) · 0 Sea level · -14,764 (-4,500) · Feet (meters)

A — Length: 4,500 km (2,800 miles) — B

KEY TO SYMBOLS
△ Mountain
▲ Volcano
Mangroves
Wetlands
Coral reef
Plate margins showing direction of movement

KEY TO NATURAL VEGETATION
Tundra · Needleleaf forest · Broadleaf forest · Cold desert · Mountain · Mediterranean-type · Temperate grassland

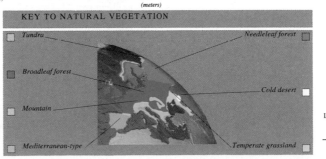

Spanish lynx
Felis lynx
Length: 4 ft (1.3 m)

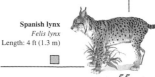

SCANDINAVIA AND FINLAND

THE SCANDINAVIAN COUNTRIES of Norway, Sweden, and Denmark and neighboring Finland are situated around the Baltic Sea in northern Europe. During past ice ages, glaciers gouged and scoured the land, leaving deep fjords, lakes, and valleys in their wake. Much of Norway and Sweden and nearly two-thirds of Finland is covered by dense forests of pine, spruce, and birch trees. In the far north, winters are long and dark, and snow falls for about eight months of the year. Most Swedish people live in the central lowlands. Norway's economy depends on its shipbuilding, fishing, and merchant fleets. Denmark is flat and low-lying, with abundant rainfall and excellent farmland. The Finnish people originally came from the east, via Russia, and consequently differ from the Scandinavians both in language and culture. All four countries have small populations, are highly industrialized, and enjoy some of the highest standards of living in the world.

Deep water enables ships to reach far inland

Rough upland grazing for sheep and goats

Fish farming of salmon in sheltered waters

Coastal fishing communities are declining

Meadow crops grown for livestock

Cultivation limited to warm, south-facing slopes

Coastal islands form natural breakwaters

A NORWEGIAN FJORD
Norway is so mountainous that only three percent of the land can be cultivated. Long inlets of sea, called fjords, cut into Norway's west coast. The best farmland is found around the head of the fjords and in the lowland areas around them. Over 70 percent of Norway's population lives in cities, many in towns situated along the sheltered fjords.

NORWAY
POP: 4,382,000

The still waters of a Norwegian fjord.

FISHING
Because Norway has little farm-land, fishing has always been a vital source of food. Today, about 95 percent of the total catch is processed; about half is made into fishmeal and oil. Fish farming is on the increase, especially of salmon in the fjords. Look for ➤

Vast schools of herring gather in the seas around Scandinavia

Fantoft Church, Bergen

LAPLAND
Lapland is a land of tundra, forests, and lakes. Here the *Samer*, or Lapps, still herd reindeer for their meat and milk. Development in the north now threatens their way of life.

STAVE CHURCHES
The wooden stave churches of Norway were built between AD 1000 and 1300. There were once 600 of them, but today only 25 are still standing. A stave church has a stone foundation with a wooden frame on top. The four wooden corner posts are called staves. Further wooden extensions can be added to the basic framework.

Lego building blocks were invented in Denmark.

SKIING
For thousands of years skiing has been the most efficient way of crossing deep snow on foot. This region is often thought to be the original home of skiing – in fact, "ski" is the Norwegian word for a strip of wood. Long-distance cross-country skiing, or *langlaufen*, is a popular sport in Norway, Finland, and Sweden.

Scrambled eggs
Prawns
Caviar
Asparagus
Smoked salmon

SMÖRGÅSBORD
Smörgåsbord means "sandwich table" in Swedish. Other countries in this region have their own versions, but the idea is the same: a great spread of local delicacies, served cold on bread, which can include dishes such as reindeer, fish, cheese, and salad.

COPENHAGEN
Copenhagen's fine natural harbor and position at the main entrance to the Baltic Sea helped it become a major port and Denmark's capital city. The city's tiny shops, cobbled streets, museums, and cafés attract more than a million tourists each year.

Danish bacon for export

DANISH AGRICULTURE
Two-thirds of the total area of Denmark is used for farming. Denmark exports agricultural products all over the world. The main products are bacon, dairy products, cereals, and beef. Cereals are widely grown, but mainly as fodder for pigs. Look for 🐖

DENMARK
POP: 5,203,000

DENMARK

Skagerrak

Kattegat

Steinkjer
Hitra
Smøla
Vanadium
Trondheim
Molde
Ålesund
Iron
Nordfjord
Rørø
Sognefjord
Heymansverk
Bergen
Hardanger Fjord
Gjøvik
L. Mjøsa
Lågen
Lilleham
Haugesund
Honefoss
Oats
OSLO
Bokna Fjord
Drammen
Kongsberg
Stavanger
Porsgrunn
Dairy
Moss
Fredrikstad
Sandnes
Titanium
Otra
Dairy
Hølden
Iron
Dairy
Arendal
Oslo Fjord
Kristiansand

Uddevalla
Trollhättan
Göteborg
Borå
Hjørring
Frederikshavn
Ålborg
Dairy
Rye
Varber
Holstebro
Randers
Halmstad
Ringkøbing
JUTLAND
Århus
Hälsingborg
Barley
Horsens
Helsingør
Esbjerg
Vejle
COPENHAGEN
Hassle
Ribe
Odense
Ma
Åbenrå
Fyn
Slagelse
Sønderborg
Naestved
Sjaelland
Nakskov
Barley
GERMANY
Nykøbing

ARCTIC OCEAN

North Cape
Magerøy
Sørøya
Hammerfest
Vardø
Vadsø
Varanger Fjord
Kirkenes
Ringvassøy
Tromsø
L. Inari
Karasjok
Iron
Senja
Harstad
Ivalo
Hinnøye
Narvik
Sodankylä
L. Torne
Kiruna
Iron
Torne
Iron
Bodø
Copper
Gällivare
Iron
Kemijärvi
Iron
Mo i Rana
Rovaniemi
Kuusamo
Donna
Iron
Lead
Jokkmokk
Chromium Kemi
Kemt
Zinc
L. Uddjaur
Tornio
Kemi
Vanadium
Arvidsjaur
Luleå
Oulu
Piteå
Oulu
Storuman
Copper
Silver
L. Oulu
Skellefteå
Lead
Zinc
Vanadium
Kajaani
Gold
Copper
Copper
Titanium
Umeå
Kokkola
Iron
Iisalmi
Jakobstad
Östersund
Örnsköldsvik
Copper
L. Pielinen
Lake Stor
Cobalt
Uranium
Vaasa
Kuopio
Joensuu
Härnösand
Seinäjoki
Nickel
Sundsvall
Varkaus
L. Ori
Jyväskylä
Savonlinna
L. Saimaa
Hudiksvall
Mikkeli
Mora
Pori
Tampere
Imatra
Rauma
Valkeakoski
Lappeenranta
Falun
Sandviken
Hämeenlinna
Kuusankoski
Iron
Borlänge
Hyvinkää
Kouvola
Iron
Barley
Åland Is.
Riihimäki
Kotka
Karlstad
Iron
Salo
Järvenpää
Barley
Uppsala
Turku
Wheat
Väster ås
Norrtälje
Maarianhamina
HELSINKI
Örebro
Dairy
Kimito
Wheat
STOCKHOLM
Huddinge
Väner
Lead
Zinc
Wheat
Mariestad
Motala
Nyköping
Skövde
Norrköping
Linköping
L. Vätter
Fårö
Jönköping
Västervik
Oats
Visby
Oskarshamn
Gotland
Växjö
Öland
Kalmar
Karlskrona
stianstad
Rønne

NORWEGIAN SEA
Lofoten
Vesterålen
Vestfjorden
KJØLEN MTS.
NORWAY
Pite
Ume
Ångerman
Indal
Ljusnan
Ljungan
SWEDEN
Dal
L. Vänern

LAPLAND
Muonio
Tana
Oanas
FINLAND
RUSSIAN FEDERATION
Gulf of Bothnia
Kvarken
Gulf of Finland
BALTIC SEA

MIDNIGHT SUN
This may look like an ordinary sunset, but this photo of Bodø in Norway was taken at midnight. In the far north of this region, the sun never sets in midsummer. The farther north you travel, the longer the period of midnight sun. In winter, in Lapland, the sun remains below the horizon for a week; in the far north, this period of darkness lasts two months.

SAUNA BATHS
Ladle
Some 1,000 years ago the Finns invented the steam bath, or *sauna,* as a way of cleansing and relaxing the body. The steam is produced by throwing water over hot stones. A plunge in an icy pool or snowdrift completes the process. The *sauna* has become a national institution.
Wooden bucket

FINLAND
POP: 5,059,000

TIMBER
Finland, Norway, and Sweden are heavily forested. The timber is used in many ways, such as building, furniture, and crafts. All three countries have large wood-pulp, paper, and board industries. Finland and Sweden are now among the world's largest exporters of these products. This Swedish child's chair is cleverly designed to grow with the child. Look for ┐

SWEDEN
POP: 8,700,000

Glass fig from Finland
Glass pear from Finland
Glass eggplant from Sweden

SCANDINAVIAN DESIGN
Scandinavians have a highly developed sense of design which extends to everyday objects like stereo equipment, furniture, and glass. Sweden and Finland are well known for their glassware, and the industry attracts many famous artists who create new designs.

Trolls are characters in Scandinavian folklore.

A forest bordering one of Finland's many lakes.

A classic Volvo sedan

CAR MANUFACTURE
For its size, Sweden has a large number of highly successful multi-national companies. Two examples are the motor manufacturers, Volvo and Saab-Scania, whose cars and trucks are widely exported. Volvo workers build cars in teams. The company pioneered this system to improve working conditions.

The carved prow of a Viking ship found in Norway.

NORWEGIAN OIL
Since oil was discovered in the North Sea in the 1970s, Norway has become self-sufficient in natural gas and oil. These account for over half the country's export earnings. It is also a world leader in drilling platforms and tankers.

Stockholm, Sweden's capital and an important seaport.

KM
0 50 100 150 200 250 300
0 50 100 150 200 MILES
N

THE BRITISH ISLES

THE BRITISH ISLES CONSIST OF TWO large islands – Great Britain and Ireland – surrounded by many smaller ones. They are divided into two countries: the United Kingdom (UK), often known as Britain, and Ireland. At the end of the 18th century, the UK became the first country in the world to undergo an industrial revolution. It became the world's leading manufacturing and trading nation and built up an empire that covered more than a quarter of the world. The UK's traditional industries, including coal mining, textiles, and car manufacturing, have declined in recent years, but service industries such as banking and insurance have been extremely successful. Ireland, which became independent from the UK in 1921, is still a mainly rural country, and many Irish people make their living from farming. However, tourism and high-tech industries like computers and pharmaceuticals are increasingly important. The UK and Ireland still have close trading links, and many Irish people go to the UK to find work.

"THE TROUBLES"

When British Protestants settled in Ireland in the 17th century, they came into conflict with Irish Catholics, whose land they had seized. In 1921, the Protestant North (Ulster) refused to join the independent South. Catholics were discriminated against in jobs and housing, and violence erupted in the 1960s. British troops were sent to police the province.

AGRICULTURE AND INDUSTRY

Farming has always been Ireland's principal source of income. Dairy products, beef, and potatoes are still important, but recently the number of high-tech industries has increased.

Irish butter

OIL

Rich reserves of both oil and natural gas were found under the North Sea in the 1960s. By the late 1970s, natural gas was being piped to most homes, factories and businesses in the UK. Massive oil rigs were moored in the North Sea, and wells were dug by drilling into the ocean bed below the platforms. Oil rigs and onshore refineries brought employment to many areas, especially in eastern Scotland. But oil reserves are being steadily used up, and oil production is now in decline. Look for

TARTAN TOURISM

Tourism is an important source of income for Scotland. People come to enjoy the beautiful highland scenery and visit the ancient castles. For centuries, Scotland was dominated by struggles between rival families, known as clans. Today one of the most popular tourist souvenirs is tartan – textiles woven in the colors of the clans.

Tartan scarf

Scottish shortbread

Bright red letter boxes are a common sight on British streets.

FISHING

The waters of the north-east Atlantic are among the world's richest fishing grounds, well stocked with mackerel, herring, cod, haddock, and shellfish. The British Isles has many fishing ports, like this one in northeastern England. But EU regulations, designed to reduce catches and conserve fish stocks, are causing widespread discontent amongst fishermen. Look for

INDUSTRY

Many Japanese companies, car and electronics manufacturers in particular, are now based in the UK, attracted by a skilled labor force and access to European markets. Britain's traditional industries – such as textiles, steel, and pottery – have been joined by newer, high-tech industries. Look for

AEROSPACE

UK firms design and build a wide range of civil and military aircraft. Perhaps the most famous is Concorde, a supersonic jet created in partnership with France. Recently, the aerospace industry has been badly hit by world recession, and UK companies have had to develop products in other areas, such as electronics and telecommunications. Look for

The Concorde supersonic jet

A deep inlet of water – or loch – in northern Scotland.

NORTH SEA

ATLANTIC OCEAN

Shetland

Lerwick

Orkney

Kirkwall

Stromness

Thurso

C. Wrath

Ullapool

Stornoway

Lewis

Harris

North Minch

Little Minch

North Uist

South Uist

Barra

Skye

Canna

Rum

Eigg

Muck

Coll

Tiree

Mull

Colonsay

Jura

Islay

Kintyre

Arran

Outer Hebrides

Fort William

Oban

Mallaig

Loch Ness

Loch Shin

Moray Firth

Inverness

Elgin

Aberdeen

Peterhead

Fraserburgh

Dundee

Perth

Stirling

Firth of Forth

Edinburgh

Glasgow

Greenock

Firth of Clyde

Loch Lomond

Loch Fyne

SCOTLAND

GRAMPIANS

SOUTHERN UPLANDS

Lough Foyle

Beef

Barley

Oats

Dee

Tweed

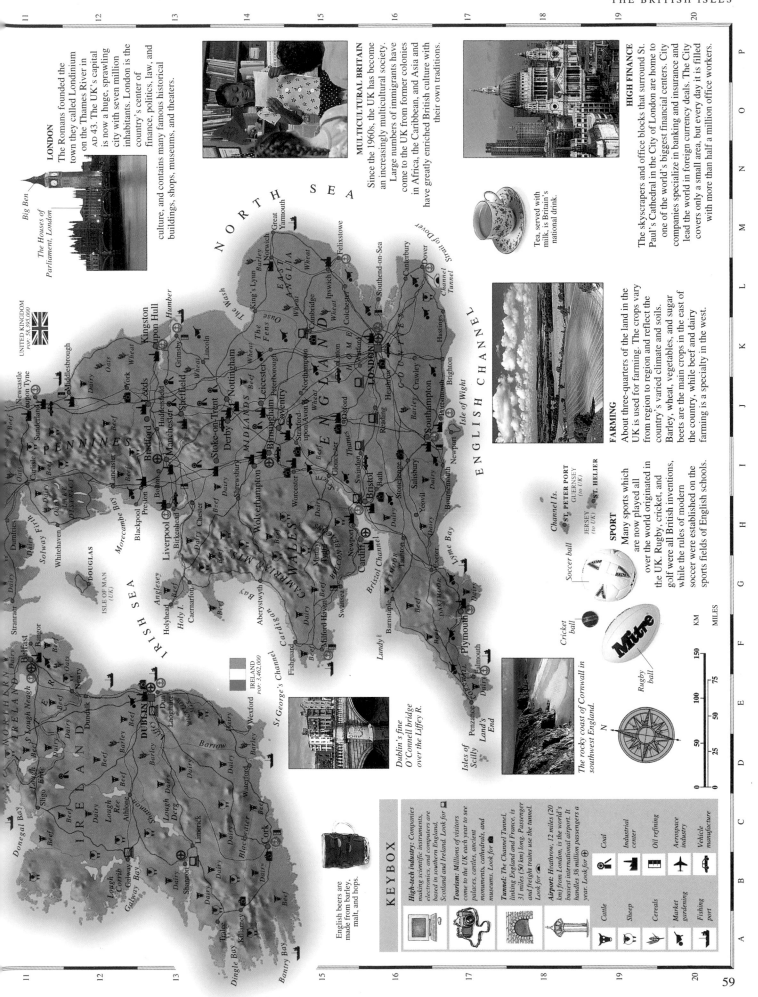

LONDON
The Romans founded the town they called Londinium on the Thames River in AD 43. The UK's capital is now a huge, sprawling city with seven million inhabitants. London is the country's center of finance, politics, law, and culture, and contains many famous historical buildings, shops, museums, and theaters.

Big Ben

The Houses of Parliament, London

MULTICULTURAL BRITAIN
Since the 1960s, the UK has become an increasingly multicultural society. Large numbers of immigrants have come to the UK from former colonies in Africa, the Caribbean, and Asia and have greatly enriched British culture with their own traditions.

HIGH FINANCE
The skyscrapers and office blocks that surround St. Paul's Cathedral in the City of London are home to one of the world's biggest financial centers. City companies specialize in banking and insurance and lead the world in foreign currency deals. The City covers only a small area, but every day it is filled with more than half a million office workers.

Tea, served with milk, is Britain's national drink.

FARMING
About three-quarters of the land in the UK is used for farming. The crops vary from region to region and reflect the country's varied climate and soils. Barley, wheat, vegetables, and sugar beets are the main crops in the east of the country, while beef and dairy farming is a specialty in the west.

SPORT
Many sports which are now played all over the world originated in the UK. Rugby, cricket, and golf were all British inventions, while the rules of modern soccer were established on the sports fields of English schools.

Soccer ball
Cricket ball
Rugby ball

The rocky coast of Cornwall in southwest England.

Dublin's fine O'Connell bridge over the Liffey R.

English beers are made from barley, malt, and hops.

UNITED KINGDOM
POP: 58,395,000

IRELAND
POP: 3,462,000

KEYBOX
High-tech industry: Companies making scientific instruments, electronics, and computers are based in southern England, Scotland and Ireland. Look for ▣

Tourism: Millions of visitors come to the UK each year to see palaces, castles, ancient monuments, cathedrals, and museums. Look for ☐

Tunnel: The Channel Tunnel, linking England and France, is 31 miles (50 km) long. Passenger and freight trains use the tunnel.

Airport: Heathrow, 12 miles (20 km) from London, is the world's busiest international airport. It handles 38 million passengers a year. Look for ✈

Coal | Cattle
Industrial center | Sheep
Oil refining | Cereals
Aerospace industry | Market gardening
Vehicle manufacture | Fishing port

NORTH SEA
IRISH SEA
ENGLISH CHANNEL
Strait of Dover
Channel Tunnel
St George's Channel
Bristol Channel
Lyme Bay
Cardigan Bay
Morecambe Bay
Solway Firth
Donegal Bay
Galway Bay
Dingle Bay
Bantry Bay

IRELAND
NORTHERN IRELAND
ENGLAND
WALES
SCOTLAND
PENNINES
CAMBRIAN MTS
BRECON BEACONS
LAKE DISTRICT
THE MIDLANDS
EAST ANGLIA
THE FENS
The Wash
DARTMOOR

Channel Is.
ST PETER PORT GUERNSEY (to UK)
ST. HELIER JERSEY (to UK)
Isle of Wight
Isle of Man (UK)
DOUGLAS
Anglesey
Holy I.
Lundy
Isles of Scilly

N

Spain and Portugal

Spain and Portugal are located on the Iberian Peninsula, which is cut off from the rest of Europe by the Pyrénées. This isolation, combined with the region's closeness to Africa and the Atlantic Ocean, has shaped the history of the two countries. The Moors, an Islamic people from North Africa, occupied the peninsula in the 8th century AD, leaving an Islamic legacy that is still evident today. In 1492 the Moors were finally expelled from Catholic Spain. The oceangoing Spanish and Portuguese took the lead in exploring and colonizing the New World, and both nations acquired substantial overseas empires. During this era, Portugal was ruled by Spain from about 1580 to 1640. Eventually, both nations lost most of their colonies, and their once-great wealth and power declined. Spain was torn apart by a vicious civil war from 1936-39, and right-wing dictators ruled both Spain and Portugal for much of the 20th century. In the 1970s, both countries emerged as modern democracies and have since experienced rapid economic growth, benefiting from their membership in the European Union. Today, their economies are dominated by tourism and agriculture, although Spanish industry is expanding rapidly.

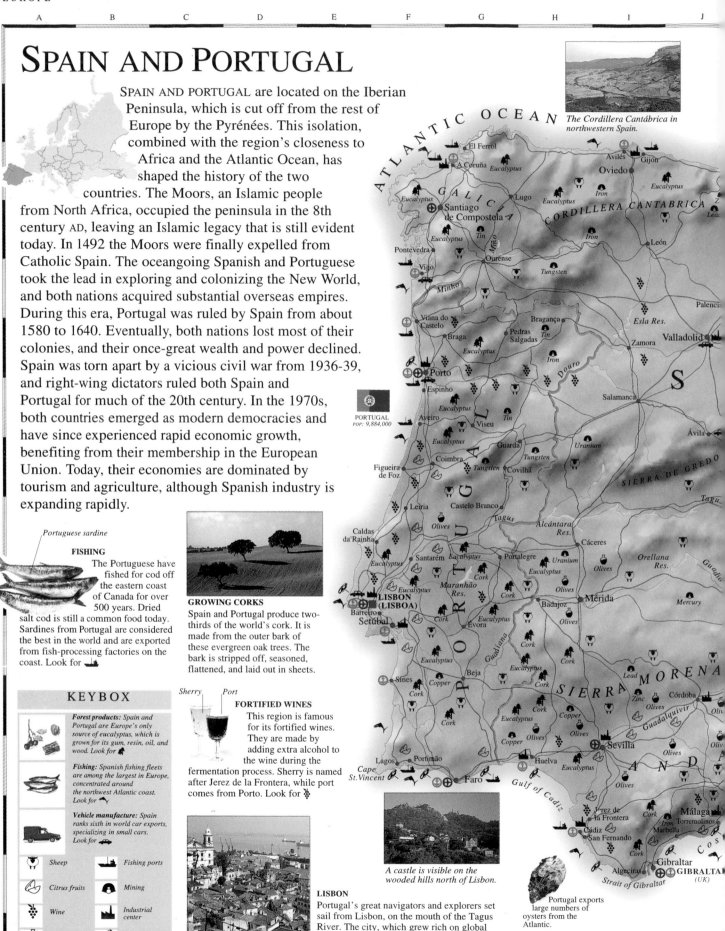

The Cordillera Cantábrica in northwestern Spain.

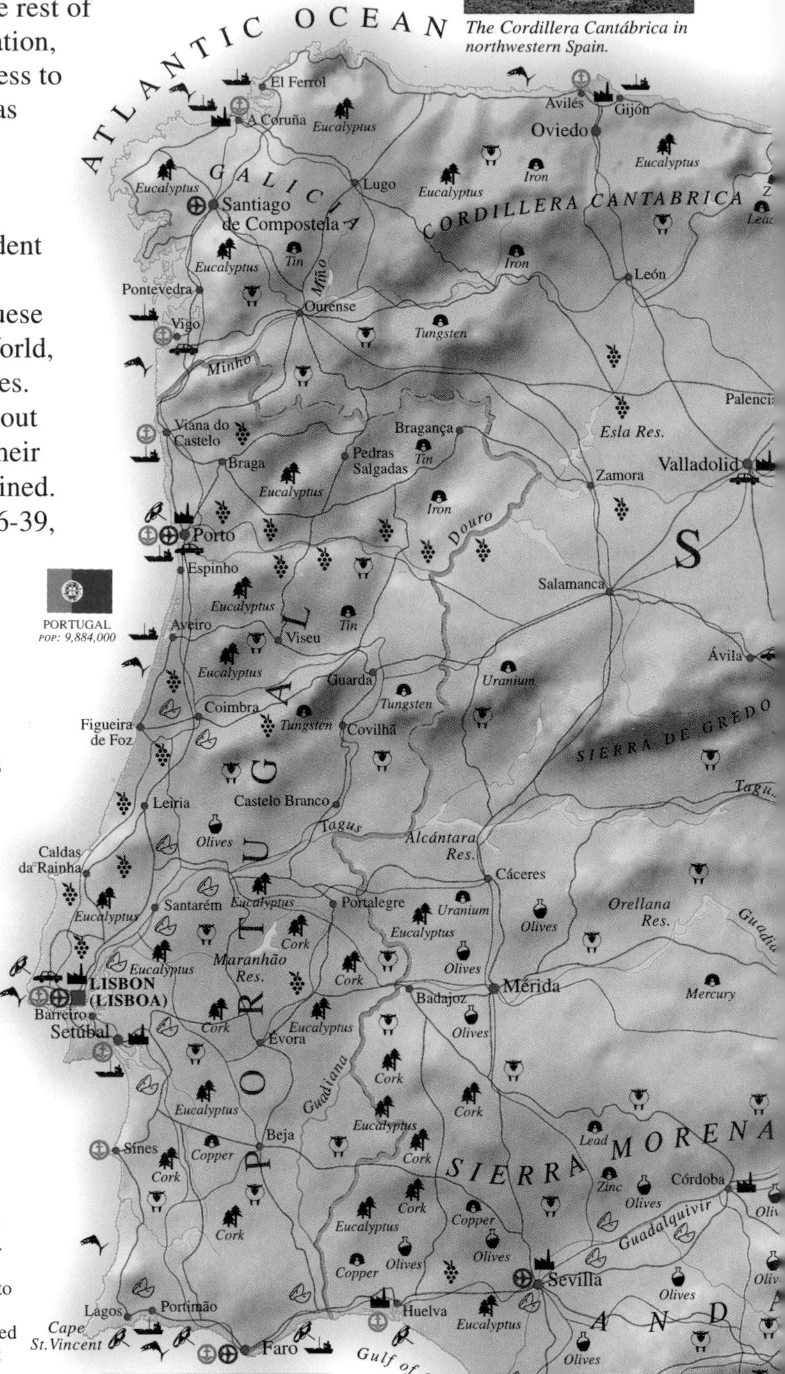

Portuguese sardine

FISHING

The Portuguese have fished for cod off the eastern coast of Canada for over 500 years. Dried salt cod is still a common food today. Sardines from Portugal are considered the best in the world and are exported from fish-processing factories on the coast. Look for [fishing port symbol]

GROWING CORKS

Spain and Portugal produce two-thirds of the world's cork. It is made from the outer bark of these evergreen oak trees. The bark is stripped off, seasoned, flattened, and laid out in sheets.

KEYBOX

Forest products: *Spain and Portugal are Europe's only source of eucalyptus, which is grown for its gum, resin, oil, and wood. Look for* [forest symbol]

Fishing: *Spanish fishing fleets are among the largest in Europe, concentrated around the northwest Atlantic coast. Look for* [fish symbol]

Vehicle manufacture: *Spain ranks sixth in world car exports, specializing in small cars. Look for* [car symbol]

Sheep	*Fishing ports*
Citrus fruits	*Mining*
Wine	*Industrial center*
Vegetable oil	*Tourism*

Sherry *Port*

FORTIFIED WINES

This region is famous for its fortified wines. They are made by adding extra alcohol to the wine during the fermentation process. Sherry is named after Jerez de la Frontera, while port comes from Porto. Look for [wine symbol]

A castle is visible on the wooded hills north of Lisbon.

LISBON

Portugal's great navigators and explorers set sail from Lisbon, on the mouth of the Tagus River. The city, which grew rich on global trade, was completely rebuilt after an earthquake destroyed two-thirds of it in 1755.

Portugal exports large numbers of oysters from the Atlantic.

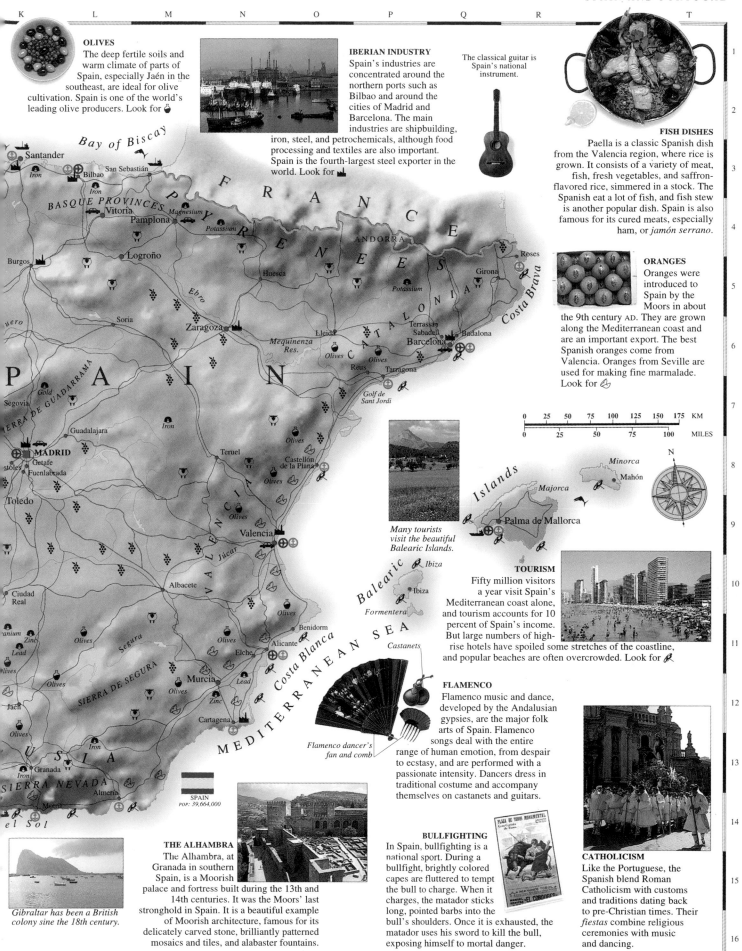

OLIVES

The deep fertile soils and warm climate of parts of Spain, especially Jaén in the southeast, are ideal for olive cultivation. Spain is one of the world's leading olive producers. Look for 🫒

IBERIAN INDUSTRY

Spain's industries are concentrated around the northern ports such as Bilbao and around the cities of Madrid and Barcelona. The main industries are shipbuilding, iron, steel, and petrochemicals, although food processing and textiles are also important. Spain is the fourth-largest steel exporter in the world. Look for 🏭

The classical guitar is Spain's national instrument.

FISH DISHES

Paella is a classic Spanish dish from the Valencia region, where rice is grown. It consists of a variety of meat, fish, fresh vegetables, and saffron-flavored rice, simmered in a stock. The Spanish eat a lot of fish, and fish stew is another popular dish. Spain is also famous for its cured meats, especially ham, or *jamón serrano*.

ORANGES

Oranges were introduced to Spain by the Moors in about the 9th century AD. They are grown along the Mediterranean coast and are an important export. The best Spanish oranges come from Valencia. Oranges from Seville are used for making fine marmalade. Look for 🍊

Many tourists visit the beautiful Balearic Islands.

TOURISM

Fifty million visitors a year visit Spain's Mediterranean coast alone, and tourism accounts for 10 percent of Spain's income. But large numbers of high-rise hotels have spoiled some stretches of the coastline, and popular beaches are often overcrowded. Look for 🏖

FLAMENCO

Flamenco music and dance, developed by the Andalusian gypsies, are the major folk arts of Spain. Flamenco songs deal with the entire range of human emotion, from despair to ecstasy, and are performed with a passionate intensity. Dancers dress in traditional costume and accompany themselves on castanets and guitars.

Castanets

Flamenco dancer's fan and comb

SPAIN
POP: 39,664,000

THE ALHAMBRA

The Alhambra, at Granada in southern Spain, is a Moorish palace and fortress built during the 13th and 14th centuries. It was the Moors' last stronghold in Spain. It is a beautiful example of Moorish architecture, famous for its delicately carved stone, brilliantly patterned mosaics and tiles, and alabaster fountains.

Gibraltar has been a British colony since the 18th century.

BULLFIGHTING

In Spain, bullfighting is a national sport. During a bullfight, brightly colored capes are fluttered to tempt the bull to charge. When it charges, the matador sticks long, pointed barbs into the bull's shoulders. Once it is exhausted, the matador uses his sword to kill the bull, exposing himself to mortal danger.

CATHOLICISM

Like the Portuguese, the Spanish blend Roman Catholicism with customs and traditions dating back to pre-Christian times. Their *fiestas* combine religious ceremonies with music and dancing.

FRANCE

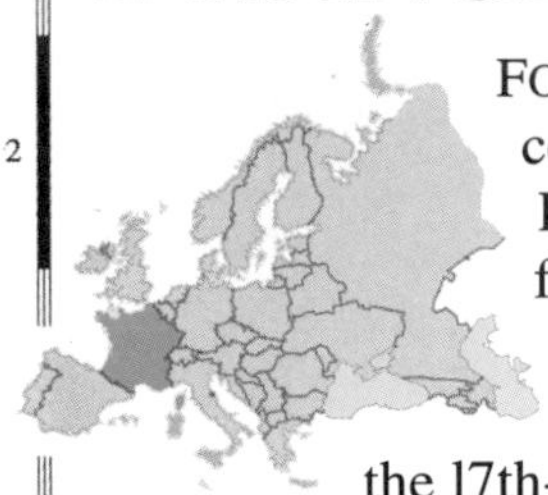

FOR CENTURIES FRANCE has played a central role in European civilization. Reminders of its long history can be found throughout the land: prehistoric cave dwellings, Roman amphitheaters, medieval cathedrals and castles, and the 17th- and 18th-century palaces of the powerful French monarchs. The French Revolution of 1789 swept away the monarchy and changed the face of France forever. The country survived the Napoleonic Wars and occupation during World Wars I and II, and now has a thriving economy based on farming and industry. France is a land of varied scenery and strong regional traditions – the only country which belongs to both northern and southern Europe. Farming is still important, but many people have moved from the country to the cities. France still administers a number of overseas territories, all that remain of its once widespread empire. Today, France's population includes immigrants from its former colonies, especially Muslims from North Africa. France is one of the most enthusiastic members of the European Union.

PARIS

Paris, the capital of France, is the largest and most important city in the country. It lies on both banks of the Seine River. One of the world's great cities, Paris contains magnificent buildings, art treasures, and elegant shops. The wrought-iron Eiffel Tower, the symbol of Paris, looms above the city.

A cyclist in the *Tour de France*, the world's most famous bicycle race.

FRANCE
POP: 57,800,000

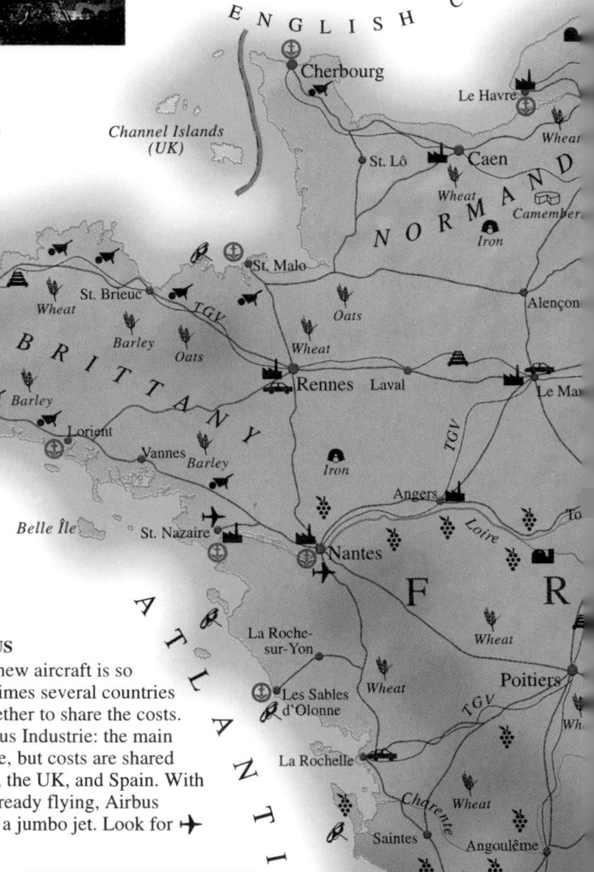

AGRICULTURE

France is a mainly rural country producing a wide range of farm products. Some farms still use traditional methods, but modern technology has transformed regions like the Paris Basin, where cereals are grown on a large scale. Look for ✹

THE AIRBUS

Developing new aircraft is so costly that sometimes several countries form a company together to share the costs. One example is Airbus Industrie: the main factory is at Toulouse, but costs are shared by France, Germany, the UK, and Spain. With successful aircraft already flying, Airbus Industrie is planning a jumbo jet. Look for ✈

KEYBOX

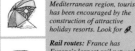
Market gardening: *In the northwest, the mild climate and sheltered conditions are ideal for growing early vegetables, called primeurs. Look for* 🛒

Nuclear power: *Lacking its own energy sources, France has developed its nuclear power industry. It now produces 70% of its electricity. Look for* ◧

Tourism: *In the underdeveloped Mediterranean region, tourism has been encouraged by the construction of attractive holiday resorts. Look for* ☂

Rail routes: *France has Europe's largest rail network. Intercity trains (TGVs) travel at speeds of up to 186 miles (300 km) per hour. Look for* 🚄

⬭	Cheese	⚑	Coal
✹	Cereals	🏭	Industrial center
🌰	Sugar beets	✈	Aerospace industry
❋	Wine	�car	Vehicle manufacturing
⛏	Mining	🎿	Skiing

CHATEAUS

France has many beautiful historic buildings. Along the banks of the Loire River and its tributaries are royal palaces, or chateaus, built by the royalty of France from the 15th-17th centuries. Chambord, once a hunting lodge, has 440 rooms and 85 staircases. Fairy-tale palaces like these attract thousands of visitors each year.

Fields of sunflowers can be seen in many areas of France.

Head of garlic   *Snail*

Clove of garlic   Snails, served with butter and garlic, are a great French delicacy.

CHEESE

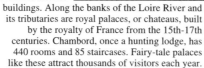
Camembert

France is famous for its cheese. Over 300 different varieties are made. Many, like Camembert, Roquefort, and Brie, are world famous and copied in many other countries. Each region has its traditional way of making and packaging its cheeses. Goat's and sheep's milk are used as well as cow's. Look for ⬭

Brie

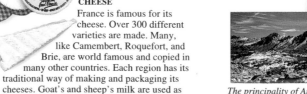
The principality of Andorra is situated in the Pyrenees.

ENGLISH CHANNEL

Cherbourg   Le Havre

Channel Islands (UK)   St. Lô   Caen   Wheat

NORMAND   Wheat   Iron   Camember

Île d'Ouessant   St. Malo   St. Brieuc   Alençon

Brest   Wheat   Oats

BRITTANY   Barley   Oats   Wheat

Quimper   Rennes   Laval   Le Man

Barley   Lorient   Vannes   Barley   Iron   Angers   Loire   To

Belle Île   St. Nazaire   Nantes   FR

La Roche-sur-Yon   Wheat

ATLANTIC   Les Sables d'Olonne   Wheat   Poitiers

La Rochelle   TGV   Wh

Charente   Wheat

OCEAN   Saintes   Angoulême

Barley

Dordogne

Bordeaux

Arcachon   Garonne

TGV   Mont-de-Marsan

Bayonne   Corn   Corn

Pau   Tarbe

PYRE   E

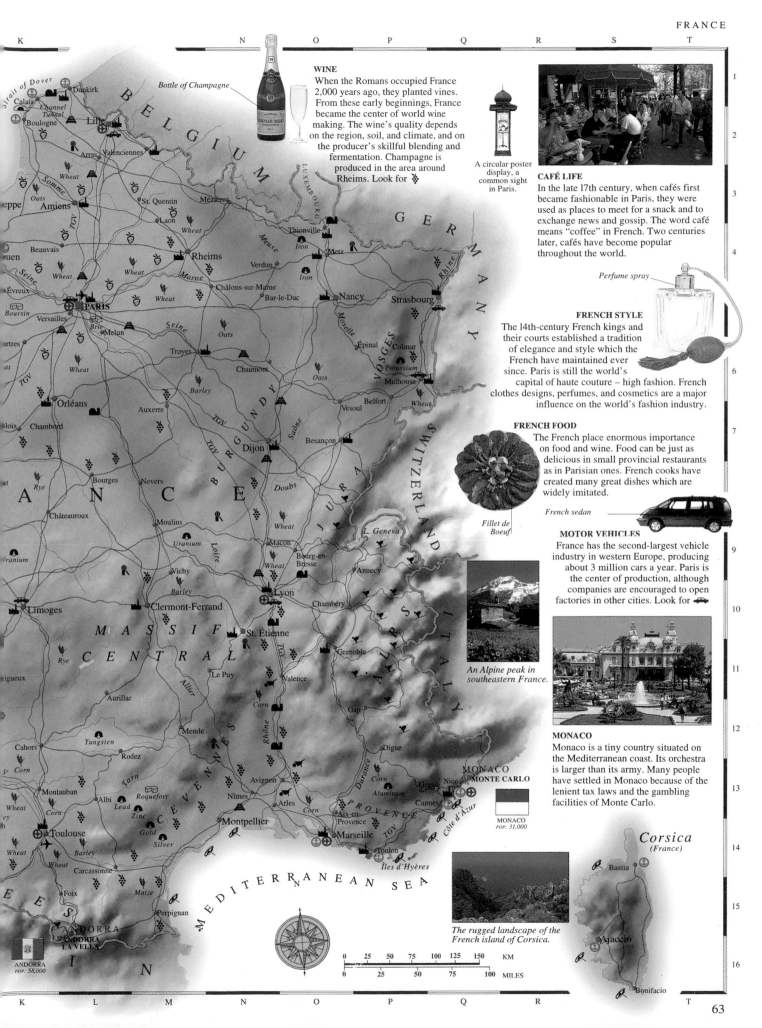

WINE

When the Romans occupied France 2,000 years ago, they planted vines. From these early beginnings, France became the center of world wine making. The wine's quality depends on the region, soil, and climate, and on the producer's skillful blending and fermentation. Champagne is produced in the area around Rheims. Look for 🍇

Bottle of Champagne

A circular poster display, a common sight in Paris.

CAFÉ LIFE

In the late 17th century, when cafés first became fashionable in Paris, they were used as places to meet for a snack and to exchange news and gossip. The word café means "coffee" in French. Two centuries later, cafés have become popular throughout the world.

Perfume spray

FRENCH STYLE

The l4th-century French kings and their courts established a tradition of elegance and style which the French have maintained ever since. Paris is still the world's capital of haute couture – high fashion. French clothes designs, perfumes, and cosmetics are a major influence on the world's fashion industry.

FRENCH FOOD

The French place enormous importance on food and wine. Food can be just as delicious in small provincial restaurants as in Parisian ones. French cooks have created many great dishes which are widely imitated.

Fillet de Boeuf

French sedan

MOTOR VEHICLES

France has the second-largest vehicle industry in western Europe, producing about 3 million cars a year. Paris is the center of production, although companies are encouraged to open factories in other cities. Look for 🚗

An Alpine peak in southeastern France.

MONACO

Monaco is a tiny country situated on the Mediterranean coast. Its orchestra is larger than its army. Many people have settled in Monaco because of the lenient tax laws and the gambling facilities of Monte Carlo.

MONACO
POP: 31,000

Corsica (France)

The rugged landscape of the French island of Corsica.

ANDORRA
POP: 58,000

KM
0   25   50   75   100   125   150

MILES
0   25   50   75   100

THE LOW COUNTRIES

BELGIUM, THE NETHERLANDS, and Luxembourg are the most densely populated countries in Europe. They are known as the "Low Countries" because much of the land is flat and low-lying. In the Netherlands, much of the land lies below sea level, and has been reclaimed from the sea over the centuries by ingenious technology. The marshy, drained soils are extremely fertile. All three countries enjoy high living standards, with well-developed industries and excellent rail, road, and waterway communications with the rest of Europe. During the course of their history, the Low Countries have often been the battleground between warring nations, and Belgium and Luxembourg only achieved independence in the 19th century. Belgium is still divided by language – Dutch is spoken in the north, while the Walloons in the south speak French. The northern Netherlands are mainly Protestant; the rest of the region is basically Roman Catholic. Today, the Low Countries are unswerving supporters of the European Union. The cities of Brussels, The Hague, and Luxembourg are all headquarters of important European institutions.

FLOWERS
The Netherlands is Europe's largest producer of flowers, and spectacular fields of spring flowers in full bloom are a major tourist attraction. Cut flowers are flown daily from the Netherlands to cities all over the world. Cultivation of bulbs such as crocuses, hyacinths, daffodils, and tulips is a speciality. Tulips have been grown here since about 1600, when they were introduced from Turkey and the Middle East. Look for 🌷

Tulip

FLOOD CONTROL
Much of the Netherlands lies below sea level, and is constantly at risk of flooding. Over the centuries, land has been painstakingly reclaimed from the sea. Barriers called dykes are built to keep the sea out, and water is drained and pumped into canals. Originally the water was pumped out by windmills, but now electric pumps are used. Sluice-gates control the flow of excess water.

The rind of Dutch Edam cheese is colored with anatto dye.

IMMIGRATION
Immigrants from the Netherlands' former colonies of Surinam, the Antilles, and Indonesia have had a strong impact on Dutch life and culture. Indonesian restaurants are a common sight in Dutch cities, and *rijstafel* (rice surrounded by side dishes of eggs, vegetables, meat, and fish) is now a national dish.

Satay (barbecued meat)

Peanuts

Beef Rendang

Egg-fried rice

Prawns and garlic

Salad in peanut sauce

Pickled vegetables

NETHERLANDS
Pop: 15,612,000

DELFT TILE
Delft pottery has been made in the Netherlands since the 17th century. The technique of glazing pottery with tin, used in Delft, came to the Netherlands from the Middle East via Spain and Italy. This Delft tile is decorated with a windmill, a familiar sight in the Netherlands. There are about 1,000 windmills still standing today, dating mainly from the 18th and 19th centuries.

CITY OF CANALS
The Dutch capital, Amsterdam, is a city of islands built on swampy land. It is criss-crossed by 160 canals. Many of the city's finest gabled houses date from the 16th-18th centuries, when merchants grew rich from trade and exploration. Amsterdam is not only the country's historic center, it is also its second-largest port.

ROTTERDAM
Rotterdam is one of the world's largest ports, lying within a massive built-up and industrialized area called Randstad Holland. Rotterdam is situated near the mouth of the Rhine River, an important trade route. Imported oil is refined locally. The port also handles minerals, grain, timber, and coal.

Both Belgium and the Netherlands are major beer exporters.

GERMANY

Delfzijl
Winschoten · Wheat
Emmen
Wheat · Beef
Groningen · Dairy
Assen
Hoogeveen
Leeuwarden · Dairy · Drachten
Heerenveen
Meppel
Zwolle
IJssel
Schiermonnikoog
Ameland
West Frisian Is.
Terschelling
Vlieland
Harlingen
WADDEN ZEE
Texel
Den Helder
Hoorn
Alkmaar
Purmerend
Zaanstad
AMSTERDAM
Velsen
IJmuiden
Haarlem
Leiden
Alphen aan
Lelystad
Flevoland
Harderwijk
Hilversum
Amersfoort
Apeldoorn
Deventer
Zutphen
Almelo
Hengelo
Enschede
IJSSELMEER
Dairy · Wheat · Beef

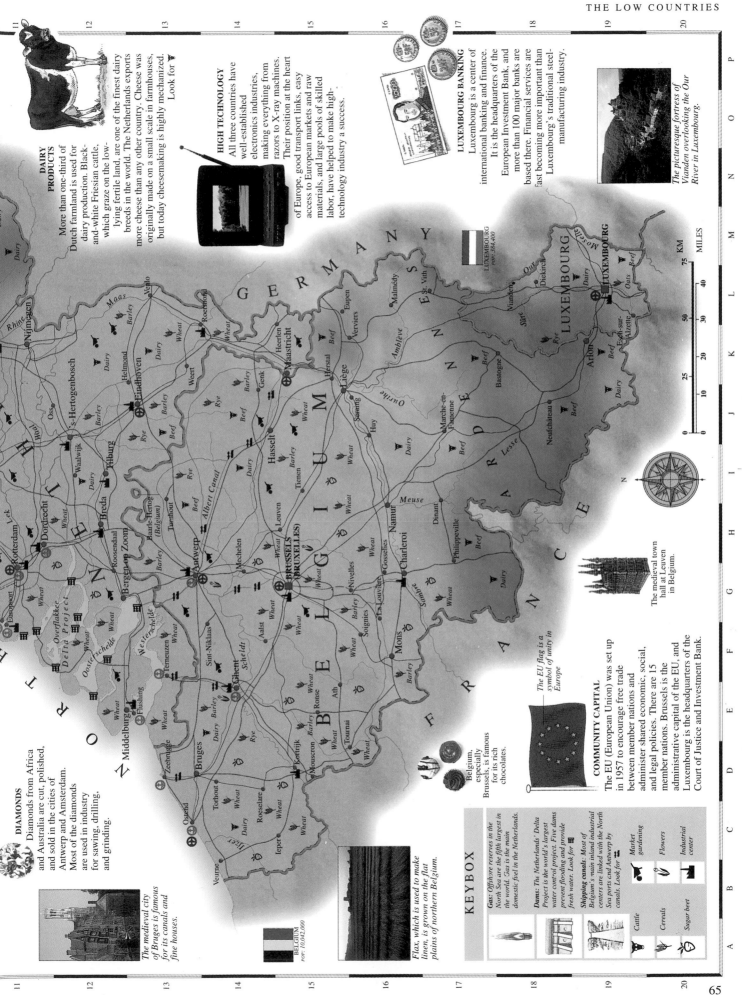

DAIRY PRODUCTS

More than one-third of Dutch farmland is used for dairy production. Black-and-white Friesian cattle, which graze on the low-lying fertile land, are one of the finest dairy breeds in the world. The Netherlands exports more cheese than any other country. Cheese was originally made on a small scale in farmhouses, but today cheesemaking is highly mechanized. Look for 🐄

HIGH TECHNOLOGY

All three countries have well-established electronics industries, making everything from razors to X-ray machines. Their position at the heart of Europe, good transport links, easy access to European markets and raw materials, and large pools of skilled labor, have helped to make high-technology industry a success.

LUXEMBOURG BANKING

Luxembourg is a center of international banking and finance. It is the headquarters of the European Investment Bank, and more than 100 major banks are based there. Financial services are fast becoming more important than Luxembourg's traditional steel-manufacturing industry.

The picturesque fortress of Vianden overlooking the Our River in Luxembourg.

LUXEMBOURG
pop: 384,400

DIAMONDS

Diamonds from Africa and Australia are cut, polished, and sold in the cities of Antwerp and Amsterdam. Most of the diamonds are used in industry for sawing, drilling, and grinding.

The medieval city of Bruges is famous for its canals and fine houses.

BELGIUM
pop: 10,042,000

Flax, which is used to make linen, is grown on the flat plains of northern Belgium.

KEYBOX

Gas: *Offshore reserves in the North Sea are the fifth largest in the world. Gas is the main domestic fuel in the Netherlands.*

Dams: *The Netherlands' Delta Project is the world's largest water control project. Five dams prevent flooding and provide fresh water. Look for* 🏛

Shipping canals: *Most of Belgium's main inland industrial centers are linked with the North Sea ports and Antwerp by canals. Look for*

Market gardening

Flowers

Industrial center

Cattle

Cereals

Sugar beet

COMMUNITY CAPITAL

The EU (European Union) was set up in 1957 to encourage free trade between member nations and administer shared economic, social, and legal policies. There are 15 member nations. Brussels is the administrative capital of the EU, and Luxembourg is the headquarters of the Court of Justice and Investment Bank.

The EU flag is a symbol of unity in Europe

Belgium, especially Brussels, is famous for its rich chocolates.

The medieval town hall at Leuven in Belgium.

GERMANY

F R A N C E

BELGIUM

L U X E M B O U R G

A R D E N N E S

Place labels (map)

Nijmegen, Rotterdam, Dordrecht, Europoort, 's-Hertogenbosch, Oss, Waalwijk, Tilburg, Breda, Eindhoven, Helmond, Weert, Roermond, Venlo, Maastricht, Heerlen, Bergen op Zoom, Roosendaal, Baarle-Hertog (Belgium), Turnhout, Antwerp, Mechelen, Genk, Hasselt, Eupen, Verviers, Liège, Seraing, Huy, Herstal, Malmédy, St. Vith, Vianden, Diekirch, LUXEMBOURG, Arlon, Esch-sur-Alzette, Bastogne, Marche-en-Famenne, Neufchâteau, Namur, Charleroi, Dinant, Philippeville, La Louvière, Gosselies, Nivelles, Soignies, Mons, Ath, Ronse, Aalst, Leuven, Tienen, BRUSSELS (BRUXELLES), Sint-Niklaas, Ghent, Terneuzen, Flushing, Middelburg, Zeebrugge, Bruges, Ostend, Torhout, Roeselare, Ieper, Veurne, Kortrijk, Mouscron, Tournai

Rhine, Maas, Waal, Lek, Westerschelde, Oosterschelde, Scheldt, Albert Canal, Meuse, Sambre, Ourthe, Amblève, Lesse, Our, Sûre, Alzette, Moselle, Ijzer

Overflakkee Delta Project

N

NORTH SEA

Compass / scale

N

KM 75 50 25 10 0

MILES 40 30 20 10 0

GERMANY

SITUATED IN THE CENTER OF EUROPE, Germany is now the continent's leading economic power. In the past it has been an area of great conflict; it was not until 1871 that a patchwork of independent states, which had fought bitterly for centuries, were united under Prussian leadership to form Germany. In this century, Germany was defeated in two world wars. By 1945 the economy was shattered and the country divided between a Soviet-dominated communist East and a democratic West. The postwar years saw an amazing recovery in West Germany's economy. Natural advantages – a central position in Europe, large reserves of coal and iron, along with the construction of an efficient transportation system and the determination to succeed – have all helped to create a dynamic economy. The East, on the other hand, lagged behind. In 1989, the Soviet Union began to disintegrate, and communism collapsed throughout Eastern Europe. The two halves of Germany were reunified in 1990, but problems soon became apparent. West Germans resented the huge amounts of money invested in the East to bring it up to their standards. East Germans became impatient with the slow pace of change. These resentments have led to violence against refugees, immigrants, and "guest workers," many of whom have lived in Germany for most of their lives.

A windmill in the fertile farmland of the northeast.

Many German towns have half-timbered buildings dating back to the Middle Ages.

CARS
Germany is Europe's largest vehicle producer, specializing in high-quality cars. American and Japanese car companies are based here, too, attracted by the skilled workforce. Look for ⊟

AGRICULTURE
Germany produces all its own food and is one of the world's main growers of sugar beets, barley, and rye. Oats, rye, and barley thrive in the mild, wet north, while wheat is grown in the warmer south. Look for ♈

This decorated stein, or mug, is used for beer.

Green pastures and woodland on the flat Baltic coast.

BERLIN
At the end of World War II, Germany's capital city, Berlin, was divided between the four victorious Allies. In 1961, the Berlin Wall was built to separate the Russian sector from the other three. In 1989, the wall came down: East Germans streamed through this gate into West Berlin.

Brandenburg Gate

DRESDEN
Once Dresden was a beautiful old city, with many 18th-century buildings. But in World War II it was devastated by Allied bombing. After extensive reconstruction, the city's historic buildings have now been restored to their former state.

Peppered salami

Salami

SAUSAGES
Sausages are Germany's favorite snack. There are many regional variations; Frankfurt has even given its name to the Frankfurter sausage. Germany also has over 200 varieties of bread.

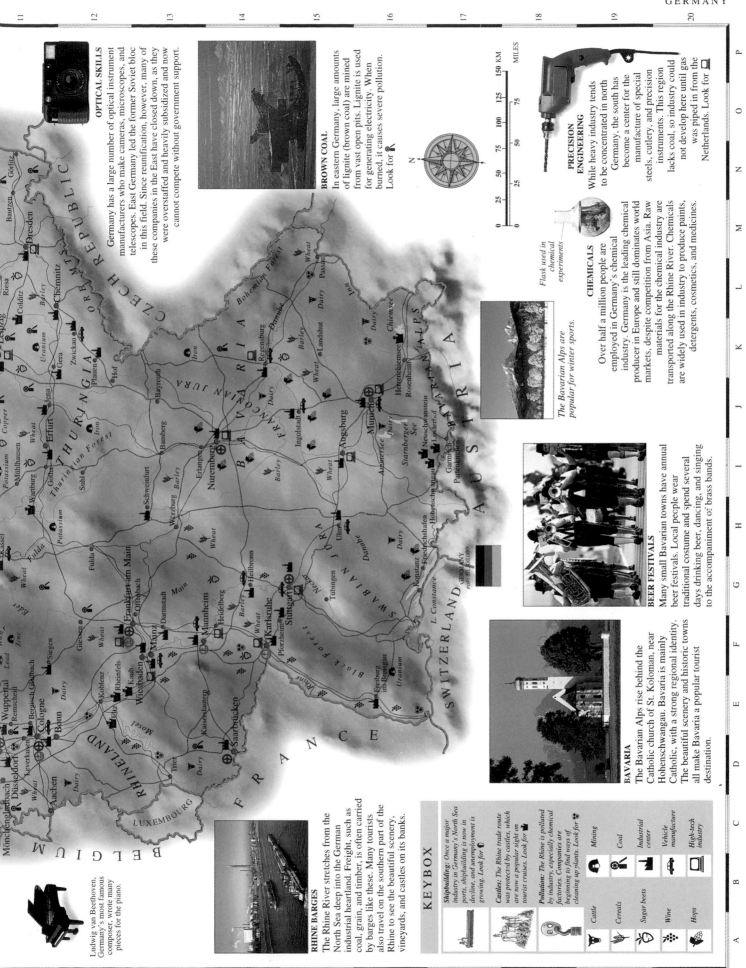

OPTICAL SKILLS

Germany has a large number of optical instrument manufacturers who make cameras, microscopes, and telescopes. East Germany led the former Soviet bloc in this field. Since reunification, however, many of these companies in the East have closed down, as they were overstaffed and heavily subsidized and now cannot compete without government support.

BROWN COAL

In eastern Germany, large amounts of lignite (brown coal) are mined from vast open pits. Lignite is used for generating electricity. When burned, it causes severe pollution. Look for ☠

PRECISION ENGINEERING

While heavy industry tends to be concentrated in north Germany, the south has become a center for the manufacture of special steels, cutlery, and precision instruments. This region lacks coal, so industry could not develop here until gas was piped in from the Netherlands. Look for ▯

Flask used in chemical experiments

CHEMICALS

Over half a million people are employed in Germany's chemical industry. Germany is the leading chemical producer in Europe and still dominates world markets, despite competition from Asia. Raw materials for the chemical industry are transported along the Rhine River. Chemicals are widely used in industry to produce paints, detergents, cosmetics, and medicines.

The Bavarian Alps are popular for winter sports.

BEER FESTIVALS

Many small Bavarian towns have annual beer festivals. Local people wear traditional costume and spend several days drinking beer, dancing, and singing to the accompaniment of brass bands.

BAVARIA

The Bavarian Alps rise behind the Catholic church of St. Koloman, near Hohenschwangau. Bavaria is mainly Catholic, with a strong regional identity. The beautiful scenery and historic towns all make Bavaria a popular tourist destination.

Ludwig van Beethoven, Germany's most famous composer, wrote many pieces for the piano.

RHINE BARGES

The Rhine River stretches from the North Sea deep into the German industrial heartland. Freight, such as coal, grain, and timber, is often carried by barges like these. Many tourists also travel on the southern part of the Rhine to see the beautiful scenery, vineyards, and castles on its banks.

KEYBOX

Shipbuilding: Once a major industry in Germany's North Sea ports, shipbuilding is now in decline, and unemployment is growing. Look for 🚢

Castles: The Rhine trade route was protected by castles, which are now a popular sight on tourist cruises. Look for 🏰

Pollution: The Rhine is polluted by industry, especially chemical factories. Companies are beginning to find ways of cleaning up plants. Look for ☢

🐄 Cattle	⛏ Mining
🌾 Cereals	⚙ Coal
🌱 Sugar beets	🏭 Industrial center
🍇 Wine	🚗 Vehicle manufacture
🌾 Hops	▯ High-tech industry

KM / MILES scale: 0 25 50 75 100 125 150 KM / 0 25 50 75 MILES

N (compass)

GERMANY
Pop: 80,500,000

67

AUSTRIA AND SWITZERLAND

RUNNING THROUGH the middle of Austria and Switzerland are the Alps, the highest mountains in Europe. Both countries lie on Europe's main north-south trading routes, with access to the heart of Europe via the great Danube and Rhine waterways. Switzerland was formed in the Middle Ages when a number of Alpine communities united in defensive leagues against their more powerful neighbors. Modern Switzerland is a confederation of 23 separate provinces, called cantons. The country has three main languages – German, French, and Italian. Austria was once the center of the Hapsburg Empire, which had vast territories in Central Europe. When the empire collapsed in 1918, Austria became an independent country. Austria has mineral resources, especially iron, and thriving industries. With few natural resources, Switzerland has concentrated instead on skilled high-technology manufacturing.

Gold bar

BANKING
Switzerland is one of the world's main financial centers. People from all over the world put their money into Swiss bank accounts as the country is well known for its political stability. Liechtenstein is also a major banking center. Look for 🪙

DAIRY FARMING
Swiss dairy cattle spend the winter in the Alpine valleys and in summer are taken up to the Alpine pastures for grazing. The milk is used to make many varieties of cheese, including Gruyère. Look for 🐂

FALSE TEETH
Liechtenstein is the headquarters of world dental manufacture. False teeth, filling materials, and plastic for crown and bridge dental work are exported to more than 100 countries.

Porcelain teeth

Liechtenstein is famous for its beautiful stamps.

The castle at Vaduz, the capital of Liechtenstein.

GENEVA
Switzerland has not been at war for 150 years and is therefore seen as a neutral meeting place. Many international organizations have their headquarters in the city of Geneva.

The Swiss consume more chocolate than any other nationality in the world.

SWITZERLAND
POP: 6,995,000

LIECHTENSTEIN
POP: 31,500

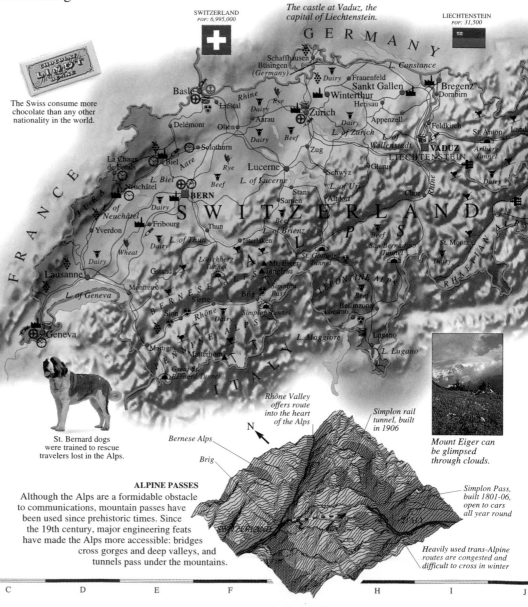

GERMANY

Schaffhausen
Büsingen (Germany)
L. Constance
Frauenfeld
Sankt Gallen
Basle
Rhine
Winterthur
Herisau
Bregenz
Dornbirn
Liestal
Dairy
Rye
Delémont
Olten
Aarau
Zürich
Appenzell
Feldkirch
Solothurn
Dairy
Beef
L. of Zurich
St. Anton
Landeck
La Chaux-de-Fonds
Biel
Zug
Rye
Lucerne
L. of Wallenstadt
Arlberg Tunnel
VADUZ
LIECHTENSTEIN
Neuchâtel
L. Biel
Beef
L. of Lucerne
Schwyz
Glarus
Dairy
Aare
FRANCE
L. of Neuchâtel
Dairy
BERN
Stans
Samen
Altdorf
L. of Uri
Chur
Yverdon
Fribourg
Thun
Rhine
Wheat
L. of Thun
L. of Brienz
Interlaken
Beef
San Bernadino Tunnel
St. Moritz
Lausanne
Dairy
Lötschberg Tunnel
Mt. Eiger
Jungfrau
St. Gotthard Tunnel
SWITZERLAND
ALPS
Beef
RHAETIAN ALPS
Montreux
BERNESE ALPS
Gstaad
Brig
Simplon Pass
LEPONTINE ALPS
Bellinzona
Beef
L. of Geneva
Sierre
Rhône
Dairy
Simplon Tunnel
Locarno
Lugano
Sion
L. Maggiore
Geneva
Martigny
PENNINE ALPS
Matterhorn
ITALY
L. Lugano
Great St. Bernard Tunnel
N
Rhône Valley offers route into the heart of the Alps

Bernese Alps

Brig

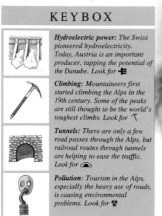

St. Bernard dogs were trained to rescue travelers lost in the Alps.

ALPINE PASSES
Although the Alps are a formidable obstacle to communications, mountain passes have been used since prehistoric times. Since the 19th century, major engineering feats have made the Alps more accessible: bridges cross gorges and deep valleys, and tunnels pass under the mountains.

Simplon rail tunnel, built in 1906

Mount Eiger can be glimpsed through clouds.

Simplon Pass, built 1801-06, open to cars all year round

Heavily used trans-Alpine routes are congested and difficult to cross in winter

KEYBOX

Hydroelectric power: The Swiss pioneered hydroelectricity. Today, Austria is an important producer, tapping the potential of the Danube. Look for ⚡

Climbing: Mountaineers first started climbing the Alps in the 19th century. Some of the peaks are still thought to be the world's toughest climbs. Look for ⛏

Tunnels: There are only a few road passes through the Alps, but railroad routes through tunnels are helping to ease the traffic. Look for 🚇

Pollution: Tourism in the Alps, especially the heavy use of roads, is causing environmental problems. Look for ☠

🌾	Cereals	🕐	Watchmaking
🐂	Cattle	💉	Pharmaceuticals
🍇	Wine	💰	Financial center
🏭	Industrial center	⛷	Skiing

VIENNA

For many centuries, Austria was ruled by the Hapsburg family. Their empire included Hungary; their capital was Vienna. The city contained many grand buildings and elegant palaces such as this one, the Schönbrunn Palace, which was the Hapsburg family's summer residence. The Hapsburg empire finally collapsed in 1918.

Cowbells help farmers locate animals in remote Alpine pastures.

AUSTRIA
POP: 7,884,000

PHARMACEUTICALS

One of Switzerland's main industries is pharmaceuticals (drugs and medicines). The industry has benefited from the Swiss emphasis on the importance of research and product development, the latest technology, and a highly skilled workforce. Perfumes, cosmetics, and drugs are all made in the Basel area. Look for ✐

WATCHMAKING

Watches and clocks have been made in Switzerland since the 16th century. Recently, however, Swiss companies have been under pressure from the Japanese and Americans, who developed quartz technology. The Swiss have saved their industry by making certain of their more famous watches less expensive. Look for ☺

The abbey at Melk in Austria was built in the 18th century.

Edelweiss is a rare Alpine flower.

AUSTRIAN INDUSTRY

Hydroelectric power from the Austrian Alps is a major source of energy for heavy industry. Iron ore deposits around Linz and Donawitz fuel the Austrian steel industry. Some Austrian steel plants have been forced to close by lower world steel prices. Look for ⛏

Iron ore

COFFEE AND CAKES

The Ottoman Turks, who besieged Vienna in 1529 and 1683, first brought coffee to the city. It was in Vienna that the first coffee shop in Western Europe was opened. There are still many cafés in Vienna, where people drink coffee and eat Austria's famous chocolate cakes. *Sachertorte* is named after the Viennese pastry shop where it is made.

Sachertorte

SWISS FOLK TRADITIONS

Swiss folk traditions are very much alive: among the annual events are carnivals during Lent, cheese and wine-makers' festivals, and celebrations marking the change of the seasons, such as the return of the cows from Alpine pasture. Colorful costumes and traditional musical instruments are used at these events.

Alpine accordion

SKI CENTER

The Alps are visited by over 100 million people each year. But ski runs, improved roads, and expanding resorts are all having a harmful effect on the environment. Huge numbers of trees have been cut down to make way for ski runs, but this can provide routes for avalanches. Look for ⚲

AUSTRIAN TOURISM

Austria's tourist industry is booming due to the attractions of its beautiful scenery, historical towns, picturesque villages, and winter sports facilities. Tourism is now one of Austria's most profitable industries. A quarter of Austria's tourists visit during the winter; many of the visitors come from nearby Germany.

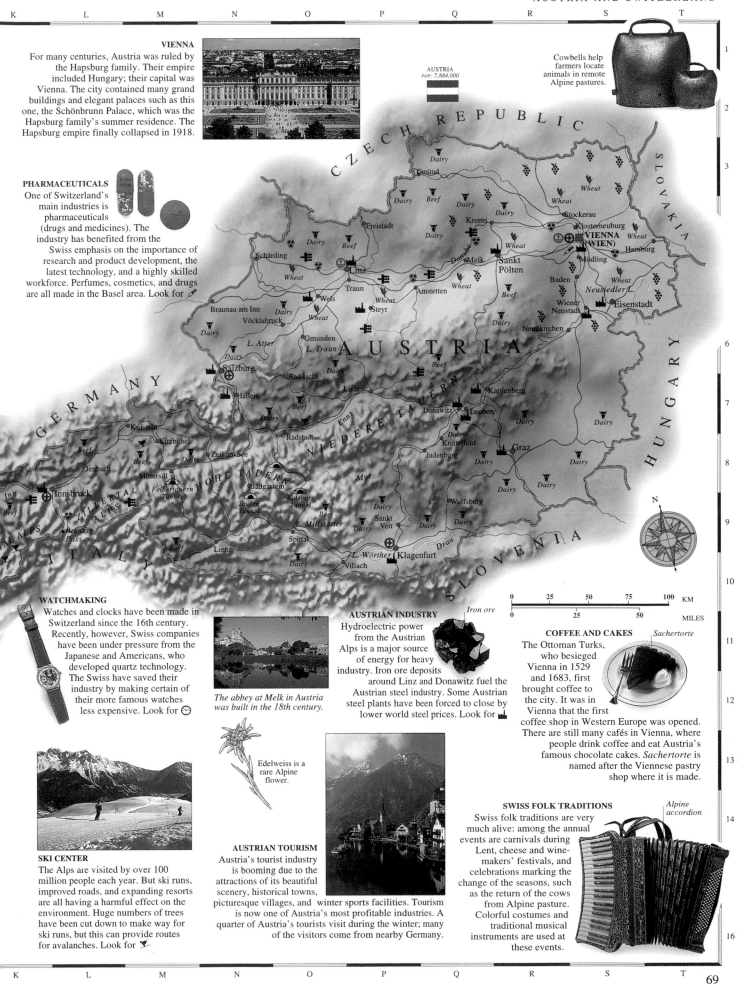

CENTRAL EUROPE

IN 1989 THE COMMUNIST governments of Central Europe collapsed and the region entered a period of momentous change. All four countries of Central Europe only became independent states earlier this century. After World War II, they were incorporated into the Soviet bloc and ruled by communist governments. These states started to industrialize rapidly, but they were heavily dependent on the former Soviet Union for their raw materials and markets. When communism collapsed in 1989, the new, democratically elected governments were faced with many problems: modernizing industry, huge foreign debts, soaring inflation, rising unemployment, and terrible pollution. In 1993 the former state of Czechoslovakia was split into two countries, the Czech Republic and Slovakia.

Grudziądz, a medieval Polish town on the Vistula River.

POLLUTION
The Czech Republic is Europe's most polluted country. The pollution comes from its own industry, but also from factories in Germany. Forests are dying because of acid rain, rivers are poisoned and the scarred landscapes will take decades to recover. Look for 💀

PUPPETS
Puppet shows are popular throughout Central Europe, but the former Czechoslovakia is acknowledged as the original home of European puppetry. Today, over a thousand Czech Republic and Slovak puppet companies perform plays.

Wooden puppet

GLASS
The Czech Republic's glass industry is centuries old. Glassware, such as this decanter and glasses, is often intricate and brightly colored. The industry uses local supplies of sand to make the glass. Bohemian crystal is manufactured principally in the northwest around Karlovy Vary and is also popular with the ever-increasing number of tourists.

PRAGUE
The Czech Republic's capital, Prague, has some of the most beautiful and well-preserved architecture in Europe. Since 1989, when the country was opened to tourists, thousands of people have flocked to the city Look for 📷

POLAND
POP: 38,500,000

CZECH REPUBLIC
POP: 10,302,215

Beautifully painted eggs are sold in the Czech Republic and Slovakia at Easter.

BEER
Some of Europe's finest beers are brewed in the Czech Republic. Pilsener lager originated in the town of Plzeň; Budweiser beer has been brewed at České Budějovice for over a century. Huge quantities of beer, the Budweiser beer in particular, are exported, principally to European countries such as Germany and the UK.

HUNGARIAN INDUSTRY
Since the end of World War II, Hungary has industrialized rapidly. It manufactures products such as aluminum, steel, electronic goods, and vehicles, especially buses. When the Soviet Union disintegrated, Hungarian manufacturers lost many of the traditional markets for their products – especially in heavy industry – and now face many problems. Look for 🏭

HUNGARY
POP: 10,518,000

KEYBOX

Mining: Poland is one of the world's largest coal producers, but recently the industry has been affected by competition from abroad. Look for ⛏

Financial center: In Hungary, the Budapest stock exchange opened in 1990, and many new banks have now opened in the city. Look for 💰

Dam: The dam built by the Slovaks on the Danube at Gabčíkovo has caused a major dispute between Hungary and Slovakia. Look for ▦

🌾	Cereals	🏭	Industrial center
🥬	Sugar beets	🗑	Shipbuilding
🍓	Mixed fruits	📷	Tourism
⚘	Timber	🌱	Spas
⚫	Mining	💀	Pollution

N

0   50   100   150   200 KM

0   25   50   75   100 MILES

A   B   C   D   E   F   G   H   I   J

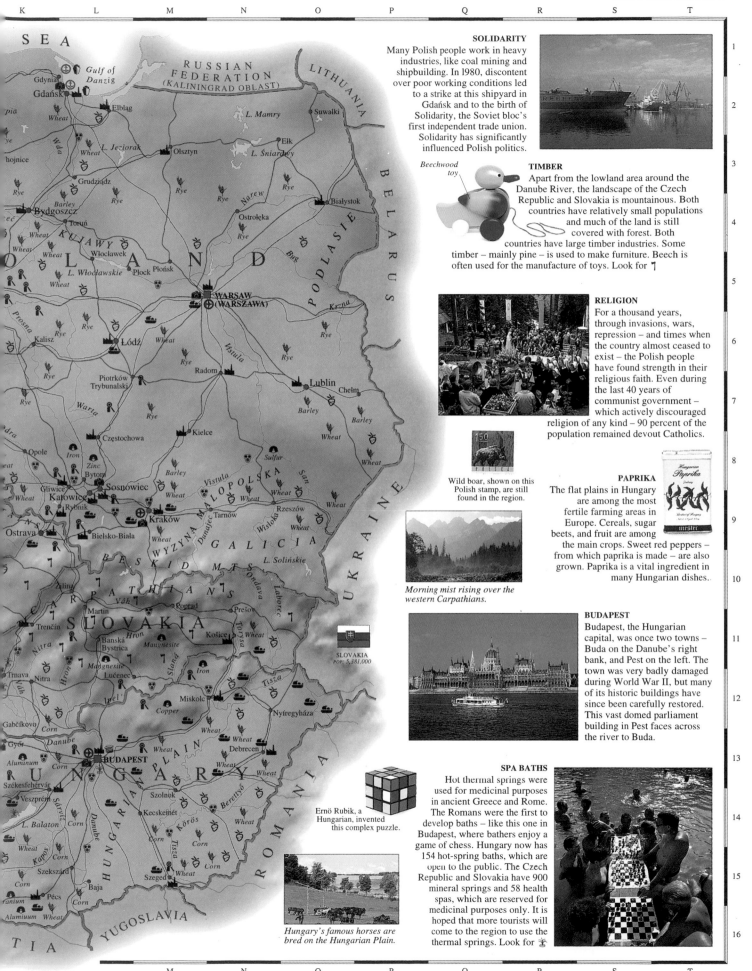

K L M N O P Q R S T

SEA

Gulf of Danzig

Gdynia

Gdańsk

RUSSIAN FEDERATION (KALININGRAD OBLAST)

LITHUANIA

Elblag

Wheat

pia

L. Mamry

Suwałki

ye

Wda

L. Jeziorak

Olsztyn

Ełk

L. Śniardwy

hojnice

Wheat

Grudziądz

BELARUS

Białystok

Rye

Rye

Narew

Rye

Rye

Rye

Barley

Bydgoszcz

Rye

KUJAWY

Ostrołęka

Toruń

Wheat

Rye

PODLASIE

Bug

Wheat

Włocławek

P O L A N D

Wheat

L. Włocławskie

Płock

Płońsk

WARSAW (WARSZAWA)

Krna

Prosna

Rye

Kalisz

Rye

Łódź

Wheat

Vistula

Rye

Rye

Rye

Piotrków Trybunalski

Radom

Lublin

Rye

Warta

Chełm

Rye

Częstochowa

Kielce

Barley

Barley

Opole

Iron

Wheat

Sulfur

Wheat

Zinc

Bytom

Barley

San

Wheat

Gliwice

Sosnowiec

VISTULA

MAŁOPOLSKA

Wheat

Wheat

Katowice

Rybnik

Kraków

Tarnów

Rzeszów

Wheat

Ostrava

Bielsko-Biała

Wheat

Dunajec

Wisłoka

Wheat

dra

BESKID MTS

GALICIA

L. Solińskie

Żilina

CARPATHIANS

Sondava

UKRAINE

Váh

Poprad

Martin

Prešov

Trenčín

SLOVAKIA

Hron

Košice

Torysa

Wheat

Nitra

Banská Bystrica

Magnesite

Slaná

Laborec

Trnava

Magnesite

Iron

Nitra

Lučenec

Tisza

Gabčíkovo

Ipel'

Miskolc

Corn

Copper

Nyíregyháza

Győr

Danube

Wheat

Wheat

BUDAPEST

Wheat

Debrecen

H U N G A R Y

Aluminum

Corn

Wheat

Székesfehérvár

HUNGARIAN PLAIN

Veszprém

Sárviz

Szolnok

ROMANIA

L. Balaton

Corn

Kecskemét

Berettyó

Wheat

Wheat

Körös

Corn

Corn

Kapos

Corn

Tisza

Corn

Szekszárd

Szeged

Wheat

Corn

Tanium

Pécs

Corn

Baja

Aluminum

Wheat

TIA

YUGOSLAVIA

1
2
3
4
5
6
7
8
9
10
11
12
13
14
15
16

SOLIDARITY

Many Polish people work in heavy industries, like coal mining and shipbuilding. In l980, discontent over poor working conditions led to a strike at this shipyard in Gdańsk and to the birth of Solidarity, the Soviet bloc's first independent trade union. Solidarity has significantly influenced Polish politics.

TIMBER

Beechwood toy

Apart from the lowland area around the Danube River, the landscape of the Czech Republic and Slovakia is mountainous. Both countries have relatively small populations and much of the land is still covered with forest. Both countries have large timber industries. Some timber – mainly pine – is used to make furniture. Beech is often used for the manufacture of toys. Look for ⊤

RELIGION

For a thousand years, through invasions, wars, repression – and times when the country almost ceased to exist – the Polish people have found strength in their religious faith. Even during the last 40 years of communist government – which actively discouraged religion of any kind – 90 percent of the population remained devout Catholics.

Wild boar, shown on this Polish stamp, are still found in the region.

Morning mist rising over the western Carpathians.

SLOVAKIA
POP: 5,381,000

PAPRIKA

The flat plains in Hungary are among the most fertile farming areas in Europe. Cereals, sugar beets, and fruit are among the main crops. Sweet red peppers – from which paprika is made – are also grown. Paprika is a vital ingredient in many Hungarian dishes.

BUDAPEST

Budapest, the Hungarian capital, was once two towns – Buda on the Danube's right bank, and Pest on the left. The town was very badly damaged during World War II, but many of its historic buildings have since been carefully restored. This vast domed parliament building in Pest faces across the river to Buda.

Ernö Rubik, a Hungarian, invented this complex puzzle.

SPA BATHS

Hot thermal springs were used for medicinal purposes in ancient Greece and Rome. The Romans were the first to develop baths – like this one in Budapest, where bathers enjoy a game of chess. Hungary now has 154 hot-spring baths, which are open to the public. The Czech Republic and Slovakia have 900 mineral springs and 58 health spas, which are reserved for medicinal purposes only. It is hoped that more tourists will come to the region to use the thermal springs. Look for ⚘

Hungary's famous horses are bred on the Hungarian Plain.

ITALY AND MALTA

AT VARIOUS TIMES in the past 2,000 years Italy has influenced the development of European civilization. From this narrow, boot-shaped peninsula the Romans established a vast empire throughout Europe and North Africa; Christianity was first adopted as an official religion by a Roman emperor, and Rome later became the center of the Catholic church. In the 14th century, an extraordinary flowering of the arts and sciences, known as the Renaissance, or "rebirth," started in Italy and transformed European thought and culture. Italy at this time was divided into independent city-states and was later ruled by foreign nations, including France and Austria. But by 1870, after centuries of foreign domination, Italy became an independent and unified country. Despite a lack of natural resources and defeat in World War II, Italy has become a major industrial power. The country has long suffered from corruption and organized crime, but recent changes show promise of more political stability in the future.

PASTA

The Italian explorer Marco Polo is said to have brought the recipe for pasta to Italy when he returned from his great journey to China. Pasta is a type of dough made by adding water to wheat flour. It has become one of the world's most popular foods. It can be made into different shapes and filled with meat or vegetables.

Cappelletti (little hats)

Orecchioni (large ears)

Round tortellini (small pies)

Pinnacles of the Dolomites in northeastern Italy.

VERONA

The ancient Romans were skillful engineers, and many of their remarkable buildings are still standing today. The foundations of much of Italy's road system was also built by the Romans. Verona is based on the Roman grid street plan. The town's ancient amphitheater seats 22,000 and is still used.

Silk scarf

Suede shoe

DESIGN

Italians place great emphasis on design and produce beautiful products. This flair for design is particularly obvious in their cars and clothes. The fashion houses of Rome, Florence, Milan, and Venice rival those of Paris, and Italian shoes and clothes are widely exported.

Masks like these are worn during the February carnival in Venice, which includes plays, masked balls, and fireworks.

VENICE

This historic city is built on a number of islands in a shallow lagoon. Many buildings stand on wooden stilts driven into the mud. Venice's future is now uncertain, threatened by flooding and pollution.

THE PO VALLEY

Between the Alps and the Apennines lies a huge triangular plain, drained by Italy's greatest river, the Po. The majority of the country's agriculture, population, and industry is concentrated in this region. Its major cities like Milan and Turin are important industrial and commercial centers.

Milan

Turin

The Alps

Farming of corn, wheat, and rice

Apennines

Po

Genoa: major seaport and industrial center

Alpine rivers supply water for HEP and irrigation

N

Mountain passes link Italy to the rest of Europe

SAN MARINO
POP: 23,000

ITALY
POP: 57,956,000

SLOVENIA

AUSTRIA

SWITZERLAND

FRANCE

ADRIATIC

LIGURIAN SEA

Trieste
Udine
Gulf of Venice
Chioggia
Piave
Corn
Corn
Corn
Venice
Mestre
Treviso
Padua
Adige
Comacchio Lagoon
Ravenna
Cervia
Ferrara
Bologna
Forlì
SAN MARINO
Rimini
Riccione
Pesaro
Ancona
Wheat
Wheat
Wheat
Wheat
Vicenza
Verona
L. Garda
L. d'Iseo
Mantova
Modena
Reggio nell'Emilia
Parma
Cremona
Piacenza
Brescia
Bergamo
Monza
Milan
Novara
Turin
Asti
Alessandria
Savona
Genoa
Gulf of Genoa
Alassio
San Remo
Cuneo
Olive
Wheat
Wheat
Wheat
Wheat
Wheat
Wheat
Corn
Corn
Corn
Po
Arno
La Spezia
Viareggio
Livorno
Pisa
Lucca
Pistoia
Prato
Florence
Siena
Arezzo
Perugia
L. Trasimeno
Potenza
TUSCANY
Pyrite
Marble
Zinc

72

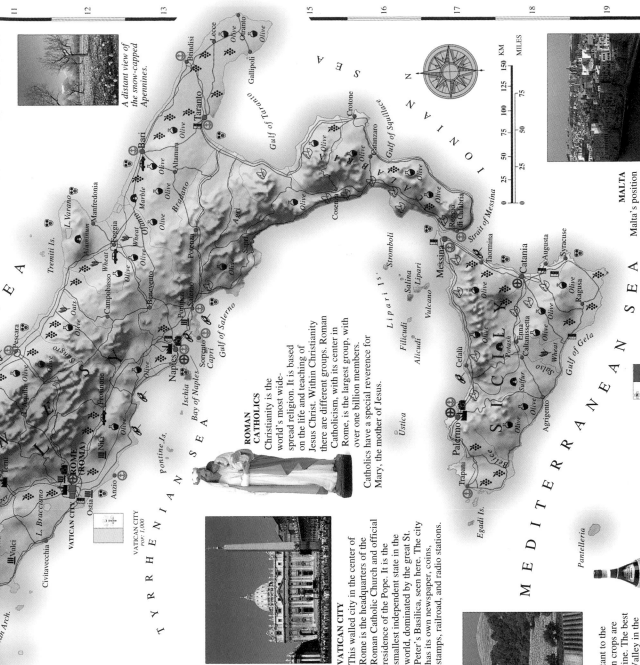

A distant view of the snow-capped Apennines.

MOTOR VEHICLES
Many Italian car manufacturers are based around the cities of Milan and Turin. Italian engineers and designers have developed some of the finest vehicles in Europe, both high-performance cars and cheaper, economical models. Look for 🚗

— Model of Ferrari car

Sardinia, a large island in the Mediterranean.

ROMAN CATHOLICS
Christianity is the world's most widespread religion. It is based on the life and teaching of Jesus Christ. Within Christianity there are different groups. Roman Catholicism, with its center in Rome, is the largest group, with over one billion members. Catholics have a special reverence for Mary, the mother of Jesus.

VATICAN CITY
This walled city in the center of Rome is the headquarters of the Roman Catholic Church and official residence of the Pope. It is the smallest independent state in the world, dominated by the great St. Peter's Basilica, seen here. The city has its own newspaper, coins, stamps, railroad, and radio stations.

VATICAN CITY
POP: 1,000

Italians are passionate soccer fans.

Italian national team shirt /

Bottles of Chianti are often sold in a wicker casing called a fiasco.

AGRICULTURE
Agriculture is very important to the Italian economy. The main crops are olives, citrus fruits, and wine. The best farming region is the Po Valley in the north. Southern Italy has always suffered from its hilly terrain and low rainfall, but thanks to irrigation and modern farming methods, agriculture has improved since the 1950s.

MALTA
Malta's position on the Mediterranean shipping routes explains its important role in the history of the region. The Romans, Arabs, French, Turks, Spanish, and British have all colonized or fought over the island. In 1964 it became independent. Today, its main income comes from tourism and its port facilities.

MALTA
POP: 370,000

KEYBOX
Wine: Italy is the world's largest wine producer. Recently, the wine industry has brought in rules for higher quality and better control. Look for 🍇

Oil refining: Italy is more dependent on imported fuel than any European country. Crude oil has to be imported and refined. Look for ▥

Sightseeing: Millions of tourists visit Italy each year to see its historic towns, famous buildings, and museums. Look for 📷

🌾 Cereals
〰 Rice
🍊 Citrus fruits
🫒 Vegetable oil
⚒ Mining

🏭 Industrial center
🚗 Vehicle manufacture
✈ Tourism
▥ Archaeological sites
☢ Pollution

Seas and places (map labels):

ADRIATIC SEA
IONIAN SEA
TYRRHENIAN SEA
MEDITERRANEAN SEA
LIGURIAN SEA

Lecce, Olive, Otranto, Brindisi, Gallipoli, Taranto, Bari, Manfredonia, L. Varano, Altamura, Foggia, Tremiti Is., Campobasso, Benevento, Potenza, Matera, Bradano, Agri, Sele, Crotone, Catanzaro, Gulf of Squillace, Cosenza, Reggio di Calabria, Strait of Messina, Stromboli, Lipari Is., Salina, Lipari, Vulcano, Filicudi, Alicudi, Ustica, Messina, Taormina, Catania, Augusta, Syracuse, SICILY, Enna, Caltanissetta, Potash, Sulfur, Ragusa, Gulf of Gela, Gela, Agrigento, Palermo, Cefalù, Trapani, Belice, Salso, Pelagie Is., Lampedusa, Linosa, Lampione, Pantelleria, Gozo, MALTA, VALLETTA, Gulf of Taranto, Gulf of Salerno, Salerno, Sorrento, Capri, Naples, Ischia, Bay of Naples, Pontine Is., ROME (ROMA), VATICAN CITY, Ostia, Anzio, Civitavecchia, L. Bracciano, Vulci, Tiber, Tuscan Arch., Pescara, Oats, Wheat, Sangro, Olive, Olive, Olive, SARDINIA, Olbia, Strait of Bonifacio, Nuoro, Sassari, Alghero, Oristano, Tirso, Mannu, Cagliari, Gulf of Cagliari, Sarroch, Zinc, Lead, Iglesias, C. Spartivento, San Pietro, Sant'Antioco, Capper, Egadi Is.

N

KM MILES
150
125
100
75
50
25
0
75
50
25
0

THE WESTERN BALKANS

THIS TROUBLED REGION of southeastern Europe consists of a wide variety of landscapes, religions, peoples and languages. The region was invaded many times, and from the 14th to 19th centuries was under foreign occupation. After World War II, both Albania and Yugoslavia were ruled by communist governments. When the Yugoslav dictator, Marshal Tito, died in 1980 the Yugoslav government became less centralized, and former republics demanded their independence. Serbia, the largest and most powerful republic, resisted the break-up of Yugoslavia. In 1991, a bloody civil war broke out between Serbia and Croatia and, eventually, between Serbs and Muslims in Bosnia. Albania was isolated by its communist government from the rest of Europe and became economically backward. The country has now shaken off its communist rulers and held democratic elections. The economy, however, is still in chaos.

SLOVENIA
POP: 2,016,000

CROATIA
POP: 4,801,000

The spectacular scenery of northern Slovenia.

YUGO
This car, the Yugo, is manufactured in former Yugoslavia at Kragujevac. It was designed for foreign export, but the economic disruption caused by the civil war has dealt a death blow to this industry. Slovenia has had more success; French cars are made there under licence, and are sold to the domestic market. Look for 🚗

UNDER FIRE
The world looked on in horror as Dubrovnik, a beautiful city with an untouched center dating back 1,000 years, came under Serbian attack in 1991. Sarajevo, the Bosnian capital, was another casualty; many of its historic churches and mosques were hit by shells. Other historic towns in Bosnia and Croatia have also suffered irreparable damage during the war.

Nugget of mercury ore

BOSNIA & HERZEGOVINA
POP: 4,446,000

Slovenia is a major producer of mercury, used in thermometers.

TOURISM
Many tourists used to visit former Yugoslavia, attracted by the country's beautiful scenery, warm climate and stunning coastline. By the late 1980s, an average of 9 million visitors were coming to Yugoslavia every year. However, the violent civil war has now virtually put an end to the tourist industry. Look for 🏖

KEYBOX

Mining: Albania has some of the world's largest chromium reserves. Exports are hampered by outdated mining equipment and frequent strikes. Look for ⛑

Refugee centres: The war in former Yugoslavia has forced over a million people to leave their homes and seek asylum in nearby countries. Look for ⛺

🌾	Cereals	⚙	Coal
🥫	Mixed fruits	⚡	Hydroelectric power
🍇	Wine	🏭	Industrial center
🚬	Tobacco	🚗	Vehicle manufacture
🎣	Fishing	🏖	Tourism

MARKETS
In peacetime, local markets in the region are packed with people and well stocked with a wide range of produce from nearby farms. Large quantities of fruit and vegetables are grown in the mild, warm climate of the Croatian coast and in western Bosnia. Look for 🥫

FOLKLORE
Variations in national costume reflect the many different traditions and peoples living in this region. In Slovenia, for example, costumes show a strong Alpine influence – leather trousers and gathered *dirndl* skirts. Further south, the Dubrovnik region is famous for its costume of white dresses, embroidered blouses and vests. Folk-music and dancing take place at religious festivals and on market-days, and are also performed for tourist groups.

N

0   50   100   150 KM
0   50   100   150 MILES

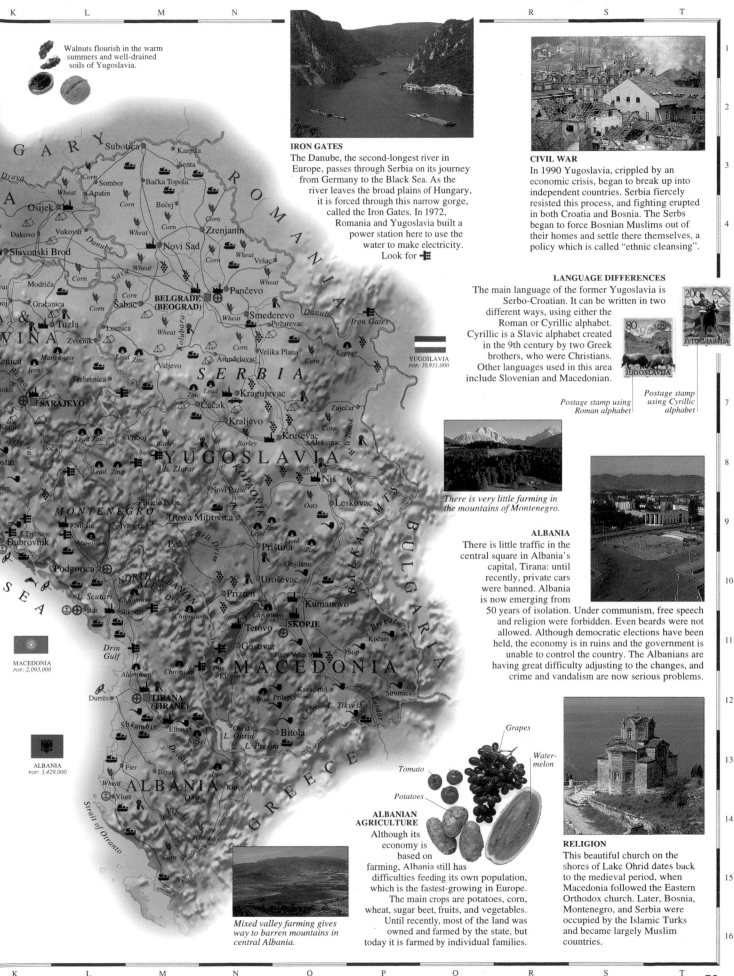

Walnuts flourish in the warm summers and well-drained soils of Yugoslavia.

IRON GATES

The Danube, the second-longest river in Europe, passes through Serbia on its journey from Germany to the Black Sea. As the river leaves the broad plains of Hungary, it is forced through this narrow gorge, called the Iron Gates. In 1972, Romania and Yugoslavia built a power station here to use the water to make electricity. Look for ▟

CIVIL WAR

In 1990 Yugoslavia, crippled by an economic crisis, began to break up into independent countries. Serbia fiercely resisted this process, and fighting erupted in both Croatia and Bosnia. The Serbs began to force Bosnian Muslims out of their homes and settle there themselves, a policy which is called "ethnic cleansing".

LANGUAGE DIFFERENCES

The main language of the former Yugoslavia is Serbo-Croatian. It can be written in two different ways, using either the Roman or Cyrillic alphabet. Cyrillic is a Slavic alphabet created in the 9th century by two Greek brothers, who were Christians. Other languages used in this area include Slovenian and Macedonian.

YUGOSLAVIA
POP: 10,931,000

Postage stamp using Roman alphabet

Postage stamp using Cyrillic alphabet

There is very little farming in the mountains of Montenegro.

ALBANIA

There is little traffic in the central square in Albania's capital, Tirana: until recently, private cars were banned. Albania is now emerging from 50 years of isolation. Under communism, free speech and religion were forbidden. Even beards were not allowed. Although democratic elections have been held, the economy is in ruins and the government is unable to control the country. The Albanians are having great difficulty adjusting to the changes, and crime and vandalism are now serious problems.

MACEDONIA
POP: 2,093,000

ALBANIA
POP: 3,429,000

Grapes

Water-melon

Tomato

Potatoes

ALBANIAN AGRICULTURE

Although its economy is based on farming, Albania still has difficulties feeding its own population, which is the fastest-growing in Europe. The main crops are potatoes, corn, wheat, sugar beet, fruits, and vegetables. Until recently, most of the land was owned and farmed by the state, but today it is farmed by individual families.

Mixed valley farming gives way to barren mountains in central Albania.

RELIGION

This beautiful church on the shores of Lake Ohrid dates back to the medieval period, when Macedonia followed the Eastern Orthodox church. Later, Bosnia, Montenegro, and Serbia were occupied by the Islamic Turks and became largely Muslim countries.

ROMANIA AND BULGARIA

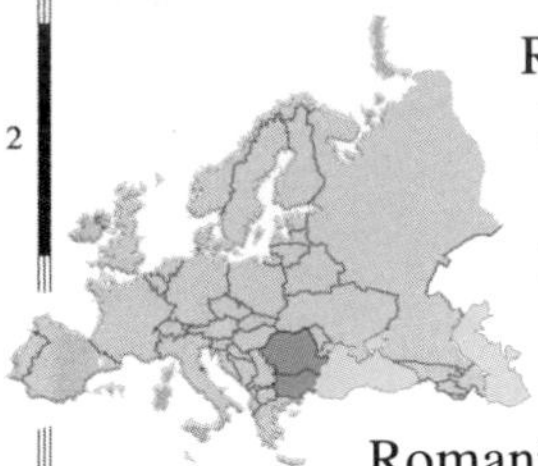

ROMANIA AND BULGARIA ARE LOCATED in southeastern Europe, on the shores of the Black Sea. The Danube River forms the border between the two countries, and the most fertile land in the region is found in the river's vast valley and delta. Forests of oak, pine, and fir trees grow on the slopes of the Carpathian and Balkan mountains.

Romania and Bulgaria were occupied by Romans, Bulgars, Hungarians, and Turkish Ottomans, but this troubled history ended when they became independent countries in the late 19th and early 20th centuries. After two world wars, both countries became part of the Soviet communist bloc. Although they are no longer communist, economic reform has been slow, and unemployment, high prices, and food shortages are still constant problems.

THE PRESIDENTIAL PALACE
Under Romania's repressive communist leader, President Ceauşescu, food and energy supplies were rationed. Despite this, the president started a series of expensive building projects, such as this presidential palace in Bucharest. In 1989, the Romanian people rose up against communism and executed their president.

Rose petal

ROSE OIL
Used in perfume, rose oil is literally worth its weight in gold. Central Bulgaria produces most of the world's supply. The world's largest rose gardens are at Kazanlŭk. Look for ⚘

TOBACCO
Bulgaria is the world's second largest exporter of cigarettes. Tobacco is grown in the fertile valleys of the Maritsa River. This woman is sorting tobacco leaves, ready for selling. Look for

Small farms in the wooded valleys of central Romania.

YOGURT
Yogurt, made from the milk of cows, sheep, or goats, is an important part of the Bulgarian diet. Many Bulgarians claim that eating yogurt helps them live to a ripe old age.

The Alexander Nevsky church in Sofia celebrates liberation from Turkish rule.

Bulgaria is the world's fourth largest wine exporter.

RILA MONASTERY
The walls of Rila monastery are decorated with no less than 1,200 superb wall paintings. The monastery became a symbol of the Bulgarians' struggle to preserve the Christian faith during centuries of Turkish rule. The monastery was originally founded in 1335 and was rebuilt after it burned to the ground in the 19th century.

KEYBOX

Vehicle manufacture: *Romanian factories make copies of French vehicles for export to China, Russia, and many Western countries. Look for*

High-tech industry: *Electronics earns Bulgaria foreign currency, although the computer industry is suffering from international competition. Look for*

Spas: *Mineral springs and health treatments are provided by many spa resorts, which are a popular tourist attraction. Look for*

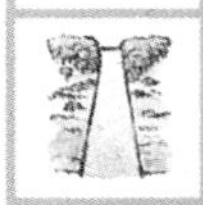

Shipping canal: *The Danube-Black Sea Canal enables ships to avoid the slow journey through the Danube Delta. Look for*

Cattle	*Mining*
Cereals	*Oil*
Wine	*Gas*
Tobacco	*Industrial center*
Roses	*Tourism*

UKR
HUNGARY
YUGOSLAVIA
MACEDONIA
GR
ROM
B
Transylvan
CARPATH
BALKA
RHODOPE MTS
Satu Mare
Baia Mare
Oradea
Cluj-Napoca
Arad
Alba Iulia
Copşa Mică
Deva
Timişoara
Reşiţa
Râmnicu Vâlce
Târgu Jiu
Băile Herculane
Drobeta-Turnu-Severin
Craiova
Vidin
Mikhaylovgrad
Vratsa
Pravets
SOFIA (SOFIYA)
Pernik
L. Iskŭr
Rila
Pazard
Velingrad
Sandanski
Mureş
Someş
Timiş
Jiu
Danube
Struma
Wheat
Corn
Beef
Dairy
Zinc
Lead
Copper
Gold
Iron
Aluminum
Manganese
Chromium

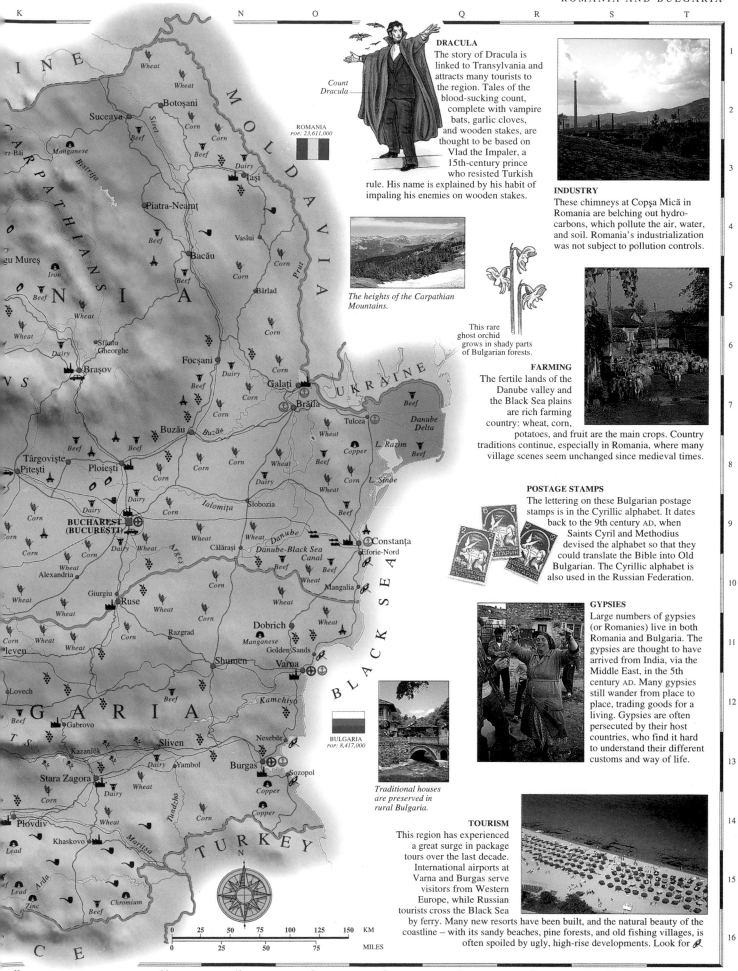

DRACULA

The story of Dracula is linked to Transylvania and attracts many tourists to the region. Tales of the blood-sucking count, complete with vampire bats, garlic cloves, and wooden stakes, are thought to be based on Vlad the Impaler, a 15th-century prince who resisted Turkish rule. His name is explained by his habit of impaling his enemies on wooden stakes.

Count Dracula

ROMANIA
POP: 23,611,000

The heights of the Carpathian Mountains.

This rare ghost orchid grows in shady parts of Bulgarian forests.

INDUSTRY

These chimneys at Copşa Mică in Romania are belching out hydro-carbons, which pollute the air, water, and soil. Romania's industrialization was not subject to pollution controls.

FARMING

The fertile lands of the Danube valley and the Black Sea plains are rich farming country: wheat, corn, potatoes, and fruit are the main crops. Country traditions continue, especially in Romania, where many village scenes seem unchanged since medieval times.

POSTAGE STAMPS

The lettering on these Bulgarian postage stamps is in the Cyrillic alphabet. It dates back to the 9th century AD, when Saints Cyril and Methodius devised the alphabet so that they could translate the Bible into Old Bulgarian. The Cyrillic alphabet is also used in the Russian Federation.

GYPSIES

Large numbers of gypsies (or Romanies) live in both Romania and Bulgaria. The gypsies are thought to have arrived from India, via the Middle East, in the 5th century AD. Many gypsies still wander from place to place, trading goods for a living. Gypsies are often persecuted by their host countries, who find it hard to understand their different customs and way of life.

BULGARIA
POP: 8,417,000

Traditional houses are preserved in rural Bulgaria.

TOURISM

This region has experienced a great surge in package tours over the last decade. International airports at Varna and Burgas serve visitors from Western Europe, while Russian tourists cross the Black Sea by ferry. Many new resorts have been built, and the natural beauty of the coastline – with its sandy beaches, pine forests, and old fishing villages, is often spoiled by ugly, high-rise developments. Look for

KM
0   25   50   75   100   125   150

MILES
0   25   50   75

GREECE

FROM THE EARLIEST TIMES, the life and economy of Greece has been shaped by its geography. It is a country of rugged mountains, isolated valleys, remote peninsulas, and more than 1,400 scattered islands. The difficulty of traveling by land has turned Greece into a seafaring nation, which owns the second largest fleet of merchant ships in the world. Ninety percent of its imports and exports are carried by sea rather than by road. Most people in Greece make their living from farming, but in recent years, tourism has become an important source of income. Tourists visit Greece not only for its warm, Mediterranean climate and beautiful landscape, but also for its ancient ruins. Many of these date from the 5th century BC, when the country was the cultural center of the Western world, the birthplace of democracy, and home of great thinkers such as Socrates, Plato, and Aristotle.

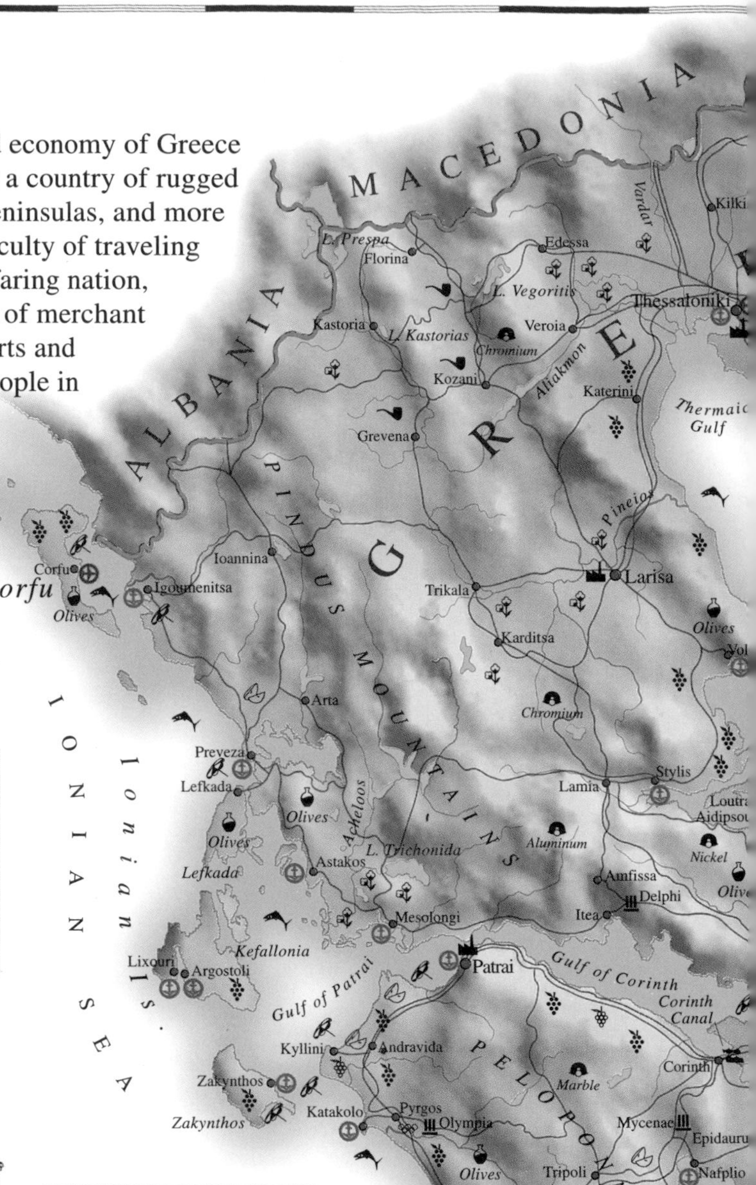

MACEDONIA
ALBANIA
GREECE
PINDUS MOUNTAINS
PELOPONNESE
IONIAN SEA
Ionian Is.
Corfu
Olives
Corfu
Igoumenitsa
Ioannina
L. Prespa
Florina
Edessa
Vardar
Kilki
L. Vegoritis
Thessaloniki
Kastoria
L. Kastorias
Chromium
Veroia
Kozani
Aliakmon
Katerini
Thermaic Gulf
Grevena
Pineios
Larisa
Trikala
Karditsa
Chromium
Olives
Arta
Preveza
Lefkada
Olives
Olives
Lefkada
Acheloos
L. Trichonida
Astakos
Aluminum
Lamia
Stylis
Loutra Aidipsou
Nickel
Amfissa
Delphi
Itea
Olives
Mesolongi
Kefallonia
Lixouri
Argostoli
Patrai
Gulf of Patrai
Gulf of Corinth
Corinth Canal
Corinth
Kyllini
Andravida
Zakynthos
Zakynthos
Katakolo
Pyrgos
Olympia
Marble
Mycenae
Epidauru
Nafplio
Tripoli
Olives
Manganese
Olives
Olives
Sparti
Leoni
Kalamata
Pilos
Olives
Gulf of Messini
Gytheio
Gulf of Laconia
Neapoli
Kythira

Greek Orthodox bishop

THE ORTHODOX CHURCH

Most Greek Christians belong to the Orthodox Church. This was founded in Constantinople (modern Istanbul) in the 4th century AD. The Eastern Orthodox Church established there still flourishes in Greece, Eastern Europe, and Russia.

ATHENS

Athens is famous for its Acropolis ("high place"), crowned by the Parthenon temple. Smog all too often obscures the Acropolis, and cars are banned from the city on certain days to reduce pollution.

Parsley
Eggplant
Cucumber
Beef tomato

GREEK SALAD

Many Greek farms are small, growing just enough vegetables and fruit for the farmer's family. Lettuces, cucumbers, tomatoes, olives, herbs, and cheese are the most common products.

The Parthenon temple (built 432 BC) was the center of religious life in classical Athens.

KEYBOX

Archaeological sites: Remains from ancient Greece are found all over the country, attracting many visitors. Look for Ⅲ	
Sultanas and currants: Greece is the world's largest exporter of these fruits. Small, black currants are named after the town of Corinth. Look for	
The Olympic Games: The event started in Olympia in 776 BC. Sports included running, wrestling, boxing, horse racing, javelin, and discus. Look for	
Citrus fruit	*Fishing*
Wine	*Mining*
Vegetable oil	*Oil*
Cotton	*Industrial center*
Tobacco	*Tourism*

THE CORINTH CANAL

Athens is separated from the Ionian Sea by a narrow neck of land called the Isthmus of Corinth. In 1893 the Greeks cut a canal through the isthmus. It is 3.9 miles (6.3 km) long, but only just wide enough for a ship to squeeze between the cliffs on either side. Look for

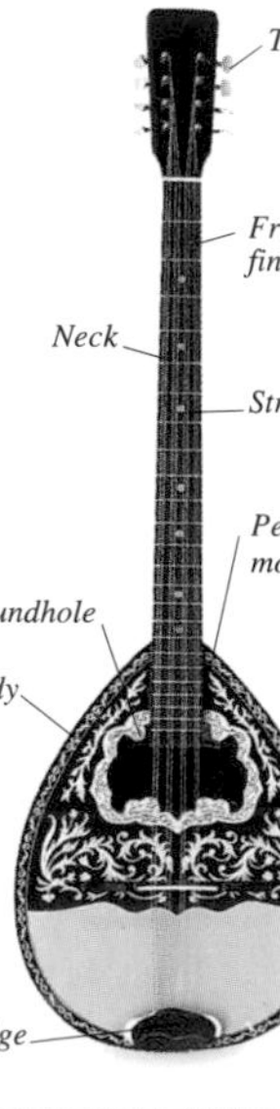

Tuning peg
Fretted fingerboard
Neck
String
Pegbox inlaid with mother-of-pearl
Soundhole
Body
Bridge

CLASSICAL MUSIC

The bouzouki is a stringed instrument, similar to a lute or a guitar, which is used in traditional Greek music. Folk dances, national costumes, and music are still very popular at religious festivals such as Easter, and on special occasions such as weddings.

Olives and cypresses grow throughout Greece.

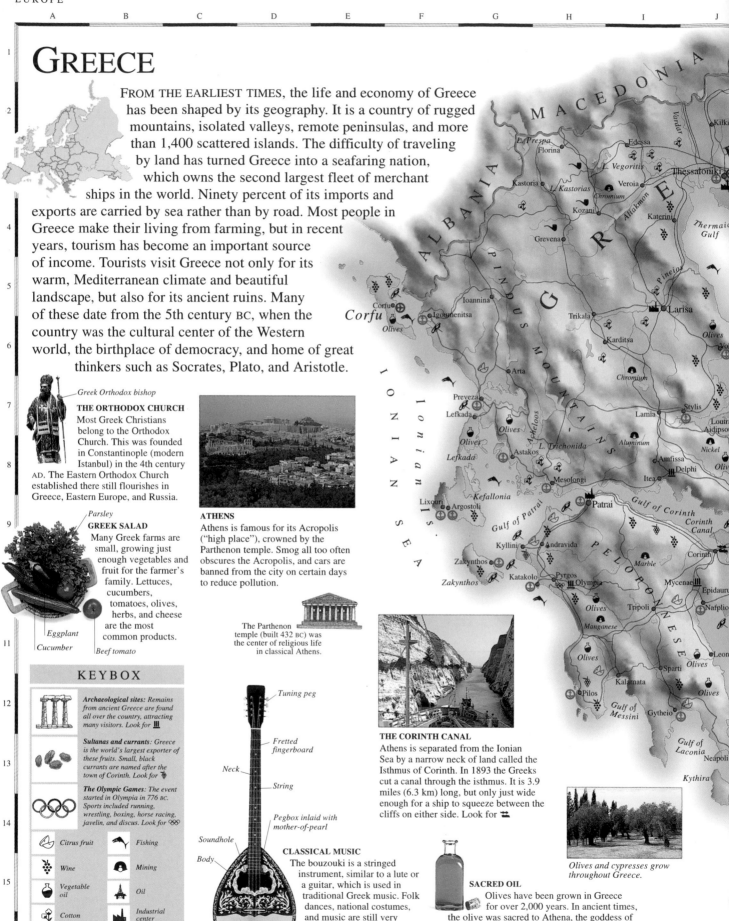

SACRED OIL

Olives have been grown in Greece for over 2,000 years. In ancient times, the olive was sacred to Athena, the goddess of war, and olive wreaths were worn as a symbol of victory. Today, olives and olive oil are major exports. Look for

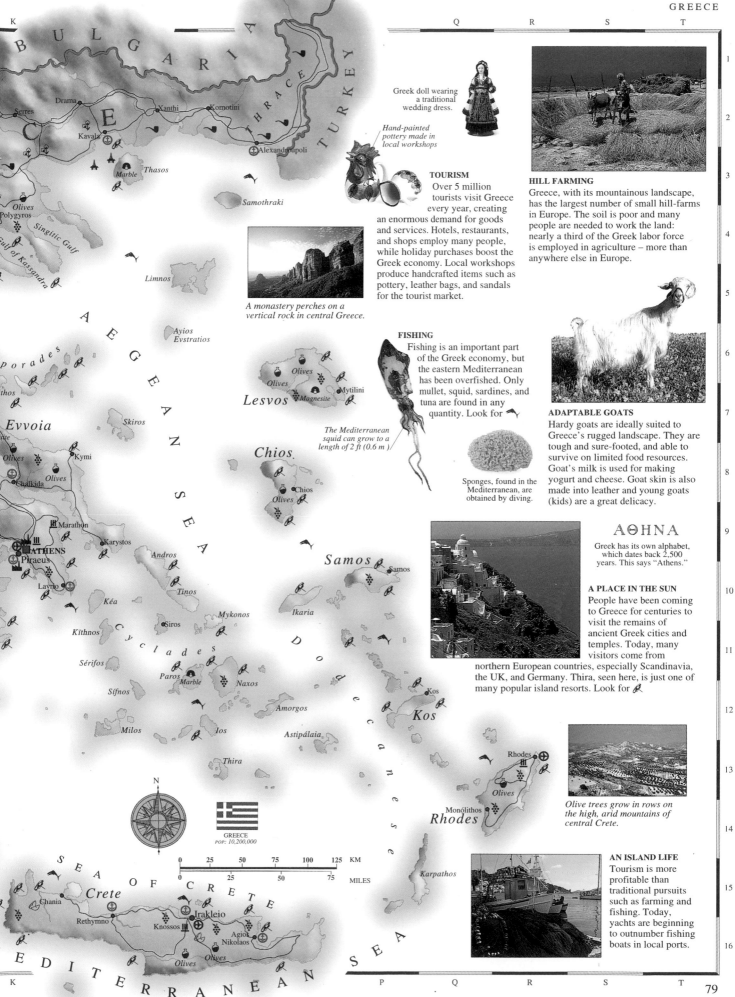

K Q R S T

BULGARIA

THRACE

TURKEY

Serres
Drama
Xanthi
Komotini
Kavala
Alexandroupoli

THRACE
Thasos
Marble
Olives
Polygyros
Singitic Gulf
Gulf of Kassandra

Samothraki

Limnos

Ayios
Evstratios

Sporades
áthos

Evvoia
Olives
Kymi
Chalkida
Olives
Marathon
Karystos
ATHENS
Piraeus
Lavrio

A E G E A N   S E A

Skiros

Lesvos
Olives
Olives
Magnesite
Mytilini

Chios
Chios
Olives

Samos
Samos

Andros
Tinos
Kéa
Mykonos
Ikaria
Kíthnos
Sérifos
Siros
Paros
Marble
Naxos
Amorgos
Astipálaia
Milos
Ios
Thira

Cyclades

D o d e c a n e s e

Kos
Kos

Rhodes
Monólithos
Olives
Rhodes

Karpathos

N

GREECE
POP: 10,200,000

0 25 50 75 100 125 KM
0 25 50 75 MILES

SEA OF CRETE

Chania
Crete
Rethymno
Knossos
Irakleio
Agios
Nikolaos
Olives
Olives

MEDITERRANEAN SEA

K P Q R S T

Greek doll wearing a traditional wedding dress.

Hand-painted pottery made in local workshops

TOURISM
Over 5 million tourists visit Greece every year, creating an enormous demand for goods and services. Hotels, restaurants, and shops employ many people, while holiday purchases boost the Greek economy. Local workshops produce handcrafted items such as pottery, leather bags, and sandals for the tourist market.

A monastery perches on a vertical rock in central Greece.

FISHING
Fishing is an important part of the Greek economy, but the eastern Mediterranean has been overfished. Only mullet, squid, sardines, and tuna are found in any quantity. Look for

The Mediterranean squid can grow to a length of 2 ft (0.6 m)

Sponges, found in the Mediterranean, are obtained by diving.

HILL FARMING
Greece, with its mountainous landscape, has the largest number of small hill-farms in Europe. The soil is poor and many people are needed to work the land: nearly a third of the Greek labor force is employed in agriculture – more than anywhere else in Europe.

ADAPTABLE GOATS
Hardy goats are ideally suited to Greece's rugged landscape. They are tough and sure-footed, and able to survive on limited food resources. Goat's milk is used for making yogurt and cheese. Goat skin is also made into leather and young goats (kids) are a great delicacy.

ΑΘΗΝΑ
Greek has its own alphabet, which dates back 2,500 years. This says "Athens."

A PLACE IN THE SUN
People have been coming to Greece for centuries to visit the remains of ancient Greek cities and temples. Today, many visitors come from northern European countries, especially Scandinavia, the UK, and Germany. Thira, seen here, is just one of many popular island resorts. Look for

Olive trees grow in rows on the high, arid mountains of central Crete.

AN ISLAND LIFE
Tourism is more profitable than traditional pursuits such as farming and fishing. Today, yachts are beginning to outnumber fishing boats in local ports.

1
2
3
4
5
6
7
8
9
10
11
12
13
14
15
16

THE BALTIC STATES AND BELARUS

THE THREE BALTIC STATES – Latvia, Lithuania, and Estonia – made history in 1990-91 when they became the first republics to declare their independence from the Soviet Union. This was the end of a long series of invasions and occupations by the Vikings, Germans, Danes, Poles, and Russians. A new era had begun, but many of the old problems – food shortages, pollution, weak economies – still remained. The region's flat landscape is well drained by lakes and rivers and is ideal for farming. The main crops are grains, sugar beets, and potatoes. In Belarus, heavy industry like machine building and metalworking is important, while the Baltic states manufacture electronics and consumer goods. Nearly half the population of the Baltic states are Russians who have moved there to work in industry. The Baltic Sea, although frozen in the winter months, gives access to the markets of northern Europe. Industrialization has left a terrible legacy. Summer resorts along the Baltic coast have been closed to visitors because of polluted seawater, and Belarus was badly hit by the nuclear accident at Chernobyl in the Ukraine in 1986, when 70 percent of the radioactive fallout landed on its territory.

ESTONIA
POP: 1,572,000

LITHUANIA
POP: 3,782,000

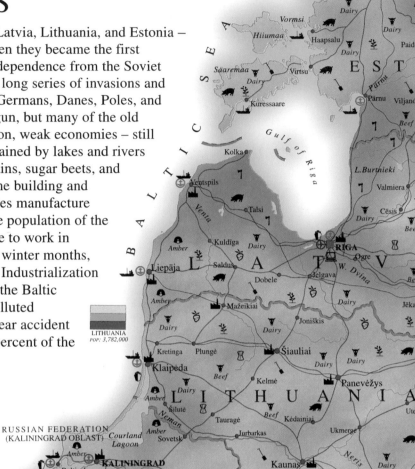

NEW CURRENCY
When the three Baltic states separated from the Soviet Union, they all stopped using the rouble and introduced their own currencies. Companies which had been owned and run by the communist state came under private ownership, and the Baltic States encouraged investment in these industries from abroad.

One of the many lakes of Lithuania.

Spider trapped in amber

BALTIC GOLD
Amber is the fossilized sap of ancient trees. The Baltic states produce two-thirds of the world's amber, most of it found along Lithuania's "amber coast." Amber has been collected and traded since prehistoric times. It is a precious stone but is also valued for its medical properties. Even today it is used to treat rheumatism. Look for 🐚

MINSK
Although Minsk was founded over 900 years ago, it has no historic buildings. The city was virtually destroyed by bombing during World War II, when half of Minsk's population is estimated to have been killed. After the war, the city was rebuilt and became one of the industrial centers of the former Soviet Union.

Sour cream

NATIONAL DISH
Draniki is the national dish of Belarus. It is made of grated potatoes fried in vegetable oil and served with sour cream. Potatoes are grown everywhere, and are one of Belarus's main products. Large numbers of dairy cattle are kept on its extensive pastureland.

Beetroot mixed with sour cream

Draniki

KEYBOX

Cattle: The Baltic states were the centers of beef and dairy production for the former Soviet Union. Look for ▼

Oil: The Baltic states used to obtain free oil by pipeline from the former Soviet Union. Now they depend on Estonia's oil shale deposits. Look for ▌

Peat: This region has large supplies of peat – a fuel made from carbonized plant material found in bogs. Look for ╲

🐖	Pigs	⛴	Fishing port
🌿	Sugar beets	⛏	Mining
🌱	Potatoes	🏭	Industrial center
⚱	Flax	🗑	Shipbuilding
🌾	Timber	💻	High-tech industry

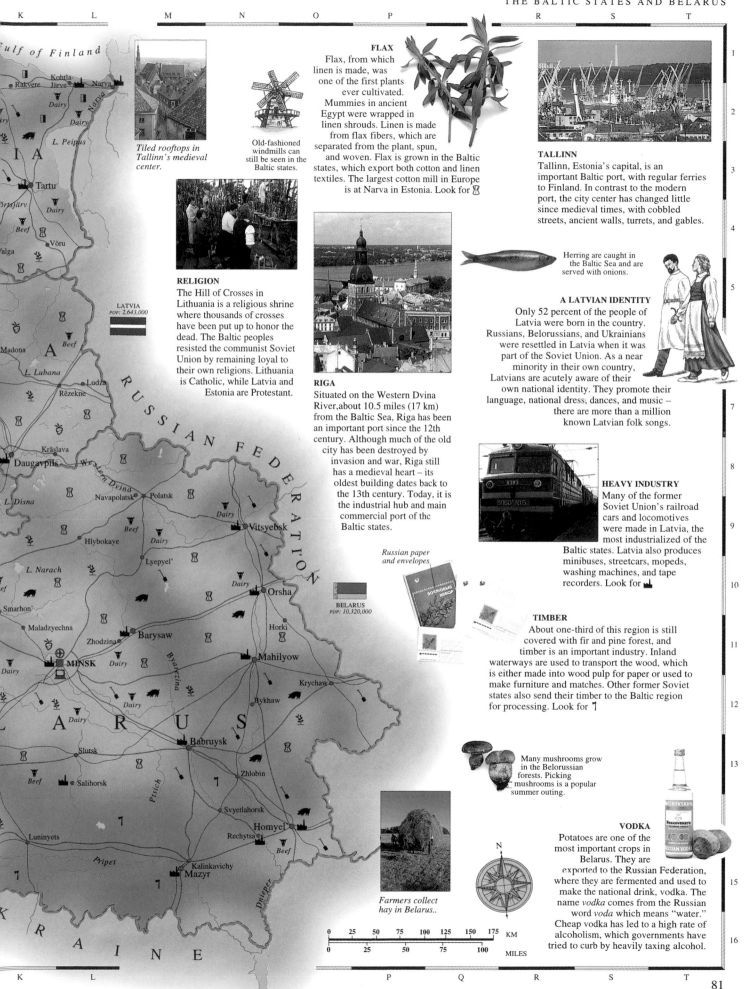

Gulf of Finland

Tiled rooftops in Tallinn's medieval center.

Old-fashioned windmills can still be seen in the Baltic states.

FLAX
Flax, from which linen is made, was one of the first plants ever cultivated. Mummies in ancient Egypt were wrapped in linen shrouds. Linen is made from flax fibers, which are separated from the plant, spun, and woven. Flax is grown in the Baltic states, which export both cotton and linen textiles. The largest cotton mill in Europe is at Narva in Estonia. Look for 🏭

TALLINN
Tallinn, Estonia's capital, is an important Baltic port, with regular ferries to Finland. In contrast to the modern port, the city center has changed little since medieval times, with cobbled streets, ancient walls, turrets, and gables.

Herring are caught in the Baltic Sea and are served with onions.

RELIGION
The Hill of Crosses in Lithuania is a religious shrine where thousands of crosses have been put up to honor the dead. The Baltic peoples resisted the communist Soviet Union by remaining loyal to their own religions. Lithuania is Catholic, while Latvia and Estonia are Protestant.

LATVIA
POP: 2,643,000

A LATVIAN IDENTITY
Only 52 percent of the people of Latvia were born in the country. Russians, Belorussians, and Ukrainians were resettled in Latvia when it was part of the Soviet Union. As a near minority in their own country, Latvians are acutely aware of their own national identity. They promote their language, national dress, dances, and music – there are more than a million known Latvian folk songs.

RIGA
Situated on the Western Dvina River, about 10.5 miles (17 km) from the Baltic Sea, Riga has been an important port since the 12th century. Although much of the old city has been destroyed by invasion and war, Riga still has a medieval heart – its oldest building dates back to the 13th century. Today, it is the industrial hub and main commercial port of the Baltic states.

HEAVY INDUSTRY
Many of the former Soviet Union's railroad cars and locomotives were made in Latvia, the most industrialized of the Baltic states. Latvia also produces minibuses, streetcars, mopeds, washing machines, and tape recorders. Look for 🏭

Russian paper and envelopes

BELARUS
POP: 10,320,000

TIMBER
About one-third of this region is still covered with fir and pine forest, and timber is an important industry. Inland waterways are used to transport the wood, which is either made into wood pulp for paper or used to make furniture and matches. Other former Soviet states also send their timber to the Baltic region for processing. Look for 🌲

Many mushrooms grow in the Belorussian forests. Picking mushrooms is a popular summer outing.

Farmers collect hay in Belarus..

N

VODKA
Potatoes are one of the most important crops in Belarus. They are exported to the Russian Federation, where they are fermented and used to make the national drink, vodka. The name *vodka* comes from the Russian word *voda* which means "water." Cheap vodka has led to a high rate of alcoholism, which governments have tried to curb by heavily taxing alcohol.

```
0   25   50   75   100  125  150  175  KM
0      25       50      75      100  MILES
```

81

EUROPEAN RUSSIA

THE RUSSIAN FEDERATION is the largest country in the world. Stretching across two continents – Europe in the west and Asia in the east – it is twice the size of the USA. The Ural Mountains form the division between the European and Asian parts of the country. The Russian Federation has fertile farmlands, vast mineral deposits, and abundant timber, oil, and other natural resources. Despite its size and natural wealth, Russia is currently in a state of political and economic turmoil. After centuries of rule by czars (emperors), the world's first communist government took power in Russia in 1917; five years later the country became the Union of Soviet Socialist Republics (USSR), which included many of the territories that were formerly parts of the Russian Empire. During 74 years of communist rule, the Soviet Union became an industrial and military superpower, but at an appalling cost to its people and environment. Economic problems led to liberal reforms beginning in the mid-1980s, but the reforms unleashed a whirlwind of change which led to the fall of the communist regime in December 1991. By then most of the non-Russian republics had declared independence. The new Russian Federation is now struggling to become a democracy.

RELIGION

Moscow is the spiritual center of the Russian Orthodox Church. For many decades, the church was persecuted in Russia; today, churches are re-opening, and many Russian people are turning back to religion. Beautiful icons (religious images painted on wood), like this one, adorn the churches and people's homes.

ST. PETERSBURG

САНКТ-ПЕТЕРБУРГ

The name "St. Petersburg," written in Russia's Cyrillic alphabet, which was devised by Christian missionaries in the 10th century.

St. Petersburg, the capital of Russia from 1712-1918, was founded by Czar Peter the Great in 1703. It is built on 12 islands linked by bridges and has many elegant 18th-century buildings.

Northern Russia is covered with coniferous forest called taiga.

Many wooden churches built in the 17th century still stand on small islands in Lake Onega.

MOSCOW

The city of Moscow was founded in the 12th century. At its center is a fortified citadel called the *Kremlin*. Its stone walls enclose the grand palace of the czars, four cathedrals, and a church. The *Kremlin* became – and remains – the country's seat of government.

St. Basil's, Moscow, built in the 16th century

RUSSIAN FEDERATION
POP: 150,638,000
(EUROPEAN RUSSIA)
POP: 108,950,000

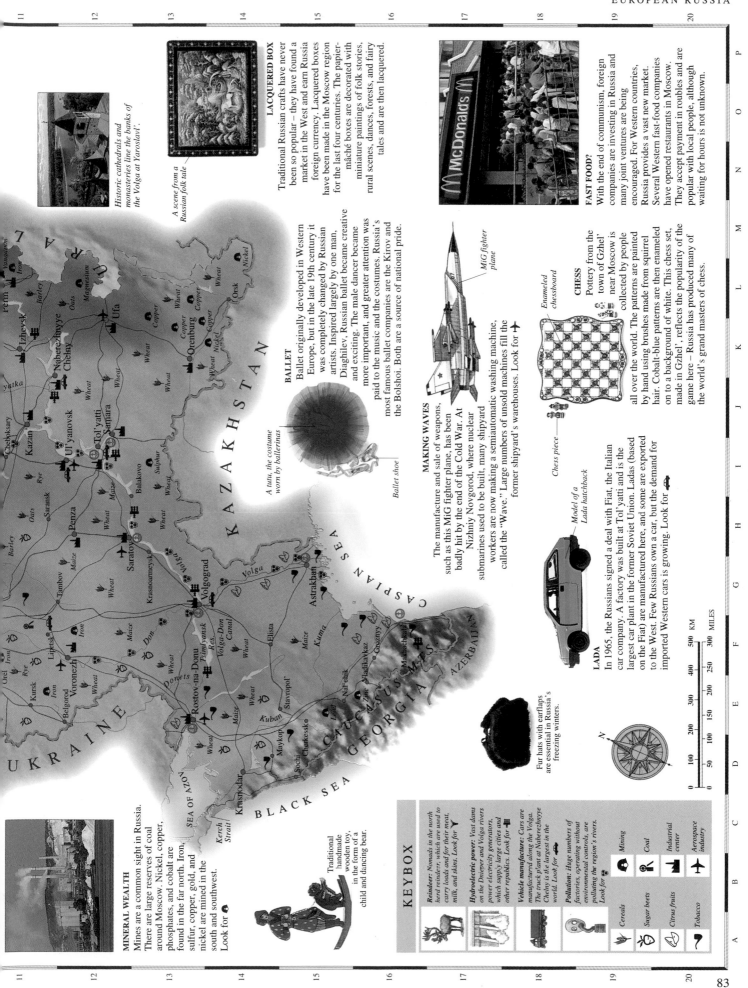

Historic cathedrals and monasteries line the banks of the Volga at Yaroslavl'.

A scene from a Russian folk tale

LACQUERED BOX

Traditional Russian crafts have never been so popular – they have found a market in the West and earn Russia foreign currency. Lacquered boxes have been made in the Moscow region for the last four centuries. The papier-mâché boxes are decorated with miniature paintings of folk stories, rural scenes, dances, forests, and fairy tales and are then lacquered.

FAST FOOD?

With the end of communism, foreign companies are investing in Russia and many joint ventures are being encouraged. For Western countries, Russia provides a vast new market. Several Western fast-food companies have opened restaurants in Moscow. They accept payment in roubles and are popular with local people, although waiting for hours is not unknown.

BALLET

Ballet originally developed in Western Europe, but in the late 19th century it was completely changed by Russian artists. Inspired largely by one man, Diaghilev, Russian ballet became creative and exciting. The male dancer became more important, and greater attention was paid to the music and the costumes. Russia's most famous ballet companies are the Kirov and the Bolshoi. Both are a source of national pride.

A tutu, the costume worn by ballerinas

Ballet shoe

MiG fighter plane

MAKING WAVES

The manufacture and sale of weapons, such as this MiG fighter plane, has been badly hit by the end of the Cold War. At Nizhniy Novgorod, where nuclear submarines used to be built, many shipyard workers are now making a semiautomatic washing machine, called the "Wave." Large numbers of unsold machines fill the former shipyard's warehouses. Look for ✈

Enameled chessboard

CHESS

Pottery from the town of Gzhel' near Moscow is collected by people all over the world. The patterns are painted by hand using brushes made from squirrel hair. Cobalt-blue patterns are then enameled on to a background of white. This chess set, made in Gzhel', reflects the popularity of the game here – Russia has produced many of the world's grand masters of chess.

Chess piece

Model of a Lada hatchback

LADA

In 1965, the Russians signed a deal with Fiat, the Italian car company. A factory was built at Tol'yatti and is the largest car plant in the former Soviet Union. Ladas (based on the Fiat) are manufactured here, and some are exported to the West. Few Russians own a car, but the demand for imported Western cars is growing. Look for 🚗

MINERAL WEALTH

Mines are a common sight in Russia. There are large reserves of coal around Moscow. Nickel, copper, phosphates, and cobalt are found in the far north. Iron, sulfur, copper, gold, and nickel are mined in the south and southwest. Look for ⛏

Fur hats with earflaps are essential in Russia's freezing winters.

Traditional handmade wooden toy, in the form of a child and dancing bear.

KEYBOX

Reindeer: Nomads in the north herd reindeer, which are used to carry loads and for their meat, milk, and skins. Look for 🦌

Hydroelectric power: Vast dams on the Dnieper and Volga rivers power electricity generators, which supply large cities and other republics. Look for 🏭

Vehicle manufacture: Cars are manufactured along the Volga. The truck plant at Naberezhnyye Chelny is the largest in the world. Look for 🚚

Pollution: Huge numbers of factories, operating without environmental controls, are polluting the region's rivers. Look for 🔧

🌾 Cereals	⛏ Mining
🍃 Sugar beets	⚒ Coal
🍊 Citrus fruits	🏭 Industrial center
🍂 Tobacco	✈ Aerospace industry

500 KM
300 MILES

N

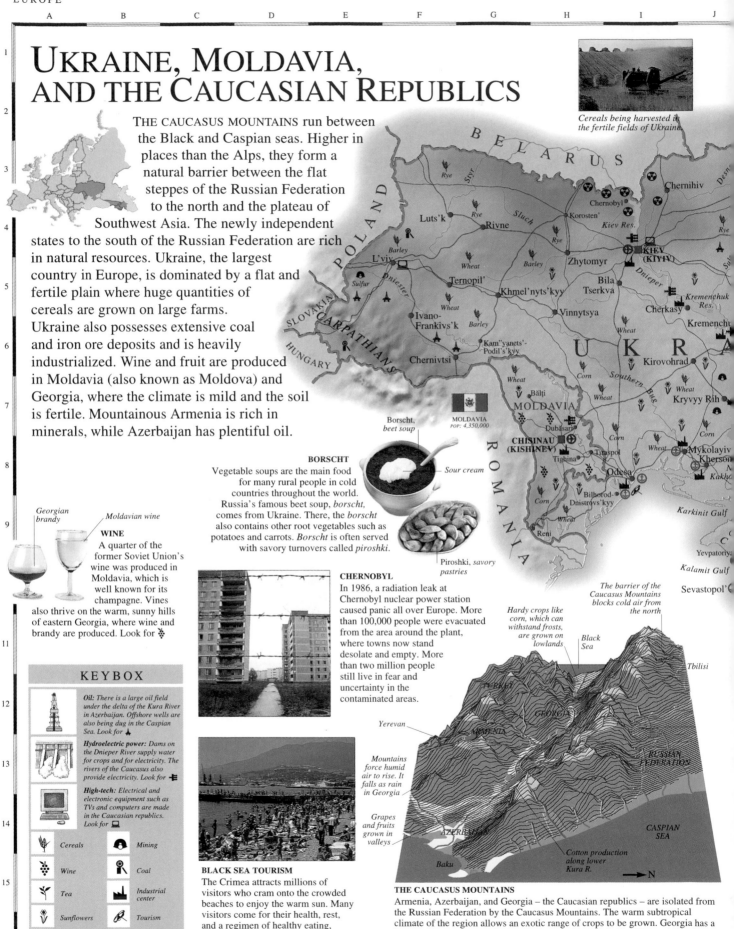

UKRAINE, MOLDAVIA, AND THE CAUCASIAN REPUBLICS

THE CAUCASUS MOUNTAINS run between the Black and Caspian seas. Higher in places than the Alps, they form a natural barrier between the flat steppes of the Russian Federation to the north and the plateau of Southwest Asia. The newly independent states to the south of the Russian Federation are rich in natural resources. Ukraine, the largest country in Europe, is dominated by a flat and fertile plain where huge quantities of cereals are grown on large farms. Ukraine also possesses extensive coal and iron ore deposits and is heavily industrialized. Wine and fruit are produced in Moldavia (also known as Moldova) and Georgia, where the climate is mild and the soil is fertile. Mountainous Armenia is rich in minerals, while Azerbaijan has plentiful oil.

Cereals being harvested in the fertile fields of Ukraine.

MOLDAVIA
POP: 4,350,000

BORSCHT
Vegetable soups are the main food for many rural people in cold countries throughout the world. Russia's famous beet soup, *borscht,* comes from Ukraine. There, the *borscht* also contains other root vegetables such as potatoes and carrots. *Borscht* is often served with savory turnovers called *piroshki.*

Borscht, beet soup

Sour cream

Piroshki, savory pastries

WINE
A quarter of the former Soviet Union's wine was produced in Moldavia, which is well known for its champagne. Vines also thrive on the warm, sunny hills of eastern Georgia, where wine and brandy are produced. Look for ❦

Georgian brandy

Moldavian wine

CHERNOBYL
In 1986, a radiation leak at Chernobyl nuclear power station caused panic all over Europe. More than 100,000 people were evacuated from the area around the plant, where towns now stand desolate and empty. More than two million people still live in fear and uncertainty in the contaminated areas.

KEYBOX

Oil: *There is a large oil field under the delta of the Kura River in Azerbaijan. Offshore wells are also being dug in the Caspian Sea. Look for* ♠

Hydroelectric power: *Dams on the Dnieper River supply water for crops and for electricity. The rivers of the Caucasus also provide electricity. Look for* ⊟

High-tech: *Electrical and electronic equipment such as TVs and computers are made in the Caucasian republics. Look for* ▭

🌾	Cereals	⛏	Mining
🍇	Wine	👷	Coal
🌿	Tea	🏭	Industrial center
🌻	Sunflowers	🎿	Tourism
🐟	Fishing	☢	Nuclear pollution

BLACK SEA TOURISM
The Crimea attracts millions of visitors who cram onto the crowded beaches to enjoy the warm sun. Many visitors come for their health, rest, and a regimen of healthy eating, massage, and exercise. Look for 🎿

The barrier of the Caucasus Mountains blocks cold air from the north

Hardy crops like corn, which can withstand frosts, are grown on lowlands

Black Sea

Mountains force humid air to rise. It falls as rain in Georgia

Grapes and fruits grown in valleys

Cotton production along lower Kura R.

N →

THE CAUCASUS MOUNTAINS
Armenia, Azerbaijan, and Georgia – the Caucasian republics – are isolated from the Russian Federation by the Caucasus Mountains. The warm subtropical climate of the region allows an exotic range of crops to be grown. Georgia has a humid climate, so tea and citrus fruits are cultivated. In the drier east, the rivers running down from the mountains are used to water the fields.

BLACK BREAD

Ukraine was known as the former Soviet Union's "breadbasket." Its broad flat steppes, with their fertile black earth, are intensively cultivated: wheat, buckwheat, potatoes, rye, and flax are grown on vast farms. Much of Ukraine's countryside consists of endless fields of cereals, the view broken only by the occasional haystack.

Matrioshka dolls are hand painted. Each is made from a single piece of wood.

UKRAINE *POP: 52,498,000*

The Ukraine is the world's largest producer of buckwheat. Although it is ground up to make flour, buckwheat is not a true cereal.

KIEV

Kiev, founded in the 9th century, is the capital of Ukraine. St. Sophia's cathedral, with its gilded domes, has been Kiev's most famous landmark since 1037. Kiev is situated on the banks of the Dnieper River, the republic's main waterway. It is within easy reach of the Black Sea ports, as well as being near Ukraine's industrial center.

COAL

About one-third of the former Soviet Union's coal came from the area around Donets'k in Ukraine, where there are about 40 deep mines. Miners working here are reasonably well paid, but gas explosions and the frequent breakdown of equipment put them at risk. Death rates in these mines are 10 times higher than in mines in the USA. Look for 🏋

INDUSTRIAL HEARTLAND

Ukraine's Donbass region, with its rich reserves of coal, iron, manganese, and other minerals, is a major industrial area. Heavy industry, such as iron- and steelworks, engineering, and chemicals, still dominate the region, but today cars, aircraft, televisions, and computers are also manufactured here. Look for ⬛

CAUCASIAN CONFLICT

When the Caucasian republics were part of the Soviet Union, many different peoples were forced to live side by side. Since these countries became independent, many pent-up resentments have been unleashed. For example, fighting has erupted between Armenian Christians and Muslim Azeris over Nagorno-Karabakh, an Armenian area within Azerbaijan's borders.

SUNFLOWERS

Sunflowers are an important crop in southern Ukraine. The seeds, which can be eaten, contain oil and protein. Sunflower oil is used for cooking. The seeds are also used in the manufacture of margarine and soap and are mixed with corn and peas for cattle feed. Look for 🌱

TEA

Tea is a popular drink throughout the former Soviet Union, and over 90 percent of the tea consumed there is grown in Georgia. Both black and green teas are grown on large tea plantations. Tea is served black and strong, with sugar or lemon. Look for 🌿

Decorated Black Sea fiddle, from Georgia.

The snow-capped peaks of the Caucasus Mountains.

AZERBAIJAN *POP: 7,507,000*

Caviar, served on toast

CAVIAR

The Russian sturgeon is a large fish which can grow up to 23 ft (7 m) in length. Sturgeon eggs, called caviar, are an expensive delicacy. Sturgeon live in the Black and Caspian seas and swim up rivers like the Dnieper to breed in fresh water. Hydroelectric dams on these rivers have disrupted the sturgeons' routes, and polluted water is causing concern about falling numbers of fish. Look for 🐟

GEORGIA *POP: 5,478,000*

TEXTILES

Georgia is famous for its silk and textiles. Brightly colored and patterned cotton fabrics are woven with gold and silver thread. Worn by women as headscarves, these fabrics are seen throughout the Caucasus.

The Swallow's Nest Castle, high on a rock near Yalta.

ARMENIA *POP: 3,816,000*

KM 0 50 100 150 200 250 300
MILES 0 50 100 150

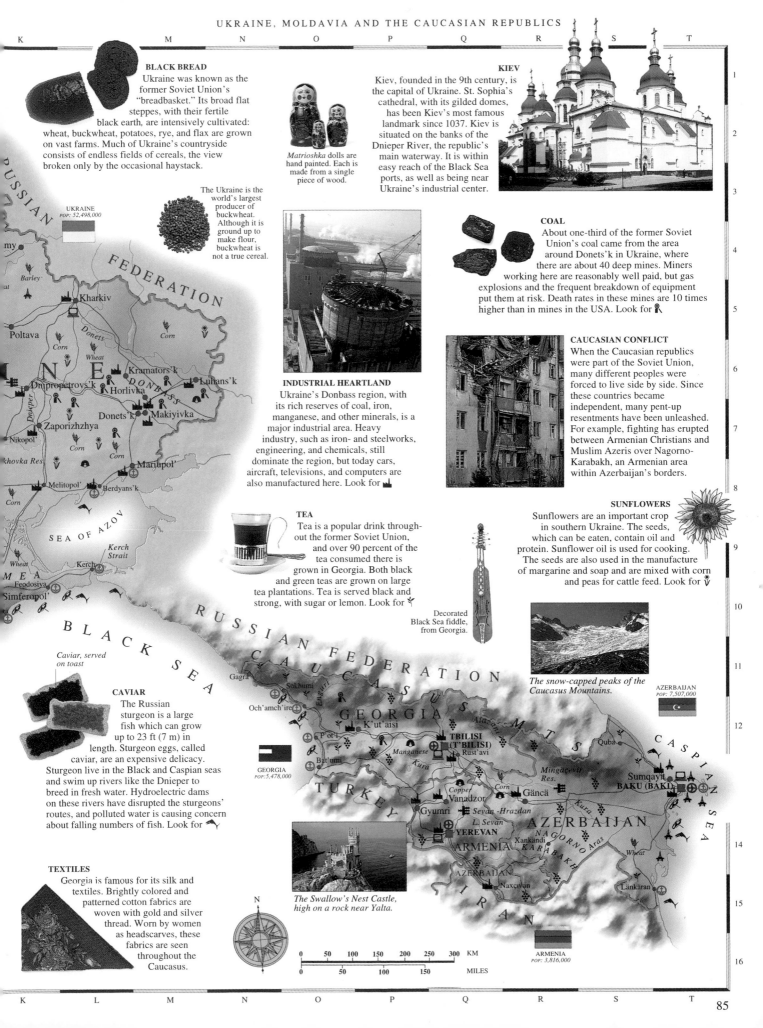

Cheetah
Acinonyx jubatus
Length: 7 ft (2.2 m)

Aye-aye
Daubentonia madagascariensis
Length: 18 in (45 cm)

White-backed vulture
Gyps bengalensis
Wingspan: 7 ft (2.2 m)

AFRICA

AFRICA IS THE SECOND largest continent after Asia, and the only one through which the Equator and both tropics run. It is also home to the world's longest river, the Nile. The climate and vegetation roughly mirror each other on either side of the Equator. In the extreme south and along the Mediterranean coast in the north, hot dry summers are followed by mild wet winters. Similarly, the land around each tropic is hot and starved of rain, so great deserts have formed. Africa's immense tropical savannah grasslands are prone to drought, but around the Equator high rainfall has produced lush tropical rain forests. The volcanoes and strangely elongated lakes in the Great Rift Valley are evidence of cracks in the Earth's crust that threaten to split Africa apart eventually.

Burchell's zebra
Equus burchelli
Height: 4 ft (1.2 m)

Umbrella thorn acacia
Acacia tortillis
Height: 60 ft (18 m)

■ HOT SAHARA
The inhospitable Sahara desert covers one-third of Africa. Temperatures can exceed 120°F (50°C).

■ MISTY RAIN FOREST
Tropical rain forests only grow where temperatures are always high and rain is abundant. Here in central Africa, it rains every day – more than 7 ft (2 m) falls each year.

Malachite is a copper-rich ore found in many parts of eastern Africa.

■ THUNDERING WATERFALL
The Zambezi River winds slowly through dry woodlands before reaching the Victoria Falls. Here it plummets 354 ft (108 m), creating so much noise and spray that it is known as "the smoke that thunders."

■ GREAT RIFT VALLEY
Cracks in the Earth's crust have made a valley 3,750 miles (6,000 km) long and up to 55 miles (90 km) wide.

The South African turban shell looks like a headdress made of coiled cloth.

■ SAND DUNES IN THE NAMIB
The intensely hot Namib Desert forms a narrow strip down Africa's southwest coast. Rainfall is less than 6 in (15 cm) a year, but sea mists from the cold currents along the coast provide enough moisture for some plants and animals to survive.

■ SERENGETI PLAIN
Savannah – grassland and open woodland – is home to huge herds of grazing animals, including wildebeest and zebra.

Shells like this black miter can be found in shallow water along the west African coast.

Gaboon viper
Bitis gabonica
Length: 7 ft (2 m)

■ ■ OKAVANGO DELTA
Not all rivers run to the sea. The Okavango River ends in a huge inland swamp that attracts thousands of water loving animals, such as hippopotamuses.

CROSS-SECTION THROUGH AFRICA

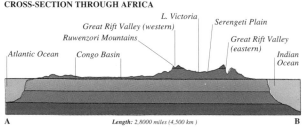

L. Victoria
Great Rift Valley (western)
Ruwenzori Mountains
Serengeti Plain
Great Rift Valley (eastern)

9,843 (3,000)
Atlantic Ocean
Congo Basin
Indian Ocean

Sea level 0

-14,764 (-4,500)

Feet (meters)
A
Length: 2,8000 miles (4,500 km)
B

■ SOUTHERN AFRICA
Rain is so low in southern Africa that for most of the year few plants show themselves above ground. As soon as the rains come, however, a barren landscape is transformed into a brilliant mass of flowers.

African elephant
Loxodonta africana
Height: 13 ft (4 m)

Desert scorpion
Androctonus australis
Length: 3 in (8 cm)

Mountain gorilla
Gorilla gorilla
Height: 6 ft (1.8 m)

BOTTLE TREES
Plants can resist drought by reducing their leaf size and enlarging their stems to store water. Here in Madagascar's dry woodlands, huge-trunked baobabs, or "bottle trees," grow alongside spiny Dideria.

Black rhinoceros
Diceros bicornis
Length: 12 ft (3.6 m)

KEY TO SYMBOLS

▲ Mountain

△ Volcano

Mangroves

Wetlands

Coral reef

Plate margins with direction of movement

KEY TO NATURAL VEGETATION

Mediterranean-type

Hot desert

Tropical grassland

Tropical rain forest

Temperate grassland

Mountain

Dry woodland

NORTHWEST AFRICA

OVER THE CENTURIES, Northwest Africa has been invaded by many peoples. The entire north coast from the Red Sea to the Atlantic was once part of the Roman Empire. Later colonization by Italy, Great Britain, Turkey, Spain, and France contributed to the culture of the countries, but it was the 7th-century Arab conquest which fundamentally changed the region. The conversion of the original peoples – the Berbers – to Islam, and the use of Arabic as a common language, gave these countries a sense of unity which remains today. In fact, the region is sometimes called the Maghreb, which means "west" in Arabic. In the northwest, the Atlas Mountains form a barrier between the wetter, cooler areas along the coast and the great Saharan Desert. This desert is the biggest on Earth and is still growing. Water shortages and lack of land for farming are problems throughout the region, especially as the population of the Maghreb is increasing rapidly. In Algeria and Libya, however, the desert has revealed hidden riches – abundant oil and natural gas.

FEZ – AN ISLAMIC CITY
This view of the city of Fez in Morocco shows the flat-roofed houses that are traditional in this region. Seen from the narrow streets, the houses look blank and windowless, but this is because they are designed to face inward onto central courtyards which are cool and private. Islamic cities may appear to be chaotic mazes of streets, but in fact they are laid out following guidelines set in the holy book of Islam, the *Koran*.

The Moroccans make a refreshing tea from the spearmint plant.

MOROCCO
POP: 28,913,000

Strait of Gibraltar   M E D

Tangier   Ceuta *(Spain)*
    Tétouan
Al Hoceima   Melilla *(Spain)*
Kénitra   Tlemcen
RABAT   Oujda
Casablanca   Meknès   Fez
Safi   Khouribga
MOROCCO   *Phosphates*   Beni Mellal
Essaouira   Figuig
Phosphates   Marrakesh   Er Rachidia
    Boumalne-Dadès   Béchar
Agadir
Tiznit   A T L A S   M T S
    Olive
Tan-Tan   A L G
EL AAIUN   Adra
(LAÂYOUNE)
    Tindouf
Phosphates   Smara   o
WESTERN SAHARA
Dakhla   MAURITANIA

WESTERN SAHARA
POP: 200,000   M A L I
S
Morocco occupied the whole of Western Sahara in 1979

Lagouira

BERBERS
Berbers were the original people of northwest Africa. When the Arabs invaded, they were driven out of the fertile coastal areas. Many Berbers still live in remote villages or towns – such as here at Boumalne-Dadès – high in the Atlas Mountains, where their lifestyle and language have remained unchanged for centuries.

Couscous is the basic ingredient of many North African dishes. It is made of tiny pellets of flour, called semolina.

KEYBOX

Mining: *Huge quantities of phosphates come from the sands of Western Sahara and Morocco. They are the vital raw material for fertilizers. Look for* ●

Gas: *Algeria has vast reserves of natural gas, much of it exported to Europe – some by pipeline to Italy across the Mediterranean Sea. Look for* ○

Archaeological sites: *Early civilizations, such as the Romans, built cities in the desert and along the coast of North Africa. Look for* ⫼

♉	Sheep	⛴	Fishing port
🍋	Citrus fruits	⚓	Oil
🌴	Dates	🏭	Industrial center
🍇	Wine	⚲	Tourism
🫙	Vegetable oil	🌴	Oases

CARPETS AND RUGS
Hand-knotted carpets and rugs, with their distinctive bold patterns and deep pile, are made throughout the region. In Morocco the most important carpet factories are in Rabat and Fez. Craftworkers often work together in cooperatives to maintain high quality and to control prices.

WESTERN SAHARA
Western Sahara is a sparsely populated desert area lying between Morocco and Mauritania. It was a Spanish colony until 1976 but is now fighting for independence from Morocco, which claims two-thirds of the country and the phosphates found there. This photo shows young members of the liberation movement.

Painted plate

Leather bag

TOURISM
Tourism is a vital source of foreign income for Morocco and Tunisia. When oil prices fell in the 1980s, tourism took the place of oil as the main source of foreign income. Modern hotels, built in traditional styles, have sprung up along the coast. Both countries produce handicrafts for tourists, such as leather and brassware. Look for ⚲

The Ahaggar Mountains, Algeria, jut up in the middle of the Sahara.

THE TUAREG
The Tuareg are a nomadic tribe who inhabit a huge area of the Sahara. In the past they controlled the great camel caravans which crossed the desert to the Mediterranean, carrying slaves, ivory, gold, and salt. Today, some Tuareg still follow the traditional desert way of life, but many have become settled farmers.

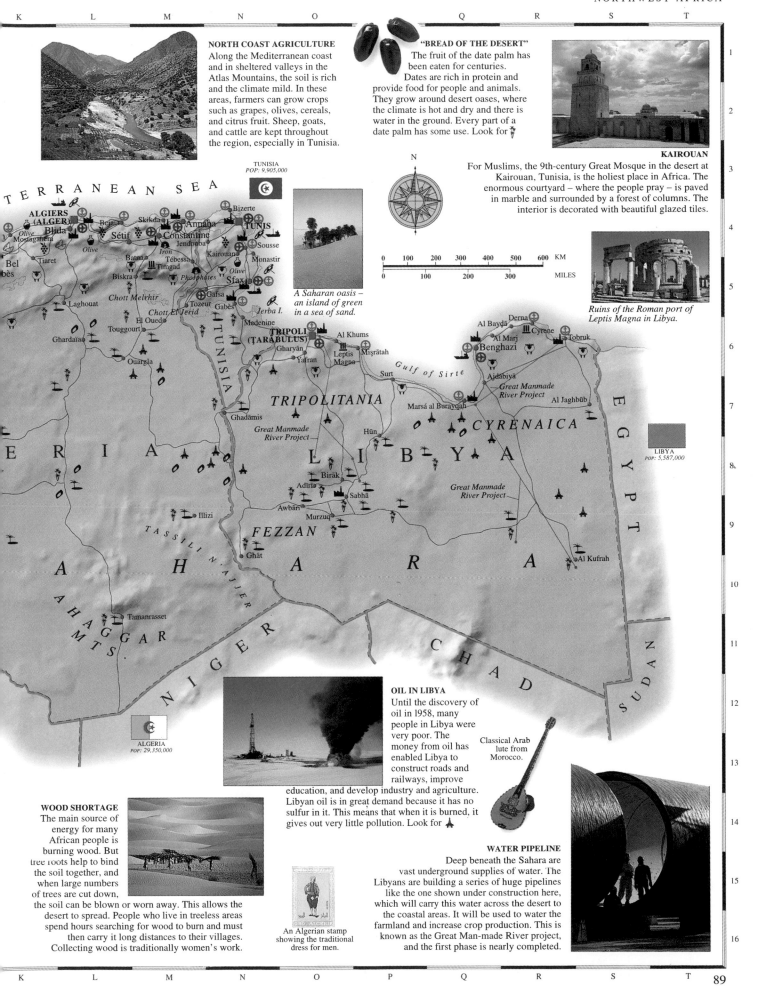

NORTH COAST AGRICULTURE
Along the Mediterranean coast and in sheltered valleys in the Atlas Mountains, the soil is rich and the climate mild. In these areas, farmers can grow crops such as grapes, olives, cereals, and citrus fruit. Sheep, goats, and cattle are kept throughout the region, especially in Tunisia.

"BREAD OF THE DESERT"
The fruit of the date palm has been eaten for centuries. Dates are rich in protein and provide food for people and animals. They grow around desert oases, where the climate is hot and dry and there is water in the ground. Every part of a date palm has some use. Look for

KAIROUAN
For Muslims, the 9th-century Great Mosque in the desert at Kairouan, Tunisia, is the holiest place in Africa. The enormous courtyard – where the people pray – is paved in marble and surrounded by a forest of columns. The interior is decorated with beautiful glazed tiles.

A Saharan oasis – an island of green in a sea of sand.

Ruins of the Roman port of Leptis Magna in Libya.

TUNISIA
POP: 9,905,000

LIBYA
POP: 5,587,000

ALGERIA
POP: 29,350,000

N

KM
0   100   200   300   400   500   600
MILES
0   100   200   300

MEDITERRANEAN SEA

ALGIERS (ALGER)
Blida
Mostaganem
Olive
Bel bès
Tiaret
Sétif
Béjaïa
Skikda
Constantine
Annaba
Bizerte
TUNIS
Jendouba
Sousse
Monastir
Batna
Tébessa
Iron
Timgad
Kairouan
Sfax
Biskra
Phosphates
Gafsa
Tozeur
Gabès
Jerba I.
Chott Melrhir
Laghouat
Chott El Jerid
El Oued
Medenine
Touggourt
Ghardaïa
Ouargla
TRIPOLI (ṬARABULUS)
Gharyān
Al Khums
Leptis Magna
Miṣrātah
Al Baydā
Derna
Cyrene
Tobruk
Al Marj
Benghazi
Ghadāmis
Yafran
Surt
Gulf of Sirte
Ajdabiya
Marsá al Burayqah
Al Jaghbūb

TUNISIA

TRIPOLITANIA

CYRENAICA

L I B Y A

Great Manmade River Project

Great Manmade River Project

Great Manmade River Project

Hūn
Birāk
Adīri
Sabhā
Awbāri
Murzuq
Al Kufrah

FEZZAN

ERIA

ALGERIA

TASSILI N'AJJER
Illizi
Ghāt

S A H A R A

AHAGGAR MTS.
Tamanrasset

NIGER

CHAD

SUDAN

EGYPT

OIL IN LIBYA
Until the discovery of oil in 1958, many people in Libya were very poor. The money from oil has enabled Libya to construct roads and railways, improve education, and develop industry and agriculture. Libyan oil is in great demand because it has no sulfur in it. This means that when it is burned, it gives out very little pollution. Look for

Classical Arab lute from Morocco.

WATER PIPELINE
Deep beneath the Sahara are vast underground supplies of water. The Libyans are building a series of huge pipelines like the one shown under construction here, which will carry this water across the desert to the coastal areas. It will be used to water the farmland and increase crop production. This is known as the Great Man-made River project, and the first phase is nearly completed.

WOOD SHORTAGE
The main source of energy for many African people is burning wood. But tree roots help to bind the soil together, and when large numbers of trees are cut down, the soil can be blown or worn away. This allows the desert to spread. People who live in treeless areas spend hours searching for wood to burn and must then carry it long distances to their villages. Collecting wood is traditionally women's work.

An Algerian stamp showing the traditional dress for men.

NORTHEAST AFRICA

WATERED AND FERTILIZED BY THE NILE, the longest river in the world, Egypt is a fertile strip running through the Sahara Desert. The first people settled there about 8,000 years ago, and by the time of the pharaohs, Egypt had become one of the world's first great civilizations. Today, Egypt is a relatively stable democracy, with a growing number of industries and control of the Suez Canal, one of the world's most important waterways. To the south are the highlands of Ethiopia and Eritrea. This area is fertile and well-watered in places, but recent droughts have made life precarious for the farmers and nomads who live there. The countries of Somalia, Sudan, and Ethiopia have been beset by terrible problems, including drought, famine, religious conflicts, and civil war. About half of Africa's 4.5 million refugees come from this area. In 1993, Eritrea gained independence from Ethiopia, after a civil war which lasted 30 years.

TOURIST SOUVENIRS
Large numbers of "ancient Egyptian" *scarabs* (beetles) and other fake antiques are made locally and sold to tourists. City streets are lined with market stalls and the small workshops where these goods are made. Tourism has stimulated this informal economy.

SUEZ CANAL
Opened in 1869, the Suez Canal is one of the world's largest artificial waterways and a vital source of income for Egypt. It connects the Red Sea with the Mediterranean, offering a shortcut from Europe through the Persian Gulf to India and the Far East. On average, 21,250 ships a year use the canal.

Coptic cross

THE COPTIC CHURCH
Although Ethiopia is surrounded by Islamic countries, about 40 per-cent of its population is Christian. The isolated Ethiopian church developed into a unique branch of Christianity, called the Coptic church.

COTTON
Egypt produces about a third of the world's high-quality cotton. Textile industries, such as spinning, weaving, and dyeing cotton, are also important. Cotton is the coolest fabric to wear during hot summers. Egyptian men often wear a long-sleeved cotton garment, or *jelaba*. Look for ⚐

Cotton jelaba

Tomb dwelling in Cairo's City of the Dead

CAIRO
Cairo is the largest city in the Islamic world and is also one of the fastest growing. Its current population is estimated at 9.5 million, but it is said to be increasing at a rate of 1,500 people a day. New arrivals live in squalid shantytowns on the outskirts of the city. The City of the Dead, a huge ancient cemetery outside Cairo, has now been occupied by the homeless.

The gold death mask of the Pharaoh Tutankhamun, c. 1352 BC

AGRICULTURE
Although there is fertile land in southern Ethiopia, farming methods are inefficient. The scratch plow is widely used but, as its name implies, it is only able to turn over the surface of the soil. After a few years, the nutrients in the soil are used up, and crops will no longer grow.

TOURISM
Visitors from all over the world go to Egypt to see the pyramids and other ancient sites. Income from tourism helps to maintain these ancient sites. The Temple of Isis at Philae would have been flooded by the Aswân Dam, so it was moved, brick by brick, to another island. Look for ⚑

The Giza pyramids were built as tombs for the pharaohs.

EGYPT
POP: 59,713,000

THE GIFT OF THE NILE
The Nile River floods in the summer, carrying rich mud from the highlands of Sudan and Ethiopia to the deserts of Egypt. This creates some of the most fertile land in the world. Nearly 99 percent of the Egyptian population lives along the banks of the Nile.

The ancient Egyptians used this reedlike plant, called *papyrus*, to make paper.

MEDITERRANEAN SEA
ISRAEL
RED SEA
Gulf of Aqaba
Gulf of Suez
SINAI
Port Said
Suez Canal
Ismâ'ilîya
Suez
Bûr Safâga
Alexandria
Tanta
El Mansûra
Helwân
Ras Gharib
CAIRO (EL QAHIRA)
Giza
Saqqara
El Faiyûm
Beni Suef
El Minya
EGYPT
Asyût
Sohâg
Abydos
Qena
Thebes
Luxor
Valley of the Kings
Idfu
Kom Ombo
Aswân
Philae
Aswân High Dam
L. Nasser
Abu Simbel
Sub Temple
Wadi Halfa
NUBIAN DESERT
Marsa Matrûh
Qattâra Depression
LIBYAN DESERT
LIBYA
Nile

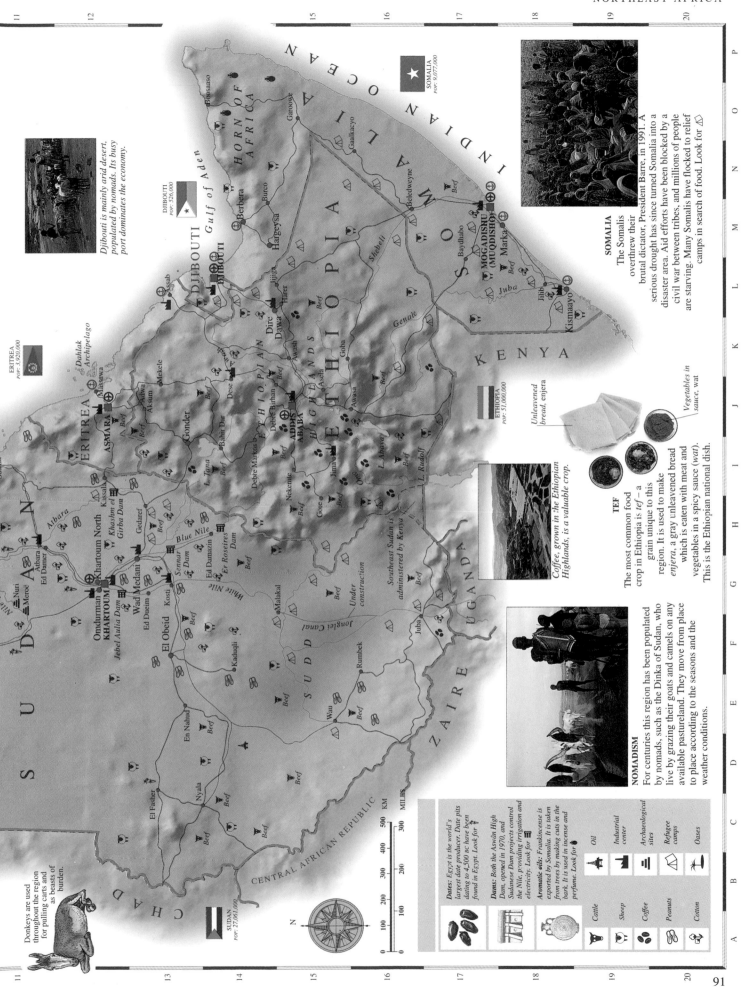

Djibouti is mainly arid desert, populated by nomads. Its busy port dominates the economy.

SOMALIA
The Somalis overthrew their brutal dictator, President Barre, in 1991. A serious drought has since turned Somalia into a disaster area. Aid efforts have been blocked by a civil war between tribes, and millions of people are starving. Many Somalis have flocked to relief camps in search of food. Look for

TEF
The most common food crop in Ethiopia is *tef* – a grain unique to this region. It is used to make *enjera*, a gray unleavened bread which is eaten with meat and vegetables in a spicy sauce (*wat*). This is the Ethiopian national dish.

Unleavened bread, enjera
Vegetables in sauce, wat

Coffee, grown in the Ethiopian Highlands, is a valuable crop.

NOMADISM
For centuries this region has been populated by nomads, such as the Dinka of Sudan, who live by grazing their goats and camels on any available pastureland. They move from place to place according to the seasons and the weather conditions.

Donkeys are used throughout the region for pulling carts and as beasts of burden.

Dates: Egypt is the world's largest date producer. Date pits dating to 4,500 BC have been found in Egypt. Look for

Dams: Both the Aswān High Dam, opened in 1970, and Sudanese Dam projects control the Nile, providing irrigation and electricity. Look for

Aromatic oils: Frankincense is exported by Somalia. It is taken from trees by making cuts in the bark. It is used in incense and perfume. Look for

Cattle
Sheep
Coffee
Peanuts
Cotton

Oil
Industrial center
Archaeological sites
Refugee camps
Oases

ERITREA POP: 3,920,000
DJIBOUTI POP: 526,000
SOMALIA POP: 9,077,000
ETHIOPIA POP: 51,000,000
SUDAN POP: 27,061,000

WEST AFRICA

THE LANDSCAPE OF WEST AFRICA ranges from the sand dunes of the Sahara through the dry grasslands of the Sahel region to the tropical rain forests in the south. There is just as much variety in the peoples of the region – more than 250 different tribes live in Nigeria alone. In the north, most people are Muslim, a legacy of the Arab traders who controlled the great caravan routes across the Sahara and brought Islam with them. It was from West Africa, particularly the coastal regions, that millions of Africans were transported to North and South America as slaves. Today many people in West Africa make their living by farming or herding animals. Crops such as coffee and cocoa are grown on large plantations. Like the logging industry, which is also a major source of earnings, these plantations are often owned by foreign multinational companies who take most of the profits out of the region. Recent discoveries of oil and minerals offer the promise of economic prosperity, but this has been prevented by falling world prices, huge foreign debts, corruption, and civil wars.

Calabash (bowl) made from a decorated gourd.

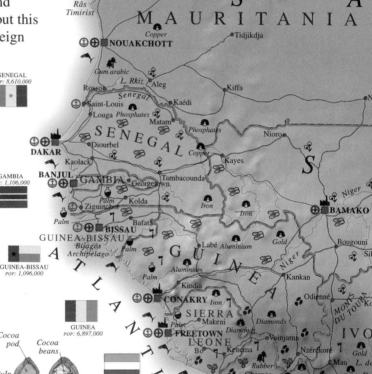

MAURITANIA
POP: 2,399,000

SENEGAL
POP: 8,610,000

DAKAR
Dakar, the capital of Senegal, is one of the main ports in West Africa. It lies on the Atlantic coast and has a fine natural harbor, large modern docks, and ship repair facilities. It is the country's main industrial center.

Kano mosque, built to serve the largely Islamic population in northern Nigeria.

GAMBIA
POP: 1,106,000

GUINEA-BISSAU
POP: 1,096,000

KEYBOX

Vegetable oil: The oil palm is widely grown throughout West Africa. Palm oil is used by people in the region and some is exported. Look for ⚗

Research center: At a center in Ibadan, Nigeria, new disease-resistant varieties of corn, cassava, and other crops have been bred. Look for ⊛

Film industry: Burkina has a large film industry, subsidized by the government, with studios in Ouagadougou and an annual film festival. Look for 🎥

Shipping registry: Many of the world's shipping countries register their ships in Liberia because of low taxes and lax employment rules. Look for 🏴

🫘	Coffee	🌲	Forest products
🥜	Cocoa	🐟	Fishing
🥜	Peanuts	⛏	Mining
🌱	Cotton	🛢	Oil
🌴	Timber	🏭	Industrial center

TOURISM
Tourism in this region has expanded rapidly. In Gambia, the number of visitors has risen from 300 in 1965 to over 100,000 a year in the 1990s. Most tourists stay along the Atlantic coast, but many also go on trips into the bush.

DEFORESTATION
The population of West Africa is growing rapidly. Vast areas of forest have been cut down, for wood or to clear farmland to feed these extra people. This problem is particularly bad in the Ivory Coast, where little forest is left. Look for 🌴

GUINEA
POP: 6,897,000

SIERRA LEONE
POP: 4,863,000

Cocoa pod
Cocoa beans
Pulp

COCOA
The ancient Aztec people of Mexico were the first to make a drink called *chocolatl* from the seeds of the cacao tree, brought to West Africa by European colonizers. The region now produces over half the world's supply of cocoa beans. Look for 🌿

LIBERIA
POP: 3,136,000

IVORY COAST
POP: 14,891,000

AFTER INDEPENDENCE
Since independence, some African countries have been plagued by many problems, such as unstable governments and foreign debts. Ivory Coast, however, is one of West Africa's most prosperous countries. Its last president built this cathedral when he had the capital moved to his family village at Yamoussoukro.

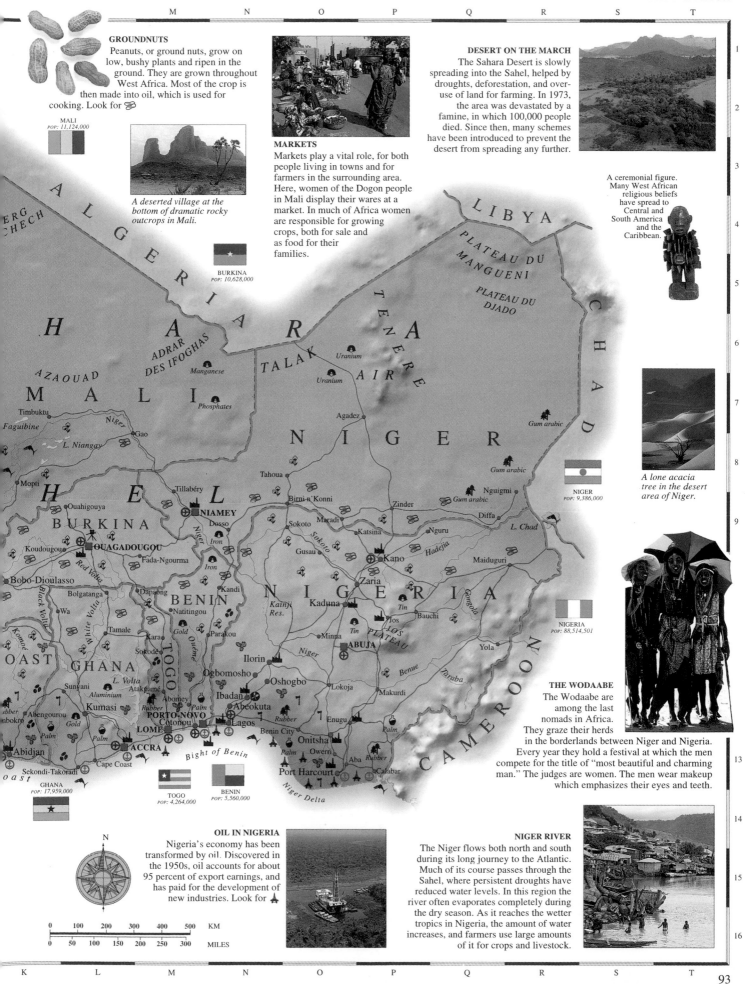

GROUNDNUTS
Peanuts, or ground nuts, grow on low, bushy plants and ripen in the ground. They are grown throughout West Africa. Most of the crop is then made into oil, which is used for cooking. Look for

MALI
POP: 11,124,000

A deserted village at the bottom of dramatic rocky outcrops in Mali.

MARKETS
Markets play a vital role, for both people living in towns and for farmers in the surrounding area. Here, women of the Dogon people in Mali display their wares at a market. In much of Africa women are responsible for growing crops, both for sale and as food for their families.

BURKINA
POP: 10,628,000

DESERT ON THE MARCH
The Sahara Desert is slowly spreading into the Sahel, helped by droughts, deforestation, and over-use of land for farming. In 1973, the area was devastated by a famine, in which 100,000 people died. Since then, many schemes have been introduced to prevent the desert from spreading any further.

A ceremonial figure. Many West African religious beliefs have spread to Central and South America and the Caribbean.

A lone acacia tree in the desert area of Niger.

NIGER
POP: 9,386,000

NIGERIA
POP: 88,514,501

THE WODAABE
The Wodaabe are among the last nomads in Africa. They graze their herds in the borderlands between Niger and Nigeria. Every year they hold a festival at which the men compete for the title of "most beautiful and charming man." The judges are women. The men wear makeup which emphasizes their eyes and teeth.

OIL IN NIGERIA
Nigeria's economy has been transformed by oil. Discovered in the 1950s, oil accounts for about 95 percent of export earnings, and has paid for the development of new industries. Look for

NIGER RIVER
The Niger flows both north and south during its long journey to the Atlantic. Much of its course passes through the Sahel, where persistent droughts have reduced water levels. In this region the river often evaporates completely during the dry season. As it reaches the wetter tropics in Nigeria, the amount of water increases, and farmers use large amounts of it for crops and livestock.

GHANA
POP: 17,959,000

TOGO
POP: 4,264,000

BENIN
POP: 5,560,000

0 100 200 300 400 500 KM
0 50 100 150 200 250 300 MILES

CENTRAL AFRICA

MUCH OF THIS REGION IS COVERED in dense tropical rain forest, drained by the great Congo (Zaire) River and its tributaries. The climate is hot and humid. All the countries have small populations, and many of them have French as their official language – a legacy from the days when they were French colonies. Zaire, the third-largest country in Africa, has rich mineral deposits, but it has declined economically since independence. In 1997 Zaire adopted the name Democratic Republic of the Congo. Chad has been torn apart by civil wars, and the Central African Republic has suffered from corrupt governments. Both countries are desperately poor. Equatorial Guinea has suffered so much from bad government that some 100,000 people have emigrated. Abundant minerals and oil have made Gabon the richest country in the region. Oil is also of major importance in the Congo, and both countries have relatively large urban populations. Relatively prosperous, Cameroon is home to more than 200 different peoples.

A wooden figure from Cameroon, made to honor an ancestor.

HEALTH CLINIC
Traditional African medicine is still widely practiced in this region. Western medicine has also been successfully used to cure or control many diseases. Medicines are often dispensed at village clinics like this one. But there are still major problems – many babies do not survive and there is a great shortage of doctors. In Chad, for example, over 40,000 people have to share one doctor.

LAKE CHAD
Lake Chad lies at the point where Chad, Cameroon, Niger, and Nigeria meet. Due to a series of droughts, the rivers that feed the lake have shrunk to little more than streams and reduced it to a tenth of its former size. Fish from Lake Chad – such as this *tilapia* – are a major source of food for the people who live in the surrounding areas. But each year the fishermen must haul their boats farther to reach the lake's receding water.

PYGMIES
Several groups of pygmies live scattered through the rain forests of Central Africa. They still survive mainly by hunting and gathering, but they also trade with neighboring peoples and have learned to speak their languages. Pygmies rarely reach a height of more than 4 ft (125 cms). This pygmy hut, made of banana fronds, is in a forest clearing in the Central African Republic.

Forested valleys and hills around Loubomo, Congo.

CHAD
pop: 6,537,000

CENTRAL AFRICAN REPUBLIC
pop: 3,026,000

CAMEROON
pop:13,651,000

RELIGION
The main religion in this region is Christianity, but many Africans follow the traditional religions of their ancestors. They believe in many gods and spirits, who are often associated with natural forces or the elements, such as trees and thunder. This photo shows a ritual dance from Cameroon.

Dancer dressed as a leopard spirit

River flowing through dense rain forest in Cameroon.

TRADITIONAL HOUSING
Traditional African houses vary from area to area, according to the building materials available locally. The walls of these houses in Cameroon are made of mud and the roofs of straw. Building a house is one of the regular family tasks. As the family grows, new houses are added to the group.

LIBYA

SUDAN

TIBESTI

NIGER

CHAD

Faya

Mao

Bol
L. Chad

N'DJAMENA
Kousseri

Biltine

Abéché

Ati

Mongo

Am Timan

Salamat

Sarh

Moundou

Bongor
Logone
Lai
Goe
Chari
Erguig

Maroua
Guider
Garoua
L. Lagdo

Ngaoundéré

Bunyo
Aluminum
Tin

Bafoussam
Baoenda

CAMEROON

NIGERIA

Birao

Ndélé

Kaga-Bandoro

Bossangoa

Bouar

CENTRAL
AFRICAN REPUBLIC

Sibut

Bria
Bambari

Obo

Copper
Chromium

Diamonds
Diamonds
Uranium
Kono

Gold

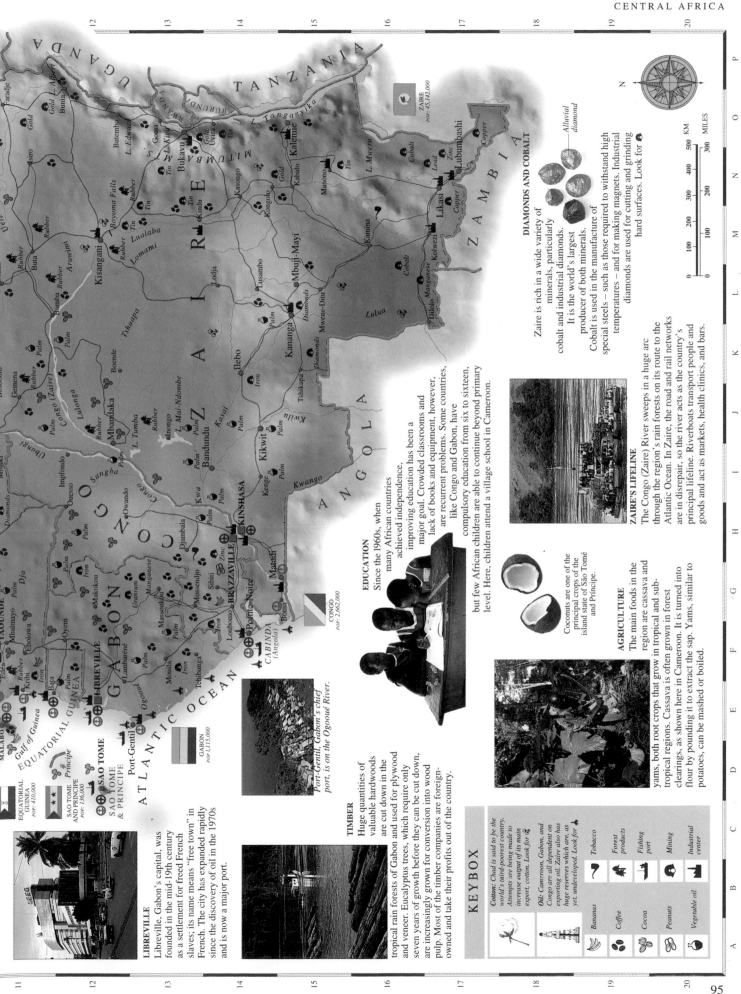

ZAIRE POP: 45,142,000

CONGO POP: 2,662,000

GABON POP: 1,115,000

SAO TOME AND PRINCIPE POP: 136,000

EQUATORIAL GUINEA POP: 410,000

DIAMONDS AND COBALT

Zaire is rich in a wide variety of minerals, particularly cobalt and industrial diamonds. It is the world's largest producer of both minerals. Cobalt is used in the manufacture of special steels – such as those required to withstand high temperatures – and for making magnets. Industrial diamonds are used for cutting and grinding hard surfaces. Look for

Alluvial diamond

ZAIRE'S LIFELINE

The Congo (Zaire) River sweeps in a huge arc through the region's rain forests on its route to the Atlantic Ocean. In Zaire, the road and rail networks are in disrepair, so the river acts as the country's principal lifeline. Riverboats transport people and goods and act as markets, health clinics, and bars.

EDUCATION

Since the 1960s, when many African countries achieved independence, improving education has been a major goal. Crowded classrooms and lack of books and equipment, however, are recurrent problems. Some countries, like Congo and Gabon, have compulsory education from six to sixteen, but few African children are able to continue beyond primary level. Here, children attend a village school in Cameroon.

Coconuts are one of the principal crops of the island state of São Tomé and Príncipe.

AGRICULTURE

The main foods in the region are cassava and yams, both root crops that grow in tropical and sub-tropical regions. Cassava is often grown in forest clearings, as shown here in Cameroon. It is turned into flour by pounding it to extract the sap. Yams, similar to potatoes, can be mashed or boiled.

LIBREVILLE

Libreville, Gabon's capital, was founded in the mid-19th century as a settlement for freed French slaves; its name means "free town" in French. The city has expanded rapidly since the discovery of oil in the 1970s and is now a major port.

TIMBER

Huge quantities of valuable hardwoods are cut down in the tropical rain forests of Gabon and used for plywood and veneer. Eucalyptus trees, which require only seven years of growth before they can be cut down, are increasingly grown for conversion into wood pulp. Most of the timber companies are foreign-owned and take their profits out of the country.

Port-Gentil, Gabon's chief port, is on the Ogooué River.

KEYBOX

Cotton: Chad is said to be the world's third-poorest country. Attempts are being made to increase exports of its main export, cotton. Look for

Oil: Cameroon, Gabon, and Congo are all dependent on exporting oil. Zaire also has huge reserves which are, as yet, undeveloped. Look for

Bananas	Tobacco
Coffee	Forest products
Cocoa	Fishing port
Peanuts	Mining
Vegetable oil	Industrial center

95

A B C D E F G H I J

1

CENTRAL EAST AFRICA

EAST AFRICA'S WEALTH lies in its land. Most people make their living from farming or cattle herding. Large areas covered with long grass, scrub, and scattered trees, called savannah, provide grazing for domestic and wild animals alike. But some land, especially in Uganda and Zambia, cannot be used because of tsetse fly, which is dangerous to both animals and humans. Tea, coffee, and tobacco are grown as cash crops throughout the area, especially in Kenya and Malawi. Uganda has great potential for farming, but for the last 20 years it has been crippled by civil wars. Zambia, Rwanda, Burundi, and Uganda all suffer from having no seaports. Industry is poorly developed in the region, except in Kenya, and only Zambia is rich in minerals. Burundi and Rwanda are densely populated, and Kenya now has the world's fastest-growing population. After economic decline in the 1980s, Tanzania is slowly recovering.

THE SAMBURU
In Kenya's northern plateau region, tribes like the Samburu continue to follow the traditional way of life of their ancestors. They live by grazing their herds of cattle, sheep, and goats on the savannah. This *moran*, or warrior, wears numerous strings of beads, distinctive ivory earrings, and always carries two spears and a knife.

TRAINS
Countries with no coastline are very dependent on road and rail transport to link them to industrial centers and main ports. Although the African rail network is expanding, tracks are often poorly maintained. Here, people board a train at Kampala in Uganda.

PREDATORY FISH
Thirty years ago the Nile perch was introduced into Lake Victoria to increase fish production. Although the lake is vast, this fish now occupies every corner and is killing off the original fish population. Look for ✦

POACHING
Africa's wildlife parks have helped preserve the animals, but poaching remains a major problem. Recently, in an attempt to save the elephants, a worldwide ban on the sale of ivory was imposed. But policing the parks is very costly; poachers are armed and dangerous. Here, in Tanzania, wardens are burning a poacher's hut.

AIDS
AIDS is a worldwide problem, but it is particularly widespread in Africa. Many people on the continent already suffer from diseases and malnutrition, which makes them more vulnerable to the illnesses associated with AIDS.

WILDLIFE RESERVES
Africa's great plains contain some of the world's most spectacular species of wildlife. All the countries in the region have set aside huge areas as national parks where animals are protected. Wildlife safaris attract thousands of tourists and provide countries with much needed foreign income. Look for ⚑

Tsetse fly carries a disease that can kill cattle and humans.

Copper bracelets

COPPER
There are huge deposits of copper in central Africa, centered around Ndola in Zambia. This region is often called the Copperbelt. Copper accounts for 90 percent of Zambia's export earnings, but low prices in recent years and the discovery of cheaper substitutes have badly affected the industry. Supplies of copper are nearly used up, which could mean disaster for the Zambian economy. The Copperbelt now has improved transport links, such as the Tanzam Railway, which take the refined copper to various destinations. Look for ⬤

Vultures cluster in a lone tree on the Tanzanian grasslands.

KEYBOX

Coffee: A valuable cash crop, coffee is grown in Uganda, Kenya, Tanzania, and Rwanda. Kenya plans to triple production by the year 2000. Look for ♨

Market gardening: Kenya has ideal conditions for growing vegetables and fruit, which are exported in large quantities, mainly to Europe. Look for 🗡

Hydroelectric power: The Kariba Dam on the Zambezi River, built by Zambia and Zimbabwe, supplies both nations with electricity. Look for ▦

Refugee camps: Warfare in neighboring countries has caused thousands of refugees to flee to temporary camps in the region. Look for △

⚓	Sugarcane	🌲	Forest products
🥥	Coconuts	🐟	Fishing
🌾	Tea	⛏	Mining
🌿	Cotton	🏭	Industrial center
🍃	Tobacco	⚑	Wildlife reserves

AFRICAN VILLAGE
East African villages usually consist of a series of huts enclosed by thorn fences. This aerial photo shows a village belonging to the Masai tribe. A Masai man may have several wives. Each wife has her own huts, enclosed by a fence. The livestock is taken out to graze by day and driven into the fenced enclosure at night.

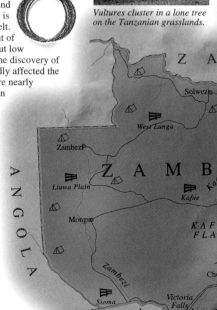

N

```
0     100   200   300   400   500  KM
|--|--|--|--|--|--|--|--|--|--|--|
0   50   100  150  200  250  300  MILES
```

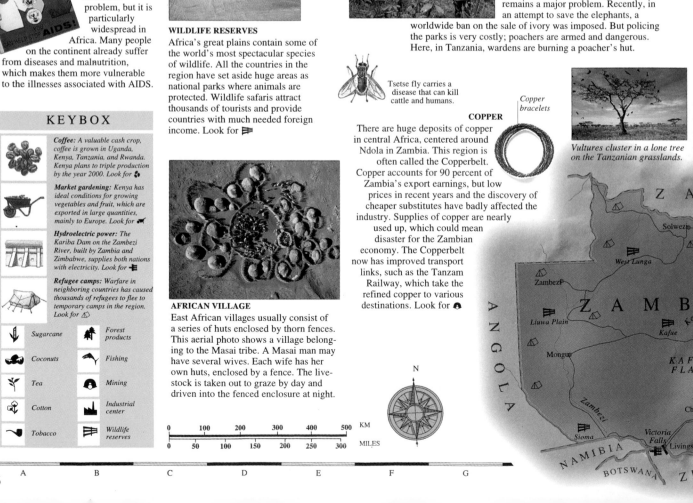

ZA

Solwezi

West Lunga

Zambezi

Liuwa Plain   Kafue

Mongu   Kafue

ZAMB

KAFU FLA

A N G O L A

Zambezi

Sioma   Victoria Falls   Livingsto

NAMIBIA   BOTSWANA   ZI

Chor

A B C D E F G

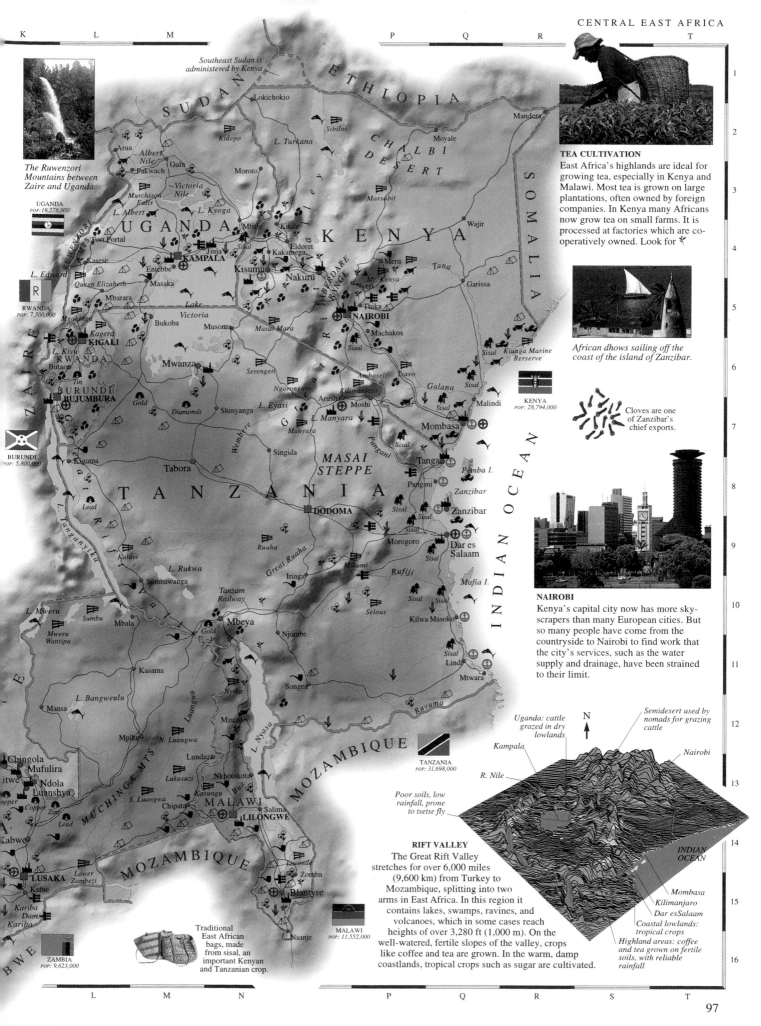

TEA CULTIVATION
East Africa's highlands are ideal for growing tea, especially in Kenya and Malawi. Most tea is grown on large plantations, often owned by foreign companies. In Kenya many Africans now grow tea on small farms. It is processed at factories which are co-operatively owned. Look for 🌱

African dhows sailing off the coast of the island of Zanzibar.

Cloves are one of Zanzibar's chief exports.

NAIROBI
Kenya's capital city now has more sky-scrapers than many European cities. But so many people have come from the countryside to Nairobi to find work that the city's services, such as the water supply and drainage, have been strained to their limit.

RIFT VALLEY
The Great Rift Valley stretches for over 6,000 miles (9,600 km) from Turkey to Mozambique, splitting into two arms in East Africa. In this region it contains lakes, swamps, ravines, and volcanoes, which in some cases reach heights of over 3,280 ft (1,000 m). On the well-watered, fertile slopes of the valley, crops like coffee and tea are grown. In the warm, damp coastlands, tropical crops such as sugar are cultivated.

The Ruwenzori Mountains between Zaire and Uganda.

Southeast Sudan is administered by Kenya.

UGANDA POP: 19,278,000
RWANDA POP: 7,500,000
BURUNDI POP: 5,800,000
KENYA POP: 28,794,000
TANZANIA POP: 31,698,000
MALAWI POP: 11,552,000
ZAMBIA POP: 9,623,000

Traditional East African bags, made from sisal, an important Kenyan and Tanzanian crop.

Uganda: cattle grazed in dry lowlands
Semidesert used by nomads for grazing cattle
Kampala
Nairobi
R. Nile
Poor soils, low rainfall, prone to tsetse fly
INDIAN OCEAN
Mombasa
Kilimanjaro
Dar esSalaam
Coastal lowlands: tropical crops
Highland areas: coffee and tea grown on fertile soils, with reliable rainfall

SOUTHERN AFRICA

THE WEALTHIEST and most dominant country in this region is South Africa. Black African lands were gradually settled in the 19th century by Dutch colonists, their descendants – the Afrikaners – and the British. When vast deposits of gold and diamonds were discovered in the late 19th century, the country became rich. In 1948 the government introduced a system of "separate development," called *apartheid*, which separated people according to their color and gave political power to whites only. This policy led to isolation and sanctions from the rest of the world's nations, which only ended after the abolition of apartheid. The first democratic elections were held in 1994. After years of conflict, South Africa has now become a more integrated society. Most of the countries around South Africa rely on its industries for trade and work. After 30 years of unrest, Namibia has won independence from South Africa. Mozambique and Angola are both struggling for survival after years of civil war. Zimbabwe has a relatively diverse economy, based on agriculture and its rich mineral resources.

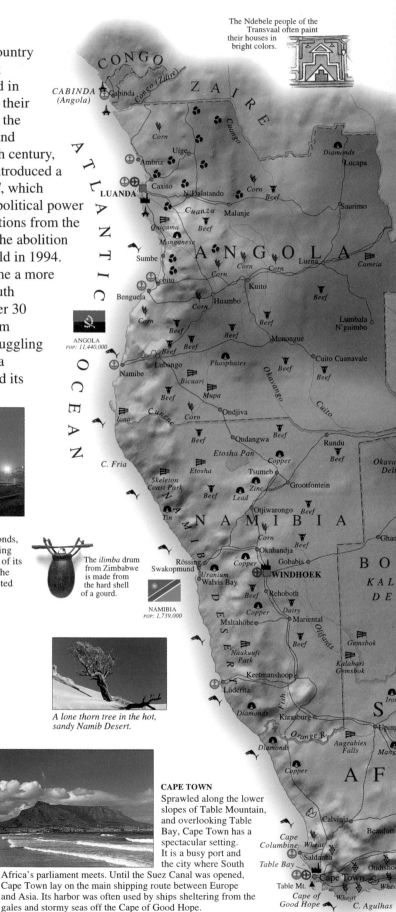

The Ndebele people of the Transvaal often paint their houses in bright colors.

ANGOLA
POP: 11,440,000

The *ilimba* drum from Zimbabwe is made from the hard shell of a gourd.

NAMIBIA
POP: 1,739,000

INDUSTRY
South Africa is the region's industrial leader. Johannesburg, the country's largest city, is seen here behind the huge mounds of earth excavated from the gold mines. Look for ⛏

URANIUM
Namibia is rich in copper, diamonds, tin, and other minerals. The mining industry accounts for 90 percent of its export earnings. At Rössing, in the Namib Desert, uranium is extracted from a huge open-pit mine and exported abroad. Look for ☢

KEYBOX

🐟	**Fishing:** Overfishing by both foreign and local fleets is a major threat to Namibia's once-rich fishing grounds. Controls are in operation. Look for ⌐
🛢	**Oil:** Civil war in Angola has disrupted industry, but its oil reserves – the only major ones in the region – so far have been little affected. Look for ⚒
🦒	**Wildlife reserves:** Most of the region's countries have set aside large areas as wildlife parks, which are popular tourist attractions. Look for ⚑

🐂	Cattle	🌱	Tea
🌾	Cereals	🚬	Tobacco
🍋	Citrus fruits	⛏	Mining
🍇	Wine	⚒	Coal
☕	Coffee	🏭	Industrial center

BUSHMEN
Bushmen – or *San* – are one of the few groups of hunter-gatherers left in Africa. These people can be traced far back into African history. Today, some 1,000 bushmen still live in the harsh environment of the Kalahari Desert.

A lone thorn tree in the hot, sandy Namib Desert.

CAPE TOWN
Sprawled along the lower slopes of Table Mountain, and overlooking Table Bay, Cape Town has a spectacular setting. It is a busy port and the city where South Africa's parliament meets. Until the Suez Canal was opened, Cape Town lay on the main shipping route between Europe and Asia. Its harbor was often used by ships sheltering from the gales and stormy seas off the Cape of Good Hope.

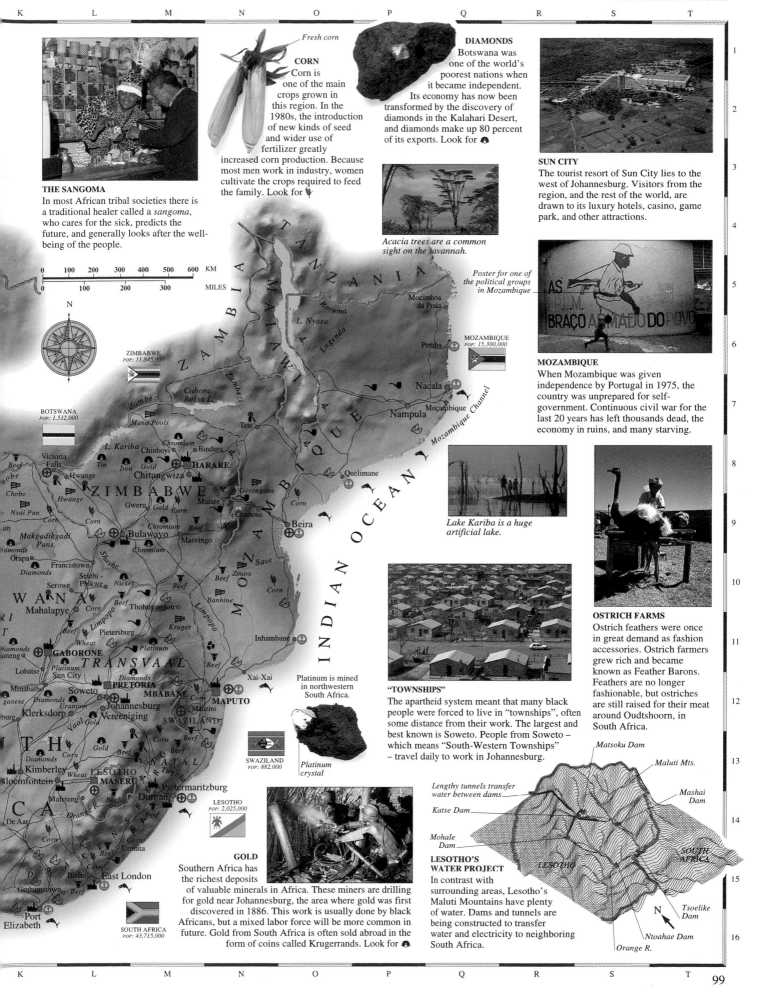

THE SANGOMA
In most African tribal societies there is a traditional healer called a *sangoma*, who cares for the sick, predicts the future, and generally looks after the well-being of the people.

Fresh corn

CORN
Corn is one of the main crops grown in this region. In the 1980s, the introduction of new kinds of seed and wider use of fertilizer greatly increased corn production. Because most men work in industry, women cultivate the crops required to feed the family. Look for 🌾

Acacia trees are a common sight on the savannah.

Poster for one of the political groups in Mozambique

DIAMONDS
Botswana was one of the world's poorest nations when it became independent. Its economy has now been transformed by the discovery of diamonds in the Kalahari Desert, and diamonds make up 80 percent of its exports. Look for ◈

SUN CITY
The tourist resort of Sun City lies to the west of Johannesburg. Visitors from the region, and the rest of the world, are drawn to its luxury hotels, casino, game park, and other attractions.

MOZAMBIQUE
When Mozambique was given independence by Portugal in 1975, the country was unprepared for self-government. Continuous civil war for the last 20 years has left thousands dead, the economy in ruins, and many starving.

Lake Kariba is a huge artificial lake.

OSTRICH FARMS
Ostrich feathers were once in great demand as fashion accessories. Ostrich farmers grew rich and became known as Feather Barons. Feathers are no longer fashionable, but ostriches are still raised for their meat around Oudtshoorn, in South Africa.

"TOWNSHIPS"
The apartheid system meant that many black people were forced to live in "townships", often some distance from their work. The largest and best known is Soweto. People from Soweto – which means "South-Western Townships" – travel daily to work in Johannesburg.

Platinum is mined in northwestern South Africa.

Platinum crystal

GOLD
Southern Africa has the richest deposits of valuable minerals in Africa. These miners are drilling for gold near Johannesburg, the area where gold was first discovered in 1886. This work is usually done by black Africans, but a mixed labor force will be more common in future. Gold from South Africa is often sold abroad in the form of coins called Krugerrands. Look for ◈

LESOTHO'S WATER PROJECT
In contrast with surrounding areas, Lesotho's Maluti Mountains have plenty of water. Dams and tunnels are being constructed to transfer water and electricity to neighboring South Africa.

Lengthy tunnels transfer water between dams

Matsoku Dam
Maluti Mts.
Mashai Dam
Katse Dam
Mohale Dam
LESOTHO
SOUTH AFRICA
Tsoelike Dam
Ntoahae Dam
Orange R.

Map labels
ZIMBABWE POP: 11,845,000
BOTSWANA POP: 1,532,000
MOZAMBIQUE POP: 15,300,000
SWAZILAND POP: 882,000
LESOTHO POP: 2,025,000
SOUTH AFRICA POP: 43,715,000

TANZANIA
ZAMBIA
MALAWI
Rovuma
L. Nyasa
Lugenda
Mocimboa da Praia
Pemba
Nacala
Moçambique
Nampula
Zambezi
Cabora Bassa L.
Tete
Zambezi
Mana Pools
Victoria Falls
Hwange
Chinhoyi
Chromium
Bindura
L. Kariba
Tin
Iron
Gold
HARARE
Chitungwiza
ZIMBABWE
Gweru
Gold
Corn
Mutare
Gorongosa
Quelimane
Chromium
Chimoio
Beira
Bulawayo
Masvingo
Chromium
Beef
MOZAMBIQUE
Save
Zinave
Corn
INDIAN OCEAN
Mozambique Channel
Nickel
Selebi-Phikwe
Serowe
Francistown
Diamonds
Orapa
Makgadikgadi Pans
Diamonds
Nxai Pan
Chobe
Beef
Corn
Banhine
Beef
Mahalapye
Thohoyandou
Corn
Limpopo
Pietersburg
Kruger
Beef
Inhambane
Wheat
GABORONE
Platinum
Xai-Xai
Lobatse
Platinum
Sun City
Diamonds
TRANSVAAL
PRETORIA
Mmabatho
Diamonds
Uranium
MBABANE
MAPUTO
Manzini
Soweto
Johannesburg
Klerksdorp
Vereeniging
SWAZILAND
Vaal
Gold
Corn
Beef
NATAL
Gold
Beef
Diamonds
Corn
Kimberley
Wheat
LESOTHO
MASERU
Bloemfontein
Pietermaritzburg
Mafeteng
Durban
De Aar
Orange R.
Beef
Corn
Umtata
Bisho
Corn
Grahamstown
East London
Port Elizabeth

Scale
0 100 200 300 400 500 600 KM
0 100 200 300 MILES
N

THE INDIAN OCEAN

THE INDIAN OCEAN is the smallest of the world's oceans, but some 5,000 islands – many of them surrounded by coral reefs – are scattered across its area. Beneath its surface, three great mountain ranges converge toward the ocean's center – an area of strong seismic and volcanic activity. The ocean reaches its greatest depth – 24,400 ft (7,440 m) – in the Java Trench. More than one billion people – about a fifth of the world's population – live in the countries around the Indian Ocean, representing an immense range of cultures and religions. Heavy monsoon rain and tropical storms cause flooding along the ocean's northern coasts. The world's largest oil fields are located around the Persian Gulf.

Sugar cane

SUGAR

Sugar was first brought to Mauritius by the Dutch in the 1600s. Ninety percent of the island's arable farmland is covered by sugar plantations. But today sugar has been replaced in importance by textiles, which now account for nearly half the island's exports. Look for ↓

TOURISM

The Indian Ocean islands are great tourist attractions. The islands welcome the money this brings, but the sheer number of visitors threatens to destroy the islands' environment. Look for ↓

Hotel complex on an island in Mauritius

Once thought extinct, the coelacanth has been found, alive and well, off southeast Africa.

KARACHI

In the mid-19th century a railroad was built along the Indus River valley to Karachi, which developed into a large port and industrial city. When Pakistan became an independent nation in 1947, Karachi became the country's capital. It has now been replaced by the new city of Islamabad in the north.

FISHING

Large-scale fishing is far less developed in the Indian Ocean than in either the Atlantic or Pacific. Fishing is difficult because there are relatively few areas of shallow sea. Small-scale fishing, however, provides a valuable source of food. Many fishermen, like these Sri Lankans, use basic and often inefficient methods. Tuna is the most important catch in the area. Look for ↑

ISLANDS

The islands of the Indian Ocean include enormous ones like Madagascar, coral atolls like the Maldives, and volcanic islands like Réunion. All are threatened by rising sea levels, which reduce the area of land available. Coral reefs are being eroded, leaving islands increasingly exposed to ocean tides and flooding.

The loggerhead turtle is one of the Indian Ocean's many endangered species.

MONSOON

Farmers in the lands around the Indian Ocean are wholly dependent on the coming of the monsoon rains. In May or June, the western arm of the monsoon sweeps in from the Arabian Sea, bringing torrential downpours which move north through India. At the same time, the monsoon's eastern arm curves out of the Bay of Bengal, driving north as far as the Himalayan foothills. About 85 percent of India's annual rainfall occurs during the monsoon periods.

COMOROS
POP. 676,000

Mangroves grow along many of the Indian Ocean's coasts.

ASHMORE & CARTIER IS. (Australia)

Map labels

Nile
Suez
Suez Canal
Port Said
RED SEA
Kuwait City
Basra
Tigris
Euphrates
Manama
Persian Gulf
ARABIA
Djibouti
Gulf of Aden
Aden
Salālah
Maṣīrah
Ra's al Ḥadd
Chāh Bahār
Gulf of Oman
Socotra (Yemen)
C. Xaafuun
ASIA
Indus
Ganges
Karachi
Bombay
ARABIAN SEA
Vishakhapatnam
Madras
Cochin
C. Comorin
Calcutta
Bay of Bengal
Mekong
Irrawaddy
Rangoon
ANDAMAN SEA
Andaman Is. (India)
Nicobar Is. (India)
Gulf of Thailand
SOUTH CHINA SEA
George Town
Melaka
Singapore
Tin
Strait of Malacca
Sumatra
Java Trench
Java
JAVA SEA
Borneo
CHRISTMAS I. (Australia)
COCOS IS. (Keeling)
Trincomalee
Sri Lanka
Colombo
Dondra Head
Laccadive Is. (India)
MALDIVES
POP. 255,000
MALE
Maldive Ridge
Carlsberg Ridge
BRITISH INDIAN OCEAN TERRITORY (UK)
Diego Garcia
INDIAN
OCEAN
Somali Basin
Mascarene Plateau
MADAGASCAR
SEYCHELLES
VICTORIA
Mahé
Amirante Is. (Seychelles)
Aldabra Is. (Seychelles)
Grande Comore
MORONI
COMOROS
MAYOTTE (France)
C. Bobaomby
Antsiranana
Mombasa
Dar es Salaam
AFRICA

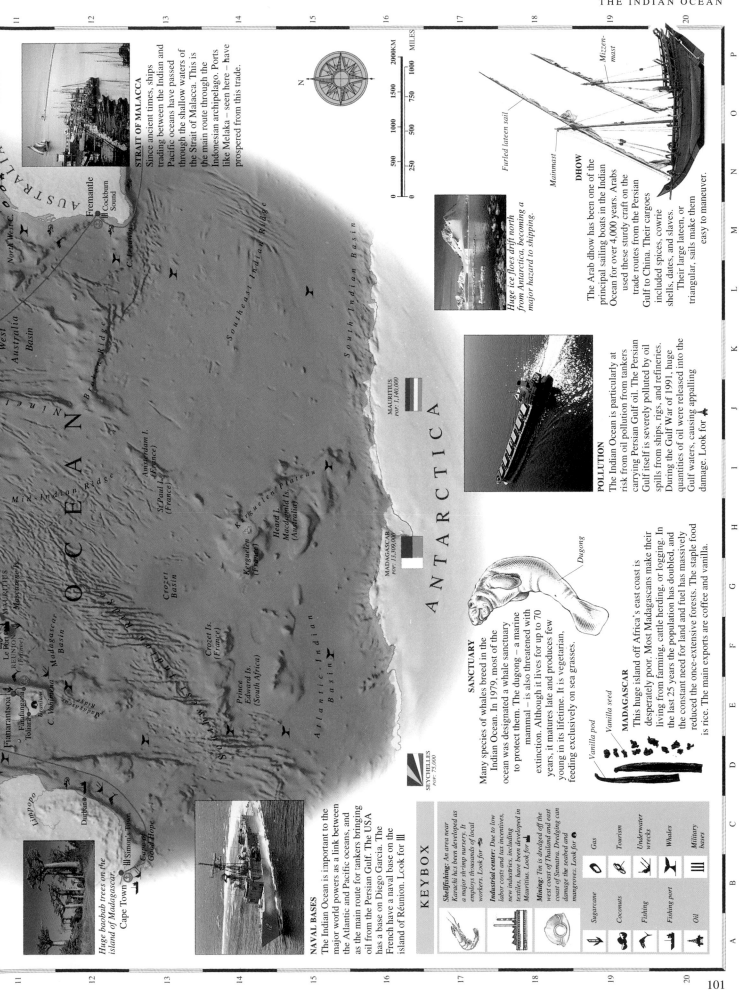

STRAIT OF MALACCA

Since ancient times, ships trading between the Indian and Pacific oceans have passed through the shallow waters of the Strait of Malacca. This is the main route through the Indonesian archipelago. Ports like Melaka – seen here – have prospered from this trade.

Furled lateen sail

Mizzen-mast

Mainmast

DHOW

The Arab dhow has been one of the principal sailing boats in the Indian Ocean for over 4,000 years. Arabs used these sturdy craft on the trade routes from the Persian Gulf to China. Their cargoes included spices, cowrie shells, dates, and slaves. Their large lateen, or triangular, sails make them easy to maneuver.

Huge ice floes drift north from Antarctica, becoming a major hazard to shipping.

POLLUTION

The Indian Ocean is particularly at risk from oil pollution from tankers carrying Persian Gulf oil. The Persian Gulf itself is severely polluted by oil spills from ships, rigs, and refineries. During the Gulf War of 1991, huge quantities of oil were released into the Gulf waters, causing appalling damage. Look for ⚓

SANCTUARY

Many species of whales breed in the Indian Ocean. In 1979, most of the ocean was designated a whale sanctuary to protect them. The dugong – a marine mammal – is also threatened with extinction. Although it lives for up to 70 years, it matures late and produces few young in its lifetime. It is vegetarian, feeding exclusively on sea grasses.

Dugong

MADAGASCAR

This huge island off Africa's east coast is desperately poor. Most Madagascans make their living from farming, cattle herding, or logging. In the last 25 years the population has doubled, and the constant need for land and fuel has massively reduced the once-extensive forests. The staple food is rice. The main exports are coffee and vanilla.

Vanilla seed

Vanilla pod

NAVAL BASES

The Indian Ocean is important to the major world powers as a link between the Atlantic and Pacific oceans, and as the main route for tankers bringing oil from the Persian Gulf. The USA has a base on Diego Garcia. The French have a naval base on the island of Réunion. Look for ⫿⫿⫿

Huge baobab trees on the island of Madagascar.

KEYBOX

Shellfishing: An area near Karachi has been developed as a major shrimp nursery. It employs thousands of local workers. Look for 🦐

Industrial center: Due to low labor costs and tax incentives, new industries, including textiles, have been developed in Mauritius. Look for ▦

Mining: Tin is dredged off the west coast of Thailand and east coast of Sumatra. Dredging can damage the seabed and mangroves. Look for 🪨

〰	Sugarcane	⚙	Gas
🥥	Coconuts	✿	Tourism
🐟	Fishing	⚓	Underwater wrecks
🐋	Fishing port	🐋	Whales
⚓	Oil	⫿⫿⫿	Military bases

MAURITIUS
POP. 1,140,000

MADAGASCAR
POP. 13,300,000

SEYCHELLES
POP. 75,000

N

2000KM
1000 MILES
1500
750
1000
500
500
250
0 0

OCEAN

ANTARCTICA

AUSTRALIA

North West C.
Fremantle
Cockburn Sound
C. Leeuwin

West Australia Basin

Broken Ridge

Southeast Indian Ridge

Ninety East Ridge

Amsterdam I. (France)
St Paul I. (France)

Mid-Indian Ridge

Crozet Basin

Kerguelen Plateau

Heard I.
Macdonald Is. (Australia)

Kerguelen (France)

Crozet Is. (France)

Prince Edward Is. (South Africa)

South Indian Basin

Atlantic-Indian Basin

Madagascar Basin

MAURITIUS
Mauritius
Le Port
REUNION (France)

Fianarantsoa
Fianarantsoa
Toliara
C. Vohimena
uranium

Madagascar Ridge

Limpopo
Durban
Cape of Good Hope
Cape Town
Simon's Town

Cedar of Lebanon
Cedrus libani
Height: 130 ft (40 m)

Arabian oryx
Oryx leucoryx
Height: 4 ft (1.2 m)

Baikal seal
Phoca sibirica
Length: 5 ft (1.5 m)
Found only in Lake Baikal

Darkling beetle
Sternodes species
Length: 1 in (2 cm)

Reindeer
Rangifer tarandus
Body length: 7 ft (2.2 m)

Common hamster
Cricetus cricetus
Length: 12 in (30 cm)

Waxwing
Bombycilla garrulus
Length: 8 in (18 cm)

NORTH AND WEST ASIA

NORTH AND WEST ASIA contains some of the world's most inhospitable environments. In the south, the Arabian Peninsula is almost entirely a baking hot desert where no plants can grow. To the north, a belt of rugged, snow-capped mountains and high plateaus cross the continent. The climate becomes drier and more extreme toward the center of the continent. Dry hot summers contrast with bitterly cold winters. Cold deserts give way to treeless plains known as steppe, then to huge marshes, and to the world's largest needleleaf forest. In the extreme north, both land and sea are frozen for most of the year. Only in summer do the top layers of soil thaw briefly allowing plants of the tundra, such as moss and lichen, to cover the land.

COLD FOREST
Strong but flexible trunks and a tentlike shape help needleleaf trees withstand the great weight of snow that covers them throughout the long winter.

HOT BATHS
These strange white terraces formed in southwestern Asia in much the same way that a kettle develops scale. Underground water heated by volcanic activity dissolves minerals in rocks. These are deposited when the water reaches the surface and cools.

DROUGHT-TOLERANT TREES
Plants growing near the Black Sea minimize water loss during the long hot summers. Most have wax-covered leaves through which little water can escape.

Blue turquoise, a semiprecious stone mainly found in cold areas of north Asia.

REGENERATING FOREST
Unlike many plants, juniper trees are able to withstand the acid soils of needleleaf forests. Here junipers cover the floor of a dense pine forest.

The fossilized head of *Gallimimus*, an ostrichlike dinosaur that once lived in Asia.

SINAI'S ROCK "MUSHROOMS"
In deserts, sand particles whipped along by high-speed winds create natural sculptures. Rock at the base of the "mushroom" has been more heavily eroded than rock above, leading to these unusual landforms.

▲ VOLCANO
There are more than 30 active volcanoes on the Kamchatka peninsula, part of the Pacific Ocean's "Ring of Fire." Volcanic activity is due to the deep underground movements of the Eurasian plate.

FROZEN RIVER
The Lena River rises near Lake Baikal, the world's deepest and oldest freshwater lake. Like other Siberian rivers, it flows into the Arctic Ocean and is frozen over for eight or nine months of the year.

HOT DESERTS
The Arabian Desert is one of the hottest and driest places in the world. Temperatures frequently reach 120°F (45°C) and very little rain falls.

CROSS-SECTION THROUGH NORTH AND WEST ASIA

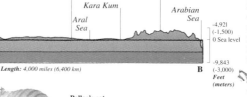

Ural Mts

Kirghiz Steppe

Arctic Ocean

Kara Sea

Kara Kum

Aral Sea

Iranian Plateau

Arabian Sea

-4,921 (-1,500)
0 Sea level
-9,843 (-3,000)
Feet (meters)

A   *Length: 4,000 miles (6,400 km)*   B

COLD WINTER DESERT
Large parts of Central Asia are covered in deserts that are hot in summer but very cold in winter. A river has been naturally dammed to form this lake, which is unusual in this dry region.

Pallas's cat
Felis manul
Length: 26 in (65 cm)

Gray wolf
Canis lupus
Length: 5 ft (1.4 m)

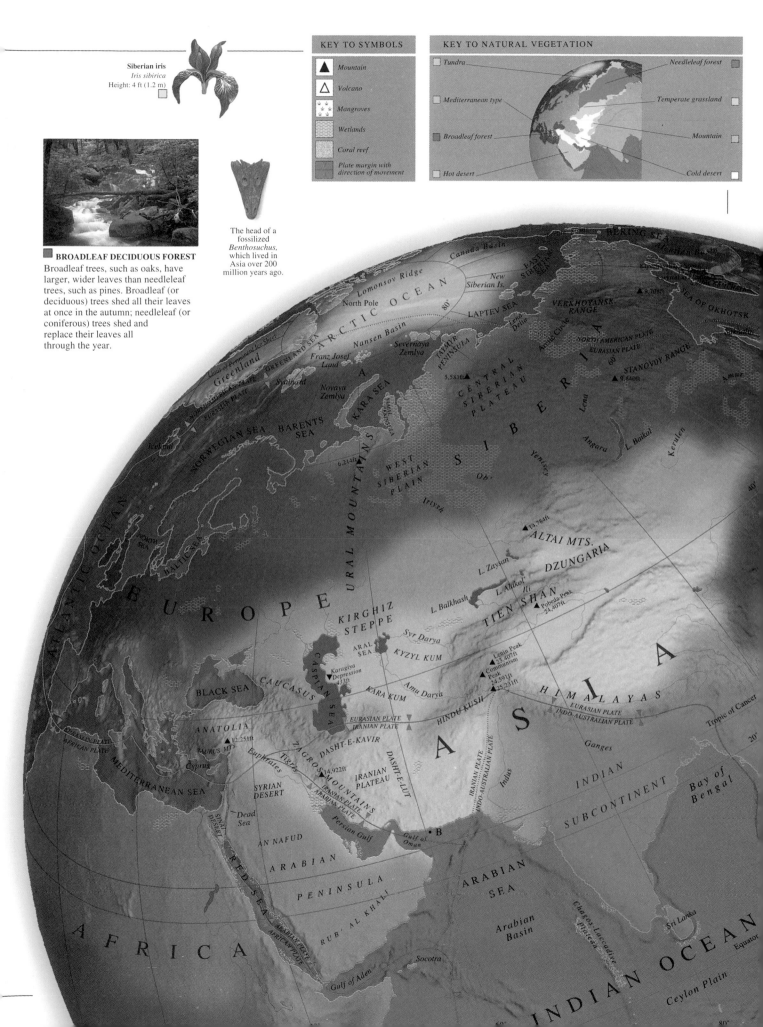

Siberian iris
Iris sibirica
Height: 4 ft (1.2 m)

The head of a fossilized *Benthosuchus*, which lived in Asia over 200 million years ago.

BROADLEAF DECIDUOUS FOREST

Broadleaf trees, such as oaks, have larger, wider leaves than needleleaf trees, such as pines. Broadleaf (or deciduous) trees shed all their leaves at once in the autumn; needleleaf (or coniferous) trees shed and replace their leaves all through the year.

TURKEY AND CYPRUS

SITUATED PARTLY IN EUROPE and partly in Asia, Turkey is also balanced between modern Europe and its Islamic past. For 600 years, the Ottoman Turks ruled over a great empire covering a quarter of Europe, but by the early 20th century their empire had disappeared. In the 1920s, Mustapha Kemal Atatürk forcibly modernized Turkish society. Today, Turkey is becoming increasingly industrialized; textile and food-processing industries dominate the economy. In the central plateau, however, farmers and herders live as they have done for centuries, adapting their lives to the harsh environment. To the north, the Black Sea is rich in fish, and the fertile areas around its shores are well suited to farming. The beautiful western and southern coasts are strewn with the remains of ancient Greek settlements, attracting 1.5 million tourists to Turkey every year.

ISTANBUL
Istanbul is divided in two by a strait of water called the Bosporus. One part of the city is in Europe, the other in Asia. Its buildings are also a mix of East and West: grand mosques, graceful minarets, and exotic bazaars rub shoulders with modern shops, offices, and restaurants.

TURKEY
POP: 63,204,000

The harbor and castle of St. Peter at Bodrum.

STREET TRADERS
Large numbers of people from the countryside go to Turkey's cities to try to make a living. Many of them sell goods, food, or drink on the streets or from makeshift market stalls. Others work as shoeshiners, carrying their equipment in highly decorated brass cases.

A CLASSICAL LEGACY
The temple of Athena in Priene is one of Turkey's many ancient treasures. The Aegean coast was colonized by the ancient Greeks as early as 700 BC. Many people go to Turkey to visit the dramatic remains of Greek cities and temples. Look for ▥

KEYBOX

 Tobacco: *Turkey is a major producer. Dark Turkish tobacco is grown around the Black Sea and Aegean coasts. Look for* ⬎

 Tourism: *Coastal resorts are developing rapidly. Airports cater for growing numbers of visitors from northern Europe. Look for* 🏖

 Dams: *Ambitious dam-building programs, especially in the southeast, are being used for hydroelectric power and for watering farmland. Look for* ▦

🌾	Cereals	🌿	Cotton
	Sugar beet	🐟	Fishing
	Citrus fruit		Carpet weaving
	Wine	🏭	Industrial center
	Vegetable oil	▥	Archaeological site

Blue Mosque, Istanbul

MOSQUE
Modern Turkey does not have a state religion. It was once an Islamic country, but earlier this century reforms limited the powers of the clerics and introduced civil law. Recently, however, there has been an Islamic revival, and modern Turks are going back to many customs from their rich Islamic past.

ANKARA
Ankara has been the capital of Turkey since 1923. It is a planned modern city with boulevards, parks, and many high-rise apartments. Until recently, the city suffered from terrible pollution, caused by people burning brown coal, or lignite, for heating. Now, clean natural gas is piped into the city from the Russian Federation.

This strange landscape is in Cappadocia, central Turkey.

Dried apricot

Almond

Hazelnut

Peach

Fig

AGRICULTURE
Turkey has a varied landscape and climate. This means that many different types of crop can be grown there, and the Turks are able to produce all their own food. Cereals, sugar beet, grapes, nuts, cotton, and tobacco are all major exports. Hazelnuts are grown along the shores of the Black Sea. Figs, peaches, olives, and grapes are grown along the Mediterranean coast and in the coastal lowlands. Cereals are cultivated on the central plateau. Farms are still relatively small and only gradually being modernized, but despite this productivity is high.

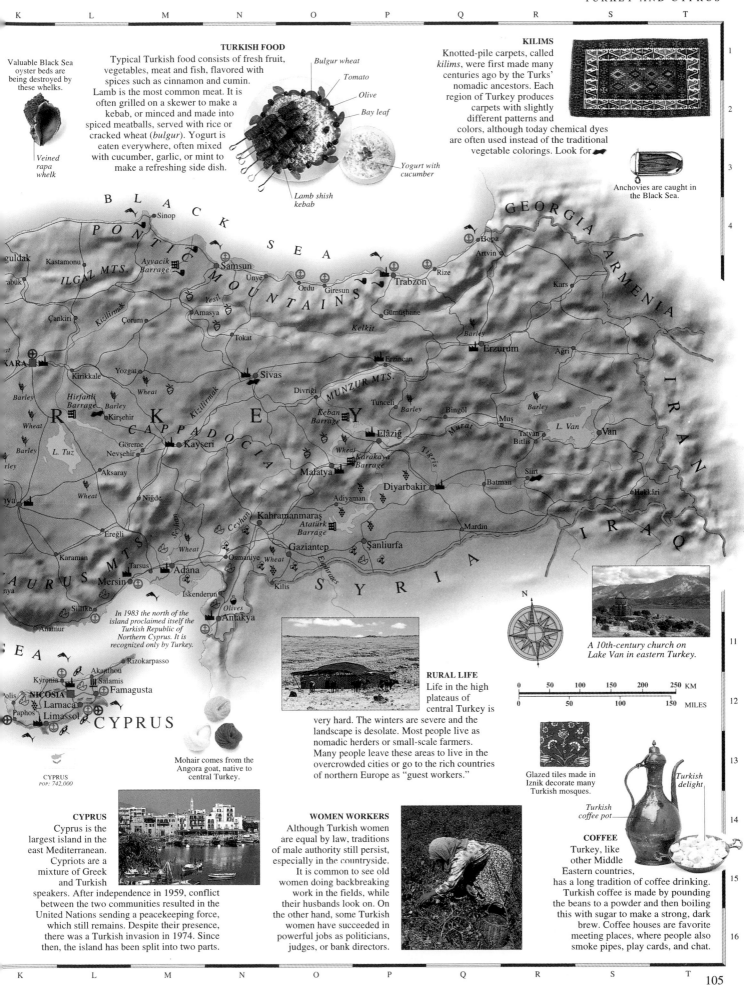

Valuable Black Sea oyster beds are being destroyed by these whelks.

Veined rapa whelk

TURKISH FOOD

Typical Turkish food consists of fresh fruit, vegetables, meat and fish, flavored with spices such as cinnamon and cumin. Lamb is the most common meat. It is often grilled on a skewer to make a kebab, or minced and made into spiced meatballs, served with rice or cracked wheat (*bulgur*). Yogurt is eaten everywhere, often mixed with cucumber, garlic, or mint to make a refreshing side dish.

Bulgur wheat
Tomato
Olive
Bay leaf
Yogurt with cucumber
Lamb shish kebab

KILIMS

Knotted-pile carpets, called *kilims*, were first made many centuries ago by the Turks' nomadic ancestors. Each region of Turkey produces carpets with slightly different patterns and colors, although today chemical dyes are often used instead of the traditional vegetable colorings. Look for

Anchovies are caught in the Black Sea.

A 10th-century church on Lake Van in eastern Turkey.

RURAL LIFE

Life in the high plateaus of central Turkey is very hard. The winters are severe and the landscape is desolate. Most people live as nomadic herders or small-scale farmers. Many people leave these areas to live in the overcrowded cities or go to the rich countries of northern Europe as "guest workers."

Glazed tiles made in Iznik decorate many Turkish mosques.

Turkish delight
Turkish coffee pot

COFFEE

Turkey, like other Middle Eastern countries, has a long tradition of coffee drinking. Turkish coffee is made by pounding the beans to a powder and then boiling this with sugar to make a strong, dark brew. Coffee houses are favorite meeting places, where people also smoke pipes, play cards, and chat.

In 1983 the north of the island proclaimed itself the Turkish Republic of Northern Cyprus. It is recognized only by Turkey.

Mohair comes from the Angora goat, native to central Turkey.

CYPRUS
POP: 742,000

CYPRUS

Cyprus is the largest island in the east Mediterranean. Cypriots are a mixture of Greek and Turkish speakers. After independence in 1959, conflict between the two communities resulted in the United Nations sending a peacekeeping force, which still remains. Despite their presence, there was a Turkish invasion in 1974. Since then, the island has been split into two parts.

WOMEN WORKERS

Although Turkish women are equal by law, traditions of male authority still persist, especially in the countryside. It is common to see old women doing backbreaking work in the fields, while their husbands look on. On the other hand, some Turkish women have succeeded in powerful jobs as politicians, judges, or bank directors.

KM
MILES

THE NEAR EAST

CAUGHT BETWEEN the continents of Europe and Asia, the Near East is bordered on the west by the fertile coasts of the Mediterranean Sea, and on the east by the arid deserts of Arabia. Some of the world's earliest civilizations were born here, while the history of three of the world's greatest religions – Judaism, Christianity, and Islam – is closely bound up with the region. Imperial conquerors, crusaders, and Muslim warriors battled fiercely over this territory, and by the 17th century much of the region was part of the Turkish Ottoman Empire. In 1918, the region came under the control of Britain and France; a dangerous mixture of religions and passionate nationalism plunged the area into conflict. Today, Lebanon is just beginning to emerge from a fierce civil war between Christians and Muslims. Israel, which became a Jewish state in 1948, has been involved in numerous wars with its neighbors, and there is considerable unrest among its Palestinian population. Many Palestinian refugees, who have left Israel, are living in camps in Jordan and Lebanon. Despite these problems, the Near East continues to survive economically. Israel is highly industrialized and a world leader in advanced farming techniques. Syria has its own reserves of oil and is gradually becoming more industrialized.

Carnation
Rose
Grapefruit
Orange
Lemon
Lime

FARMING

Although about half of Israel is desert, it is self-sufficient in most food, and actually exports agricultural produce, especially citrus fruits and flowers. Israeli farming uses advanced irrigation techniques and is highly mechanized. Many farms are run as *kibbutzim*; the land is owned by members, who share work and profits. Look for

JERUSALEM THE GOLDEN

The historic city of Jerusalem is held sacred by three major religions: Judaism, Christianity, and Islam. Throughout its history, it has been the object of pilgrimage and religious crusades. For Jews, the Wailing Wall, seen here, is the holiest site, while the Dome of the Rock is sacred to Muslims.

Skullcap, yarmulke

JUDAISM

Judaism is one of the oldest religions in the world. Jews believe in one God and follow codes of behavior based on the Torah, the first part of the Old Testament, which is written in Hebrew, plus other scriptures. Modern Hebrew is the language of Israel.

The Torah

Prayer shawl

UZI GUNS

Israel is a major arms producer, developing weapons for its own army, such as this Uzi gun, as well as medium-range missiles to deter Arab enemies. Military service in the Israel Defence Force (IDF) is compulsory for all Israeli citizens. Men must serve three years, unmarried women two years.

Lake Tiberias, known in the Bible as the Sea of Galilee.

WATER WARS

Water is in very short supply throughout this region. Where water resources are shared (for example, Israel and Jordan share the Jordan River), disputes can occur. Israel leads the way in irrigation techniques. Fields are watered by drip irrigation – holes in pipes dispense exactly the right amount of water required, avoiding wastage.

DEAD SEA MUD

The Dead Sea, 1,300 ft (400 m) below sea level, is an enclosed salt lake. Salt levels are six times higher than in other seas, so no fish live in these waters. The Dead Sea is rich in minerals, some of which have medical properties.

Dead Sea mud is used as a skin conditioner and cure for arthritis

Soap made from Dead Sea mud

KEYBOX

Cotton: Syria's most profitable cash crop is cotton. The area of land devoted to cotton has been expanded in recent years. Look for

Tourism: People come to this region from all over the world to visit archaeological sites, ancient cities, and holy places. Look for

Refugee camps: Palestinian refugees have fled from Israel to Jordan and Lebanon. Many fled to Jordan from Kuwait after the 1991 Gulf War. Look for

🌾 Cereals		⛏ Mining	
Sugar beets		🗼 Oil	
Citrus fruits		🏭 Industrial center	
Vegetable oil		Tourism	
Tobacco		Irrigated agriculture	

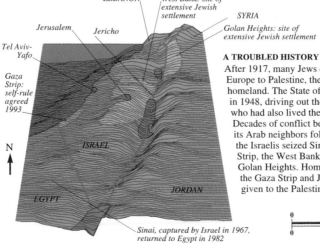

LEBANON
West Bank: site of extensive Jewish settlement
Jerusalem
Jericho
SYRIA
Golan Heights: site of extensive Jewish settlement
Tel Aviv-Yafo
Gaza Strip: self-rule agreed 1993
ISRAEL
JORDAN
EGYPT
N
Sinai, captured by Israel in 1967, returned to Egypt in 1982

A TROUBLED HISTORY

After 1917, many Jews emigrated from Europe to Palestine, their ancient homeland. The State of Israel was created in 1948, driving out the Palestinian Arabs who had also lived there for centuries. Decades of conflict between Israel and its Arab neighbors followed. In 1967 the Israelis seized Sinai, the Gaza Strip, the West Bank, and the Golan Heights. Home rule of the Gaza Strip and Jericho was given to the Palestinians in 1994.

S I N
Gulf of Suez

N

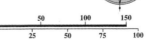

0	50	100	150	
				KM
0	25	50	75	100
				MILES

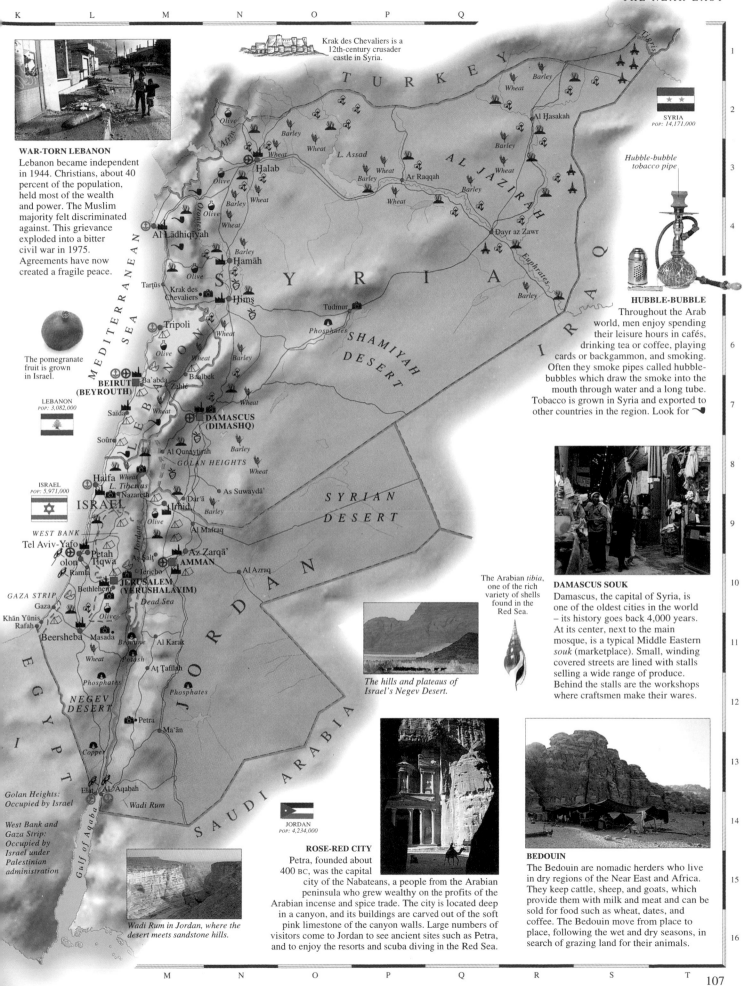

K L M N O P Q

Krak des Chevaliers is a
12th-century crusader
castle in Syria.

T U R K E Y

Barley

Wheat

Al Hasakah

Barley

SYRIA
POP: 14,171,000

A L J A Z I R A H

Olive

Barley

Wheat

L. Assad

Wheat

Ar Raqqah

Wheat

Barley

Barley

Halab

Olive

Barley

Wheat

Wheat

*Hubble-bubble
tobacco pipe*

Al Lādhiqīyah

Olive

Barley

Wheat

Hamāh

Dayr az Zawr

I R A Q

Tartūs

Olive

Krak des
Chevaliers

Hims

Tudmur

S Y R I A

Euphrates

Tripoli

Phosphates

Barley

Wheat

Olive

SHAMIYAH

DESERT

HUBBLE-BUBBLE
Throughout the Arab
world, men enjoy spending
their leisure hours in cafés,
drinking tea or coffee, playing
cards or backgammon, and smoking.
Often they smoke pipes called hubble-
bubbles which draw the smoke into the
mouth through water and a long tube.
Tobacco is grown in Syria and exported to
other countries in the region. Look for ⤳

The pomegranate
fruit is grown
in Israel.

BEIRUT
(BEYROUTH)

Ba'abda
Zahlé
Baalbek

Wheat

Barley

DAMASCUS
(DIMASHQ)

Barley

Al Quņaytirah

Wheat

LEBANON
POP: 3,082,000

Saïda

Soûr

GOLAN HEIGHTS

Wheat

SYRIAN

DESERT

ISRAEL
POP: 5,971,000

Haifa
L. Tiberias
Nazareth

Wheat

Dar'ā

Barley

Irbid

As Suwaydā'

ISRAEL

WEST BANK

Tel Aviv-Yafo

Olive

Al Mafraq

Holon

Petah
Tiqwa

As Salt

Az Zarqā'

Ramla

AMMAN

Al Azraq

J O R D A N

Jericho

JERUSALEM
(YERUSHALAYIM)

Bethlehem

Dead Sea

DAMASCUS SOUK
Damascus, the capital of Syria, is
one of the oldest cities in the world
– its history goes back 4,000 years.
At its center, next to the main
mosque, is a typical Middle Eastern
souk (marketplace). Small, winding
covered streets are lined with stalls
selling a wide range of produce.
Behind the stalls are the workshops
where craftsmen make their wares.

GAZA STRIP

Gaza

Khān Yūnis
Rafah

Olive

Beersheba

Masada

Brome

Al Karak

Wheat

Potash

At Ţafīlah

The Arabian *tibia*,
one of the rich
variety of shells
found in the
Red Sea.

N E G E V

DESERT

Phosphates

Phosphates

The hills and plateaus of
Israel's Negev Desert.

Petra

Ma'ān

J O R D A N

Copper

Elat
Al 'Aqabah

Golan Heights:
Occupied by Israel

West Bank and
Gaza Strip:
Occupied by
Israel under
Palestinian
administration

Wadi Rum

S A U D I A R A B I A

JORDAN
POP: 4,234,000

E G Y P T

MEDITERRANEAN SEA

Gulf of Aqaba

Wadi Rum in Jordan, where the
desert meets sandstone hills.

ROSE-RED CITY
Petra, founded about
400 BC, was the capital
city of the Nabateans, a people from the Arabian
peninsula who grew wealthy on the profits of the
Arabian incense and spice trade. The city is located deep
in a canyon, and its buildings are carved out of the soft
pink limestone of the canyon walls. Large numbers of
visitors come to Jordan to see ancient sites such as Petra,
and to enjoy the resorts and scuba diving in the Red Sea.

BEDOUIN
The Bedouin are nomadic herders who live
in dry regions of the Near East and Africa.
They keep cattle, sheep, and goats, which
provide them with milk and meat and can be
sold for food such as wheat, dates, and
coffee. The Bedouin move from place to
place, following the wet and dry seasons, in
search of grazing land for their animals.

WAR-TORN LEBANON
Lebanon became independent
in 1944. Christians, about 40
percent of the population,
held most of the wealth
and power. The Muslim
majority felt discriminated
against. This grievance
exploded into a bitter
civil war in 1975.
Agreements have now
created a fragile peace.

1
2
3
4
6
7
8
9
10
11
12
13
14
15
16

M N O P Q R S T

107

THE MIDDLE EAST

THE WORLD'S FIRST cities developed about 5,500 years ago in the area between the Tigris and Euphrates rivers. The land in this region is dry, but these early people created ingenious irrigation techniques to direct the river water onto their fields of crops. In AD 570, the Prophet Mohammed, founder of the Islamic religion, was born in Mecca in modern-day Saudi Arabia. Islam soon spread throughout the Middle East, where it is now the dominant religion, and then to the rest of the world. In recent years, the discovery of oil has brought great wealth to the region, and with it, rapid industrial and social change. Both Iran and Iraq earn huge revenues from oil, but they have been troubled by dictatorship and political unrest, as well as by a ten-year war. In 1991, the region was devastated by the Gulf War, which brought UN troops to the Middle East to fight against Iraq.

Pistachio nuts   *Aduki beans*   *Green lentils*

Red lentils

Dates

MIDDLE EASTERN FOOD

Chickpeas

Farming in the Arabian peninsula has been transformed by new irrigation methods. Saudi Arabia now exports wheat; the United Arab Emirates exports vegetables. Elsewhere, lentils and chickpeas are the main food crops.

BAGHDAD
Baghdad, Iraq's capital since 1918, has grown dramatically over the last 20 years but was badly damaged during the Gulf War. The city has been rebuilt. Massive monuments to President Hussein once again adorn its streets.

For centuries, Marsh Arabs have lived in the swampy delta of the Tigris and Euphrates.

ARAB DRESS
Kufiyah, *male headdress*   Khimar, *veil worn by women*

In summer, when temperatures in the Gulf reach 122° F (50° C), layers of loose robes and a headdress are worn to make the heat bearable.

Hirz, *amulet charm case*

Aqaal, *used to secure headdress*

ISLAM
Mecca is Islam's holiest place; according to Islamic teaching, every Muslim should make a pilgrimage to the city. Believers should also pray five times a day, give alms to the poor, and fast during the month-long period of *Ramadan*.

MAKING THE DESERT BLOOM
Water, scarce all over this region, is carefully managed. More than 60 percent of the world's desalination plants are on the Arabian peninsula. They are used to extract the salt from seawater to make it drinkable. Look for ◊

KEYBOX

Archaeological sites: *The ancient cities of the Middle East, such as Ur, date back to 3,500 BC. They are the oldest cities in the world. Look for* ▲

Dams: *A series of dams and barrages have been built along the Tigris and Euphrates to provide water for the dry plains of southern Iraq. Look for* ▦

Industrial center: *Saudi Arabia's economy has been dominated by oil. It is seeking to widen its range of industries. Look for* ■

🌾	Cereals	⚒	Oil
🥕	Dates	◊	Gas
🌾	Rice	✚	Carpet weaving
🐟	Fishing	◊	Desalination plants

Camels, known as "ships of the desert," can go for days without water. They are used to carry loads.

YEMEN
Unlike the rest of the Arabian peninsula, Yemen has enough rainfall to water its crops. Most crops are grown on mountain terraces in the highlands. The country is self-sufficient in barley, lentils, sorghum, corn, and coffee. Look for ✦

The minaret of the Great Mosque at Sāmarrā, Iraq.

Yemen's capital, San'ā, dates back to the 7th century.

YEMEN
POP: 14,361,000

IRAQ
POP: 21,882,000

'Annah
Al Ḩadīth
Wādī Ḩawran

JORDAN   SYRIA

SYRIAN DESERT

Wādī al Ghâ

An Nabk

Wādī Ar

EGYPT

Gulf of Aqaba

'Ar 'ar

Tabūk

Al Jawf   *Sakākah*

AN NAFUD

Wheat

Ha'il

HEJAZ

Wheat

Wheat

SAUDI ARABIA
POP: 18,171,000

Yanbu al Baḩr

Wheat

Medina

NEJD

Buraydah

RED SEA

Mecca

Jedda

Tā'if

SA

ARA

Al Bāḩah

ASIR

Wheat

Khaybar

Barley

Abhā

Khamīs Mushayţ

RU

Najrān

Jīzān

Sa'dah

RAMLAT

Kamarān I.

Barley

Ḩajjah

Barley

Ma'rib

SAN'Ā

YE

Ḩodeida

Millet

Al Maḩwīt

Dhamār

HA

Ibb

Ta'izz

Al Bayda

Ataq

Al Mukhā

Labij

Zinjibar

Aden

Bab el Mandeb

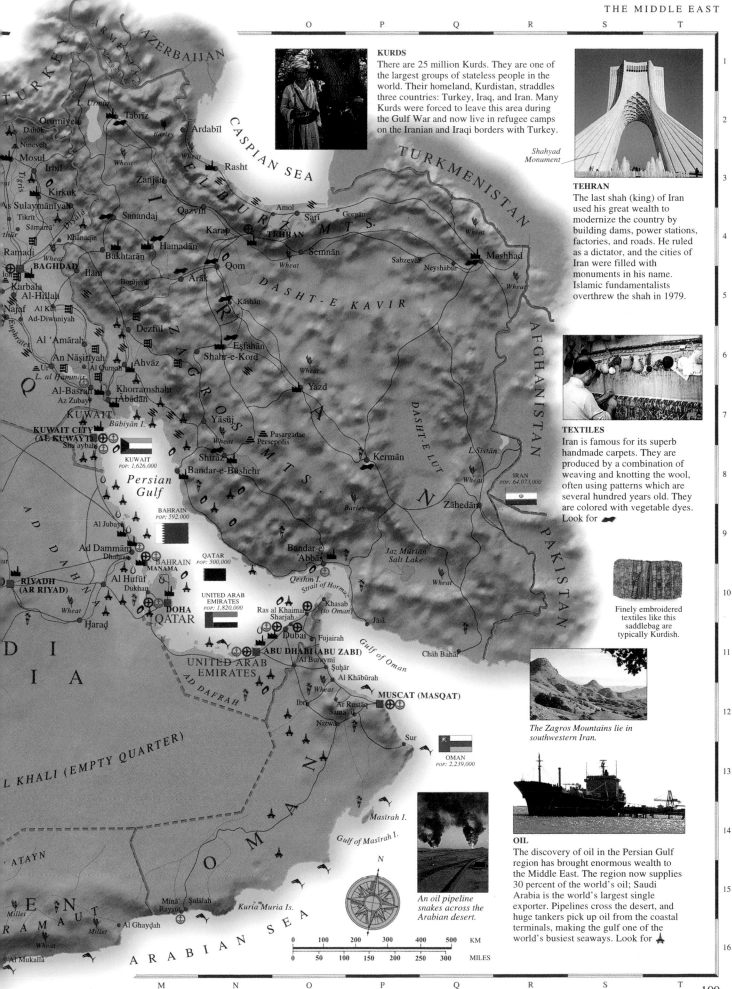

O P Q R S T

KURDS
There are 25 million Kurds. They are one of the largest groups of stateless people in the world. Their homeland, Kurdistan, straddles three countries: Turkey, Iraq, and Iran. Many Kurds were forced to leave this area during the Gulf War and now live in refugee camps on the Iranian and Iraqi borders with Turkey.

Shahyad Monument

TEHRAN
The last shah (king) of Iran used his great wealth to modernize the country by building dams, power stations, factories, and roads. He ruled as a dictator, and the cities of Iran were filled with monuments in his name. Islamic fundamentalists overthrew the shah in 1979.

TEXTILES
Iran is famous for its superb handmade carpets. They are produced by a combination of weaving and knotting the wool, often using patterns which are several hundred years old. They are colored with vegetable dyes. Look for

Finely embroidered textiles like this saddlebag are typically Kurdish.

The Zagros Mountains lie in southwestern Iran.

OIL
The discovery of oil in the Persian Gulf region has brought enormous wealth to the Middle East. The region now supplies 30 percent of the world's oil; Saudi Arabia is the world's largest single exporter. Pipelines cross the desert, and huge tankers pick up oil from the coastal terminals, making the gulf one of the world's busiest seaways. Look for

An oil pipeline snakes across the Arabian desert.

TURKEY
ARMENIA
AZERBAIJAN
CASPIAN SEA
TURKMENISTAN
AFGHANISTAN
PAKISTAN

Orūmīyeh
Dahūk
Nineveh
Mosul
Irbil
Kirkuk
As Sulaymānīyah
Tikrīt
Sāmarrā'
Khānaqīn
Ramadi
BAGHDAD
Karbalā
Al-Hillah
Najaf
Ad-Dīwānīyah
An Nāṣirīyah
Ur
L. al Ḥammār
Al-Basrah
Az Zubayr
Khorramshahr
Ābādān

Tābrīz
Ardabīl
Rasht
Zanjān
Qazvīn
Sanandaj
Hamadān
Bakhtārān
Ilām
Borūjerd
Arāk
Dezfūl
Eṣfahān
Shahr-e-Kord
Yāsūj
Shīrāz
Bandar-e-Būshehr

L. Urmia
ELBURZ MTS.
Amol
Sari
Karaj
TEHRAN
Semnān
Qom
Kāshān
DASHT-E KAVIR
Yazd
Pasargadae
Persepolis
Kermān
Zāhedān
ZAGROS MTS.
DASHT-E LUT
Jaz Mūriān Salt Lake
Bandar-e 'Abbās
Qeshm I.
Strait of Hormuz
Jāsk
Chāh Bahār
L. Sīstān

Gorgān
Sabzevār
Neyshābūr
Mashhad

IRAN
POP: 64,073,000

KUWAIT
KUWAIT CITY (AL KUWAYT)
Shuʻaybah
Būbiyān I.
KUWAIT
POP: 1,626,000

Persian Gulf

BAHRAIN
POP: 592,000
Al Jubayl
Ad Dammām
Dhahran
BAHRAIN
MANAMA
Al Hufūf
Dukhān
QATAR
POP: 500,000
DOHA
QATAR
Ḥaraḍ

RIYADH (AR RIYAD)
AD DAHNA

UNITED ARAB EMIRATES
POP: 1,820,000
Ras al Khaimah
Sharjah
Dubai
Fujairah
ABU DHABI (ABU ZABI)
Al Buraymī
AD DAFRAH
UNITED ARAB EMIRATES

Khasab (to Oman)
Gulf of Oman
Ṣuḥār
Al Khābūrah
Ibri
MUSCAT (MASQAT)
Al Rustāq
Samā'il
Nizwā
Sur

OMAN
POP: 2,239,000

L KHALI (EMPTY QUARTER)
DIA
'ATAYN
E
N
RAMAUT
Minā' Raysūt
Ṣalālah
Al Ghaydah
Al Mukallā

ARABIAN SEA

Masīrah I.
Gulf of Masīrah I.
Kuria Muria Is.

Wheat
Barley
Millet

0 100 200 300 400 500 KM
0 50 100 150 200 250 300 MILES

1 2 3 4 5 6 7 8 9 10 11 12 13 14 15 16

M N O P Q R S T

CENTRAL ASIA

THE CENTRAL ASIAN REPUBLICS lie on the ancient Silk Road between Asia and Europe, and their historic cities grew up along this route. Afghanistan controlled the trade route south into Pakistan and India, through the Khyber Pass in the Hindu Kush mountains. The hot, dry deserts of Central Asia and high, rugged mountain ranges of the Pamirs and Tien Shan were not suited to agriculture. For centuries people lived as nomads, herding sheep across the empty plains, or settled as merchants and traders in the Silk Road cities. When Central Asia became part of the Soviet Union everything changed: local languages and the Islamic religion (which had come to the region from the Middle East in the 8th century) were restricted; irrigation schemes made farming the arid land possible; oil, gas, and other minerals were exploited; industry was developed. Today, these newly independent republics are returning to the languages, religion, and traditions of their past. Afghanistan, independent since 1750, has recently suffered terrible conflict and economic collapse.

Akhal-Teke racehorse

HORSEMEN OF THE STEPPES
The nomadic peoples of the steppes travel great distances on horseback, and horse fairs and races are important events in their calendar. Ashgabat in Turkmenistan is the main breeding center for the Akhal-Teke, a much prized racehorse, which is able to maintain its speed in desert conditions.

UZBEKISTAN
POP: 23,308,000

TURKMENISTAN
POP: 4,260,000

USTYURT PLATEAU

ARAL SEA

Muynak•

L. Sarykamysh

Sulfur

Khodzheyli • Nukus

Zaliv Kara-Bogaz-Gol

Sulfur

Dashkhovuz

Urgench

Krasnovodsk

Cheleken

Nebitdag

Kizyl-Arbat

TURKMENISTAN

Bezmein

Kizyl-Atrek•

ASHGABAT (ASHKHABAD)

IRAN

Tedzhen

CASPIAN SEA

AGRICULTURE
Farming in this dry region depends on irrigation. The Karakum Canal is 683 miles (1,100 km) long – the longest canal in the world. It carries water from the Amu Darya toward the Caspian Sea and waters vast areas of land. Draining the river, however, has reduced the size of the Aral Sea.

Opium poppies are grown all over the region. They provide illegal money for many farmers, who supply the international drug trade.

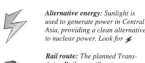

SULFUR
Turkmenistan's sulfur deposits are among the largest in the world. Sulfur is used in the manufacture of gunpowder, medicine, ointment, and drugs. Turkmenistan also has large reserves of oil and gas, but has yet to make money from its substantial resources.

MARKETS
Towns such as Samarkand have changed little since the days of the Silk Road, and are still full of merchants and traders. Bazaars and streetside stalls sell local fruit and vegetables, herbs, spices, silk, and cotton.

Kowl-e-Namaksār

KEYBOX

⚡ **Alternative energy:** *Sunlight is used to generate power in Central Asia, providing a clean alternative to nuclear power. Look for* ⚡

🚂 **Rail route:** *The planned Trans-Asian Railway will connect Beijing and Istanbul via Central Asia and the Caspian Sea. Look for* 🚂

🐂	Cattle	⛑	Mining
🐑	Sheep	🛢	Oil
🍈	Fruit	◖	Natural gas
🌿	Tobacco	〰	Carpet weaving
⚓	Cotton	🏭	Industrial center

Carrots were first grown for food in Afghanistan.

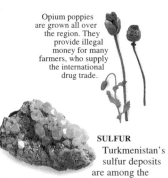

CARPETS
Carpets from Uzbekistan, Turkmenistan, northern Afghanistan, and other parts of this region are world-famous. They are made by hand-knotting and are woven from fine Karakul wool in a range of red, brown, and maroon colors. They follow distinctive geometric patterns. Carpets are used as saddle blankets, tent hangings, and prayer mats. Look for 〰

KARAKUL SHEEP
Karakul sheep are bred for their distinctive curly fleece. They are especially important in Afghanistan. Nomadic people have herded sheep in this region for many centuries. Each summer they take their flocks up to the lush mountain pastures, and in winter they are herded down onto the plains. Look for 🐑

Hāmūn-e-Sā

Gowd-e-Zere

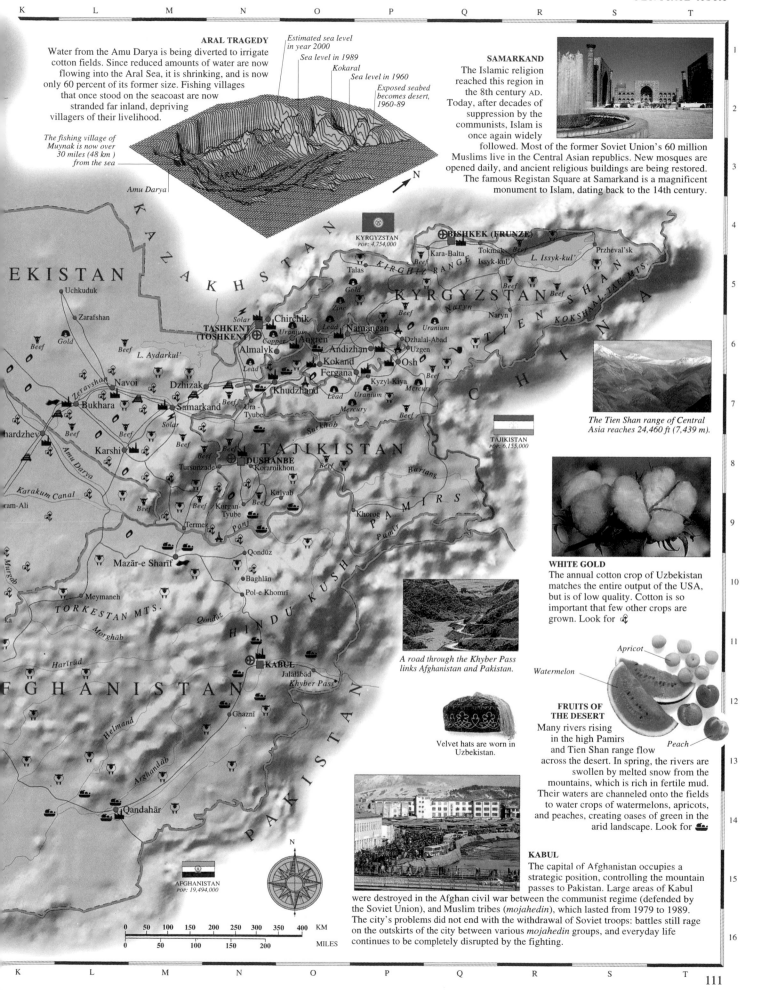

ARAL TRAGEDY

Water from the Amu Darya is being diverted to irrigate cotton fields. Since reduced amounts of water are now flowing into the Aral Sea, it is shrinking, and is now only 60 percent of its former size. Fishing villages that once stood on the seacoast are now stranded far inland, depriving villagers of their livelihood.

Estimated sea level in year 2000
Sea level in 1989
Kokaral
Sea level in 1960
Exposed seabed becomes desert, 1960-89

The fishing village of Muynak is now over 30 miles (48 km) from the sea

Amu Darya

N

SAMARKAND

The Islamic religion reached this region in the 8th century AD. Today, after decades of suppression by the communists, Islam is once again widely followed. Most of the former Soviet Union's 60 million Muslims live in the Central Asian republics. New mosques are opened daily, and ancient religious buildings are being restored. The famous Registan Square at Samarkand is a magnificent monument to Islam, dating back to the 14th century.

The Tien Shan range of Central Asia reaches 24,460 ft (7,439 m).

WHITE GOLD

The annual cotton crop of Uzbekistan matches the entire output of the USA, but is of low quality. Cotton is so important that few other crops are grown. Look for ❧

Apricot
Watermelon
Peach

FRUITS OF THE DESERT

Many rivers rising in the high Pamirs and Tien Shan range flow across the desert. In spring, the rivers are swollen by melted snow from the mountains, which is rich in fertile mud. Their waters are channeled onto the fields to water crops of watermelons, apricots, and peaches, creating oases of green in the arid landscape. Look for 🚣

KABUL

The capital of Afghanistan occupies a strategic position, controlling the mountain passes to Pakistan. Large areas of Kabul were destroyed in the Afghan civil war between the communist regime (defended by the Soviet Union), and Muslim tribes (*mojahedin*), which lasted from 1979 to 1989. The city's problems did not end with the withdrawal of Soviet troops: battles still rage on the outskirts of the city between various *mojahedin* groups, and everyday life continues to be completely disrupted by the fighting.

A road through the Khyber Pass links Afghanistan and Pakistan.

Velvet hats are worn in Uzbekistan.

Map labels:

KAZAKHSTAN

EKISTAN
Uchkuduk
Zarafshan
Beef
Gold
L. Aydarkul'
Navoi
Dzhizak
Zeravshan
Bukhara
Samarkand
Karshi
chardzhev
Beef
Amu Darya
Karakum Canal
ram-Ali
Muynak

TASHKENT (TOSHKENT)
Chirchik
Almalyk
Angren
Uranium
Lead
Copper
Solar
Kokand
Fergana
Khudzhand
Ura Tyube
Lead
Uranium
Mercury
Solar

KYRGYZSTAN
POP: 4,754,000
BISHKEK (FRUNZE)
Kara-Balta
Tokmak
Issyk-kul'
L. Issyk-kul'
Przheval'sk
Talas
KIRGHIZ RANGE
Beef
Gold
Zinc
Namangan
Andizhan
Dzhalal-Abad
Uzgen
Osh
Kyzyl-Kiya
Mercury
Naryn
Naryn
KYRGYZSTAN
TIEN SHAN
KOKSHAAL TAU MTS.
CHINA

TAJIKISTAN
POP: 6,155,000
DUSHANBE
Korarnikhon
Tursunzade
Kulyab
Kurgan Tyube
Termez
Panj
Surkhob
Bartang
Khorog
Pamir
PAMIRS
Beef

AFGHANISTAN
POP: 19,494,000
Mazar-e Sharif
Qonduz
Baghlan
Pol-e Khomri
Meymaneh
TORKESTAN MTS.
Morghab
Harirud
Helmand
Arghandab
Qonduz
HINDU KUSH
KABUL
Jalalabad
Khyber Pass
Ghazni
Qandahar
PAKISTAN
Muryab
Ka

N

0 50 100 150 200 250 300 350 400 KM
0   50   100   150   200 MILES

RUSSIA AND KAZAKHSTAN

THE URAL MOUNTAINS FORM a natural barrier between the European and the Asian parts of Russia. Although over 77 per cent of the country lies in Asia, only 27 per cent of the population live here. Siberia dominates Russia east of the Urals, stretching to the Pacific Ocean and northwards into the Arctic. The climate is severe, parts of Siberia are colder in winter than the North Pole.

Siberia has huge deposits of gold, coal, diamonds, gas, and oil, but workers had to be offered high wages and housing to work there. Today, both Russia and Kazakhstan have great economic potential, but are still coping with a legacy of severe industrial pollution.

HYDROELECTRIC POWER

Siberia's rivers provide 80 per cent of Russia's hydroelectric power, fuelling industry throughout eastern Russia. Massive dams, such as this one on the River Angara, provide the power for the aluminium industry. Look for ⊞

Ear of wheat

VIRGIN LANDS

In the 1950s, the Soviet Union tried to increase grain production. The empty steppes of Kazakhstan, known as the "Virgin Lands", were ploughed up to grow crops. Today, much of this farmland is reverting to steppe. Look for ⸸

KEYBOX

Industrial center: *This region produces one-third of the former USSR's iron and steel. Timber processing is also very important. Look for* 🏭

Pollution: *Nearly 500 Soviet nuclear devices were detonated in Kazakhstan from 1949-1989. Many children in this area are malformed at birth. Look for* ☢

Military bases: *Russia's far East is a highly militarized area. The Russian Pacific fleet is based at Vladivostok. ICBM bases line the southeast border. Look for* ⫴

🌾	*Cereals*	⛏	*Coal*
🔆	*Timber*	🛢	*Oil*
🐟	*Fishing*	🔘	*Gas*
⛏	*Mining*	⊞	*Hydro-electric power*

KAZAKHSTAN
POP: 17,575,000

KAZAKH HORSEMEN

The first inhabitants of the steppe were a nomadic people who travelled on horseback, herding their sheep with them. They slept in felt tents like these, called *yurts*. Their descendants, the Kazakhs, still place great value on horses and riding skills, and horse racing is a popular sport. The Kazakh national drink is *kumiss* – fermented mare's milk. The traditional nomadic lifestyle of the steppe has gradually been replaced by large-scale agriculture and industry.

SPACE CENTER

The Russian space programme is based at Baykonur in Kazakhstan, where this Buran unmanned shuttle was launched in 1988. Russia's achievements in space technology started with the launch of the Sputnik satellite in 1957. Since then, Russia has been responsible for the first man in space, the first woman cosmonaut, and the first space walk. The Mir orbital station has now been in space for over five years.

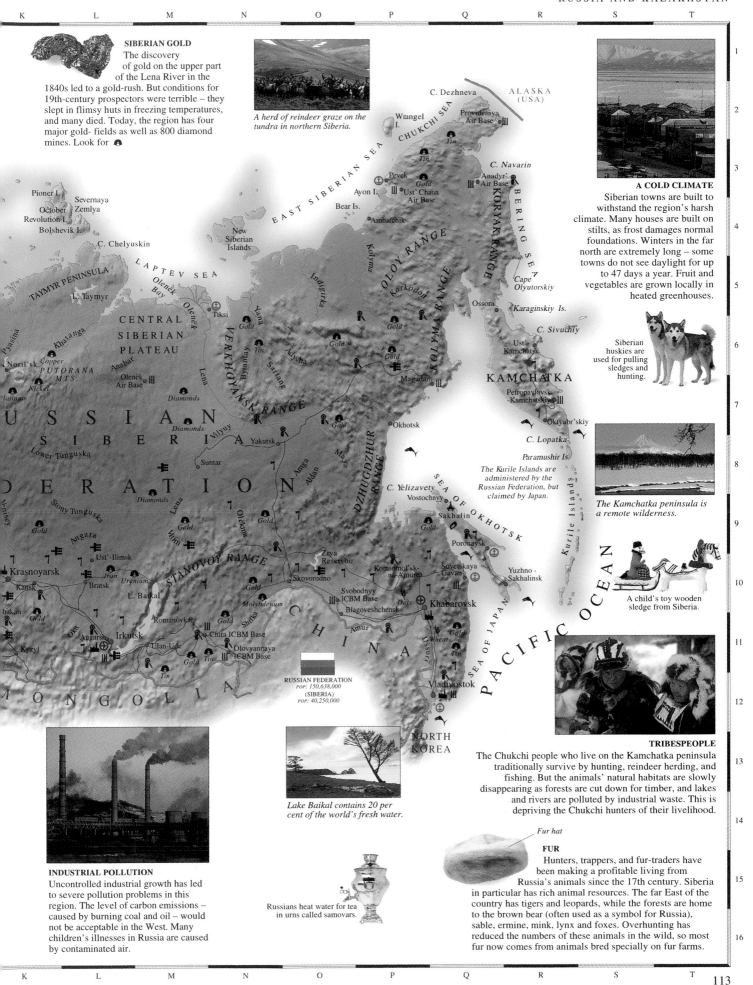

SIBERIAN GOLD
The discovery of gold on the upper part of the Lena River in the 1840s led to a gold-rush. But conditions for 19th-century prospectors were terrible – they slept in flimsy huts in freezing temperatures, and many died. Today, the region has four major gold-fields as well as 800 diamond mines. Look for 🪙

A herd of reindeer graze on the tundra in northern Siberia.

A COLD CLIMATE
Siberian towns are built to withstand the region's harsh climate. Many houses are built on stilts, as frost damages normal foundations. Winters in the far north are extremely long – some towns do not see daylight for up to 47 days a year. Fruit and vegetables are grown locally in heated greenhouses.

Siberian huskies are used for pulling sledges and hunting.

The Kamchatka peninsula is a remote wilderness.

A child's toy wooden sledge from Siberia.

TRIBESPEOPLE
The Chukchi people who live on the Kamchatka peninsula traditionally survive by hunting, reindeer herding, and fishing. But the animals' natural habitats are slowly disappearing as forests are cut down for timber, and lakes and rivers are polluted by industrial waste. This is depriving the Chukchi hunters of their livelihood.

Fur hat

FUR
Hunters, trappers, and fur-traders have been making a profitable living from Russia's animals since the 17th century. Siberia in particular has rich animal resources. The far East of the country has tigers and leopards, while the forests are home to the brown bear (often used as a symbol for Russia), sable, ermine, mink, lynx and foxes. Overhunting has reduced the numbers of these animals in the wild, so most fur now comes from animals bred specially on fur farms.

INDUSTRIAL POLLUTION
Uncontrolled industrial growth has led to severe pollution problems in this region. The level of carbon emissions – caused by burning coal and oil – would not be acceptable in the West. Many children's illnesses in Russia are caused by contaminated air.

Russians heat water for tea in urns called samovars.

Lake Baikal contains 20 per cent of the world's fresh water.

RUSSIAN FEDERATION
POP: 150,638,000
(SIBERIA)
POP: 40,250,000

Map labels:
ALASKA (USA)
C. Dezhneva
CHUKCHI SEA
Wrangel I.
Providentiya Air Base
Pevek
Ayon I.
Gold
Ust' Chaun Air Base
Bear Is.
Ambarchik
Anadyr' Air Base
C. Navarin
KORYAK RANGE
BERING SEA
Cape Olyutorskiy
Ossora
Karaginskiy Is.
C. Sivuchiy
Ust-Kamchatsk
KAMCHATKA
Petropavlovsk-Kamchatskiy
Oktyabr'skiy
C. Lopatka
Paramushir Is.
The Kurile Islands are administered by the Russian Federation, but claimed by Japan.
Kurile Islands
PACIFIC OCEAN
EAST SIBERIAN SEA
Pioner I.
Severnaya Zemlya
October Revolution I.
Bolshevik I.
C. Chelyuskin
New Siberian Islands
TAYMYR PENINSULA
LAPTEV SEA
L. Taymyr
Olenëk Bay
Tiksi
CENTRAL SIBERIAN PLATEAU
Pyasina
Khatanga
Anabar
Olenëk
Olenëk Air Base
Noril'sk
Copper
PUTORANA MTS.
Nickel
Platinum
Lower Tunguska
Diamonds
Lena
Vilyuy
Yakutsk
Diamonds
Suntar
Diamonds
Stony Tunguska
Yenisey
Gold
Gold
Angara
Ust'-Ilimsk
Krasnoyarsk
Kansk
Iron
Bratsk
Uranium
L. Baikal
Romanovka
Molybdenum
Shilka
Chita ICBM Base
Olovyannaya ICBM Base
Gold
Tin
Irkutsk
Angarsk
Ulan-Ude
Kyzyl
Oka
MONGOLIA
Gold
Tin
VERKHOYANSK RANGE
Gold
Yana
Adycha
Indigirka
Sartang
Aldan
Amga
Maya
Olëkma
Vitim
Gold
STANOVOY RANGE
Zeya Reservoir
Svobodnyy ICBM Base
Blagoveshchensk
Skovorodno
Komsomol'sk-na-Amure
Oats
Amur
CHINA
Ussuri
Wheat
Tin
Vladivostok
NORTH KOREA
Khabarovsk
Sovetskaya Gavan
Yuzhno-Sakhalinsk
Poronaysk
Sakhalin
Vostochnyy
C. Yelizavety
SEA OF OKHOTSK
Okhotsk
Magadan
Gold
DZHUGDZHUR RANGE
Korkodon
Kolyma
KOLYMA RANGE
OLOY RANGE
Gold
Tin
Tin
SEA OF JAPAN

113

Komodo dragon
Varanus komodoensis
Length: 10 ft (3 m)

Golden pheasant
Chrysolophus pictus
Length: 3ft (1 m)

King cobra
Ophiophagus hannah
Length: 18 ft (5.5 m)

SOUTH AND EAST ASIA

THE WORLD'S 10 HIGHEST PEAKS, including Mount Everest, are all found in the Himalayas and other mountain ranges in the center of this region. At these altitudes, monsoon rains fall as snow on mountain tops. The melted snow from the mountains feeds some of the largest rivers in the world, such as the Ganges and Irrawaddy, which have created huge deltas where they enter the sea. Fingers of land stretch into tropical seas, and volcanic island chains border the continent. In tropical areas high rainfall and temperatures support vast areas of forest. Inland, a climate of extremes prevails, with baking hot summers and long harsh winters. Cold desert and grassy plains cover much of the interior.

■ ▲ **VOLCANIC ROCK**
This huge granite rock on Sri Lanka was formed in the mouth of a volcano. It is surrounded by forest.

Gingko
Gingko biloba
Height: 100 ft (30 m)

The tiger cowrie is found on coral reefs.

■ ▲ **YOUNG MOUNTAINS**
Himalaya is the Nepalese word for "home of the snows." The range began to form about 40 million years ago – recent in the Earth's history.

■ △ **ISLAND VOLCANOES**
Plants are growing again on the scorched slopes of Bromo in Java, one of a chain of active volcanoes around the southeast Pacific.

■ **TROPICAL RAIN FOREST**
Rain forests grow in layers: an understory with creepers and the main canopy through which tallest trees protrude.

Giant panda
Ailuropoda melanoleuca
Length: 5 ft (1.5 m)

■ **HIDDEN CAVES**
This maze of limestone caves along the Gulf of Thailand has been carved by rainwater.

■ △ **SACRED MOUNTAIN**
Mount Fuji, Japan's highest peak, is surrounded by temperate broadleaf trees. Once an active volcano, Mount Fuji has not erupted for 300 years. The snow-capped summit is the rim of a volcanic crater.

The royal cloak scallop shell is found in the waters of the Pacific Ocean.

■ **MANGROVES IN SILHOUETTE**
Mangroves grow along many coastlines, giving some protection during tropical storms.

Rafflesia
Rafflesia pricei
Width: 3 ft (1 m)

▨ **TROPICAL ISLAND**
There are thousands of tiny coral islands in this region. Many are volcanic in origin, like this one in the South China Sea.

CROSS-SECTION THROUGH SOUTH AND EAST ASIA

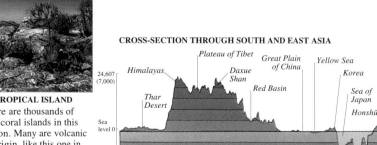

24,607 (7,000)

Sea level 0

-14,764 (-4,500) **A**

Feet (meters)

Himalayas

Thar Desert

Plateau of Tibet

Daxue Shan

Great Plain of China

Red Basin

Yellow Sea

Korea

Sea of Japan

Honshū

Length: 5,000 miles (8,000 km) **B**

□ **COLD HIGH NEPAL**
No trees are to be found above 10,000 ft (3,000 m) in the Himalayas, although dwarf shrubs and grasses can withstand the harsher conditions up to 15,000 ft (4,500 m). Higher still, the rock is bare or covered in snow.

Wild yak
Bos grunniens
Length: 9 ft (3 m)

Gulf of Aden

Somali Basin

Chinese river dolphin
Lipotes vexillifer
Length: 8 ft (2.4 m)

Siberian tiger
Panthera tigris
Length: 8 ft (2.4 m)

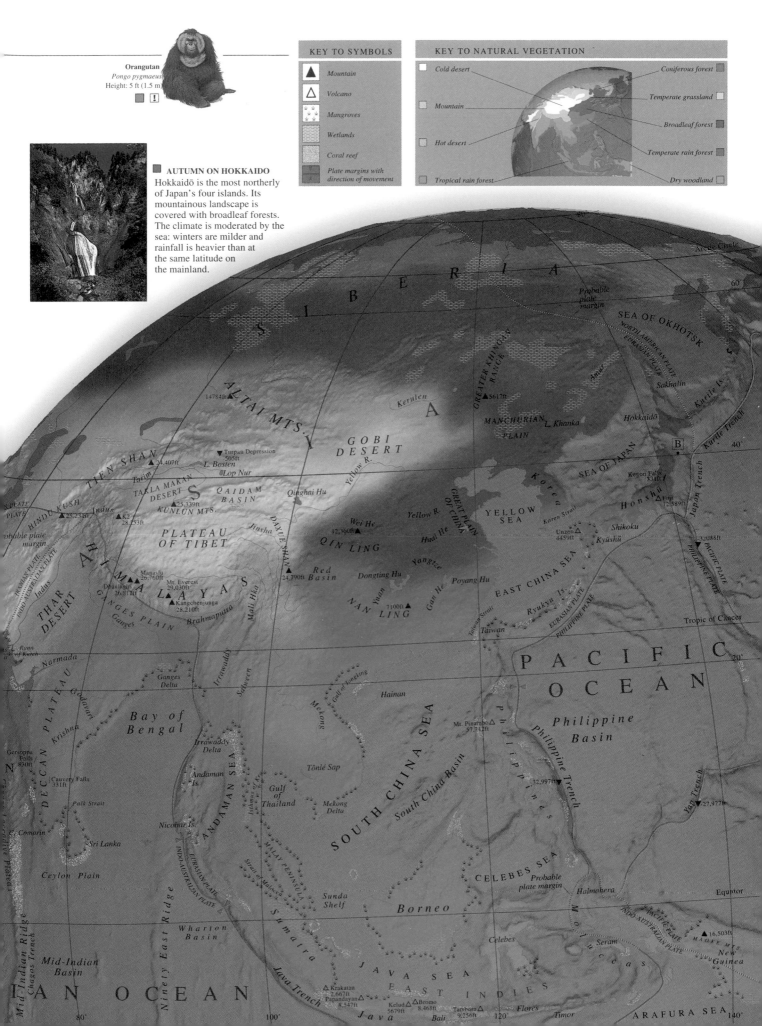

Orangutan
Pongo pygmaeus
Height: 5 ft (1.5 m)
□ !

AUTUMN ON HOKKAIDO
Hokkaidō is the most northerly
of Japan's four islands. Its
mountainous landscape is
covered with broadleaf forests.
The climate is moderated by the
sea: winters are milder and
rainfall is heavier than at
the same latitude on
the mainland.

KEY TO SYMBOLS

▲ Mountain
△ Volcano
🌿 Mangroves
▦ Wetlands
▦ Coral reef
▦ Plate margins with
direction of movement

KEY TO NATURAL VEGETATION

□ Cold desert
□ Mountain
□ Hot desert
□ Tropical rain forest

□ Coniferous forest
□ Temperate grassland
□ Broadleaf forest
□ Temperate rain forest
□ Dry woodland

SIBERIA

Arctic Circle
60

Probable
plate
margin

SEA OF OKHOTSK

NORTH AMERICAN PLATE
EURASIAN PLATE

Sakhalin
Kurile Is.

GREATER KHINGAN RANGE

▲5617ft

Kerulen

MANCHURIAN
PLAIN

L. Khanka

Amur

Kurile Trench

Hokkaidō

B
40

14784ft▲

ALTAI MTS.

GOBI
DESERT

Yellow R.

Korea

SEA OF JAPAN

TIEN SHAN

24,407ft▲
Tarim
L. Bosten
Lop Nur

▼ Turpan Depression
-505ft

TAKLA MAKAN
DESERT

QAIDAM
BASIN

Qinghai Hu

Wei He

Yellow R.

GREAT PLAIN OF CHINA

YELLOW
SEA

Korea Strait

Honshū

Kegon Falls
331ft

Fuji
12,389ft

Japan Trench

▲25,253ft
HINDU KUSH
Indus

▲25,339ft
KUNLUN MTS.

Jinsha

DAXUE SHAN

12,360ft▲

QIN LING

Huai He

Unzen △
4459ft

Shikoku

Kyūshū

PACIFIC PLATE

12,388ft▲

PHILIPPINE PLATE

PLATE

▲K2
28,753ft

PLATEAU
OF TIBET

Red
Basin

Yangtze

EAST CHINA SEA

Probable plate
margin

Manaslu
26,760ft

Mt. Everest
29,030ft

24,790ft▲

Dongting Hu

Yuan

Gan He Poyang Hu

Ryukyu Is.

EURASIAN PLATE

PHILIPPINE PLATE

HIMALAYAS

Dhaulagiri
26,812ft

Kangchenjunga
28,210ft

NAN LING

7100ft▲

Tropic of Cancer

THAR
DESERT

Ganges

GANGES PLAIN

Brahmaputra

Mali Hka

Taiwan

Taiwan Strait

IRANIAN PLATE
INDO-AUSTRALIAN PLATE

Indus

Rann
of Kutch

Narmada

Ganges
Delta

Irrawaddy

Salween

Gulf of Tongking

Hainan

PACIFIC

OCEAN

20

DECCAN PLATEAU

Godavari

Krishna

Mekong

SOUTH CHINA SEA

Mt. Pinatubo △
57,712ft

Philippine
Basin

Gersoppa
Falls
830ft

Cauvery Falls
331ft

Irrawaddy
Delta

Andaman
Is.

Gulf
of
Thailand

Tônlé Sap

South China Basin

Philippines

Philippine Trench

Palk Strait

Nicobar Is.

ANDAMAN SEA

Mekong
Delta

32,997ft▼

C. Comorin

Sri Lanka

MALAY PENINSULA

Yap Trench
-27,977ft

Ceylon Plain

EURASIAN PLATE
INDO-AUSTRALIAN PLATE

Strait of Malacca

CELEBES SEA

Probable
plate margin

Halmahera

Equator

Mid-Indian Ridge

Chagos Trench

Ninety East Ridge

Wharton
Basin

Sumatra

Sunda
Shelf

Borneo

Celebes

Moluccas

Seram

PACIFIC PLATE
INDO-AUSTRALIAN PLATE

MAOKE MTS.

▲16,503ft

New
Guinea

Mid-Indian
Basin

IAN OCEAN

80

JAVA SEA

EAST INDIES

Krakatau
-2,667ft
Papandayan
-8,547ft

Kelud△ △Bromo
5679ft 8,468ft

Java

100

Tambora △
9,256ft

Bali

120

Flores

Timor

ARAFURA SEA

140

THE INDIAN SUBCONTINENT

SOUTH OF THE HIMALAYAS, the world's highest mountains, lies the Indian subcontinent. In the north of the region, the Buddhist kingdoms of Nepal and Bhutan cling to the slopes of the Himalayas. In the south, the island state of Sri Lanka hangs like a teardrop from the tip of India. The subcontinent has been invaded many times: the first invaders were Aryan tribes from the north, whose beliefs and customs form the basis of the Hindu religion. During the 16th century India was united and ruled by the Islamic Mogul emperors. Two centuries later it became a British colony. In 1947 India gained independence, but religious differences led to the creation of two countries – Hindu India and Muslim Pakistan. Eastern Pakistan became Bangladesh in 1971. Today India is an industrial power, but most of the people still live in villages and make their living from tiny farms. In spite of terrible poverty and a population of about 850 million people, India remains a relatively stable democracy.

PAKISTAN
POP: 138,672,000

The Thar Desert, a vast, arid region in India and Pakistan.

Sitar

MOOD MUSIC
Most traditional Indian music is improvised. Its aim is to create a mood, such as joy or sorrow. One of the main instruments is the *sitar*, which is played by plucking seven of its strings. Other strings, which are not plucked, vibrate to give the distinctive sound of Indian music.

PAKISTAN
This bus illustrates a big problem in Pakistan: overpopulation. 95 percent of the people are Muslim, and traditional Islam rejects contraception, so the birthrate is high. 3 million refugees, displaced by the war in Afghanistan, have stretched resources further.

A MARBLE MEMORIAL
The Taj Mahal at Agra in northern India was built in the 17th century by the Mogul emperor, Shah Jahan, as a tomb for his beloved wife. She was the mother of 14 children. Built of the finest white marble, the Taj Mahal is a supreme example of Islamic architecture and one of the world's most beautiful buildings.

KEYBOX

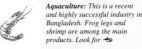

Aquaculture: This is a recent and highly successful industry in Bangladesh. Frog legs and shrimp are among the main products. Look for 🦐

Hiking: Every year some 250,000 hikers visit Nepal, boosting its economy. But the extra visitors are damaging the environment. Look for 👟

Dams: Irrigation on a vast scale in the Indus Valley in Pakistan has sustained and increased the country's food production. Look for 🏯

Cereals		Cotton
Rice		Mining
Sugarcane		Coal
Tea		Industrial center

INDUSTRY
After independence, India started to modernize. It is now one of the most industrialized countries in Asia. Factories make a wide range of goods, from cement to cars. Recently, the manufacture of products like machine tools and electronic equipment has increased. Local cotton is processed in mills like these in Ahmadabad. Look for 🏭

INDIAN FILMS
More films are produced in India than anywhere else in the world – including Hollywood. Bombay is the center of the Indian film industry.

Jewelry, especially silver, is one of India's main exports.

Traditional fishing boats on the coast of Sri Lanka.

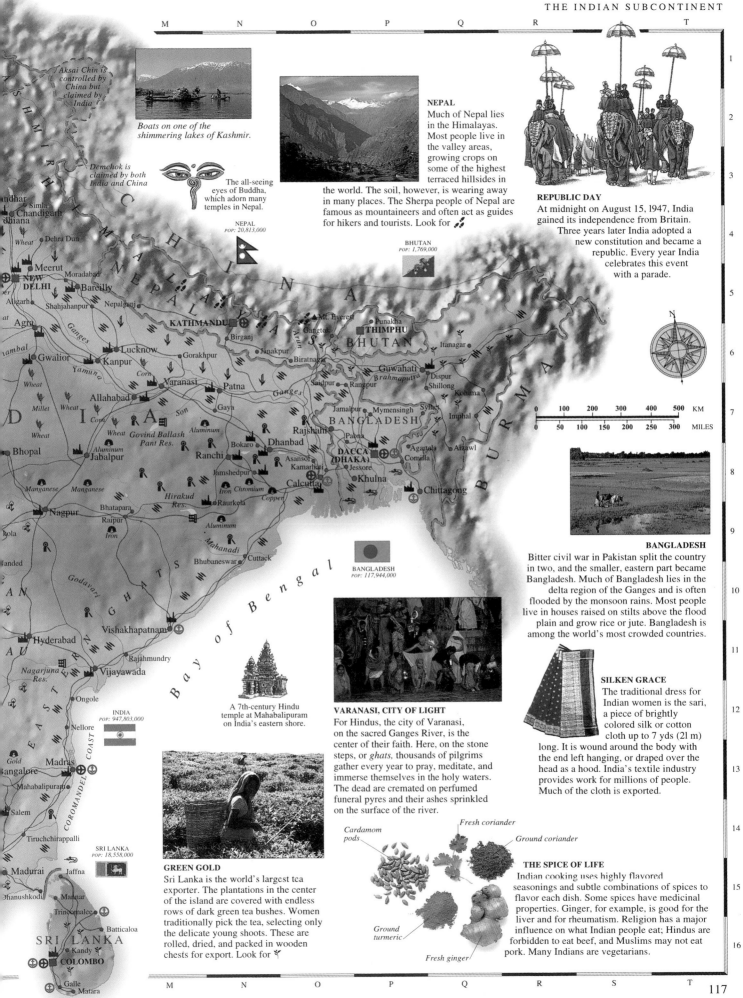

Aksai Chin is controlled by China but claimed by India

Boats on one of the shimmering lakes of Kashmir.

Demchok is claimed by both India and China

The all-seeing eyes of Buddha, which adorn many temples in Nepal.

NEPAL
Much of Nepal lies in the Himalayas. Most people live in the valley areas, growing crops on some of the highest terraced hillsides in the world. The soil, however, is wearing away in many places. The Sherpa people of Nepal are famous as mountaineers and often act as guides for hikers and tourists. Look for

NEPAL
POP: 20,813,000

BHUTAN
POP: 1,769,000

REPUBLIC DAY
At midnight on August 15, 1947, India gained its independence from Britain. Three years later India adopted a new constitution and became a republic. Every year India celebrates this event with a parade.

KASHMIR

andhar
Simla
dhiana
Chandigarh
Wheat
Dehra Dun
Meerut
Moradabad
NEW DELHI
Bareilly
Aligarh
Shahjahanpur
Nepalganj
at Agra
Ganges
Lucknow
Gorakhpur
Gwalior
Kanpur
Yamuna
Corn
Varanasi
Patna
Wheat
Allahabad
Son
Gaya
D I A
Millet
Wheat
Corn
Wheat
Bhopal
Govind Ballash Pant Res.
Aluminum
Jabalpur
Aluminum
Bokaro
Dhanbad
Ranchi
Jamshedpur
Manganese
Manganese
Iron
Chromium
Hirakud Res.
Raurkela
Coppe
Nagpur
Bhatapara
Raipur
Iron
Aluminum
Bhubaneswar
Cuttack
Mahanadi
Godavari
Nagarjuna Res.
Hyderabad
Vishakhapatnam
Rajahmundry
Vijayawada
Ongole
Nellore
Gold
Madras
angalore
Mahabalipuram
Salem
Tiruchirappalli
Madurai
Jaffna
Dhanushkodi
Mannar
Trincomalee
SRI LANKA
Batticaloa
Kandy
COLOMBO
Galle
Matara

KATHMANDU
Birganj
Janakpur
Biratnagar
Mt. Everest
Gangtok
Punakha
THIMPHU
BHUTAN
Itanagar
Saidpur
Rangpur
Dispur
Shillong
Kohima
Guwahati
Brahmaputra
Jamalpur
Mymensingh
Sylhet
Imphal
BANGLADESH
Rajshahi
Pabna
Agartala
DACCA (DHAKA)
Comilla
Asansol
Jessore
Kamarhati
Calcutta
Khulna
Chittagong

B U R M A

Arun
Ganges

BANGLADESH
POP: 117,944,000

N
0 100 200 300 400 500 KM
0 50 100 150 200 250 300 MILES

BANGLADESH
Bitter civil war in Pakistan split the country in two, and the smaller, eastern part became Bangladesh. Much of Bangladesh lies in the delta region of the Ganges and is often flooded by the monsoon rains. Most people live in houses raised on stilts above the flood plain and grow rice or jute. Bangladesh is among the world's most crowded countries.

SILKEN GRACE
The traditional dress for Indian women is the sari, a piece of brightly colored silk or cotton cloth up to 7 yds (21 m) long. It is wound around the body with the end left hanging, or draped over the head as a hood. India's textile industry provides work for millions of people. Much of the cloth is exported.

Bay of Bengal

A 7th-century Hindu temple at Mahabalipuram on India's eastern shore.

VARANASI, CITY OF LIGHT
For Hindus, the city of Varanasi, on the sacred Ganges River, is the center of their faith. Here, on the stone steps, or *ghats,* thousands of pilgrims gather every year to pray, meditate, and immerse themselves in the holy waters. The dead are cremated on perfumed funeral pyres and their ashes sprinkled on the surface of the river.

INDIA
POP: 947,803,000

SRI LANKA
POP: 18,558,000

EASTERN GHATS
COROMANDEL COAST

GREEN GOLD
Sri Lanka is the world's largest tea exporter. The plantations in the center of the island are covered with endless rows of dark green tea bushes. Women traditionally pick the tea, selecting only the delicate young shoots. These are rolled, dried, and packed in wooden chests for export. Look for

Cardamom pods
Fresh coriander
Ground coriander
Ground turmeric
Fresh ginger

THE SPICE OF LIFE
Indian cooking uses highly flavored seasonings and subtle combinations of spices to flavor each dish. Some spices have medicinal properties. Ginger, for example, is good for the liver and for rheumatism. Religion has a major influence on what Indian people eat; Hindus are forbidden to eat beef, and Muslims may not eat pork. Many Indians are vegetarians.

CHINA AND MONGOLIA

THE REMOTE MOUNTAINS, deserts, and steppes of Mongolia and the northwestern part of China are harsh landscapes; temperatures are extreme, the terrain is rugged, and distances between places are vast. Three large autonomous regions of China lie here – Inner Mongolia, Xinjiang, and Tibet. Remote Tibet, situated on a high plateau and ringed by mountains, was invaded by China in 1950. The Chinese have systematically destroyed Tibet's traditional agricultural society and Buddhist monasteries. Most of China's ethnic minorities and Muslims (a legacy of Silk Road trade with the Middle East) are located in Inner Mongolia and Xinjiang. Roads and railroads are being built to make these secluded areas accessible, and rich resources of coal are being exploited. Mongolia is a vast, isolated country. It became a communist republic in 1924 but has now reestablished democracy. Most people still live by herding animals, although new industries have begun to develop.

In Tibet, written prayers are placed in prayer wheels. These small cylinders are rotated by hand.

Cylinder containing written prayer

MONGOLIAN STEPPES
About half the Mongolian population still live in the countryside, many as nomadic herders. Nomads live in *gers* – circular tents made of felt and canvas stretched over a wooden frame. They herd yaks, sheep, goats, cattle, and camels and travel great distances on horseback.

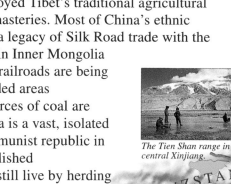

The Tien Shan range in central Xinjiang.

KASHI MARKET
The city of Kashi is located in the far west of China. With its Muslim mosques, minarets, and lively bazaar, it is more like a city in the Middle East than China. Its Sunday market, the biggest in Asia, attracts up to 60,000 visitors. A vast array of goods are sold there: horses, camels, livestock, grains, spices, and cloth.

KEYBOX

Timber: Forests in eastern Tibet have been cut down by the Chinese. Bare hillsides encourage flooding, landslides, and soil erosion. Look for 🌲

Coal: Mongolia is a major exporter of coal to the Russian Federation. There are also open-pit mines in Xinjiang and Inner Mongolia. Look for ⛏

Pollution: Nuclear tests in Xinjiang have caused radiation fallout, pollution, and many birth defects. Look for ☢

🐂	Cattle and yaks	⛏	Mining
🐑	Sheep	🛢	Oil
🌾	Cereals	🏭	Industrial center
🍈	Mixed fruit	🌴	Oases

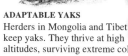

ADAPTABLE YAKS
Herders in Mongolia and Tibet keep yaks. They thrive at high altitudes, surviving extreme cold and even burrowing under snow for grass. Yaks provide milk, butter, meat, wool, and leather. In Tibet, yak butter is served with tea. Look for 🐃

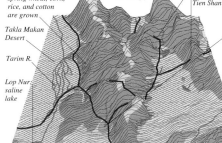

N →

Oases: winter and spring wheat, corn, rice, and cotton are grown

Takla Makan Desert

Tarim R.

Lop Nur: saline lake

Passes through Tien Shan range

Turpan oasis: fruit and cotton are grown on irrigated land

SILK ROAD OASES
The oases of Xinjiang lie on the edge of the Takla Makan Desert in the foothills of the Tien Shan range. They are watered by melted snow from the mountains and sheltered by warm winds coming down the mountain slopes. Towns grew up next to the oases, which lie along the ancient Silk Road.

The high plateau of Tibet, known as "the roof of the world."

KAZAKHSTAN
ALTAI MTS.
L. Uvs
Ulaangom
L. Hyarga
Beef
Ölgiy
Altay
Wheat
Irtysh
Yaks
Hovd
Har Us L.
Beef
Karamay
Beef
XINJIANG UIGHUR
Shihezi
Yining
Wheat
Kuytun
Ürümqi
Turpan
Beef
Hami
KYRGYZSTAN
TIEN SHAN
AUTONOMOUS
Wheat
Aksu
Wheat
Korla
L. Bosten
Wheat
Corn
Iron
TAJIKISTAN
Kashi
Wheat
Corn
Tarim
Corn
REGION
Lop Nur
AFGHANISTAN
Shache
Wheat
Tarim Basin
TAKLA MAKAN DESERT
C
H
PAKISTAN
KARAKORUM MTS.
Beef
Hotan
Wheat
Wheat
ALTUN MTS.
Lenghu
Da Qai
Beef
KUNLUN MTS.
Golmu
Aksai Chin is controlled by China but claimed by India
Yaks
Iro
Zongtian He
INDIA
Demchok is claimed by both China and India
Yaks
TIBETAN
TANGGULA MTS.
Gar
Yaks
AUTONOMOUS
Tangra Yumco
Siling Co
Yaks
Nam Co
Nagqu
Yaks
GANGDISE RANGE
REGION
Lhasa
Brahmaputra (Yarlung Zangbo)
Wheat
Beef
Xigazê
Nyingchi
Gyangzê
Yamzho Yumco
HIMALAYAS
Nylam
Mt. Everest
Yaks
NEPAL
BHUTAN
IND

N O P Q R S T

NATIONAL GAMES
Horse racing, archery, and wrestling competitions are held all over Mongolia every July 11, the day of the national Nadam festival. Mongols are among the most accomplished riders in the world. They learn to ride as children, and some of the jockeys are only three years old.

MONGOLIA
POP: 2,560,000

STEEL CITY
Railroads were built in the 1950s to transport coal and iron from the north of the country. Baotou is the center of iron and steel production in Inner Mongolia. Look for ⚒

R U S S I A N   F E D E R A T I O N

L. Hövsgöl
Mörön
Egiyn
Copper
Sühbaatar
Darhan
Erdenet
Gold
Orhon
Uldz
Manzhouli
Hulun Nur
Beef
Yakeshi
Hailar
Zalantun
Amur
Argun
G R E A T E R   K H I N G A N   R A N G E

**ULAN BATOR
(ULAANBAATAR)**
Choybalsan
Kerulen
Wheat
Wheat
Zinc
Lead
Ulanhot
Beef
Ondörhaan
Tungsten
Tsetserleg Yaks
Wheat
Yaks
Tungsten
Arvayheer
Saynshand
I N N E R   M O N G O L I A
Beef
Tongliao
Beef

M O N G O L I A
G O B I   D E S E R T
Erenhot
Xilinhot
Chifeng
Beef
Great Wall

Beef
Wheat
Jining
E A S T E R N   C H I N A
N O R T H   K O R E A

Wheat
Iron
Oats
Hohhot
Baotou
Great Wall
BAIDAN JARAN DESERT
Linhe
Wheat
Dongsheng
Wuhai
Wheat
ORDOS DESERT
Yellow R.
CHINA
POP: 1,252,188,000
(NORTHWEST CHINA)
POP: 43,099,600
Y E L L O W   S E A
S O U T H   K O R E A

Great Wall
Great Wall
Wheat
Great Wall
Wheat
Delingha
Qinghai Hu
Gonghe
Xining
Q I N G H A I
B A Y A N   H A R   M T S.
Yaks
ushu
Mekong
Qando
Salween
iks
E A S T E R N   C H I N A
BURMA

THIS MAP SHOWS THE NORTH-WESTERN PART OF CHINA ONLY. THE REST OF CHINA IS SHOWN ON PAGES 120-121.

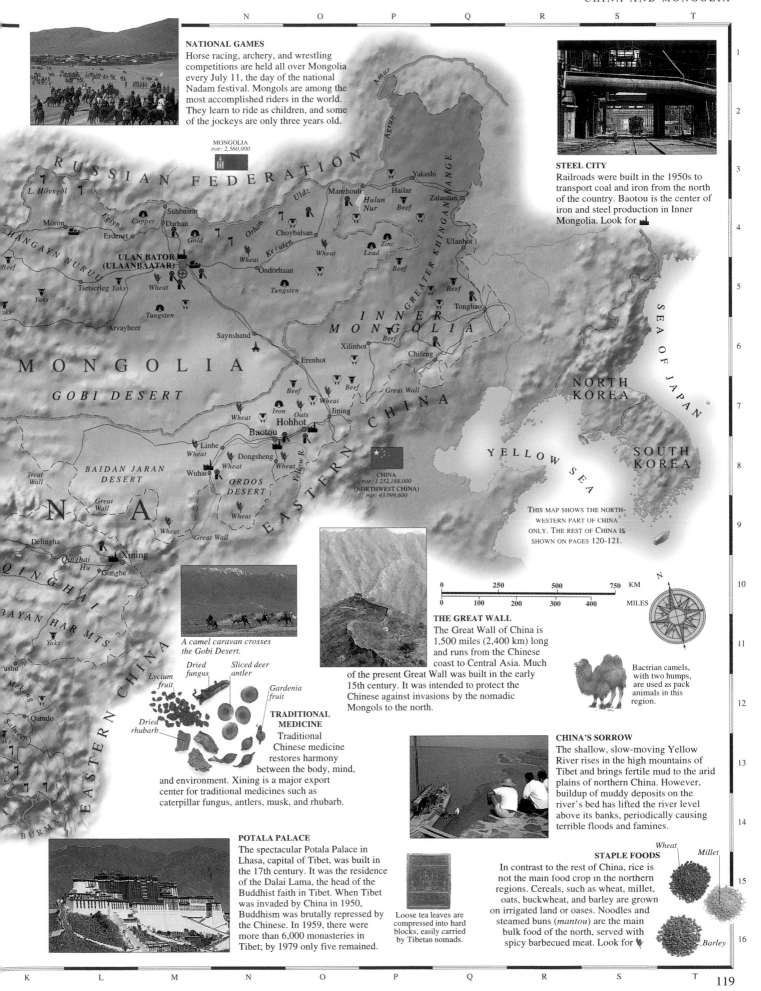

A camel caravan crosses the Gobi Desert.

Dried fungus
Sliced deer antler
Lycium fruit
Gardenia fruit
Dried rhubarb

TRADITIONAL MEDICINE
Traditional Chinese medicine restores harmony between the body, mind, and environment. Xining is a major export center for traditional medicines such as caterpillar fungus, antlers, musk, and rhubarb.

KM
0   250   500   750
0   100   200   300   400
MILES
N

THE GREAT WALL
The Great Wall of China is 1,500 miles (2,400 km) long and runs from the Chinese coast to Central Asia. Much of the present Great Wall was built in the early 15th century. It was intended to protect the Chinese against invasions by the nomadic Mongols to the north.

Bactrian camels, with two humps, are used as pack animals in this region.

CHINA'S SORROW
The shallow, slow-moving Yellow River rises in the high mountains of Tibet and brings fertile mud to the arid plains of northern China. However, buildup of muddy deposits on the river's bed has lifted the river level above its banks, periodically causing terrible floods and famines.

POTALA PALACE
The spectacular Potala Palace in Lhasa, capital of Tibet, was built in the 17th century. It was the residence of the Dalai Lama, the head of the Buddhist faith in Tibet. When Tibet was invaded by China in 1950, Buddhism was brutally repressed by the Chinese. In 1959, there were more than 6,000 monasteries in Tibet; by 1979 only five remained.

Loose tea leaves are compressed into hard blocks, easily carried by Tibetan nomads.

Wheat
Millet
Barley

STAPLE FOODS
In contrast to the rest of China, rice is not the main food crop in the northern regions. Cereals, such as wheat, millet, oats, buckwheat, and barley are grown on irrigated land or oases. Noodles and steamed buns (*mantou*) are the main bulk food of the north, served with spicy barbecued meat. Look for 🌾

CHINA AND KOREA

THE LANDSCAPE OF SOUTHEASTERN CHINA ranges from mountains and plateaus to wide river valleys and plains. One-fifth of all the people on Earth live in China, and most Chinese live in the eastern part of the country. For centuries, China was isolated from the rest of the world, ruled by powerful emperors and known only to a handful of traders. In the 19th century, the European powers and Japan forced China to open its borders to trade, starting a period of rapid change. In 1949, after a long struggle between nationalists and communists, the People's Republic of China was established as a communist state. Taiwan became a separate country. The communist government has encouraged foreign investment, technological innovation, and private enterprise, although calls for democracy have been suppressed. Korea was dominated by its powerful Chinese and Japanese neighbors for many years. After World War II, Korea was divided in two. North Korea became one of the most isolated and repressive communist regimes in the world. South Korea transformed itself into a highly industrialized nation.

PEKING OPERA
Traditional Chinese opera dates back 2,000 years and combines many different elements – songs, dance, mime, and acrobatics. The stories are based on folktales. Makeup shows the characters' personalities – kind, loyal, or wicked, for example.

Sesame oil

Dried mushroom

FOOD
Chinese food varies widely from region to region. Its most famous cuisine comes from the area around Canton and uses a huge range of ingredients – it is said that people from this region will "eat anything with wings except airplanes and anything with legs except the table". Chinese food has become popular all over the world.

Soy sauce

Dried prawn

INDUSTRY
Although China has extensive reserves of coal, iron ore, and oil, its heavy industry is state-run, old-fashioned, and inefficient. 70 percent of China's energy is provided by coal. About half of China's coal comes from large, well-equipped mines; the rest is extracted from small local pits. These mines are notorious for their high accident rates. Look for 🏔

THIS MAP SHOWS THE SOUTH-EASTERN PART OF CHINA ONLY. THE REST OF CHINA IS SHOWN ON PP. 118-119.

The Great Wild Goose pagoda at Xi'an was built in the 7th century AD. It formed part of a Buddhist monastery.

KEYBOX

Hydroelectric power: China's rivers have great potential; dams, lakes, and canals provide flood control and irrigation as well as electricity. Look for ▦

Economic zones: The Chinese government has set up special industrial zones, encouraging foreign investment through tax incentives. Look for 🏭

Refugees: Vietnamese refugees come to Hong Kong by boat. In 1991, there were over 61,000 Vietnamese in Hong Kong's detention camps. Look for ⛺

Borders: The most militarized border in the world divides Korea into communist North and democratic South. Look for ⚔

🌾 Cereals	⬤ Mining
🌾 Rice	🏔 Coal
🌿 Tea	⚓ Oil
🌲 Timber	🏭 Industrial center
🐟 Fishing	⚒ Shipbuilding

BABY BOOM
China's population is now over a billion, stretching resources such as land, food, and education to the limit. Couples with only one child receive various benefits. If a second child is born, these benefits are withdrawn.

Tea, China's national drink, is grown on terraced hillsides in the south of the country.

AGRICULTURE
China feeds its vast population from only 7 percent of the world's farmland. In the fertile southern part of the country, the fields can yield three harvests every year – two crops of rice and a third crop of vegetables or cereals. Look for 🌾

RACIAL MINORITIES
This woman comes from the Hani people, one of the many different ethnic minorities who live in southwest China. Most minority groups live in remote, sparsely inhabited regions. Many still follow traditional lifestyles based on herding, hunting, or growing food for their families.

MONGOLIA

WEST

Yumen

Great Wall

WESTERN CHINA

Wuwei   Yinchuan

NINGXIA HUI AUTONOMOUS REGION

Lanzhou

Wheat

Wheat

Yalong   Dadu He

Litang

Mianyang

Chengdu   Corn

Leshan   Jinsha   Chongqing
Zigong

Xichang

Zunyi

Panzhihua Copper Aluminum Guiyang
           Dongchuan

Dali

Kunming   Corn
           Hongshui He

Gejiu   Corn

Tin   Corn

LAOS   VIETNAM   Pingxiang

MYANMAR (BURMA)

Salween

Mekong

N

| 0 | 100 | 200 | 300 | 400 | 500 | 600 | KM |
| 0 | 100 | 200 | | 300 | | | MILES |

THE DRAGON THRONE
The Hall of Supreme Harmony houses the Dragon Throne, seat of the former emperors of China. It is the largest building in Beijing's Forbidden City and dates back to the 15th century. Ordinary citizens were banned from this area, which was reserved for the emperor and his courtiers. Today, the Forbidden City has been restored and opened to the public; it attracts millions of tourists every year.

北京
The word *Beijing*, written in Chinese. Each symbol stands for a word or an idea.

A jade vase. Jade is China's most precious stone.

COMMUNISM
In the 1960s, China suffered a campaign of terror against artists, politicians, and intellectuals. Although the regime is now more liberal, political messages displayed on walls are often the only way of challenging the government.

GINSENG
Korea exports this precious root, which is widely used in traditional Asian medicine. It is also popular in the West where it is thought to improve health and promote long life and vigor.

Ginseng roots are grown for 4-6 years, then steamed and dried

Rice fields in South Korea. Rice thrives in the mild south.

NORTH KOREA
POP: 24,307,000

CHINA
POP: 1,252,188,000
(SOUTHEAST CHINA)
POP: 1,090,583,000

SOUTH KOREA
POP: 44,516,000

Playing Ping-Pong is a national passion in China.

LAND OF MIRACLES
The Korean economy was devastated by World War II, but during the last 40 years South Korea has undergone an economic miracle. Today, it has a major shipbuilding industry and modern steelworks; cars, computers, televisions, and VCRs pour off production lines. A quarter of all South Koreans live in the capital, Seoul, which has become one of the world's largest cities.

SHANGHAI
The port of Shanghai is the largest city in China. In the 19th century, foreign countries who were involved in trade with China claimed sections of the city. They established commercial buildings and warehouses, giving central Shanghai the appearance of a European city. Today, Shanghai has become important as a center of heavy industry.

The roofs of Wen-wu Temple, on Taiwan's Sun Moon Lake.

THE LITTLE DRAGON
Taiwan has one of Asia's wealthiest economies. The country produces about 10 per-cent of the world's computers and also specializes in textiles and shoe manufacturing. The Taiwanese refer to their country as the Republic of China, but China does not recognize the country under this name.

TAIWAN
POP: 20,800,000

HONG KONG
The rocky island of Hong Kong became a British Crown Colony in the 19th century. In 1997 it will be returned to China, when it will become a "special administrative region." Hong Kong has the busiest container port in the world and is a center of trade, finance, manufacturing, and tourism.

JAPAN

THE LAND OF THE RISING SUN, as Japan is sometimes called, was ruled for centuries by powerful warlords called *shōguns*, who discouraged any contact with the outside world. When traders from America and Europe arrived, Japan's isolation suddenly ended, the *shōgun* was overthrown, and an emperor ruled the country. Over the next century, Japan transformed itself into one of the world's richest nations, a change in fortune all the more remarkable considering the country's geography. Japan consists of four main islands and 4,000 smaller islands. The majority of its 123 million people live closely packed together around the coast, since two-thirds of the land is mountainous and thickly forested. Japan has few natural resources and has to import most of its fuel and raw materials. The Japanese have concentrated on improving and adapting technology imported from abroad. Today, Japanese companies are world leaders in many areas of research and development, a success partly due to their management techniques, which ensure a well paid and loyal workforce.

The Japanese are skilled at bonsai – the art of producing miniature trees and shrubs.

The Kurile Islands are administered by the Russian Federation, but claimed by Japan.

The Hidaka Mountains on the large island of Hokkaido.

FOOD

The Japanese eat a lot of fish because there is not enough farmland to keep cattle for meat or dairy produce.

Lacquer dish

Rice

Seaweed

Marinated raw fish

SHIPBUILDING

A large number of the ships sailing the world today were made in Japan. Countries such as South Korea can now build ships more cheaply, however, and Japan's industry is declining. To remain competitive, Japanese shipbuilders are building specialized ships such as cruise liners and developing new products like oil-drilling platforms. Look for ⚓

JAPAN
POP: 126,320,000

RICE CULTIVATION

Rice is Japan's main food. Although only about 11 percent of the land is suitable for farming, Japan produces enough rice for its own needs. The crop is intensively cultivated on small plots of land using fertilizers and sophisticated machinery, like this rice planter. The warm, wet summers in southern Japan are ideal for growing rice. Look for ⚘

FISHING

Fish is a very popular food in Japan. Huge quantities are caught each year by the country's fishing fleet – the world's largest. One million tons of fish and shellfish are also bred every year on fish farms. These tuna are on sale in Tokyo's fish market. Look for 🐟

KABUKI THEATER

There are two forms of traditional Japanese theater: Noh and Kabuki. Noh is very old: the plays are based on myths of the gods and contain music and symbolic dancing. Kabuki theaters have plays based on stories of great heroes of the past. This photo shows a scene from a Kabuki play.

A miniature television produced in Japan.

TRADITIONAL DRESS

Until the 19th century, Japanese traditional dress varied greatly between the social classes. In the royal courts, long-sleeved robes called *kimonos* were worn. Made of silk, these were wound around the body and tied with a sash. *Kimonos* are still worn on special occasions.

Silk kimono

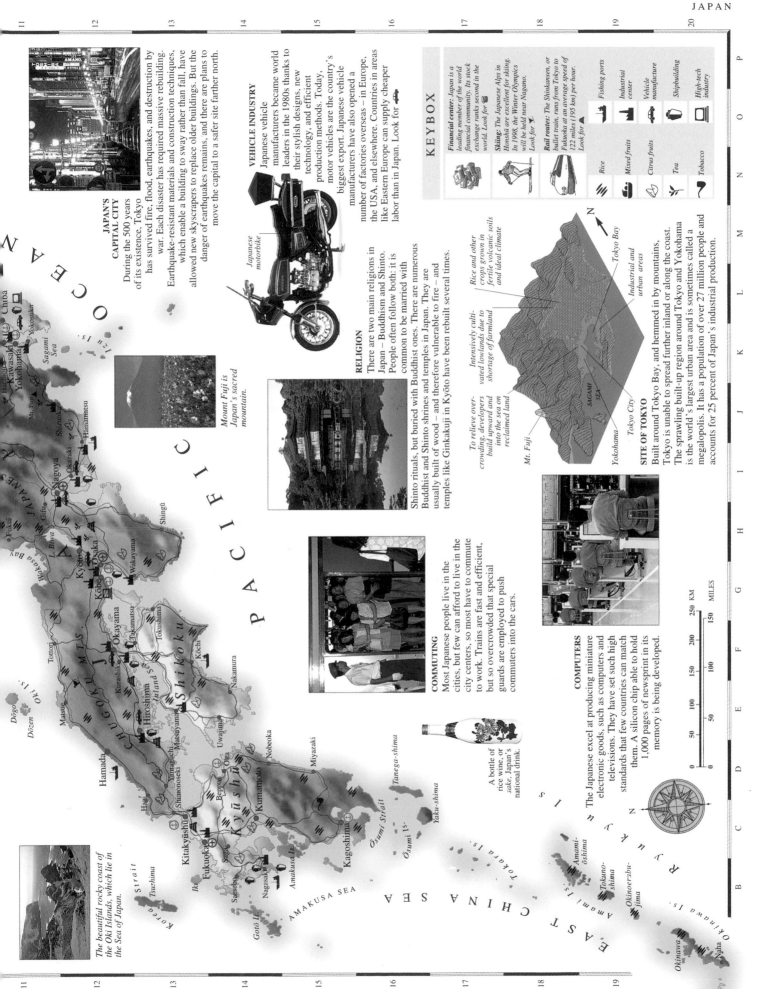

JAPAN'S CAPITAL CITY

During the 500 years of its existence, Tokyo has survived fire, flood, earthquakes, and destruction by war. Each disaster has required massive rebuilding. Earthquake-resistant materials and construction techniques, which enable a building to sway rather than fall, have allowed new skyscrapers to replace older buildings. But the danger of earthquakes remains, and there are plans to move the capital to a safer site farther north.

VEHICLE INDUSTRY

Japanese vehicle manufacturers became world leaders in the 1980s thanks to their stylish designs, new technology, and efficient production methods. Today, motor vehicles are the country's biggest export. Japanese vehicle manufacturers have also opened a number of factories overseas – in Europe, the USA, and elsewhere. Countries in areas like Eastern Europe can supply cheaper labor than in Japan. Look for 🏍

Japanese motorbike

RELIGION

There are two main religions in Japan – Buddhism and Shinto. People often follow both: it is common to be married with Shinto rituals, but buried with Buddhist ones. There are numerous Buddhist and Shinto shrines and temples in Japan. They are usually built of wood – and therefore vulnerable to fire – and temples like Ginkakuji in Kyōto have been rebuilt several times.

Mount Fuji is Japan's sacred mountain.

COMMUTING

Most Japanese people live in the cities, but few can afford to live in the city centers, so most have to commute to work. Trains are fast and efficient, but so overcrowded that special guards are employed to push commuters into the cars.

COMPUTERS

The Japanese excel at producing miniature electronic goods, such as computers and televisions. They have set such high standards that few countries can match them. A silicon chip able to hold 1,000 pages of newsprint in its memory is being developed.

A bottle of rice wine, or sake, Japan's national drink.

SITE OF TOKYO

Built around Tokyo Bay, and hemmed in by mountains, Tokyo is unable to spread further inland or along the coast. The sprawling built-up region around Tokyo and Yokohama is the world's largest urban area and is sometimes called a megalopolis. It has a population of over 27 million people and accounts for 25 percent of Japan's industrial production.

Rice and other crops grown in fertile volcanic soils and ideal climate

Intensively cultivated lowlands due to shortage of farmland

To relieve overcrowding, developers build upward and into the sea on reclaimed land

Industrial and urban areas

Mt. Fuji

Yokohama

Tokyo City

Tokyo Bay

SAGAMI SEA

N

KEY BOX

Financial center: Japan is a leading member of the world financial community. Its stock exchange ranks second in the world. Look for 💻

Skiing: The Japanese Alps in Honshu are excellent for skiing. In 1998, the Winter Olympics will be held near Nagano. Look for ⛷

Rail routes: The Shinkansen, or bullet train, runs from Tokyo to Fukuoka at an average speed of 122 miles (195 km) per hour. Look for 🚄

Fishing ports

Industrial center

Vehicle manufacture

Shipbuilding

High-tech industry

Rice

Mixed fruits

Citrus fruits

Tea

Tobacco

The beautiful rocky coast of the Oki Islands, which lie in the Sea of Japan.

PACIFIC OCEAN

SEA OF JAPAN

EAST CHINA SEA

AMAKUSA SEA

Korea Strait

Izu Is.

Sagami Sea

JAPANESE ALPS

CHUGOKU MTS.

Shikoku

Inland S.

Kyūshū

Ōsumi Strait

Ōsumi Is.

Tanega-shima

Yaku-shima

Ryukyu Is.

Tokara Is.

Amami Is.

Okinawa Is.

Oki Is.

Dōgo
Dōzen

Tsushima

Gotō Is.

Amakusa Is.

Amami-ōshima

Tokuno-shima

Okinoerabu-jima

Okinawa

Chiba
Yokosuka
Kawasaki
Yokohama
Hachioji
Mt. Fuji
Shizuoka
Hamamatsu
Nagoya
Okazaki
Gifu
L. Biwa
Fukui
Wakasa Bay
Kyōto
Ōsaka
Kōbe
Wakayama
Shingū
Okayama
Kurashiki
Hiroshima
Takamatsu
Matsuyama
Tokushima
Kōchi
Nakamura
Tottori
Matsue
Hamada
Yamaguchi
Hagi
Shimonoseki
Kitakyushu
Fukuoka
Saga
Sasebo
Nagasaki
Beppu
Ōita
Kumamoto
Miyazaki
Nobeoka
Uwajima
Kagoshima
Naha

KM
0   50   100   150   200   250
0   50   100   150
MILES

N

MAINLAND SOUTHEAST ASIA

MUCH OF THIS REGION is mountainous and covered with forest. Most of the people live in the great river valleys, plateaus, or fertile plains. Farming is the main occupation, with rice the principal crop. Of the seven countries, only Thailand was not a British or French colony. Thais are deeply devoted to their royal family and the Buddhist faith. The Federation of Malaysia includes 11 states on the mainland, joined in 1963 by Sabah and Sarawak in Borneo. This union of east and west has produced one of the world's most successful developing countries. Singapore, at first part of Malaysia, became a republic in 1965. The island controls the busy shipping routes between the Indian and Pacific oceans. Cambodia, Laos, and Vietnam have all suffered from many years of warfare. Cambodia's future is still uncertain, but the other two countries show signs of economic recovery. Myanmar (Burma) has become increasingly isolated from the world by its repressive government.

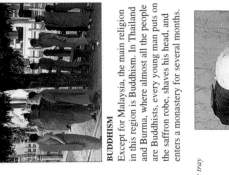

BUDDHISM
Except for Malaysia, the main religion in this region is Buddhism. In Thailand and Burma, where almost all the people are Buddhists, every young man puts on the saffron robe, shaves his head, and enters a monastery for several months.

TIMBER
Thailand was once a major producer of teak, but so much of the country's forests have been cut down that commercial logging was banned in 1989 – until forests recover. Myanmar is now the world's principal teak exporter. Here, huge logs float down the Irrawaddy River. Look for

Lacquer tray

Making lacquer ware is a traditional craft in Thailand.

RUBIES
Several types of precious stones are mined in northeastern Myanmar. The glowing red rubies from this region are considered the finest in the world. Many people in Asia believe that wearing a ruby protects you from harm. Today Myanmar has a virtual monopoly over the ruby trade. Look for

Ruby   *Calcite*

Boats on the Irrawaddy, the great river of Burma.

MYANMAR (BURMA)
pop: 47,502,000

OPIUM
For the poor hill tribes of the "Golden Triangle" – the remote area where Burma, Laos, and Thailand meet – growing opium poppies is one of the few sources of income. Useful painkillers can be made from the poppies, but so too are dangerous drugs such as heroin. Governments are encouraging people in this area to grow other crops, including flowers and tobacco.

Poppy seeds

Dried opium poppy

LAOS
pop: 5,015,000

VIETNAM
Rice is the principal crop in this country. As Vietnam is so mountainous, most people live in the two main river deltas. Two-thirds of the farmed land is devoted to growing rice. The wet field, or *paddy*, is planted by women. Look for

Durian fruit is grown throughout the region.

FISHING
Fish is one of the main foods in this area. Thailand has a thriving fish canning industry. Fish farming on the inland lake of Tônlé Sap, Cambodia, is also successful. Here, in Myanmar, fish are caught from small huts built over the water. Look for

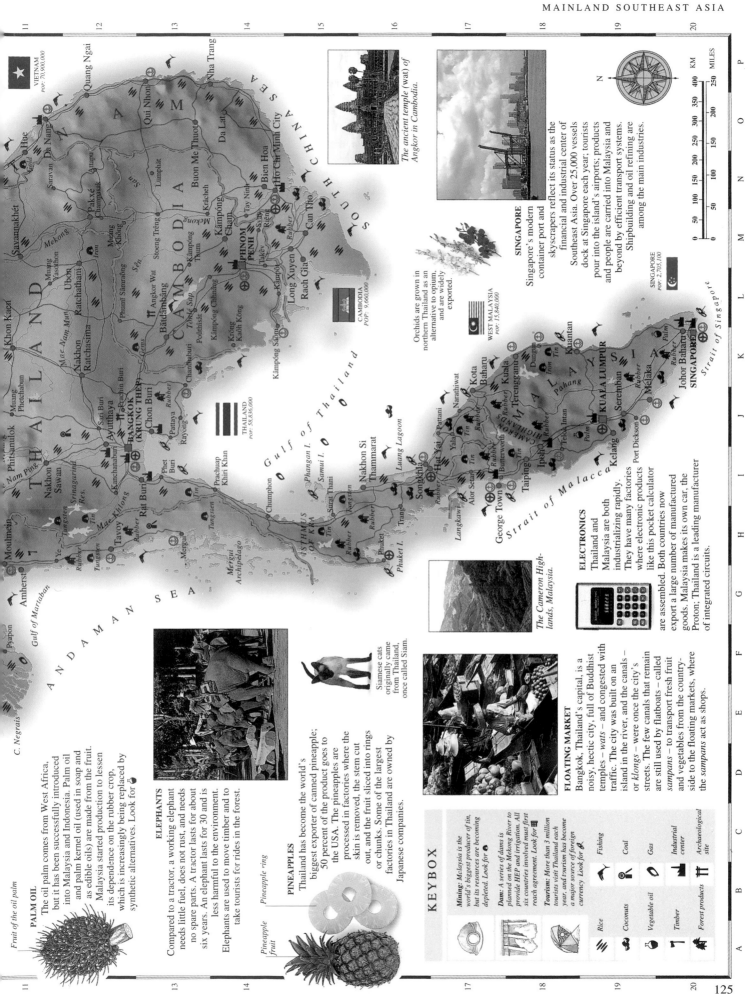

The ancient temple (wat) of Angkor in Cambodia.

SINGAPORE

Singapore's modern container port and skyscrapers reflect its status as the financial and industrial center of Southeast Asia. Over 25,000 vessels dock at Singapore each year; tourists pour into the island's airports; products and people are carried into Malaysia and beyond by efficient transport systems. Shipbuilding and oil refining are among the main industries.

Orchids are grown in northern Thailand as an alternative to opium, and are widely exported.

ELECTRONICS

Thailand and Malaysia are both industrializing rapidly. They have many factories where electronic products like this pocket calculator are assembled. Both countries now export a large number of manufactured goods. Malaysia makes its own car, the Proton; Thailand is a leading manufacturer of integrated circuits.

The Cameron Highlands, Malaysia.

FLOATING MARKET

Bangkok, Thailand's capital, is a noisy, hectic city, full of Buddhist temples – *wats* – and congested with traffic. The city was built on an island in the river, and the canals – or *klongs* – were once the city's streets. The few canals that remain are still used by flatboats – called *sampans* – to transport fresh fruit and vegetables from the country-side to the floating markets, where the *sampans* act as shops.

Fruit of the oil palm

PALM OIL

The oil palm comes from West Africa, but it has been successfully introduced into Malaysia and Indonesia. Palm oil and palm kernel oil (used in soap and as edible oils) are made from the fruit. Malaysia started production to lessen its dependence on the rubber crop, which is increasingly being replaced by synthetic alternatives. Look for ⬤

ELEPHANTS

Compared to a tractor, a working elephant needs little fuel, does not rust, and needs no spare parts. A tractor lasts for about six years. An elephant lasts for 30 and is less harmful to the environment. Elephants are used to move timber and to take tourists for rides in the forest.

Siamese cats originally came from Thailand, once called Siam.

Pineapple ring

Pineapple fruit

PINEAPPLES

Thailand has become the world's biggest exporter of canned pineapple; 50 percent of the product goes to the USA. The pineapples are processed in factories where the skin is removed, the stem cut out, and the fruit sliced into rings or chunks. Some of the largest factories in Thailand are owned by Japanese companies.

KEYBOX

Mining: Malaysia is the world's biggest producer of tin, but its resources are becoming depleted. Look for ⬤

Dam: A series of dams is planned on the Mekong River to provide HEP and irrigation. All six countries involved must first reach agreement. Look for ⬤

Tourism: More than 3 million tourists visit Thailand each year, and tourism has become a major source of foreign currency. Look for ⬤

Rice	Fishing
Coconuts	Coal
Vegetable oil	Gas
Timber	Industrial center
Forest products	Archaeological site

VIETNAM
POP: 70,900,000

CAMBODIA
POP: 9,660,000

THAILAND
POP: 58,836,000

WEST MALAYSIA
POP: 15,840,000

SINGAPORE
POP: 2,705,100

SOUTH CHINA SEA

ANDAMAN SEA

Gulf of Thailand

Gulf of Martaban

Strait of Malacca

Strait of Singapore

ISTHMUS OF KRA

Mergui Archipelago

Map labels:

VIETNAM, CAMBODIA, THAILAND, MALAYSIA, SINGAPORE

Quang Ngai, Qui Nhon, Nha Trang, Da Nang, Hue, Saravan, Pakxé, Champasak, Savannakhet, Buon Me Thuot, Da Lat, Bien Hoa, Tay Ninh, Ho Chi Minh City, Kracheh, Kâmpóng Cham, Can Tho, Stoeng Treng, Kâmpóng Thum, PHNOM PENH, Takêv, Kâmpóng Saôm, Kâmpôt, Long Xuyen, Rach Gia, Kompong Chhnang, Krong Kaoh Kong, Phumi Sâmraông, Bâtdâmbâng, Tônlé Sap, Angkor Wat, Siem Reap, Muang Khong, Ubon Ratchathani, Nakhon Ratchasima, Khon Kaen, Phitsanulok, Nakhon Sawan, Muang Phetchabun, Lomphat, Mae Nam Mun, Chanthaburi, Chon Buri, BANGKOK (KRUNG THEP), Ayutthaya, Pattaya, Rayong, Phet Buri, Prachuap Khiri Khan, Chumphon, Surat Thani, Phangan I., Samui I., Nakhon Si Thammarat, Luang Lagoon, Trang, Phuket I., Hat Yai, Songkhla, Pattani, Yala, Narathiwat, Kota Bharu, Kuala Terengganu, Dungun, Kuantan, Alor Setar, Langkawi, George Town, Butterworth, Taiping, Ipoh, Telok Intan, Kelang, KUALA LUMPUR, Seremban, Port Dickson, Melaka, Johor Baharu, SINGAPORE, Moulmein, Amherst, Ye, Tavoy, Mergui, Pyapon, Srinagarind Res., Phrae, Kanchanaburi, Sări Buri, Prachin Buri, Rāt Buri, Mae Khlong, Nam Ping

C. Negrais

N

KM / MILES
0 50 100 150 200 250 300 350 400
0   50   100   150   200   250

MARITIME SOUTHEAST ASIA

SCATTERED between the Indian and Pacific oceans lies a huge crescent of mountainous tropical islands – the East Indies. The largest country in this region is Indonesia, which was ruled by the Dutch for nearly 350 years. Over half its 13,677 islands are still uninhabited. The island of Borneo is shared between Indonesia, the Malaysian enclaves of Sabah and Sarawak, and the Sultanate of Brunei. Indonesia's national motto, "Unity in diversity," ideally suits a country made up of 362 different peoples speaking over 250 dialects and languages. Indonesia's seizure of East Timor in 1975 has resulted in a long and bloody resistance by the islanders. Java, the main island, is so crowded that thousands of people have been moved to less populated islands. The Philippines, ruled for three centuries by Spain, then for about 50 years by the USA, consists of over 7,000 islands. It is the only mainly Christian country in Asia. Much of the region is covered by forests, which contain some of the finest timber in the world.

COCONUTS
Indonesia and the Philippines are the world's major coconut growers. Every part of the tree has its uses, even the leaves. The kernel is dried to make copra, from which a valuable oil is obtained. Look for 🥥
Kernel

STILT VILLAGES
Many of the villages in this region are built over water. The houses are made of local materials like wood and bamboo and built on stilts to protect them from vermin and flooding. For houses built on land, raised floors also provide shelter for the owner's animals which live underneath.

Helicopter

AIRCRAFT INDUSTRY
Indonesia has developed a thriving aircraft industry. About 12,000 workers assemble helicopters and aircraft at Bandung in Java. The factories are jointly owned by five international aircraft manufacturers. The first solely Indonesian-designed aircraft will soon be completed.

BRUNEI
The Sultanate of Brunei became rich when oil was discovered in 1929. This golden-domed mosque, built with the country's newfound wealth, towers above the capital, Bandar Seri Begawan. The small, predominantly Muslim population pays no taxes and enjoys free education and health care.

MALAYSIA
POP: 17,567,000
(EAST MALAYSIA:
SABAH AND SARAWAK)
POP: 3,360,000

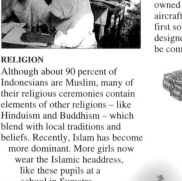
RELIGION
Although about 90 percent of Indonesians are Muslim, many of their religious ceremonies contain elements of other religions – like Hinduism and Buddhism – which blend with local traditions and beliefs. Recently, Islam has become more dominant. More girls now wear the Islamic headdress, like these pupils at a school in Sumatra.

Borobudur, the great 8th-century Buddhist temple on Java.

BRUNEI
POP: 288,000

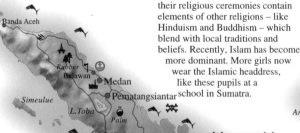
Dense rain forest on Sumatra is home to elephants and tigers.

KEYBOX

Vegetable oil: *Indonesia is now one of the world's major producers of palm oil. It has many uses, from hydraulic brake fluids to cooking oil. Look for* 🫗

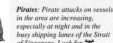
Research center: *Near Manila in the Philippines, the Rice Research Institute has developed many of the world's modern high-yield types of rice. Look for* 🔬

Pirates: *Pirate attacks on vessels in the area are increasing, especially at night and in the busy shipping lanes of the Strait of Singapore. Look for* ☠

	Rice		Fishing
	Coconuts		Mining
	Timber		Oil
	Forest products		Industrial center

JAKARTA
Situated on the island of Java, Indonesia's capital, Jakarta, has the largest population of any city in Southeast Asia – and it is still growing rapidly. It was once the center of the region's Dutch trading empire, and many typical Dutch buildings still stand in the old part of the city. At night, skyscrapers glitter above the city's modern center.

Banda Aceh
Rubber
Balawan
Medan
Pematangsiantar
L. Toba
Palm
Simeulue
Sibolga
Nias
Pini
Padang
Siberut
Batu Is.
Batanghari
Sipura
North Pagai
South Pagai
Rubber
Jambi
Rubber
Enggano
Bengkulu
Rubber
Palm
Tanjungkarang

S u m a t r a
BARISAN MTS

Pakambaru
Lingga
Singkep
Tanjungpinang
Bintan
Strait of Singapore
Bangka
Pangkalpinang
Palembang
Belitung
Tin

Natuna
Natuna Is.
Anambas Is.
Karimata

SOUTH CHINA SEA

Kota Kinabalu
BANDAR SERI BEGAWAN
Miri
Kuala Belait
BRUNEI
MALAYSIA (EAST)
Sibu
Sarikei
Kuching
S A R A W A K
Rajang
TAMADO RANGE
B o r n e o
MULLER MTS
Pontianak
Kapuas
SCHWANER MTS
Rubber
Rubber
Rubber
Rubber
Mendawai
Barito
Rubber
Rubber
Palm
Kualakapuas
Banjarmasin
Rubber

I N D

JAVA SEA
Bawean

JAKARTA
Bogor
Sukabumi
Bandung
Cirebon
Semarang
Borobudur
Yogyakarta
Kediri
Malang
Madura
Surabaya
Jember
Banyuwangi
Kangean
Denpasar
Bali
J a v a

INDIAN OCEAN

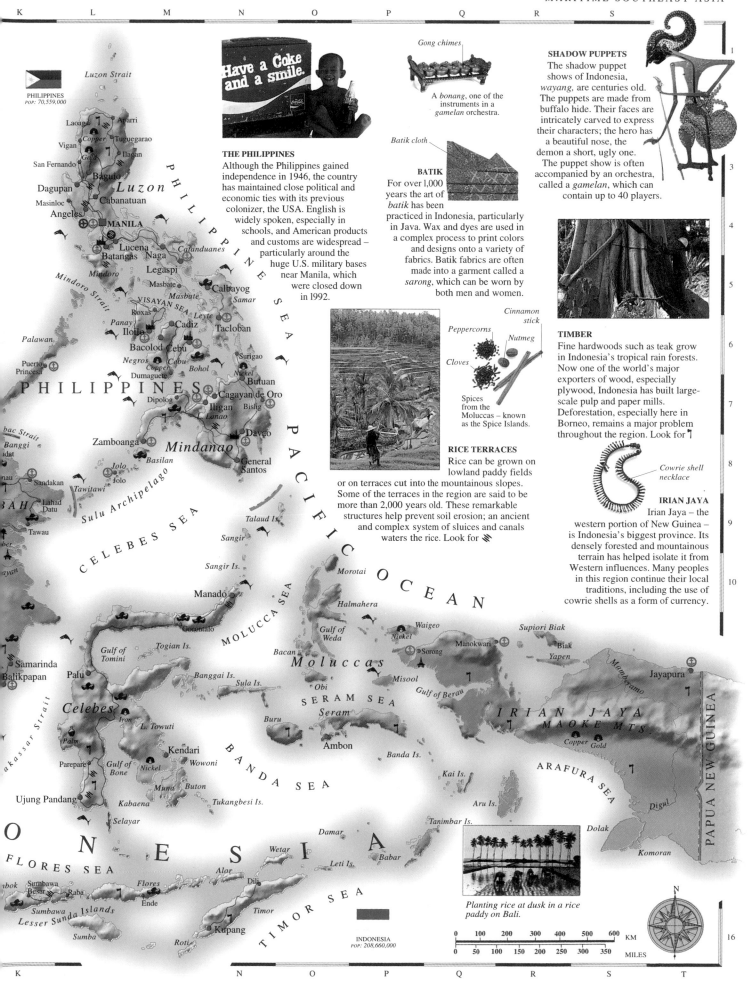

PHILIPPINES
POP: 70,559,000

Luzon Strait

Laoag · Aparri
Vigan · Tuguegarao
· Ilagan
San Fernando
Baguio
Dagupan · Cabanatuan
Masinloc
Angeles · MANILA
Lucena
Batangas · Naga · *Catanduanes*
Legaspi
Mindoro
Masbate
Masbate
Samar
Calbayog
VISAYAN SEA
Roxas · *Leyte*
Panay · Cadiz · Tacloban
Iloilo
Bacolod · Cebu
Negros · Copper Cebu · *Bohol*
Dumaguete · Surigao
Nickel
Dipolog · Butuan
Cagayan de Oro
Iligan · Bislig
Lanao
Davao
Zamboanga · *Mindanao*
General Santos
Iolo · *Basilan*
Iolo
Sandakan
Lahad Datu
Tawau
Sulu Archipelago
Talaud Is.
Sangir
Sangir Is.

Luzon
Mindoro Strait
Palawan
Puerto Princesa
PHILIPPINES
Banggi

PHILIPPINE SEA

CELEBES SEA

Manado
Gorontalo
Togian Is.
Gulf of Tomini
Palu
Samarinda
Balikpapan
Celebes
Iron
L. Towuti
Palu
Kendari
Parepare
Gulf of Bone · Nickel · *Wowoni*
Ujung Pandang
Muna · *Buton*
Kabaena
Tukangbesi Is.
Selayar
Makassar Strait

MOLUCCA SEA

Morotai
Halmahera
Waigeo
Nickel
Bacan
Moluccas
Obi
Sula Is.
SERAM SEA
Seram
Buru
Ambon
Banggai Is.
BANDA SEA
Banda Is.
Kai Is.
Aru Is.
Tanimbar Is.

PACIFIC OCEAN

Sorong
Manokwari · *Supiori Biak*
Biak
Yapen
Misool
Gulf of Berau
ARAFURA SEA
Jayapura
IRIAN JAYA
MAOKE MTS
Copper · Gold
Mamberamo
Digul
Dolak
Komoran

PAPUA NEW GUINEA

I N D O N E S I A
FLORES SEA
Lombok · Sumbawa · Besar · Raba
Flores
Sumbawa · Ende
Lesser Sunda Islands
Sumba
Alor · Dili
Wetar · *Damar*
Babar
Leti Is.
Timor · *Roti*
Kupang
TIMOR SEA

THE PHILIPPINES
Although the Philippines gained independence in 1946, the country has maintained close political and economic ties with its previous colonizer, the USA. English is widely spoken, especially in schools, and American products and customs are widespread – particularly around the huge U.S. military bases near Manila, which were closed down in 1992.

Gong chimes

A *bonang*, one of the instruments in a *gamelan* orchestra.

Batik cloth

BATIK
For over 1,000 years the art of *batik* has been practiced in Indonesia, particularly in Java. Wax and dyes are used in a complex process to print colors and designs onto a variety of fabrics. Batik fabrics are often made into a garment called a *sarong*, which can be worn by both men and women.

Cinnamon stick
Peppercorns
Nutmeg
Cloves

Spices from the Moluccas – known as the Spice Islands.

RICE TERRACES
Rice can be grown on lowland paddy fields or on terraces cut into the mountainous slopes. Some of the terraces in the region are said to be more than 2,000 years old. These remarkable structures help prevent soil erosion; an ancient and complex system of sluices and canals waters the rice. Look for ≈

SHADOW PUPPETS
The shadow puppet shows of Indonesia, *wayang,* are centuries old. The puppets are made from buffalo hide. Their faces are intricately carved to express their characters; the hero has a beautiful nose, the demon a short, ugly one. The puppet show is often accompanied by an orchestra, called a *gamelan*, which can contain up to 40 players.

TIMBER
Fine hardwoods such as teak grow in Indonesia's tropical rain forests. Now one of the world's major exporters of wood, especially plywood, Indonesia has built large-scale pulp and paper mills. Deforestation, especially here in Borneo, remains a major problem throughout the region. Look for ⌐

Cowrie shell necklace

IRIAN JAYA
Irian Jaya – the western portion of New Guinea – is Indonesia's biggest province. Its densely forested and mountainous terrain has helped isolate it from Western influences. Many peoples in this region continue their local traditions, including the use of cowrie shells as a form of currency.

Planting rice at dusk in a rice paddy on Bali.

INDONESIA
POP: 208,660,000

0 100 200 300 400 500 600 KM
0 50 100 150 200 250 300 350 MILES

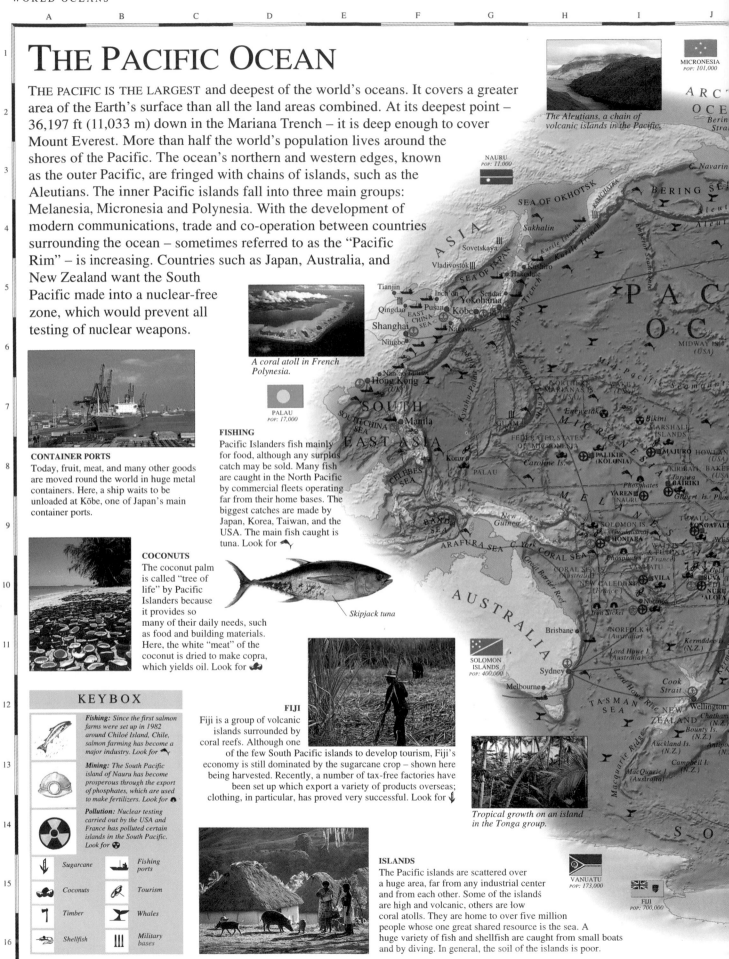

THE PACIFIC OCEAN

THE PACIFIC IS THE LARGEST and deepest of the world's oceans. It covers a greater area of the Earth's surface than all the land areas combined. At its deepest point – 36,197 ft (11,033 m) down in the Mariana Trench – it is deep enough to cover Mount Everest. More than half the world's population lives around the shores of the Pacific. The ocean's northern and western edges, known as the outer Pacific, are fringed with chains of islands, such as the Aleutians. The inner Pacific islands fall into three main groups: Melanesia, Micronesia and Polynesia. With the development of modern communications, trade and co-operation between countries surrounding the ocean – sometimes referred to as the "Pacific Rim" – is increasing. Countries such as Japan, Australia, and New Zealand want the South Pacific made into a nuclear-free zone, which would prevent all testing of nuclear weapons.

MICRONESIA
POP: 101,000

The Aleutians, a chain of volcanic islands in the Pacific.

NAURU
POP: 11,000

A coral atoll in French Polynesia.

PALAU
POP: 17,000

CONTAINER PORTS
Today, fruit, meat, and many other goods are moved round the world in huge metal containers. Here, a ship waits to be unloaded at Kōbe, one of Japan's main container ports.

FISHING
Pacific Islanders fish mainly for food, although any surplus catch may be sold. Many fish are caught in the North Pacific by commercial fleets operating far from their home bases. The biggest catches are made by Japan, Korea, Taiwan, and the USA. The main fish caught is tuna. Look for

COCONUTS
The coconut palm is called "tree of life" by Pacific Islanders because it provides so many of their daily needs, such as food and building materials. Here, the white "meat" of the coconut is dried to make copra, which yields oil. Look for

Skipjack tuna

KEYBOX

Fishing: Since the first salmon farms were set up in 1982 around Chiloé Island, Chile, salmon farming has become a major industry. Look for

Mining: The South Pacific island of Nauru has become prosperous through the export of phosphates, which are used to make fertilizers. Look for

Pollution: Nuclear testing carried out by the USA and France has polluted certain islands in the South Pacific. Look for

Sugarcane		Fishing ports
Coconuts		Tourism
Timber		Whales
Shellfish		Military bases

FIJI
Fiji is a group of volcanic islands surrounded by coral reefs. Although one of the few South Pacific islands to develop tourism, Fiji's economy is still dominated by the sugarcane crop – shown here being harvested. Recently, a number of tax-free factories have been set up which export a variety of products overseas; clothing, in particular, has proved very successful. Look for

Tropical growth on an island in the Tonga group.

SOLOMON ISLANDS
POP: 400,000

VANUATU
POP: 173,000

FIJI
POP: 700,000

ISLANDS
The Pacific islands are scattered over a huge area, far from any industrial center and from each other. Some of the islands are high and volcanic, others are low coral atolls. They are home to over five million people whose one great shared resource is the sea. A huge variety of fish and shellfish are caught from small boats and by diving. In general, the soil of the islands is poor.

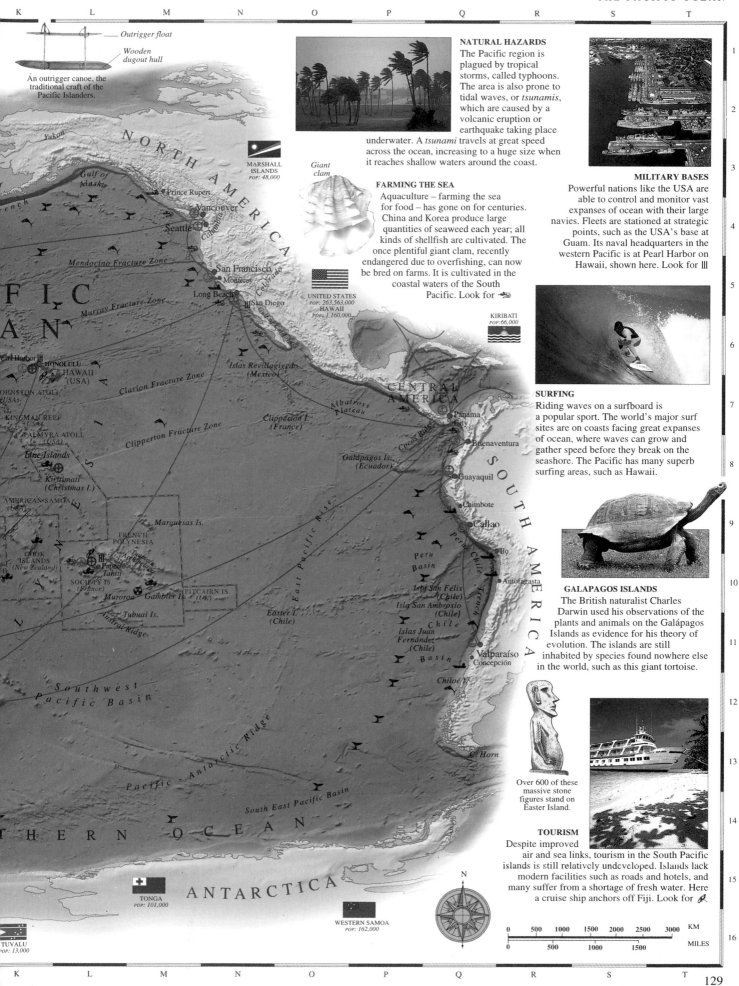

— Outrigger float

Wooden dugout hull

An outrigger canoe, the traditional craft of the Pacific Islanders.

NATURAL HAZARDS

The Pacific region is plagued by tropical storms, called typhoons. The area is also prone to tidal waves, or *tsunamis*, which are caused by a volcanic eruption or earthquake taking place underwater. A *tsunami* travels at great speed across the ocean, increasing to a huge size when it reaches shallow waters around the coast.

Giant clam

FARMING THE SEA

Aquaculture – farming the sea for food – has gone on for centuries. China and Korea produce large quantities of seaweed each year; all kinds of shellfish are cultivated. The once plentiful giant clam, recently endangered due to overfishing, can now be bred on farms. It is cultivated in the coastal waters of the South Pacific. Look for 🐚

MILITARY BASES

Powerful nations like the USA are able to control and monitor vast expanses of ocean with their large navies. Fleets are stationed at strategic points, such as the USA's base at Guam. Its naval headquarters in the western Pacific is at Pearl Harbor on Hawaii, shown here. Look for ⚓

SURFING

Riding waves on a surfboard is a popular sport. The world's major surf sites are on coasts facing great expanses of ocean, where waves can grow and gather speed before they break on the seashore. The Pacific has many superb surfing areas, such as Hawaii.

GALAPAGOS ISLANDS

The British naturalist Charles Darwin used his observations of the plants and animals on the Galápagos Islands as evidence for his theory of evolution. The islands are still inhabited by species found nowhere else in the world, such as this giant tortoise.

Over 600 of these massive stone figures stand on Easter Island.

TOURISM

Despite improved air and sea links, tourism in the South Pacific islands is still relatively undeveloped. Islands lack modern facilities such as roads and hotels, and many suffer from a shortage of fresh water. Here a cruise ship anchors off Fiji. Look for ⚓

MARSHALL ISLANDS
POP: 48,000

UNITED STATES
POP: 263,563,000
HAWAII
POP: 1,160,000

KIRIBATI
POP: 66,000

TONGA
POP: 101,000

WESTERN SAMOA
POP: 162,000

TUVALU
POP: 13,000

| 0 | 500 | 1000 | 1500 | 2000 | 2500 | 3000 | KM |

| 0 | 500 | 1000 | 1500 | MILES |

NORTH AMERICA

Yukon

Gulf of Alaska

Prince Rupert

Vancouver

Seattle

Columbia

Mendocino Fracture Zone

San Francisco
Monterey

Long Beach
San Diego

Colorado

PACIFIC OCEAN

Murray Fracture Zone

Pearl Harbor
HONOLULU
HAWAII
(USA)

JOHNSTON ATOLL
(USA)

KINGMAN REEF
(USA)

PALMYRA ATOLL
(USA)

Line Islands

Kiritimati
(Christmas I.)

AMERICAN SAMOA
(USA)

COOK ISLANDS
(New Zealand)

Papeete
Tahiti
SOCIETY IS.
(France)

FRENCH POLYNESIA

Marquesas Is.

Mururoa
Gambier Is.

PITCAIRN IS.
(UK)

Tubuai Is.

Austral Ridge

MICRONESIA

POLYNESIA

Clarion Fracture Zone

Islas Revillagigedo
(Mexico)

Clipperton Fracture Zone

Clipperton I.
(France)

Albatross Plateau

Galápagos Is.
(Ecuador)

East Pacific Rise

CENTRAL AMERICA

Panama City

Cocos Ridge

Buenaventura

Guayaquil

SOUTH AMERICA

Chimbote

Callao

Ilo

Peru Basin

Peru Chile Trench

Antofagasta

Isla San Félix
(Chile)

Isla San Ambrosio
(Chile)

Islas Juan Fernández
(Chile)

Chile Basin

Valparaíso
Concepción

Chiloé I.

C. Horn

Easter I.
(Chile)

Southwest Pacific Basin

Pacific - Antarctic Ridge

South East Pacific Basin

SOUTHERN OCEAN

ANTARCTICA

N

Koala
Phascolarctos cinereus
Length: 31 in (80 cm)

Funnel-web spider
Atrax robustus
Length: 1 in (3 cm)

Raggiana's bird of paradise
Paradisaea raggiana
Length: 4 ft (1.4 m)

OCEANIA

OCEANIA INCLUDES AUSTRALIA, New Zealand, and numerous island groups in the Pacific. Australia – the smallest, flattest, and driest continent – has been worn down by 3,000 million years of exposure to wind and rain. Away from Australia, along the edges of the continental plates, volcanic activity is common because the plates are still moving. These plate movements greatly affect New Guinea, the Pacific Islands, and New Zealand. Elsewhere in the Pacific Ocean, thousands of tiny coral islands have grown on the tops of undersea volcanic mountains. Climates vary greatly across the region, from the wet tropical climates of the islands in the outer Pacific to the hot, dry deserts of central Australia. Tropical rain forest can be found in northern Australia and on New Guinea.

Cider gum tree
Eucalyptus gunnii
Height: 76 ft (25 m)

Taipan
Oxyuranuus scutellatus
Length: 12 ft (3.6 m)

Giant white buttercup
Ranunculus lyalii
Size: 3 ft (1 m)

SURF AND SAND
Powerful waves from the Tasman Sea wash the southeast coast of Australia, creating long, sandy beaches.

AUSTRALIA'S RAIN FOREST
Over 600 different types of trees grow in the tropical rain forest on the Cape York Peninsula. Mists often hang over the forest.

DESERT MOUNTAINS
For millions of years, erosion has scoured the center of Australia. Mountains like Mount Olga have been reduced to stumps of sandstone.

TROPICAL GRASSLAND
Three great deserts dominate the center of Australia. On the desert margins, some rain falls, enabling scattered trees and grasses to grow.

DRY WOODLAND
Gum trees – otherwise known as eucalyptus – abound in Australia. Many species are adapted to dry conditions, with leaves that hang straight down to avoid the full heat of the sun.

TEMPERATE RAIN FOREST
Far from other land and surrounded by ocean, much of New Zealand has high rainfall and is warm all year round. These conditions encourage the unique plants of the temperate rain forest.

Black opal, a precious stone found in Australia.

△ **HOT NEW ZEALAND**
Steam rises from pools of sulfurous boiling water and mud, signs of volcanic activity along the plate margins. The heat comes from deep within the earth.

THE PINNACLES
Western Australia's weird limestone pinnacles stand out in the sandy desert. Rain and plant roots have shaped the pillars over the last 25,000 years.

CROSS-SECTION THROUGH AUSTRALIA AND OCEANIA

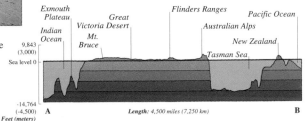

Exmouth Plateau
Indian Ocean
Mt. Bruce
Great Victoria Desert
Flinders Ranges
Australian Alps
Pacific Ocean
New Zealand
Tasman Sea

9,843 (3,000)
Sea level 0
-14,764 (-4,500)
Feet (meters)
A
Length: 4,500 miles (7,250 km)
B

▲ **NEW ZEALAND'S ALPS**
Rising steeply from the coast, the Southern Alps cover 80 percent of South Island. Glaciers moving down the mountains carved deep inlets – fjords – along the southwest coast.

Red kangaroo
Macropus rufus
Height: 6 ft (2 m)

Brown kiwi
Apteryx australis
Height: 14 in (35 cm)

Giant clam
Tridacna gigas
Shell: 5 ft (1.5 m)
!

Butterfly fish
Chaetodon auriga
Length: 8 in (20 cm)

PACIFIC OCEAN

Philippine Basin
Philippine Trench
32,997ft
Yap Trench 27,977ft
Caroline Ridge
Melanesian Basin
Gilbert Ridge
Equator

CELEBES SEA
Celebes Basin
Halmahera
Celebes
Serang
Sumba Flores Timor
Bali

EURASIAN PLATE
PHILIPPINE PLATE
PACIFIC PLATE
Probable plate margin

BISMARCK SEA
New Ireland
Manam 6004ft
Mt. Ulawun 7,861ft
New Britain
Mt. Bagana 5,590ft
29,332ft
Solomon Islands
SOLOMON SEA
BISMARCK RANGE
Mt. Wilhelm 14,784ft
OWEN STANLEY RANGE
New Britain Trench
13,242ft

New Guinea

INDO-AUSTRALIAN PLATE
PACIFIC PLATE
Vanuatu
New Hebrides Trench
West Fiji Basin
Fiji
20,103ft
Probable plate margin

ARAFURA SEA
Torres Strait
CAPE YORK PENINSULA
Great Barrier Reef
Coral Sea Basin
CORAL SEA
New Caledonia
Tropic of Capricorn
South Fiji Basin

TIMOR SEA
ARNHEM LAND
Gulf of Carpentaria
Victoria
Flinders

EURASIAN PLATE
INDO-AUSTRALIAN PLATE

North Australian Basin

KIMBERLEY PLATEAU 2,994ft

TANAMI DESERT

Exmouth Plateau
GREAT SANDY DESERT
Mt. Bruce 4,023ft
GIBSON DESERT
L. Mackay
MACDONNELL RANGES 4,954ft
SIMPSON DESERT
Mt. Olga 3,507ft Uluru 2,848ft
GREAT VICTORIA DESERT
Great Artesian Basin
GREAT DIVIDING RANGE
5,299ft

Lord Howe Seamounts
Lord Howe Rise
New Caledonia Basin
North Island

AUSTRALIA
-52ft L. Eyre
Darling
NULLARBOR PLAIN
L. Torrens
FLINDERS RANGES
Murray

L. Taupo
Ruapehu 9,177ft 40°
New Zealand
SOUTHERN ALPS
Cook Strait

Perth Basin
Pinnacles Desert
Great Australian Bight
Mt. Kosciusko 7,317ft AUSTRALIAN ALPS
Bass Strait
Tasmania

TASMAN SEA

South Australian Basin
South Tasman Rise

Probable plate margin
Sutherland Falls 1,903ft
INDO-AUSTRALIAN PLATE
PACIFIC PLATE
Mt. Cook 12,250ft
South Island
Macquarie Ridge
Campbell Plateau

INDO-AUSTRALIAN PLATE
ANTARCTIC PLATE

SOUTHERN OCEAN

Kerm Trench
PACIFIC PLATE
ANTARCTIC PLATE
Probable plate margin

South Indian Basin
Probable plate margin
Antarctic Circle
ROSS SEA

ANTARCTICA

CORAL ISLAND
Coral grows in warm shallow seas.
Coral reefs surround many Pacific
islands, like this one in Fiji, and
form Australia's Great Barrier Reef.

The southern triton
is common in
Australian waters.

Frilled lizard
Chlamydosaurus kingii
Length: 3 ft (1 m)

KEY TO SYMBOLS
▲ Mountain
△ Volcano
Mangroves
Wetlands
Coral reef
Plate margins with direction of movement

KEY TO NATURAL VEGETATION
Dry woodland
Tropical grassland
Hot desert
Temperate grassland
Tropical rain forest
Mediterranean-type
Temperate rain forest

AUSTRALIA AND PAPUA NEW GUINEA

AUSTRALIA IS A LAND OF EXTREMES. It is the world's smallest, flattest continent, with the lowest rainfall. The landscape ranges from rain forest along the north coast, to arid desert, called the Outback, in the center, to snowfields in the southeast. It is also one of the most urbanized countries; 70 percent of the population lives in towns and cities in the coastal regions, while much of the interior remains sparsely inhabited. Until two centuries ago this vast land was solely occupied by Aboriginal peoples, but in 1788 convict settlers from Britain established a colony on the southeast coast. Since then immigration, especially from Europe, has played a vital part in Australia's development. Australia is a wealthy and politically stable country with rich natural resources, steady population growth, and increasingly strong trade links in the Pacific area, especially with Japan and the USA. Papua New Guinea, the eastern half of the mountainous island of New Guinea, was once an Australian colony, but became independent in 1975.

FLYING DOCTOR
In the Australian Outback, the nearest neighbor can live vast distances away. For a doctor to cover such huge areas by road would be impossible. About 60 years ago, the Royal Flying Doctor Service was established. In an emergency, a caller can contact the service by radio, 24 hours a day, and receive medical treatment within hours.

MINING
Australia has large deposits of minerals such as gold, uranium, coal, and diamonds. The mining of these minerals played an important part in the early development of the continent. Improved mining techniques have led to a resurgence in gold mining in Western Australia. Look for 🪙

Quartz — *Gold*

THE GREAT OUTDOORS
Australia's climate is ideal for watersports and other outdoor activities. But Australians are increasingly aware of the danger of skin cancer because of the hole in the ozone layer above the Antarctic, and are learning to take precautions when in the sun.

Yam

Cassava

Cassava and yam are staple foods in Papua New Guinea.

KEYBOX

Cattle: Australia has about 24 million cattle and exports beef and veal to over 100 countries, especially Japan and the USA. Look for 🐄

Mining: Papua New Guinea has recently become a major producer of gold, which is mined on the mainland and on one of the outlying islands. Look for ⛑

Pearls: Large South Sea pearls are cultivated in oysters in the waters along Australia's northwest coast. These are called "cultured" pearls. Look for 🦪

Symbol	Meaning	Symbol	Meaning
🐑	Sheep		Fishing ports
	Cereals		Coal
	Sugarcane		Industrial center
	Timber		Major airstrips
	Wine		Tourism

FIRST INHABITANTS
Aboriginal peoples believe they have occupied Australia since "before time began." Early Aboriginal societies survived by hunting and gathering. They had their own traditions of storytelling, ceremonies, and art. Today, 66 percent of Aboriginal peoples live in towns. Here, 200 years after the first European settlement, activists march through Sydney demanding land rights. The government has introduced programs to improve Aboriginal standards of living, education, and employment.

The world's finest opals come from northern New South Wales.

WINE PRODUCTION
When Europeans began to settle in Australia, they brought with them skills including winemaking. The British first began to grow grapes in South Australia, which now produces over half the country's wines and brandies. With the continued arrival of Europeans, other grapes were added, including the famous French and German varieties. Grapes are now grown throughout the country, most notably in Western Australia in recent years. Australia is now producing vintages of international quality. Look for 🍇

TIMOR SEA

INDIAN OCEAN

Melville I.
Bathurst I.
Clarence Strait
DARWIN
C. Londonderry
Joseph Bonaparte Gulf
Beef
Wyndham
Victoria
Beef
Collier Bay
C. Leveque
KIMBERLEY PLATEAU
Diamonds
KING LEOPOLD RANGES
Iron
Beef
Beef
Broome
Fitzroy
Halls Creek
Beef
Beef
NOR
Copp
Port Hedland
GREAT SANDY DESERT
TER
Monte Bello Is.
Dampier
Iron
Barrow I.
North West C.
HAMERSLEY RANGE
Iron
Manganese
Ashburton
Iron
L. Mackay
MACDONNE
L. Macleod
W E S T E R N
L. Disappointment
Carnarvon
Gold
GIBSON DESERT
Ulur
Shark Bay
Dirk Hartog I.
Murchison
Gold
Meekatharra
L. Carnegie
L. Wells
A U S T R A L I A
Gold
Gold
GREAT VICTORIA DESERT
Geraldton
Gold
Mount Magnet
Nickel
Nickel
A
Zinc
L. Barlee
Gold
Nickel
Oats
L. Moore
Gold
Kalgoorlie
NULLARBOR PLAIN
Dair
Wheat
Gold
Gold
Nickel
PERTH
Fremantle
Rockingham
Dairy
Gold
Esperance
Great Australian Bight
C. Naturaliste
Dairy
Bunbury
C. Pasley
Augusta
Barley
C. Leeuwin
Albany

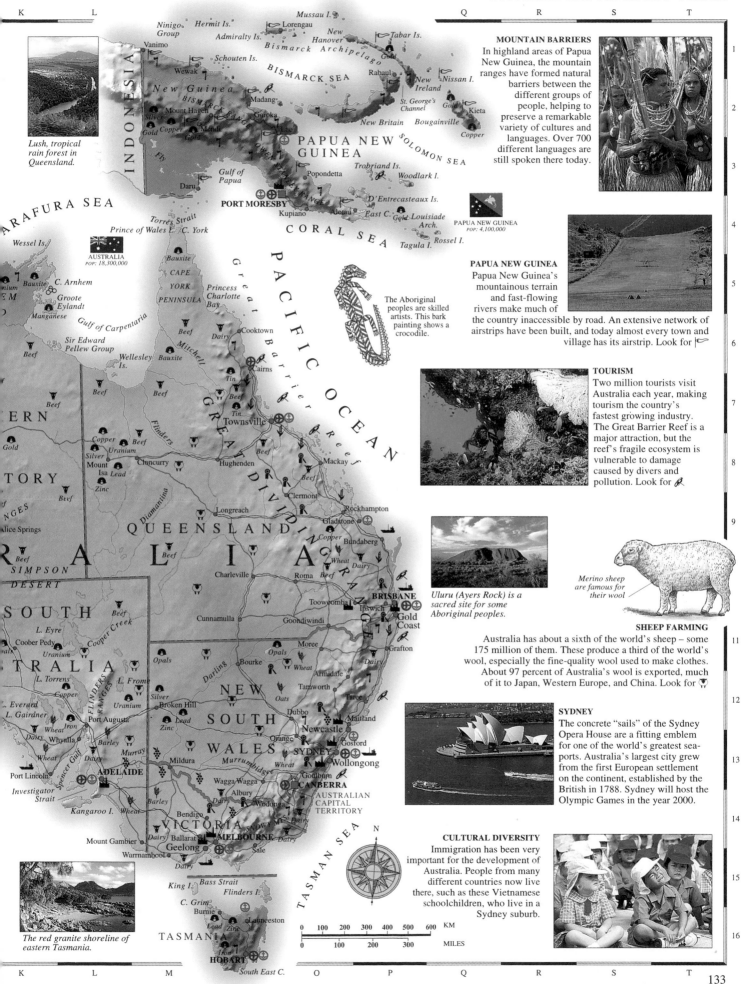

Lush, tropical rain forest in Queensland.

PORT MORESBY

AUSTRALIA POP: 18,300,000

PAPUA NEW GUINEA POP: 4,100,000

The Aboriginal peoples are skilled artists. This bark painting shows a crocodile.

MOUNTAIN BARRIERS

In highland areas of Papua New Guinea, the mountain ranges have formed natural barriers between the different groups of people, helping to preserve a remarkable variety of cultures and languages. Over 700 different languages are still spoken there today.

PAPUA NEW GUINEA

Papua New Guinea's mountainous terrain and fast-flowing rivers make much of the country inaccessible by road. An extensive network of airstrips have been built, and today almost every town and village has its airstrip. Look for ⌐

TOURISM

Two million tourists visit Australia each year, making tourism the country's fastest growing industry. The Great Barrier Reef is a major attraction, but the reef's fragile ecosystem is vulnerable to damage caused by divers and pollution. Look for ✦

Uluru (Ayers Rock) is a sacred site for some Aboriginal peoples.

Merino sheep are famous for their wool

SHEEP FARMING

Australia has about a sixth of the world's sheep – some 175 million of them. These produce a third of the world's wool, especially the fine-quality wool used to make clothes. About 97 percent of Australia's wool is exported, much of it to Japan, Western Europe, and China. Look for ♈

SYDNEY

The concrete "sails" of the Sydney Opera House are a fitting emblem for one of the world's greatest sea-ports. Australia's largest city grew from the first European settlement on the continent, established by the British in 1788. Sydney will host the Olympic Games in the year 2000.

CULTURAL DIVERSITY

Immigration has been very important for the development of Australia. People from many different countries now live there, such as these Vietnamese schoolchildren, who live in a Sydney suburb.

The red granite shoreline of eastern Tasmania.

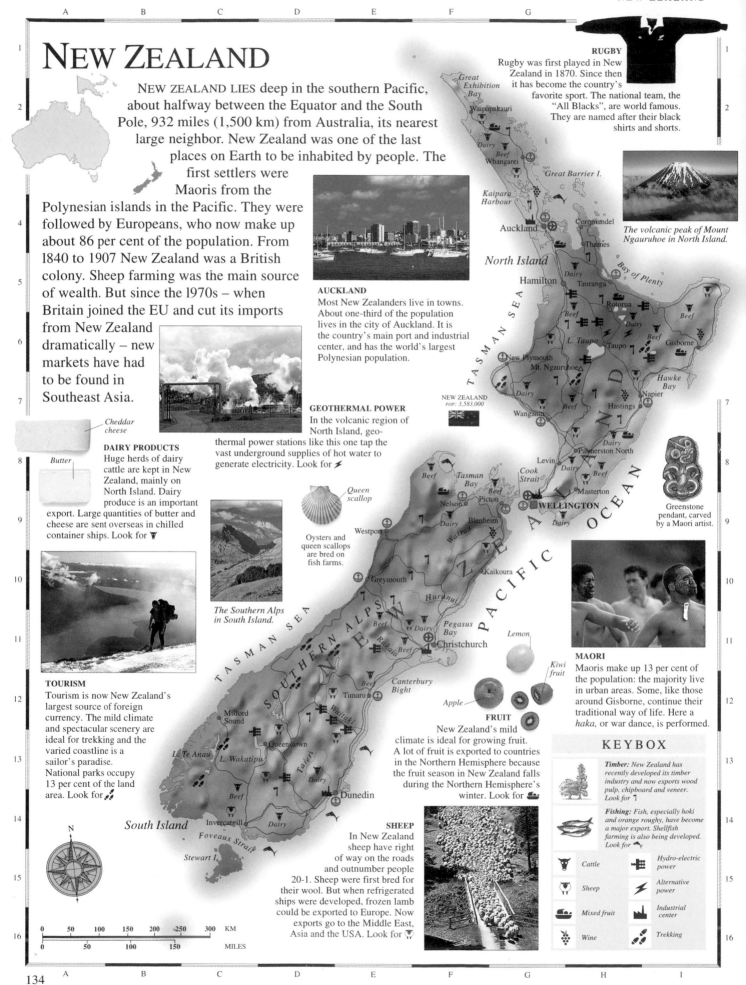

NEW ZEALAND

NEW ZEALAND LIES deep in the southern Pacific, about halfway between the Equator and the South Pole, 932 miles (1,500 km) from Australia, its nearest large neighbor. New Zealand was one of the last places on Earth to be inhabited by people. The first settlers were Maoris from the Polynesian islands in the Pacific. They were followed by Europeans, who now make up about 86 per cent of the population. From 1840 to 1907 New Zealand was a British colony. Sheep farming was the main source of wealth. But since the 1970s – when Britain joined the EU and cut its imports from New Zealand dramatically – new markets have had to be found in Southeast Asia.

RUGBY
Rugby was first played in New Zealand in 1870. Since then it has become the country's favorite sport. The national team, the "All Blacks", are world famous. They are named after their black shirts and shorts.

The volcanic peak of Mount Ngauruhoe in North Island.

AUCKLAND
Most New Zealanders live in towns. About one-third of the population lives in the city of Auckland. It is the country's main port and industrial center, and has the world's largest Polynesian population.

NEW ZEALAND
POP: 3,583,000

Cheddar cheese

Butter

DAIRY PRODUCTS
Huge herds of dairy cattle are kept in New Zealand, mainly on North Island. Dairy produce is an important export. Large quantities of butter and cheese are sent overseas in chilled container ships. Look for ▼

GEOTHERMAL POWER
In the volcanic region of North Island, geothermal power stations like this one tap the vast underground supplies of hot water to generate electricity. Look for ⚡

Queen scallop

Oysters and queen scallops are bred on fish farms.

The Southern Alps in South Island.

TOURISM
Tourism is now New Zealand's largest source of foreign currency. The mild climate and spectacular scenery are ideal for trekking and the varied coastline is a sailor's paradise. National parks occupy 13 per cent of the land area. Look for 👣

Greenstone pendant, carved by a Maori artist.

MAORI
Maoris make up 13 per cent of the population: the majority live in urban areas. Some, like those around Gisborne, continue their traditional way of life. Here a *haka*, or war dance, is performed.

Lemon

Kiwi fruit

Apple

FRUIT
New Zealand's mild climate is ideal for growing fruit. A lot of fruit is exported to countries in the Northern Hemisphere because the fruit season in New Zealand falls during the Northern Hemisphere's winter. Look for 🍱

SHEEP
In New Zealand sheep have right of way on the roads and outnumber people 20-1. Sheep were first bred for their wool. But when refrigerated ships were developed, frozen lamb could be exported to Europe. Now exports go to the Middle East, Asia and the USA. Look for ☖

KEYBOX

Timber: New Zealand has recently developed its timber industry and now exports wood pulp, chipboard and veneer. Look for ⌐

Fishing: Fish, especially hoki and orange roughy, have become a major export. Shellfish farming is also being developed. Look for ◥

🐄 Cattle	╬	Hydro-electric power
♈ Sheep	⚡	Alternative power
🍱 Mixed fruit	🏭	Industrial center
🍇 Wine	👣	Trekking

Map labels:
North Island, South Island, Great Exhibition Bay, Waipapakauri, Whangarei, Great Barrier I., Kaipara Harbour, Auckland, Coromandel, Thames, Hamilton, Bay of Plenty, Tauranga, Rotorua, L. Taupo, Taupo, Gisborne, New Plymouth, Mt. Ngauruhoe, Hawke Bay, Napier, Hastings, Wanganui, Palmerston North, Levin, Masterton, Cook Strait, WELLINGTON, Tasman Bay, Nelson, Picton, Blenheim, Westport, Wairau, Greymouth, Hurunui, Kaikoura, Pegasus Bay, Christchurch, Rakaia, Canterbury Bight, Timaru, Waitaki, Milford Sound, Queenstown, L. Te Anau, L. Wakatipu, Taieri, Dunedin, Invercargill, Foveaux Strait, Stewart I., TASMAN SEA, PACIFIC OCEAN, SOUTHERN ALPS

Beef, Dairy

N

| 0 | 50 | 100 | 150 | 200 | 250 | 300 | KM |
| 0 | 50 | 100 | 150 | | | MILES |

GLOSSARY

This list provides clear and simple meanings for certain geographical and technical terms used in this atlas.

Acid rain Rain which has been made poisonous by industrial pollution.

AIDS (Acquired Immune Deficiency Syndrome). A fatal condition spread by infected blood and certain body fluids.

Alliance A union of nations, which has been agreed by treaty for economic, political, or military purposes.

Alluvium Loose material, such as **silt**, sand, and gravel, carried by rivers.

Alternative energy Sources of energy which can be renewed – including solar or wind power. These forms of energy, unlike fossil fuel energy from coal and oil, do not produce pollution.

Apartheid The policy, developed in South Africa, of separating peoples by race. Non-whites did not have the same democratic rights, and many public institutions were restricted to one race only.

Aquaculture Cultivation of fish and shellfish in lakes, **estuaries**, rivers, or the sea.

Archipelago A group of islands.

Atoll A circular or horseshoe-shaped coral reef enclosing a shallow area of water.

Bilingual Speaking two languages.

Biotechnology The use of living organisms in the manufacture of food, drugs, and other products. Yeast, for example, is used to make beer and bread.

Buddhism A religion that began in India in about 500 BC. It is based on the teachings of Buddha, who believed that good or evil deeds can be rewarded or punished in this life, or in other lives that will follow. Buddhists aim to achieve inner peace by living their lives according to the example set by Buddha.

Cash crop Agricultural produce grown for sale, often for foreign export, rather than to be consumed by the country or locality where it was grown.

Christianity A religion that began in the 1st century BC. Christians believe in one God and follow the teachings of Jesus Christ, whom they believe was the Son of God.

Civil war A war between rival groups of people who live in the same country.

Classical Art, architecture, or literature which originated in the time of the ancient Greeks and Romans.

Colony A territory which belongs to another country. Also a group of people living separately within a country.

Communism An economic and political system of the 19th and 20th centuries in which farms, factories, and the goods they produce, are owned by the state.

Coniferous Trees or shrubs, like pines and firs, which have needles instead of leaves. Most are evergreen.

Conquistador The word is Spanish for "conqueror," and was applied to the Spanish explorers and invaders of Mexico and parts of South America in the 16th century.

Consumer goods Objects such as food, clothing, furniture, cars, and televisions which are purchased by people for their personal and private use.

Continental plates The huge interlocking plates which make up the Earth's surface. A plate margin is an area where two plates meet, and is the point at which **earthquakes** occur most frequently.

Continental shelf The edge of a landmass which forms a shallow, raised shelf in the sea.

Cosmopolitan Influenced by foreign cultures.

Cottage industry The manufacture of products – often traditional ones like textiles or pottery – by people in their own homes.

Crude oil Oil in its original state, before chemicals and other products have been removed by various processes in a refinery.

Crusades A series of wars from the 11th to 13th centuries when Christian European armies fought against non Christian, often Islamic, armies for possession of the Holy Land, or Palestine.

Cultural heritage Anything handed down from a country's past, such as its traditions, art, and architecture.

Currency The money of a particular country.

Deforestation The cutting of trees for timber or clearing of forest for farmland. The land is often left bare, leading to soil erosion and increasing the risk of flooding and landslides.

Democracy A political system in which everyone above a certain age has the right to vote for the election of his or her representatives in the national and local governments.

Desertification The creation of deserts either by changes in climate or by overgrazing, over-population, **deforestation,** or overcultivation.

Developing world Parts of the world which are still undergoing the process of industrialization.

Dictator A political leader who assumes absolute rule of a nation.

Earthquake A trembling or more violent movement of the ground caused by **seismic activity.** Earthquakes occur most frequently along **continental plate** margins.

Economy The organization of a country's finances, exports, imports, industry, agriculture, and services.

Ecosystem A community of plants and animals dependent on each other and on the habitat in which they live.

Electronics The use of electricity to produce signals that carry information and control devices such as telephones or computers.

Emigrant A person who has moved from one country or region to settle in another country or region.

Empire A large group of countries ruled by one person – an emperor.

Equator An imaginary East-West line that circles the middle of the Earth at equal distance from the **Poles.** The Equator also marks the nearest point on the Earth's surface to the Sun, so it has a consistently hot climate.

Estuary The mouth of a river, where the tide's salt water meets the fresh water of the river.

Ethnic diversity People of several different cultures living in the same region.

Ethnic minority A group of people who share a culture and are outnumbered by others living in the same region.

European Union (EU) (or European Community, EC) A group of European countries linked together by treaty to promote trade, industry, and agriculture within a **free-market economy.**

Exports Goods produced in a country but sold abroad.

Fauna Animals of a region.

Flora Plants of a region.

Foreign debt The money owed by one country to the government, banks, or institutions of one or more other countries.

Foreign exchange Money brought into a country from abroad, usually by the sale of **exports,** by **service industries,** or by tourism.

Free-market economy An economy which is regulated by the price of goods bought and sold freely in national and international markets.

Geothermal energy Electricity produced from hot rocks under the Earth's surface. These heat water and produce steam, which can then be used to generate electricity.

Geyser A fountain of hot water or steam that erupts periodically as a result of underground streams coming into contact with hot rocks.

Greenhouse effect A rise in the global temperature caused as heat, reflected and radiated from the Earth's surface, is trapped in the atmosphere by a build up of "greenhouse" gases, such as carbon dioxide. Also called "global warming."

Habitat A place or region where a certain animal or plant usually lives.

Heavy industry Industry that uses large amounts of energy and raw materials to produce heavy goods, such as machinery, ships, or locomotives.

Hunter-gatherers People who do not grow their food, but obtain it by hunting and gathering it from their environment. There are few hunter-gatherer groups left in the world today.

Hydroelectric power (HEP) Electricity produced by harnessing the force of falling water.

ICBM (Intercontinental Ballistic Missile) A missile, usually with a nuclear warhead, that can be fired from one continent to land in another.

Immigrant A person who has come to live in a country from another country or region.

Incentives Something that arouses or encourages people to greater efforts.

Inflation The rate at which a country's prices increase.

Informal economy An economy in which people buy and sell from each other, not through shops or markets.

Infrastructure The buildings, transportation, and communication links that enable goods to be produced and then moved around within a country.

Irrigation A system of watering dry areas. Water is carried or pumped to the area through pipes or ditches.

Islam A religion founded in the Middle East in the 7th century AD by the prophet Mohammed. Its followers, called Muslims (or Moslems), believe in one God – called Allah. The rules and beliefs of Islam are contained in its holy book, the *Koran.*

Islamic fundamentalist A person who strictly follows the rules and beliefs of Islam contained in the holy book, the Koran. See **Islam.**

Isthmus A narrow piece of land connecting two larger bodies of land, surrounded on two sides by water.

Labor intensive An activity which requires large amounts of work or large numbers of workers to accomplish it.

Lent A period of time lasting 40 days observed by Christians during which they fast and prepare for the festival of Easter.

Lignite Woody or brown coal.

Living standards The quality of life in a country, usually measured by income, material possessions, and levels of education and health care.

Malnutrition A prolonged lack of adequate food.

Market gardening Farms and **smallholdings** growing fruit and vegetables for sale.

Megalopolis A very large or continuous urban area in which several large towns or cities have joined as their urban areas have spread.

Metropolis A major city, often the capital.

Militarized zone An area occupied by armed military forces

Multinational company A company which has branches, or factories, in several countries.

Nationalists Groups of people united in their wish for independence from a government or from foreign rule.

Neutral country A country which refrains from taking part in international conflicts.

Nomad A person who does not settle in one place for any length of time, but moves in search of hunting or grazing land.

Oil shale Flaky rock containing oil.

Pastoralist A person who makes a living from grazing livestock.

Peat Decomposed vegetation found in bogs. It can be dried and used as fuel.

Peninsula A strip of land surrounded on three sides by water.

Permafrost Permanently frozen ground. The surface thaws in summer, but water cannot drain away through the frozen subsurface. Typical of **subarctic** areas.

Pharmaceuticals The manufacture of medicinal drugs.

Plantation A large farm on which only one crop is usually grown.

Plate margin See **Continental plates.**

Polar regions The regions around the North and South Poles which are permanently frozen, and where the temperature only rises above the freezing point for a few months of the year.

Poles, the The term applied to the North and South Poles, the northernmost and southernmost points of the Earth's axis or rotation.

Prairie A Spanish/American term for a large area of grassland.

Privatization When state-owned activities and companies are taken over by private firms.

Protestant A member of one of the main Christian religions founded in the 16th century by those who did not agree with all aspects of the Roman Catholic Church. Protestantism became one of the main branches of **Christianity**.

Quota A maximum quantity imposed on the number of goods produced, imported, or exported by a country.

Rain forest Dense forest found in hot and humid equatorial regions; often called tropical rain forest.

Raw materials Substances in a natural or unrefined state used in the manufacture of goods, like cotton for textiles and bauxite for aluminum.

Refugees People who flee their own country or region because of political, religious, or racial persecution.

Republic The form of government in a country that has no monarch. The head of state is usually a president, like the President of the USA.

Reservation An area of land set aside for occupation by specific people, plants, or animals.

Revenue Money paid to a government, like taxes.

Roman Catholic A Christian who accepts the Pope as his or her spiritual leader.

Rural In, or belonging to, the countryside.

Savannah Tropical grasslands where an annual dry season prevents the growth of most trees.

Seismic activity Tremors and shocks in the Earth's crust usually caused by the movement of plates along a fault.

Service industry An industry that supplies services, such as banking, rather than producing manufactured goods.

Shantytown An area in or around a city where people live in temporary shacks, usually without basic facilities such as running water.

Silt Small particles, finer than sand, often carried by water and deposited on riverbanks, at river mouths and harbors. See also **alluvium.**

Smallholding A plot of agricultural land smaller than a farm.

Socialism Political system in which the economy is owned and controlled by the state and not by private companies or individuals.

Soviet bloc All those countries which were ruled directly or indirectly by the communist government of the former USSR.

Staple crop The main crop grown in a region.

Staple food The basic part of a diet, such as rice or bread.

Steppes An extensive, grass-covered and virtually treeless plain, such as those found in Siberia.

Stock Exchange A place where people buy and sell government bonds, **currency,** stocks, and financial shares in large private companies.

Strategic Carefully planned or well placed from a military point of view.

Subarctic The climate in **polar** regions, characterized by extremely cold temperatures and long winters.

Technological The application of science through the use of machines.

Temperate The mild, variable climate found in areas between the **tropics** and cold **polar** regions.

Tropic of Cancer, Capricorn Two imaginary lines of latitude drawn on the Earth's surface above and below the Equator. The hottest parts of the world are between these two lines.

Tropics, the An area between the **Equator** and the **tropics of Cancer and Capricorn** that has heavy rainfall, high temperatures, and lacks any clear seasonal variation.

Tundra Vegetation found in areas within the Arctic Circle, such as dwarf bushes, very short grasses, mosses, and lichens.

United Nations (UN) An association of countries established to work together to prevent wars and to supply aid, advice, and research on an international basis.

Urban area Town, city or extensive built-up area.

West, the Those countries in Europe and North America with **free-market economies** and **democratic** governments.

Western The economic, cultural, and political values shared by countries belonging to **the West**.

Dorling Kindersley would like to thank the following for their help supplying objects for photography: Catherine Lucas, Clare Carolin, Dina Adkins, Clive Webster; Russian Connections for supplying the *draniki* on p.5 and p.80; Mexicolore, London, for skeleton and *sarape* on p.38; Fiat Auto SpA for Fiat Tempra on p.47; Uruguayan Embassy for scarf on p.49; Rosenthal Studio Haus Ltd., London, for glass fruit on p.57; Heal's, London, for child's chair on p.57; Minans Restaurant, London, for *rijstafel* on p.64; Philips Consumer Electronics, London, for television on p.65; BMW (GB) Ltd., Bracknell, for car on p.66; Leica UK, London, for camera on p.67; Watches of Switzerland Ltd., London, for watch on p.69; Hannah Kodicek for puppet on p.70; Henry Marchant Ltd., London, for Bohemian glass on p.70 and ballet costume on p.83; Exico Ltd., London, for wooden duck on p.71; The Greek Shop, London, for doll on p.79; Soccer Scene, London for football shirt on p.73 and rugby shirt on p.134; Gucci, London, for shoes and scarf on p. 72; Embassy of Latvia for currency on p.80; Embassy of Lithuania for currency on p.80; The Russian Shop, London, for chess set, child's toy, lacquered box on p.83, Georgian scarf and Russian dolls on cover and p.85, *samovar* and doll on p.112 and mink hat on p.113; Liberty's, London, for rug on p.88; African Centre, London, for African sculptures on p.93, cover and p.94; Sofra Restaurant, London, for coffee pot and dish on cover and p.123; Covent Garden Oriental Carpets for carpet and saddle cloth on p.110; Ranger Arms Co. Ltd. for gun on p.106; Sandra Schneider for *yarmulke*, prayer book, shawl, etc. on p.106; Saree Emporium, London, for saris on p.117; East West Herb Shop, London, for herbal medicines on p.119; Chuntex (UK) Ltd. for computer monitor on p.121; Tourism Authority of Thailand for lacquer work on p.124.

Map symbols designed by: Kenny Laurenson

Other help supplied by: Crispian Martin St. Valery, Alastair Owens, Janet Oswald, Rosemary Cowan, Jane Lewis, Judy Chamberlain, Michael Capon and George Heritage.

Antarctic terrain supplied by Mullard Space Science Laboratory, University College London, using data from the radar altimeter aboard the European Space Agency's ERS-1 satellite

PICTURE CREDITS:

Heather Angel: 86ct. **B. and C. Alexander**: 25tl, 25tr, 51ct. **Max Alexander**: 63tcr. **P. and G. Bowater**: 69cb. **Chris Branfield**: front cover cl. **Duncan Brown**: 117bl. **J Allan Cash**: front cover bl, 31tr, 36tc, 38cr, 42cl, 42bc, 44bc, 49tcr, 56cr, 56bcl, 57bc, 57bl, 57br, 58tr, 60bl, 61c, 61bl, 61bc, 62cl, 71c, 74ct, 76c, 76bc, 78br, 92 c, 93br, 94bl, 100br, 104ct, 104cl, 105bc, 108bl, 108br, 109tr, 109bcr, 110br, 114tcr, 117cr, 120cbr, 123c, 127tc. **Cephas**: 49ctr. **Mark Chapman**: 93tcl. **J.R.Chapman**: 88cr, 88br, 96tr, 116cr, 117tl. **Oliver Crimmon**: 96ctr. **Ann Clarke**: 49bc. **John Cleare/Mountain Camera**: 40bcl. **Stephanie Colasanti**: 106cr. **Bruce Coleman**: 65br, 118br; Gene Ahrens 26cb, 27tl, 27cr; Alain Compost 126cr, 126bl; Gerald Cubitt 13bl, 98cl, 99bc, 99cb, 114ct, 114ctr, 114cbl, 126cl, Francisco J.Erize 50cl; M. P. L Fogden 35c; Jeff Foott Productions 20ct; Christer Fredriksson 86ctr; Dr. Charles Henneghien 93tc; Hans Gerd Heyer 121cbr; Udo Hirsch 129cbr; David Houston 89tl; Johnny Johnson 50cr; Herbert Kranawetter 75br; O. Langrand 95tl; Wayne Lankinen 30bcl; Thor Larsen 51bc; Leonard Lee Rue 21cbr; Luiz C. Marigo 13cbl, 40ctr; Larry Mulvehill/Black Star 120ct; John Murray 114cl, 128cbl; Orion Press 122cr; Charlie Ott 20tl; Dieter and Mary Plage 40ctl; Dr. Eckhart Pott 38c; Dr. Sandro Prato 73cl, 128cb; Fritz Prenzel 128cb, 128br; Hans Reinhard 50bl, 71bc; N.Tomalin 35tr; Konrad Wothe 101tl; Jonathan T. Wright 32c, 83tl; J. Zwanepoel 65cl. **Colorific**: Linda Bartlett 75c; Steve Benbow 75bc; Marcus Brooke 102ctl; David Burnett/Contact Press 33ctr; Paul Conklin 32cl; John Dominis 74cl; Enrico Ferorelli 33ct; Frank Hermann 94tr; Anthony Joyce 133bl; Sarah Meltzoff/Black Star 139tr; Christopher Morris/Blackstar 75tr; Peter Nacke/Picture Group 84clb; Lehtikuva Ov 14cb; Reza/Black Star 15tl; Malcolm Sanders 133tl; Michael St. Maur Sheil 99c; Peter Turnley/Blackstar 84tr. **Comstock**: 72ct. **Steven J. Cooling**: 99ct, 134cbl. **Lupe Cuhna**: 48tc. **James Davis/Worldwide**: 24bc, 46br, 52bl, 53cr, 69bl, 89ct, 107bl; WVF/Maarten Udema 112cl. **Ecoscene**: Peter Hulme back cover tr, 55tl. **Lynn Edelman**: 45bc. **Tor Eigeland**: 96cl. **Environmental Picture Library**: 92 tr, 102ctr. **Robert Estall**: 23bc. **Chris Fairclough**: 90c, 106c, 116cl, 117c; P. George 117tc. **Sydney Freelance**: 132bl. **Ronald Grant Archive**: 116bl. **Sonia Halliday**: Jane Taylor 107br. **R. Hanbury Tennison**: 77cbr. **Robert Harding**: front cover cr, 11tr, 13tr, 14cr, 15tc, 23cb, 26cr, 27bcl, 35cr, 39cb, 39bl, 45cl, 46tcr, 46tr, 49cr, 49br, 52cl, 56tcr, 56cl, 56c, 61tc, 63cbr, 65tl, 65bl, 68tr, 68cl, 68br, 76cl, 78cl, 79tr, 80cr, 89tr, 89tcr, 90br, 91bl, 93bc, 98cbl, 100tc, 111bc, 116br, 117bcr, 125tcl, 125cr, 125bcl, 125cb, 125br, 127tcr; Mohamed Amin 108cl; Bildagentur Schuster/Eckhardt 66cl, 66tr, 67cl, 78cbr; Bildagentur Schuster/Scholz 85tr; Graham Birch 126tr; C.E.Clark 99cr; C.Delu 95ctl; F.Dubes 63bc; Alan L.Durand 85cbr; Explorer/J. P. Nacivet 62c; Robert Fereck 45tc; Fournie 124cr; Robert Francis 13cl, 39c, 39bcr; Lee Frost 78c; James Green 79bcr; Ian Griffiths 94cr, 133tcr; Gavin Heller 43bl, 115tl; Michael Jenner 104cb, 107cr; Paolo Koch 126tcr; David Lomax 42cr, 43tc; Claude Martine 63cb; Photri 10tr, 10ctr, 10br, 27c; Chris Rennie 39cr, 77tr, 77ct, 110cl; Rolf Richardson 77bc; Sassoon 124tc; M. Short 79cb, 105cb, 105bl; Julia Thorne 51br; David Tokeley 116ct; Adina Tovy 29bl; Vaduz 68cr; A. C.Waltham 34c, 34bcr; Elizabeth Weiland 119tl; G. M.Wilkins 99tl; Adam Woolfitt 53cl, 64tr, 64c, 75tc, 102ct, 104br. **Paul Harris**: 24ct, 24cb, 25br, 82cl, 83br, 113tr, 113cb, 113bcr, 118tcr, 119cl, 122c. **J. Henderson**: 76cb. **John Heseltine**: 59tr. **Leila Hilland**: 133br. **Jimmy Holmes /Himalayan Images**: 118c, 118cl, 119c, 122cl, 123tl. **Pippa Hurst**: 88cl. **Hutchison Library**: 24cl, 43br, 92bl, 95cl, 107cb, 113cr; Robert Aberman 104bl; John Egan 79cr; Sarah Errington 100cr, 112bc; J.G.Fuller 129tc; John Hatt 102br; Richard House 47ctl; Victoria Ivleva 81c; Joan Klatchko 104c; R. Ian Lloyd 101tr; Michael Macintyre 121ctr, 129tr; Stephen Pern 49cr; R. Reeve 52ctr; Bernard Regent 130ctl; Kirsten Rodgers 44tc; Prue Rankin Smith 42tr; Andrei Solomonov 85ct; Tony Souter 73bl. **A. Hyman**: 110c. **ICCE**: S. M. Andrews 86ctl, 89bl. **Image Bank**: 9ccl; Peter Hendrie, 85bc; H.J.Aders 50ct; Gio Barto 88tr; Vladimir Birgos 81tcl; Ira Block 22c; David Brownell 35tcr; P. and G. Bowater 123tr; Edward W. Bower 28cl; Luis Castaneda 29bc; Gerard Champlong 34cl; Gary S. Chapman 42bcr; S. Costa 47bc; Melchior Di Giacomo 15bl, 43c; Wendy Dison 119bl; Tom Owen Edwards 51cbl, 75cr; Grant V. Faint 69tc, 122cbl; David W. Hamilton 60br; David Hiser 128ct; Don Klumpp 74c; Steve Krongard 111cr; Patti McConville 37tr; Fong Siu Nang 120bc; Nick Nicholson 129br; Albert Normandin 22bcr; Francisco Onatanon 61br; John R. Ramey 35bl; Guido Alberto Rossi front cover bcl, 43tr, 43cr, 100bcl; Steve Satushek 23tl, 36cbl, 12cb; Erik Leigh Simmons 31bc; John Lewis Stage 47tr; Peter Turner 28cb; Frank Wing 120tr; Hans Wolf 67bcr. **Images**: 61cr, 130cbl; Andris Apse 130cbr; Horizon 127br. **Impact**: B. Babanov/Vika 113tcl; A. Bradshaw/Visions 113bc; Piers Cavendish 96ct, 97ctr; Rupert Conant 71tr; Anita Corbin 126c; John Denhan 66tl; Colin Jones 28bl; Mike McQueen 114br; M. Milivojevic 70bl; Paul O'Driscoll 99tcr. **Ann Jousiffe**: 89br. **Kaleidescope**: Victor Englebert 93cbr. **Frank Lane**: D.Hoadley 12 tr; W. Wisniewski 53bl, 102cbr. **Anthony Lambert**: 77cr. **Nicki Liddiard**: 58cr. **Life File**: 48bl; Sue Davies 29c, 44tr; Juliet Highet 79br; Eddy Tan 60tr; Sergei Verein 113bl. **Catherine Lucas**: 96c. **Magnum**: Abbas 45tcr, 95bc; Eve Arnold 90bl; Bruno Barbey 92cl, 109cr, 123cl, 124bl; Rene Burri 34bl; M. Franck 91tr; S. Franklin 90ctr, 108tr; Thomas Hoepker 66cr, 67cr; David Hurn/J.Hillelson 89cb; Hiroji Kubota 119cbr; Fred Mayer 102cr; Gideon Mendel 92bc; Eli Reed 107tl; Marc Riboud 102bl, 109bc; Dennis Stock 26c, 28br; Kryn Taconis/John Hillelson 22br; Chris Steele-Perkins 91br, 98c; Dennis Stock 53tr. **Military and Research Services**/Todd Shipyards: 101tcl. **Tim Motion**: 60c, 62cr. **National Maritime Museum**: 101br. **Natural History Photographic Agency**: ANT 133ct; Anthony Bannister 86bcl; Stephen Krasemann 128tr; Dr. Ivan Polunin 114cbr; John Shaw 134cl. **Nature Photographers**: Peter Craig Cooper 98cbr; Mark Pidgeon 87bl; Roger Tidman 97tl. **New Zealand Tourist Office**: 134cr. **Nissan**: 58br. **Oxford Scientific Films**: I. Bernard 40cbr; Tony Bomford 49bcr; Lon E Lauber 11br;; Ted Mead 45c; Larry Ulrich 20tc; Konrad Wothe 40cr. **Panos**: 46cbr; Heidi Bradner 70ct; Matthew Boysons 52cr; Alain le Garsmeur 119tr. **Philips CED Publicity**: 65tcr. **Pictor**: back cover tl, 12ctr, 13cr, 14c, 22bl, 23tr, 28c, 31br, 32br, 33cbl, 47cr, 48tr, 55ctr, 59cl, 86cb, 86bcr, 90tr, 98bc, 101bc, 102cbl, 124c, 129ctr, 130bl. **John Pilkington**: 111tcr. **Pirelli Cables**: 53br. **Planet Earth Pictures**: 20tr, 20cl; Yuri Shibnev 102tr, 103tr; John Eastcott/Yva Momatiuk 13tc; William M. Smithey Jr. 21cbl. **Philip Powell**: front cover cbl. **Quadrant**: 45tr. **Donna Rispoli** 127c. **Science Photo Library**: Martin Bond 9ccr; David Parker 9 cr; Ray Ellis 13br; Simon Frazer 55cr; John Heseltine 55cbl; Michael Martin 55tcl; Novosti Press Agency 112ct. **South American Pictures**: 44cr, 45bl, 49tcr. **Spectrum**: 55ctl, 55cb; Jean Paul Nacivet 55tr. **Frank Spooner**: Tordai 88c. **John Massey Stewart**: 81tl. **Still Pictures**: 25tc; Doug Armand 100tr; Mark Edwards 38bc, 93tr, 95c, 95bl; Edward Parker 94cl; Hjalte Tin 113tl. **Tony Stone**: 10cbr 37bl, 55cbr, 58c, 67bcl, 79ct, 86tcr, 114ctl, 114cb, 123tc, 128cl, 130cb, 130br; Glen Allison 32tr; Doug Armand 69bc, 73c; John Beatty 53bc, 101bcr; Oliver Benn 40tr; Ken Biggs 12tcr; Allan Bramley 130ct; Doug Boult 24c; Michael Buselle 59bc; Julian Calder 111c, 121tl; Mike Caldwell 74bl; John Callahan 121bc; Hubert Camille 62tc; Bryn Campbell 52tc; Paul Chesley 121cr, 130ctr, 134br; Paul Damien 33tl; Nicholas De Vore 40cb; Doris De Witt 28tr; Sepp Dietrich 71cb; Richard Elliot 134cb; John Garrett 132 cl; Margaret Gowan 120bl; David Hanson 36bl, 37cbl, 71br; David Hiser 21cb, 51cl, 128bl; Ernst Hohne 67bl; Gary Irving 30bc, 30bcr; Geoff Johnson 111tr; H. Richard Johnson 11ctr; Chris Kaploka 130cr; Oldrich Karasek 70c; Mitch Kezan 96cl; Jim Kingshott 74br; Thia Konig 37ctr; Bob Krist 82tc; Hideo Kurihara 52tr, 134tc, 134ctr; Peter Lamberti 11cbr; John Lawlor 37tl; Alan Levenson 123bc; Lukasseck 34cb; Angus Mackillop 15cbl; Mike McQueen 55cl; Roger Mear 50br; Lawrence Migdale 59cr; Ian Murphy 59br, 64bl; Donald Nausbaum 41bl; Nicholas Parfitt 86cbr,96br; Tom Raymond 29cr; Mitch Reardon 2c,133cb; Steven Rothfeld 14br; David Schultz 33tr; Mark Segal 30c; Hugh Sitton 90cl, 100tcr, 104tr; Adam Smith 47cl; P. and K. Smith 36cr; Robin Smith 131bl; Bill Staley 21ctr; Alena Vikova 72tr; Charlie Waite 59bl, 73tr; Ken Wilson 133bc. **Ina Strading**: 81ct. **Survival Anglia**: 82c; Ross Bray 107bc; Andrew Park 108c. **Sygma**: Bernard Bisson 85ctr; Fabian 112tr. **Telegraph Colour Library**: 58cl, 99tr; J. C. Davies 72cbr; N. MacIntyre 122br; J. C. Meauxsoone 53tcl; P.Wadey 121tr. **Travel Photo International**: 71ct, 120cbl. **Tony Waltham**: 9cl. **Alan Watson**: 40ct. **Chris Whitwell**: 109tc, 124tr. **David Woodfall**: 81bc. **World Wildlife Fund**: 40bcr; John Newby 93cr; Mauri Rautkari 94bcl. **Zefa**: 20ctl, 29cbr, 51ctl, 66bl, 70tc, 73br, 80c, 81tr, 94br, 106ctr; P. W. Bading 22tr; Jim Brandenburg 31tl; Damm front cover br, 97cr; P. Fera 57tr, 109br; K. Goebel 27bcr, 108ct; Jens Herrman 91cb; Hunter 22cl; Janicek 105cr; Minden 96bl; Sonak 84bl; Steenmans 83tr.

INDEX

Throughout the Atlas, population figures have been taken from the latest official estimates.

HOW TO USE THE GRID

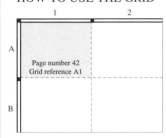

Page number 42
Grid reference A1

Grid references in the Index help you to find places on the map. For example, if you look up Nairobi in the Index, you will see the reference 97 O5. The first number, 97, is the page number of the map on which Nairobi appears. Find the letters and numbers which border the page, and trace a line across from the letter and down from the number. This directs you to the exact grid square in which Nairobi is located.

The numbers that appear after the names are the page numbers, followed by the grid references.

There are two sorts of factbox in the index. Countries that are more important economically or politically in their area have a larger factbox.

In the factboxes, many statistics are not yet available for the new states of the world. When we have been unable to find the correct figure, N/A is given, which stands for not available.

Population density
This is the total population divided by the land area of a country.

Average life expectancy
This is the average life expectancy at birth, barring war or natural disasters.

Literacy
This is the percentage of people over the age of 15 years who can read and write a simple sentence. When figures for male (m) and female (f) have not been available, we have used an average (av.).

Death penalty
The countries with Yes use the death penalty regularly. Some of the states with No still have a law permitting the death penalty but do not use it.

Percentage of urban population
This is the percentage of the total population who live in towns or cities.

Calories consumed daily
The recommended daily number for a healthy life is about 2500 calories; the inhabitants of some countries consume far more than others.

The following abbreviations have been used in the index:

anc. = ancient name
Arch. = Archipelago
C. = Cape
E. = East
Ft. = Fort
I. = Island
Is. = Islands
L. = Lake
Mt. = Mountain
Mts. = Mountains
N. = North
N.P. = National Park
Pen. = Peninsula
prev. = previously
Pt. = Point
Res. = Reservoir
R. = River
S. = South
St. = Saint
var. = variant name
W. = West

A

A Coruña (var. La Coruña) Spain 52 J8, 60 G3
Aachen Germany 67 C11
Aalst Belgium 65 F14
Aarau Switzerland 68 F9
Aare *River* Switzerland 68 E9
Aba Nigeria 93 O13
Ābādān Iran 109 L7
Abajo Mountains *Mountain range* Utah, USA 35 K5
Abakan Russian Federation 112 J11
Abashiri Japan 122 M3
Abaya, L. *Lake* Ethiopia 91 J16
Abéché Chad 94 K7
Abengourou Ivory Coast 93 K12
Åbenrå Denmark 56 H16
Abeokuta Nigeria 93 N12
Aberdare Range *Mountain range* Kenya 97 O5
Aberdeen Scotland, UK 52 K7, 58 J8
Aberdeen South Dakota, USA 33 N6
Aberdeen Washington, USA 36 G7
Aberystwyth Wales, UK 59 G14
Abhā Saudi Arabia 108 H13
Abidjan Ivory Coast 93 K13
Abilene Texas, USA 35 P10
Abitibi, L. *Lake* Ontario/Quebec, Canada 25 K11
Abomey Benin 93 M12
Abu Dhabi (var. Abū Zabī) United Arab Emirates 109 N11
Abū Zabī *see* Abu Dhabi
Abu Simbel *Archaeological site* Egypt 90 F9
Abuja Nigeria 93 O11
Abydos *Archaeological site* Egypt 90 G8
Abyssinia *see* Ethiopia
Acapulco Mexico 39 M14
Accra Ghana 93 L13
Acheloos *River* Greece 78 H7
Achinsk Russian Federation 112 J10
Acklins I. *Island* Bahamas 43 M5
Aconcagua *Mountain* Argentina 41
Ad Dafrah *Desert region* United Arab Emirates 109 N12
Ad Dahna *Desert region* Saudi Arabia 109 L10
Ad Dammām Saudi Arabia 109 M9
Ad Dawhah *see* Doha
Ad-Diwaniyah Iraq 109 K5
Adak I. *Island* Aleutian Is. Alaska, USA 22 A6
Adamawa Highlands *Physical region* Cameroon 87
Adana Turkey 105 M10
Adapazari Turkey 104 I5
Adare, C. *Cape* Victoria Land, Antarctica 50 E12
Addis Ababa Ethiopia 91 J15
Adelaide South Australia, Australia 133 L13
Aden Yemen 100 E7, 108 I16
Aden, Gulf of *Sea feature* Arabia/E Africa 87, 91 N14, 100 E7, 103, 114
Adige *River* Italy 72 H7
Adīrī Libya 89 O8
Adirondack Mts. *Mountain range* New York, USA 27 L7
Adiyaman Turkey 105 O9
Admiralty Is. *Island group* Papua New Guinea 133 N1
Adrar Algeria 88 J8
Adrar des Ifôghas *Mountain range* Mali 93 M6
Adrian Michigan, USA 31 O10
Adriatic Sea S Europe 54, 72 K10, 74 I9
Adwa Ethiopia 91 J13
Adycha *River* Russian Federation 113 N6
Aegean Sea Greece/Turkey 54, 79 M7, 104 F7
Ağri (var. Karaköse) Turkey 105 R6
Afghanistan *Country* C Asia 110-111

Afghanistan 110-111

a Dari, Pashto • ▪ Afghani • ♦ 66 • ● 42 • ○ £7.03 • ▶ (m) 44% (f) 14% • ⬚ 8 • ✚ 5148 • ❀ Yes • ⬛ 18% • ⍦ 2022

Africa *Continent* 8, 11, 12, 13, 15, 87, 103
African Plate *Physical feature* 8, 20, 41, 54, 87, 103, 115
'Afrīn *River* Syria/Turkey 107 N2
Afyon Turkey 104 J8
Agadez Niger 93 P7
Agadir Morocco 88 G6
Agartala India 117 P8
Agattu I. *Island* Aleutian Is. Alaska, USA 22 A4
Agen France 62 J13
Agios Nikolaos Crete, Greece 79 N16
Agra India 117 K5
Agri *River* Italy 73 M14
Agrigento Sicily 73 J18
Aguarico *River* Ecuador 44 D8
Aguascalientes Mexico 39 L10
Agulhas Basin *Sea feature* Atlantic/ Indian Ocean 87
Agulhas, C. *Cape* South Africa 87, 98 J16
Agulhas current *Ocean current* Indian Ocean 12
Agulhas Ridge *Sea feature* Atlantic Ocean 87
Ahaggar *Mountain range* Algeria 87, 89 L11
Ahmadabad India 116 I8
Ahvāz Iran 109 M6
Aïr *Mountain range* Niger 93 P9
Aix-en-Provence France 63 O13
Aizawl India 117 Q8
Ajaccio Corsica 63 S16

Ajdābiyā Libya 89 Q7
Ajmer India 116 J6
Akanthou Cyprus 105 L12
Akhisar Turkey 104 H7
Akimiski I. *Island* Canada 24 J8
Akita Japan 122 K7
Akmola (var. Akmolinsk, Tselinograd) Kazakhstan 122 G11
Akmolinsk *see* Akmola
Akola India 117 K9
Akpatok I. *Island* Canada 25 N3
Akron Ohio, USA 31 Q10
Aksai Chin *Disputed region* China/India 16, 117 L1, 118 F10
Aksaray Turkey 105 L8
Akseki Turkey 104 J10
Aksu China 118 F7
Aksum Ethiopia 91 J13
Aktau (var. Shevchenko) Kazakhstan 112 D10
Aktyubinsk (var. Aqtöbe) Kazakhstan 112 E10
Akyab *see* Sittwe
Al 'Amārah Iraq 109 L6
Al 'Aqabah (var. Aqaba) Jordan 107 L14
Al Azraq Jordan 107 N10
Al Bāḩah Saudi Arabia 108 H12
Al Baṣrah Iraq 109 L7
Al Baydā Libya 89 R6
Al Baydā' Yemen 108 I16
Al Buraymī Oman 109 O11
Al Ghaydah Yemen 109 L16
Al Hoceima Morocco 88 J4
Al Hudaydah *see* Hodeida
Al Hufūf Saudi Arabia 109 L10
Al Hadīthah Iraq 108 J4
Al Hasakah Syria 107 R2
Al Hillah Iraq 109 K5
Al Jaghbūb Libya 89 S7
Al Jawf Saudi Arabia 108 I6
Al Jubayl Saudi Arabia 109 L9
Al-Juf *see* El Djouf
Al Karak Jordan 107 M11
Al Khābūrah Oman 109 O11
Al Khums Libya 89 O6
Al Kufrah Libya 89 S10
Al Kūt Iraq 109 L6
Al Kuwayt *see* Kuwait City
Al Lādhiqīyah (var. Latakia) Syria 107 M4
Al Madīnah *see* Medina
Al Mafraq Jordan 107 M9
Al Mahwīt Yemen 108 I15
Al Manāmah *see* Manama
Al Marj Libya 89 Q6
Al Mukallā Yemen 109 K16
Al Mukhā (var. Mocha) Yemen 108 H16
Al Qunayṭirah Syria 107 M8
Al Qurnah Iraq 109 L6
Alabama *River* Alabama, USA 29 K8
Alabama *State* USA 29
Alajuela Costa Rica 42 E13
Alakol', L. *Lake* Kazakhstan 103
Alamogordo New Mexico, USA 35 M10
Åland Is. *Island group* Finland 57 M11
Alanya Turkey 105 K10
Alapaha *River* Georgia, USA 29 N9
Alaska *State* USA 22, 51
Alaska, Gulf of *Sea feature* Alaska, USA 10, 20, 22 G9, 129 L3
Alaska Peninsula *Physical feature* 20
Alaska Range *Mountain range* Alaska, USA 10, 20, 22 G7
Alassio Italy 72 C9
Alazani *River* Azerbaijan/Georgia 85 Q12
Alba Iulia Romania 76 I6
Albacete Spain 61 M10
Albania *Country* SE Europe 75

Albania 75

a Albanian • ▪ Lek • ♦ 312 • ● 73 • ○ £0.22 • ▶ (av.) 15% • ⬛ 35%

Albany Georgia, USA 29 M9
Albany New York, USA 26-27
Albany Oregon, USA 36 G9
Albany Western Australia, Australia 132 G14
Albany *River* Ontario, Canada 24 J9
Albatross Plateau *Sea feature* Pacific Ocean 129 O7
Albert *Waterway* Belgium 65 I14
Albert, L. *Lake* Uganda/Zaire 87, 97 L3, 95 P12
Albert Lea Minnesota, USA 30 H8
Albert Nile *River* Uganda 97 M2
Alberta *Province* Canada 23
Albertville *see* Kalemie
Albi France 63 L13
Albina Suriname 44 O6
Ålborg Denmark 56 I14
Albuquerque New Mexico, USA 35 L8
Albury New South Wales, Australia 133 N14
Alcántara Res. *Reservoir* Spain 60 H9
Aldabra Is. *Island group* Seychelles, Indian Ocean 100 E9
Aldan *River* Russian Federation 113 N9
Aleg Mauritania 92 G7
Aleksinac Serbia, Yugoslavia 75 O8
Alençon France 62 J6
Aleppo *see* Ḩalab
Alert *Research center* Canada 51 O11
Alessandria Italy 72 D7
Ålesund Norway 52 L7, 56 H8
Aleutian Basin *Sea feature* Bering Sea 103
Aleutian Is. *Island group* Alaska, USA 22 B6, 128 J4
Aleutian Trench *Sea feature* Pacific Ocean 20, 128 J4

Alexander Arch. *Island group* Alaska, USA 22 H11
Alexandretta *see* Iskenderun
Alexandria (var. El Iskandarīya) Egypt 90 F6
Alexandria Louisiana, USA 28 H8
Alexandria Romania 77 L10
Alexandria Virginia, USA 29 R3
Alexandroupoli Greece 79 N2
Aleysk Air Base *Military center* Russian Federation 112 I11
Algeciras Spain 60 I15
Alger *see* Algiers
Algeria *Country* N Africa 88-89

Algeria 88-89

a Arabic • ▪ Dinai • ♦ 28 • ● 66 • ○ £0.64 • ▶ (m) 70% (f) 45% • ⬚ 74 • ✚ 43 • ❀ Yes • ⬛ 52% • ⍦ 2866

Alghero Sardinia 73 G13
Algiers (var. Alger; anc. Icosium) Algeria 52 K9, 89 L4
Aliakmon *River* Greece 78 I4
Alicante Spain 61 N11
Alice Springs Northern Territory, Australia 133 K9
Alicudi *Island* Lipari Is., Sicily 73 K16
Aligarh India 117 K5
Alkmaar Netherlands 64 H8
Allahabad India 117 M7
Allegheny Mts. *Mountain range* West Virginia, USA 29 Q3
Allentown Pennsylvania, USA 27 K12
Allier *River* France 63 M11
Alma-Ata (var. Almaty) Kazakhstan 112 G13
Almaty *see* Alma-Ata
Almalyk Uzbekistan 111 N6
Almelo Netherlands 64 M9
Almería Spain 61 L14
Alor *Island* Indonesia 127 N15
Alor Setar Malaysia 125 I17
Alotau Papua New Guinea 133 O4
Alpena Michigan, USA 31 O6
Alphen aan den Rijn Netherlands 64 H10
Alps *Mountain range* C Europe 8, 11, 54, 63 P11, 68 G11, 72 D6
Altai Mts. *Mountain range* Asia 103, 105, 118 I5
Altamura Italy 73 N13
Altay Mongolia 118 J5
Altdorf Switzerland 68 G10
Altiplano *Physical region* Bolivia 41
Alton Illinois, USA 31 J13
Altoona Pennsylvania, USA 26 I12
Altun Ha *Archaeological site* Belize 42 C6
Altun Mts. *Mountain range* China 118 H9
Alturas California, USA 37 I12
Alytus Lithuania 80 I10
Am Timan Chad 94 K8
Amakusa Is. *Island group* Japan 123 C15
Amakusa Sea Japan 123 B15
Amami Is. *Island group* Japan 123 B19
Amami-ōshima *Island* Amami Is., Japan 123 B18
Amarapura Burma 124 G7
Amarillo Texas, USA 35 O8
Amasya Turkey 105 M5
Amazon *River* S America 41, 44 G9, 46 H7, 53 F12
Amazon Basin *Physical region* Brazil 11, 41
Amazonia *Physical region* S America 44 G8, 46 C8
Ambarchik Russian Federation 51 R5, 113 O4
Ambato Ecuador 44 C9
Amblève *River* Belgium 65 K16
Ambon Ambon, Indonesia 127 O13
Amboseli *National park* Kenya 97 P6
Ambre, Cap d' *see* Bobaomby, C.
Ambriz Angola 98 G4
Ameland *Island* West Frisian Is. Netherlands 64 K6
American Samoa *Dependent territory* Polynesia, Pacific Ocean 129 K9
Amersfoort Netherlands 64 J10
Amery Ice Shelf *Coastal feature* Indian Ocean Coast, Antarctica 50 G8
Ames Iowa, USA 33 Q9
Amfissa Greece 78 I8
Amga *River* Russian Federation 113 N9
Amherst Burma 125 G11
Amiens France 63 L3
Amirante Is. *Island group* Seychelles 100 F9
Amistad Res. *Reservoir* Mexico/Texas, USA 35 O13
Amlia I. *Island* Aleutian Is., Alaska, USA 22 B7
Amman (var. Rabbah Ammon; anc. Philadelphia) Jordan 107 M10
Ammassalik Greenland 51 N15
Ammersee *Lake* Germany 67 I16
Amol Iran 109 O4
Amorgos *Island* Cyclades, Greece 79 O12
Amritsar India 116 J3
Amstelveen Netherlands 64 I10
Amsterdam Netherlands 64 I9
Amsterdam New York, USA 27 L9
Amsterdam I. *Island* Indian Ocean 101 I13
Amstetten Austria 69 P5
Amu Darya *River* C Asia 103, 111 L8
Amundsen Gulf *Sea feature* Northwest Territories, Canada 23 K6
Amundsen-Scott *Research center* Antarctica 50 E9
Amundsen Sea Pacific Ocean, Antarctica 50 C10

a Language (official or most commonly spoken) • ▪ Currency • ♦ Population density per square mile • ● Average life expectancy • ○ Price of 1 dozen hen's eggs • ▶ Literacy • ⬚ Number of TVs per 1,000 people • ✚ Number of people per doctor • ❀ Death penalty • ⬛ Percentage of urban-based population • ⍦ Average number of calories consumed daily per person

137

Amur – Balkhash, L.

Amur (var. Heilong Jiang) *River* China/Russian Federation 103, 113 O11, 115, 121 O1
An Nabk Saudi Arabia 108 H5
An Nafūd *Desert region* Saudi Arabia 103, 108 I6
An-Najaf Iraq 109 K5
An Nāṣirīyah Iraq 109 L6
Anabar *River* Russian Federation 113 L6
Anaconda Montana, USA 32 G6
Anadyr' Air Base *Military center* Russian Federation 113 Q3
Anambas Is. *Island group* Indonesia 126 F10
Anamur Turkey 105 K11
Anatolia *Region* Turkey 54, 103
Anchorage Alaska, USA 22 G8
Ancona Italy 52 L8, 72 J9
Ancyra *see* Ankara
Andalusia *Region* Spain 60-61
Andaman Is. *Island group* India, Indian Ocean 100 K7, 115
Andaman Sea Indian Ocean 100 K7, 115, 125 F12
Andautonia *see* Zagreb
Anderson Indiana, USA 31 N12
Andes *Mountain range* S America 11, 41, 44 E7, 48 H8
Andizhan Uzbekistan 111 P6
Andorra *Country* SW Europe 63

Andorra 63

a Catalan • Franc and Peseta • 297 • 77 • £1.12 • (m) 100% (f) 100% • 95%

Andorra la Vella Andorra 63 L16
Andravida Greece 78 H9
Andros *Island* Cyclades, Greece 79 M9
Andros I. *Island* Bahamas 43 K3
Angara *River* Russian Federation 103, 113 K10
Angarsk Russian Federation 113 L11
Ángel de la Guarda I. *Island* Mexico 38 G4
Angel Falls *Waterfall* Venezuela 41
Angeles Luzon, Philippines 127 L4
Ångerman *River* Sweden 57 L8
Angers France 62 I7
Angkor Wat *Archaeological site* Cambodia 125 L13
Anglesey *Island* Wales, UK 59 G13
Angol Chile 49 G12
Angola *Country* Southern Africa 98

Angola 98

a Portuguese • Kwanza • 21 • 46 • £1.63 • (m) 55% (f) 28% • 28%

Angola Basin *Sea feature* Atlantic Ocean 53 K13, 87
Angora *see* Ankara
Angoulême France 62 J10
Angren Uzbekistan 111 O6
Anguilla *Dependent territory* West Indies 43 S9
Ankang China 121 K10
Ankara (prev. Angora; anc. Ancyra) Turkey 105 K6
Ann Arbor Michigan, USA 31 O9
Annaba Algeria 89 M4
'Annah Iraq 108 J4
Annam *see* Vietnam
Annapolis Maryland, USA 29 S3
Annecy France 63 P9
Anshan China 121 O6
Antakiyah *see* Antakya
Antakya (var. Antakiyah; anc. Antioch) Turkey 105 N11
Antalya Turkey 104 J10
Antananarivo Madagascar 101 E11
Antarctic Circumpolar current *Ocean current* Southern Ocean 12
Antarctic Plate *Physical feature* 8, 41, 87, 131
Antarctica *Continent* 8, 11, 12, 13, 41, 50, 131
Anticosti, Île d' *Island* Quebec, Canada 25 Q9
Antigua *Island* Antigua & Barbuda 43 T11
Antigua and Barbuda *Country* West Indies 43 T10

Antigua and Barbuda 43

a English • Dollar • 471 • 74 • £1.29 • (m) 90% (f) 88% • 31%

Antioch *see* Antakya
Antipodes Is. *Island group* New Zealand, Pacific Ocean 128 J13
Antofagasta Chile 48 F6, 129 R10
Antsirañana (prev. Diégo-Suarez) Madagascar 100 F10
Antwerp (var. Anvers) Belgium 65 G13
Antwerp I. *see* Anvers I.
Anvers I. (prev. Antwerp I.) *Island* Pacific Ocean, Antarctica 50 B8
Anvers *see* Antwerp
Anzio Italy 73 I12
Aomori Japan 122 K6
Aosta Italy 72 B6
Aparri Luzon, Philippines 127 L2
Apatin Serbia, Yugoslavia 75 L3
Apeldoorn Netherlands 64 K10
Apennines *Mountain range* Italy 54, 72 I10
Aphrodisias *Archaeological site* Turkey 104 H9
Apia Western Samoa, Pacific Ocean 128 J9
Appalachian Mts. *Mountain range* USA 10, 20, 26 I13, 29 P4
Appenzell Switzerland 68 H9
Appleton Wisconsin, USA 31 K7
Apure *River* Venezuela 44 H5
Aqaba *see* Al 'Aqabah
Aqaba, Gulf of *Sea feature* SW Asia 90 H7, 107 L14, 108 G6
Aqtöbe *see* Aktyubinsk
Ar-Ramadi Iraq 109 K4
Ar Raqqah Syria 107 P3
Ar Riyāḍ *see* Riyadh
Ar Rustāq Oman 109 O12
Arabian Basin *Sea feature* Arabian Sea 103, 114-115
Arabian Desert *Desert region* SW Asia 11
Arabian Peninsula *Peninsula* SW Asia 87, 103
Arabian Plate *Physical feature* 8, 54, 87, 103, 115
Arabian Sea Arabia/India 100 G6,103, 109 N15, 114-115, 116 H10
Aracaju Brazil 46 N10
Arad Romania 76 G5
Arafura Sea Australia/Indonesia 131, 133 K4, 127 S13, 128 G9
Araguaia *River* Brazil 41, 46 J10
Arāk Iran 109 M5
Aral Sea *Lake* Kazakhstan/Uzbekistan 103, 110 I3, 112 E11
Aram *see* Syria
Aranđelovac Serbia, Yugoslavia 75 N6
'Ar'ar Saudi Arabia 108 I5
'Ar'ar, Wādī *Seasonal watercourse* Iraq/Saudi Arabia 108 J5
Aras *River* Azerbaijan/Iran 85 S14
Arauca Colombia 44 G6
Arauca *River* Colombia/Venezuela 44 G5
Arcachon France 62 I12
Arctic Ocean 10, 20, 51, 54, 103
Arda *River* Bulgaria/Greece 77 K15
Ardabīl Iran 109 M2
Ardennes *Physical region* Belgium 65 K17
Arendal Norway 56 I12
Arequipa Peru 45 G15
Arezzo Italy 72 H10
Argentina *Country* S America 48-49

Argentina 48-49

a Spanish • Peso • 31 • 71 • £0.67 • (m) 94% (f) 95% • 222 • 328 • No • 86% • 3113

Argentine Basin *Sea feature* Atlantic Ocean 53 G15
Argentino, L. *Lake* Argentina 49 I18
Argeş *River* Romania 77 M10
Arghandāb *River* Afghanistan 111 M13
Argostoli Kefallonia, Greece 78 F9
Århus Denmark 56 I15
Arica Chile 48 F3
Arizona *State* USA 34-35
Arkalyk Kazakhstan 112 F11
Arkansas *River* USA 20, 28 I5, 33 N13, 35 O5
Arkansas *State* USA 28
Arkansas City Kansas, USA 33 P13
Arkhangel'sk Russian Federation 82 J7
Arlberg Tunnel *Tunnel* Austria 68 I9
Arles France 63 N13
Arlon Belgium 65 K19
Armenia Colombia 44 E6
Armenia *Country* SW Asia 85

Armenia 85

a Armenian • Dram • 292 • 73 • £2.12 • N/A • 68%

Armidale New South Wales, Australia 133 O12
Arnhem Netherlands 65 K11
Arnhem Land *Physical region* Northern Territory, Australia 131, 132 J5
Arnhem, C. *Cape* Northern Territory, Australia 133 L5
Arno *River* Italy 72 F9
Arran *Island* Scotland, UK 58 G10
Arras France 63 L2
Arta Greece 78 G6
Artesia New Mexico, USA 35 M10
Artigas Uruguay 48 N8
Artvin Turkey 105 Q4
Aru Is. *Island group* Indonesia 127 Q14
Arua Uganda 97 L2
Aruba *Dependent territory* Caribbean Sea 43 N13
Arun *River* India/Nepal 117 O6
Arusha Tanzania 97 O7
Aruwimi *River* Zaire 95 M12
Arvayheer Mongolia 119 L6
Arvidsjaur Sweden 57 M6
Aş Şalţ Jordan 107 M10
As Sulaymānīyah Iraq 109 L3
As Suwaydā' Syria 107 N8
Asahikawa Japan 122 L3
Asansol India 117 O8
Ascension I. *Dependent territory* Atlantic Ocean 53 J12
Asela Ethiopia 91 J15
Ashburton *River* Western Australia, Australia 132 F9
Asheville North Carolina, USA 29 O5
Ashgabat (prev. Ashkhabad) Turkmenistan 110 I8
Ashkhabad *see* Ashgabat
Ashland Oregon, USA 37 H11
Ashmore & Cartier Is. *Dependent territory* Indian Ocean 100 N10
Ashtabula Ohio, USA 31 Q9
Asia *Continent* 8, 10, 11, 12, 15, 20, 87, 103, 130
Asir *Province* Saudi Arabia 108 I12
Asmara Eritrea 91 J12
Aspen Colorado, USA 35 L4
Assab Eritrea 91 L13
Assad, L. (var. Buḩayrat al Asad) *Lake* Syria 107 P3
Assen Netherlands 64 M7
Assisi Italy 72 I10
Astakos Greece 78 G8
Asti Italy 72 C7
Astipálaia *Island* Dodecanese, Greece 79 O12
Astoria Oregon, USA 36 G7
Astrakhan Russian Federation 83 G15
Asunción Paraguay 48 M6
Aswân Egypt 90 G9
Aswân High Dam *Dam* Egypt 90 G9
Asyût Egypt 90 F8
Aţ Ţafīlah Jordan 107 M11
Atacama Desert *Desert region* Chile 12, 22, 41, 48 G5
Atakpamé Togo 93 M12
Ataq Yemen 108 J16
Atar Mauritania 92 H5
Atatürk Barrage *Dam* Turkey 105 O9
Atbara Sudan 91 H11
Atbara *River* Sudan 91 H12
Ath Belgium 65 E15
Athabasca Alberta, Canada 23 L13
Athabasca *River* Canada 23 L12
Athabasca, L. *Lake* Alberta/Saskatchewan Canada 20, 23 L11
Athens Georgia, USA 29 N7
Athens Greece 79 K9
Athlone Ireland 59 C12
Ati Chad 94 J7
Atka I. *Island* Aleutian Is. Alaska, USA 22 B7
Atlanta Georgia, USA 29 M7
Atlantic City New Jersey, USA 27 L14
Atlantic-Indian-Antarctic Basin *Sea feature* Atlantic Ocean 53 M16
Atlantic-Indian Basin *Sea feature* Indian Ocean 101 E15
Atlantic Indian Ridge *Sea feature* Atlantic Ocean 53 M15
Atlantic Ocean 8, 10, 13, 20, 41, 52-53, 54, 86-87, 103
Atlas Mts. *Mountain range* Morocco 88 I6
Atlixco Mexico 39 N12
Attapu Laos 125 N12
Attawapiskat Ontario, Canada 24 J8
Attawapiskat *River* Ontario, Canada 24 I8
Atter, L. *Lake* Austria 69 O6
Attu I. *Island* Aleutian Is. Alaska, USA 22 A4
Atyrau (prev. Gur'yev) Kazakhstan 112 D10
Auburn New York, USA 26 J8
Auch France 63 K14
Auckland New Zealand 134 G4
Auckland Is. *Island group* New Zealand, Pacific Ocean 128 I13
Augrabies Falls N.P. *National park* South Africa 98 I13
Augsburg Germany 67 I15
Augusta Georgia, USA 29 O8
Augusta Maine, USA 27 P6
Augusta Sicily 73 L18
Augusta Western Australia, Australia 132 F13
Aurillac France 63 L11
Aurora Colorado, USA 35 M4
Aurora Illinois, USA 31 L10
Austin Minnesota, USA 30 H8
Austin Texas, USA 35 Q12
Austral Ridge *Sea feature* Pacific Ocean 129 L11
Australia *Country* Oceania 132-133

Australia 132-133

a English • Dollar • 5 • 77 • £0.87 • (m) 99% (f) 99% • 486 • 438 • No • 85% • 3216

Australia *Continent* 8, 11, 12, 15, 131
Australian Alps *Mountain range* Australia 11, 131
Australian Capital Territory *Territory* (prev. Federal Capital Territory) Australia 133
Australian Desert *Desert region* Australia 11
Austria *Country* C Europe 68-69

Austria 68-69

a German • Schilling • 242 • 76 • £1.88 • (m) 99% (f) 99% • 481 • 336 • No • 58% • 3495

Auxerre France 63 M7
Aveiro Portugal 60 F7
Avignon France 63 O13
Ávila Spain 60 J7
Avilés Spain 60 I3
Awasa Ethiopia 91 J16
Awash Ethiopia 91 K15
Awash *River* Ethiopia 91 K14
Awbārī Libya 89 O9
Axel Heiberg I. *Island* Northwest Territories, Canada 20, 23 N3, 51 O10
Axios *see* Vardar
Ayacucho Peru 45 E13
Aydarkul', L. *Lake* Kazakhstan/Uzbekistan 111 M6
Aydin Turkey 104 G9
Ayers Rock *see* Uluru
Ayios Evstratios *Island* Greece 79 M6
Ayon Is. *Island group* Russian Federation 113 O3
Ayr Scotland, UK 58 G10
Ayutthaya Thailand 125 J12
Ayvacik Barrage *Dam* Turkey 105 M5
Ayvalik Turkey 104 G7
Az Zahrān *see* Dhahran
Az Zarqā' Jordan 107 M9
Az Zubayr Iraq 109 L7
Azaouâd *Physical region* Mali 93 L7
Azerbaijan *Country* SW Asia 85

Azerbaijan 85

a Azerbaijani • Ruble • 216 • 71 • £0.66 • (av.) 99% • 53%

Azores *Island group* Atlantic Ocean 8, 52 I9
Azov, Sea of (var. Azovs'ke More) Russian Federation/Ukraine 54, 83 C13, 85 L9
Azovs'ke More *see* Azov, Sea of
Azul Argentina 49 M11

B

Ba'abda Lebanon 107 M7
Baalbek Lebanon 107 M6
Bab el Mandeb *Channel* Yemen 108 H16
Babahoyo Ecuador 44 C9
Babar *Island* Indonesia 127 P15
Babruysk (var. Bobruysk) Belarus 81 M13
Babylon *Archaeological site* Iraq 109 K5
Bacan *Island* Indonesia 127 O11
Bacău Romania 77 M4
Bačka Topola Serbia, Yugoslavia 75 M3
Bacolod Negros, Philippines 127 M6
Bad Ischl Austria 69 O7
Badain Jaran Desert *Desert region* China 119 L8
Badajoz Spain 60 H10
Badalona Spain 61 Q6
Baden Austria 69 S5
Badgastein Austria 69 N8
Bādiyat ash Shām *see* Syrian Desert
Badlands *Physical region* North Dakota, USA 33 L5
Bafatá Guinea-Bissau 92 G9
Baffin *Region* Northwest Territories, Canada 23 P6
Baffin Bay *Sea feature* Canada/Greenland 10, 20, 23 P4, 51 N12, 52 F6
Baffin I. *Island* Northwest Territories, Canada 10, 20, 23 Q5, 51 M12
Bafia Cameroon 94 F10
Bafoussam Cameroon 94 F10
Bagana, Mt. *Volcano* Solomon Is. Pacific Ocean 131
Baghdad Iraq 109 K4
Baghlān Afghanistan 111 N10
Baguio Luzon, Philippines 127 L3
Bahamas *Country* West Indies 43

Bahamas 43

a English • Dollar • 67 • 69 • £0.79 • (m) 90% (f) 89% • 75%

Bahamas *Island group* West Indies 20, 41
Bahawalpur Pakistan 116 I4
Bahía Blanca Argentina 49 L12, 53 F14
Bahir Dar Ethiopia 91 I14
Bahr el Azraq *see* Blue Nile
Bahr el Jebel *see* White Nile
Bahrain (anc. Tylos) *Country* SW Asia 109

Bahrain 109

a Arabic • Dinar • 1973 • 69 • £0.96 • (m) 82% (f) 69% • 83%

Bahrat Lut *see* Dead Sea
Baia Mare Romania 76 I2
Baidoa *see* Baydhabo
Baikal, L. *Lake* Russian Federation 103, 113 L11
Baile Atha Cliath *see* Dublin
Băile Herculane Romania 76 H8
Bairiki Tarawa Kiribati, Pacific Ocean 128 I8
Baja Hungary 71 L15
Baja California *Peninsula* Mexico 20, 38 G5, 41
Baker City Oregon, USA 36 L9
Baker I. *Dependent territory* Polynesia, Pacific Ocean 128 J8
Bakersfield California, USA 37 K17
Bakhtarān (var. Kermanshah) Iran 109 L4
Bakı *see* Baku
Baku (var. Bakı) Azerbaijan 85 T13
Balabac Strait *Channel* Borneo/Philippines 127 K7
Balakovo Russian Federation 83 I12
Balaton, L. *Lake* Hungary 54, 71 K14
Balbina Res. *Reservoir* Brazil 46 F7
Balearic Islands *Island group* Spain 54, 61
Bali *Island* Indonesia/SE Asia 115, 126 J16, 131
Balikesir Turkey 104 H6
Balikpapan Borneo, Indonesia 127 K12
Balkan Mts. *Mountain range* SE Europe 54, 76 J13, 75 P9
Balkhash, L. *Lake* Kazakhstan 103, 112 G12

Ballarat – Bologna

Ballarat Victoria, Australia 133 M14
Balleny Is. *Island group* Pacific Ocean, Antarctica 50 F12
Balsas *River* Mexico 39 M12
Baltic Sea N Europe 52 M7, 54-55, 57 M13, 70 J1, 80 G4, 103
Baltimore Maryland, USA 29 S3
Baltimore Virginia, USA 52 D9
Baltiysk Russian Federation 80 E9
Bălţi Moldavia 84 G7
Bamako Mali 92 I9
Bambari Central African Republic 94 K10
Bamenda Cameroon 94 E10
Ban Houayxay Laos 124 J9
Banda Is. *Island group* Indonesia 127 P13
Banda Sea SE Asia 127 N13, 128 F9
Bandar-e Abbās Iran 109 O9
Bandar-e Būshehr Iran 109 M8
Bandar Seri Begawan (var. Brunei Town) Brunei 126 J9
Bandirma Turkey 104 H6
Bandon Oregon, USA 36 F10
Bandundu (prev. Banningville) Zaire 95 I14
Bandung Java, Indonesia 126 G15
Bangalore India 117 K13
Bangassou Central African Republic 94 L10
Banggai Is. *Island group* Indonesia 127 N12
Banggi *Island* Malaysia 127 K8
Bangka *Island* Indonesia 126 G12
Bangkok (var. Krung Thep) Thailand 125 J12
Bangladesh (prev. East Pakistan) *Country* S Asia 117

Bangladesh 117

a Bengali • Taka • 2103 • 52 • £0.68 • (m) 47% (f) 22% • 5 • 6219 • Yes • 16% • 2021

Bangor Maine, USA 27 Q6
Bangor Northern Ireland, UK 59 F11
Bangui Central African Republic 94 J10
Bangweulu, L. *Lake* Zambia 97 L12
Banhine N.P. *National park* Mozambique 99 N10
Bani *River* Mali 92 J9
Banja Luka Bosnia and Herzegovina 74 J5
Banjarmasin Borneo, Indonesia 126 J13
Banjul (prev. Bathurst) Gambia 92 F9
Banks I. *Island* Northwest Territories, Canada 20, 23 L5, 51 N8
Banks L. *Lake* Washington, USA 36 J6
Banningville *see* Bandundu
Banská Bystrica Slovakia 71 L11
Bantry Bay *Sea feature* Ireland 59 A14
Banyo Cameroon 94 F10
Banyuwangi Java, Indonesia 126 J15
Baoji China 121 K9
Baotou China 119 N8
Bar Montenegro, Yugoslavia 75 L10
Bar-le-Duc France 63 N5
Baranavichy (var. Baranovichi) Belarus 80 J13
Baranovichi *see* Baranavichy
Barbados *Country* West Indies 43 T14

Barbados 43

a English • Dollar • 1554 • 75 • £1.65 • (m) 99% (f) 99% • 45%

Barbados *Island* West Indies 41
Barbuda *Island* Antigua & Barbuda 43 T10
Barcelona Spain 61 Q6
Barcelona Venezuela 44 J4
Bareilly India 117 L5
Barents Sea Arctic Ocean 51 R12, 54, 82 L5, 103
Bari Italy 73 N13
Barinas Venezuela 44 G5
Barisan Mts. *Mountain range* Sumatra, Indonesia 126 E12
Barito *River* Borneo, Indonesia 126 J11
Bârlad Romania 77 N5
Barlee, L. *Lake* Western Australia, Australia 132 G12
Barnaul Russian Federation 112 I11
Barnstaple England, UK 59 G16
Baroda *see* Vadodara
Barquisimeto Venezuela 44 H4
Barra *Island* Scotland, UK 58 E8
Barranquilla Colombia 44 E4
Barreiras Brazil 47 K11
Barreiro Portugal 60 F10
Barrie Ontario, Canada 25 K14
Barrow Alaska, USA 22 H4
Barrow *River* Ireland 59 D13
Barrow I. *Island* Western Australia, Australia 132 E8
Barstow California, USA 37 M18
Bartang *River* Tajikistan 111 P8
Bartica Guyana 44 M6
Barysaw (var. Borisov) Belarus 81 M11
Basel *see* Basle
Basilan *Island* Philippines 127 M8
Basle (var. Basel) Switzerland 68 F8
Basque Provinces *Region* Spain 61 L4
Basra Iraq 100 E4
Bass Strait *Channel* Australia 131, 133 N15
Basse-Terre Guadeloupe 43 S12
Basse Terre *Island* Guadeloupe 43 S12
Bassein Burma 124 E10
Basseterre St Kitts & Nevis 43 S10
Bastia Corsica 63 S14
Bastogne Belgium 65 K18
Basutoland *see* Lesotho
Bata Equatorial Guinea 95 E11
Batangas Luzon, Philippines 127 L4
Batanghari *River* Sumatra, Indonesia 126 E12
Batavia New York, USA 26 I8
Batavia *see* Jakarta
Bătdâmbâng Cambodia 125 K13
Bath England, UK 59 I16
Bathurst I. *Island* Northern Territory, Australia 132 I5
Bathurst I. *Island* Northwest Territories, Canada 23 M4
Bathurst New Brunswick, Canada 25 P11
Bathurst *see* Banjul
Batman Turkey 105 Q8
Batna Algeria 89 M4
Baton Rouge Louisiana, USA 28 I9
Batticaloa Sri Lanka 117 L16
Battle Creek Michigan, USA 31 N9
Batu Is. *Island group* Indonesia 126 D11
Bat'umi Georgia 85 O13
Bauchi Nigeria 93 P11
Bautzen Germany 67 N11
Bavaria *Region* Germany 67 J14
Bavarian Alps *Mountain range* Austria/Germany 67 J17
Bawean *Island* Indonesia 126 I14
Bay City Michigan, USA 31 O8
Bayamo Cuba 43 K6
Bayan Har Mts. (var. Bayan Har Shan) *Mountain range* China 119 K11
Bayan Har Shan *see* Bayan Har Mts.
Baydarata Bay *Sea feature* Russian Federation 82 O6, 112 I6
Baydhabo (var. Baidoa) Somalia 91 M17
Baykonur Kazakhstan 112 F11
Bayonne France 62 H14
Bayram-Ali Turkmenistan 111 K9
Bayreuth Germany 67 J13
Beagle Channel *Channel* Argentina 49 L20
Bear Is. *Island group* Russian Federation 113 O4
Bear L. *Lake* Idaho/Utah, USA 34 J2
Beaufort Sea Arctic Ocean 10, 20, 22 J6, 51 N7
Beaufort West South Africa 98 J15
Beaumont Texas, USA 35 T12
Beauvais France 63 L4
Beaver I. *Island* Michigan, USA 31 M5
Bečej Serbia, Yugoslavia 75 M4
Béchar Algeria 88 J6
Bedford Indiana, USA 31 M13
Be'er Sheva' *see* Beersheba
Beersheba (var. Be'er Sheva') Israel 107 L11
Bei'an China 121 P3
Beijing *see* Peking
Beira Mozambique 99 O9, 101 D11
Beirut (var. Beyrouth; anc. Berytus) Lebanon 107 M7
Beja Portugal 60 G12
Bejaïa Algeria 89 L4
Belarus (var. Belorussia) *Country* NE Europe 80-81

Belarus 80-81

a Belorussian • Ruble • 129 • 73 • £2.31 • (m) 99% (f) 99% • 268 • 246 • Yes • 66% • N/A

Belawan Sumatra, Indonesia 126 D9
Belaya Tserkov *see* Bila Tserkva
Belcher Islands *Island group* Canada 25 K5
Beledweyne Somalia 91 M16
Belém Brazil 46 J7
Belfast Northern Ireland UK 59 F11
Belfort France 63 P6
Belgaum India 116 I11
Belgian Congo *see* Zaire
Belgium *Country* W Europe 65

Belgium 65

a Dutch, French • Franc • 787 • 76 • £1.25 • (m) 99% (f) 99% • 452 • 309 • No • 97% • 3902

Belgorod Russian Federation 83 E12
Belgorod-Dnestrovskiy *see* Bilhorod-Dnistrovs'kyy
Belgrade (var. Beograd) Serbia, Yugoslavia 75 N5
Belgrano II *Research center* Antarctica 50 D7
Beli Drim *River* Serbia, Yugoslavia 75 N9
Beli Timok *River* Serbia, Yugoslavia 75 P8
Belice *River* Sicily 73 I18
Belitung *Island* Indonesia 126 G13
Belize *Country* C America 42

Belize 42

a English • Dollar • 22 • 68 • £0.92 • (m) 93% (f) 93% • 50%

Belize *River* Belize 42 C6
Belize City Belize 42 C6
Belle Fourche *River* Wyoming, USA 33 K7
Belle Île *Island* France 62 G8
Belle Isle *Island* Newfoundland, Canada 25 R7
Belle Isle, Strait of *Channel* Newfoundland, Canada 25 R8
Bellevue Washington, USA 36 H6
Bellingham Washington, USA 36 H5
Bellingshausen Plain *Sea feature* Pacific Ocean 41
Bellingshausen Sea Pacific Ocean, Antarctica 50 B9
Bellinzona Switzerland 68 H12
Bello Colombia 44 E6
Belluno Italy 72 H6
Belmopan Belize 42 C6
Belo Horizonte Brazil 47 L13
Beloit Wisconsin, USA 31 K9
Belorussia *see* Belarus
Belyy Is. *Island group* Russian Federation 112 I5
Bemidji Minnesota, USA 30 G3
Benares *see* Varanasi
Bend Oregon, USA 36 I9
Bendery *see* Tighina
Bendigo Victoria, Australia 133 M14
Benevento Italy 73 L13
Bengal, Bay of *Sea feature* India/SE Asia 103, 100 J6, 115, 117 P9, 124 D9
Benghazi Libya 89 Q6
Bengkulu Sumatra, Indonesia 126 E13
Benguela Angola 98 G6
Benguela current *Ocean current* S Atlantic Ocean 12
Beni *River* Bolivia 45 H13
Beni Mellal Morocco 88 I6
Beni Suef Egypt 90 F7
Benidorm Spain 61 O11
Benin (prev. Dahomey) *Country* W Africa 93

Benin 93

a French • Franc • 114 • 51 • £0.86 • (m) 32% (f) 16% • 38%

Benin, Bight of *Sea feature* W Africa 93 N13
Benin City Nigeria 93 O12
Bennington Vermont, USA 27 M9
Benton Harbor Michigan, USA 31 M10
Benue *River* Cameroon/Nigeria 87, 93 P12
Beograd *see* Belgrade
Beppu Japan 123 D14
Berat Albania 75 M13
Berau, Gulf of *Sea feature* Irian Jaya, Indonesia 126 Q12
Berbera Somalia 91 M14
Berbérati Central African Republic 95 H11
Berbice *River* Guyana 44 M7
Berdyans'k Ukraine 85 L8
Berettyő *River* Hungary/Romania 71 N14
Bereza *see* Byaroza
Bergama *see* Pergamon
Bergamo Italy 72 E6
Bergen Norway 52 K7, 56 H10
Bergen *see* Mons
Bergen op Zoom Netherlands 65 G12
Bergisch Gladbach Germany 67 E11
Bering Sea Pacific Ocean 10, 20, 22 C7, 103, 113 R5, 128 J3
Bering Strait *Channel* Arctic Ocean/Pacific Ocean 20, 22 E4, 103, 128 J2
Berlin Germany 66 L9
Bermejo *River* Argentina/Bolivia 48 K5
Bermuda *Dependent territory* Atlantic Ocean 52 F9
Bermuda *Island* Atlantic Ocean 20
Bermuda Rise *Sea feature* Atlantic Ocean 20
Bern Switzerland 68 E10
Bernese Alps *Mountain range* Switzerland 68 F12
Beroea *see* Ḩalab
Berry Is. *Island group* Bahamas 43 K2
Bertoua Cameroon 94 G10
Beruni Uzbekistan 110 J5
Berytus *see* Beirut
Besançon France 63 O7
Beskid Mts. *Mountain range* C Europe 71 L9
Bethel Alaska, USA 22 E7
Bethlehem West Bank 107 L10
Beykoz Turkey 104 I5
Beyrouth *see* Beirut
Beyşehir Turkey 104 J9
Beyşehir, L. *Lake* Turkey 104 J9
Bezmein Turkmenistan 110 H8
Bhamo Burma 124 H6
Bhatapara India 117 M9
Bhavnagar India 116 I8
Bhopal India 117 K8
Bhubaneswar India 117 N9
Bhumiphol Res. *Reservoir* Thailand 124 H10
Bhutan *Country* S Asia 117

Bhutan 117

a Dzongkha • Ngultrum • 80 • 49 • £0.56 • (m) 51% (f) 25% • 5%

Biak *Island* Indonesia 127 R11
Białystok Poland 71 O4
Bicuari N.P. *National park* Angola 98 G7
Biddeford Maine, USA 27 O8
Biel Switzerland 68 E9
Biel, L. *Lake* Switzerland 68 E10
Bielefeld Germany 66 F10
Bielsko-Biała Poland 71 L9
Bien Hoa Vietnam 125 N14
Big Spring Texas, USA 35 O11
Bighorn *River* Montana/Wyoming, USA 32 J6
Bighorn Mts. *Mountain range* Wyoming, USA 32 J7
Bihać Bosnia and Herzegovina 74 I5
Bijagós Archipelago *Island group* Guinea-Bissau 92 F10
Bijelo Polje Montenegro, Yugoslavia 75 M9
Bikini *Island* Marshall Islands, Pacific Ocean 128 I7
Bila Tserkva (var. Belaya Tserkov) Ukraine 84 I5
Bilbao Spain 61 L3
Bilecik Turkey 104 I6
Bilhorod-Dnistrovs'kyy (var. Belgorod-Dnestrovskiy) Ukraine 84 I8
Billings Montana, USA 32 I6
Biloxi Mississippi, USA 28 J9
Biltine Chad 94 K7
Bindura Zimbabwe 99 M8
Binghamton New York, USA 27 K10
Bingöl Turkey 105 Q7
Bintan *Island* Indonesia 126 F11
Bío-Bío *River* Chile 49 H12
Birāk *Oasis* Libya 89 O8
Birao Central African Republic 94 L8
Biratnagar Nepal 117 O6
Birganj Nepal 117 N6
Birkenhead England, UK 59 H13
Birmingham Alabama, USA 29 L7
Birmingham England, UK 59 I14
Birni n'Konni Niger 93 O9
Biscay, Bay of *Sea feature* Spain 54, 61 L3
Biscay Plain *Sea feature* Atlantic Ocean 54
Bishkek (prev. Frunze) Kyrgyzstan 111 Q4
Bisho South Africa 99 L15
Bishop California, USA 37 K15
Biskra Algeria 89 L5
Bislig Mindanao, Philippines 127 N7
Bismarck North Dakota, USA 33 M5
Bismarck Arch. *Island group* Papua New Guinea 133 O1
Bismarck Range *Mountain range* Papua New Guinea 131, 133 N2
Bismarck Sea Papua New Guinea 131, 132 O1
Bissau Guinea-Bissau 92 F10
Bistriţa Romania 76 J3
Bitlis Turkey 105 R8
Bitola Macedonia 75 O13
Bitterroot Range *Mountain range* Idaho/Montana USA 32 G6
Biysk Russian Federation 112 I11
Bizerte Tunisia 89 N4
Bjelovar Croatia 74 J3
Black Forest (var. Schwarzwald) *Physical region* Germany 67 F15
Black Hills *Mountain range* South Dakota/Wyoming, USA 33 L7
Black R. (var. Song Da) *River* China/Vietnam 124 L8
Black R. *River* Arkansas/Missouri USA 28 J4
Black Rock Desert *Desert region* Nevada, USA 20, 34 F1
Black Sea (var. Chernoye More, Kara Deniz) Asia/Europe 52 N8, 54, 77 P11, 85 M11, 103, 105 N4
Black Volta *River* West Africa 87, 93 K10
Blackpool England, UK 59 H12
Blackwater *River* Ireland 59 C14
Blagoveshchensk Russian Federation 113 O11
Blanca, Bahía *Sea feature* Argentina 49 L12
Blanca, Costa *Coastal region* Spain 61 O11
Blanco, Cape *see* Nouadhibou, Râs
Blanice *River* Czech Republic 70 H10
Blantyre Malawi 97 O15
Blenheim New Zealand 134 G9
Blida Algeria 89 L4
Bloemfontein South Africa 99 K13
Blois France 63 K7
Bloomington Illinois, USA 31 K12
Bloomington Indiana, USA 31 M13
Bloomington Minnesota, USA 30 H6
Blue Mesa Dam *Dam* Colorado, USA 35 L5
Blue Mountains *Mountain range* Oregon/Washington USA 36 K9
Blue Nile (var. Bahr el Azraq) *River* Ethiopia/Sudan 87, 91 H13
Blue Nile *River* 87
Bluefields Nicaragua 42 E11
Bo Sierra Leone 92 H12
Bo Hai *Sea feature* China 121 N7
Boa Vista Brazil 46 F6
Boaco Nicaragua 42 D10
Bobaomby, C. (var. Cap d' Ambre) *Cape* Madagascar 100 E10
Bobo-Dioulasso Burkina 93 K10
Bóbr *River* Poland 70 I6
Bobruysk *see* Babruysk
Bocas del Toro Panama 42 F14
Bochum Germany 66 E10
Bodensee *see* Constance, L.
Bodø Norway 57 L4
Bodrum Turkey 104 G9
Boende Zaire 95 K12
Bogor Java, Indonesia 126 G14
Bogotá (prev. Santa Fe) Colombia 44 E6
Bohemian Forest (var. Böhmerwald) *Physical region* Czech Republic/Germany 67 L14
Böhmerwald *see* Bohemian Forest
Bohol *Island* Philippines 127 M6
Boise Idaho, USA 32 F8
Bokaro India 117 N8
Bokna Fjord *Coastal feature* Norway 56 H11
Bol Chad 94 H7
Bolgatanga Ghana 93 L10
Bolivia *Country* S America 45

Bolivia 45

a Aymara, Quechua, Spanish • Boliviano • 18 • 60 • £0.52 • (m) 85% (f) 70% • 163 • 2100 • No • 51% • 1916

Bologna Italy 72 G8

a Language (official or most commonly spoken) • Currency • Population density per square mile • Average life expectancy • Price of 1 dozen hen's eggs • Literacy • Number of TVs per 1,000 people • Number of people per doctor • Death penalty • Percentage of urban-based population • Average number of calories consumed daily per person

Bolsena, L. – Carlsberg Ridge

Bolsena, L. *Lake* Italy 73 H11
Bolshevik I. *Island* Severnaya Zemlya, Russian Federation 113 K4
Bolton England, UK 59 I13
Bolu Turkey 104 J5
Bolvadin Turkey 104 J8
Bolzano (var. Bozen) Italy 72 G5
Boma Zaire 95 G15
Bombay India 15, 100 H6, 116 I10
Bomu *River* Central African Republic/Zaire 94 M10
Bon, C. *Cape* Tunisia 87
Bonaire *Island* Netherlands Antilles 43 O14
Bondo Zaire 95 L11
Bone, Gulf of *Sea feature* Celebes, Indonesia 127 L13
Bongor Chad 94 H8
Bonifacio Corsica, France 63 S16
Bonifacio, Strait of *Channel* Sardinia 73 D12
Bonn Germany 67 E11
Boosaaso Somalia 91 O14
Boothia, Gulf of *Sea feature* Northwest Territories, Canada 23 O6
Borås Sweden 56 J13
Bordeaux France 62 I12
Borger Texas, USA 35 O8
Borisov *see* Barysaw
Borlänge Sweden 57 K11
Borneo *Island* SE Asia 100 M8, 115, 126 J11, 131
Bornholm *Island* Denmark 57 K16
Borobudur *Archaeological site* Java, Indonesia 126 H15
Borūjerd Iran 109 M5
Bosanska Gradiška Bosnia and Herzegovina 74 J5
Bosanska Krupa Bosnia and Herzegovina 74 I5
Bosna *River* Bosnia and Herzegovina 75 K7
Bosnia and Herzegovina *Country* SE Europe 74-75

Bosnia and Herzegovina 74-75

a Serbo-Croat • Dinar • 213 • 72 • £8.20 • (av.) 93% • 36%

Bosobolo Zaire 95 J11
Bosporus *Channel* Turkey 104 I5
Bossangoa Central African Republic 94 I10
Bosten, L. *Lake* China 115, 118 H7
Boston Massachusetts, USA 27 O10
Boston Mts. *Mountain range* Arkansas, USA 28 H4
Bothnia, Gulf of *Sea Feature* Finland/Sweden 54, 57 N8
Botoşani Romania 77 M2
Botswana *Country* Southern Africa 98-99

Botswana 98-99

a English • Pula • 5 • 68 • £0.87 • (m) 84% (f) 65% • 28%

Bouaké Ivory Coast 92 J12
Bouar Central African Republic 94 H10
Bougainville *Island* Papua New Guinea 133 Q2
Bougouni Mali 92 J10
Boulder Colorado, USA 35 M4
Boulogne France 52 K8, 63 K2
Boumalne-Dadès Morocco 88 I6
Bountiful Utah, USA 34 J3
Bounty Is. *Island group* New Zealand, Pacific Ocean 128 J12
Bourg-en-Bresse France 63 O9
Bourges France 63 L8
Bourke New South Wales, Australia 133 N11
Bournemouth England, UK 59 I17
Bouvet I. *Dependent territory* Atlantic Ocean 53 K16
Bowling Green Kentucky, USA 29 M4
Boyoma Falls (prev. Stanley Falls) *Waterfall* Zaire 95 M12
Bozeman Montana, USA 32 H6
Bozen *see* Bolzano
Brač *Island* Croatia 74 I8
Bracciano, L. *Lake* Italy 72 H11
Bradano *River* Italy 73 M13
Bradford England, UK 59 J13
Braga Portugal 60 F6
Bragança Portugal 60 H6
Brahmaputra (var. Yarlung Zangbo) *River* India/China 115, 117 P6, 118 G13
Brăila Romania 77 O7
Brainerd Minnesota, USA 30 H5
Branco *River* Brazil 41
Brandenburg Germany 66 K9
Brandon Manitoba, Canada 23 O15
Brasília Brazil 47 J12
Braşov Romania 77 L6
Bratislava (prev. Posonium) Slovakia 70 J12
Bratsk Russian Federation 113 K10
Brattleboro Vermont, USA 27 N9
Braunau am Inn Austria 69 N5
Braunschweig Germany 66 I9
Brava, Costa *Coastal region* Spain 61 R5
Bravo del Norte *River* Mexico 39 K3
Brawley California, USA 37 N19
Brazil *Country* S America 46-47

Brazil 46-47

a Portuguese • Cruzeiro • 47 • 67 • £0.63 • (m) 83% (f) 80% • 213 • 852 • No • 75% • 2751

Brazil Basin *Sea feature* Atlantic Ocean 53 I12
Brazil current *Ocean current* Atlantic Ocean 12
Brazilian Highlands *Mountain range* Brazil 41, 47 L12
Brazos *River* Texas, USA 35 R11
Brazzaville Congo 95 H14
Brecon Beacons *Mountain range* Wales, UK 59 H15
Breda Netherlands 65 H12
Bregalnica *River* Macedonia 75 P11
Bregenz Austria 68 I8
Bremen Germany 66 G8
Bremerhaven Germany 52 L8, 66 G7
Bremerton Washington, USA 36 H6
Brenner Pass Austria/Italy 69 L9
Brescia Italy 72 F7
Breslau *see* Wroclaw
Brest Belarus 80 H15
Brest France 62 F6
Breton Sound *Inlet* Louisiana, USA 28 J10
Bria Central African Republic 94 K10
Bridgeport Connecticut, USA 27 M11
Bridgetown Barbados 43 T14
Brienz, L. of *Lake* Switzerland 68 G11
Brig Switzerland 68 F12
Brigham City Utah, USA 34 J2
Bright Angel Point *Physical feature* Arizona, USA 34 J2
Brighton England, UK 59 K17
Brindisi Italy 73 P13
Brisbane Queensland, Australia 128 H11, 133 P10
Bristol England, UK 59 H16
Bristol Bay *Sea feature* Alaska, USA 22 E8
Bristol Channel *Sea feature* England/Wales, UK 59 G16
Britain *Island* W Europe 54
British Columbia *Province* Canada 22
British Guiana *see* Guyana
British Indian Ocean Territory *Dependent territory* Indian Ocean 100 H9
British Virgin Islands *Dependent territory* West Indies 43 R9
Brittany *Region* France 62 G6
Brno Czech Republic 70 J10
Broken Arrow Oklahoma, USA 33 P14
Broken Hill New South Wales, Australia 133 M12
Broken Ridge *Sea feature* Indian Ocean 101 K12
Brokopondo Suriname 44 O6
Bromo *Volcano* Java, Indonesia 115
Brooks Range *Mountain range* Alaska, USA 10, 20, 22 H5
Broome Western Australia, Australia 132 G7
Brownsville Texas, USA 35 R16
Bruce, Mt. *Mountain* Australia 131
Bruges (var. Brugge) Belgium 65 D13
Brugge *see* Bruges
Brunei *Country* Borneo, SE Asia 126

Brunei 126

a Malay • Dollar • 130 • 76 • £0.97 • (m) 91% (f) 79% • 81%

Brunei Town *see* Bandar Seri Begawan
Brunswick Georgia, USA 29 O10
Brunswick Maine, USA 27 P7
Brussels (var. Bruxelles) Belgium 65 G15
Bruxelles *see* Brussels
Bryansk Russian Federation 82 E10
Bryce Canyon *Physical feature* Arizona, USA 34 I5
Bua *River* Malawi 97 N13
Būbiyān I. *Island* Kuwait 109 L7
Bucaramanga Colombia 44 F6
Buchanan Liberia 92 H13
Bucharest (var. Bucureşti; anc. Cetatea, Dambovitei) Romania 77 L9
Bucureşti *see* Bucharest
Budapest Hungary 71 L13
Buenaventura Colombia 44 D7, 129 Q8
Buenos Aires Argentina 14, 48 M10, 53 F14
Buenos Aires, L *Lake* Argentina/Chile 49 I16
Buffalo New York, USA 26 H8
Bug *River* Poland/Ukraine 71 O5
Buḥayrat al Asad *see* Assad, L.
Bujumbura Burundi 97 K7
Bukavu Zaire 95 O13
Bukhara (var. Bukhoro) Uzbekistan 111 L7
Bukhoro *see* Bukhara
Bukoba Tanzania 97 M5
Bulawayo Zimbabwe 99 L9
Bulgaria *Country* E Europe 76-77

Bulgaria 76-77

a Bulgarian • Lev • 206 • 73 • £0.33 • (m) 94% (f) 93% • 250 • 324 • Yes • 68% • 3707

Bumba Zaire 95 L11
Bunbury Western Australia, Australia 132 F13
Bundaberg Queensland, Australia 133 P9
Bunia Zaire 95 O12
Buon Me Thuot Vietnam 125 O13
Bûr Safâga Egypt 90 G8
Bûr Sa'îd *see* Port Said
Burao *see* Burco
Buraydah Saudi Arabia 108 J9
Burco (var. Burao) Somalia 91 M14
Burdur Turkey 104 I9
Burgas Bulgaria 77 N13
Burgos Spain 61 K5
Burgundy *Region* France 63 N7
Burkina (var. Burkina Faso; prev. Upper Volta) *Country* W Africa 93

Burkina 93

a French • Franc • 88 • 48 • N/A • (m) 28% (f) 9% • 9%

Burkina Faso *see* Burkina
Burlington Iowa, USA 33 R10
Burlington Vermont, USA 27 M6
Burma (var. Myanmar) *Country* SE Asia 124-125

Burma 124-125

a Burmese • Kyat • 168 • 62 • £4.26 • (m) 89% (f) 72% • 2 • 43 • Yes • 25% • 2440

Burnie Tasmania, Australia 133 N16
Burns Oregon, USA 36 K10
Bursa Turkey 104 H6
Burtnieki, L. *Lake* Latvia 80 J4
Buru *Island* Indonesia 127 N12
Burundi *Country* C Africa 97

Burundi 97

a French, Kirundi • Franc • 565 • 47 • £0.98 • (m) 61% (f) 40% • 6%

Büsingen Germany 68 G8
Buta Zaire 95 M11
Butare Rwanda 97 L6
Butembo Zaire 95 O12
Butler Pennsylvania, USA 26 G11
Buton *Island* Indonesia 127 M13
Butte Montana, USA 32 H6
Butterworth Malaysia 125 I17
Butuan Mindanao, Philippines 127 N7
Buyo Res. *Reservoir* Ivory Coast 92 J12
Buzău Romania 77 M7
Buzău *River* Romania 77 N7
Byarezina *River* Belarus 81 M11
Byaroza (var. Bereza) Belarus 80 I14
Bydgoszcz Poland 71 K4
Bykhaw (var. Bykhov) Belarus 81 N12
Bykhov *see* Bykhaw
Bytantay *River* Russian Federation 113 N7
Bytom Poland 71 L8
Byzantium *see* Istanbul

C

Caazapá Paraguay 48 N6
Caballo Res. *Reservoir* New Mexico, USA 35 L10
Cabanatuan Luzon, Philippines 127 L4
Cabimas Venezuela 44 G4
Cabinda *Region* Angola 95 F14, 98 F2
Cabora Bassa L. *Reservoir* Mozambique 99 N7
Cabot Strait *Channel* Canada 25 R10
Čačak Serbia, Yugoslavia 75 N7
Cáceres Spain 60 H9
Cachapoal *River* Chile 49 G11
Cadiz Negros, Philippines 127 M6
Cádiz Spain 60 H14
Cádiz, Gulf of *Sea feature* Spain 60 H13
Caen France 62 I4
Caernarfon Wales, UK 59 G13
Cagayan de Oro Mindanao, Philippines 127 N7
Cagliari Sardinia 73 D15
Cagliari, Gulf of *Sea feature* Sardinia 73 D16
Cahors France 63 K12
Caicos Is. *Island group* Turks & Caicos Islands 41, 43 N6
Cairns Queensland, Australia 133 N6
Cairo (var. El Qâhira) Egypt 15, 90 F6
Cajamarca Peru 45 C11
Čakovec Croatia 74 I2
Calabar Nigeria 93 P13
Calafate Argentina 49 I18
Calais France 63 K1
Calais Maine, USA 27 R5
Calama Chile 48 G5
Călăraşi Romania 77 N9
Calbayog Samar, Philippines 127 N5
Calcutta India 15, 100 J5, 117 O8
Caldas da Rainha Portugal 60 F9
Caleta Olivia Argentina 49 J16
Calgary Alberta, Canada 23 L14
Cali Colombia 44 D7
Calicut India 116 J14
California *State* USA 37
California current *Ocean current* Pacific Ocean 12
California, Gulf of *Sea feature* Mexico 10, 20, 41, 38 H6, 129 O6
Callao Peru 45 D13, 129 Q9
Callipolis *see* Gallipoli
Caltanissetta Sicily 73 K18
Calvinia South Africa 98 J15
Camagüey Cuba 42 J5
Cambodia (prev. Kampuchea) *Country* SE Asia 125

Cambodia 125

a Khmer • Riel • 127 • 51 • £0.99 • (m) 48% (f) 22% • 9 • 43 • No • 12% • 2166

Cambrian Mts. *Mountain range* Wales, UK 59 G14
Cambridge England, UK 59 K15
Camden New Jersey, USA 27 K13
Cameia N.P. *National park* Angola 98 J5
Cameron Highlands *Mountain range* Malaysia 125 J18
Cameroon *Country* C Africa 94-95

Cameroon 94-95

a English, French • Franc • 67 • 57 • £1.72 • (m) 66% (f) 43% • 41%

Cameroon, Mt. *Volcano* Cameroon 8, 87
Campbell I. *Island* New Zealand, Pacific Ocean 128 J13
Campbell Plateau *Sea feature* Pacific Ocean 131
Campbell River Vancouver I. British Columbia, Canada 22 I14
Campeche Mexico 39 S12
Campeche, Bay of *Sea feature* Mexico 39 Q12
Campina Grande Brazil 47 H13
Campinas Brazil 47 K14
Campobasso Italy 73 K12
Can Tho Vietnam 125 M15
Canada *Country* N America 22-23, 24-25

Canada 22-25

a English, French • Dollar • 8 • 78 • £0.78 • (m) 96% (f) 96% • 641 • 452 • No • 41% • 3482

Canada Basin *Sea Feature* Arctic Ocean 20, 103
Canadian River *River* USA 25 N8, 33 P15
Canadian Shield *Physical feature* Canada 20
Çanakkale Turkey 104 G6
Canaries current *Ocean current* Atlantic Ocean 12
Canary Basin *Sea feature* Atlantic Ocean 52 H10
Canary Islands *Island group* Atlantic Ocean 52 I9, 87
Canaveral, Cape *Cape* Florida, USA 29 O12
Canberra Australian Capital Territory, Australia 133 O13
Cancún Mexico 39 T11
Caniapiscau *River* Quebec, Canada 25 N5
Caniapiscau Res. *Reservoir* Quebec, Canada 25 M7
Çankiri Turkey 105 L6
Canna *Island* Scotland, UK 58 F8
Cannes France 63 Q13
Canterbury England, UK 59 L16
Canterbury Bight *Sea feature* New Zealand 134 E12
Canton (var. Guangzhou) China 121 L14
Canton Illinois, USA 30 J11
Canton Ohio, USA 31 Q11
Canyon De Chelly *National monument* Arizona, USA 35 K7
Canyon Ferry L. *Lake* Montana, USA 32 H5
Cap-Haïtien Haiti 43 M7
Cape Basin *Sea feature* Atlantic Ocean 53 L14, 87
Cape Coast Ghana 93 L13
Cape Cod *Peninsula* Massachusetts, USA 10, 20, 27 P10
Cape Girardeau Missouri, USA 33 T12
Cape Town South Africa 53 M14, 98 I16, 101 B12
Cape Verde *Country* Atlantic Ocean 52 I10

Cape Verde 52

a Portuguese • Escudo • 246 • 66 • £1.31 • (m) 61% (f) 29% • 65%

Cape Verde Basin *Sea feature* Atlantic Ocean 53 H11
Cape Verde Is. *Island group* Atlantic Ocean 87
Cape York Peninsula *Physical feature* Queensland, Australia 131, 133 M5
Cappadocia *Physical region* Turkey 105 M7
Capri *Island* Italy 73 K14
Caquetá *River* Brazil/Colombia 44 G8
Caracas Venezuela 44 I4
Caratasca Lagoon *Coastal feature* Honduras 42 F9
Carbondale Illinois, USA 31 K15
Carcassonne France 63 L14
Cardiff Wales, UK 59 H16
Cardigan Bay *Sea feature* Wales, UK 59 G14
Caribbean Plate *Physical feature* 8, 20, 41
Caribbean Sea Atlantic Ocean 10, 13, 20, 41, 52 D10
Caribou Maine, USA 27 Q2
Carlisle England, UK 59 I11
Carlisle Pennsylvania, USA 26 J13
Carlsbad New Mexico, USA 35 N10
Carlsberg Ridge *Sea feature* Indian Ocean 100 G8

Carlyle L. – Corfu

Carlyle L. *Lake* Illinois, USA 31 K14
Carmen I. *Island* Mexico 38 H7
Carnarvon Western Australia, Australia 132 E10
Carnegie, L. *Lake* Western Australia, Australia 132 H10
Carolina Brazil 46 K9
Caroline Is. *Island group* Federated States of Micronesia, Pacific Ocean 128 H8
Caroline Ridge *Sea feature* Pacific Ocean 131
Carpathians *Mountain range* E Europe 54, 71 L10, 77 L4, 84 E6
Carpentaria, Gulf of *Sea feature* Northern Territory/Queensland, Australia 131, 133 L6
Carson City Nevada, USA 34 E3
Cartagena Colombia 44 E4, 53 D11
Cartagena Spain 61 N12
Cartago Costa Rica 42 E13
Cartwright Newfoundland, Canada 25 R6
Casa Grande Arizona, USA 34 I10
Casablanca Morocco 52 K9, 88 H5
Cascade Range *Mountain range* USA 20, 36 I8
Caseyr, C. *Cape* Somalia 87
Casper Wyoming, USA 33 K9
Caspian Sea *Lake* Asia/Europe 54-55, 83 G16, 85 T13, 103, 109 N2, 110 F7, 112 C10
Castellón de la Plana Spain 61 O8
Castelo Branco Portugal 60 G9
Castries St Lucia 43 T13
Castro Chile 49 G15
Cat I. *Island* Bahamas 43 L3
Catalonia *Region* Spain 61 P6
Catamarca Argentina 48 I8
Catanduanes *Island* Philippines 127 M4
Catania Sicily 73 L18
Catanzaro Italy 73 N16
Catskill Mts. *Mountain range* New York, USA 27 L10
Cauca *River* Colombia 44 E5
Caucasus Mts. *Mountain range* Europe/Asia 54, 83 E16, 85 P11, 103
Cauquenes Chile 48 G12
Cauvery Falls *Waterfall* India 115
Cavally *River* Ivory Coast 92 I13
Caxito Angola 98 G4
Cayenne French Guiana 44 P7, 53 F11
Cayman Brac *Island* Cayman Islands 42 I6
Cayman Islands *Dependent territory* Caribbean Sea 42 H6
Ceará Plain *Sea feature* Atlantic Ocean 41
Cebu Cebu, Philippines 127 M6
Cebu *Island* Philippines 127 M6
Cedar *River* Iowa, USA 33 Q8
Cedar Rapids Iowa, USA 33 R9
Cedros I. *Island* Mexico 38 F5
Cefalù Sicily 73 K17
Celaya Mexico 39 M11
Celebes (var. Sulawesi) *Island* Indonesia 115, 127 L12, 131
Celebes Basin *Sea feature* SE Asia 131
Celebes Sea SE Asia 115, 127 M9, 128 F8, 131
Celje Slovenia 74 H2
Celle Germany 66 H9
Celtic Shelf *Sea Feature* Atlantic Ocean 54
Central African Republic *Country* C Africa 94-95

Central African Republic (C.A.R.) 94-95

a French • Franc • 13 • 49 • £4.30 • (m) 52% (f) 25% • 47%

Central America *Region* 20, 41
Central Arizona Project *Irrigation project* Arizona, USA 34 I9
Central Siberian Plateau *Physical region* Russian Federation 103, 113 L6
Centralia Illinois, USA 31 K14
Cerralvo I. *Island* Mexico 38 I8
Cerro Bonete *Mountain* Chile 41
Cerro de Pasco Peru 44 D12
Cēsis Latvia 80 J5
České Budějovice Czech Republic 70 H10
Česma *River* Croatia 74 I3
Cetatea *see* Bucharest
Ceuta *Spanish enclave* NW Africa 88 I4
Cévennes *Mountain range* France 63 M13
Ceyhan *River* Turkey 105 N9
Ceylon *see* Sri Lanka
Ceylon Plain *Sea feature* Indian Ocean 103, 115
Chad *Country* C Africa 94

Chad 94

a Arabic, French • Franc • 12 • 48 • £2.15 • (m) 42% (f) 18% • 30%

Chad, L. *Lake* C Africa 87, 93 R9, 94 H7
Chagai Hills *Mountain range* Pakistan 116 F4
Chagos-Laccadive Plateau *Sea feature* Indian Ocean 103, 115
Chagos Trench *Sea feature* Indian Ocean 115
Chāh Bahār Iran 100 G5, 109 Q11
Chaitén Chile 49 H15
Chalbi Desert *Desert region* Kenya 97 P2
Chalcis *see* Chalkida
Chalkida (var. Chalcis) Greece 79 K8
Châlons-sur-Marne France 63 N5
Chambal *River* India 117 K6
Chambéry France 63 O10
Chambord France 63 K7
Champaign Illinois, USA 31 L12
Champasak Laos 125 M12
Champlain, L. *Lake* New York/Vermont, USA 27 M6
Chañaral Chile 48 G7
Chandigarh India 117 K4
Changchun China 121 P5
Changsha China 121 L12
Changzhi China 121 L8
Chania Crete, Greece 79 L15
Channel Islands *Island group* UK 59 H18, 62 G4
Channel-Port-aux-Basques Newfoundland, Canada 25 R10
Chanthaburi Thailand 125 K13
Chapala, L. *Lake* Mexico 39 L11
Chardzhev (prev. Chardzhou) Turkmenistan 111 K8
Chardzhou *see* Chardzhev
Charente *River* France 62 I10
Chari *River* Chad 94 H8
Chariton *River* Iowa/Missouri, USA 33 R10
Charleroi Belgium 65 G16
Charles, Cape *Cape* Virgina, USA 29 S5
Charleston South Carolina, USA 29 P8
Charleston West Virginia, USA 29 P3
Charleville Queensland, Australia 133 N10
Charlotte North Carolina, USA 29 P6
Charlotte Amalie Virgin Islands (US) 43 R9
Charlottesville Virginia, USA 29 Q4
Charlottetown Prince Edward Island, Canada 25 Q11
Chartres France 63 K5
Chashma Barrage *Dam* Pakistan 116 I2
Châteauroux France 63 K8
Chatham Is. *Island group* New Zealand, Pacific Ocean 128 J12
Chattahoochee *River* Alabama/Georgia, USA 29 M7
Chattanooga Tennessee, USA 29 M6
Chauk Burma 124 F8
Chaumont France 63 N6
Cheboksary Russian Federation 83 I11
Cheboygan Michigan, USA 31 N5
Cheju South Korea 121 P9
Chelan, L. *Lake* Washington, USA 36 I6
Cheleken Turkmenistan 110 F6
Chełm Poland 71 P7
Chelyabinsk Russian Federation 112 G9
Chelyuskin, C. *Cape* Russian Federation 113 L4
Chemnitz Germany 67 L11
Chenab *River* India/Pakistan 116 J3
Chengdu China 120 J10
Chequamegon Bay *Physical feature* Wisconsin, USA 30 J4
Cherbourg France 62 H4
Cherepovets Russian Federation 82 H9
Cherkasy Ukraine 84 J5
Cherkessk Russian Federation 83 E15
Chernigov *see* Chernihiv
Chernihiv Ukraine 84 I3
Chernivtsi (var. Chernivtsi) Ukraine 84 F6
Chernobyl Ukraine 84 I4
Chernovtsy *see* Chernivtsi
Chernoye More *see* Black Sea
Chernyakhovsk Russian Federation 80 G10
Chesapeake Bay Maryland/Virginia, USA 29 S4
Chesha Bay *Sea feature* Russian Federation 82 L6
Chester England, UK 59 H13
Chesterfield Inlet *Sea feature* Northwest Territories, Canada 23 O9
Chesuncook L. *Lake* Maine, USA 27 P4
Chetumal Mexico 39 T12
Cheyenne Wyoming, USA 33 K10
Cheyenne *River* South Dakota/Wyoming, USA 33 M7
Chi-lung Taiwan 121 O13
Chiang Jiang *see* Yangtze
Chiang Mai Thailand 124 I9
Chiang Rai Thailand 124 I9
Chiba Japan 123 L11
Chibougamau Quebec, Canada 25 L10
Chicago Illinois, USA 31 L10
Chichén Itzá *Archaeological site* Mexico 39 T11
Chiclayo Peru 45 C11
Chico California, USA 37 H13
Chicoutimi Quebec, Canada 25 N11
Chidley, C. *Cape* Quebec, Canada 25 O2
Chiemsee *Lake* Germany 67 K16
Chifeng (var. Ulanhad) China 119 Q6
Chihuahua Mexico 39 K5
Chile *Country* S America 48-49

Chile 48-49

a Spanish • Peso • 46 • 72 • £0.67 • (m) 94% (f) 93% • 205 • 2383 • Yes • 86% • 2581

Chile Basin *Sea feature* Pacific Ocean 41, 129 Q12
Chile Chico Chile 49 I16
Chile Rise *Sea feature* Pacific Ocean 41
Chillán Chile 49 G12
Chillicothe Ohio, USA 31 P13
Chiloé I. *Island* Chile 41, 49 G15, 129 Q13
Chilpancingo Mexico 39 N13
Chimborazo *Mountain* Ecuador 41
Chimbote Peru 45 C12, 129 Q9
Chimkent *see* Shymkent
Chimoio Mozambique 99 N9
Chin Hills *Mountain range* Burma/India 124 E7
China *Country* E Asia 9, 118-119, 120-121

China 118-121

a Mandarin • Yuan • 319 • 70 • £0.37 • (m) 84% (f) 62% • 31 • 1077 • Yes • 33% • 2639

China Lake Naval Weapons Center *Military center* California, USA 37 L17
Chinandega Nicaragua 42 C10
Chindwin *River* Burma/India 124 F6
Chingola Zambia 97 K13
Chinhoyi (var. Sinoia) Zimbabwe 99 M8
Chioggia Italy 72 H7
Chios Chios, Greece 79 O8
Chios *Island* Greece 79 O8
Chipata Zambia 97 M13
Chippewa L. *Lake* Wisconsin, USA 30 J5
Chirchik Uzbekistan 111 N6
Chiriquí, Gulf of *Sea feature* Panama 42 E15
Chişinău (var. Kishinev) Moldavia 84 H8
Chita ICBM Base *Military center* Russian Federation 113 M11
Chitré Panama 42 G15
Chittagong Bangladesh 117 P8
Chitungwiza Zimbabwe 99 M8
Chobe *River* Botswana/Namibia 99 K8
Chobe N.P. *National park* Botswana 99 K8
Chojnice Poland 71 K3
Cholula *Archaeological site* Mexico 39 N12
Choluteca Honduras 42 C9
Choma Zambia 96 J16
Chon Buri Thailand 125 J13
Ch'ŏngjin North Korea 121 Q5
Chongqing China 120 J11
Chott El Jerid *Physical region* Algeria 87 M6
Choybalsan Mongolia 119 O4
Christchurch New Zealand 134 F11
Christiania *see* Oslo
Christianstad Virgin Islands 43 R10
Christmas I. *Dependent territory* Indian Ocean 100 M10
Chu *River* Kazakhstan/Kyrgyzstan 112 F12
Chubut *River* Argentina 49 I15
Chūgoku Mountains *Mountain range* Japan 123 E12
Chukchi Sea Arctic Ocean 51 P5, 113 P2
Chumphon Thailand 125 H14
Chuquicamata Chile 48 G5
Chur Switzerland 68 I10
Churchill Manitoba, Canada 23 O11
Churchill *River* Manitoba, Canada 23 O11
Churchill Falls Newfoundland, Canada 25 P7
Cienfuegos Cuba 42 I4
Cincinnati Ohio, USA 31 O13
Cirebon Java, Indonesia 126 H15
Citlaltépetl, Mt. *Mountain* Mexico 20
Ciudad Bolívar Venezuela 44 J5
Ciudad del Este Paraguay 48 O6
Ciudad Guayana Venezuela 44 K5
Ciudad Juárez Mexico 39 K3
Ciudad Madero Mexico 39 O10
Ciudad Obregón Mexico 38 I5
Ciudad Real Spain 61 K10
Ciudad Victoria Mexico 39 N9
Čiovo *Island* Croatia 74 I8
Civitavecchia Italy 73 H11
Clair Eagle L. *Lake* California, USA 37 H12
Claremont New Hampshire, USA 27 N8
Clarence Strait *Channel* Northern Territory, Australia 132 I5
Clarenville Newfoundland, Canada 25 T9
Clarion Facture Zone *Sea feature* Pacific Ocean 129 M7
Clarksville Tennessee, USA 29 L4
Clearwater Florida, USA 29 N13
Clermont Queensland, Australia 133 O9
Clermont-Ferrand France 63 M10
Cleveland Ohio, USA 31 P10
Clipperton Fracture Zone *Sea feature* Pacific Ocean 129 M7
Clipperton I. *Dependent territory* C. America, Pacific Ocean 129 O7
Cloncurry Queensland, Australia 133 M8
Clovis New Mexico, USA 35 N9
Cluj-Napoca Romania 76 I4
Clyde *River* Scotland, UK 58 H10
Coast Ranges *Mountain range* N America 10, 20, 37 G13
Coatzacoalcos Mexico 39 Q13
Cobán Guatemala 42 B7
Cobija Bolivia 45 H13
Cochabamba Bolivia 45 I15
Cochin India 100 I7, 116 J15
Cochrane Chile 49 I17
Cochrane Ontario, Canada 24 J11
Cockburn Sound Australia 101 M12
Coco *River* Honduras 42 E9
Cocos Is. *Dependent territory* Indian Ocean 100 L10
Cocos Plate *Physical feature* 8, 20, 41
Cocos Ridge *Sea feature* Pacific Ocean 41, 129 P8
Cody Wyoming, USA 32 I7
Coeur d'Alene Idaho, USA 32 F4
Coiba I. *Island* Panama 42 F15
Coihaique Chile 49 H16
Coimbatore India 116 J14
Coimbra Portugal 60 F8
Colbeck, C. *Cape* Pacific Ocean Coast, Antarctica 50 D11
Colchester England, UK 59 L15
Colditz *Castle* Germany 67 L11
Colhué Huapí, L *Lake* Argentina 49 J16
Colima Mexico 39 K12
Colima *Volcano* Mexico 20
Coll *Island* Scotland, UK 58 F8
Collier Bay *Sea feature* Western Australia, Australia 132 H6
Colmar France 63 P6
Cologne (var. Köln) Germany 67 E11
Colombia *Country* S America 44

Colombia 44

a Spanish • Peso • 82 • 69 • £0.54 • (m) 88% (f) 86% • 115 • 1102 • No • 70% • 2598

Colombian Basin *Sea feature* Caribbean Sea 41
Colombo Sri Lanka 100 I7, 117 K16
Colombus Nebraska, USA 33 O10
Colón Argentina 48 M9
Colón Panama 42 G14
Colonia Uruguay 48 N10
Colonsay *Island* Scotland, UK 58 F9
Colorado *River* Argentina 49 K13
Colorado *River* Mexico/USA 20, 35 K5, 37 O18, 38 G1, 41, 129 N5
Colorado *State* USA 35
Colorado Plateau *Physical region* Arizona, USA 34 I7
Colorado Project *Irrigation project* Colorado, USA 34 H10
Colorado Springs Colorado, USA 35 M5
Columbia Missouri, USA 33 R11
Columbia South Carolina, USA 29 P7
Columbia *River* Canada/USA 20, 23 K14, 36 K5, 129 N4
Columbine, C. *Cape* South Africa 98 I15
Columbus Georgia, USA 29 M8
Columbus Indiana, USA 31 N13
Columbus Mississippi, USA 29 K7
Columbus Ohio, USA 31 P12
Colville *River* Alaska, USA 22 H5
Comacchio Lagoon *Lake* Italy 72 H8
Comayagua Honduras 42 C8
Comilla Bangladesh 117 P8
Communism Peak (var. Pik Kommunizma, prev. Mt. Stalin) *Peak* Tajikistan 103
Como, L. *Lake* Italy 72 E6
Comodoro Rivadavia Argentina 49 K16
Comorin, C. *Cape* India 100 I7, 115
Comoros *Country* Indian Ocean 100 E10

Comoros 100

a Arabic, French • Franc • 571 • 56 • £1.19 • (m) 56% (f) 40% • 28%

Comoros Is. *Island group* Indian Ocean 87
Conakry Guinea 92 G11
Concepción Chile 49 G12, 129 Q12
Concepción Paraguay 48 M5
Conchas L. *Lake* New Mexico, USA 35 M10
Conchos *River* Mexico 38 J5
Concord California, USA 37 H15
Concord New Hampshire, USA 27 N8
Concordia Argentina 48 M9
Congo *Country* C Africa 95

Congo 95

a French • Franc • 18 • 53 • £1.43 • (m) 70% (f) 44% • 41%

Congo (var. Zaire) *River* C Africa 11, 53 M12, 87, 95, J12, 98 G2, 95 I13
Congo Basin *Physical region* Congo/Zaire 11, 87
Connecticut *River* USA 27 N7
Connecticut *State* USA 27 M10
Constance, L. (var. Bodensee) *Lake* C Europe 54, 67 G17, 68 H8
Constantine Algeria 89 M4
Constantinople *see* Istanbul
Constanța Romania 77 P9
Contwoyto L. *Lake* Northwest Territories, Canada 23 M9
Coober Pedy South Australia, Australia 133 K11
Cook Islands *Dependent territory* Polynesia, Pacific Ocean 129 K10
Cook, Mt. *Mountain* South I. New Zealand 131
Cook Strait *Channel* New Zealand 128 I12, 131, 134 G8
Cooktown Queensland, Australia 133 N6
Cooper Creek *River* Queenland/South Australia, Australia 133 L11
Coos Bay Oregon, USA 36 F10
Copán *Archaeological site* Honduras 42 C8
Copenhagen Denmark 56 J15
Copiapó Chile 48 G7
Coppermine Northwest Territories, Canada 23 L8
Coppermine *River* Northwest Territories, Canada 23 L8
Copşa Mică Romania 76 J6
Coquilhatville *see* Mbandaka
Coquimbo Chile 48 G9
Corabia Romania 76 J10
Coral Sea Pacific Ocean 128 H10, 131, 133 O4
Coral Sea Basin *Sea feature* Pacific Ocean 131
Coral Sea Is. *Dependent territory* Pacific Ocean 128 H10
Cordillera Cantábrica *Mountain range* Spain 54, 60 I4
Córdoba Argentina 48 J9
Córdoba Spain 60 J12
Cordova Alaska, USA 22 G9
Corfu Corfu, Greece 78 F5

a Language (official or most commonly spoken) • Currency • Population density per square mile • Average life expectancy • Price of 1 dozen hen's eggs • Literacy • Number of TVs per 1,000 people • Number of people per doctor • Death penalty • Percentage of urban-based population • Average number of calories consumed daily per person

141

Durango – Fort Smith

Durango Mexico 39 K8
Durazno Uruguay 48 N10
Durban South Africa 99 M14, 101 C12
Durham North Carolina, USA 29 Q5
Durrës Albania 75 L12
Dushanbe (prev. Stalinabad) Tajikistan 111 N8
Düsseldorf Germany 67 D11
Dutch East Indies *see* Indonesia
Dutch Guiana *see* Suriname
Dutch Harbor Unalaska I. Aleutian Is. Alaska, USA 22 C8
Dvina *see* Dvina, Northern or Dvina, Western
Dvina, Northern *River* Russian Federation 54, 82 J8
Dvina, Western (var. Daugava) *River* NE Europe 54, 80 I6, 81 M8
Dzhalal-Abad Kyrgyzstan 111 P6
Dzhambul *see* Zhambyl
Dzhezkazgan *see* Zhezkazgan
Dzhizak Uzbekistan 111 M7
Dzhugdzhur Range *Mountain range* Russian Federation 113 O9
Dzungaria *Mountain range* China/Kazakhstan 103

E

Eagle L. *Lake* California, USA 37 I12
Eagle L. *Lake* Maine, USA 27 P3
Eagle Mountain L. *Lake* Texas, USA 35 Q10
Eagle Pass Texas, USA 35 P14
East African Plateau *Physical feature* Kenya/Uganda 87
East Anglia *Region* England, UK 59 M14
East C. *Cape* Papua New Guinea 133 P4
East China Sea China 115, 121 O12, 123 B17, 128 F6
East Frisian Is. *Island group* Germany 66 E7
East Greenland current *Ocean current* Atlantic Ocean 12
East Indies (var. Indonesia) *Island group* SE Asia 115, 131
East Liverpool Ohio, USA 31 Q11
East London South Africa 99 L15
East Pacific Ridge *Sea feature* Pacific Ocean 41
East Pacific Rise *Sea feature* Pacific Ocean 129 O9
East Pakistan *see* Bangladesh
East St. Louis Illinois, USA 30 J14
East Siberian Sea Arctic Ocean 51 R6, 103, 113 O3
Easter I. *Island* Polynesia, Pacific Ocean 129 O10
Eastern Ghats *Mountain range* India 117 L11
Eastmain *River* Quebec, Canada 25 M8
Eastport Maine, USA 27 R5
Eau Claire Wisconsin, USA 30 I6
Eblana *see* Dublin
Ebolowa Cameroon 95 F11
Ebro *River* Spain 54, 61 M5
Ecuador *Country* S America 44

Ecuador 44

a Spanish • Sucre • 98 • 66 • £0.31 • (m) 88% (f) 84% • 56%

Ed Damazin Sudan 91 H14
Ed Damer Sudan 91 H11
Ed Dueim Sudan 91 G13
Ede Netherlands 64 K10
Edéa Cameroon 95 F11
Eder *River* Germany 67 G11
Edessa Greece 78 I3
Edinburgh Scotland, UK 58 I10
Edirne Turkey 104 G4
Edmonds Washington, USA 36 H6
Edmonton Alberta, Canada 23 L13
Edward, L. *Lake* Uganda/Zaire 95 O12, 97 K4
Edwards Air Base *Military center* California, USA 37 L18
Edwards Plateau *Physical region* Texas, USA 35 P12
Eforie-Nord Romania 77 P9
Egadi Is. *Island Group* Sicily 73 H17
Egiyn *River* Mongolia/Russian Federation 119 L4
Eğridir, L. *Lake* Turkey 104 J8
Egypt *Country* NE Africa 90

Egypt 90

a Arabic • Pound • 138 • 61 • £0.52 • (m) 63% (f) 34% • 109 • 5092 • Yes • 47% • 3336

Eiger, Mt. *Mountain* Switzerland 68 F11
Eigg *Island* Scotland, UK 58 F8
Eindhoven Netherlands 65 J13
Eire *see* Ireland
Eisenstadt Austria 69 S5
El Aaiún (var. Laâyoune) Western Sahara 88 F7
El Faiyûm Egypt 90 F7
El Fasher Sudan 91 D13
El Ferrol Spain 60 G3
El Iskandariya *see* Alexandria
El Jerid, Chott *Salt lake* Tunisia 89 M5
El Juf *see* El Djouf
El Khartûm *see* Khartoum
El Mansûra Egypt 90 F6
El Minya Egypt 90 F7
El Obeid Sudan 91 F13
El Oued Algeria 89 M6
El Paso Texas, USA 35 L11
El Qâhira *see* Cairo
El Salvador *Country* C America 42

El Salvador 42

a Spanish • Colon • 663 • 64 • £0.59 • (m) 76% (f) 70% • 44%

El Suweis *see* Suez
Elat Israel 107 L14
Elâziğ Turkey 105 P8
Elba *Island* Italy 72 F10
Elbasan Albania 75 M12
Elbe *River* Germany 54, 66 I8
Elbe *see* Laba
Elbert, Mt. *Mountain* Colorado, USA 20
Elbląg Poland 71 L2
El'brus *Mountain* Russian Federation 54
Elburz Mts. *Mountain range* Iran 109 N4
Elche Spain 61 N11
Eldoret Kenya 97 O4
Elephant Butte Res. *Reservoir* New Mexico, USA 35 L10
Elephant I. *Island* South Shetland Is. Antarctica 50 B6
Eleuthera *Island* Bahamas 43 L2
Elgin Scotland, UK 58 I7
Elisabethville *see* Lubumbashi
Elista Russian Federation 83 F14
Ełk Poland 71 N3
Elko Nevada, USA 34 H2
Ellensburg Washington, USA 36 I7
Ellesmere I. *Island* Northwest Territories, Canada 20, 23 N1, 51 O11
Ellsworth Mountains *Mountain range* Antarctica 50 C9
Elmira New York, USA 26 J10
Eltz *Castle* Germany 67 E12
Elwell, L. *Lake* Montana, USA 32 I4
Ely Nevada, USA 34 H4
Elyria Ohio, USA 31 P10
Emba *River* Kazakhstan 112 E10
Emden Germany 66 E7
Emerson (Trimmu) Barrage *Dam* Pakistan 116 I3
Emmen Netherlands 64 N8
Emona *see* Ljubljana
Emperor Seamounts *Sea feature* Pacific Ocean 128 I5
Emporia Kansas, USA 33 P12
Empty Quarter *see* Rub 'al Khali
Ems *River* Germany 66 E9
En Nahud Sudan 91 E13
Encarnación Paraguay 48 N7
Ende Flores, Indonesia 127 M15
Enderby Land *Region* Antarctica 50 G7
Enewetak *Island* Marshall Islands, Pacific Ocean 128 H7
Enggano *Island* Indonesia 126 E14
England *Country* UK 59
English Channel France/UK 54, 59 J17, 62 I3
Enguri *River* Azerbaijan/Georgia 85 O11
Enid Oklahoma, USA 33 O14
Enna Sicily 73 K18
Enns *River* Austria 69 P7
Enriquillo, L. *Lake* Dominican Republic 43 N8
Enschede Netherlands 64 N10
Ensenada Mexico 38 F2
Entebbe Uganda 97 M4
Enugu Nigeria 93 O12
Ephesus *Archaeological site* Turkey 104 G8
Epidaurus *Archaeological site* Greece 78 J10
Épinal France 63 P6
Equatorial Current *Ocean current* Pacific Ocean 12
Equatorial Guinea *Country* C Africa 95

Equatorial Guinea 95

a Spanish • Franc • 39 • 47 • £2.15 • (m) 64% (f) 37% • 27%

Er Rachidia Morocco 88 I6
Er Roseires Dam *Dam* Sudan 91 H14
Erdenet Mongolia 119 L4
Ereğli Turkey 105 L9
Erenhot China 119 O6
Erfurt Germany 67 I11
Erg Chech *Desert region* Algeria/Mali 93 K4
Erguig *River* Chad 94 I8
Erie Pennsylvania, USA 26 G10
Erie, L. *Lake* Canada/USA 20, 24 J15, 26 G9, 31 P9
Erie Canal *Waterway* New York, USA 26 I8
Eritrea *Country* E Africa 91

Eritrea 91

a Amharic • Birr • 97 • 48 • N/A • (av.) 71% • N/A

Erivan *see* Yerevan
Erlangen Germany 67 I13
Ernakulam India 116 J14
Erne, Lough *Lake* Northern Ireland, UK 59 D11
Ertix He *see* Irtysh
Erzincan Turkey 105 P6
Erzurum Turkey 105 Q6
Es Semara *see* Smara
Esbjerg Denmark 52 L7, 56 H15
Escanaba Michigan, USA 31 L5
Esch-sur-Alzette Luxembourg 65 L19
Escuintla Guatemala 42 A8
Eşfahān Iran 109 N6
Eskimo Pt. Northwest Territories, Canada 23 O10
Eskişehir Turkey 104 J6
Esla Res. *Reservoir* Spain 60 I6
Esmeraldas Ecuador 44 C8
Esperance Western Australia, Australia 132 H13
Espinho Portugal 60 F7
Espíritu Santo I. *Island* Mexico 38 H8
Esquel Argentina 49 H15
Essaouira Morocco 88 G6
Essen Germany 66 E10
Essequibo *River* Guyana 44 M7
Estelí Nicaragua 42 D10
Estevan Saskatchewan, Canada 23 N15
Estonia (var. Estonskaya SSR) *Country* NE Europe 80-81

Estonia 80-81

a Estonian • Kroon • 91 • 48 • £0.38 • (m) 99% (f) 99% • 71%

Estonskaya SSR *see* Estonia
Ethiopia (var. Abyssinia) *Country* E Africa 91

Ethiopia 91

a Amharic • Birr • 124 • 48 • £0.50 • (av.) 29% • 2 • 38359 • Yes • 13% • 1667

Ethiopian Highlands *Mountain range* Ethiopia 87, 91 J15
Etna *Volcano* Sicily
Etosha N.P. *National park* Namibia 98 H9
Etosha Pan *Salt basin* Namibia 98 H8
Euboea *see* Evvoia
Eugene Oregon, USA 36 G9
Eupen Belgium 65 L15
Euphrates *River* SW Asia 100 E4, 103, 105 O10, 107 R5, 109 K6
Eurasian Plate *Physical feature* 8, 20, 54, 87, 103, 115, 131
Eureka California, USA 37 F12
Europe *Continent* 8, 10, 11, 12, 13, 15, 20, 103
Europoort Netherlands 65 G11
Evanston Illinois, USA 31 L10
Evansville Indiana, USA 31 L14
Everard, L. *Lake* South Australia, Australia 133 K12
Everest, Mt. (var. Qomolangma Feng) *Mountain* China/Nepal 115, 117 O5
Everett Washington, USA 35 H6
Everglades, The *Swamp region* Florida, USA 20, 29 O14
Évora Portugal 60 G11
Évreux France 63 K5
Evvoia (var. Euboea) *Island* Greece 79 K7
Exeter England, UK 59 G16
Exmoor *Physical region* England, UK 59 G16
Exmouth Plateau *Sea feature* Indian Ocean 131
Eyasi, L. *Lake* Tanzania 97 N7
Eyre, L. *Lake* South Australia, Australia 131, 133 L11

F

Fada-Ngourma Burkina 93 M10
Faeroe Islands *Dependent territory* Atlantic Ocean 52 J7
Faeroe Islands *Island group* Atlantic Ocean 54
Faeroe Shelf *Sea feature* Atlantic Ocean 54
Faguibine, L. *Lake* Mali 93 K7
Fairbanks Alaska, USA 22 H7
Fairmont Minnesota, USA 30 G8
Faisalabad Pakistan 116 I3
Falkland Escarpment *Sea feature* Atlantic Ocean 41
Falkland Is. *Dependent territory* Atlantic Ocean 53 F15
Falkland Is. *Island group* Atlantic Ocean 41
Fall River Massachusetts, USA 27 O11
Falmouth England, UK 59 E17
Falun Sweden 57 L11
Famagusta Cyprus 105 L12
Faradje Zaire 95 O11
Farafangana Madagascar 101 E11
Farewell, Cape Greenland 52 H7
Fargo North Dakota, USA 33 O5
Faribault Minnesota, USA 30 H7
Farmington New Mexico, USA 35 K6
Faro Portugal 60 G13
Faro Yukon Territory, Canada 22 I9
Fårö *Island* Sweden 57 M13
Farvel, Cape (var. Kap Farvel) *Cape* Greenland 51 M16
Fax *River* Sweden 57 K8
Faya (var. Faya Largeau) Chad 94 J5
Faya Largeau *see* Faya
Fayetteville Arkansas, USA 28 H3
Fayetteville North Carolina, USA 29 Q6
Fdérik Mauritania 92 H4
Fear, Cape *Cape* North Carolina, USA 29 Q8
Federal Capital Territory *see* Australian Capital Territory
Fehmarn *Island* Germany 66 J6
Feira de Santana Brazil 47 N11
Felbertauern Tunnel *Tunnel* Austria 69 M8
Feldkirch Austria 68 I9
Felixstowe England, UK 59 M15
Femund, L. *Lake* Norway 56 J9
Fens, The *Physical region* England, UK 59 K14
Feodosiya Ukraine 85 K10
Fergana Uzbekistan 111 P6
Fergus Falls Minnesota, USA 30 F5
Fernando de Noronha I. *Island* Atlantic Ocean 53 I12
Fernando Póo *Island* Equatorial Guinea 87
Ferrara Italy 72 H8
Fethiye Turkey 105 H10
Feuilles, Rivère aux *River* Quebec, Canada 25 M4
Fez Morocco 88 I5
Fezzan *Physical region* Libya 89 O9
Fianarantsoa Madagascar 101 E11
Fier Albania 75 L13
Figueira de Foz Portugal 60 F8
Figuig Morocco 88 J6
Fiji *Country* Melanesia, Pacific Ocean 128 J10

Fiji 128

a English • Dollar • 106 • 65 • £1.17 • (m) 90% (f) 84% • 39%

Fiji *Island group* Melanesia, Pacific Ocean 131
Filadelphia Paraguay 48 L4
Filchner Ice Shelf *Coastal feature* Atlantic Ocean Coast, Antarctica 50 D8
Filicudi *Island* Lipari Is. Sicily 73 K16
Fimbul Ice Shelf *Coastal feature* Atlantic Ocean Coast, Antarctica 50 E6
Findlay Ohio, USA 31 O11
Finger Lakes *Physical region* New York, USA 26 J9
Finisterre, C. *Coastal feature* Spain 54
Finland *Country* N Europe 57

Finland 57

a Finnish, Swedish • Markka • 43 • 76 • £1.54 • (m) 99% (f) 99% • 497 • 515 • No • 60% • 3253

Finland, Gulf of *Sea feature* Baltic Sea 54, 57 O12, 81 K1, 82 E7
Firenze *see* Florence, Italy
Firth of Clyde *Sea feature* Scotland, UK 58 G10
Firth of Forth *Sea feature* Scotland, UK 58 I9
Fish *River* Namibia 98 I13
Fishguard Wales, UK 59 F15
Fitzroy *River* Western Australia, Australia 132 H7
Flagstaff Arizona, USA 34 I7
Flaming Gorge Dam *Dam* Utah, USA 35 K3
Flaming Gorge Res. *Reservoir* Utah/Wyoming, USA 32 I10
Flathead L. *Lake* Montana, USA 32 G4
Flin Flon Manitoba, Canada 23 N13
Flinders *River* Queensland, Australia 131, 133 M7
Flinders I. *Island* Tasmania, Australia 133 N15
Flinders Ranges *Mountain range* South Australia, Australia 131, 133 L12
Flint Michigan, USA 31 O8
Flint *River* Florida/Georgia 29 M9
Florence (var. Firenze) Italy 72 G9
Florence Alabama, USA 29 K5
Florence South Carolina, USA 29 P7
Florencia Colombia 44 E8
Flores Guatemala 42 B6
Flores *Island* Indonesia 115, 131, 127 M15
Flores Sea Indonesia 127 K15
Florianópolis Brazil 47 J15
Florida Uruguay 48 N10
Florida *State* USA 29 N11
Florida Keys *Island group* Florida, USA 29 O16
Florida, Straits of *Channel* Cuba/USA 29 P15
Florina Greece 78 H3
Flushing (var. Vlissingen) Netherlands 65 E13
Fly *River* Papua New Guinea 133 M3
Foča Bosnia and Herzegovina 75 L8
Focşani Romania 77 N6
Foggia Italy 73 M12
Föhr *Island* North Frisian Is. Germany 66 G5
Foix France 63 L15
Fond du Lac Wisconsin, USA 31 K8
Fongafale Tuvalu, Pacific Ocean 128 J9
Forlì Italy 72 H8
Formentera *Island* Balearic Islands 61 P11
Formosa Argentina 48 M6
Fort Bliss Military Reservation *Military center* New Mexico, USA 35 L11
Fort Collins Colorado, USA 35 M3
Fort-de-France Martinique 43 T13
Fort Dodge Iowa, USA 33 Q8
Fort-Foureau *see* Kousseri
Fort Lamy *see* N'Djamena
Fort Lauderdale Florida, USA 29 O15
Fort McMurray Alberta, Canada 23 L12
Fort McPherson Northwest Territories, Canada 22 J7
Fort Myers Florida, USA 29 N14
Fort Nelson British Columbia, Canada 23 J11
Fort Peck L. *Lake* Montana, USA 32 J4
Fort Portal Uganda 97 L4
Fort Resolution Northwest Territories, Canada 23 L10
Fort Shevchenko Kazakhstan 112 D10
Fort Simpson Northwest Territories, Canada 23 K10
Fort Smith Arkansas, USA 28 H4
Fort Smith Northwest Territories, Canada 23 L11

a Language (official or most commonly spoken) • Currency • Population density per square mile • Average life expectancy • Price of 1 dozen hen's eggs • Literacy • Number of TVs per 1,000 people • Number of people per doctor • Death penalty • Percentage of urban-based population • Average number of calories consumed daily per person

Fort Smith *Region* Northwest Territories, Canada 23 L9
Fort St John British Columbia, Canada 23 K12
Fort Vermilion Alberta, Canada 23 L11
Fort Victoria *see* Masvingo
Fort Wayne Indiana, USA 31 N11
Fort Wellington Guyana 44 M6
Fort William Scotland, UK 58 G8
Fort Worth Texas, USA 35 R10
Fortaleza Brazil 46 N8, 53 H12
Forth *River* Scotland, UK 58 H9
Foveaux Strait *Channel* New Zealand 134 C14
Foxe Basin *Sea feature* Northwest Territories, Canada 23 P7
Foyle, Lough *Lake* Northern Ireland/Ireland 58 E10
France *Country* W Europe 62-63

France 62-63

a French • 🪙 Franc • ♟ 267 • ● 77 • ◒ £1.61 • 📖 (m) 99% (f) 99% • 📺 406 • ✚ 381 • ☢ No • ⌂ 74% • 🍴 3465

Franceville *see* Massoukou
Francis Case, L. *Lake* South Dakota, USA 33 N8
Francistown Botswana 99 L10
Franconian Jura *Mountain range* Germany 67 J14
Frankfort Indiana, USA 31 M12
Frankfort Kentucky, USA 29 N3
Frankfurt am Main Germany 67 F12
Frankfurt an der Oder Germany 66 N9
Franz Josef Land *Island group* Russian Federation 51 R11, 54, 103
Fraser *River* British Columbia, Canada 20, 22 J13
Fraserburgh Scotland, UK 58 J7
Frauenfeld Switzerland 68 H8
Fray Bentos Uruguay 48 N9
Fredericton New Brunswick, Canada 25 P12
Frederikshåb (var. Paamiut) Greenland 51 M15
Frederikshavn Denmark 56 I13
Fredrikstad Norway 56 J12
Freeport Bahamas 43 K1
Freeport Illinois, USA 31 K9
Freeport Texas, USA 35 S13
Freetown Sierra Leone 92 G11
Freiburg im Breisgau Germany 67 E16
Freistadt Austria 69 P4
Fremantle Western Australia, Australia 101 M12, 132 F12
French Guiana *Dependent territory* S America 44
French Polynesia *Dependent territory* Polynesia, Pacific Ocean 129 M9
French Sudan *see* Mali
French Togo *see* Togo
Fresno California, USA 37 J16
Fria, C. *Cape* Namibia 87, 98 F9
Fribourg Switzerland 68 E10
Friedrichshafen Germany 67 G16
Frobisher Bay Baffin I. Northwest Territories, Canada 23 S7
Frobisher Bay *see* Iqaluit
Frobisher L. *Lake* Saskatchewan, Canada 23 M12
Frome, L. *Lake* South Australia, Australia 133 L12
Frontera Mexico 39 Q13
Frosinone Italy 73 J12
Frunze *see* Bishkek
Fuenlabrada Spain 61 K8
Fuerte Olimpo Paraguay 48 M4
Fujairah United Arab Emirates 109 O11
Fuji, Mt. *Mountain* Japan 115, 123 J11
Fukui Japan 123 H11
Fukuoka Japan 123 C13
Fukushima Japan 122 K5
Fukushima Japan 122 K9
Fulda Germany 67 H12
Fulda *River* Germany 67 H11
Fundy, Bay of *Sea feature* Canada 25 P13, 52 F8
Funen *see* Fyn
Furnas Res. *Reservoir* Brazil 47 K13
Fushun China 121 O6
Fuzhou China 121 N13
Fyn (var. Funen) *Island* Denmark 56 I16

G

Gaalkacyo Somalia 91 N16
Gabčíkovo Slovakia 71 K12
Gabès Tunisia 89 N5
Gabon *Country* C Africa 95

Gabon 95

a French • 🪙 Franc • ♟ 12 • ● 54 • ◒ £2.57 • 📖 (m) 74% (f) 49% • ⌂ 46%

Gaborone Botswana 99 K11
Gabrovo Bulgaria 77 L12
Gadsden Alabama, USA 29 L6
Gafsa Tunisia 89 N5
Gagnoa Ivory Coast 92 J13
Gagra Georgia 85 N11
Gainesville Florida, USA 29 N11
Gairdner, L.144 *Lake* South Australia, Australia 133 K12
Galana *River* Kenya 97 Q6
Galapagos Is. *Island group* Pacific Ocean 41, 129 P8
Galați Romania 77 O7
Galesburg Illinois, USA 30 J11
Galicia *Region* Poland 71 N9
Galicia *Region* Spain 60 G3
Galilee, Sea of *see* Tiberias, L.
Galle Sri Lanka 117 L16
Gallego Rise *Sea feature* Pacific Ocean 41
Gallia *see* Paris
Gallipoli Italy 73 P14
Gallipoli (var. Gelibolu; anc. Callipolis) Turkey 104 G5
Gällivare Sweden 57 N5
Gallup New Mexico, USA 35 K7
Galveston Texas, USA 35 S13
Galway Ireland 59 B12
Galway Bay *Sea feature* Ireland 59 B12
Gambia *Country* W Africa 92

Gambia 92

a English • 🪙 Dalasi • ♟ 233 • ● 45 • ◒ £1.81 • 📖 (m) 39% (f) 16% • ⌂ 23%

Gambier Is. *Island group* French Polynesia, Pacific Ocean 129 M10
Gan He *River* 115
Gäncä (var. Gyandzha; prev. Kirovabad) Azerbaijan 85 R13
Gander Newfoundland, Canada 25 S9
Gandi Res. *Reservoir* India 116 J7
Ganga *see* Ganges
Gangdise Range *Mountain range* China 118 G12
Ganges (var. Ganga) *River* India 100 J5, 115, 117 O7
Ganges *River basin* India 11
Ganges Delta *Delta* Bangladesh 115
Ganges Plain *Physical region* India 115
Gangtok India 117 O6
Ganzhou China 121 M13
Gao Mali 93 L8
Gap France 63 P12
Gar China 118 F11
Garda, L. *Lake* Italy 72 F6
Garden City Kansas, USA 33 M13
Garissa Kenya 97 Q5
Garmisch-Partenkirchen Germany 67 I17
Garonne *River* France 54, 62 J12
Garoowe Somalia 91 O15
Garoua Cameroon 94 G9
Garry L. *Lake* Northwest Territories, Canada 23 N8
Gary Indiana, USA 31 L10
Gaspé Quebec, Canada 25 P10
Gastonia North Carolina, USA 29 P6
Gatineau Quebec, Canada 25 L13
Gävle Sweden 57 L11
Gaya India 117 N7
Gaza Gaza Strip 107 K10
Gaza Strip *Occupied by Israel* SW Asia 107 K10
Gaziantep Turkey 105 O9
Gbarnga Liberia 92 H12
Gdańsk (prev. Danzig) Poland 71 L2
Gdynia Poland 71 K2
Gedaref Sudan 91 H13
Geelong Victoria, Australia 133 M14
Gejiu China 120 I14
Gela, Gulf of *Sea feature* Sicily 73 K19
Gelibolu *see* Gallipoli
Gelsenkirchen Germany 66 E10
Gemena Zaire 95 J11
Gemlik Turkey 104 I6
Gemsbok N.P. *National park* Botswana 98 J11
Genale *River* Ethiopia 91 K16
General Eugenio A. Garay Paraguay 41 K4
General Santos Mindanao, Philippines 127 N8
Genesee *River* New York/Pennsylvania, USA 26 I9
Geneva (var. Genève) Switzerland 68 C12
Geneva New York, USA 26 J9
Geneva, L. *Lake* France/Switzerland 54, 63 P9, 68 D12
Genève *see* Geneva, Switzerland
Genk Belgium 65 J14
Genoa (var. Genova) Italy 72 D8
Genoa, Gulf of *Sea feature* Italy 72 D8
Genova *see* Genoa
Gent *see* Ghent
Georg van Neumayer *Research center* Antarctica 50 D6
Georgetown Delaware, USA 27 K15
Georgetown Gambia 92 G9
Georgetown Grand Cayman, Cayman Islands 42 H6
Georgetown Guyana 44 M6, 53 F11
George Town (var. Pinang)Malaysia 100 L7, 125 I17
Georgia *Country* SW Asia 85

Georgia 85

a Georgian • 🪙 Ruble • ♟ 204 • ● 73 • ◒ N/A • 📖 N/A • ⌂ 56%

Georgia *State* USA 29
Gera Germany 67 K11
Geraldton Western Australia, Australia 132 E11
Germany *Country* C Europe 66-67

Germany 66-67

a German • 🪙 Mark • ♟ 590 • ● 77 • ◒ £1.33 • 📖 (m) 99% (f) 99% • 📺 570 • ✚ 345 • ☢ No • ⌂ 86% • 🍴 3665

Gerona *see* Girona
Gersoppa Falls *Waterfall* India 115
Getafe Spain 61 K8
Gettysburg Pennsylvania, USA 26 I13
Getz Ice Shelf *Coastal feature* Pacific Ocean Coast, Antarctica 50 C10
Ghadaf, Wādī al *Seasonal watercourse* Iraq 108 J5
Ghadāmis Libya 89 N7
Ghana (prev. Gold Coast) *Country* W Africa 93

Ghana 93

a English • 🪙 Cedi • ♟ 173 • ● 55 • ◒ £0.76 • 📖 (m) 70% (f) 51% • ⌂ 33%

Ghanzi Botswana 98 J10
Ghardaïa Algeria 89 L6
Gharyān Libya 89 O6
Ghāt *Oasis* Libya 89 N10
Ghaznī Afghanistan 111 N12
Ghent (var. Gent) Belgium 65 E14
Ghulam Muhammad Barrage *Dam* Pakistan 116 G6
Gibraltar Gibraltar 60 I15
Gibraltar *Dependent territory* Mediterranean Sea 52 K9, 60 I15
Gibraltar, Strait of *Channel* Morocco/Spain 54, 87, 88 I4, 60 I15
Gibson Desert *Desert region* Western Australia, Australia 131, 132 H10
Giessen Germany 67 F12
Gifu Japan 123 I11
Giganta, Sierra de la *Mountain range* Mexico 39 H7
Gijón Spain 60 I3
Gila *River* Arizona/New Mexico, USA 35 K10
Gilbert Is. *Island group* Kiribati, Pacific Ocean 128 J9
Gilbert Ridge *Sea feature* Pacific Ocean 131
Gillette Wyoming, USA 33 K7
Giresun Turkey 105 O5
Girona (var. Gerona) Spain 61 Q5
Gisborne New Zealand 134 I6
Giurgiu Romania 77 L10
Giza Egypt 90 F6
Gjøvik Norway 56 J10
Gladstone Queensland, Australia 133 O9
Glåma *River* Norway 56 J9
Glarus Switzerland 68 H9
Glasgow Montana, USA 33 K4
Glasgow Scotland, UK 58 H10
Glen Canyon Dam *Dam* Utah, USA 34 J6
Glendale Arizona, USA 34 I9
Glendale California, USA 37 K18
Glendive Montana, USA 33 K5
Glens Falls New York, USA 27 M8
Gliwice Poland 71 L8
Gloucester England, UK 59 I15
Gloucester Massachusetts, USA 27 O9, 52 E8
Glubokoye *see* Hlybokaye
Gmünd Austria 69 P3
Gmunden Austria 69 O6
Gnjilane Serbia, Yugoslavia 75 O10
Goba Ethiopia 91 K15
Gobabis Namibia 98 I10
Gobi Desert *Desert region* C Asia 11, 115, 119 L7
Godavari *River* India 115, 117 L10
Godhavn Greenland 51 N13
Godoy Cruz Argentina 48 H10
Godthåb (var. Nuuk) Greenland 51 M14
Goiânia Brazil 47 J12
Golan Heights *Physical region occupied by Israel* Syria 107 M8
Gold Coast Queensland, Australia 133 P11
Gold Coast *see* Ghana
Golden Sands Bulgaria 77 O11
Golmud China 118 J10
Goma Zaire 95 O13
Gomel' *see* Homyel'
Gómez Palacio Mexico 39 L7
Gonaïves Haiti 43 M7
Gonâve, Île de la *Island* Haiti 43 M8
Gonder Ethiopia 91 I13
Gonghe China 119 L10
Gongola *River* Nigeria 93 Q10
Good Hope, Cape of *Cape* South Africa 53 M14, 87, 98 I16, 101 B12
Goondiwindi Queensland, Australia 133 O11
Goose Bay Newfoundland, Canada 25 Q7
Goose L. *Lake* California/Oregon, USA 37 I11
Gorakhpur India 117 M6
Goré Chad 94 I9
Gore Ethiopia 91 H15
Göreme Turkey 105 M8
Gorgān Iran 109 O4
Gorki *see* Horki
Görlitz Germany 67 N11
Gorlovka *see* Horlivka
Gorodets Russian Federation 82 H10
Goroka Papua New Guinea 133 N2
Gorongosa N.P. *National park* Mozambique 99 N8
Gorontalo Celebes, Indonesia 127 M11
Gorzów Wielkopolski Poland 70 I4
Gosford New South Wales, Australia 133 O13
Gospić Croatia 74 H5
Gosselies Belgium 65 G16
Gostivar Macedonia 75 N11
Göteborg Sweden 56 J13
Gotha Germany 67 I11
Gotland *Island* Sweden 57 L14
Gotō Is. *Island group* Japan 123 B14
Göttingen Germany 66 H10
Gouda Netherlands 65 H11
Gough Island *Island* Atlantic Ocean 53 K14
Gouin Res. *Reservoir* Quebec, Canada 25 L11
Goulburn New South Wales, Australia 133 O13
Govind Ballash Pant Res. *Reservoir* India 117 M7
Gowd-e-Zereh *Salt pan* Afghanistan 110 J15
Gozo *Island* Malta 73 K20
Gračanica Bosnia and Herzegovina 75 K5
Grafton New South Wales, Australia 133 P11
Grahamstown South Africa 99 L15
Grampian Mts. *Mountain range* Scotland, UK 54, 58 M8
Gran Chaco *Physical region* Argentina 41, 48 K6
Granada Nicaragua 42 D11
Granada Spain 61 K13
Grand Bahama *Island* Bahamas 43 K1
Grand Banks *Sea feature* Newfoundland, Canada 25 T10, 52 G8
Grand Canal (var. Da Yunhe) *Waterway* China 121 N9
Grand Canyon *Physical feature* Arizona, USA 20, 34 I6
Grand Cayman *Island* Cayman Islands 42 H6
Grand Falls New Brunswick, Canada 25 O11
Grand Falls Newfoundland, Canada 25 S9
Grand Forks North Dakota, USA 33 O4
Grand Island Nebraska, USA 33 O10
Grand Junction Colorado, USA 35 K4
Grand Rapids Michigan, USA 31 M8
Grand Teton Mts. *Mountain range* Wyoming, USA 32 I8
Grand Turk Turks & Caicos Islands 43 N6
Grande, Bahía *Sea feature* Argentina 49 K18
Grande, Serra *Mountain range* Brazil 46 M8
Grande Comore *Island* Comoros 100 E10
Grande Prairie Alberta, Canada 23 K13
Grande Rivière de la Baleine *River* Quebec, Canada 25 L6
Grande Terre *Island* Guadeloupe 43 T11
Grangemouth Scotland, UK 58 H9
Grants Pass Oregon, USA 37 G11
Grasse France 63 Q13
Graz Austria 69 R8
Great Abaco *Island* Bahamas 43 K1
Great Artesian Basin *Physical feature* Australia 131
Great Australian Bight *Sea feature* Australia 131, 132 J13
Great Bahama Bank *Sea feature* West Indies 42 J2
Great Barrier I. *Island* New Zealand 134 H3
Great Barrier Reef *Coral reef* Queensland, Australia 128 H10, 131, 133 O7
Great Basin *Physical region* SW USA 10, 11, 20, 34 G2
Great Bear L. *Lake* Northwest Territories, Canada 20, 23 K8
Great Bend Kansas, USA 33 O12
Great Dividing Range *Mountain range* Queensland, Australia 131, 133 O9
Great Exhibition Bay *Sea feature* New Zealand 134 F2
Great Exuma *Island* Bahamas 43 L4
Great Falls Montana, USA 32 H5
Great Inagua *Island* Bahamas 43 M6
Great Plain of China *Physical region* China 115
Great Plains *Physical region* USA 20, 33 L7
Great Rift Valley *Physical feature* SE Africa/SW Asia 8, 87, 97 O6
Great Ruaha *River* Tanzania 97 O9
Great St. Bernard Tunnel *Tunnel* Switzerland 68 E13
Great Salt Desert *see* Dasht-e-Kavir
Great Salt L. *Salt lake* Utah, USA 20, 34 I2
Great Salt Lake Desert *Desert region* Utah, USA 34 I3
Great Sandy Desert *Desert region* Western Australia, Australia 131, 132 H8
Great Slave L. *Lake* Northwest Territories, Canada 20, 23 L10
Great Victoria Desert *Desert region* Western Australia, Australia 131, 132 I11
Great Yarmouth England, UK 59 M14
Greater Antilles *Island group* Caribbean Sea 20, 41, 43 N9
Greater Khingan Range *Mountain range* China 115, 119 Q4
Gredos, Sierra de *Mountain range* Spain 60 J8
Greece *Country* S Europe 78-79

Greece 78-79

a Greek • 🪙 Drachma • ♟ 200 • ● 77 • ◒ £1.11 • 📖 (m) 98% (f) 89% • 📺 196 • ✚ 300 • ☢ No • ⌂ 62% • 🍴 3825

Greeley Colorado, USA 35 N3
Green Bay Wisconsin, USA 31 L7
Green R. *River* Kentucky, USA 29 M3
Green R. *River* W USA 32 I9, 35 K3
Greenfield Massachusetts, USA 27 N9
Greenland *Dependent territory* Arctic Ocean 10, 51, 52 H6
Greenland *Island* Arctic Ocean 20, 103
Greenland Sea Arctic Ocean 51 P14, 52 J6, 103
Greenock Scotland, UK 58 G9
Greensboro North Carolina, USA 29 P5

Greenville – Igoumenitsa

Greenville Liberia 92 I13
Greenville Mississippi, USA 28 I6
Greenville South Carolina, USA 29 O6
Greifswald Germany 66 L6
Grenada *Country* Caribbean Sea 43 S15

Grenada 43

a English • ≋ Dollar • ♦ 693 • ♥ 70 • ◒ £3.10 • ✎ (av.) 90% • ⌂ 34%

Grenadines, The *Island group* St Vincent & The Grenadines 43 S14
Grenoble France 63 O11
Grevena Greece 78 H4
Greymouth New Zealand 134 E10
Grim, C. *Cape* Tasmania, Australia 133 M15
Grimsby England, UK 52 K8, 59 K13
Grodno *see* Hrodna
Groningen Netherlands 64 M6
Groote Eylandt *Island* Northern Territory, Australia 133 L5
Grootfontein Namibia 98 I9
Grosseto Italy 72 G10
Groznyy Russian Federation 83 F16
Grudziądz Poland 71 L3
Gstaad Switzerland 68 E11
Guacanayabo, Gulf of *Sea feature* Cuba 42 J6
Guadalajara Mexico 39 L11
Guadalajara Spain 61 L8
Guadalcanal *Island* Solomon Islands, Pacific Ocean 128 I9
Guadalquivir *River* Spain 54, 60 I12
Guadalupe Mexico 39 L9
Guadarrama, Sierra de *Mountain range* Spain 61 K7
Guadeloupe *Dependent territory* Caribbean Sea 43 S11
Guadiana *River* Portugal/Spain 60 G11
Gualeguaychu Argentina 48 M9
Guallatiri *Volcano* Chile 41
Guam *Dependent territory* Micronesia, Pacific Ocean 128 G7
Guanare Venezuela 44 H5
Guangxi Zhuang Autonomous Region China 121 K14
Guangzhou *see* Canton
Guantánamo Cuba 43 L6
Guantánamo Bay *Sea feature* Cuba 43 L7
Guarda Portugal 60 H8
Guatemala *Country* C America 42

Guatemala 42

a Spanish • ≋ Quetzal • ♦ 226 • ♥ 64 • ◒ £0.51 • ✎ (m) 63% (f) 47% • ⌂ 39%

Guatemala Basin *Sea feature* Pacific Ocean 41
Guatemala City Guatemala 42 B8
Guaviare *River* Colombia/Venezuela 44 F7
Guayaquil Ecuador 44 C9, 129 Q8
Guayaquil, Gulf of *Sea feature* Ecuador/Peru 44 B9
Guaymas Mexico 38 H5
Guddu Barrage *Dam* Pakistan 116 H4
Guernsey *Dependent territory* W Europe 59 H18
Guiana Highlands *Mountain range* South America 41
Guider Cameroon 94 G8
Guilin China 121 K13
Guinea *Country* W Africa 92

Guinea 92

a French • ≋ Franc • ♦ 62 • ♥ 44 • ◒ £1.21 • ✎ (m) 35% (f) 13% • ▭ 7 • ✚ 10300 • ✪ Yes • ⌂ 26% • ⍊ 2132

Guinea, Gulf of *Sea feature* C Africa 53 L11, 87, 95 E11
Guinea Basin *Sea feature* Gulf of Guinea, Atlantic Ocean 53 K12, 87
Guinea-Bissau (prev. Portuguese Guinea) *Country* W Africa 92

Guinea-Bissau 92

a Portuguese • ≋ Peso • ♦ 92 • ♥ 41 • ◒ £1.53 • ✎ (m) 50% (f) 24% • ⌂ 20%

Guiyang China 120 J12
Gujranwala Pakistan 116 J3
Gujrat Pakistan 116 J3
Gulf Stream current *Ocean current* Atlantic Ocean 12
Gulf, The *see* Persian Gulf
Gulfport Mississippi, USA 28 J9
Gulja *see* Yining
Gulu Uganda 97 M2
Gümüşhane Turkey 105 P5
Gur'yev *see* Atyrau
Gusau Nigeria 93 O10
Gusev Russian Federation 80 G10
Guwahati India 117 P6
Guyana (prev. British Guiana) *Country* S America 44

Guyana 44

a English • ≋ Dollar • ♦ 11 • ♥ 65 • ◒ £2.11 • ✎ (m) 97% (f) 95% • ⌂ 35%

Guyana Basin *Sea feature* Atlantic Ocean 53 G11
Gwalior India 117 K6
Gwelo *see* Gweru
Gweru (prev. Gwelo) Zimbabwe 99 M9
Gyandzha *see* Gäncä
Gyangzê China 118 I13
Gyda Peninsula *Physical feature* Russian Federation 112 I6
Győr Hungary 71 K13
Gytheio Greece 78 I12
Gyumri (var. Kumayri; var. Leninakan) Armenia 85 P13
Gzhel' Russian Federation 82 G10

H

Ha Giang Vietnam 124 M7
Haapsalu Estonia 80 I2
Haarlem Netherlands 64 H9
Ḩabbān Yemen 108 J16
Habomai Is. *Island group* Japan 122 O2
Hachinohe Japan 122 L6
Hachiōji Japan 123 K11
Hadejia *River* Nigeria 93 Q9
Hadhramaut *Region* Yemen 109 K16
Haeju North Korea 121 P7
Hagen Germany 67 E11
Hagi Japan 123 D13
Hague, The Netherlands 64 G10
Hai Phong Vietnam 124 N8
Haifa (var. Ḩefa) Israel 107 L8
Haikou China 121 K15
Hā'il Saudi Arabia 108 I8
Hailar China 119 P3
Hainan *Island* China 115, 121 K16
Hainburg Austria 69 T4
Haines Alaska, USA 22 I10
Haines Junction Yukon Territory, Canada 22 H9
Haiti *Country* Caribbean Sea 43

Haiti 43

a French, Creole • ≋ Gourde • ♦ 621 • ♥ 54 • ◒ £0.55 • ✎ (m) 59% (f) 47% • ⌂ 28%

Ḩajjah Yemen 108 H15
Hakkâri Turkey 105 S8
Hakodate Japan 122 K5, 128 G5
Ḩalab (var. Aleppo; anc. Beroea) Syria 107 N3
Halden Norway 56 J12
Halicarnassus Turkey 104 G9
Halifax Nova Scotia, Canada 25 Q13, 52 F8
Halle Germany 66 K10
Hallein Austria 69 N7
Halley *Research center* Antarctica 50 D7
Halls Creek Western Australia, Australia 132 I7
Halmahera *Island* Indonesia 115, 131, 127 P10
Halmstad Sweden 56 J14
Hälsingborg Sweden 56 J15
Hamada Japan 123 D12
Hamadān Iran 109 M4
Ḩamāh Syria 107 N5
Hamamatsu Japan 123 J12
Hamar Norway 56 J10
Hamburg Germany 66 H7
Hameenlinna Finland 57 O10
Hamersley Range *Mountain range* Western Australia, Australia 132 F9
Hamhŭng North Korea 121 P6
Hami (var. Kumul) China 118 J7
Hamilton New Zealand 134 G5
Hamilton Ontario, Canada 25 K14
Hamm Germany 66 F10
Ḩammār, L. al *Lake* Iraq 109 L6
Hammerfest Norway 57 O1
Hāmūn-e-Şāberī *Salt pan* Afghanistan/Iran 110 J14
Handan China 121 M8
Hangayn Nuruu *Mountain range* Mongolia 119 K4
Hangzhou China 121 O11
Hannover *see* Hanover
Hanoi Vietnam 124 M8
Hanover (var. Hannover) Germany 66 H9
Har Us L. *Lake* Mongolia 118 J5
Ḩaraḑ Saudi Arabia 109 L10
Harare (prev. Salisbury) Zimbabwe 99 M8
Harbin China 121 P4
Hardanger Fjord *Sea feature* Norway 56 H10
Harderwijk Netherlands 64 J10
Harer Ethiopia 91 L15
Hargeysa Somalia 91 M14
Harīrūd *River* C Asia 111 L11
Harlan County L. *Lake* Nebraska, USA 33 N11
Harlingen Netherlands 64 J7
Harney L. *Lake* Oregon, USA 36 K10
Härnösand Sweden 57 M9
Harper Liberia 92 I13
Harris *Island* Scotland, UK 58 F7
Harrisburg Pennsylvania, USA 26 J13
Harry S. Truman Res. *Reservoir* Missouri, USA 33 Q12
Harstad Norway 57 M3
Hartford Connecticut, USA 27 M11
Hasselt Belgium 65 J14
Hässleholm Sweden 56 J15
Hastings England, UK 59 L17
Hastings Nebraska, USA 33 O10
Hastings New Zealand 134 H7
Hat Yai Thailand 125 I16
Hatteras, Cape *Cape* North Carolina, USA 20, 29 S6
Hatteras Plain *Sea feature* Atlantic Ocean 20
Hattiesburg Mississippi, USA 28 J8
Haugesund Norway 52 K7, 56 H11
Havana (var. La Habana) Cuba 42 H3
Havre Montana, USA 32 I4
Havre-Saint-Pierre Quebec, Canada 25 P9
Hawaii *Island* Pacific Ocean 12
Hawaii *State* USA, Pacific Ocean 129 L6
Hawaiian Is. *Island group* Polynesia, Pacific Ocean 8, 129 K7
Hawke Bay *Sea feature* New Zealand 134 I7
Ḩawran, Wādī *Seasonal watercourse* Iraq 108 J4
Hay River Northwest Territories, Canada 23 L10
Hayes *River* Manitoba, Canada 23 P12
Hays Kansas, USA 33 N13
Hazleton Pennsylvania, USA 27 K12
Heads, The *Cape* Oregon, USA 36 F10
Heard and MacDonald Islands *Dependent territory* *see* Heard I, MacDonald Is
Heard I. *Island* Indian Ocean 50 I7, 101 H15
Heathrow *Airport* England, UK 59 K16
Heerenveen Netherlands 64 K7
Heerlen Netherlands 65 K15
Hefa *see* Haifa
Hefei China 121 N10
Heidelberg Germany 67 F14
Heilbronn Germany 67 G14
Heilong Jiang *see* Amur
Hejaz *Region* Saudi Arabia 108 H9
Helena Montana, USA 32 H5
Helgoland Bay (var. Helgoländer Bucht) *Sea feature* Germany 66 G6
Helgoländer Bucht *see* Helgoland Bay
Helmand *River* Afghanistan/Iran 111 L12
Helmond Netherlands 65 K12
Helsingør Denmark 56 J15
Helsinki Finland 57 O11
Helwân Egypt 90 F7
Henderson Nevada, USA 34 H7
Hengelo Netherlands 64 N10
Henrietta Maria, C. *Cape* Canada 24 J6
Henzada Burma 124 F10
Herāt Afghanistan 110 J12
Herisau Switzerland 68 H8
Herlen Gol *see* Kerulen
Hermansverk Norway 56 I9
Hermit Is. *Island group* Papua New Guinea 133 N1
Hermosillo Mexico 38 H4
Herrenchiemsee *Castle* Germany 67 K16
Herstal Belgium 65 K15
Hialeah Florida, USA 29 O15
Hibbing Minnesota, USA 30 H3
Hidaka Mts. *Mountain range* Japan 122 L4
Hidalgo del Parral Mexico 39 K6
Hierosolyma *see* Jerusalem
Hiiumaa *Island* Estonia 80 H2
Hildesheim Germany 66 H9
Hillsboro Oregon, USA 36 H8
Hilversum Netherlands 64 I10
Himalayas *Mountain range* S Asia 8, 11, 103, 115, 117 M5, 118 H14
Ḩimş Syria 107 N5
Hindu Kush *Mountain range* 103, 111 O10, 115
Hinnøya *Island* Norway 57 L3
Hirakud Res. *Reservoir* India 117 M9
Hirfanli Barrage *Dam* Turkey 105 L7
Hiroshima Japan 123 E13
Hispania *see* Spain
Hispaniola *Island* Caribbean Sea 20, 41
Hīt Iraq 108 J4
Hitachi Japan 122 L10
Hitra *Island* Norway 56 I7
Hjørring Denmark 56 I13
Hjort Trench *Sea feature* 131
Hlybokaye (var. Glubokoye) Belarus 81 L9
Ho Chi Minh City (prev. Saigon) Vietnam 125 N14
Hobart Tasmania, Australia 133 N16
Hobbs New Mexico, USA 35 N10
Hodeida (var. Al Hudaydah) Yemen 108 H15
Hoek van Holland Netherlands 65 G11
Hof Germany 67 J12
Hohe Tauern *Mountain range* Austria 69 N8
Hohenschwangau *Castle* Germany 67 I17
Hohhot China 119 O7
Hokkaidō *Island* Japan 115, 122 L3
Holguín Cuba 43 K6
Holland Michigan, USA 31 M9
Hollywood California, USA 37 K18
Hollywood Florida, USA 29 O15
Holon Israel 107 L10
Holstebro Denmark 56 H14
Holy I. *Island* Wales, UK 59 G13
Holyhead Wales, UK 59 G13
Home Counties *Region* England, UK 59 K16
Homer Alaska, USA 22 F8
Homyel' (var. Gomel') Belarus 81 O14
Honduras *Country* C America 42

Honduras 42

a Spanish • ≋ Lempira • ♦ 122 • ♥ 65 • ◒ £0.56 • ✎ (m) 75% (f) 70% • ⌂ 44%

Honduras, Gulf of *Sea feature* C America 42 C7
Hønefoss Norway 56 I11
Hong Gai Vietnam 124 N8
Hong Kong *Dependent territory* SE China 121 M14 128 E7
Hongshui He *River* China 120 J13
Hongze Hu *Lake* China 121 N9
Honiara Guadalcanal Solomon Islands, Pacific Ocean 128 I9
Honolulu Oahu Hawaiian Islands, Pacific Ocean 129 K6
Honshū *Island* Japan 115, 122 J9
Hoogeveen Netherlands 64 M8
Hoorn Netherlands 64 I8
Hoover Dam *Dam* Arizona/Nevada, USA 34 H7
Hopa Turkey 105 Q4
Hopedale Newfoundland, Canada 25 P5
Hopkinsville Kentucky, USA 29 L3
Horki (var. Gorki) Belarus 81 O11
Horlivka (var. Gorlovka) Ukraine 85 M6
Hormuz, Strait of *Channel* Iran/Oman 109 O10
Horn of Africa *Physical region* Somalia 91 O14
Horn, Cape *Cape* Chile 49 L20, 56 F16, 129 Q14
Horsens Denmark 56 I15
Hot Springs Arkansas, USA 28 H5
Hotan China 118 F9
Houlton Maine, USA 27 Q3
Houston Texas, USA 35 S13
Hovd Mongolia 118 I5
Hövsgöl, L. *Lake* Mongolia 119 L3
Howland I. *Dependent territory* Polynesia, Pacific Ocean 128 J8
Hradec Králové Czech Republic 70 I8
Hrodna (var. Grodno) Belarus 80 I12
Hron *River* Slovakia 71 L11
Hrvatska *see* Croatia
Huai He *River* China 115
Huainan China 121 N10
Huambo (var. Nova Lisboa) Angola 98 H6
Huancayo Peru 45 E13
Huang He *see* Yellow R.
Huánuco Peru 45 D12
Huascarán *Mountain* Peru 41
Huddersfield England, UK 59 J13
Huddinge Sweden 57 L12
Hudiksvall Sweden 57 L10
Hudson *River* New York, USA 27 M10
Hudson Bay *Sea feature* Canada 10, 20, 23 P10, 24 I5, 52 D7
Hudson-Mohawk Gap *Physical feature* New York/Vermont, USA 27 M9
Hudson Strait *Channel* Canada 20, 23 R8, 25 M2
Hue Vietnam 125 N11
Huehuetenango Guatemala 42 A7
Huelva Spain 60 H13
Huesca Spain 61 N5
Hughenden Queensland, Australia 133 N8
Hulun Nur *Lake* China 119 P4
Humber *River* England, UK 59 K13
Humboldt *River* Nevada, USA 34 H2
Hūn Libya 89 P7
Hungarian Plain *Physical region* Hungary 54, 71 L14
Hungary *Country* C Europe 70-71

Hungary 70-71

a Hungarian • ≋ Forint • ♦ 295 • ♥ 71 • ◒ £0.44 • ✎ (m) 99% (f) 99% • ▭ 410 • ✚ 330 • ✪ No • ⌂ 61% • ⍊ 3644

Huntington West Virginia, USA 29 O3
Huntington Beach California, USA 37 L19
Huntsville Alabama, USA 29 L6
Huron Ohio, USA 31 P10
Huron, Lake *Lake* Canada/USA 20, 24 J13, 31 O6
Hurunui *River* New Zealand 134 F10
Husum Germany 66 G6
Hutchinson Kansas, USA 33 O12
Huy Belgium 65 J16
Hvar *Island* Croatia 74 I8
Hwange (prev. Wankie) Zimbabwe 99 L8
Hwange N.P. *National park* Zimbabwe 99 L9
Hyargas, L. *Lake* Mongolia 118 J4
Hyderabad India 117 K11
Hyderabad Pakistan 116 H6
Hyères, Îles d' *Island* France 63 P14
Hyparis *see* Southern Bug
Hyvinkää Finland 57 O11

I

Ialomiţa *River* Romania 77 N9
Iaşi Romania 77 N3
Ibadan Nigeria 93 N12
Ibagué Colombia 44 E7
Ibar *River* Serbia, Yugoslavia 75 N9
Ibarra Ecuador 44 C8
Ibb Yemen 108 I16
Iberian Pen. *Physical region* SW Europe 54
Ibiza Ibiza, Balearic Islands, Spain 61 P10
Ibiza *Island* Balearic Islands, Spain 61 P10
Ibotirama Brazil 47 L11
Ibrī Oman 109 O12
Ica Peru 45 E14
Iceland *Country* Atlantic Ocean 51, 52 J7

Iceland 52

a Icelandic • ≋ Krona • ♦ 7 • ♥ 78 • ◒ £2.72 • ✎ (m) 100% (f) 100% • ▭ 320 • ✚ 376 • ✪ No • ⌂ 91% • ⍊ 3611

Iceland *Island* Atlantic Ocean 8, 10, 20, 103
Icosium *see* Algiers
Idaho *State* USA 32
Idaho Falls Idaho, USA 32 H8
Idfu Egypt 90 G8
Ieper Belgium 65 C15
Iglesias Sardinia 73 C15
Igoumenitsa Greece 78 F5

a Language (official or most commonly spoken) • ≋ Currency • ♦ Population density per square mile • ♥ Average life expectancy • ◒ Price of 1 dozen hen's eggs • ✎ Literacy • ▭ Number of TVs per 1,000 people • ✚ Number of people per doctor • ✪ Death penalty • ⌂ Percentage of urban-based population • ⍊ Average number of calories consumed daily per person

145

Iguaçu – Kâmpôt

Iguaçu *River* Argentina/Brazil 47 H15
Iguaçu Falls *Waterfall* Brazil 41, 47 H14
Iisalmi Finland 57 P8
IJmuiden Netherlands 64 H9
IJssel *River* Netherlands 64 K9
IJsselmeer *Man-made lake* Netherlands 64 J8
Ijzer *River* Belgium/France 65 C14
Ikaria *Island* Greece 79 O10
Iki *Island* Japan 123 B13
Ilagan Luzon, Philippines 127 L3
Ilām Iran 109 L5
Ilebo Zaire 95 K14
Ilgaz Mts. *Mountain range* Turkey 104 L5
Ilha Solteira Res. *Reservoir* Brazil 47 I13
Ili *River* Kazakhstan 103, 112 G13
Iliamna L. *Lake* Alaska, USA 22 F8
Iligan Mindanao, Philippines 127 N7
Ilium *see* Troy
Illapel Chile 48 G10
Illinois *River* Illinois, USA 31 J13
Illinois *State* USA 30-31
Illizi Algeria 89 M9
Ilo Peru 129 Q9
Iloilo Panay, Philippines 127 M6
Ilorin Nigeria 93 N11
Imatra Finland 57 Q10
Imperial Dam *Dam* Arizona/California USA 34 H9
Impfondo Congo 95 I12
Imphal India 117 Q7
Inari, L. *Lake* Finland 57 P2
Inch'ŏn South Korea 121 P7, 128 F5
Independence Missouri, USA 33 Q11
India *Country* S Asia 116-117

India 116-117

a Hindi, English • Rupee • 754 • 59 • £0.39 • (m) 64% (f) 39% • 32 • 2400 • Yes • 27% • 2229

India *Subcontinent* 8, 9, 103
Indian Desert *see* Thar Desert
Indian Ocean 87, 91, 100-101, 103, 114-115, 130-131
Indiana Pennsylvania, USA 26 H12
Indiana *State* USA 31
Indianapolis Indiana, USA 31 N12
Indigirka *River* Russian Federation 113 O5
Indo-Australian Plate *Physical feature* 8, 103, 115, 131
Indonesia (prev. Dutch East Indies) *Country* SE Asia 126-127

Indonesia 126-127

a Bahasa Indonesia • Rupiah • 259 • 62 • £0.41 • (m) 84% (f) 68% • 60 • 7372 • Yes • 31% • 2750

Indore India 116 J8
Indus *River* Asia 100 H5, 103, 115, 116 G7
Indus Delta *Delta* Pakistan 115
Ingolstadt Germany 67 J15
Inhambane Mozambique 99 O11
Inland Sea Japan 123 F13
Inle, L. *Lake* Burma 124 G8
Inn *River* Austria/Germany/Switzerland 67 L15, 69 K8
Inner Mongolia (var. Nei Mongol) *Region* China 119 P6
Innsbruck Austria 69 L8
Inongo Zaire 95 J13
Insein Burma 124 F10
Interlaken Switzerland 68 F11
Inukjuak Quebec, Canada 25 K4
Inuvik Northwest Territories, Canada 22 J7
Inuvik *Region* Northwest Territories, Canada 22 J8
Invercargill New Zealand 134 C14
Inverness Scotland, UK 58 H8
Investigator Strait *Channel* South Australia, Australia 133 K14
Ioannina Greece 78 G5
Iona N.P. *National park* Angola 98 F8
Ionian Is. *Island group* Greece 78 F8
Ionian Sea Greece/Italy 54, 73 O17, 78 F8
Ios *Island* Cyclades, Greece 79 N12
Iowa *State* USA 33
Iowa City Iowa, USA 33 R9
Ipel' *River* Hungary/Slovakia 71 L12
Ipoh Malaysia 125 I18
Ipswich England, UK 59 L15
Ipswich Queensland, Australia 133 P10
Iqaluit (var. Frobisher Bay) Baffin I. Northwest Territories, Canada 23 R7
Iquique Chile 49 F4
Iquitos Peru 44 F9
Iracoubo French Guiana 44 O6
Irakleio Crete, Greece 79 M16
Iran (prev. Persia) *Country* SW Asia 109

Iran 109

a Farsi • Rial • 91 • 63 • £6.09 • (m) 65% (f) 44% • 247 • 2821 • Yes • 57% • 3181

Iranian Plate *Physical feature* 8, 54, 87, 103, 115
Iranian Plateau *Physical feature* Iran 103
Irapuato Mexico 39 M11
Iraq (anc. Mesopotamia) *Country* SW Asia 108-109

Iraq 108-109

a Arabic • Dinar • 116 • 63 • N/A • (m) 70% (f) 49% • 69 • 1732 • Yes • 71% • 2887

Irbid Jordan 107 M9
Irbil Iraq 109 K3
Ireland (var. Eire) *Country* W Europe 58-59

Ireland 58-59

a Irish, English • Punt • 132 • 75 • £1.27 • (m) 98% (f) 98% • 276 • 633 • No • 57% • 3778

Ireland *Island* W Europe 54
Irian Jaya *Region* Indonesia 127 S12
Iringa Tanzania 97 O10
Irish Sea Ireland/UK 59 F13
Irkutsk Russian Federation 113 L12
Iron Gates *HEP station* Serbia, Yugoslavia 75 P6
Irrawaddy *River* Burma 100 K5, 115, 124 G7
Irrawaddy Delta *Delta* Burma 115
Irtysh (var. Ertix He) *River* N Asia 103, 112 H9, 118 H5
Ischia *Island* Italy 72 J13
Isea, L. d' *Lake* Italy 72 F6
Ishikari *River* Japan 122 K4
Ishikari Bay *Sea feature* Japan 122 K4
Ishikari Mts. *Mountain range* Japan 122 L3
Ishim *River* Kazakhstan/Russian Federation 112 G10
Isiro Zaire 95 N11
Iskenderun (anc. Alexandretta) Turkey 105 N10
Iskŭr *River* Bulgaria 76 J11
Iskŭr, L. *Lake* Bulgaria 76 I13
Islam Barrage *Dam* Pakistan 116 I4
Islamabad Pakistan 116 J2
Islay *Island* Scotland, UK 58 F10
Isle Royale *Island* Michigan, USA 31 K3
Ismâ 'ilîya Egypt 90 G6
Isparta Turkey 104 J9
Israel *Country* SW Asia 107

Israel 107

a Hebrew, Arabic • Shekel • 623 • 76 • £0.98 • (m) 98% (f) 96% • 266 • 339 • No • 92% • 3174

Issyk-kul' (prev. Rybach'ye) Kyrgyzstan 111 R5
Issyk-kul', L. *Lake* Kyrgyzstan 111 R5
Istanbul (prev. Constantinople; anc. Byzantium) Turkey 104 H5
Itaipú Res. *Reservoir* Brazil 41, 47 H14
Itaipú Dam *Dam* Brazil/Paraguay 48 O6
Italy *Country* S Europe 9, 72-73

Italy 72-73

a Italian • Lira • 508 • 78 • £1.32 • (m) 98% (f) 96% • 424 • 233 • No • 69% • 3504

Itanagar India 117 Q6
Itatka ICBM Base *Military center* Russian Federation 112 J10
Itea Greece 78 I8
Ithaca New York, USA 26 J9
Iturup *Island* Japan 122 P1
Ivalo Finland 57 P3
Ivangrad Montenegro, Yugoslavia 75 M9
Ivano-Frankivs'k Ukraine 84 F5
Ivanovo Russian Federation 82 H10
Ivory Coast (var. Côte d'Ivoire) *Country* W Africa 92-93

Ivory Coast 92-93

a French • Franc • 100 • 55 • £1.42 • (m) 67% (f) 40% • 40%

Ivory Coast *Physical region* W Africa 92 J13
Iwaki Japan 122 L9
Izabal, L. *Lake* Guatemala 42 B7
Izhevsk Russian Federation 83 K11
Izhma *River* Russian Federation 82 L8
Izmir Turkey 104 G8
Izmit Turkey 104 I5
Iznik Turkey 104 I6
Iztaccíhuatl *Mountain* Mexico 39 N12
Izu Is. *Island group* Japan 123 K12

J

Jabalpur India 116 L8
Jackson Michigan, USA 31 N9
Jackson Mississippi, USA 28 J7
Jackson Tennessee, USA 29 K5
Jackson L. *Lake* Wyoming, USA 32 I7
Jacksonville Florida, USA 29 O10
Jacksonville Illinois, USA 30 J12
Jacmel Haiti 43 M8
Jadotville *see* Likasi
Jaén Spain 61 K12
Jaffna Sri Lanka 117 L15
Jaipur India 116 J6
Jaisalmer India 116 I5
Jajce Bosnia and Herzegovina 74 J6
Jakarta (var. Batavia) Indonesia 15, 126 G14
Jakobstad Finland 57 N8
Jalālābād Afghanistan 111 O12
Jalandhar India 117 K3
Jalapa Mexico 39 O12
Jamaica *Country* Caribbean Sea 14, 42-43

Jamaica 42-43

a English • Dollar • 584 • 73 • £0.54 • (m) 98% (f) 99% • 52%

Jamaica *Island* Caribbean Sea 20, 41
Jamalpur Bangladesh 117 P7
Jambi Sumatra, Indonesia 126 F12
James *River* South Dakota/North Dakota, USA 33 O7
James Bay *Sea feature* Canada 24 J7
Jamestown New York, USA 26 H10
Jamestown North Dakota, USA 33 N5
Jamnagar India 116 H8
Jamshedpur India 116 N8
Jan Mayen *Dependent territory* Arctic Ocean 51 P15
Janakpur Nepal 117 N6
Janesville Wisconsin, USA 31 K9
Japan (var. Nippon, Nihon) *Country* E Asia 122-123

Japan 122-123

a Japanese • Yen • 853 • 79 • £1.38 • (m) 99% (f) 99% • 620 • 608 • Yes • 77% • 2956

Japan, Sea of E Asia 100 M9, 113 Q12, 115, 122 H9, 128 G5
Japan Trench *Sea feature* Pacific Ocean 9, 115, 128 G5
Japanese Alps *Mountain range* Japan 123 I11
Jardines de la Reina *Island group* Cuba 42 I5
Jari *River* Brazil/Suriname 46 H6
Järvenpää Finland 57 O11
Jāsk Iran 109 P10
Jasper Alberta, Canada 23 K13
Java *Island* Indonesia 100 M9, 115, 127 H15, 130-131
Java Sea Indonesia 100 M9, 115, 126 H14, 131
Java Trench *Sea feature* Indian Ocean 8, 100 L9, 115, 130
Jayapura Irian Jaya, Indonesia 127 T11
Jaz Mūrīān Salt Lake *Salt lake* Iran 109 P9
Jazīrah, Al *Region* Syria 107 R3
Jebel Aulia Dam *Dam* Sudan 91 G12
Jedda (var. Jiddah) Saudi Arabia 108 G11
Jefferson City Missouri, USA 33 R12
Jēkabpils Latvia 80 J7
Jelgava Latvia 80 I6
Jember Java, Indonesia 126 J15
Jena Germany 67 J11
Jenbach Austria 69 L8
Jendouba Tunisia 89 N4
Jerba I. *Island* Tunisia 89 N5
Jérémie Haiti 43 L8
Jerez de la Frontera Spain 60 H14
Jericho West Bank 107 M10
Jersey *Dependent territory* W Europe 59 H19
Jerusalem (var. Yerushalayim; anc. Hierosolyma) Israel 107 L10
Jesenice Slovenia 74 G2
Jessore Bangladesh 117 O8
Jeziorak, L. *Lake* Poland 71 L3
Jhelum Pakistan 116 J2
Jiamusi China 121 Q3
Jiddah *see* Jedda
Jihlava Czech Republic 70 I10
Jihlava *River* Czech Republic 70 I10
Jijiga Ethiopia 91 L14
Jilib Somalia 91 L18
Jilin China 121 P5
Jima Ethiopia 91 I15
Jinan China 121 M8
Jingdezhen China 121 N11
Jingmen China 121 L11
Jining China 119 O7
Jinja Uganda 97 M4
Jinnah Barrage *Dam* Pakistan 116 I2
Jinotega Nicaragua 42 D10
Jinsha *River* China 115, 120 H11
Jiu *River* Romania 76 J10
Jixi China 121 Q4
Jīzān Saudi Arabia 108 H14
Jizera *River* Czech Republic 70 H8
João Pessoa Brazil 46 P9
Jodhpur India 116 I6
Joensuu Finland 57 Q9
Johannesburg South Africa 99 L12
John Day *River* Oregon/Washington USA 36 J9
Johnson City Tennessee, USA 29 O5
Johnston Atoll *Dependent territory* Polynesia, Pacific Ocean 129 K7
Johnstown Pennsylvania, USA 26 H12
Johor Baharu Malaysia 125 K20
Joinville Brazil 47 J15
Jokkmokk Sweden 57 M5
Joliba *see* Niger *River*
Joliet Illinois, USA 31 L10
Jolo *Island* Philippines 127 L8
Jolo Jolo, Philippines 127 L8
Jonglei Canal *Waterway* Sudan 91 F15
Joniškis Lithuania 80 I7
Jönköping Sweden 57 K13
Jonquière Quebec, Canada 25 N11
Joplin Missouri, USA 33 Q13
Jordan (prev. Transjordan) *Country* SWAsia 107

Jordan 107

a Arabic • Dinar • 99 • 68 • £0.47 • (m) 89% (f) 70% • 68%

Jordan *River* SW Asia 107 M9
Jorge, Golfo de *Sea feature* Spain 61 P7
Jos Nigeria 93 P11
Jos Plateau *Physical feature* Nigeria 93 P11
Joseph Bonaparte Gulf *Sea feature* Northern Territory/Western Australia, Australia 132 I5
Juan de Fuca, Strait of *Channel* Canada/USA 36 G6
Juan Fernández, Islas *Island group* Pacific Ocean 129 P11
Juàzeiro Brazil 46 M10
Juba *River* Somalia 91 L18
Juba Sudan 91 F16
Júcar *River* Spain 61 N10
Judenburg Austria 69 Q8
Juigalpa Nicaragua 42 D11
Juiz de Fora Brazil 47 L14
Juliaca Peru 45 G14
Julianehåb Greenland 51 M15
Juneau Alaska, USA 22 I10
Jungfrau *Mountain* Switzerland 68 F11
Junín Argentina 48 L10
Jura *Island* Scotland, UK 58 F9
Jura *Mountain range* France/Switzerland 63 O8, 68 D10
Jurbarkas Lithuania 80 H9
Juruá *River* Brazil/Peru 41, 46 B9
Juticalpa Honduras 42 D9
Jutland *Peninsula* Denmark 54, 56 H14
Juventud, I. de la (var. I. of Pines) *Island* Cuba 42 G4
Jwaneng Botswana 99 K11
Jyväskylä Finland 57 O9

K

K2 *Mountain* Tibet 115
Kabaena *Island* Indonesia 127 M14
Kabaledo Res. *Reservoir* Suriname 44 N7
Kabalo Zaire 95 N15
Kabul Afghanistan 111 N11
Kabwe Zambia 97 K14
Kaduna Nigeria 93 O10
Kaduqli Sudan 91 F14
Kaédi Mauritania 92 G7
Kaesŏng North Korea 121 P7
Kafue Zambia 97 K15
Kafue *National park* Zambia 96 J14
Kafue *River* Zambia 96 J14
Kafue Flats *Physical region* Zambia 96 J15
Kaga-Bandoro Central African Republic 94 J10
Kagera *National park* Rwanda 97 L5
Kagoshima Japan 123 C15
Kahramanmaraş Turkey 105 N9
Kai Is. *Island group* Indonesia 127 Q13
Kaikoura New Zealand 134 F10
Kainji Res. *Reservoir* Nigeria 93 N10
Kaipara Harbour *Coastal feature* New Zealand 134 G4
Kairouan Tunisia 89 N4
Kaiserslautern Germany 67 E14
Kajaani Finland 57 P7
Kakamega Kenya 97 N4
Kakhovka Res. *Reservoir* Ukraine 85 K7
Kalahari Desert *Desert region* Botswana 11, 87, 98 J11
Kalahari Gemsbok *National park* Botswana/South Africa 98 J12
Kalamata Greece 78 I12
Kalamazoo Michigan, USA 31 N9
Kalamit Gulf *Sea feature* Ukraine 84 J10
Kalemie (prev. Albertville) Zaire 95 O15
Kalgoorlie Western Australia, Australia 132 H12
Kaliningrad (prev. Königsberg) Russian Federation 80 F9
Kaliningrad Oblast *Region* Russian Federation 80
Kalinkavichy Belarus 81 M15
Kalispell Montana, USA 32 G4
Kalisz Poland 71 K6
Kalmar Sweden 57 K15
Kaluga Russian Federation 82 F10
Kama *River* Russian Federation 82 L10
Kama Res. *Reservoir* Russian Federation 82 L10
Kamarān I. *Island* Yemen 108 H15
Kamarhati India 117 O8
Kamchatka *Peninsula* Russian Federation 103, 113 Q7, 128 I3
Kamchiya *River* Bulgaria 77 O12
Kamenets-Podol"skiy *see* Kam'yanets'-Podil's'kyy
Kamenjak, C. *Cape* Croatia 74 F5
Kamina Zaire 95 M16
Kamloops British Columbia, Canada 22 J14
Kampala Uganda 97 M4
Kâmpóng Cham Cambodia 125 M14
Kâmpóng Chhnăng Cambodia 125 L14
Kâmpóng Saôm Cambodia 125 L14
Kâmpóng Thum Cambodia 125 M13
Kâmpôt Cambodia 125 L14

Kampuchea – Kuito

Kampuchea *see* Cambodia
Kam'yanets'-Podil's'kyy (var. Kamenets-Podol"skiy) Ukraine 84 G6
Kananga (prev. Luluabourg) Zaire 95 K15
Kanazawa Japan 122 H10
Kanchanaburi Thailand 125 I12
Kandahar *see* Qandahār
Kandi Benin 93 N10
Kandla India 116 H7
Kandy Sri Lanka 117 L16
Kangaroo I. *Island* South Australia, Australia 133 L14
Kangchenjunga *Mountain* China 115
Kangean *Island* Indonesia 126 J14
Kanggye North Korea 121 P6
Kangnŭng South Korea 121 Q7
Kanjiža Serbia, Yugoslavia 75 M3
Kankakee Illinois, USA 31 L11
Kankan Guinea 92 I10
Kano Nigeria 93 P10
Kanpur India 117 L6
Kansas *State* USA 33
Kansas City Kansas, USA 33 Q11
Kansas City Missouri, USA 33 Q11
Kansk Russian Federation 113 K10
Kao-hsiung Taiwan 121 O14
Kaolack Senegal 92 F8
Kap Farvel *see* Farvel, Cape
Kapchagay Kazakhstan 112 H13
Kapfenberg Austria 69 Q7
Kapos *River* Hungary 71 K15
Kapuas *River* Borneo, Indonesia 126 I11
Kara Togo 93 M11
Kara-Balta Kyrgyzstan 111 Q4
Kara-Bogaz-Gol, Zaliv *Bay* Turkmenistan 110 F5
Kara Deniz *see* Black Sea
Kara Kum *Desert region* Turkmenistan 11, 103
Kara Sea Russian Federation 51 S11, 54, 82 O5, 103, 112 I5
Kara Strait *Channel* Russian Federation 82 N6
Karabük Turkey 105 K5
Karachi Pakistan 100 H5, 116 G6
Karaganda (var. Qaraghandy) Kazakhstan 112 G11
Karaginskiy Is. *Island Group* Russian Federation 113 Q5
Karagiya Depression *Physical region* Asia 103
Karaj Iran 109 N4
Karakaya Barrage *Dam* Turkey 105 P8
Karakinit Gulf *Sea feature* Ukraine 84 J9
Karakorum Mts. *Mountain range* C Asia 118 E9
Karaköse *see* Ağri
Karakum Canal *Waterway* Turkmenistan 111 K9
Karaman Turkey 105 K9
Karamay China 118 H5
Karasburg Namibia 98 I13
Karasjok Norway 57 O2
Karbala Iraq 109 K5
Karditsa Greece 78 I6
Kariba Dam *Dam* Zambia/Zimbabwe 97 K15
Kariba, L. *Reservoir* Zambia/Zimbabwe 87, 97 K15, 99 L8
Karimata *Island* Indonesia 126 H12
Karisimbi, Mt. *Volcano* Zaire 87
Karlovac Croatia 74 H4
Karlovy Vary Czech Republic 70 G8
Karlskrona Sweden 57 K15
Karlsruhe Germany 67 F14
Karlstad Sweden 57 K12
Karpathos *Island* Dodecanese, Greece 79 Q15
Kars Turkey 105 R5
Karshi Uzbekistan 111 L8
Karymskaya Sopka *Volcano* Siberia 103
Karystos Greece 79 L9
Kasai *River* Angola/Zaire 95 J14
Kasama Zambia 97 M11
Kasese Uganda 97 L4
Kāshān Iran 109 N5
Kashgar *see* Kashi
Kashi (var. Kashgar) China 118 E8
Kashmir *Region* S Asia 117 K2
Kaskaskia *River* Illinois, USA 31 K13
Kasongo Zaire 95 N14
Kassala Sudan 91 I12
Kassandra, Gulf of *Sea feature* Greece 79 K4
Kassel Germany 67 H11
Kastamonu Turkey 105 L5
Kastoria Greece 78 H3
Kastorias, L. *Lake* Greece 78 H3
Kasumi Lagoon *Coastal feature* Japan 122 L10
Kasungu *National park* Malawi 97 M13
Kasur Pakistan 116 J3
Katakolo Greece 78 H10
Katar *see* Qatar
Katavi *National park* Tanzania 97 M9
Katerini Greece 78 I4
Katha Burma 124 G6
Kathmandu Nepal 117 N5
Katowice Poland 71 L9
Katsberg Tunnel *Tunnel* Austria 69 O9
Katsina Nigeria 93 P9
Kattegat *Channel* Denmark/Sweden 56 I14
Kaub *Castle* Germany 67 E12
Kaufmann Peak *see* Lenin Peak
Kaunas Lithuania 80 I9
Kavadarci Macedonia 75 O12
Kavala Greece 79 L2
Kawa *Archaeological site* Sudan 91 F11
Kawasaki Japan 123 K11
Kayan *River* Borneo, Indonesia 127 K10
Kayes Mali 92 H8
Kayseri Turkey 105 M8
Kazakh Uplands *Physical region* Kazakhstan 112 G11
Kazakhstan *Country* C Asia 112

Kazakhstan 112

a Kazakh • Afghani • 16 • 69 • N/A • N/A • 58%

Kazan' Russian Federation 83 J11
Kazanlŭk Bulgaria 77 L13
Kéa *Island* Cyclades, Greece 79 L10
Keban Barrage *Dam* Turkey 105 O7
Kecskemét Hungary 71 M14
Kėdainiai Lithuania 80 I9
Kediri Java, Indonesia 126 I15
Keetmanshoop Namibia 98 I12
Keewatin *Region* Northwest Territories, Canada 23 N9
Kefallonia *Island* Ionian Is. Greece 78 G8
Kegon Falls *Waterfall* Japan 115
Kelang Malaysia 125 J19
Kelkit *River* Turkey 105 P6
Kellett, Cape *Cape* Canada 51 N8
Kelmė Lithuania 80 H8
Kelud *Volcano* Java, Indonesia 115
Kem' Russian Federation 82 I6
Kemerovo Russian Federation 112 I10
Kemi Finland 57 O6
Kemi *River* Finland 57 O5
Kemijärvi Finland 57 P5
Kenai Alaska, USA 22 G8
Kendari Celebes, Indonesia 127 M13
Kenema Sierra Leone 92 H12
Kenge Zaire 95 I14
Kénitra Morocco 88 I5
Kennebec *River* Maine, USA 27 P5
Kennedy Space Center Florida, USA 29 O12
Kennewick Washington, USA 36 K8
Kenora Ontario, Canada 24 F9
Kenosha Wisconsin, USA 31 L9
Kentucky *River* Kentucky, USA 29 N3
Kentucky *State* USA 29
Kenya *Country* E Africa 97

Kenya 97

a Swahili • Shilling • 114 • 59 • £0.46 • (m) 80% (f) 59% • 9 • 6552 • Yes • 24% • 2163

Kenya, Mt. *National park* Kenya 97 P5
Kerch Ukraine 85 L9
Kerch Strait (var. Kerchens'ka Protoka) *Channel* Russian Federation/Ukraine 54, 83 C14, 85 L9
Kerchens'ka Protoka *see* Kerch Strait
Kerguelen *Island group* Indian Ocean 101 H14
Kerguelen I. *Island* Indian Ocean, Antarctica 50 I7
Kerguelen Plateau *Sea feature* Indian Ocean 101 H14
Kermadec Is. *Island group* Polynesia, Pacific Ocean 128 J11
Kermadec Trench *Sea feature* Pacific Ocean 128 J11
Kermān Iran 109 P8
Kermanshah *see* Bakhtarān
Kerulen (var. Herlen Gol) *River* Mongolia/China 103, 114, 119 N4
Ket' *River* Russian Federation 112 I10
Ketchikan Alaska, USA 22 I12
Kewanee Illinois, USA 30 J11
Keweenaw Bay *Physical feature* Michigan, USA 31 L4
Key West Florida, USA 29 N16
Khabarovsk Russian Federation 113 P11
Khambhat, Gulf of *Sea feature* India 116 I9
Khamīs Mushayţ Saudi Arabia 108 I13
Khān Yūnis Gaza Strip 107 K11
Khānaqīn Iraq 109 L4
Khanka, Lake *Lake* 115
Khankendy *see* Xankändi
Kharkiv (var. Kharkov) Ukraine 85 L5
Kharkov *see* Kharkiv
Khartoum (var. El Kharṭûm) Sudan 91 G12
Khartoum North Sudan 91 G12
Khasab Oman 109 O10
Khashm el Girba Dam Sudan 91 I12
Khaskovo Bulgaria 77 L14
Khatanga *River* Russian Federation 113 K6
Khaybar Saudi Arabia 108 I13
Kherson Ukraine 84 J8
Khmel'nyts'kyy Ukraine 84 G5
Khodzheyli Uzbekistan 110 I5
Khon Kaen Thailand 125 K11
Khorog Tajikistan 111 P9
Khorramshahr Iran 109 L7
Khouribga Morocco 88 H5
Khudzhand (prev. Leninabad) Tajikistan 111 O7
Khulna Bangladesh 117 P8
Khyber Pass *Physical feature* Afghanistan/Pakistan 111 O12
Kičevo Macedonia 75 N12
Kidepo *National park* Uganda 97 N2
Kiel Germany 66 H6
Kiel Canal *Waterway* Germany 66 G6
Kielce Poland 71 M7
Kieta Bougainville, Papua New Guinea 133 Q2
Kiev (var. Kiyiv) Ukraine 84 I4
Kiev Res. *Reservoir* Ukraine 84 I4
Kiffa Mauritania 92 H7
Kigali Rwanda 97 L6
Kigoma Tanzania 97 L8
Kikwit Zaire 95 J14
Kilimanjaro *National park* Kenya/Tanzania 97 P6
Kilimanjaro *Volcano* Tanzania 87
Kilis Turkey 105 N10
Kilkis Greece 78 J2
Killarney Ireland 59 B14
Kilwa Masoko Tanzania 97 Q10
Kimberley South Africa 99 K13
Kimberley Plateau *Physical region* Western Australia, Australia 131, 132 I6
Kimito *Island* Finland 57 N11
Kindu Zaire 95 M13
King I. *Island* Tasmania, Australia 133 M15
King Leopold Ranges *Mountain range* Western Australia, Australia 132 H7
King William I. *Island* Northwest Territories, Canada 23 N7
King's Lynn England, UK 59 L14
Kingman Reef *Dependent territory* Polynesia, Pacific Ocean 129 K7
Kingston Jamaica 42 J8
Kingston New York, USA 27 L10
Kingston Ontario, Canada 25 L14
Kingston-upon-Hull England, UK 59 K13
Kingstown St Vincent & The Grenadines 43 T14
Kinshasa (prev. Léopoldville) Zaire 95 H14
Kintyre *Peninsula* Scotland, UK 58 F10
Kirghiz Range *Mountain range* Kazakhstan/Kyrgyzstan 111 P5
Kirghiz Steppe *Physical Region* Kazakhstan 103, 112 F10
Kiribati *Country* Micronesia/Polynesia, Pacific Ocean 128 J8

Kiribati 128

a English, I Kiribati • Dollar • 259 • 56 • £2.45 • (av.) 10% • 36%

Kirikkale Turkey 105 L6
Kirinyaga *Volcano* Kenya 87
Kiritimati (var. Christmas Island) *Dependent territory* Pacific Ocean 128 L8
Kirkenes Norway 57 P2
Kirklareli Turkey 104 G4
Kirksville Missouri, USA 33 R10
Kirkuk Iraq 109 K3
Kirkwall Orkney Scotland, UK 58 J6
Kirov Russian Federation 82 J10
Kirovabad *see* Gäncä
Kirovakan *see* Vanadzor
Kirovohrad (var. Yelyzavethrad) Ukraine 84 J6
Kiruna Sweden 57 N4
Kirşehir Turkey 105 L7
Kisangani (prev. Stanleyville) Zaire 95 M12
Kishinev *see* Chişinău
Kiska I. *Island* Aleutian Is. Alaska, USA 22 A5
Kismaayo Somalia 91 L18
Kisumu Kenya 97 N4
Kitakyūshū Japan 123 C13
Kitale Kenya 97 N4
Kitami Japan 122 M3
Kitchener Ontario, Canada 25 K14
Kíthnos *Island* Cyclades, Greece 79 L11
Kitikmeot *Region* Northwest Territories, Canada 23 M7
Kitimat British Columbia, Canada 23 I12
Kitwe Zambia 97 K13
Kitzbühel Austria 69 M8
Kiunga Marine Reserve *Nature reserve* Kenya 97 R6
Kivu, L. *Lake* Rwanda/Zaire 95 O13, 97 L6
Kiyiv *see* Kiev
Kizilirmak *River* Turkey 105 M7
Kizyl-Arbat Turkmenistan 110 H7
Kizyl-Atrek Turkmenistan 110 G8
Kjølen Mts. *Mountain range* Norway/Sweden 54, 57 K6
Klagenfurt Austria 69 P9
Klaipėda Lithuania 80 G8
Klamath Falls Oregon, USA 37 H11
Klerksdorp South Africa 99 K12
Ključ Bosnia and Herzegovina 74 I6
Klosterneuburg Austria 69 S4
Kluane L. *Lake* Yukon Territory, Canada 22 H9
Klyuchevskaya Sopka *Volcano* Siberia 103
Knin Croatia 74 I6
Knittelfeld Austria 69 Q8
Knossos *Archaeological site* Crete, Greece 79 M16
Knoxville Tennessee, USA 29 N5
Knud Rasmussen Land *Physical region* Greenland 51 O12
Ko Phangan *see* Phangan I.
Ko Phuket *see* Phuket I.
Ko Samui *see* Samui I.
Kōbe Japan 15, 123 G12, 128 G5
Koblenz Germany 67 E12
Kobryn Belarus 80 I14
Kočani Macedonia 75 P11
Kōchi Japan 123 F13
Kodiak Kodiak I. Alaska, USA 22 F9
Kodiak I. *Island* Alaska, USA 20, 22 F9
Kohima India 117 Q7
Kohtla-Järve Estonia 81 L2
Kokand Uzbekistan 111 O6
Kokchetav (var. Kökshetaū) Kazakhstan 112 G10
Kokkola Finland 57 N8
Kokomo Indiana, USA 31 M11
Kokshaal-Tau Mts. *Mountain range* China/Kyrgyzsta 111 S5
Kökshetaū *see* Kokchetav
Kola Peninsula *Physical feature* Russian Federation 54, 82 J6
Kolda Senegal 92 G9
Kolguyev I. *Island* Russian Federation 82 M6
Kolka Latvia 80 H4
Köln *see* Cologne
Kolonia *see* Palikir
Kolubara *River* Serbia, Yugoslavia 75 M6
Kolwezi Zaire 95 M17
Kolyma *River* Russian Federation 113 O5
Kolyma Range *Mountain range* Russian Federation 113 P6
Kom Ombo *Archaeological site* Egypt 90 G9
Kommunizma, Pik *see* Communism Peak
Komoé *River* Ivory Coast 93 K11
Komoran *Island* Indonesia 127 T15
Komotini Greece 79 N2
Komsomol'sk-na-Amure Russian Federation 113 P10
Kongolo Zaire 95 N14
Kongsberg Norway 56 I11
Königsberg *see* Kaliningrad
Konjic Bosnia and Herzegovina 75 K7
Konstanz Germany 67 G16
Konya Turkey 105 K9
Kopaonik *Mountain range* Serbia, Yugoslavia 75 N8
Koper Slovenia 74 F3
Koprivnica Croatia 74 J2
Korarnikhon Tajikistan 111 N8
Korčula *Island* Croatia 74 I9
Korçë Albania 75 N13
Korčulanski Kanal *Channel* Croatia 74 I8
Korea *Region* E Asia 115
Korea Bay *Sea feature* Korea/China 121 O7
Korea Strait *Channel* Korea/Japan 115, 121 Q9, 123 B13
Korhogo Ivory Coast 92 J11
Kōriyama Japan 122 K9
Korkodon *River* Russian Federation 113 P5
Korla China 118 H7
Kornat *Island* Croatia 74 H7
Koror Palau, Pacific Ocean 128 G8
Körös *River* Hungary 71 M14
Korosten' Ukraine 84 H4
Kortrijk (var. Courtrai) Belgium 65 D15
Koryak Range *Mountain range* Russian Federation 113 Q4
Kos Kos, Greece 79 Q12
Kos *Island* Dodecanese, Greece 79 Q12
Kosciusko, Mt. *Mountain* Australia 131
Košice Slovakia 71 N11
Kossou, L. de *Lake* Ivory Coast 92 J12
Kosti Sudan 91 G13
Kostroma Russian Federation 82 H9
Koszalin Poland 70 J2
Kota India 116 J6
Kota Baharu Malaysia 125 J17
Kota Kinabalu Borneo, Malaysia 126 J8
Kotka Finland 57 P11
Kotlas Russian Federation 82 J9
Kotto *River* Central African Republic/Zaire 94 L9
Kotzebue Alaska, USA 22 G5
Kotzebue Sound *Sea feature* Alaska, USA 22 F4
Koudougou Burkina 93 L9
Kourou French Guiana 44 P6
Kousseri (prev. Fort-Foureau) Cameroon 94 H7
Kouvola Finland 57 P11
Kowl-e-Namaksār *Salt pan* Afghanistan/Iran 110 J12
Kowloon Hong Kong 121 M14
Kozani Greece 78 H4
Kra, Isthmus of *Physical region* Thailand 115, 125 H15
Krâcheh Cambodia 125 M13
Kragujevac Serbia, Yugoslavia 75 N7
Krak des Chevaliers Syria 107 M5
Krakatau *Volcano* Indonesia 9, 114
Kraków (var. Cracow) Poland 71 M9
Kralendijk Netherlands Antilles 43 O14
Kraljevo Serbia, Yugoslavia 75 N7
Kramators'k Ukraine 85 L6
Kranj Slovenia 74 G2
Krāslava Latvia 81 K8
Krasnoarmeysk Russian Federation 82 H13
Krasnodar Russian Federation 83 D14
Krasnovodsk Turkmenistan 110 F6
Krasnoyarsk Russian Federation 112 J10
Krefeld Germany 67 D11
Kremenchuk Ukraine 84 J6
Kremenchuk Res. *Reservoir* Ukraine 84 J5
Krems Austria 69 Q4
Kretinga Lithuania 80 G7
Kribi Cameroon 95 E11
Krichev *see* Krychaw
Krishna *River* India 115, 116 J11
Kristiansand Norway 56 H12
Kristianstad Sweden 57 K15
Kristiansund Norway 52 L7
Krivoy Rog *see* Kryvyy Rih
Krk *Island* Croatia 74 G4
Krka *River* Croatia 74 H7
Krŏng Kaôh Kŏng Cambodia 125 K14
Kruger N.P. *National park* South Africa 99 M11
Krung Thep *see* Bangkok
Kruševac Serbia, Yugoslavia 75 O8
Krychaw (var. Krichev) Belarus 81 O12
Krym *see* Crimea
Kryvyy Rih (var. Krivoy Rog) Ukraine 84 J7
Krzna *River* Belarus/Poland 71 O5
Kuala Belait Brunei 126 J9
Kuala Lumpur Malaysia 125 J19
Kuala Terengganu Malaysia 125 K18
Kualakapuas Borneo, Indonesia 126 J13
Kuantan Malaysia 125 K18
Kuba *see* Quba
Kuban *River* Russian Federation 83 E14
Kuching Borneo, Malaysia 126 H10
Kudat Borneo, Malaysia 127 K8
Kufstein Austria 69 M7
Kuito Angola 98 H6

a Language (official or most commonly spoken) • Currency • Population density per square mile • Average life expectancy • Price of 1 dozen hen's eggs • Literacy • Number of TVs per 1,000 people • Number of people per doctor • Death penalty • Percentage of urban-based population • Average number of calories consumed daily per person

Londinium *see* London
London (anc. Londinium) England, UK 14, 59 K16
London Ontario, Canada 24 J15
Londonderry Northern Ireland, UK 58 E10
Londonderry, C. *Cape* Western Australia, Australia 132 H5
Londrina Brazil 47 I14
Long Beach California, USA 37 K19, 129 N5
Long Branch New Jersey, USA 27 L13
Long I. *Island* Bahamas 43 L4
Long I. *Island* New York, USA 27 N12
Long Xuyen Vietnam 125 M15
Longmont Colorado, USA 35 M4
Longreach Queensland, Australia 133 N9
Longview Washington, USA 36 H8
Longyearbyen Svalbard, Arctic Ocean 51 Q13
Lop Nur *Lake* China 115, 118 I8
Lopatka, C. *Cape* Russian Federation 113 R8
Lord Howe I. *Island* Australia, Pacific Ocean 128 I11
Lord Howe Rise *Sea feature* Pacific Ocean 128 I12, 131
Lord Howe Seamounts *Sea feature* Pacific Ocean 131
Lorengau Admiralty Is. Papua New Guinea 133 O1
Lorient France 52 K8, 62 G7
Los Alamos New Mexico, USA 35 L7
Los Angeles California, USA 14, 37 K18
Los Angeles Chile 49 G12
Los Mochis Mexico 38 I7
Lošinj *Island* Croatia 74 G5
Lot *River* France 63 K12
Lötschberg Tunnel *Tunnel* Switzerland 68 F11
Louang Namtha Laos 124 J8
Louang Phrabang Laos 124 K9
Loubomo Congo 95 G14
Louga Senegal 92 F8
Louise, L. *Lake* Alberta, Canada 23 L14
Louisiade Archipelago *Island group* Papua New Guinea 133 P4
Louisiana *State* USA 28
Louisville Kentucky, USA 29M3
Lourenço Marques *see* Maputo
Loutra Aidipsou Greece 78 J7
Louvain *see* Leuven
Lovech Bulgaria 77 K12
Lowell Massachusetts, USA 27 O9
Lower Red L. *Lake* Minnesota, USA 30 G3
Lower Tunguska *River* Russian Federation 113 L9
Lower Zambezi *National park* Zambia 97 L14
Loznica Serbia, Yugoslavia 75 L6
Lualaba *River* Zaire 95 M13
Luanda (prev. Loanda) Angola 98 G4
Luang Lagoon *Coastal feature* Thailand 125 I16
Luangwa *River* Zambia 97 M12
Luangwa, N. *National park* Zambia 97 M12
Luangwa, S. *National park* Zambia 97 M13
Luanshya Zambia 97 K13
Lubana, L. *Lake* Latvia 81 K6
Lubango Angola 98 G7
Lubbock Texas, USA 35 O9
Lübeck Germany 66 I7
Lublin Poland 71 O7
Lubumbashi (prev. Elisabethville) Zaire 95 N17
Lucapa Angola 98 I4
Lucca Italy 72 F9
Lucena Luzon, Philippines 127 L4
Lučenec Slovakia 71 L12
Lucerne (var. Luzern) Switzerland 68 G10
Lucerne, L. of *Lake* Switzerland 68 G10
Lucknow India 117 L6
Lüderitz Namibia 53 M14, 98 H12
Ludhiana India 117 K4
Ludza Latvia 81 L7
Luena Angola 98 I5
Lugano Switzerland 68 H12
Lugano, L. *Lake* Italy/Switzerland 68 H12
Lugansk *see* Luhans'k
Lugenda *River* Mozambique 99 O6
Lugo Spain 60 G3
Luhans'k (var. Lugansk; prev. Voroshilovgrad) Ukraine 85 M6
Luik *see* Liège
Luke Air Force Range *Military center* Arizona, USA 34 H10
Lukusuzi *National park* Zambia 97 M13
Lule *River* Sweden 57 M4
Luleå Sweden 57 N6
Lulonga *River* Zaire 95 J12
Lulua *River* Angola/Zaire 95 L16
Luluabourg *see* Kananga
Lumbala N'guimbo Angola 98 J6
Lumphat Cambodia 125 N13
Lundazi Zambia 97 N13
Lundy *Island* England, UK 59 F16
Lüneburg Germany 66 I8
Luninyets Belarus 81 K14
Luoyang China 121 L9
Lusaka Zambia 97 K15
Lusambo Zaire 95 L14
Luton England, UK 59 K15
Luts'k Ukraine 84 F4
Lutzow-Holm Bay *Sea feature* Indian Ocean Coast, Antarctica 50 G6
Luxembourg *Country* W Europe 65

Luxembourg 65

a French, German, Litzebuergish • Franc • 379 • 75 • £1.67 • (m) 100% (f) 100% • 255 • 529 • No • 84% • 3902

Luxembourg Luxembourg 65 L19
Luxor Egypt 90 G8
Luzern *see* Lucerne
Luzon *Island* Philippines 127 M3
Luzon Strait *Channel* Philippines 127 L1
Lužnice *River* Czech Republic 70 H10
L'viv (var. L'vov) Ukraine 84 F5
L'vov *see* L'viv
Lyepyel' (var. Lepel') Belarus 81 M10
Lyme Bay *Sea feature* England, UK 59 H17
Lynchburg Virginia, USA 29 Q4
Lynn Massachusetts, USA 27 O9
Lynn Lake Manitoba, Canada 23 N12
Lyon France 63 N10

M

Ma'ān Jordan 107 M12
Maarianhamina Finland 57 M11
Maas *River* Germany/Netherlands 65 L12
Maastricht Netherlands 65 K15
Mabaruma Guyana 44 L5
Macao *Dependent territory* SE China 121 M14
Macao Macao, SE China 121 M14
Macapá Brazil 46 I7
Macdonald Is. *Island group* Indian Ocean 101 H15
Macdonnell Ranges *Mountain range* Northern Territory, Australia 131, 132 J9
Macedonia (var. Makedonija) *Country* SE Europe 75

Macedonia 75

a Macedonian • Denar • 191 • 72 • N/A • (av.) 93% • 54%

Maceió Brazil 46 O10
Machakos Kenya 97 P5
Machala Ecuador 44 B9
Machu Picchu *Archaeological site* Peru 45 F13
Mackay Queensland, Australia 133 O8
Mackay, L. *Lake* Northern Territory/Western Australia, Australia 131, 132 I9
Mackenzie *River* Northwest Territories, Canada 10, 20, 23 K9
Mackenzie *River basin* N America 11
Mackenzie Bay *Sea feature* Indian Ocean Coast, Antarctica 50 G8
Mackenzie Bay *Sea feature* Northwest territories/Yukon Territory, Canada 22 J6
Mackenzie King I. *Island* Northwest Territories, Canada 23 L4
Mackenzie Mts. *Mountain range* Northwest Territories, Canada 22 J9
Mackinac, Strait of *Channel* Michigan, USA 31 N5
Macleod, L. *Lake* Western Australia, Australia 132 E9
Macomb Illinois, USA 30 J12
Mâcon France 63 N9
Macon Georgia, USA 29 N8
Macoraba *see* Mecca
Macquarie I *Island* Pacific Ocean 128 I13
Macquarie Ridge *Sea feature* Pacific Ocean 128 I13, 131
Madagascâr *Country* Indian Ocean 100

Madagascar 100

a French, Malagasy • Franc • 54 • 51 • £1.09 • (m) 88% (f) 73% • 24%

Madagascar *Island* Indian Ocean 87
Madagascar Basin *Sea feature* Indian Ocean 87, 101 F11
Madagascar Ridge *Sea feature* Indian Ocean 87, 101 E12
Madang Papua New Guinea 133 N2
Madeira *Island* Atlantic Ocean 52 J9
Madeira *Island group* Atlantic Ocean 87
Madeira *River* Bolivia/Brazil 41, 46 F8
Madeira Ridge *Sea feature* Atlantic Ocean 54, 87
Madeleine, Îles de la (var. Magdalen Is.) *Island group* Quebec, Canada 26 Q10
Madison Wisconsin, USA 31 K8
Madona Latvia 81 K6
Madras India 100 I7, 117 L13
Madre de Dios *River* Bolivia/Peru 45 H13
Madrid Spain 61 K8
Madura *Island* Indonesia 126 I14
Madurai India 117 K15
Mae Khlong (var. Meklong) *River* Thailand 125 H12
Maebashi Japan 122 J10
Mafeteng Lesotho 99 L14
Mafia I. *Island* Tanzania 97 Q10
Magadan Russian Federation 113 P7
Magdalen Is. *see* Madeleine, Îles de la
Magdalena *River* Colombia 41, 44 E5
Magdeburg Germany 66 J9
Magellan, Strait of *Channel* Chile 41, 49 I20
Magerøy *Island* Norway 57 P1
Maggiore, L. *Lake* Italy/Switzerland 68 G12, 72 D6
Magnitogorsk Russian Federation 112 F9
Mahabalipuram India 117 L13
Mahajanga Madagascar 100 E10
Mahalapye Botswana 99 L10
Mahanadi *River* India 117 N9
Mahé *Island* Seychelles 100 F9
Mahilyow (var. Mogilev) Belarus 81 N11
Mahón Minorca, Spain 61 S8
Mai-Ndombe, L *Lake* Zaire 95 J13
Maiduguri Nigeria 93 R10
Main *River* Germany 67 G13
Maine *State* USA 27 P4
Mainz Germany 67 F13
Maitland New South Wales, Australia 133 P12
Majorca (var. Mallorca) *Island* Balearic Islands, Spain 61 R8
Majuro Marshall Islands, Pacific Ocean 128 I8
Makarikari *see* Makgadikgadi Pans
Makassar *see* Ujung Pandang
Makassar Strait *Channel* Borneo/Celebes, Indonesia 127 K13
Makedonija *see* Macedonia
Makeni Sierra Leone 92 H11
Makeyevka *see* Makiyivka
Makgadikgadi Pans (var. Makarikari, Soa Salt Pan) *Salt basin* Botswana 99 K9
Makhachkala Russian Federation 83 F16
Makiyivka (var. Makeyevka) Ukraine 85 M7
Makkah *see* Mecca
Makkovik Newfoundland, Canada 25 Q6
Makokou Gabon 95 G12
Makran *Physical region* Pakistan 116 F5
Makurdi Nigeria 93 P12
Malabar Coast *Coastal region* India 116 I14
Malabo Equatorial Guinea 95 E11
Malacca *see* Melaka
Malacca, Strait of *Channel* SE Asia 100 L8, 115, 130
Maladzyechna (var. Molodechno) Belarus 81 K11
Málaga Spain 60 J14
Malakal Sudan 91 G15
Malang Java, Indonesia 126 I15
Malanje Angola 98 H4
Malatya Turkey 105 O8
Malawi *Country* C Africa 97

Malawi 97

a English • Kwacha • 242 • 46 • £0.68 • (m) 34% (f) 12% • 12%

Malay Pen. *Peninsula* SE Asia 115
Malaya *see* Malaysia
Malaysia (prev. Malaya) *Country* SE Asia 125

Malaysia 125

a Malay • Ringgit • 144 • 70 • £0.65 • (m) 87% (f) 70% • 148 • 2708 • Yes • 43% • 2774

Malaysia (East) Borneo, SE Asia 126
Maldive Ridge *Sea feature* Indian Ocean 100 H9
Maldives *Country* Indian Ocean 100 I8

Maldives 100

a Divehi • Rufiyya • 1908 • 62 • £1.33 • (m) 91% (f) 92% • 30%

Male Maldives 100 I8
Malheur L. *Lake* Oregon, USA 36 K10
Mali (prev. French Sudan) *Country* W Africa 92-93

Mali 92-93

a French • Franc • 18 • 48 • £1.41 • (m) 41% (f) 24% • 19%

Mali Hka *River* Burma 115
Malindi Kenya 97 Q7
Malines *see* Mechelen
Mallaig Scotland, UK 58 G8
Mallorca *see* Majorca
Malmédy Belgium 65 L16
Malmö Sweden 56 J15
Malta (var. Melita) *Country* Europe 73

Malta 73

a Maltese, English • Lira • 2881 • 74 • £0.78 • (m) 96% (f) 96% • 87%

Maltahöhe Namibia 98 H11
Maluku *see* Moluccas
Mamberamo *River* Indonesia 127 S12
Mamoré *River* Bolivia 45 J14
Mamry, L. *Lake* Poland 71 N3
Man Ivory Coast 92 I12
Man, Isle of *Dependent territory* W Europe 59 G12
Manado Celebes, Indonesia 127 N10
Managua Nicaragua 42 D11
Managua, L. *Lake* Nicaragua 42 D10
Manam *Volcano* New Guinea 131
Manama (var. Al Manamah) Bahrain 100 F5, 109 M9
Manaslu *Mountain* China 115
Manaus Brazil 46 F8
Manchester England, UK 59 I13
Manchester New Hampshire, USA 27 N9
Manchuria *Region* China 121 P4
Manchurian Plain *Physical region* China 115
Mandalay Burma 124 G7
Mandera Kenya 97 R2
Mangalia Romania 77 P10
Mangalore India 116 J13
Mangla Res. *Reservoir* India/Pakistan 116 J2
Manguéni, Plateau du *Physical region* Niger 93 R5
Manhattan Kansas, USA 33 P11
Manicouagan Res. *Reservoir* Quebec, Canada 25 N9
Manila Philippines 15, 127 L4, 128 F7
Manisa Turkey 104 G8
Manistee Michigan, USA 31 M7
Manistee *River* Michigan, USA 31 M7
Manitoba *Province* Canada 23
Manitoba, L. *Lake* Manitoba, Canada 20
Manitowoc Wisconsin, USA 31 L7
Manizales Colombia 44 E6
Mankato Minnesota, USA 30 H7
Mannar Sri Lanka 117 K15
Mannheim Germany 67 F13
Mannu *River* Sardinia 73 D15
Manokwari Irian Jaya, Indonesia 127 Q11
Manono Zaire 95 N15
Mansa Zambia 97 K12
Mansel I. *Island* Canada 25 K2
Mansfield Ohio, USA 31 P11
Manta Ecuador 44 B9
Mantova (var. Mantua) Italy 72 F7
Mantua *see* Mantova
Manyara *National park* Tanzania 97 O7
Manyara, L. *Lake* Tanzania 97 O7
Manzanillo Mexico 39 K12
Manzhouli China 119 P3
Manzini Swaziland 99 M12
Mao Chad 94 H7
Maoke Mts. New Guinea 115
Maputo (prev. Lourenço Marques) Mozambique 99 N12
Mar Chiquita, L. *Salt lake* Argentina 48 K8
Mar del Plata Argentina 49 N12, 53 F14
Maracaibo Venezuela 44 G4
Maracaibo, L. *Sea feature* Venezuela 41, 44 G5
Maracay Venezuela 44 I4
Maradi Niger 93 O9
Marajó I. *Island* Brazil 41
Maramba *see* Livingstone
Maranhão Res. *Reservoir* Portugal 60 G10
Marañón *River* Peru 41, 44 D10
Marathon *Archaeological site* Greece 79 L9
Marbella Spain 60 J14
Marche-en-Famenne Belgium 65 J17
Mardan Pakistan 116 I2
Mardin Turkey 105 Q9
Margarita Island *Island* Venezuela 44 J4
Margherita Peak *Volcano* Uganda 87
Mariana Trench *Sea feature* Pacific Ocean 8, 128 G6
Marías Is. *Island group* Mexico 38 J10
Ma'rib *Archaeological site* Yemen 109 I15
Maribor Slovenia 74 H2
Marie Byrd Land *Region* Antarctica 50 C10
Marie Galante *Island* Guadeloupe 43 T12
Mariental Namibia 98 I11
Mariestad Sweden 57 K12
Marijampolė Lithuania 80 H10
Marinette Wisconsin, USA 31 L6
Marion Indiana, USA 31 N11
Marion Ohio, USA 31 P11
Marion, L. *Lake* South Carolina, USA 29 P8
Maritsa *River* SE Europe 77 M14
Mariupol' Ukraine 85 L8
Marka Somalia 91 M18
Marmara, Sea of Turkey 104 H5
Marmaris Turkey 104 H10
Marne *River* France 63 M4
Maroua Cameroon 94 H8
Marowijne *River* French Guiana/Suriname 44 O7
Marquesas Is. *Island group* French Polynesia, Pacific Ocean 129 M9
Marquette Michigan, USA 31 L4
Marrakesh Morocco 88 H6
Marsá al Burayqah Libya 89 Q7
Marsa Matrûh Egypt 90 E6
Marsabit *National park* Kenya 97 P3
Marseille France 52 L8, 63 O14
Marsh I. *Island* Louisiana, USA 28 H10
Marshall Islands *Country* Micronesia, Pacific Ocean 128 I7

Marshall Islands 128

a English, Marshallese • Dollar • 687 • 65 • £1.28 • (av.) 7% • N/A

Marshfield Wisconsin, USA 30 J7
Martaban, Gulf of *Sea feature* Burma 125 G11
Martha's Vineyard *Island* Massachusetts, USA 27 O11
Martigny Switzerland 68 E12
Martin Slovakia 71 L10
Martinique *Dependent territory* Caribbean Sea 43 T13
Martre, Lac la *Lake* Northwest Territories, Canada 23 K9
Mary (prev. Merv) Turkmenistan 110 J9
Maryland *State* USA 29
Maryville Missouri, USA 33 Q10
Masada Israel 107 L11
Masai Mara *Nature reserve* Kenya 97 N5
Masai Steppe *Physical region* Tanzania 97 O8
Masaka Uganda 97 M5
Masbate Masbate, Philippines 127 M5
Masbate *Island* Philippines 127 M5
Mascarene Is. *Island group* Indian Ocean 101 G11
Mascarene Plateau *Sea feature* Indian Ocean 100 G10
Maseru Lesotho 99 L13
Mashhad Iran 109 Q4

a Language (official or most commonly spoken) • Currency • Population density per square mile • Average life expectancy • Price of 1 dozen hen's eggs • Literacy • Number of TVs per 1,000 people • Number of people per doctor • Death penalty • Percentage of urban-based population • Average number of calories consumed daily per person

Masinloc – Mozambique Channel

Masinloc Luzon, Philippines 127
Maşīrah Oman 100 G6
Masīrah, Gulf of *Sea feature* Oman 109 P14 L4
Masīrah I. *Island* Oman 109 P14
Mason City Iowa, USA 33 Q8
Masqat *see* Muscat
Massachusetts *State* USA 27
Massawa Eritrea 91 J12
Massena New York, USA 27 L6
Massif Central *Physical feature* France 54, 63 M11
Massillon Ohio, USA 31 Q11
Massina *Physical region* 87
Massoukou (prev. Franceville) Gabon 95 G13
Masterton New Zealand 134 H8
Masvingo (prev. Fort Victoria, Nyanda) Zimbabwe 99 M9
Matadi Zaire 95 G15
Matagalpa Nicaragua 42 D10
Matam Senegal 92 G8
Matamoros Mexico 39 O7
Matanzas Cuba 42 H3
Matara Sri Lanka 117 L16
Mato Grosso, Plateau of *Physical region* Brazil 41, 46 G10
Matsue Japan 123 E12
Matsuyama Japan 123 E13
Matterhorn (var. Monte Cervino) *Mountain* Switzerland 54, 68 F13
Mattoon Illinois, USA 31 L13
Maturín Venezuela 44 K5
Maumee *River* Indiana/Ohio, USA 31 O10
Maun Botswana 99 K9
Mauritania *Country* W Africa 92

Mauritania 92

a Arabic • Ouguiya • 5 • 47 • £1.87 • (m) 47% (f) 21% • 47%

Mauritius *Country* Indian Ocean 101 G11

Mauritius 101

a English • Rupee • 1516 • 70 • £0.98 • (m) 89% (f) 77% • 41%

Mawson *Research center* Antarctica 50 G7
Maya *River* Russian Federation 113 O8
Mayaguana *Island* Bahamas 43 M5
Mayagüez Puerto Rico 43 P9
Maykop Russian Federation 83 D14
Mayor Pablo Lagerenza Paraguay 48 K3
Mayotte *Dependent territory* Indian Ocean 100 E10
Mazār-e Sharīf Afghanistan 111 M10
Mazaruni *River* Guyana 44 L6
Mazatenango Guatemala 42 A8
Mazatlán Mexico 38 J9
Mažeikiai Lithuania 80 H7
Mazyr (var. Mozyr') Belarus 81 M15
Mbabane Swaziland 99 M12
Mbaïki Central African Republic 95 I11
Mbala Zambia 97 M10
Mbale Uganda 97 N4
Mbalmayo Cameroon 95 F11
Mbandaka (prev. Coquilhatville) Zaire 95 J12
Mbarara Uganda 97 L5
Mbeya Tanzania 97 N10
Mbuji-Mayi Zaire 95 L15
McAllen Texas, USA 35 Q16
McClellan Air Base *Military center* California, USA 37 I14
McClintock Channel *Channel* Northwest Territories, Canada 23 M6
McClure Strait *Channel* Banks I./Melville I. Northwest Territories, Canada 23 L5
McKinley, Mt. *see* Denali
McMurdo Sound *Sea feature* Pacific Ocean Coast, Antarctica 50 E11
Mead, L. *Lake* Arizona/Nevada USA 34 H6
Meadville Pennsylvania, USA 26 G10
Mecca (var. Makkah; anc. Macoraba) Saudi Arabia 108 H11
Mechelen (var. Malines) Belgium 65 G14
Mecklenburg Bay *Sea feature* Germany 66 J6
Medan Sumatra, Indonesia 127 D10
Medellín Colombia 44 E6
Medenine Tunisia 89 N6
Medford Oregon, USA 37 G11
Medicine Hat Alberta, Canada 23 L15
Medina (var. Al Madinah; prev. Yathrib) Saudi Arabia 108 H9
Medina L. *Lake* Texas, USA 35 Q13
Mediterranean Sea Africa/Europe 11, 13, 54, 52 L9, 73 J19, 87, 90 E6, 103
Meekatharra Western Australia, Australia 132 G10
Meerut India 117 K5
Mekele Ethiopia 91 J13
Meklong *see* Mae Khlong
Meknès Morocco 88 I5
Mekong (var. Lancang Jiang) *River* Asia 100 L6, 115, 119 K12, 120 H14, 125 M13
Mekong Delta *Delta* Vietnam 115
Melaka (var. Malacca) Malaysia 100 M8 125 J19
Melanesia *Region* Pacific Ocean 128 I9
Melanesian Basin *Sea feature* Pacific Ocean 131
Melbourne Florida, USA 29 O13
Melbourne Victoria, Australia 128 H12, 133 N14
Melilla *Spanish enclave* NW Africa 88 J4
Melita *see* Malta
Melitopol' Ukraine 85 K8
Melk Austria 69 Q5
Melo Uruguay 48 O9
Melrhir, Chott *Salt lake* Algeria 89 M5
Melun France 63 L5
Melville Saskatchewan, Canada 23 N14
Melville I. *Island* Northern Territory, Australia 132 J4
Melville I. *Island* Northwest Territories, Canada 23 L4, 51 N9
Memphis Tennessee, USA 28 J5
Mendawai *River* Borneo, Indonesia 126 J12
Mende France 63 M12
Mendeleyev Ridge *Sea feature* Arctic Ocean 20
Mendi Papua New Guinea 133 M2
Mendocino, C. *Cape* California, USA 20
Mendocino Fracture Zone *Sea feature* Pacific Ocean 129 L5
Mendoza Argentina 48 H10
Menongue Angola 98 H7
Menorca *see* Minorca
Mensk *see* Minsk
Meppel Netherlands 64 L8
Mequinenza Res. *Reservoir* Spain 61 O6
Merced California, USA 37 I15
Mercedario *Mountain* Argentina 41
Mercedes Argentina 48 J10
Mercedes Uruguay 48 N9
Mergui Burma 125 H13
Mergui Archipelago *Island group* Burma 125 H14
Mérida Mexico 39 S11
Mérida Spain 60 H10
Mérida Venezuela 44 G5
Meridian Mississippi, USA 28 J8
Meroë *Archaeological site* Sudan 91 G11
Mersin Turkey 105 L10
Merthyr Tydfil Wales, UK 59 H15
Meru Kenya 97 P4
Merv *see* Mary
Mesa Arizona, USA 34 I9
Meseta *Physical region* Spain 54
Mesolongi Greece 78 H8
Mesopotamia *see* Iraq
Messina Sicily 73 M17
Messina, Strait of *Channel* Italy/Sicily 54, 73 M17
Messini, Gulf of *Sea feature* Greece 78 I12
Mestre Italy 72 H7
Meta *River* Colombia/Venezuela 44 G6
Metković Croatia 74 J8
Metz France 63 O4
Meuse *River* W Europe 54, 63 N4, 65 I16
Mexicali Mexico 38 F1
Mexican Plateau *Physical feature* Mexico 20
Mexico *Country* S America 38-39

Mexico 38-39

a Spanish • Peso • 119 • 70 • £0.46 • (m) 90% (f) 85% • 139 • 613 • No • 73% • 3052

Mexico Basin *Sea feature* Gulf of Mexico 20, 41
Mexico City Mexico 14, 39 N12
Mexico, Gulf of *Sea feature* Mexico/USA 10, 20, 29 L11, 39 Q12, 41, 52 C10
Meymaneh Afghanistan 111 L10
Mezen' *River* Russian Federation 82 K7
Mézières France 63 N3
Mgahinga *National park* Uganda 97 L5
Miami Florida, USA 29 O15
Mianyang China 120 J10
Michigan *State* USA 30-31
Michigan City Indiana, USA 31 M10
Michigan, L. *Lake* USA 20, 24 H14, 31 M6
Micronesia *Region* Pacific Ocean 128 I8

Micronesia 128

a English • Dollar • 376 • 70 • £1.42 • (m) 90% (f) 85% • N/A

Micronesia, Federated States of *Country* Micronesia, Pacific Ocean 128 H8
Mid-Atlantic Ridge *Sea feature* Atlantic Ocean 20, 53 H11, 86-87
Mid-Indian Basin *Sea feature* Indian Ocean 115
Mid-Indian Ridge *Sea feature* Indian Ocean 101 I12, 115
Mid-Pacific Seamounts *Sea feature* Pacific Ocean 128 J7
Middelburg Netherlands 65 E12
Middle America Trench *Sea feature* Pacific Ocean 41
Middle Loup *River* Nebraska, USA 33 M9
Middlesbrough England, UK 59 J12
Middletown New York, USA 27 L11
Midland Michigan, USA 31 N7
Midland Texas, USA 35 O11
Midlands *Region* England, UK 59 J14
Midway Is. *Dependent territory* Polynesia, Pacific Ocean 128 J6
Mikhaylovgrad Bulgaria 76 I11
Mikkeli Finland 57 P10
Mikumi *National park* Tanzania 97 P9
Milagro Ecuador 44 C9
Milan (var. Milano) Italy 72 E7
Milano *see* Milan
Milâs Turkey 104 G9
Mildura Victoria, Australia 133 M13
Miles City Montana, USA 33 K5
Miletus *Archaeological site* Turkey 104 G9
Milford Delaware, USA 27 K15
Milford Haven Wales, UK 59 F15
Milford Sound New Zealand 134 C12
Mille Lacs L. *Lake* Minnesota, USA 30 H5
Millstätter, Lake *Lake* Austria 69 O9
Milos *Island* Cyclades, Greece 79 L12
Milwaukee Wisconsin, USA 31 L8
Mīnā' Raysūt Oman 109 M15
Minatitlán Mexico 39 P13
Minbu Burma 124 F8
Mindanao *Island* Philippines 127 M8
Minden Germany 66 G9
Mindoro *Island* Philippines 127 L5
Mindoro Strait *Channel* Philippines 127 L5
Mingäçevir Res. (var. Mingechaur Res.) *Reservoir* Azerbaijan 85 R13
Mingechaur Res. *see* Mingäçevir Res.
Minho (var. Miño) *River* Portugal 60 G5
Minna Nigeria 93 O11
Minneapolis Minnesota, USA 30 H6
Minnesota *State* USA 30
Miño (var. Minho) *River* Spain 60 G4
Minorca (var. Menorca) *Island* Balearic Islands, Spain 61 S8
Minot North Dakota, USA 33 M4
Minsk (var. Mensk) Belarus 80 L11
Miri Borneo, Malaysia 126 J9
Mirim Lagoon *Lake* Brazil/Uruguay 41, 47 I17, 48 P9
Mirimar Naval Air Station *Military center* California, USA 37 M19
Mirnyy *Research center* Antarctica 50 G9
Mirpur Khas Pakistan 116 H6
Miskolc Hungary 71 N12
Misool *Island* Indonesia 127 P12
Mişrātah Libya 89 P6
Mississippi *River* USA 10, 20, 28 H8, 30 H4, 33 R10, 52 C9
Mississippi *River basin* N America 11
Mississippi *State* S USA 28-29
Mississippi Delta *Delta* Louisiana, USA 20, 28 I10
Missoula Montana, USA 32 G5
Missouri *River* USA 10, 20, 33 N8
Missouri *State* USA 33
Mistassini, L. *Lake* Quebec, Canada 25 M9
Mitchell South Dakota, USA 33 O8
Mitchell *River* Queensland, Australia 133 M6
Mito Japan 122 L10
Mittelland Canal *Waterway* Germany 66 J9
Mittersill Austria 69 M8
Mitú Colombia 44 G8
Mitumba Mts. *Mountain range* Zaire 95 N13
Miyazaki Japan 123 D15
Mjøsa, L. *Lake* Norway 56 J10
Mljet *Island* Croatia 74 J9
Mmabatho South Africa 99 K12
Mo i Rana Norway 56 L5
Mobile Alabama, USA 29 K9
Moçambique Mozambique 99 Q7
Mocha *see* Al Mukhā
Mocimboa da Praia Mozambique 99 Q5
Mocoa Colombia 44 D8
Modena Italy 72 G8
Modesto California, USA 37 I15
Mödling Austria 69 S5
Modriča Bosnia and Herzegovina 75 K5
Moeskroen *see* Mouscron
Mogadishu (var. Muqdisho) Somalia 91 M17
Mogilev *see* Mahilyow
Mohawk *River* New York, USA 27 L8
Mojave California, USA 37 L17
Mojave Desert *Desert region* California, USA 20, 37 M17
Molat *Island* Croatia 74 G6
Moldavia (var. Moldova) *Country* E Europe 84

Moldavia 84

a Romanian • Lew • 337 • 69 • N/A • (av.) 99% • 48%

Molde Norway 56 I8
Moldova *see* Moldavia
Mollendo Peru 45 F15
Molodechno *see* Maladzyechna
Molucca Sea Indonesia 127 N11
Moluccas (var. Maluku) *Island group* Indonesia 115, 127 O11, 131
Mombasa Kenya 97 Q7, 110 D9
Mona Passage *Channel* Dominican Republic/Puerto Rico 43 P9
Monaco *Country* W Europe 63

Monaco 63

a French • Franc • 39454 • 76 • £1.86 • (m) 100% (f) 100% • 100%

Monaco Basin *Sea feature* Atlantic Ocean 87
Monastir Tunisia 89 N4
Mönchengladbach Germany 67 D11
Monclova Mexico 39 M6
Moncton New Brunswick, Canada 25 P12
Monessen Pennsylvania, USA 26 G13
Mongo Chad 94 J7
Mongolia *Country* E Asia 119

Mongolia 119

a Khalka Mongol • Tugrik • 4 • 63 • £3.56 • (m) 93% (f) 86% • 52%

Mongu Zambia 96 H15
Mono L. *Lake* California, USA 37 K15
Monólithos Rhodes, Greece 79 Q14
Monroe Louisiana, USA 28 H7
Monroe Michigan, USA 31 O0
Monrovia Liberia 92 H12
Mons (var. Bergen) Belgium 65 F16
Monsoon current *Ocean current* Indian Ocean 12
Mont Blanc *Mountain* France 54
Mont-de-Marsan France 62 I13
Montana *State* USA 32-33
Montauban France 63 K13
Monte Albán *Archaeological site* Mexico 39 O14
Monte Bello Is. *Island group* Western Australia, Australia 132 E8
Monte Carlo Monaco 63 Q13
Monte Cervino *see* Matterhorn
Monte Rosa *Mountain* Italy 54
Montecristi Dominican Republic 43 N7
Montecristi Ecuador 44 B9
Montego Bay Jamaica 42 J7
Montenegro *Republic* Yugoslavia 75 L9
Monterey California, USA 37 H16, 129 N5
Montería Colombia 44 E5
Monterrey Mexico 39 M7
Montevideo Uruguay 48 O10
Montgomery Alabama, USA 29 L8
Montpelier Vermont, USA 27 M7
Montpellier France 63 N14
Montreal Quebec, Canada 25 M13
Montreux Switzerland 68 E12
Montserrat *Dependent territory* Caribbean Sea 43 S11
Monument Valley *Physical feature* Arizona/Utah USA 34 J6
Monywa Burma 124 F7
Monza Italy 72 E7
Moore, L. *Lake* Western Australia, Australia 132 F12
Moorhead Minnesota, USA 30 F4
Moose Jaw Saskatchewan, Canada 23 M15
Moosehead L. *Lake* Maine, USA 27 P4
Moosonee Ontario, Canada 24 J9
Mopti Mali 93 K8
Mora Sweden 57 K10
Moradabad India 117 L5
Morava *River* Czech Republic 70 J11
Moravia *Region* Czech Republic 70 J10
Moray Firth *Sea feature* Scotland, UK 58 I7
Moreau *River* South Dakota, USA 33 M6
Morecambe Bay *Sea feature* England, UK 59 H12
Moree New South Wales, Australia 133 O11
Morehead City North Carolina, USA 29 R7
Morelia Mexico 39 M12
Morena, Sierra *Mountain range* Spain 60 I12
Morgantown West Virginia, USA 29 Q2
Morghāb *River* Afghanistan 111 L11
Morioka Japan 122 L7
Mornington Plain *Sea feature* Pacific Ocean 41
Morocco *Country* NW Africa 88-89

Morocco 88-89

a Arabic • Dirham • 149 • 62 • £0.85 • (m) 61% (f) 38% • 74 • 4763 • Yes • 48% • 3020

Morogoro Tanzania 97 P9
Mörön Mongolia 119 L4
Moroni Comoros 100 E10
Morotai *Island* Indonesia 127 P10
Moroto Uganda 97 N3
Moscow (var. Moskva) Russian Federation 15, 82 F10
Moscow-Volga Canal *Waterway* Russian Federation 82 G10
Mosel (var. Moselle) *River* Germany 67 E13
Moselle (var. Mosel) *River* W Europe 63 O5, 65 M19
Moses Lake Washington, USA 36 J7
Moshi Tanzania 97 P7
Moskva *see* Moscow
Mosquito Gulf *Sea feature* Panama 42 F14
Moss Norway 56 J12
Mossendjo Congo 95 G13
Mossoró Brazil 46 O9
Mostaganem Algeria 89 K4
Mostar Bosnia and Herzegovina 75 K8
Móstoles Spain 61 K8
Mosul Iraq 109 K3
Motala Sweden 57 K13
Motril Spain 61 K14
Mouila Gabon 95 F13
Mould Bay *Research center* Canada 51 O9
Moulins France 63 M9
Moulmein Burma 125 H11
Moundou Chad 94 H9
Mount Gambier South Australia, Australia 133 L14
Mount Hagen Papua New Guinea 133 M2
Mount Isa Queensland, Australia 133 L8
Mount Magnet Western Australia, Australia 132 G11
Mount Pleasant Michigan, USA 31 N8
Mount St. Helens *Volcano* Washington, USA 20
Mount Vernon Illinois, USA 31 K14
Mouscron (var. Moeskroen) Belgium 65 D15
Mouse River *see* Souris
Moyale Kenya 97 Q2
Mozambique *Country* Southern Africa 99

Mozambique 99

a Portuguese • Metical • 53 • 47 • £0.58 • (m) 45% (f) 21% • 27%

Mozambique Channel *Channel* Madagascar/Mozambique 87, 99 Q7

Mozyr' – North Albanian Alps

Mozyr' *see* Mazyr
Mpika Zambia 97 M12
Mtwara Tanzania 97 Q11
Muang Khammouan (var. Thakhek) Laos 124 M10
Muang Không Laos 125 M12
Muang Lampang Thailand 124 I10
Muang Loei Thailand 124 K10
Muang Nan Thailand 124 J9
Muang Pakxan Laos 124 L10
Muang Phetchabun Thailand 125 J11
Muang Phitsanulok Thailand 125 I11
Muang Xaignabouri Laos 124 K9
Muang Yasothon Thailand 125 L11
Muchinga Mts. *Mountain range* Zambia 97 L13
Muck *Island* Scotland, UK 58 F8
Mufulira Zambia 97 K13
Muğla Turkey 104 H9
Mühlhausen Germany 67 I11
Mulhouse France 63 P6
Mull *Island* Scotland, UK 58 F9
Muller Mts. *Mountain range* Indonesia 126 I11
Multan Pakistan 116 I4
Mun, Mae Nam *River* Thailand 125 K12
Muna *Island* Indonesia 127 M13
München *see* Munich
Muncie Indiana, USA 31 N12
Munich (var. München) Germany 67 J16
Münster Germany 66 E10
Munzur Mts. *Mountain range* Turkey 105 P7
Muonio *River* Sweden 57 N3
Mupa N.P. *National park* Angola 98 H7
Muqdisho *see* Mogadishu
Mur (var. Mura) *River* Austria 69 P8
Mura (var. Mur) *River* Slovenia 74 I1
Murat *River* Turkey 105 Q7
Murchison *River* Western Australia, Australia 132 F10
Murchison Falls *National park* Uganda 97 M3
Murcia Spain 61 M12
Mureş *River* Romania 76 H6
Murfreesboro Tennessee, USA 29 L5
Murgab *River* Turkmenistan 111 K10
Müritz, L. *Lake* Germany 66 L7
Murmansk Russian Federation 52 M7, 82 J5
Murmansk Rise *Sea feature* Barents Sea 54
Muroroa *Island* French Polynesia, Pacific Ocean 129 L10
Murray *River* New South Wales/South Australia, Australia 131, 133 L13
Murray Fracture Zone *Sea feature* Pacific Ocean 129 L5
Murrumbidgee *River* New South Wales, Australia 133 N13
Murzuq Libya 89 O9
Muş Turkey 105 R7
Muscat (var. Masqat) Oman 109 P12
Muscat and Oman *see* Oman
Muskegon Michigan, USA 31 M8
Muskegon *River* Michigan, USA 31 N7
Muskogee Oklahoma, USA 33 Q14
Musoma Tanzania 97 N5
Mussau I. *Island* Papua New Guinea 133 O1
Mutare (prev. Umtali) Zimbabwe 99 N9
Muynak Uzbekistan 110 I3
Mwanza Tanzania 97 M6
Mweru, L. *Lake* Zaire/Zambia 87, 95 O16, 97 K10
Mwene-Ditu Zaire 95 L15
Mweru Wantipa *National park* Zambia 97 K11
Myanmar *see* Burma
Mycenae *Archaeological site* Greece 78 J10
Myingyan Burma 124 F8
Myitkyina Burma 124 H5
Mykolayiv (var. Nikolayev) Ukraine 84 J8
Mykonos *Island* Cyclades, Greece 79 N10
Mymensingh Bangladesh 117 P7
Mysore India 116 J13
Mytilini Lesvos, Greece 79 O7
Mzuzu Malawi 97 N12

N

Naberezhnyye Chelny Russian Federation 83K11
Nacala Mozambique 99 Q7
Naestved Denmark 56 I16
Nafplio Greece 78 J10
Naga Cebu, Philippines 127 M4
Nagano Japan 122 J10
Nagarjuna Res. *Reservoir* India 117 K11
Nagasaki Japan 123 B14, 128 F6
Nagercoil India 116 J16
Nagorno-Karabakh *Region* Azerbaijan 85 R14
Nagoya Japan 123 I11
Nagpur India 117 K9
Nagqu China 118 I12
Nagykanizsa Hungary 70 J15
Naha Okinawa, Japan 123 A20
Nahuel Huapí, L *Lake* Argentina 49 H14
Nain Newfoundland, Canada 25 P5
Nairobi Kenya 97 O5
Naissaar *Island* Estonia 80 I1
Najrān Saudi Arabia 108 I14
Nakamura Japan 123 E14
Nakhichevan' *see* Naxçıvan
Nakhodka Russian Federation 112 I7
Nakhon Ratchasima Thailand 125 K12
Nakhon Sawan Thailand 125 I11
Nakhon Si Thammarat Thailand 125 I16
Nakina Ontario, Canada 24 H10
Nakskov Denmark 56 I16
Nakuru Kenya 97 O4
Nal'chik Russian Federation 83 E15
Nam Co *Lake* China 118 I12
Nam Dinh Vietnam 124 N9
Nam Ngum Dam Laos 124 K10
Nam Theun *River* Laos 124 M10
Namangan Uzbekistan 111 O6
Namen *see* Namur
Namib Desert *Desert region* SW Africa 11, 87, 98 H11
Namibe Angola 98 F7
Namibia (prev. South-West Africa) *Country* Southern Africa 98

Namibia 98

a English • Rand • 6 • 58 • £2.44 • (m) 74% (f) 71% • 28%

Nampa Idaho, USA 32 F8
Namp'o North Korea 121 P7
Nampula Mozambique 99 P7
Namur (var. Namen) Belgium 65 H16
Nan Ling *Mountain range* 115
Nan'ao China 128 E6
Nanchang China 121 M12
Nancy France 63 O5
Nanded India 117 K10
Nanjing China 121 N10
Nanning China 121 K14
Nanping China 121 N12
Nansen Basin *Sea feature* Arctic Ocean 54, 103
Nantes France 62 H8
Nantucket I. *Island* Massachusetts, USA 27 P11
Napa Valley *Physical feature* California, USA 37 H14
Napier New Zealand 134 H7
Naples (var. Napoli) Italy 52 L9 73 K13
Naples, Bay of *Sea feature* Italy 73 K13
Napo *River* Ecuador/Peru 44 E9
Napoli *see* Naples
Narach, L. *Lake* Belarus 81 K10
Narathiwat Thailand 125 J17
Nares Plain *Sea feature* Atlantic Ocean 20
Nares Strait *Channel* Northwest Territories, Canada 23 O1
Narew *River* Poland/Belarus 71 N4
Narmada *River* India 115, 116 J8
Narsarsuaq Greenland 51 M15
Narva Estonia 81 L2
Narva *River* Estonia/Russian Federation 81 L2
Narvik Norway 57 M3
Naryn Kyrgyzstan 111 R5
Naryn *River* Kyrgyzstan 111 Q5
Nashua New Hampshire, USA 27 N9
Nashville Tennessee, USA 29 L4
Nasik India 116 I9
Nassau Bahamas 43 K2
Nasser, L. *Reservoir* Egypt/Sudan 87, 90 G9
Natal Brazil 46 O9
Natal *Region* South Africa 99 M13
Natal Basin *Sea feature* Indian Ocean 87
Natitingou Benin 93 M11
Natuna *Island* Natuna Is. Indonesia 126 H9
Natuna Is. *Island group* Indonesia 126 G10
Naturaliste, C. *Cape* Western Australia, Australia 132 F13
Naukuuft Park *National park* Namibia 98 H12
Nauru *Country* Micronesia, Pacific Ocean 128 I9

Nauru 128

a Nauruan • Dollar • 1122 • 67 • £1.68 • (m) 99% (f) 99% • 100%

Navajo Dam *Dam* New Mexico, USA 35 L7
Navajo Indian Reservation *Reservation* USA 35 K8
Navapolatsk (var. Novopolotsk) Belarus 81 M8
Navarin, C. *Cape* Russian Federation 113 Q3, 128 J3
Navoi Uzbekistan 111 L7
Nawabshah Pakistan 116 H6
Naxçıvan (var. Nakhichevan') Azerbaijan 85 Q15
Naxos *Island* Cyclades, Greece 79 N12
Nazareth Israel 107 L8
Nazca *Archaeological site* Peru 45 E14
Nazca Plate *Physical feature* 41
Nazilli Turkey 104 H9
N'Dalatando Angola 98 G4
Ndélé Central African Republic 94 K9
N'Djamena (prev. Fort Lamy) Chad 94 H7
Ndola Zambia 97 K13
Neagh, Lough *Lake* Northern Ireland, UK 59 E11
Neapoli Greece 78 J13
Nebitdag Turkmenistan 110 G7
Nebraska *State* USA 33
Nechako *River* Alberta/British Columbia, Canada 22 J13
Neches *River* Texas, USA 35 S11
Neckar *River* Germany 67 G15
Necochea Argentina 49 M12
Negev Desert *Desert region* Israel 107 L12
Negrais, Cape *Cape* Burma 125 E11
Negro *River* Argentina 49 K13
Negro *River* Brazil/Uruguay 48 O9
Negro, Rio *River* S America 41, 46 D7
Negros *Island* Philippines 127 M6
Nei Mongol *see* Inner Mongolia
Neiva Colombia 44 E7
Nejd *Region* Saudi Arabia 108 I9
Nekemte Ethiopia 91 I15
Nellis Air Force Range *Military center* Nevada, USA 34 G5
Nellore India 117 L12
Nelson New Zealand 134 F9
Nelson *River* Manitoba, Canada 23 O12
Néma Mauritania 92 J7
Neman (var. Nemunas) *River* Belarus/Lithuania 80 G9
Nemunas *see* Neman
Nemuro Japan 122 O3
Neosho *River* Kansas/Oklahoma, USA 33 P12
Nepal *Country* S Asia 117

Nepal 117

a Nepali • Rupee • 367 • 52 • £0.38 • (m) 38% (f) 13% • 10%

Nepalganj Nepal 117 M5
Neretva *River* Bosnia and Herzegovina 75 K8
Neris *River* Belarus/Lithuania 80 I9
Nesebŭr Bulgaria 77 O13
Ness, Loch *Lake* Scotland, UK 58 H8
Netherlands *Country* Europe 64-65

Netherlands 64-65

a Dutch • Guilder • 1147 • 77 • £1.08 • (m) 99% (f) 99% • 495 • 414 • No • 89% • 3151

Netherlands Antilles *Dependent territory* Caribbean Sea 20, 43 O14
Neubrandenburg Germany 66 L7
Neuchâtel Switzerland 68 E10
Neuchâtel, L. of *Lake* Switzerland 68 D10
Neufchâteau Belgium 65 J18
Neumünster Germany 66 H6
Neunkirchen Austria 69 R6
Neuquén Argentina 49 I13
Neuschwanstein *Castle* Germany 67 I16
Neusiedler L. *Lake* Austria/Hungary 69 S5
Nevada *State* USA 34
Nevada, Sierra *Mountain range* Spain 61 K13
Nevada Test Site *Military center* Nevada, USA 34 G6
Nevel' Russian Federation 82 E9
Nevers France 63 M8
Nevşehir Turkey 105 M8
New Albany Indiana, USA 31 N14
New Amsterdam Guyana 44 N6
New Amsterdam *see* New York City
New Bedford Massachusetts, USA 27 O11
New Britain *Island* Papua New Guinea 131, 133 P2
New Britain Trench *Sea feature* Pacific Ocean 131
New Brunswick New Jersey, USA 27 L12
New Brunswick *Province* Canada 25
New Caledonia *Dependent territory* Melanesia, Pacific Ocean 128 H10
New Caledonia *Island* Melanesia, Pacific Ocean 131
New Caledonia Basin *Sea feature* Pacific Ocean 131
New Castle Pennsylvania, USA 26 G11
New Delhi India 117 K5
New England *Physical region* USA 27 O6
New Guinea *Island* Indonesia/Papua New Guinea 115, 128 G9, 131, 133 M2
New Hampshire *State* USA 27
New Hanover *Island* Papua New Guinea 133 O1
New Haven Connecticut, USA 27 M11
New Hebrides Trench *Sea feature* Pacific Ocean 131
New Ireland *Island* Papua New Guinea 131, 133 P1
New Jersey *State* USA 27
New London Connecticut, USA 27 N11
New Mexico *State* USA 35
New Orleans Louisiana, USA 28 I9, 52 C9
New Plymouth New Zealand 134 G6
New Providence *Island* Bahamas 43 K2
New R. *River* Virginia/West Virginia, USA 29 P3
New Siberian Is. (var. Novosibirskiye Ostrova) *Island group* Russian Federation 51 R7, 103, 113 N4
New South Wales *State* Australia 133
New Ulm Minnesota, USA 30 G7
New York *State* NE USA 27 K9
New York City (prev. New Amsterdam) New York, USA 14, 52 E9, 27 L12
New Zealand *Country* Polynesia, Pacific Ocean 8, 131, 134

New Zealand 134

a English, Maori • Dollar • 33 • 76 • £0.88 • (m) 99% (f) 99% • 442 • 373 • No • 84% • 3362

Newark Delaware, USA 27 K14
Newark New Jersey, USA 27 L12
Newark Ohio, USA 31 P12
Newburgh New York, USA 27 L11
Newcastle New South Wales, Australia 133 O12
Newcastle upon Tyne England, UK 59 J11
Newfoundland *Island* Newfoundland, Canada 10, 20, 25 R9, 52 F8
Newfoundland *Province* Canada 25
Newfoundland Basin *Sea feature* Atlantic Ocean 52 G8
Newport Isle of Wight England, UK 59 J17
Newport Oregon, USA 36 G9
Newport Rhode Island, USA 27 N11
Newport Wales, UK 59 H15
Newport News Virginia, USA 29 S5
Newry Northern Ireland, UK 59 E12
Neyshābūr Iran 109 Q4
Ngaoundéré Cameroon 94 G9
Ngauruhue, Mt. *Volcano* North Island, New Zealand 134 H6
Ngorongoro *Conservation area* Tanzania 97 O6
Ngorongoro Crater *Physical feature* Tanzania 87
Nguigmi Niger 93 R8
Nguru Nigeria 93 P9
Nha Trang Vietnam 125 P14
Niagara Falls New York, USA 26 H8
Niagara Falls Ontario, Canada 25 K14
Niagara Falls *Waterfall* Canada/USA 20
Niagara Peninsula *Physical feature* Canada 25 K15
Niamey Niger 93 M9
Niangay, L. *Lake* Mali 92 L8
Nias *Island* Indonesia 126 C11
Nicaragua *Country* C America 42

Nicaragua 42

a Spanish • Cordoba • 87 • 65 • £0.64 • (av.) 66% • 60%

Nicaragua, L. *Lake* Nicaragua 41, 42 D11
Nice France 63 Q13
Nicobar Is. *Island group* India, Indian Ocean 100 K7, 115
Nicosia (var. Lefkosa; prev. Levkosia) Cyprus 105 L12
Nicoya, Gulf of *Sea feature* Costa Rica 42 D13
Niedere Tauern *Mountain range* Austria 69 P7
Nifa *Archaeological site* Italy 73 I12
Niğde Turkey 105 M9
Niger *Country* W Africa 93

Niger 93

a French • Franc • 16 • 46 • £1.72 • (m) 40% (f) 17% • 20%

Niger (var. Joliba, Kworra) *River* W Africa 53 F11, 87, 93 M9
Niger Delta *Delta* Nigeria 87, 93 O14
Nigeria *Country* W Africa 93

Nigeria 93

a English • Naira • 252 • 52 • £0.39 • (m) 62% (f) 40% • 32 • 6134 • Yes • 35% • 2312

Nihon *see* Japan
Niigata Japan 122 J9
Nijmegen Netherlands 65 K11
Nikolayev *see* Mykolayiv
Nikopol' Ukraine 85 K7
Nikšić Montenegro, Yugoslavia 75 L9
Nile *River* Africa 52 N10, 87, 91 G11, 100 C5
Nile *River basin* Africa 11
Nile Delta *Delta* Egypt 87
Niles Michigan, USA 31 M10
Nîmes France 63 N13
Ninety East Ridge *Sea feature* Indian Ocean 100 J10, 115, 130
Nineveh *Archaeological site* Iraq 109 K2
Ningbo China 121 O11, 128 F6
Ningxia Hui Autonomous Region China 120 J8
Ninigo Group *Island Group* Papua New Guinea 133 M1
Niobrara *River* Nebraska, USA 33 M9
Nioro Mali 92 I8
Nipigon, L. *Lake* Ontario, Canada 24 H10
Nippon *see* Japan
Niš Serbia, Yugoslavia 75 O8
Nissan I. *Island* Papua New Guinea 133 Q1
Nitra Slovakia 71 K12
Nitra *River* Slovakia 71 K11
Niue *Dependent territory* Polynesia, Pacific Ocean 129 K10
Nivelles Belgium 65 G16
Nizhnevartovsk Russian Federation 112 I9
Nizhniy Novgorod Russian Federation 82 H10
Nizhniy Tagil Russian Federation 112 G8
Nizwā Oman 109 O12
Njombe Tanzania 97 N10
Nkhotakota Malawi 97 N13
Nkongsamba Cameroon 94 E10
Nobeoka Japan 123 D14
Nogales Mexico 38 H3
Nome Alaska, USA 22 F5
Nonacho L. *Lake* Northwest Territories, Canada 23 M10
Nordfjord *Coastal feature* Norway 56 H9
Nordhausen Germany 66 I10
Nordstrand *Island* North Frisian Is. Germany 66 G6
Nordvik *Research center* Russian Federation 51 T9
Norfolk Nebraska, USA 33 O9
Norfolk Virginia, USA 29 S5
Norfolk I. *Dependent territory* Pacific Ocean 128 I11
Norge *see* Norway
Noril'sk Russian Federation 112 J7
Norman Oklahoma, USA 33 O15
Normandy *Region* France 62 J5
Norman Wells Northwest Territories, Canada 22 J8
Norrköping Sweden 57 L13
Norrtälje Sweden 56 M12
North Albanian Alps *Mountain range* Albania/Yugoslavia 75 M10

a Language (official or most commonly spoken) • Currency • Population density per square mile • Average life expectancy • Price of 1 dozen hen's eggs • Literacy • Number of TVs per 1,000 people • Number of people per doctor • Death penalty • Percentage of urban-based population • Average number of calories consumed daily per person

Panama, Gulf of – Ptuj

Panama, Gulf of *Sea feature* Panama 41, 42 G15
Panama, Isthmus of *Physical feature* Panama 41
Panay *Island* Philippines 127 L6
Pančevo Serbia, Yugoslavia 75 N5
Panevėžys Lithuania 80 I8
Pangaea *Ancient Continent* 8
Pangani Tanzania 97 Q8
Pangani *River* Tanzania 97 P7
Pangkalpinang Bangka, Indonesia 126 G12
Pangnirtung Baffin I. Northwest Territories, Canada 23 R6, 51 M13
Panj (var. Pyandzh) *River* Afghanistan/Tajikistan 111 N9
Panjnad Barrage *Dam* Pakistan 116 H4
Pantelleria *Island* Italy 73 H19
Panuco *River* Mexico 39 M10
Panzhihua China 120 I12
Papandayan *Volcano* Java, Indonesia 115
Papeete Tahiti French Polynesia, Pacific Ocean 129 L10
Paphos Cyprus 105 K12
Papua, Gulf of *Sea feature* Papua New Guinea 133 N3
Papua New Guinea *Country* Australasia 133

Papua New Guinea (P.N.G.) 133

a English • Kina • 23 • 55 • £2.23 • (m) 65% (f) 38% • 16%

Paraguarí Paraguay 48 N6
Paraguay *Country* S America 48

Paraguay 48

a Spanish • Kina • 29 • 67 • £0.37 • (m) 92% (f) 88% • 48%

Paraguay *River* S America 41, 47 G13, 48 N5
Parakou Benin 93 N11
Paramaribo Suriname 44 O6
Paramushir Is. *Island Group* Russian Federation 113 R8
Paraná Argentina 48 L9
Paraná *River* Argentina/Paraguay 41, 47 H14, 48 M10
Paraná *River basin* S America 11
Paranaíba *River* Brazil 46 K10
Pardubice Czech Republic 70 I9
Parecis, Serra dos *Mountain range* Brazil 47 F11
Parepare Celebes, Indonesia 127 L13
Paris (anc. Gallia) France 63 L5
Parker Dam *Dam* Arizona, USA 34 H8
Parkersburg West Virginia, USA 29 P2
Parma Italy 72 F8
Parnaíba Brazil 46 M8
Parnaíba *River* Brazil 41
Pärnu Estonia 80 J3
Pärnu *River* Estonia 80 J3
Paros *Island* Cyclades, Greece 79 M11
Parry Is. *Island group* Northwest Territories, Canada 23 M4
Pas, The Manitoba, Canada 23 N13
Pasadena California, USA 37 L18
Pasadena Texas, USA 35 S13
Pasargadae *Archaeological site* Iran 109 N7
Pasley, C. *Cape* Western Australia, Australia 132 H13
Passau Germany 67 M15
Passo Fundo Brazil 47 I16
Pasto Colombia 44 D8
Patagonia *Physical region* Argentina 41, 49 J16
Paterson New Jersey, USA 27 L12
Pathfinder Res. *Reservoir* Wyoming, USA 32 J9
Patna India 117 N7
Patos Lagoon *Lake* Brazil 47 I16
Patrai Greece 78 H9
Patrai, Gulf of *Sea feature* Greece 78 G9
Pattani Thailand 125 J17
Pattaya Thailand 125 J13
Patuca *River* Honduras 42 E9
Pátzcuaro, L. *Lake* Mexico 39 L12
Pau France 62 J14
Pavlodar Kazakhstan 112 H11
Paysandú Uruguay 48 N9
Pazardzhik Bulgaria 76 J14
Peć Serbia, Yugoslavia 75 M9
Pearl *River* Louisiana/Mississippi, USA 28 J8
Pearl Harbor Oahu Hawaiian Is. Pacific Ocean 129 K6
Peary Land *Physical region* Greenland 51 P12
Pechora *River* Russian Federation 54, 82 L7
Pecos Texas, USA 35 N11
Pecos *River* New Mexico/Texas, USA 35 O12
Pécs Hungary 71 K15
Pedras Salgadas Portugal 60 G6
Pedro Juan Caballero Paraguay 48 N4
Pee Dee *River* North Carolina/South Carolina, USA 29 Q8
Pegasus Bay *Sea feature* New Zealand 134 F11
Pegu Burma 124 G10
Peipus, L. *Lake* Estonia/Russian Federation 81 L3
Peking (var. Beijing) China 15, 121 M7
Pelada, Serra *Mountain range* Brazil 46 J8
Pelagie Is. *Island group* Italy 73 H20
Pelée, Mt. *Volcano* Martinique, Caribbean Sea 9, 41
Pelješac *Peninsula* Croatia 74 J9
Pelly *River* Yukon Territory, Canada 22 I8
Peloponnese *Region* Greece 78 I10
Pelotas Brazil 47 I17
Pematangsiantar Sumatra, Indonesia 126 D10
Pemba Mozambique 99 Q6
Pemba I. *Island* Tanzania 97 Q8
Pendleton Oregon, USA 36 K8
Pennine Alps *Mountain range* Switzerland 68 F12
Pennines *Mountain range* England, UK 54, 59 I12
Pennsylvania *State* USA 26
Penobscot *River* Maine, USA 27 Q5
Penonomé Panama 42 G15
Pensacola Florida, USA 29 K10
Penticton British Columbia, Canada 23 K15
Penza Russian Federation 83 H12
Penzance England, UK 59 E17
Peoria Illinois, USA 31 K11
Pereira Colombia 44 E6
Pergamon (var. Bergama) *Archaeological site* Turkey 104 G7
Perge *Archaeological site* Turkey 104 J10
Périgueux France 63 K11
Perito Moreno Argentina 49 I16
Perm' Russian Federation 83 L11
Pernik Bulgaria 76 I13
Perpignan France 63 M15
Persepolis *Archaeological site* Iran 109 N7
Persia *see* Iran
Persian Gulf (var. The Gulf) *Sea feature* Arabia/Iran 87, 100 F5, 103, 109 M8
Perth Scotland, UK 58 I9
Perth Western Australia, Australia 132 F12
Perth Basin *Sea feature* Indian Ocean 131
Peru *Country* S America 9, 45-46

Peru 45-46

a Spanish, Quechua • Sol • 45 • 63 • £0.25 • (m) 92% (f) 79% • 97 • 966 • No • 70% • 2186

Peru Basin *Sea feature* Pacific Ocean 129 P10
Peru-Chile Trench *Sea feature* Pacific Ocean 8, 129 Q11
Peru Current *Ocean current* Pacific Ocean 12
Peruć, L. *Lake* Croatia 74 I7
Perugia Italy 72 H10
Pesaro Italy 72 I9
Pescara Italy 73 K11
Peshawar Pakistan 116 I2
Petah Tiqwa Israel 107 L9
Petaluma California, USA 37 G15
Peter the First I. *Dependent territory* Pacific Ocean, Antarctica 50 B9
Peterborough England, UK 59 K14
Peterborough Ontario, Canada 25 K14
Peterhead Scotland, UK 58 J8
Petersburg Alaska, USA 22 I11
Petersburg Virginia, USA 29 R4
Petra Jordan 107 M12
Petropavl *see* Petropavlovsk
Petropavlovsk (var. Petropavl) Kazakhstan 112 G10
Petropavlovsk-Kamchatskiy Russian Federation 113 R7
Petrozavodsk Russian Federation 82 H7
Pevek Russian Federation 51 Q5, 113 P3
Pforzheim Germany 67 F15
Phangan I. (var. Ko Phangan) *Island* Thailand 125 I15
Phet Buri Thailand 125 I13
Philadelphia, Jordan *see* Amman
Philadelphia Pennsylvania, USA 27 K13
Philae *Archaeological site* Egypt 90 G9
Philippeville Belgium 65 H17
Philippine Basin *Sea feature* Pacific Ocean 115, 131
Philippine Plate *Physical feature* 8, 115, 131
Philippine Sea Philippines 127 N4
Philippine Trench *Sea feature* Pacific Ocean 115, 131
Philippines *Country* SE Asia 127

Philippines 127

a English, Filipino • Peso • 545 • 65 • £0.79 • (m) 90% (f) 90% • 48 • 6413 • No • 43% • 2375

Philippines *Island group* SE Asia 115, 131
Phnom Penh Cambodia 125 M14
Phoenix Arizona, USA 34 I9
Phoenix Is. *Island group* Kiribati, Pacific Ocean 128 J9
Phôngsali Laos 124 K8
Phuket Thailand 125 H16
Phuket I. (var. Ko Phuket) *Island* Thailand 125 H16
Phumĭ Sâmraông Cambodia 125 L12
Piacenza Italy 72 E7
Piatra-Neamţ Romania 77 M4
Piave *River* Italy 72 H6
Pichilemu Chile 49 G11
Picos Brazil 46 M9
Picton New Zealand 134 G9
Piedras Negras Mexico 39 M5
Pielinen, L. *Lake* Finland 57 P8
Pierre South Dakota, USA 33 N7
Pietermaritzburg South Africa 99 M13
Pietersburg South Africa 99 M11
Piła Poland 70 J4
Pilar Paraguay 48 M6
Pilcomayo *River* Bolivia/Paraguay 48 M5
Pilos Greece 78 H12
Pilsen *see* Plzeň
Pinang *see* Georgetown
Pinar del Río Cuba 42 G3
Pinatubo Mt. *Volcano* Philippines 115
Pindus Mountains *Mountain range* Greece 54, 78 H6
Pine Bluff Arkansas, USA 28 I5
Pinega *River* Russian Federation 82 K8
Pineios *River* Greece 78 I5
Pines, I. of *see* Juventud, Isla de la
Ping, Mae Nam *River* Thailand 125 I11
Pingxiang China 120 J14, 121 M12
Pini *Island* Indonesia 126 C11
Pinnacles Desert *Desert region* Australia 131
Pinsk Belarus 80 J15
Pioner I. *Island* Severnaya Zemlya, Russian Federation 113 K3
Piotrków Trybunalski Poland 71 L7
Piqua Ohio, USA 31 O12
Piraeus Greece 79 K9
Pisa Italy 72 F9
Pisác *Archaeological site* Peru 45 G13
Pistoia Italy 72 G9
Pitcairn Is. *Dependent territory* Polynesia, Pacific Ocean 129 M10
Pite *River* Sweden 57 M5
Piteå Sweden 57 N6
Piteşti Romania 77 K8
Pittsburg Kansas, USA 33 Q13
Pittsburgh Pennsylvania, USA 26 G12
Pittsfield Massachusetts, USA 27 M9
Piura Peru 44 B10
Placentia Bay *Sea feature* Newfoundland, Canada 25 T10
Plainview Texas, USA 35 O9
Plate *River* Argentina/Uruguay 41, 48 N10
Platte *River* Nebraska, USA 20, 33 N10
Platte, North *River* Nebraska, USA 33 L10
Plattsburgh New York, USA 27 M6
Plauen German 67 K12
Plenty, Bay of *Sea feature* New Zealand 134 I5
Pleven Bulgaria 77 K11
Ploča, C. *Cape* Croatia 74 H8
Płock Poland 71 L5
Ploieşti Romania 77 L8
Płońsk Poland 71 M5
Plovdiv Bulgaria 77 K14
Plungė Lithuania 80 G7
Plymouth England, UK 59 G17
Plymouth Montserrat 43 S11
Plzeň (var. Pilsen) Czech Republic 70 G9
Po *River* Italy 54, 72 C7
Po Delta *Delta* Italy 54
Pobeda Peak (var. Pik Pobedy) *Peak* China/Kyrgyzstan 103
Pobedy, Pik *see* Pobeda Peak
Pocatello Idaho, USA 32 H8
Podgorica (prev. Titograd) Montenegro, Yugoslavia 75 L10
Podlasie *Region* Poland 71 O5
Poinsett, C. *Cape* Wilkes Land, Antarctica 50 G10
Pointe-à-Pitre Guadeloupe 43 T11
Pointe-Noire Congo 95 F14
Poitiers France 62 J9
Pol-e Khomrī Afghanistan 111 N10
Poland *Country* C Europe 70-71

Poland 70-71

a Polish • Zloty • 326 • 71 • £0.42 • (av.) 99% • 293 • 479 • Yes • 62% • 3505

Polatsk (var. Polotsk) Belarus 81 M8
Polis Cyprus 105 K12
Polotsk *see* Polatsk
Poltava Ukraine 85 K5
Polygyros Greece 79 K4
Polynesia *Region* Pacific Ocean 129 K10
Pomerania *Region* Germany/Poland 70 I3
Pomeranian Bay *Sea feature* Germany/Poland 70 H2
Pompeii *Archaeological site* Italy 73 K13
Ponca City Oklahoma, USA 33 P13
Ponce Puerto Rico 43 Q9
Pontchartrain, L. *Lake* Louisiana, USA 28 I9
Pontevedra Spain 60 F4
Pontiac Michigan, USA 31 O9
Pontianak Borneo, Indonesia 126 H11
Pontic Mountains *Mountain range* Turkey 105 N5
Pontine Is. *Island group* Italy 73 I13
Poona *see* Pune
Poopó, L. *Lake* Bolivia 41, 45 H15
Popayán Colombia 44 D7
Poplar Bluff Missouri, USA 33 S13
Popocatépetl *Volcano* Mexico 20, 39 N12
Popondetta Papua New Guinea 133 O3
Poprad Slovakia 71 M10
Porbandar India 116 H8
Porcupine *River* Canada/Alaska, USA 22 H6
Pori Finland 57 N10
Poronaysk Russian Federation 113 Q10
Porpoise Bay *Sea feature* Wilkes Land, Antarctica 50 G11
Porsangen *Coastal feature* Norway 57 O1
Porsgrunn Norway 56 I12
Port Alice Vancouver I. British Columbia, Canada 22 I14
Port Angeles Washington, USA 36 G6
Port Antonio Jamaica 43 K8
Port Arthur Texas, USA 35 T13
Port-au-Prince Haiti 43 M8
Port Augusta South Australia, Australia 133 L12
Port-de-Paix Haiti 43 M7
Port Dickson Malaysia 125 J19
Port Elizabeth South Africa 99 K16
Port-Gentil Gabon 95 E13
Port Harcourt Nigeria 93 O13
Port Hedland Western Australia, Australia 132 F8
Port Hope Simpson Newfoundland, Canada 25 R7
Port Huron Michigan, USA 31 P8
Port Lincoln South Australia, Australia 133 K13
Port Louis Mauritius 101 G11
Port Moresby Papua New Guinea 133 N4
Port Nolloth South Africa 53 M14
Port of Spain Trinidad & Tobago 43 S16
Port Said (var. Bûr Sa'îd) Egypt 52 N9, 90 G6, 100 D4
Port Sudan Sudan 91 I11
Portalegre Portugal 60 G10
Portales New Mexico, USA 35 N9
Portimão Portugal 60 F13
Portland Maine, USA 27 O8, 52 E8
Portland Oregon, USA 36 H8
Porto (var. Oporto) Portugal 52 J9, 60 F6
Pôrto Alegre Brazil 47 I16
Porto-Novo Benin 93 M12
Pôrto Velho Brazil 46 D9
Portoviejo Ecuador 44 B9
Portsmouth England, UK 59 J17
Portsmouth New Hampshire, USA 27 O8
Portsmouth Ohio, USA 31 P13
Portugal *Country* SW Europe 60

Portugal 60

a Portuguese • Escudo • 293 • 75 • £0.95 • (m) 89% (f) 82% • 177 • 381 • No • 34% • 3495

Portuguese Guinea *see* Guinea-Bissau
Porvenir Chile 49 J19
Posadas Argentina 48 N7
Posonium *see* Bratislava
Potash Italy 73 K18
Potenza Italy 73 M13
Potenza *River* Italy 72 J10
P'ot'i Georgia 85 O12
Potosí Bolivia 45 I16
Potsdam Germany 66 L9
Poughkeepsie New York, USA 27 L11
Poŭthĭsăt Cambodia 125 L13
Powder *River* Montana/Wyoming, USA 33 K6
Powell, L. *Lake* Utah, USA 34 J5
Poyang Hu *Lake* China 115, 121 M11
Poza Rica Mexico 39 O11
Požarevac Serbia, Yugoslavia 75 O6
Poznań Poland 70 J5
Pozo Colorado Paraguay 48 M5
Prachin Buri *Archaeological site* Thailand 125 J12
Prachin Buri Thailand 125 J12
Prachuap Khiri Khan Thailand 125 I14
Prague (var. Praha) Czech Republic 70 H9
Praha *see* Prague
Praia Cape Verde, Atlantic Ocean 52 I10
Prato Italy 72 G9
Pratt Kansas, USA 33 O13
Pravats (var. Pravets) Bulgaria 76 J12
Pravets *see* Pravats
Prešov Slovakia 71 N11
Prescott Arizona, USA 34 I8
Prespa, L. *Lake* SE Europe 75 N13, 78 G2
Presque Isle Maine, USA 27 Q2
Preston England, UK 59 I13
Pretoria South Africa 99 L12
Preveza Greece 78 G7
Priene *Archaeological site* Turkey 104 G9
Prijedor Bosnia and Herzegovina 75 I5
Prilep Macedonia 75 O12
Prince Albert Saskatchewan, Canada 23 M13
Prince Charles I. *Island* Northwest Territories, Canada 23 Q6
Prince Edward Island *Province* Canada 25
Prince Edward Is. *Island group* South Africa, Indian Ocean 101 E14
Prince George British Columbia, Canada 22 J13
Prince of Wales I. *Island* Northwest Territories, Canada 23 N5
Prince of Wales I. *Island* Queensland, Australia 133 M4
Prince Patrick I. *Island* Canada 51 N8
Prince Rupert British Columbia, Canada 22 I12, 129 M3
Princess Charlotte Bay *Sea feature* Queensland, Australia 133 N5
Princeton New Jersey, USA 27 L13
Príncipe *Island* Sao Tome & Principe 87, 95 D12
Pripet *River* E Europe 81 L15
Priština Serbia, Yugoslavia 75 N9
Prizren Serbia, Yugoslavia 75 N10
Progreso Mexico 39 S11
Prome Burma 124 F9
Prosna *River* Poland 71 K6
Provence *Region* France 63 P13
Providence Rhode Island, USA 27 O10
Provideniya Air Base *Military center* Russian Federation 113 Q2
Provo Utah, USA 34 J3
Prudhoe Bay Alaska, USA 51 O6
Prudhoe Bay *Sea feature* Alaska, USA 22 I5
Prut *River* E Europe 77 O5
Pruzhany Belarus 80 I14
Prydz Bay *Sea feature* Indian Ocean Coast, Antarctica 50 G8
Przheval'sk Kyrgyzstan 111 S4
Pskov Russian Federation 82 E8
Ptsich *River* Belarus 81 M13
Ptuj Slovenia 74 I2

a Language (official or most commonly spoken) • Currency • Population density per square mile • Average life expectancy • Price of 1 dozen hen's eggs • Literacy • Number of TVs per 1,000 people • Number of people per doctor • Death penalty • Percentage of urban-based population • Average number of calories consumed daily per person

St Laurent-du-Maroni – Shenandoah

St Laurent-du-Maroni French Guiana 44 O6
St Lawrence *River* Canada 10, 20, 25 O11, 52 E8
St. Lawrence, Gulf of *Sea feature* Canada 20, 25 Q10
St Lawrence I. *Island* Alaska, USA 22 E5
St. Lawrence Seaway *Waterway* Ontario, Canada 25 L13
St. Lô France 62 I4
St. Louis Missouri, USA 33 S11
St-Louis Senegal 92 F7
St Lucia *Country* Caribbean Sea 43 T13

St. Lucia 43

a English • Dollar • 645 • 72 • £1.47 • (m) 81% (f) 82% • 46%

St. Malo France 62 H5
Ste Marie, Cap *see* Vohimena, C.
St Martin *Island* Guadeloupe 43 S10
St Matthew I. *Island* Alaska, USA 22 D5
St. Moritz Switzerland 68 I11
St. Nazaire France 62 H8
St Paul Minnesota, USA 30 H6
St Paul I. *Island* Indian Ocean 101 I13
St. Peter Port Guernsey, UK 59 H18
St Petersburg Florida, USA 29 N13
St. Petersburg (prev. Leningrad) Russian Federation 82 F7
St Pierre St Pierre & Miquelon 25 S10
St Pierre & Miquelon *Dependent territory* SE Canada 25 S10
St. Quentin France 63 M3
St Vincent *Island* St Vincent & The Grenadines 43 S14
St Vincent and the Grenadines *Country* Caribbean Sea 43 T14

St Vincent and the Grenadines 43

a English • Dollar • 823 • 71 • £1.47 • (m) 96% (f) 96% • 27%

St. Vincent, Cape *Coastal feature* Portugal 54, 60 E13
St Vith Belgium 65 L17
Saintes France 62 I10
Sajama *Mountain* Bolivia 41
Sakākah Saudi Arabia 108 I6
Sakakawea, L. *Lake* North Dakota, USA 33 M4
Sakarya *River* Turkey 104 J6
Sakhalin *Island* Russian Federation 113 Q9, 28 H4
Sala y Gomez Ridge *Sea feature* Pacific Ocean 41
Salado *River* Argentina 41, 48 K8
Şalālah Oman 100 F6, 109 M15
Salamanca Spain 60 I7
Salamat *River* Chad/Sudan 94 I8
Salamis *Archaeological site* Cyprus 105 L12
Saldanha South Africa 98 I15
Saldus Latvia 80 H6
Sale Victoria, Australia 133 N14
Salekhard Russian Federation 112 H7
Salem India 117 K14
Salem Oregon, USA 36
Salerno Italy 73 L13
Salerno, Gulf of *Sea feature* Italy 73 K14
Salihorsk (var. Soligorsk) Belarus 81 L13
Salima Malawi 97 N13
Salina Kansas, USA 33 O12
Salina Utah, USA 34 J4
Salina *Island* Lipari Is. Italy 73 L16
Salinas California, USA 37 H16
Salinas Mexico 39 P12
Salinas Grandes Salt Marsh *Physical feature* Argentina 41
Salisbury England, UK 59 I16
Salisbury *see* Harare
Salisbury I. *Island* Northwest Territories, Canada 25 K1
Salmon *River* Idaho.Washington, USA 32 F6
Salo Finland 57 O11
Salonika *see* Thessaloniki
Salso *River* Italy 73 K18
Salt *River* Arizona, USA 34 J9
Salt Lake City Utah, USA 34 J3
Salta Argentina 48 I6
Saltillo Mexico 39 M7
Salto Uruguay 48 N9
Salto del Guairá Paraguay 48 O5
Salton Sea *Lake* California, USA 20, 37 N19
Salvador Brazil 47 N11, 53 H12
Salween (var. Nu Jiang) *River* China 119 K12, 120 H13, 124 H9
Salzburg Austria 69 N6
Salzgitter Germany 66 I9
Samā'il Oman 109 P12
Samaná Dominican Republic 43 O8
Samar *Island* Philippines 127 N5
Samara Russian Federation 83 J12
Samarinda Borneo, Indonesia 127 K11
Samarkand (var. Samarqand) Uzbekistan 111 M7
Samarqand *see* Samarkand
Sāmarrā' Iraq 109 K4
Sambre *River* Belgium/France 65 G16
Samobor Croatia 74 H3
Samos Samos, Greece 79 P10
Samos *Island* Greece 79 P10
Samothraki *Island* Greece 79 N3
Samsun Turkey 105 N5
Samui I. (var. Ko Samui) *Island* Thailand 125 I15
San Ambrosio, Isla *Island* Chile 129 Q11
San Andreas Fault *Physical feature* USA 8
San Andrés Colombia 44 F6
San Andres Mts. *Mountain range* New Mexico, USA 35 L10
San Angelo Texas, USA 35 P11
San Antonio Chile 48 G10
San Antonio Texas, USA 35 Q13
San Antonio *River* Texas, USA 35 Q13
San Antonio Oeste Argentina 49 K13
San Benedetto del Tronto Italy 72 J10
San Bernadino Tunnel *Tunnel* Switzerland 68 H11
San Bernardino California, USA 37 L18
San Bernardo Chile 48 H10
San Carlos Nicaragua 42 E12
San Carlos Venezuela 44 H5
San Carlos de Bariloche Argentina 49 H14
San Clemente California, USA 37 L19
San Cristóbal Venezuela 44 F5
San Diego California, USA 37 L19, 129 N5
San Felipe Chile 48 G10
San Felipe Venezuela 44 H4
San Félix, Isla *Island* Chile 129 Q11
San Fernando Chile 49 H11
San Fernando Luzon, Philippines 127 L3
San Fernando Spain 60 H14
San Fernando Trinidad & Tobago 43 S16
San Fernando de Apure Venezuela 44 I5
San Francisco California, USA 9, 37 H15, 129 N5
San Francisco de Macorís Dominican Republic 43 O8
San Gorgonia Pass *Mountain pass* California, USA 37 L18
San Ignacio Belize 42 C6
San Joaquin *River* California, USA 37 I16
San Jorge, Gulf of *Sea feature* Argentina 49 K16
San Jose California, USA 37 H15
San José Costa Rica 42 E13
San José del Guaviare Colombia 44 F7
San José I. *Island* Mexico 38 H7
San José I. *Island* Panama 42 G15
San Juan Argentina 48 H9
San Juan Peru 45 E14
San Juan Puerto Rico 43 Q9
San Juan *River* Nicaragua 42 E12
San Juan *River* New Mexico/Utah, USA 35 K6
San Juan Bautista Paraguay 48 N6
San Juan de los Morros Venezuela 44 I5
San Juan Is. *Island group* Washington, USA 36 H5
San Juan Mts. *Mountain range* Colorado, USA 35 M6
San Lorenzo Honduras 42 C9
San Luis Argentina 48 J10
San Luis Obispo California, USA 37 I17
San Luis Potosí Mexico 39 M10
San Marino San Marino 72 I9
San Marino *Country* S Europe 72 I9

San Marino 72

a Italian • Lira • 849 • 76 • £1.02 • (m) 98% (f) 98% • 90%

San Matías, Gulf of *Sea feature* Argentina 49 K14
San Miguel El Salvador 42 C9
San Miguel *River* Bolivia 45 K14
San Miguel de Tucumán Argentina 48 I7
San Nicolás de los Arroyos Argentina 48 L10
San Pedro Paraguay 48 N5
San Pedro Sula Honduras 42 C8
San Pietro *Island* Italy 73 C15
San Rafael Argentina 48 I11
San Remo Italy 72 C9
San *River* Cambodia/Vietnam 125 N12
San *River* Poland/Ukraine 71 O8
San Salvador El Salvador 42 B9
San Salvador *Island* Bahamas 43 M3
San Salvador de Jujuy Argentina 49 I6
San Sebastián (var. Donostia) Spain 61 M3
San'ā Yemen 108 I15
Sanaga *River* Cameroon 94 F10
Sanandaj Iran 109 L4
Sandakan Borneo, Malaysia 127 K8
Sandanski Bulgaria 76 I15
Sandnes Norway 56 H12
Sandoway Burma 124 E9
Sandviken Sweden 57 L11
Sanford Maine, USA 27 O8
Sângeorz-Băi *Spa* Romania 77 K3
Sangha *River* Congo 95 I12
Sangir *Island* Indonesia 127 N9
Sangir Is. *Island group* Indonesia 127 N10
Sangre de Cristo Mts. *Mountain range* Colorado/New Mexico, USA 35 M6
Sangro *River* Italy 73 K12
Sankt Gallen Switzerland 68 H8
Sankt Pölten Austria 69 R5
Sankt Veit Austria 69 P9
Şanliurfa Turkey 105 P9
Sant' Antioco Sardinia 73 C16
Santa Ana California, USA 37 L19
Santa Ana El Salvador 42 B9
Santa Barbara California, USA 37 J18
Santa Catalina I. *Island* Mexico 38 H7
Santa Clara Cuba 42 I4
Santa Clara Valley *Physical feature* California, USA 37 H15
Santa Cruz Bolivia 44 J15
Santa Cruz California, USA 37 H16
Santa Cruz *River* Arizona, USA 34 I11
Santa Elena Venezuela 44 L7
Santa Fe Argentina 48 L9
Santa Fe New Mexico, USA 35 M8
Santa Fe *see* Bogotá
Santa Maria Brazil 47 H16
Santa Maria California, USA 37 I17
Santa Maria *Volcano* Guatemala 41
Santa Marta Colombia 44 F4
Santa Rosa Argentina 49 K11
Santa Rosa California, USA 37 H14
Santa Rosa Honduras 42 C8
Santa Rosalia Mexico 38 G5
Santander Spain 61 K3
Santarém Brazil 46 H8
Santarém Portugal 60 F10
Santee *River* South Carolina, USA 29 P8
Santiago Chile 48 H10
Santiago Dominican Republic 43 N8
Santiago Panama 42 F15
Santiago de Compostela Spain 60 F4
Santiago de Cuba Cuba 43 K6
Santiago del Estero Argentina 48 J7
Sant Jordi, Golf de *Sea feature* Spain 61 O7
Santo Domingo Dominican Republic 43 O9
Santo Domingo de los Colorados Ecuador 44 C8
Santorini *Volcano* Greece 54
Santos Brazil 47 K14
Santos Plateau *Sea feature* Atlantic Ocean 41
Sanya China 121 K16
São Francisco *River* Brazil 41, 47 L11
São José dos Campos Brazil 47 K14
São Luís Brazil 46 L8
São Paulo Brazil 14, 47 K14
São Roque, Cabo de *Cape* Brazil 46 P8
São Tomé Sao Tome & Principe 95 D12
Sao Tome and Principe *Country* C Africa 52 L12, 95

Sao Tome and Principe 95

a Portuguese • Dobra • 322 • 67 • £0.63 • (m) 73% (f) 42% • 33%

São Tomé, Cabo de *Cape* Brazil 47 M14
São Tomé I. *Island* 87
Saône *River* France 63 O7
Sapporo Japan 122 K4
Sapri Italy 73 M14
Saqqara *Archaeological site* Egypt 90 F7
Sara Buri Thailand 125 J12
Saragossa *see* Zaragoza
Sarajevo Bosnia and Herzegovina 75 K7
Saransk Russian Federation 83 H11
Saratoga Springs New York, USA 27 M9
Saratov Russian Federation 83 H12
Saravan Laos 125 N11
Sarawak *Region* Borneo, Malaysia 126 I10
Sardinia *Island* Italy 54, 73
Sargasso Sea Atlantic Ocean 52 G10
Sargodha Pakistan 116 I3
Sarh Chad 94 J9
Sarī Iran 109 O4
Sarikei Borneo, Malaysia 126 I10
Sariyer Turkey 104 I5
Sarnen Switzerland 68 G10
Sarnia Ontario, Canada 24 J14
Sarroch Sardinia 72 D16
Sartang *River* Russian Federation 113 N7
Sárvíz *River* Hungary 71 K14
Sarykamysh, L. *Lake* Turkmenistan/Uzbekistan 110 H5
Saskatchewan *Province* Canada 23
Saskatchewan *River* Canada 23 N13
Saskatoon Saskatchewan, Canada 23 M14
Satu Mare Romania 76 I2
Saudi Arabia *Country* SW Asia 108-109

Saudi Arabia 108-109

a Arabic • Riyal • 19 • 65 • £0.62 • (m) 73% (f) 48% • 283 • 633 • Yes • 77% • 2874

Sault Sainte Marie Ontario, Canada 24 I12
Sault Ste. Marie Michigan, USA 31 N4
Saurimo Angola 98 I4
Sava *River* SE Europe 74 J4
Savanna-la-Mar Jamaica 42 J7
Savannah Georgia, USA 29 O9
Savannah *River* Georgia, USA 29 O8
Savannakhét Laos 125 M11
Save *River* Mozambique/Zimbabwe 99 N10
Savona Italy 72 D8
Savonlinna Finland 57 Q9
Saxony *Region* Germany 66 H8
Saynshand Mongolia 119 N6
Scandinavia *Region* N Europe 54, 56-57
Scarborough Trinidad & Tobago 43 T16
Schaffhausen Switzerland 68 G8
Schärding Austria 69 N5
Schefferville Quebec, Canada 25 O6
Scheldt *River* W Europe 65 F14
Schenectady New York, USA 27 L9
Schiermonnikoog *Island* West Frisian Is. Netherlands 64 L5
Schleswig Germany 66 H6
Schouten Is. *Island group* Papua New Guinea 133 N1
Schwaner Mts. *Mountain range* Indonesia 126 I12
Schwarzwald *see* Black Forest
Schweinfurt Germany 67 H13
Schwerin Germany 66 J7
Schwerin, L. *Lake* Germany 66 J7
Schwyz Switzerland 68 G10
Scilly, Isles of *Island group* England, UK 59 D17
Scioto *River* Ohio, USA 31 O11
Scoresbysund Greenland 51 O15
Scotia Plate *Physical feature* 89, 41
Scotia Sea Atlantic Ocean 50 C6, 53 G16
Scotland *Country* UK 58
Scott Base *Research center* Antarctica 50 E11
Scottsbluff Nebraska, USA 33 L9
Scottsdale Arizona, USA 34 I9
Scranton Pennsylvania, USA 27 K11
Scupi *see* Skopje
Scutari, L. *Lake* Albania/Yugoslavia 75 L10
Sea of Galilee *see* L. Tiberias
Seaford Delaware, USA 27 K16
Seal *River* Manitoba, Canada 23 O11
Seattle Washington, USA 36 H6, 129 N4
Segovia Spain 61 K7
Segozero, L. *Lake* Russian Federation 82 H7
Segura *River* Spain 61 L11
Segura, Sierra de *Mountain range* Spain 61 L12
Seikan Tunnel *Tunnel* Japan 122 K6
Seinäjoki Finland 57 N9
Seine *River* France 54, 63 M5
Sekondi-Takoradi Ghana 93 L13
Selayar *Island* Indonesia 127 L14
Selebi-Phikwe Botswana 99 L10
Selkirk Manitoba, Canada 23 O14
Selma Alabama, USA 29 L8
Selous *Game reserve* Tanzania 97 P10
Selvas *Physical region* Brazil 41
Semarang Java, Indonesia 126 H15
Semey *see* Semipalatinsk
Semipalatinsk (var. Semey) Kazakhstan 112 H12
Semnān Iran 109 O4
Sên *River* Cambodia 125 M12
Sendai Japan 122 L8, 128 G5
Senegal *Country* W Africa 92

Senegal 92

a French • Franc • 103 • 48 • £2.00 • (m) 52% (f) 25% • 38%

Senegal *River* W Africa 87, 92 G7
Senja *Island* Norway 57 M2
Sennar Dam *Dam* Sudan 91 H13
Senta Serbia, Yugoslavia 75 M3
Seoul South Korea 15, 121 P7
Sept-Îles Quebec, Canada 25 O9
Seraing Belgium 65 J16
Seram *Island* Indonesia 127 O12, 131
Seram Sea Indonesia 127 O12
Serbia *Republic* Yugoslavia 75 N6
Seremban Malaysia 125 J19
Serengeti *National park* Tanzania 97 N6
Serengeti Plain *Physical region* Tanzania 87
Sérifos *Island* Cyclades, Greece 79 L11
Serov Russian Federation 112 G8
Serowe Botswana 99 L10
Serres Greece 79 K2
Sétif Algeria 89 L4
Setúbal Portugal 60 F11
Seul, L. *Lake* Ontario, Canada 24 G9
Sevan, L. (var. Ozero Sevan) *Lake* Armenia 85 Q14
Sevan-Hrazdan *HEP scheme* Armenia 85 Q13
Sevastopol' Ukraine 84 J10
Severn *River* England, UK 59 I15
Severn *River* Ontario, Canada 24 H7
Severnaya Zemlya (var. North Land) *Island group* Russian Federation 51 S10, 103, 113 K4
Sevier L. *Lake* Utah, USA 34 I4
Sevilla (var. Seville) Spain 60 I13
Seville *see* Sevilla
Seward Alaska, USA 22 G8
Seychelles *Country* Indian Ocean 100 F9

Seychelles 100

a Seselwa • Rupee • 662 • 71 • £1.91 • (m) 55% (f) 60% • 52%

Seyhan *River* Turkey 105 M9
Sfântu Gheorghe Romania 77 L6
Sfax Tunisia 52 L9, 89 N5
Shache (var. Yarkand) China 118 E8
Shackleton Ice Shelf *Coastal feature* Indian Ocean Coast, Antarctica 50 H10
Shadehill Res. *Reservoir* South Dakota, USA 33 M6
Shahjahanpur India 117 L5
Shahr-e-Kord Iran 109 N6
Shāmīyah Desert *Desert region* Syria 107 P6
Shandong Pen. *Physical feature* China 121 O8
Shanghai China 15, 121 O10, 128 F6
Shannon Ireland 59 B13
Shannon *River* Ireland 59 C13
Shantou China 121 N14
Shaoguan China 121 M13
Shaoxing China 121 O11
Shaoyang China 121 L12
Sharjah United Arab Emirates 109 O10
Shark Bay *Sea feature* Western Australia, Australia 132 E10
Shashe *River* Botswana/Zimbabwe 99 L10
Shasta L. *Lake* California, USA 37 H12
Shebeli *River* Ethiopia/Somalia 87, 91 M16
Sheboygan Wisconsin, USA 31 L8
Sheffield England, UK 59 J13
Shelby Montana, USA 32 H4
Shelikof Strait *Channel* Alaska, USA 22 F8
Shenandoah *River* Maryland/Virginia, USA 29 Q3

a Language (official or most commonly spoken) • Currency • Population density per square mile • Average life expectancy • Price of 1 dozen hen's eggs • Literacy • Number of TVs per 1,000 people • Number of people per doctor • Death penalty • Percentage of urban-based population • Average number of calories consumed daily per person

Sumbu – Tongking, Gulf of

Sumbu *National park* Zambia 97 L10
Sumgait *see* Sumqayıt
Summer L. *Lake* Oregon, USA 36 I10
Sumqayıt (var. Sumgait) Azerbaijan 85 T13
Sumy Ukraine 85 K4
Sun City South Africa 99 L12
Sunbury Pennsylvania, USA 26 J12
Sunda Shelf *Sea feature* South China Sea 115, 130
Sunderland England, UK 59 J11
Sundsvall Sweden 57 L9
Suntar Russian Federation 113 M8
Sunyani Ghana 93 L12
Superior Wisconsin, USA 30 I4
Superior, L. *Lake* Canada/USA 20, 24 H11, 31 L3
Supiori *Island* Indonesia 127 R11
Sur Oman 109 P13
Surabaya Java, Indonesia 126 I15
Surat India 116 I9
Surat Thani Thailand 125 H15
Sûre *River* Belgium/Luxembourg 65 L18
Surigao Mindanao, Philippines 127 N6
Suriname (prev. Dutch Guiana) *Country* S America 44

Suriname 44

a Dutch • Gulden • 7 • 68 • £3.77 • (m) 5% (f) 5% • 47%

Surkhob *River* Tajikistan 111 O7
Surt Libya 89 P7
Susquehanna *River* USA 26 J11
Sutherland Falls *Waterfall* New Zealand 131
Suva Fiji 128 J10
Suwałki Poland 71 O2
Suwannee *River* Florida, USA 29 N11
Svalbard *Island group* Arctic Ocean 51 Q12, 54, 103
Svay Riĕng Cambodia 125 M14
Sverdlovsk *see* Yekaterinburg
Sverige *see* Sweden
Svetlogorsk *see* Svyetlahorsk
Svobodnyy ICBM Base *Military center* Russian Federation 113 O11
Svyetlahorsk (var. Svetlogorsk) Belarus 81 N14
Swabian Jura *Mountain range* Germany 67 G16
Swakopmund Namibia 98 G10
Swansea Wales, UK 59 G15
Swaziland *Country* Southern Africa 99

Swaziland 99

a English, Swazi • Lilangeni • 124 • 57 • £0.84 • (m) 70% (f) 66% • 33%

Sweden (var. Sverige) *Country* Scandinavia 56-57

Sweden 56-57

a Swedish • Krona • 54 • 78 • £1.98 • (m) 99% (f) 99% • 474 • 355 • No • 84% • 2960

Sweetwater Texas, USA 35 P10
Swift Current Saskatchewan, Canada 23 M15
Swindon England, UK 59 I16
Switzerland *Country* C Europe 68

Switzerland 68

a French, German, Italian • Franc • 439 • 78 • £3.03 • (m) 99% (f) 99% • 407 • 584 • No • 60% • 3562

Sydney New South Wales, Australia 15, 128 H11, 133 O13
Sydney Nova Scotia, Canada 25 R11
Syktyvkar Russian Federation 82 K9
Sylhet Bangladesh 117 P7
Sylt *Island* North Frisian Is. Germany 66 G5
Syowa *Research center* Antarctica 50 F7
Syr Darya *River* C Asia 103, 112 F13
Syracuse New York, USA 27 K8
Syracuse *see* Siracusa
Syria (var. Aram) *Country* SW Asia 107

Syria 107

a Arabic • Pound • 180 • 66 • £0.97 • (m) 78% (f) 51% • 59 • 1347 • Yes • 50% • 3003

Syrian Desert (var. Bādiyat ash Shām) *Desert region* SW Asia 103, 107 P9, 108 I5
Szczecin Poland 70 H3
Szeged Hungary 71 M15
Székesfehérvár Hungary 71 K13
Szekszárd Hungary 71 L15
Szolnok Hungary 71 M14
Szombathely Hungary 70 J13

T

Tabar Is. *Island group* Papua New Guinea 133 P1
Tabasco Mexico 39 L10
Table Bay *Sea feature* South Africa 98 I15
Table Mt. *Mountain* South Africa 98 I16
Tábor Czech Republic 70 H10
Tabora Tanzania 97 M8
Tabríz Iran 109 L2
Tabúk Saudi Arabia 108 G6
Tacloban Leyte, Philippines 127 N6
Tacna Peru 45 G15
Tacoma Washington, USA 36 H7
Tacuarembó Uruguay 48 O9
Taegu South Korea 121 Q8
Taejŏn South Korea 121 P8
Tagula I. *Island* Papua New Guinea 133 P4
Tagus (var. Tajo, Tejo) *River* Portugal/Spain 54, 60 G9
Tahiti *Island* French Polynesia, Pacific Ocean 129 L10
Tahoe, L. *Lake* California/Nevada, USA 34 E3, 37 J14
Tahoua Niger 93 O8
Tai'an China 121 N8
Taieri *River* New Zealand 134 D13
Ṭā'if Saudi Arabia 108 H11
Taipei Taiwan 121 O13
Taiping Malaysia 125 I18
Taiwan *Country* E Asia 115, 121, 128 F6

Taiwan 121

a Mandarin • Dollar • 1670 • 74 • £0.62 • (m) 96% (f) 87% • 387 • 913 • Yes • N/A • 2875

Taiwan Strait *Channel* China/Taiwan 115, 121 N14
Taiyuan China 121 L8
Ta'izz Yemen 108 I16
Tajikistan *Country* C Asia 111

Tajikistan 111

a Tajik • Ruble • 98 • 69 • N/A • N/A • 31%

Tajo *see* Tagus
Tak Thailand 124 I10
Takamatsu Japan 123 F12
Takêv Cambodia 125 M14
Takla Makan Desert *Desert region* China 11, 118 F9
Talak *Desert region* Niger 93 O6
Talas Kyrgyzstan 111 P5
Talaud Is. *Island group* Indonesia 127 N9
Talca Chile 49 G11
Talcahuano Chile 49 G12
Taldy-Kurgan (var. Taldyqorghan) Kazakhstan 112 H13
Taldyqorghan *see* Taldy-Kurgan
Tallahassee Florida, USA 29 M10
Tallinn (prev. Revel) Estonia 52 M7, 80 J1
Talsi Latvia 80 H5
Tamabo Range *Mountain range* Borneo, Malaysia 126 J10
Tamale Ghana 93 L11
Tamanrasset Algeria 89 L11
Tambacounda Senegal 92 G9
Tambora *Volcano* Sumbawa, Indonesia 9, 115
Tambov Russian Federation 83 G11
Tampa Florida, USA 29 N13
Tampere Finland 57 O10
Tampico Mexico 39 O10
Tamworth New South Wales, Australia 133 O12
Tan-Tan Morocco 88 G7
Tana *River* Kenya 97 Q4
Tana *River* Norway 57 O3
Tana, L. *Lake* Ethiopia 87, 91 I14
Tanami Desert *Desert region* Australia 131
Tanana *River* Alaska, USA 22 H8
Tanega-shima *Island* Japan 123 D16
Tanga Tanzania 97 Q8
Tanganyika, L. *Lake* C Africa 87, 95 O15, 97 L9
Tanggula Mountains *Mountain range* China 118 I11
Tangier Morocco 88 I4
Tangra Yumco *Lake* China 118 H12
Tangshan China 121 N7
Tanimbar Is. *Island group* Indonesia 127 Q14
Tanjungkarang Sumatra, Indonesia 126 F14
Tanjungpinang Bitan, Indonesia 126 F11
Tanta Egypt 90 F6
Tanzam Railway *Railway* Tanzania 97 N10
Tanzania *Country* E Africa 97

Tanzania 97

a English, Swahili • Shilling • 74 • 47 • £0.60 • (m) 62% (f) 31% • 33%

Taormina Italy 73 L17
Taos New Mexico, USA 35 M7
Tapachula Mexico 39 R15
Tapajós *River* Brazil 41, 46 G8
Tapti *River* India 116 J8
Taraba *River* Nigeria 93 Q12
Ṭarābulus *see* Tripoli
Taranto Italy 73 O14
Taranto, Gulf of *Sea feature* Italy 73 O14
Tarawa *Island* Kiribati, Pacific Ocean 128 J8
Tarbela Dam *Dam* Pakistan 116 J2
Tarbela Res. *Reservoir* Pakistan 116 J1
Tarbes France 62 J14
Taree New South Wales, Australia 133 P12
Târgovişte Romania 77 L8
Târgu Jiu Romania 76 I8
Târgu Mureş Romania 77 K5
Tarija Bolivia 45 J17
Tarim *River* China 115, 118 G8
Tarim Basin *Physical region* China 118 G8
Tarn *River* France 63 L13
Tarnów Poland 71 N9
Tarragona Spain 61 P7
Tarsus Turkey 105 M10
Tartu Estonia 81 K3
Tarṭūs Syria 107 M5
Tashauz *see* Dashkhovuz
Tashkent (var. Toshkent) Uzbekistan 111 N6
Tasman Bay *Sea feature* New Zealand 134 F8
Tasman Sea Australia/New Zealand 128 I12, 131, 133 O15, 134 D11
Tasmania *Island* Australia 131
Tasmania *State* Australia 133
Tassili n'Ajjer *Mountain range* Algeria 87, 89 M9
Tatvan Turkey 105 R7
Tauern Tunnel *Tunnel* Austria 69 N9
Taunggyi Burma 124 G8
Taunton England, UK 59 H16
Taupo New Zealand 134 H6
Taupo, L. *Lake* New Zealand 131, 134 H6
Tauragė Lithuania 80 G9
Tauranga New Zealand 134 H5
Taurus Mts. *Mountain range* Turkey 103, 105 L10
Tavoy Burma 125 H12
Tawakoni, L. *Lake* Texas, USA 35 R10
Tawau Borneo, Malaysia 127 K9
Tawitawi *Island* Philippines 127 L8
Taxco Mexico 39 N13
Tay Ninh Vietnam 125 M1
Taymyr, L. *Lake* Russian Federation 113 K5
Taymyr Peninsula *Physical feature* Russian Federation 51 T9, 103, 113 K5
Taz *River* Russian Federation 112 I8
Tbilisi (var. T'bilisi) Georgia 85 Q12
T'bilisi *see* Tbilisi
Tchibanga Gabon 95 F13
Tchien (var. Zwedru) Liberia 92 I13
Te Anau, L. *Lake* New Zealand 134 C13
Tébessa Algeria 89 M5
Tedzhen Turkmenistan 110 J9
Tedzhen *River* Iran/Turkmenistan 110 J9
Tegucigalpa Honduras 42 D9
Tehran Iran 109 N4
Tehuantepec Mexico 39 P14
Tehuantepec, Gulf of *Sea feature* Mexico 39 P15
Tejo *see* Tagus
Tekirdağ Turkey 104 G5
Tel Aviv-Yafo Israel 107 L9
Teles Pires *River* Brazil 46 G9
Telluride Colorado, USA 35 L5
Telok Intan Malaysia 125 I18
Temuco Chile 49 G13
Tengiz, L. *Lake* Kazakhstan 112 G11
Tennessee *River* SE USA 20, 29 K4
Tennessee *State* USA 28-29
Teotihuacán *Archaeological site* Mexico 39 N12
Tepic Mexico 39 K10
Tequila Mexico 39 K11
Teresina Brazil 46 M8
Termez Uzbekistan 111 M9
Terneuzen Netherlands 65 F13
Terni Italy 73 I11
Ternopil' (var. Ternopol') Ukraine 84 F5
Ternopol' *see* Ternopil'
Terrassa Spain 61 Q6
Terre Haute Indiana, USA 31 L13
Terschelling *Island* West Frisian Is. Netherlands 64 J6
Teruel Spain 61 N8
Teslin L. *Lake* Yukon Territory, Canada 22 I10
Tete Mozambique 99 N7
Tétouan Morocco 88 I4
Tetovo Macedonia 75 N11
Tevere *see* Tiber
Texas *State* USA 35
Texas City Texas, USA 35 S13
Texcoco, L. *Lake* Mexico 39 N12
Texel *Island* West Frisian Is. Netherlands 64 H7
Thac Ba, L. *Lake* Vietnam 124 M8
Thai Nguyen Vietnam 124 N8
Thailand *Country* SE Asia 124-125

Thailand 124-125

a Thai • Baht • 287 • 66 • £0.54 • (m) 96% (f) 90% • 112 • 4843 • Yes • 23% • 2316

Thailand, Gulf of *Sea feature* Thailand 100 L7, 115, 125 J15
Thakhek *see* Muang Khammouan
Thames New Zealand 134 H4
Thames *River* England, UK 54, 59 I15
Thane India 116 I9
Thanh Hoa Vietnam 124 M9
Thar Desert (var. Indian Desert) *Desert region* India/Pakistan 11, 115, 116 I5
Tharthār, L. *Lake* Iraq 109 K4
Thasos *Island* Greece 79 M3
Thaton Burma 124 G10
Thayetmyo Burma 124 F9
Thebes *Archaeological site* Egypt 90 G8
Theodore Roosevelt L. *Lake* Arizona, USA 34 I9
Thermaic Gulf *Sea feature* Greece 78 J4
Thessaloniki (var. Salonika) Greece 78 J3
Thika Kenya 97 P5
Thimphu Bhutan 117 P6
Thionville France 63 O4
Thira *Island* Cyclades, Greece 79 N13
Thiruvananthapuram *see* Trivandrum
Thohoyandou South Africa 99 M10
Thompson Manitoba, Canada 23 O12
Thrace *Region* Greece 79 N2
Thule (var. Qaanaaq) Greenland 51 O11
Thun Switzerland 68 F11
Thun, L. of *Lake* Switzerland 68 F11
Thunder Bay Ontario, Canada 24 G11
Thüringer Wald *see* Thuringian Forest
Thuringia *Region* Germany 67 J12
Thuringian Forest (var. Thüringer Wald) *Physical region* Germany 67 I12
Thurso Scotland, UK 58 I6
Tianjin China 121 N7, 128 F5
Tiaret Algeria 89 K5
Tiber (var. Tevere) *River* Italy 73 H11
Tiberias, L. (var. Sea of Galilee) *Lake* Israel 107 M8
Tibesti *Mountain range* Chad/Libya 87, 94 I4
Tibet, Plateau of *Physical feature* China 15
Tibetan Autonomous Region *Region* China 118 H12
Tiburón I. *Island* Mexico 38 G4
Tidjikdja Mauritania 92 H6
Tien Shan *Mountain range* Kyrgyzstan/China 103, 111 R6, 115, 118 G7
Tienen Belgium 65 I15
Tierra del Fuego *Island* Argentina/Chile 41, 49 K20
Tighina (var. Bendery) Moldavia 84 H8
Tigris (var. Dijlah) *River* SW Asia 100 E4, 103, 105 Q8, 107 T1, 109 K3
Tijuana Mexico 38 F1
Tikal *Archaeological site* Guatemala 42 C6
Tikrīt Iraq 109 K4
Tiksi Russian Federation 51 T7, 113 M6
Tikveško, L. *Lake* Macedonia 75 O12
Tilburg Netherlands 65 I12
Tillabéry Niger 93 M8
Timaru New Zealand 134 E12
Timbuktu (var. Tombouctou) Mali 93 K7
Timgad *Archaeological site* Morocco 89 M5
Timirist, Râs *Cape* Mauritania 92 F6
Timiş *River* Romania/Serbia 76 H7
Timişoara Romania 77 G6
Timmins Ontario, Canada 24 J11
Timor *Island* Indonesia 115, 127 N16, 131
Timor Sea Australia/Indonesia 127 O16, 131, 133 I4
Tindouf Algeria 88 H8
Tinos *Island* Cyclades, Greece 79 M10
Tirana (var. Tiranë) Albania 75 M12
Tiranë *see* Tirana
Tiraspol Moldavia 84 H8
Tiree *Island* Scotland, UK 58 E8
Tirso *River* Sardinia 73 D14
Tiruchchirappalli India 117 K14
Tisza *River* Hungary 54, 71 M14
Titicaca, L. *Lake* Peru/Bolivia 41, 45 H14
Titograd *see* Podgorica
Titov Veles Macedonia 75 O11
Titova Mitrovica Serbia, Yugoslavia 75 N9
Tiznit Morocco 88 G6
Tlaxcala Mexico 39 N12
Tlemcen Algeria 88 J5
Toamasina Madagascar 100 E10
Toba, L. *Lake* Sumatra, Indonesia 126 C10
Tobago *Island* Trinidad & Tobago 20, 41, 43 T16
Tobakakar Range *Mountain range* Pakistan/Afghanistan 116 H3
Tobruk Libya 89 R6
Tocantins *River* Brazil 41, 46 J10
Tocopilla Chile 48 F5
Togian Is. *Island group* Indonesia 127 M11
Togo (prev. French Togo) *Country* W Africa 93

Togo 93

a French • Franc • 179 • 54 • £1.43 • (m) 56% (f) 31% • 26%

Tokara Is. *Island group* Japan 123 C17
Tokat Turkey 105 N6
Tokelau *Dependent territory* Polynesia, Pacific Ocean 128 J9
Tokmak Kyrgyzstan 111 Q4
Tokuno-shima *Island* Amami Is. Japan 123 B19
Tokushima Japan 123 G13
Tokyo Japan 15, 123 K11
Tol'yatti Russian Federation 83 I12
Toledo Ohio, USA 31 O10
Toledo Spain 61 K9
Toledo Bend Res. *Reservoir* Louisiana/Texas, USA 35 T11
Toliara Madagascar 101 E11
Tomakomai Japan 122 K4
Tombigbee *River* Alabama 29 K8
Tombouctou *see* Timbuktu
Tomé Chile 48 G12
Tomini, Gulf of *Sea feature* Celebes, Indonesia 127 L11
Tomsk Russian Federation 112 I10
Tonga *Country* Polynesia, Pacific Ocean 128 J10

Tonga 128

a English, Tongan • Pa'anga • 360 • 67 • £1.83 • (m) 93% (f) 93% • 31%

Tongking, Gulf of (var. Tonkin, Gulf of) *Sea feature* China/Vietnam 115, 121 K15, 124 O9

a Language (official or most commonly spoken) • Currency • Population density per square mile • Average life expectancy • Price of 1 dozen hen's eggs • Literacy • Number of TVs per 1,000 people • Number of people per doctor • Death penalty • Percentage of urban-based population • Average number of calories consumed daily per person

ⓐ Language (official or most commonly spoken) · 💰 Currency · ♦ Population density per square mile · 🕮 Average life expectancy · 💲 Price of 1 dozen hen's eggs · 👪 Literacy · 🖵 Number of TVs per 1,000 people · ✚ Number of people per doctor · ☠ Death penalty · 🏠 Percentage of urban-based population · 🍴 Average number of calories consumed daily per person

159

NORTH AMERICA

CANADA
PAGES 22-25

UNITED STATES OF AMERICA
PAGES 26-37

MEXICO
PAGES 38-39

CENTRAL AND SOUTH AMERICA

ANTIGUA & BARBUDA
PAGES 42-43

BAHAMAS
PAGES 42-43

BARBADOS
PAGES 42-43

BELIZE
PAGES 42-43

COSTA RICA
PAGES 42-43

JAMAICA
PAGES 42-43

NICARAGUA
PAGES 42-43

PANAMA
PAGES 42-43

ST. CHRISTOPHER & NEVIS
PAGES 42-43

ST. LUCIA
PAGES 42-43

ST. VINCENT & THE GRENADINES
PAGES 42-43

TRINIDAD & TOBAGO
PAGES 42-43

BOLIVIA
PAGES 44-45

THE ATLANTIC OCEAN

EUROPE

CHILE
PAGES 48-49

PARAGUAY
PAGES 48-49

URUGUAY
PAGES 48-49

CAPE VERDE
PAGES 52-53

ICELAND
PAGES 52-53

DENMARK
PAGES 56-57

FINLAND
PAGES 56-57

NORWAY
PAGES 56-57

BELGIUM
PAGES 64-65

LUXEMBOURG
PAGES 64-65

THE NETHERLANDS
PAGES 64-65

GERMANY
PAGES 66-67

AUSTRIA
PAGES 68-69

LIECHTENSTEIN
PAGES 68-69

SWITZERLAND
PAGES 68-69

CZECH REPUBLIC
PAGES 70-71

BOSNIA & HERZEGOVINA
PAGES 74-75

CROATIA
PAGES 74-75

MACEDONIA
PAGES 74-75

SLOVENIA
PAGES 74-75

YUGOSLAVIA
PAGES 74-75

BULGARIA
PAGES 76-77

ROMANIA
PAGES 76-77

GREECE
PAGES 78-79

AFRICA

MOLDAVIA
PAGES 84-85

UKRAINE
PAGES 84-85

ALGERIA
PAGES 88-89

LIBYA
PAGES 88-89

MOROCCO
PAGES 88-89

TUNISIA
PAGES 88-89

WESTERN SAHARA
PAGES 88-89

DJIBOUTI
PAGES 90-91

GHANA
PAGES 92-93

GUINEA
PAGES 92-93

GUINEA-BISSAU
PAGES 92-93

IVORY COAST
PAGES 92-93

LIBERIA
PAGES 92-93

MALI
PAGES 92-93

MAURITANIA
PAGES 92-93

NIGER
PAGES 92-93

EQUATORIAL GUINEA
PAGES 94-95

GABON
PAGES 94-95

SAO TOME & PRINCIPE
PAGES 94-95

ZAIRE
PAGES 94-95

BURUNDI
PAGES 96-97

KENYA
PAGES 96-97

MALAWI
PAGES 96-97

RWANDA
PAGES 96-97

THE INDIAN OCEAN

SOUTH AFRICA
PAGES 98-99

SWAZILAND
PAGES 98-99

ZIMBABWE
PAGES 98-99

COMOROS
PAGES 100-101

MADAGASCAR
PAGES 100-101

MALDIVES
PAGES 100-101

MAURITIUS
PAGES 100-101

SEYCHELLES
PAGES 100-101

IRAN
PAGES 108-109

KUWAIT
PAGES 108-109

OMAN
PAGES 108-109

QATAR
PAGES 108-109

SAUDI ARABIA
PAGES 108-109

UNITED ARAB EMIRATES
PAGES 108-109

YEMEN
PAGES 108-109

AFGHANISTAN
PAGES 110-111

PAKISTAN
PAGES 116-117

NEPAL
PAGES 116-117

SRI LANKA
PAGES 116-117

CHINA
PAGES 118-121

MONGOLIA
PAGES 118-119

NORTH KOREA
PAGES 120-121

SOUTH KOREA
PAGES 120-121

TAIWAN
PAGES 120-121

THE PACIFIC OCEAN

BRUNEI
PAGES 126-127

INDONESIA
PAGES 126-127

PHILIPPINES
PAGES 126-127

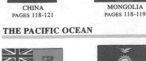
FIJI
PAGES 128-129

KIRIBATI
PAGES 128-129

MARSHALL ISLANDS
PAGES 128-129

MICRONESIA
PAGES 128-129